Equal Opportunities Handbook

LONDON BOROUGH OF
BARKING & DAGENHAM

The London Borough of
Barking & Dagenham
www.barking-dagenham.gov.uk

REFERENCE

LIBRARIES

Equal Opportunities Handbook

Fourth Edition

Martin Edwards

Head of Employment Law
and Human Resources

Mace & Jones Solicitors

Liverpool and Manchester

TOTTEL PUBLISHING, MAXWELTON HOUSE, 41–43 BOLTRO ROAD, HAYWARDS HEATH, WEST SUSSEX, RH16 1BJ

© Tottel Publishing Ltd 2007

A CIP Catalogue record for this book is available from the British Library.

ISBN 978 1 84592 223 8

Typeset by Phoenix Photosetting, Chatham, Kent
Printed and bound in Great Britain by Athenæum, Gateshead, Tyne and Wear

Preface

The aim in writing this book has been to provide a readable, practical and wide-ranging guide to one of the most important of social, political and legal issues – that of equal opportunities in employment. The remarkable pace of development of the law in this area was described in the introduction to the third edition of this book as 'little short of remarkable'. If anything, that is even truer of the changes that have taken place since that edition was published.

Amongst the key statutory developments have been a new regime outlawing age discrimination, which is arguably the most significant development in employment law for a generation. In addition, we have seen, amongst other matters:

- new equality duties in respect of gender and disability;

- changes to the law on disability discrimination;

- amendments to the legislation prohibiting discrimination on grounds of religion or belief;

- expanded parental rights;

- new statutory internal dispute resolution procedures; and

- new rules of employment tribunal procedure.

There has also been an endless flow of noteworthy practical decisions. It has been striking that, in addition to cases explaining intricacies of the more recent legislation, the *Equal Pay Act 1970*, despite having been in force for more than 30 years, is generating more litigation than in the past – much of it of a highly complex nature.

As well as covering statutory and case law changes, this book includes a good many brand new chapters, including consideration of:

- civil partnerships;

- contract compliance;

- fertility treatment;

- freedom of information;

- keeping in touch days;

- obesity;

- permanent health insurance;

- schools;

- stalking;

- veils;

- whistle-blowing; and

- without prejudice.

Each edition of this handbook has been longer than its predecessor and I have been anxious to ensure that readers should continue to find the material presented here easy to assimilate. Feedback from readers makes it clear that they want a concise A–Z handbook to utilise as a quick first point of reference, rather than yet another weighty textbook crammed with turgid minutiae. With this in mind, the fourth edition not only contains more practical checklists and appendices of guidelines on good practice that its predecessors, but also an increasing emphasis on recent cases which illustrates important points, even though some have not been widely reported. The original legislation on sex and race discrimination and equal pay continues to be discussed in depth, but less space has been devoted to points that are either familiar, uncontroversial or of limited interest to most readers. In the 2006 annual lecture of the Employment Lawyers' Association, Mr Justice Elias, the President of the Employment Appeal Tribunal concluded: 'The path of discrimination will remain strewn with difficult and intractable issues. This is hardly desirable in a jurisprudence which ought to be comprehensible to employers, unions and workers.' The aim here has been to explain those issues in a straightforward manner but without, I hope, undue distortion.

The first three editions were co-authored by Michael Malone and myself. Michael has now retired from private practice, but although this edition bears my name alone, it would not have been possible to produce it without building upon the sound foundations that he laid.

My original intention was to survey the legal rules and good practice as at 1 January 2007, but it has in the event proved possible to include reference to some developments which occurred during the early months of 2007.

I would like to thank Sarah Thomas and Kiran Goss of Tottel Publishing, successors as publishers to Tolley, for their enthusiastic support of this project, my diligent PA, Ann Geraghty, whose work on the manuscript was indispensable, and my long-suffering family for their patience as I found just how many changes were required to update the third edition, even though it appeared as recently as 2004. One safe prediction is that equal opportunities law will see continuing significant development for years to come.

Martin Edwards
Mace & Jones
Liverpool and Manchester
martin.edwards@maceandjones.co.uk
www.maceandjones.co.uk

About the Author

Martin Edwards is head of employment law at Mace & Jones Solicitors of Liverpool and Manchester. He was a founder member of the Law Society's standing committee on employment law and he acts for major employers nationwide. He has represented clients before employment tribunals throughout the country as well as before the Employment Appeal Tribunal. In addition to eight non-fiction books and many hundreds of articles, he has published eleven crime novels and a collection of short stories, as well as editing fifteen anthologies of crime fiction. His website is at www.martinedwardsbooks.com.

Contents

Contents

Contents

Contents

Contents

xiii

Contents

Contents

Table of Statutes

Table of Statutes

Table of Statutes

Table of Statutory Instruments

Table of Statutory Instruments

Table of European and other legislation

Table of Cases

Table of Cases

Table of Cases

Table of Cases

Table of Cases

1   Acts of Discrimination

1.1   THE DISCRIMINATION LAWS

The current *Discrimination Laws*, which are the main subject of this book, deal with:

(*a*)   Sex Discrimination, Marriage Discrimination and *Equal Pay*;

(*b*)   *Racial Discrimination*;

(*c*)   *Disability Discrimination*;

(*d*)   *Age Discrimination*;

(*e*)   Discrimination on the basis of *Religion or Belief*;

(*f*)   Discrimination related to *Sexual Orientation*.

The main *Discrimination Laws* defining and applying to each of the above kinds of discrimination are:

(*a*)   The *Sex Discrimination Act 1975* (the *SDA 1975*) and the *Equal Pay Act 1970* (the *EPA 1970*);

(*b*)   The *Race Relations Act 1976* (the *RRA 1976*);

(*c*)   The *Disability Discrimination Act 1995* (the *DDA 1995*);

(*d*)   The *Employment Equality (Age) Regulations 2006 (SI 2006 1031)* (the *AR 2006*);

(*e*)   The *Employment Equality (Religion or Belief) Regulations 2003 (SI 2003 No 1660)* (the *RBR 2003*);

(*f*)   The *Employment Equality (Sexual Orientation) Regulations 2003 (SI 2003 No 1661)* (the *SOR 2003*).

For convenience, in this book, the term *Discrimination Laws* is generally used to refer collectively to the above Acts and Regulations, other than the *EPA 1970*, except where in the context it is also relevant.

The law also gives rights to workers not to be subjected to discrimination by reason of their trade union membership or activities or non-membership. These rights are generally placed under the general heading of employee relations rather than equal opportunities. The legal protection afforded to people for *Whistle-blowing* is also seen as distinct from equal opportunities, but the parallels with the *Discrimination Laws* have been highlighted by the courts.

1.2   DEFINITIONS OF DISCRIMINATION

With one exception, the key provisions in each of the *Discrimination Laws* are those at or near the beginning which define the discrimination with which the particular law is concerned. The one exception is the *EPA 1970*. The *SDA 1975* deals with Sex Discrimination and (in the employment field *Marriage Discrimination*) except that the *EPA 1970* deals with *Equal Pay* issues (and also variations in other contract terms) as between men and women.

The definitions of discrimination contained in each of the other *Discrimination Laws* (except the *DDA 1995*) incorporate definitions of:

1

1.3   Acts of Discrimination

    (*a*)   *Direct Discrimination*;

    (*b*)   *Indirect Discrimination*;

    (*c*)   *Victimisation*.

In each of these *Discrimination Laws,* whenever the verb 'discriminate' is used, that verb applies to any of the above three kinds of discrimination as defined in the particular law.

The *DDA 1995* defines *Disability* and discrimination, but the definitions are on a different model from that used in the other *Discrimination Laws* – see *Disability Discrimination.*

1.3   DEFINITIONS OF HARASSMENT

Each of the *Discrimination Laws* (except the *EPA 1970*) also contains a definition of *Harassment.*

1.4   RIGHTS AND DUTIES

Each of the *Discrimination Laws* (except the *EPA 1970*) makes it unlawful for various categories of individuals and organisations to discriminate against other, specified, categories of person, although the detailed rules are not identical in each case and need, therefore, to be studied with care when a question arises.

Most (but by no means all) complaints about discrimination are by employees or job applicants against *Employers.* The law imposes not a blanket duty not to discriminate but a duty not to discriminate in relation to particular acts (or *Omissions*). For example, under the *RRA 1976* it is unlawful for an employer to discriminate (as defined in the Act) in relation to employment by the employer at an establishment in Great Britain when selecting employees for redundancy or when omitting to offer an employee an opportunity for promotion. The matters in relation to which the employer must not discriminate are, however, so comprehensively defined as to cover probably every act or omission which could be beneficial or detrimental to an employee.

The *RRA 1976, DDA 1995, RBR 2003, SOR 2003,* and *AR 2006* also contain provisions making it unlawful for *Employers* (and others) to harass employees (and others). The categories of persons to whom some or all of the *Discrimination Laws* give rights include not only employees and job applicants, but also:

    (*a*)   *Contract Workers*;

    (*b*)   *Office-holders*;

    (*c*)   *Police* officers;

    (*d*)   partners;

    (*e*)   civil servants;

    (*f*)   a wide variety of other persons seeking or undertaking work or vocational training.

The categories of persons who are under a duty not to discriminate against or harass other, specified, persons include not only *Employers* but also:

    (*a*)   *Trade Unions*;

(*b*)   other *Trade Organisations*;

(*c*)   *Qualifying Bodies*;

(*d*)   persons or organisations providing vocational training;

(*e*)   *Employment Agencies*.

1.5   OMISSIONS

Whenever discrimination is unlawful in relation to a particular act, it is also unlawful in relation to a deliberate *Omission* (as in the above example relating to an opportunity for promotion).

1.6   EMPLOYEES AND AGENTS

Each of the *Discrimination Laws* (except the *EPA 1970*) contains provisions under which *Employers* are normally legally accountable for acts of discrimination by their employees and under which principals are normally legally accountable for acts of discrimination by their *Agents*.

1.7   EXCEPTIONS

Each of the *Discrimination Laws* specifies the exceptional circumstances in which an act of discrimination is lawful – see *Exceptions*.

2   Advertisements

2.1   **GENERAL**

Advertisements play an important part in the recruitment process and there are provisions in the *SDA 1975*, the *RRA 1976* and the *DDA 1995* specifically directed at advertisements, which are broadly defined to include:

(*a*)   a job advertisement in a local, national or specialist newspaper;

(*b*)   a vacancy notice on the factory or office notice board;

(*c*)   job details in a bulletin to staff; and

(*d*)   a vacancy notice at a factory gate or in a shop window.

The detailed rules in the different statutes are not identical and discrimination in advertisements is not specifically addressed in the *RBR 2003*, the *SOR 2003* or the *AR 2006*, although the provisions of those regulations do provide those who suffer discrimination in the recruitment process with a remedy.

The questions of how and where posts should be advertised (as opposed to the content of the advertisement) are considered in relation to *Positive Discrimination* and *Recruitment*.

2.2   **ADVICE ON WORDING OF ADVERTISEMENTS**

Employers need to take great care in the way in which jobs are advertised, whether formally in a newspaper or, for example, in a staff bulletin or on a notice board. The employer must not:

(*a*)   describe the job using a term which has a sexual connotation, unless the advertisement clearly indicates that the post is open to candidates of both sexes;

(*b*)   use any other language which indicates or suggests an intention to discriminate directly;

(*c*)   include requirements or conditions which have an indirectly discriminatory effect under the *SDA 1975*, the *RRA 1976*, the *RBR 2003*, the *SOR 2003* or the *AR 2006* and which cannot be justified;

(*d*)   use language which suggests that a disabled person, or a candidate with a particular disability, would not be appointed; or

(*e*)   use language which suggests that any disabled person who applies will have to take the job as he or she finds it and that no *Reasonable Adjustments* will be made.

3   Advocates and Barristers

The *SDA 1975*, the *RRA 1976*, the *DDA 1995*, the *RBR 2003*, the *SOR 2003* and the *AR 2006* all place duties on barristers and barristers' clerks in England and Wales and on advocates in Scotland. Corresponding rights are given, in England and Wales, to pupils and barristers and to persons seeking a pupillage or tenancy; and in Scotland to pupils and persons seeking a pupillage.

For example, in England and Wales, it is unlawful for a barrister or barrister's clerk to discriminate against a person:

(*a*)   in the arrangements which are made for the purpose of determining to whom a pupillage or tenancy should be offered;

(*b*)   in respect of any terms on which it is offered; or

(*c*)   by refusing or deliberately not offering it to him.

It is also unlawful for a barrister or barrister's clerk to discriminate against an existing pupil or tenant in the set of chambers in question:

(*a*)   in respect of any terms applicable to him as a pupil or tenant;

(*b*)   in the opportunities for training, or gaining experience, which are afforded or denied to him;

(*c*)   in the benefits which are afforded or denied to him; or

(*d*)   by terminating his pupillage, or by subjecting him to any pressure to leave the chambers or other detriment.

4 Age Discrimination

4.1 INTRODUCTION

Until 1 October 2006, there was no general statutory prohibition of age discrimination in employment within England and Wales. However the *Council Directive 2000/78/EC*, known as the *Framework Directive,* requires legislation on age discrimination by 2 December 2006, and this led to the introduction of the *AR 2006*, an overview of which is set out in *Age Regulations.*

4.2 UNFAIR DISMISSAL AND REDUNDANCY

The House of Lords ruled in *Rutherford v Secretary of State for Trade and Industry (No 2) [2006] IRLR 551* that the sections of the *Employment Rights Act 1996* which provided that an employee who has reached 65 did not have the right either to claim unfair dismissal or receive a redundancy payment did not have a disparate impact on men. The rule applied to the same proportion of women over 65 as it applied to men.

By the time this long-running litigious saga had reached a conclusion, however, the *AR 2006* had rendered it largely irrelevant for the future. The *AR 2006* not only adjust the rules in respect of redundancy payment entitlement but also contain detailed rules with regard to the *Duty to Consider* and *Retirement and Dismissal.*

4.3 AGE DISCRIMINATION AND SEX DISCRIMINATION

Different treatment of men and women on the ground of age is unlawful even where the intention is to deal with apparent inconsistencies created by the fact that women are entitled to the state pension at 60, whereas men are entitled to the state pension at 65. *James v Eastleigh Borough Council [1990] IRLR 288,* concerned a local authority's concession for pensioners seeking admission to its swimming pools, which was related to the pensionable age of 60 for women and 65 for men. A man's complaint of sex discrimination was upheld because entitlement to discount was determined by sex.

Provided that there is no direct or indirect discrimination, it is possible for an employer to have a variety of retiring ages for different jobs. In *Bullock v Alice Ottley School [1992] IRLR 564,* the employer operated a retirement age of 60 for administrative and domestic staff and of 65 for maintenance and ground staff. All the latter were male and the vast majority of the administrative and domestic staff were female. A female employee complained of sex discrimination when her employment was terminated at the age of 61. Overturning a decision of the EAT, the Court of Appeal ruled that there was no evidence of discrimination. The reason for the differential in retirement ages was objectively justified on a ground unrelated to sex, i.e. the difficulty in recruiting skilled maintenance workers.

In *Price v Civil Service Commission and the Society of Civil and Public Servants [1977] IRLR 291,* the EAT held that a maximum age limit of 35 for appointment as an executive officer in the Civil Service was, in practice, harder for women to comply with as they were more likely to have interrupted their careers to start or look after a family. The complaint of indirect sex discrimination was successful in that case.

4.4   **AGE DISCRIMINATION AND RACE DISCRIMINATION**

Age discrimination may overlap with unlawful racial discrimination, as in *Perera v Civil Service Commission and another (No 2) [1982] ICR 350*. A 39-year-old VAT officer who came from Sri Lanka wished to become an administrative trainee. However, there was an upper age limit for trainees of 32. At the office where he worked there were 34 white officers, of whom 22 were under the age of 32. There were 13 ethnic minority officers, none of whom were under 32. The EAT ruled that the evidence justified a finding of indirect racial discrimination.

4.5   **CONTRACTUAL BAR ON AGE DISCRIMINATION**

It is possible for an employer to undertake a contractual obligation not to discriminate against an employee on the ground of age. In *Secretary of State for Scotland v Taylor [1997] IRLR 608*, the EAT upheld a finding that the terms of the Scottish Prison Service's equal opportunities policy, which stated that employees would be afforded opportunities on an equal basis 'regardless of gender, race, religion, sexual preference, disability or age', were incorporated into a prison officer's contractual terms of employment. The employer's argument that the policy should be regarded as a 'mission statement' which was not legally binding was rejected.

The Court of Session (*[1999] IRLR 363*), however, subsequently confirmed that the decision compulsorily to retire the prison officer before he reached the age of 60 was not in breach of his contract, notwithstanding the contractual prohibition on age discrimination. Even if the operation of a contract involves factors dependent on age, that does not necessarily signify that there has been a breach of an equal opportunities policy which prohibits age discrimination. The Court of Session pointed out that it would be impossible to deprive a retirement age policy of all age discrimination content, since any retirement policy almost inevitably results in the retiring person being replaced by someone younger. It was only if the discretion to impose retirement before 60 was operated in an inappropriate discriminatory manner that a breach of contract would result. The employers had retained a discretion with regard to retirement which, the Court of Session concluded, could not have been intended by the parties to be fettered by age considerations.

The House of Lords (*[2000] IRLR 502*) rejected a further appeal; the introduction of the equal opportunities policy did not remove the contractual provisions about the minimum retirement age. The conditions for continued service were not discriminatory and there was no indication that the officer had been singled out because of his age.

5   Age Regulations

5.1   **KEY PRINCIPLES**

The *AR 2006*, implementing provisions of the *Framework Directive*, came into force on 1 October 2006. The new regime renders unlawful the following types of discrimination on the ground of age:

(*a*)   direct discrimination;

(*b*)   indirect discrimination;

(*c*)   victimisation;

(*d*)   instructions to discriminate;

(*e*)   harassment.

Justification is relevant both to *Direct Discrimination* and *Indirect Discrimination*.

The *AR 2006* cover:

(*a*)   applicants;

(*b*)   persons in employment (widely defined to include a contract personally to do any work but confined to employment at an establishment in Great Britain);

(*c*)   agency workers;

(*d*)   members of occupational pension schemes (subject to various exceptions);

(*e*)   office-holders (to whom the *Default Retirement Age* does not apply);

(*f*)   the police;

(*g*)   barristers, pupils and tenants;

(*h*)   partners (again, the *Default Retirement Age* does not apply);

(*i*)   members of trade organisations;

(*j*)   qualification bodies;

(*k*)   persons in vocational training;

(*l*)   persons in further and higher education;

(*m*)   civil servants;

(*n*)   certain civilians working for the armed forces (but not members of the armed forces generally – the position is similar to that under the *DDA 1995* but different from that under the *SDA 1975* and the *RRA 1977*).

Regulation 24 provides that it is unlawful to discriminate against or harass a former employee if the discrimination arises out of or is connected with the relevant relationship.

Employment tribunals have general jurisdiction to deal with age discrimination claims and the principles familiar from other areas of discrimination law are again broadly relevant. As regards *Time Limits*, time begins to run when the act complained of is committed, not when the relationship ends.

The campaigning group Heyday challenged the *AR 2006*, arguing that the new regime fails to implement the *Framework Directive* correctly, since people aged 65 or over are given 'second-class status', as they could be retired without explanation. A High Court judge referred the case to the European Court of Justice. As this book went to press, the Advocate General gave an opinion in a comparable Spanish case, *Palacios de la Villa Cortefiel Servicios SA Case C-411 C5*, recommending that the ECJ find no breach of the age strand of the Framework Directive or, alternatively, that setting a retirement age is justified discrimination.

5.2   DIRECT DISCRIMINATION

Regulation 3(1) provides that person A discriminates against person B if, on grounds of B's age, A treats B less favourably than he treats or would treat other persons . . . and A cannot show the treatment . . . to be a proportionate means of achieving a legitimate aim.

Thus direct discrimination on the ground of age is capable of being justified – this is not true of other forms of unlawful direct discrimination.

To establish direct discrimination, B must show *Less Favourable Treatment*. Accordingly, B's case has to be compared with that of another person, where the relevant circumstances in the one case are the same as, or not materially different from, the other. The concept of the comparator is thus, in essentials, that familiar from other areas of discrimination law. But identifying a suitable comparator in an age case may be less straightforward than in other forms of discrimination.

Regulation 3(3)(b) provides that reference to 'age' may include B's 'apparent age'. If, therefore, a job candidate who appears older than he or she really is is rejected for an apparently more youthful person, the rejected candidate may be able to establish a case of direct discrimination.

5.3   INDIRECT DISCRIMINATION

Regulation 3(1)(b) provides that there is indirect discrimination on the ground of age where:

(*a*)   A applies to B a provision, criterion or practice;

(*b*)   that provision, criterion or practice applies equally to others;

(*c*)   it puts persons of B's age group at a particular disadvantage; and

(*d*)   B suffers that disadvantage.

Defining the correct 'pool' for comparison is important. The *AR 2006* introduce the new concept of an 'age group' which is defined in *Regulation 3(3)(a)* as 'a group of persons defined by reference to age, whether by reference to a particular age or a range of ages'.

5.4   VICTIMISATION

Regulation 4 provides that victimisation occurs where:

(*a*)   A treats B less favourably than he treats or would treat someone in the same circumstances;

(*b*)   by reason that B has committed a protected act.

'Protected acts' are: bringing proceedings under or by virtue of the *AR 2006*; giving evidence or information in connection with such proceedings; doing anything under or by reference to the *AR 2006*; and alleging that anyone has committed an act which would contravene the *AR 2006*.

5.5   **INSTRUCTIONS TO DISCRIMINATE**

Regulation 5 makes it unlawful for A to:

(a)   treat B less favourably than he treats or would treat someone in the same circumstances;

(b)   by reason that B has either:

    (i)   not carried out (wholly or in part) an instruction to do an act which is unlawful under the *AR 2006*; or

    (ii)   having been given an instruction, has complained to A or anyone else about it.

Regulation 5 does not provide a defence of justification, since if the original act was justified, *regulation 5* would be irrelevant.

5.6   **HARASSMENT**

Regulation 6 defines harassment as occurring where:

(a)   A engages in unwanted conduct;

(b)   that conduct has the purpose or effect of:

    (i)   violating B's dignity; or

    (ii)   creating an intimidating, hostile, degrading, humiliating or offensive environment for B.

Conduct is only to be regarded as having such an effect if, having regard to all the circumstances, including particular B's perception, it should reasonably be considered as having that effect. This proviso does not apply where it is the purpose of the conduct that is being relied upon.

5.7   **LIABILITY OF THE EMPLOYER**

The general principles in discrimination law considered in relation to *Liability for Employees and Agents* are relevant in the context of age discrimination. *Regulation 25(1)* renders an employer liable for any acts of age discrimination committed by his employee in the course of his employment. Similarly, a principal is liable for unlawful discrimination of his agent and the employer's defence of having taken reasonably practicable steps is not available to a principal in respect of an agent's acts.

A person who harasses or discriminates against a fellow employee is treated as aiding his employer to do such an act if the employer would be liable under *Regulation 25*. Principals have a similar liability for their agents.

5.8   **AIDING UNLAWFUL ACTS**

Regulation 26 provides that someone who knowingly helps another to do an act which is unlawful under the *AR 2006* is himself treated as having done such an act.

5.9   **EXCLUSIONS FROM COVERAGE**

The main exclusions from the scope of the *AR 2006* are:

(*a*)   genuine occupational requirement;

(*b*)   statutory authority;

(*c*)   national security;

(*d*)   positive action;

(*e*)   an exemption for employers to permit a maximum age for recruitment (see 5.10 below);

(*f*)   the *Default Retirement Age*;

(*g*)   an exception related to the national minimum wage;

(*h*)   an exception for benefits based upon seniority (see 5.11 below);

(*i*)   an exception for enhanced redundancy payments (see 5.11 below);

(*j*)   an exception for life assurance cover after retirement.

For an employer to be able to rely on a genuine occupational requirement, *Regulation 8* provides that the following conditions must be met:

(*a*)   possessing a characteristic related to age must be a genuine and determining occupational requirement;

(*b*)   it must be proportionate to apply the requirement to the case in question; and

(*c*)   either:

          (i)   the person to whom the requirement is applied does not meet it; or

          (ii)   the employer is not satisfied, and it is reasonable for him not to be satisfied, that the person meets it.

The genuine occupational requirement is not age itself, but rather a 'characteristic related to age'. Accordingly, it would cover the personal appearance of the individual in question.

Where a genuine occupational requirement has been established, an employer is entitled to:

(*a*)   treat the recruitment of job applicants differently on grounds of age;

(*b*)   deal with promotion, training and transfer differently on grounds of age;

(*c*)   rely on the exception when dismissing an employee.

However, the genuine occupational requirement defence is not available where different terms and conditions are offered to employees, or their different terms are offered to prospective employees. It does not apply to victimisation, harassment or unfavourable treatment meted out to those who fail to carry out (or complain about) instructions to discriminate.

Regulation 29 permits certain forms of *Positive Discrimination*. Otherwise, positive discrimination is prohibited in relation to age, as with other areas of discrimination law. The provisions dealing with positive action, like those in respect of *Sexual Orientation* and *Religion or Belief* based upon *Article 7.1* and are wider in scope than the positive action permissible under the *SDA 1975* and the *RRA 1976*.

5.10   **RECRUITMENT AND SELECTION**

Regulation 7(1) provides that it is unlawful for an employer, in relation to employment by him at an establishment in Great Britain, to discriminate against a person:

(a)   in the arrangements he makes for the purpose of determining to whom he should offer employment;

(b)   in the terms in which he offers that person employment; or

(c)   by refusing to offer, or deliberately not offering him employment.

It seems likely that many of the queries that will arise in connection with the *AR 2006* will concern issues of recruitment and selection. The ACAS guide on *Age and the Workplace* (see *Appendix 1*) provides useful guidance on a range of practical issues, e.g. the desirability of removing details of age/date of birth from the main application form and including that information in a diversity monitoring form to be retained by those responsible for human resources/personnel matters in the organisation. The guidance provides a number of useful signposts for employers seeking to comply with the statutory regime.

It is not, however, unlawful for an employer to discriminate in the selection process against a person who:

(a)   is over the employer's normal retirement age if that is over 65;

(b)   is over 65 if the employer has no normal retirement age;

(c)   within six months of the date of his application reaches the employer's normal retirement age, if that is over 65;

(d)   within six months of the date of his application reaches 65 if the employer has no normal retirement age.

This exception is restricted to employees engaged under a contract of service, together with civil servants and the staff of Parliament.

5.11   **TERMS AND CONDITIONS OF EMPLOYMENT, SENIORITY-RELATED BENEFITS AND ENHANCED REDUNDANCY PAY**

Regulation 7(2) provides that it is unlawful for an employer, in relation to a person whom he employs at an establishment in Great Britain to discriminate against that person:

(a)   in the terms of employment which he affords him;

(b)   in the opportunities which he affords him for promotion, a transfer, training or receiving any other benefit;

(c)   by refusing to forward him, or deliberately not affording him any such opportunity.

In relation to the national minimum wage, quite apart from the exception in relation to statutory authority, *Regulation 31* allows an employer to pay:

(a)   employees aged 22 and over more than those under 22, even where they are doing the same job, provided that those under 22 are paid less than the adult rate;

(b)   employees aged between 18 and 21 more than those under 18, even where they are doing the same job, provided that those under 18 are paid less than the adult rate.

The rationale is that employers should be encouraged to take on younger workers and pay them the minimum wage, whilst paying adult workers more, without breaching the bar on age discrimination. Accordingly, an employer may not rely on this exception if he does not base the pay structure upon the national minimum wage band.

A very important exception to the general bar on age discrimination in relation to terms of employment concerns seniority-related benefits. *Regulation 32* provides:

(1) Subject to paragraph (2), nothing in Part 2 or 3 shall render it unlawful for a person ('A'), in relation to the award of any benefit by him, to put a worker ('B') at a disadvantage when compared with another worker ('C'), if and to the extent that the disadvantage suffered by B is because B's length of service is less than that of C.

(2) Where B's length of service exceeds five years, it must reasonably appear to A that the way in which he uses the criterion of length of service, in relation to the award in respect of which B is put at a disadvantage, fulfils a business need of his undertaking (for example, by encouraging the loyalty or motivation, or rewarding the experience, of some or all of his workers).

The rationale for the exception is that, if employers have to justify benefits based on seniority on a case-by-case basis, they might be tempted to 'level down' benefits generally to the disadvantage of various employees.

Where a potential claimant's service exceeds five years, a critical question is whether the criterion of length of service fulfils a business need of the employer's undertaking. If it reasonably appears to the employer that it does, the exception applies and it should be lawful to put the potential claimant (B) at a disadvantage. It is noteworthy that this test is likely to be easier to satisfy than that of *Justification*, since the employer does not need to establish a legitimate aim or that the means of achieving the aim is 'proportionate'.

In calculating length of service for these purposes, there are two alternatives, i.e.:

(*a*) the length of time that workers have been working for the employer doing work at or above a particular level; or

(*b*) the time that they have been working for the employer in total.

Where the employer calculates the length of time on the former basis, the particular level should be assessed in relation to demands made upon the worker. The employer has some discretion in calculating length of service under the detailed rules. However, it is foreseeable that, given the increasing value of worker-related benefits, the exception in respect of seniority-related benefits will soon become the subject of case law interpretation.

The *AR 2006* also seek to avoid penalising employers who offer redundancy payments more generous than the statutory sums. An employer is permitted to make an 'enhanced redundancy payment' to any 'qualifying employee', i.e. who:

(*a*) is entitled to a redundancy payment in accordance with the statutory scheme; or

(*b*) would be entitled to such a payment if he had two years' continuous employment; or

(*c*) was not dismissed (whether after two years' continuous employment or not), but agreed to the termination of his employment in circumstances where, had he been dismissed, the dismissal would have been by reason of redundancy.

5.12   Age Regulations

An enhanced redundancy payment must first be calculated in accordance with the statutory formula, currently set out in *section 162* of the *Employment Rights Act 1996* (*ERA 1996*). Once that calculation has been made, the employer may:

(*a*)   pay the amount in question to any qualifying employee; or

(*b*)   enhance the resulting amount by multiplying it by a figure in excess of one; or

(*c*)   raise or remove the maximum amount for a week's pay as set out in *section 227* of the *ERA 1996*; or

(*d*)   do a combination of the above.

An enhanced redundancy payment meeting the above criteria need not be objectively justified.

5.12   **PENSION SCHEMES**

The *AR 2006* apply to employers' pension arrangements with effect from 1 December 2006. Benefits accrued before 1 December 2006 are exempt. The final version of the Regulations was issued shortly before 1 December 2006, but no extension was granted of the time period for pension arrangements to comply.

The rules are detailed, but briefly, with effect from 1 December 2006:

(*a*)   it is unlawful for trustees or managers of occupational pension schemes to discriminate against members or prospective members of a scheme on the basis of age where members are in the same circumstances or their circumstances are not materially different;

(*b*)   it is unlawful for employers to discriminate (in relation to provision of pensions via an occupational pension scheme or making contributions to a personal pension scheme) on the basis of age;

(*c*)   discrimination (direct or indirect) will only be lawful if one of the specific exemptions applies or if it can be objectively justified;

(*d*)   trustees or managers of occupational pension schemes will be obliged to disapply any discriminatory rules under their scheme and are also given power to amend any scheme rules which allow unlawful discrimination;

(*e*)   workers who suffer unlawful discrimination on grounds of age in relation to pensions can bring a claim to an employment tribunal, or before the Pensions Ombudsman, against the trustees/managers and/or the employer.

6   Agreements

The *Discrimination Laws* each contain provisions to make certain contractual terms void or unenforceable if they are in furtherance of or provide for unlawful discrimination or purport to take away a person's rights under any of these laws.

The only exceptions to the rule against contracting out are the normal exceptions relating to *Conciliation* and compromise agreements. Where there is a particular complaint the parties may settle that complaint and exclude the jurisdiction of the employment tribunal, so long as the prescribed conditions for compromise agreements are satisfied, including the requirement for the complainant to have independent advice.

Where a binding agreement is reached, questions sometimes arise if the respondent wishes to keep the terms of the agreement confidential – a so-called 'gagging clause'. Whether such a clause is appropriate – or, in practice, even enforceable – will need careful consideration in each case.

The *SDA Discrimination Laws* also make provision for a party to a contract to apply to a county court (or sheriff court in Scotland) for an order removing or modifying a term of a contract, where that term, for example, provides for unlawful discrimination against the party making the application. The case of *Meade-Hill v British Council [1995] IRLR 478*, referred to under *Mobility*, was an example of such an application.

Further, the *Discrimination Laws* provide that an application may be made to remove or modify a term contained in a collective agreement, works rules or the rules of *Trade Organisations* and *Qualifying Bodies*. These applications are made to an employment tribunal.

A point of general significance emerges from the decision of the EAT in *Clarke v Redcar & Cleveland Borough Council [2006] IRLR 324*. The two main ways of achieving a binding settlement of a statutory employment protection claim are either by way of an ACAS COT3 agreement or by way of a compromise agreement. The statutory requirements that need to be met in order for a compromise agreement to be valid are detailed and technical. The question for the EAT in this case was whether an ACAS conciliation officer preparing a settlement agreement on form COT3 is under any duty to advise on the merits of a claim before the employee entered into a binding agreement. The EAT held that the officer is under no such duty. Indeed, the ACAS officer must never advise as to the merits of a case. It would be quite wrong to say that an ACAS officer is obliged to go through the framework of the legislation – this might defeat the officer's very function. ACAS officers perform a very useful function, but there is no substitute for expert professional advice on the particular case (and it is fair to add that, equally, study of a textbook is no substitute for such advice either).

15

7   Aircraft and Hovercraft

Employment on an aircraft or hovercraft is covered for the purposes of the *Discrimination Laws* (except for the *RRA 1976*), unless the work is done wholly outside Great Britain (i.e. in the case of aircraft, on flights which do not depart from or return to British airfields and do not cross British airspace) if the following conditions are satisfied:

(*a*)   The aircraft or hovercraft is registered in the United Kingdom.

(*b*)   The principal place of business or ordinary residence of the operator is in Great Britain.

There is no specific reference to aircraft and hovercraft in the relevant section (*s 8*) of the *RRA 1976*. This presumably means that, wherever the aircraft or hovercraft is registered, and wherever the operator is mainly based, the Act applies as long as:

(*a*)   The work is not done wholly outside Great Britain.

(*b*)   There is an establishment in Great Britain from which the work is done or with which it has the closest connection, such as the base from which the employee flies or the office to which he or she reports.

There are circumstances in which the work need not be done wholly outside Great Britain – see *Territorial Extent*.

8   Alternative Dispute Resolution

8.1   **THE EMPLOYMENT CONTEXT**

An employment dispute with a legal element can be resolved in various ways. The traditional formal method of resolving a dispute concerning an alleged wrongful dismissal, for instance, was by way of litigation in the civil courts. The judicial system provides established court procedures, rules of evidence, and the application of substantive law and precedents. With the emergence of statutory employment rights, came alternative possibilities, intended to be more appropriate to the modern employment context. In particular, the Advisory, Conciliation and Arbitration Service (ACAS) was established in 1975. ACAS exists to improve industrial relations and employment practice, as well as to minimise conflict. Although financed by Government, it is independent in the sense that its operations are not directed by Government. ACAS prizes its unique and impartial role and, although its functions are regulated by statute, it prefers to operate by using voluntary methods.

In recent years, pressure for fresh options has grown. There has been increasing concern that tribunals have departed from their original aims of providing a readily accessible and cost-effective means of redress with the minimum of formality and delay. The caseloads of tribunals have risen dramatically, reflecting the tribunal's extending jurisdiction and a growing propensity to litigate in defence of employment rights. At the same time, developing case law, both at home and in Europe, has added to the complexity of cases coming before tribunals. The result has been perceived as increasing 'legalism' in tribunal proceedings.

Meanwhile, general awareness has arisen of the potential value of different forms of alternative dispute resolution (ADR). The Gibbons Review into the dispute resolution process, which reported in March 2007, highlighted the potential value of ADR, but stopped short of recommending that ADR be made compulsory. At the time of writing, the Department of Trade and Industry was consulting on the Gibbons recommendations. Mediation, in particular, is likely to become ever more important as a means of addressing disputes in respect of equal opportunities issues.

8.2   **CHOICE OF PROCESS**

Litigation through the courts (or, where appropriate, binding arbitration) may be preferable or even essential in certain cases. For example:

(*a*)   ADR cannot be used unless all the parties so agree;

(*b*)   where an issue of fundamental principle is involved which necessitates a binding and public precedent, for example a civil rights issue, litigation is appropriate;

(*c*)   sometimes, a substantial and serious power imbalance between the parties may be a contra-indication to ADR;

(*d*)   if a case turns solely on legal issues which need to be decided, or if credibility plays a pivotal role, litigation may be indicated; and

(*e*)   in cases where the immediate enforcement of a court order is essential, litigation is appropriate.

Conversely, ADR may be indicated in some or all of the following circumstances:

(*a*)   where the parties have a continuing employment relationship;

(*b*)   where the issues in dispute arise from a breakdown in communications or differences of respective perceptions of fairness;

(*c*)   where the outcome could possibly be enhanced by a creative business-like solution between the parties;

(*d*)   where the standards and criteria to be applied to the dispute are unclear and elements of judgement, discretion and perhaps even personal preferences are required;

(*e*)   where confidentiality is required; and

(*f*)   where, as is often the case, possible escalation of costs is a matter of concern.

The most economical way of resolving a dispute is likely to be negotiation, but negotiations may fail for reasons such as:

(*a*)   personal antagonism between the parties;

(*b*)   distrust of the other party;

(*c*)   poor communications;

(*d*)   unrealistic expectations; or

(*e*)   tactical naiveté.

8.3   **MEDIATION**

Mediation is a non-adjudicatory process, in which the parties engage a neutral mediator to help them to resolve a dispute themselves. The mediator is a facilitator who has no authority to make any decision binding on the parties. The broad objectives of mediation are:

(*a*)   to allow the parties to be directly involved in the dispute resolution process;

(*b*)   to avoid the risks and costs of litigation;

(*c*)   to provide a private forum for testing the strengths and weaknesses of the parties' cases, with input from a neutral expert who may help to bring a sense of realism into the matter; and

(*d*)   to enhance rather than damage the possibility of the continuing employment relationship.

Mediation may be particularly valuable in cases of alleged harassment and bullying or other forms of discrimination. It is a flexible tool which can be used when formal legal proceedings have not been issued. In the United States, many employers require employees, in their contracts, to engage in mediation, especially in relation to disputes arising from relationships at work (see *Relationships at Work*) prior to issuing court proceedings. This is not, however, appropriate in England, Wales and Scotland because of the statutory bar on contracting out of statutory employment protection rights.

If the parties decide to mediate, they will need to appoint an appropriately trained mediator. The form taken by mediation is highly variable. Typically, parties deliver their statement of events and relevant documents to the mediator and to each other. Confidential matters are sometimes submitted to the mediator by way of a private side letter. Often, the mediator will introduce the process and, after opening statements are presented by the parties, the mediator will meet privately with each party.

Those discussions should be frank and confidential. The mediator will seek to identify the key issues and the true interests of the parties. Bargaining will follow, with the mediator acting as a channel of communication between the parties. The individual personality, style and approach of the mediator often shapes the course of the process. The aim is to secure a solution agreed by the parties which will then become binding upon them.

At the time of writing, the employment tribunals were piloting a judicial mediation scheme for certain types of discrimination cases in certain employment tribunal regions. The tribunal will decide whether an offer of judicial mediation should be made in any particular case. To proceed, the offer must be accepted by all parties. Mediation is entirely confidential. Mediations are normally scheduled to take no more than two days and the possibility of mediation may be raised by a tribunal chairman at a case management discussion. If mediation takes place, then the chairman of the mediation will play no further part in the case if it proceeds to a hearing before the tribunal.

9   Amendments

It is possible under the Rules of Procedure for amendments to be made to both claims and responses in tribunal proceedings, in various circumstances. The need to amend a claim might arise (for instance) if only the employer has been named as respondent in a harassment case and the claimant wishes to add the name of the employee responsible for the harassment to the claim.

Leave to amend is not, however, always readily given. It is extremely important in practice to devote care and attention to the drafting of a claim or a response so as to minimise the likelihood of leave to amend later needing to be sought.

Guidance on the principles to be adopted in considering applications for leave to amend was given in the cases of *Cocking v Sandhurst (Stationers) Ltd [1974] ICR 650* and *Selkent Bus Co Ltd v Moore [1996] ICR 836*. A key issue, when a tribunal is considering an application for leave to amend, is that of injustice or hardship. Would the injustice or hardship caused to the applicant if leave were to be refused exceed that caused to the respondent if leave were to be granted? Where the application is one for leave to add a new party, the question of injustice or hardship to that party must also be considered.

10   Appeals

Complaints of employment discrimination made pursuant to the *Discrimination Laws* are heard by employment tribunals.

The tribunal's findings of fact are final (except in the extreme case where a decision can properly be said to be perverse), but there is an appeal on a point of law to the Employment Appeal Tribunal (the EAT).

There is a time limit of 42 days for appeal to the EAT. This time runs from the date on which the decision of the tribunal is sent to the parties (not the date when it is actually received).

An unsuccessful party (whether the complainant or the respondent) who wishes to appeal to the EAT does not need leave, or consent, to do so. There is, however, a sifting process, under which the EAT holds a preliminary hearing in most cases at which only the appellant is present or represented. The purpose of this preliminary hearing is to identify arguable appeals and weed out the unarguable cases.

Any appeal from the decision of the EAT goes to the Court of Appeal (or Court of Session in Scotland), but there is no automatic right of appeal. The leave of the EAT or the Court of Appeal (or Court of Session) is required.

The final court of appeal is the House of Lords, but, again, leave to appeal is required. Leave is given in only a small number of cases.

There is no right of appeal at any stage to the European Court of Justice (the ECJ), but an employment tribunal or (more commonly) the EAT, the Court of Appeal, the Court of Session or the House of Lords may refer to the ECJ a question or questions on the interpretation and application of *European Law* (or Community law).

11   Appraisals

Regular (usually annual) appraisals form an important part of the employment arrangements in many organisations; see also *Assessments*.

Often they are carried out by comparatively junior employees who have received no adequate guidance or training. Giving untrained employees responsibility for carrying out appraisals can lead to complaints of direct discrimination, because of the risk that appraisals will be subjective and inconsistent. Clearly an employee who receives a poor appraisal will be able to complain that he or she has been subjected to a detriment or denied access to a benefit or facility, because appraisals can play an important part in career development and can also be taken into account in decisions relating to:

(*a*)   pay increases;

(*b*)   promotion; and

(*c*)   selection for redundancy.

Ideally, employers should limit responsibility for appraisals to those managers who have received guidance and training on how to carry out appraisals objectively and consistently. As a minimum, guidance should be given to all appraisers and appraisals should be subject to spot checks to identify those who are not competent to carry them out.

Where the performance of job duties is adversely affected by a disability, consideration should be given to a *Reasonable Adjustment* both of the appraisal and of the job duties themselves.

12   Aptitude Tests

Where work requires a particular skill or aptitude, there is no objection in principle to the use of tests to measure a job applicant's or employee's aptitude for the work. If the test is properly designed and carried out, that would usually be an objective and non-discriminatory way of selecting for the post.

Care should be taken, however, and if necessary specialist advice should be obtained, to ensure that the test does not incorporate requirements or conditions which would tend to disqualify candidates of either sex or of any particular *Racial Group*. For example, if candidates taking a test are required to read written instructions, this requirement could exclude candidates from particular racial groups (such as candidates from other European Union or Eastern European countries) for whom English is not their first language.

Employers must also be alert to the need to carry out *Reasonable Adjustments* in order to modify any test which places a disabled candidate at a disadvantage. Depending on the kind of test and the nature of the disability, the adjustments required could include:

(*a*)   modifying the test itself;

(*b*)   allowing the candidate more time;

(*c*)   providing special equipment; or

(*d*)   permitting assistance with certain aspects of the test.

13   Armed Forces

Members of the armed forces are in the service of the Crown. They are not conventional employees.

Legislation may nevertheless provide for members of the armed forces to be treated as employees and to be given the right to present complaints of discrimination and equal pay claims. However, not all the rules in the various *Discrimination Laws* are identical and, in particular, the *DDA 1995* and the *AR 2006* exclude from their coverage members of the armed forces.

14   Assessments

The way in which workers are assessed is a key concern of the discrimination laws, particularly – but by no means only – the assessment of job applicants and candidates for promotion. Many employers give (and all should give) training to interviewers and others concerned in the selection process or in performance appraisals, to help them to avoid discriminating unlawfully or giving the impression of so doing.

Many employers overlook, however, the need to instruct and train managers in carrying out assessments for other purposes. A particularly important issue is that of redundancy selection. Increasingly, employers have moved away from exclusive reliance on length of service and other objective criteria and instead place the greatest weight on subjective criteria such as capability and motivation.

The use of these subjective criteria increases the risk of unfair selection and hence of unfair dismissal claims. It also increases the risk of direct sex or racial discrimination or disability discrimination.

Employers should give careful consideration to the arrangements for assessments, including *Appraisals*, to be carried out. The following are key elements:

(*a*)   Assessments should be carried out by more than one person, to minimise the risk of favouritism or prejudice.

(*b*)   Alternatively, all assessments should be checked by a senior person who has some knowledge of the employees being assessed.

(*c*)   Consultation with the employees must take place as part of the assessment process.

(*d*)   Guidance and training should be given to the assessors.

The training for assessors should include at least the need:

(*a*)   for consistency;

(*b*)   for impartiality;

(*c*)   to rely on verifiable facts and not on instinct;

(*d*)   to carry out assessments which can be explained and defended; and

(*e*)   to give special consideration to and take advice on the assessment of disabled employees.

15   Assistance

A claimant or prospective claimant can apply for assistance to the relevant Commission and the assistance granted can include:

(*a*)   advice at any stage;

(*b*)   assistance in settling the claim; or

(*c*)   representation at the hearing.

Claimants or prospective claimants should apply for assistance as soon as possible. There are two reasons:

(*a*)   Advice may be needed at an early stage to set the case off on the right footing and, for example, to make effective use of the *Questionnaire* procedure.

(*b*)   Applications for representation need to be investigated and reported on and considered by a committee, which can all take some considerable time.

There are many cases which the Commissions are unable to assist because of financial constraints. The cases which are most likely to receive assistance are those which raise a question of principle. Where the relevant Commission is unable or unwilling to provide representation, other possible sources include:

(*a*)   any trade union to which the complainant belongs;

(*b*)   a Law Centre, if there is one available;

(*c*)   a CAB; or

(*d*)   the Bar's Free Representation Unit and solicitors' firms.

Legal Aid for representation at tribunal hearings has never been available.

The Commissions do not have the power to assist respondents with representation, although respondents, like any other member of the public, can make enquiries about the legislation and its implications.

16   Associated Employers

It can be relevant to ascertain whether two employers are associated, because in an *Equal Pay* claim the comparator of the opposite sex who is named by the claimant need not have the same employer as the claimant in certain circumstances, including where the two employers are associated, provided that at both establishments *Common Terms and Conditions* are observed. The key concept of *Same Employment* in equal pay cases is far from straightforward, as cases such as *Armstrong v Newcastle upon Tyne NHS Hospital Trust [2006] IRLR 124*, illustrate.

Two corporate employers are associated if:

(a)   one is a company of which the other (directly or indirectly) has control; or

(b)   both are companies of which a third person (directly or indirectly) has control.

In both the above cases, the person having control could be, for example, one or more individuals or another company. If John Smith has control of both X Limited and Y Limited, then they are all three associated employers for the purposes of the *EPA 1970* and it may be possible for a claimant to argue that employees of the associated employers are in the *Same Employment* and are thus legitimate comparators.

17 Assumptions

Acts of direct discrimination frequently occur because employers, managers or interviewers base selection and other decisions on lazy assumptions, without taking the trouble to investigate the true position.

Married women, for example, may be turned down for jobs or promotion because it is assumed, without enquiry, that their childcare and other family responsibilities will prevent them from accepting jobs, promotions or transfers which will involve:

(*a*)   working unsocial hours;

(*b*)   relocating; or

(*c*)   travelling overseas.

If a decision to turn down a woman's application or ignore her claims is based on any such assumption, then that is a clear case of sex and marriage discrimination.

An example of direct discrimination under the *RRA 1976* would be turning down an application from a job applicant with a foreign sounding name on the assumption that he or she would be unable to meet the standards of written or spoken English required for the post.

The danger of basing employment decisions on uninformed assumptions is considerable in relation to disability discrimination. Many employers and managers are ignorant of the wide range of jobs which can be undertaken, with or without *Reasonable Adjustments*, by workers who have most severe disabilities. Where a disabled candidate would meet the required standard to be shortlisted and interviewed if the disability were to be disregarded, then that candidate should always be offered an interview. The questions whether the disability will make it difficult for the candidate to carry out the job, and if so whether a *Reasonable Adjustment* could help the candidate to overcome the difficulties, can then be explored positively and constructively at the interview.

Similarly, inappropriate assumptions often arise in the context of age discrimination. Following the guidance provided by ACAS in 'Age and the Workplace' (*Appendix 1*) will help to minimise the risks.

18   Asylum Seekers and Refugees

A great deal of publicity and controversy attends much of the debate about asylum seekers and refugees. Briefly, for the purposes of the *Geneva Convention* of 1951, a 'refugee' is a person who has fled his or her country of origin due to a 'well-founded fear of persecution'. In effect, an 'asylum seeker' is someone who has applied for recognition of his or her status as a refugee and who is awaiting either an initial decision or the outcome of an appeal against rejection of the application. It would be unwise to underestimate the contribution that refugee workers can make to many organisations and welcoming applications from refugees is often a valuable element of a *Diversity Strategy*. However, it is important for employers to comply with the increasingly strict legal rules with regard to *Immigration Control*.

19   Back Pay

19.1   **CASE LAW**

Equal Pay claims are usually about pay (including not only hourly pay or salary but also, for example, contractual bonus schemes and contractual terms for the payment of commission), although they can also be about other contract terms.

When a claim is about pay, the purpose is normally twofold:

(*a*)   to obtain increased pay for the future; and

(*b*)   to obtain back pay at the higher rate.

Under the *EPA 1970*, the period for which back pay can be awarded was formerly limited to the period starting two years before the application to tribunal was presented.

That limitation was overridden as a result of the decision of the ECJ in *Levez v T H Jenning (Harlow Pools) Ltd [1999] IRLR 36*. It was held by the ECJ that the two-year limitation was contrary to the principle of equal pay under *Article 141* (formerly 119) of the Treaty establishing the European Community. The reason for the decision was that the two-year limitation was not a general one applying to equal pay claims and to other claims, unrelated to equal pay or sex discrimination – it was peculiar to the *EPA 1970*.

When the case of *Levez* came back to the EAT together with another appeal which was heard at the same time, in the case of *Hicking v Basford Group Ltd [1999] IRLR 764*, the EAT had to consider, in the light of the ECJ decision, whether it makes a difference, in claims for back pay going back more than two years, whether the employee has been misled by the employer. Mrs Levez could have been awarded the extra back pay on that narrower ground; Mrs Hicking's claim for the extra back pay could succeed only if the two-year limit were to be struck down altogether.

The EAT allowed both appeals. Equal pay claims were compared with claims for moneys due under a contract, claims for unlawful deduction from wages and claims of unlawful discrimination in terms of employment on grounds of race or disability. It was held that *section 2(5)* of the *EPA 1970* (restricting claims for back pay to a period of two years):

'... represents a unique limitation on compensation which applies only when the applicant is relying upon an equality clause. There are no compensating advantages... *s 2(5)* is a restriction on the right to have a full and effective remedy for breach of *Article 119* and the Equal Pay Directive. It is a breach of the principle of equivalence.'

Accordingly:

'*s 2(5)* is no bar to the recovery of monies held to be due for a period of six years from the date of the commencement of proceedings.'

In the *Pensions* cases, where there has been past discrimination (notably against part-time workers) in relation to access to pension schemes, it has been possible for complainants to go much further back.

19.2   **THE STATUTORY POSITION**

Statutory effect was given to the six-year period by the *Equal Pay Act 1970 (Amendments) Regulations 2003 (SI 2003 No 1656)*. Arrears of remuneration or damages cannot be awarded in respect of any time earlier than the 'arrears date'. In most cases, the arrears date will be the date which is six years before the day on which the complaint to the tribunal is presented. There is, however, special provision for any case which is 'a concealment case' or 'a disability case'.

A concealment case is one in which:

(*a*)   the employer deliberately concealed from the claimant a relevant fact without knowledge of which the claimant could not reasonably have been expected to institute the proceedings; and

(*b*)   the claimant did institute the proceedings within six years of the day on which he discovered that fact (or could with reasonable diligence have discovered it).

A disability case is one in which:

(*a*)   the claimant was under a disability (i.e. a minor or of unsound mind) at the time of the contravention to which the proceedings relate; and

(*b*)   the claimant instituted the proceedings within six years of the date on which he or she ceased to be under a disability.

In a concealment case or a disability case, as defined above, arrears of remuneration or damages can be awarded with effect from the date of the contravention.

20   Bankruptcy

In *Khan v Trident Safeguards Ltd [2004] IRLR 961*, the Court of Appeal ruled that a bankrupt claimant was entitled to pursue an appeal against the finding that he had not been discriminated against, or victimised, on grounds of race. In principle, the claim vests in the trustee in bankruptcy. However, there is a public interest in claims of race discrimination being fully examined. Therefore, a bankrupt should be permitted to limit their claim for relief to a declaration and compensation for injury to feelings only. Similar arguments might be advanced in respect of other strands of discrimination law.

21   Beards

At face value (if the use of that expression can be forgiven), a requirement by an employer that job applicants, or existing employees, should be beardless is both an eccentric requirement and one which has nothing to do with discrimination.

There have, however, been cases about such requirements, not where the employer has prohibited beards for aesthetic reasons, but where there are concerns about hygiene, in chocolate and other food factories.

A requirement to shave off a beard, if employment is to be granted or retained, has a discriminatory effect against at least one ethnic group, the Sikhs. The requirement is not unlawful if it can be justified, but it is important that any employer minded to impose the requirement should in the first instance fully explore alternative methods which would not have a discriminatory effect (such as the use of some kind of protective covering). Unless this has been done, it will be difficult if not impossible to justify the requirement.

In *Mohmed v West Coast Trains Ltd [2006] All ER (D) 224 (Nov)*, an employee challenged a policy that beards be neatly trimmed and smart for all employees under the *RBR 2003*. The EAT ruled that the policy did not discriminate against employees whose religious beliefs require them to have a beard of at least one fist's length.

It is also arguable, at least in theory, that it is direct sex discrimination for an employer to require that job applicants or employees should not have beards. The argument would be that this is a gender-based criterion and the use of it is direct sex discrimination against men, in the same way that pregnancy discrimination is direct discrimination against women. Perhaps this is one of the rare cases where (if there is no question of indirect racial discrimination in relation to the actual complainant) the concept of *de minimis* may be taken out and dusted down. See also *Gender Based Criteria*.

22 Benefits

22.1 THE STATUTORY PROVISIONS

Opportunities for promotion and training are amongst the most important benefits which can be afforded to employees, but employees should also beware of discriminating in relation to any other benefits, facilities or services, whether such benefits are contractual entitlements or discretionary.

Section 6(6) SDA 1975 provides that the Act 'does not apply to benefits consisting of the payment of money when the provision of those benefits is regulated by the woman's contract of employment'. This is intended to prevent an overlap between the *EPA 1970* and the *SDA 1975*. The exclusion is significant since, unlike a sex discrimination claim, an equal pay claim requires an actual (rather than hypothetical) comparator and one who is employed on equal work. The editor of the IRLR has suggested that *section 6(6)* should be repealed and the claims of sex discrimination in pay should be heard under the *SDA 1975*. However, the Court of Session ruled in *Hoyland v ASDA Stores Ltd [2006] IRLR 468* that for *section 6(6)* to apply in a particular situation, the entitlement in question need not be part of the formal contract of employment. If the subject matter is 'regulated' by the contract, it must be brought under the *EPA 1970*.

22.2 SERVICE AND SENIORITY

Benefits and facilities are sometimes linked to length of service or *Seniority*. The complexities of the ECJ's ruling in *Cadman v Health & Safety Executive [2006] IRLR 969*, discussed in the chapter on *Seniority*, illustrate the pitfalls in this area of the law.

22.3 REASONABLE ADJUSTMENTS

There are circumstances in which a disabled employee may be placed at a substantial disadvantage in comparison with employees who are not disabled, because the employee's disability prevents him or her from enjoying a particular benefit or facility. In such circumstances, the employer must consider making reasonable adjustments. The following are possible examples:

(a) An employee is entitled to be provided with a *Company Car*, but a disability prevents the employee from driving.

(b) An employee would normally be provided with private medical insurance, but the employee's disability makes the cost prohibitively expensive.

(c) The employer would pay for the employee to join a golf club, but the employee is unable to play golf, and therefore unable or unwilling to join a club, because of a disability.

In all these examples, one possible adjustment would be for the employer to make payments to the employee, equivalent to the cost which would have been incurred by the employer in providing the benefit. In the first case, consideration should also be given to assistance with alternative transport arrangements, particularly where the disability makes it difficult for the employee either to perform certain duties or to travel between home and work.

22.4   **BENEFITS AND AGE DISCRIMINATION**

The *AR 2006* contain an important exception to the general principle that there should be no age discrimination in relation to terms and conditions of employment. *Regulation 32* provides that in certain circumstances, seniority-related benefits will not be treated as age-discriminatory. The rules are discussed in the chapter on *Age Regulations.*

23   Breastfeeding at Work

There are (at present) no dedicated regulations which protect a woman who continues to breastfeed after returning to work following the birth of a child. The principal protections relate to matters of *Health and Safety at Work*. Thus an employer is obliged to provide a woman who is breastfeeding with suitable rest facilities. An employer must also carry out a risk assessment to ensure that there are no health and safety risks to a woman who has given birth in the last six months or who is breastfeeding. In May 2003, the Government recommended that women should breastfeed for the first six months of a child's life.

Despite the absence of a statutory right to breastfeed at work, a refusal to allow a woman to do so might constitute indirect sex discrimination if the employer cannot justify the refusal. Further, a woman who suffers a detriment or is dismissed as a result of breastfeeding may be able to bring a claim of sex discrimination.

In *Williams v Ministry of Defence (2003) 153 NLJ 1670*, an RAF engineer resigned from her post in the light of her employer's policy that, if she wished to continue breastfeeding beyond her maternity leave period, she would have to take unpaid occupational maternity absence. She had wished to return to work after maternity leave and continue to breastfeed. Her employer told her that if she came back to work, she would have to carry out her usual range of duties and in practice this prevented her from combining work with breastfeeding. An employment tribunal upheld her claim of sex discrimination, taking the view that there was a 'free-standing' protection for breastfeeding mothers at work. On appeal, the engineer accepted that was not correct. The protection afforded to new mothers was limited to the maternity leave period or, thereafter, to matters of health and safety. As she was outside her maternity leave period and the tribunal had not addressed health and safety issues, the issue would need to be reconsidered by another tribunal. She argued, however, that the requirement to undertake her full duties on returning to work had a detrimental impact on women and that she had suffered a detriment herself as she had had to resign. She claimed that the employers could not justify this treatment on objective grounds. The EAT directed that this issue too should be remitted to a different tribunal.

An employer wishing to observe good practice when an employee returns to work but wishes to continue breastfeeding should first consider whether this would involve any risk to the employee or her child's health. The employer should also make reasonable attempts to accommodate her requests. In the light of recommendations of the HSE, this would include providing her with:

(*a*)   adequate and private facilities to express milk and to rest;

(*b*)   time away from her workstation to allow her to express milk; and

(*c*)   refrigeration facilities to allow her to store the milk.

The HSE takes the view that asking her to use toilet facilities would not be sufficient.

In addition, an employer should consider any request for *Flexible Working* made to facilitate the continuation of breastfeeding.

24   Burden of Proof

24.1   BACKGROUND

Few issues of discrimination law have proved as vexed in recent years as that concerning the burden of proof. Proving discrimination is often difficult and this gave rise to the *European Burden of Proof Directive (1997/80/EC)* which was introduced to 'ensure that the measures taken by the Member States to implement the principle of equal treatment are made more effective . . .'

The Directive was extended to apply to the UK in 1998. Subsequently, the concept of 'shifting' the burden of proof in certain circumstances was extended to cover not merely sex discrimination, but also discrimination based on racial or ethnic origin; disability; sexual orientation; religion or belief; and age. The requirements of the Directive have now been incorporated into the appropriate *Discrimination Laws*. The body of case law which has grown up on the subject of the burden of proof prior to the changes now needs to be considered with caution. Fortunately, the Court of Appeal has provided updated guidance.

24.2   COURT OF APPEAL GUIDANCE

In *Igen Ltd v Wong [2005] IRLR 258*, a sex discrimination case, the Court of Appeal emphasised that the statutory amendments to the burden of proof altered the pre-existing position established by the case law relating to *Direct Discrimination*. The amendments require an employment tribunal to go through a two-stage process.

The first stage requires the claimant to prove facts from which the tribunal could conclude in the absence of an adequate explanation that the respondent has committed, or is to be treated as having committed, the unlawful act of discrimination against the complainant. The words 'in the absence of an adequate explanation', followed by 'could', indicate that the tribunal is required to make an assumption at the first stage which may be contrary to reality, the plain purpose being to shift the burden of proof at the second stage so that unless the respondent provides an adequate explanation, the claimant will succeed. It would be inconsistent with that assumption to take account of an adequate explanation by the respondent at the first stage.

The second stage, which only comes into effect if the claimant has proved those facts, requires the respondent to prove that he did not commit or is not to be treated as having committed the unlawful act, if the claim is not to be upheld. If the second stage is reached, and the respondent's explanation is adequate, it will be not merely legitimate but also necessary for the tribunal to conclude that the complaint should be upheld.

The guidance issued by the EAT in *Barton v Investec Henderson Crosthwaite Securities Ltd [2003] IRLR 332* in respect of sex discrimination cases, which had been applied in relation to race and disability discrimination, would be approved in amended form, as set out below.

(1)   Pursuant to *Section 63A* of the *SDA*, it is for the claimant who complains of sex discrimination to prove on the balance of probabilities facts from which the tribunal could conclude, in the absence of an adequate explanation, that the respondent has committed an act of discrimination against the claimant which is unlawful by virtue of Part II or which by virtue of *Section 41* or *Section 42* of the *SDA* is to be treated as having been committed against the claimant. These are referred to below as 'such facts.'

(2)   If the claimant does not prove such facts he or she will fail.

(3)   It is important to bear in mind in deciding whether the claimant has proved such facts that it is unusual to find direct evidence of sex discrimination. Few employers would be prepared to admit such discrimination, even to themselves. In some cases the discrimination will not be an intention but merely based on the assumption that 'he or she would not have fitted in'.

(4)   In deciding whether the claimant has proved such facts, it is important to remember that the outcome at this stage of the analysis by the tribunal will therefore usually depend on what inferences it is proper to draw from the primary facts found by the tribunal.

(5)   It is important to note the word 'could' in *Section 63A(2)*. At this stage the tribunal does not have to reach a definitive determination that such facts would lead it to the conclusion that there was an act of unlawful discrimination. At this stage a tribunal is looking at the primary facts before it to see what inferences of secondary fact could be drawn from them.

(6)   In considering what inference or conclusions can be drawn from the primary facts, the tribunal must assume that there is no adequate explanation of those facts.

(7)   The inferences can include, in appropriate cases, any inferences that it is just and equitable to draw in accordance with *section 74(2)(b)* of the *SDA 1975* from an evasive or equivocal reply to a questionnaire or any other questions that fall within *section 74(2)* of the *SDA 1975*.

(8)   Likewise, the tribunal must decide whether any provision of any relevant code of practice is relevant and if so, take it into account in determining, such facts pursuant to *section 56A(10)* of the *SDA*. This means that inferences may also be drawn from any failure to comply with any relevant code of practice.

(9)   Where the claimant has proved facts from which conclusions could be drawn that the respondent has treated the claimant less favourably on the ground of sex, then the burden of proof moves to the respondent.

(10)   It is then for the respondent to prove that he did not commit, or as the case may be, is not to be treated as having committed, that act.

(11)   To discharge that burden if it is necessary for the respondent to prove, on the balance of probabilities, that the treatment was in no sense whatsoever on the grounds of sex, since 'no discrimination whatsoever' is compatible with the Burden of Proof Directive.

(12)   That requires a tribunal to assess not merely whether the respondent has proved an explanation for the facts from which such inferences can be drawn, but further that it is adequate to discharge the burden of proof on the balance of probabilities that sex was not a ground for the treatment in question.

(13)   Since the facts necessary to prove an explanation would normally be in the possession of the respondent, a tribunal would normally expect cogent evidence to discharge that burden of proof. In particular, the tribunal will need to examine carefully explanations for failure to deal with the questionnaire procedure and/or code of practice.

This guidance is relevant to claims of discrimination on grounds other than sex.

24.3   APPLYING THE GUIDANCE

In *Laing v Manchester City Council and others [2006] IRLR 748*, the EAT gave further guidance on the allocation of proof in the light of the judgment in *Igen Ltd v Wong*. This was a race discrimination case. A claimant, of black West Indian origin, contended that he was subjected to bullying and harassment on racial grounds by a manager. An employment tribunal held that the manager did not act appropriately, but nevertheless took the view that a *prime facie* case of racial discrimination had not been made out. The tribunal took into account evidence from the employers that the manager in question treated all subordinates abruptly.

The EAT upheld the tribunal's decision. The employee's argument, that the evidence that management concerned treated all subordinates in the same was part of the employer's explanation, and thus should have been ignored at the stage of considering whether a *prima facie* case is made out, was rejected. According to the EAT, a tribunal should have regard to all facts at the first stage to see what proper inferences can be drawn. The onus lies on the claimant to show potentially less favourable treatment from which an inference of discrimination could properly be drawn. Typically, this will involve identifying an actual comparator treated differently or, in the absence of such a comparator, a hypothetical one who would have been treated more favourably. This involves a consideration of all material facts, as opposed to any explanation. This interpretation is, in the EAT's judgment, supported by the guidance in *Igen Ltd v Wong*, which focuses on all primary facts before the tribunal. The obligation on the employer to provide an explanation once a *prima facie* case has been established strongly suggests that the employer is expected to provide a reason for the treatment. The employer must explain why he has done what could be considered to be a discriminatory act. It follows that if a manager acts rudely to a black employee, that will not necessarily raise a *prime facie* case if there is evidence that such conduct is manifest to everyone indiscriminately, regardless of race.

The EAT suggested that, in most cases, it would be sensible for a tribunal formally to analyse a case by reference to the two stages. However, it is not necessarily an error of law for a tribunal to fail to adopt the two-stage approach. The focus of the tribunal's analysis must at all times be the question whether or not they can properly and fairly infer discrimination. There are some cases where it might be sensible for a tribunal to go straight to the second stage of considering the subjective reasons which caused the employer to act as he did. The reason for the two-stage approach is that there may be circumstances where it would be to the detriment of the employee if there were a *prime facie* case and no burden was placed on the employer, because that would be imposing a burden on the employee which he cannot fairly be expected to discharge and which, evidentially, should have shifted to the employer. However, where the tribunal has in effect acted at least on the assumption that the burden may have shifted, and has considered the explanation put forward by the employer, there is no prejudice to the employee whatsoever.

As this Handbook was going to press, *Laing* was approved by the Court of Appeal in *Madarassy v Nomura International plc [2007] IRLR 246*, where it was held that the burden of proof under the *SDA 1975* did not shift simply on the claimant establishing the facts of a difference in status and in the treatment of her.

25 'But For' Test

This is an outdated test for identifying cases of *Direct Discrimination*. For example, would the complainant have received the treatment complained of from the respondent:

(*a*)   but for his colour;

(*b*)   but for her national origin;

(*c*)   but for being a woman;

(*d*)   but for being a man; or

(*e*)   but for her marital status?

The test was adopted by the House of Lords in the non-employment case of *James v Eastleigh Borough Council [1990] IRLR 288*. This was the case in which a man complained about having to pay for admission to a local authority swimming pool, while his wife, who was the same age but in receipt of a state pension, was allowed in free.

The use of the 'but for' test may also suggest, perhaps misleadingly, that there is liability in a case where *Less Favourable Treatment* is not in any sense intended – see *Unintentional Discrimination*. In *Chief Constable of West Yorkshire Police v Khan [2001] IRLR 830* the House of Lords found the test to be inappropriate – see *Victimisation*.

26   Capability Dismissals

A reason relating to the capability of the employee is one of the substantial reasons for which an employee may be fairly dismissed under *section 98* of the *Employment Rights Act 1996*. In this context, there may be a lack of capability because of inability to perform the job to a satisfactory standard or because of sickness, leading to an unacceptable level of absence (whether a long-term absence or repeated short-term absences).

It is of course essential that employers dismissing for capability, as for any other reason, should avoid any unlawful discrimination. If a dismissal is discriminatory, then whether or not it is also unfair there will be no limit on the compensation, which can include a figure for injury to feelings.

So far as disabled employees are concerned, see *Disciplining and Dismissing Disabled Employees.*

Many employers include in the contract of employment, a term under which the disciplinary procedure does not apply during the probationary period of employment or for the first year of the employment, so that employees can be dismissed without formality for poor performance before they have acquired unfair dismissal rights. There is, however, no qualifying period for rights under the discrimination legislation and there is an enhanced danger of discrimination whenever an employee is dismissed without formality. In particular:

(*a*)   Employers will live to regret hasty dismissals in cases where performance or attendance has been or could have been adversely affected by a disability.

(*b*)   A consistent approach is essential in order to minimise complaints of direct discrimination.

(*c*)   A dismissal for absences which are wholly or partly pregnancy related is an act of direct sex discrimination and is also an automatically unfair dismissal, there being no qualifying period in such cases.

27   Career Breaks

The availability of career breaks can be an important benefit or facility for employees, particularly those who have childcare responsibilities. Under the best schemes, the employer maintains links with the employee by, for example, sending him or her copies of newsletters and bulletins and inviting the employee to social events and even team meetings.

It must not be forgotten, however, that it is not only women who have childcare and other family responsibilities (such as caring for sick or elderly relatives). It is direct sex discrimination for an employer to refuse or fail to offer a career break to a man in circumstances in which it would be offered to a woman.

28   Case Law

All the Discrimination Laws give rise to difficult questions of interpretation.

Any party or advocate presenting or defending a case needs to select the decided cases on which reliance will be placed in support of legal submissions. The following are some suggested guidelines:

(*a*)   Where there are conflicting appeal decisions, Court of Appeal decisions outrank EAT decisions and they must both bow to House of Lords decisions.

(*b*)   The ECJ has the last word on questions of *European Law* (but sometimes gives the last word more than once in different terms) but it is then necessary to consider how the ECJ ruling is applied when the case comes back to the EAT, the Court of Appeal or the House of Lords.

(*c*)   It is not usually necessary or helpful to cite several authorities in support of the same proposition, especially where one particular appeal decision has become the established authority.

(*d*)   Decisions on the interpretation of one of the discrimination laws are generally recognised as authoritative on corresponding provisions in the other Acts from that contained in the *SDA 1975,* the *RRA 1976,* the *RBR 2003* and the *SOR 2003.*

There is an understandable and sensible tendency to rely, where possible, on a recent appeal decision, particularly where the House of Lords or the Court of Appeal has considered earlier authorities and summarised the state of the law on a particular issue. There are, however, early cases which are still sometimes referred to, such as:

(*a*)   the EAT decision in *Capper Pass Ltd v Lawton [1976] IRLR 366 (Like Work)* and;

(*b*)   the House of Lords decision in *Nassé v Science Research Council [1979] IRLR 465 (Documents).*

There are also many early appeal decisions on which reliance can no longer be placed, even where they have not been expressly overruled in later cases. This may arise, for instance, where an appeal decision reflecting particular attitudes becomes outdated (and is quietly ignored) because of changed social attitudes and employment practices. An example is the EAT decision in *Clymo v London Borough of Wandsworth [1989] IRLR 241 (Job Share).*

29   Case Management

29.1   KEY PRINCIPLE

The *Employment Tribunals (Constitution & Rules of Procedure) Regulations 2004 (SI 2004 No 1861)* made significant changes to the rules regarding the management of tribunal cases. The key principle is that the power to make interim or case management orders is given to a tribunal chairman acting alone and there are increased powers to make orders without the need for a hearing, or even without giving the parties an opportunity to make representations.

29.2   CASE MANAGEMENT DISCUSSIONS

Case management discussions are interim hearings, conducted by a chairman sitting alone. They may deal with procedural issues and questions relating to how the proceedings should be managed. They may be convened by a chairman on his or her own initiative, or as a result of an application by a party to the proceedings, and will be held in private. Examples of specific orders that may be made include:

(*a*)   the manner in which the proceedings are to be conducted, including any time limit to be observed;

(*b*)   the provision of additional information by the parties;

(*c*)   the attendance of a person to give evidence or produce documents or information;

(*d*)   the disclosure and inspection of documents and information;

(*e*)   the extension of time limits;

(*f*)   the provision of written answers to questions put by a tribunal or chairman;

(*g*)   staying proceedings;

(*h*)   ordering that part of the proceedings be dealt with separately;

(*i*)   ordering that different claims be considered together;

(*j*)   ordering that a person who is liable for the remedy should be made a respondent to the proceedings;

(*k*)   dismissing a claim against a respondent who is no longer directly interested in the claim;

(*l*)   postponing or adjourning any hearing;

(*m*)   varying or revoking orders;

(*n*)   giving notice to parties of a pre-hearing review or the hearing;

(*o*)   giving leave to amend claim or response;

(*p*)   the preparation and exchange of witness statements;

(*q*)   use of experts or interpreters;

(*r*)   case management discussions are sometimes conducted by telephone rather than by attendance at the tribunal office.

29.3   **RECONSIDERING CASE MANAGEMENT DECISIONS**

The scope of the power of employment tribunals to reconsider case management decisions was expressed in detail by the EAT in *Hart v English Heritage [2006] IRLR 915*. The EAT noted that, in theory, there is no limit to the number of times such decisions may be reconsidered. In practice, however, it would be very rare for it to be appropriate to vary or amend an order unless there has been some change in circumstances.

30   Charities

The general principle is that persons employed by charities have the same rights as any other employees.

The *SDA 1975*, the *RRA 1976* and the *DDA 1995* each contain, however, an exception to cover the following cases, where:

(*a*)   employment is provided pursuant to the provisions of a charitable instrument; and

(*b*)   there are provisions in that instrument which provide for discrimination in the benefits to be conferred.

A charitable instrument is an enactment or other instrument passed or made for charitable purposes.

31 Childcare

There are some households in which the male partner has an equal or even the main responsibility for childcare. There are also some lone parent households which consist of a father and children.

These cases are, however, a minority. In society as a whole, it is still women who have the main responsibilities for childcare. In some households (and not only lone parent households) it is a responsibility which they undertake without any support at all from a male partner.

The main practical implication, in the employment context, is that many women are able to undertake only part-time work. Childcare responsibilities also make it impossible for some women to comply with requirements to:

(*a*)   work unsociable hours;

(*b*)   attend residential courses in order to receive training; or

(*c*)   go on overnight business trips.

Employers need to be able to justify a requirement of full-time working and these other requirements in order to defeat complaints of *Indirect Discrimination*. Employers must be as flexible as business needs permit in relation to all these matters.

There are various circumstances in which employers can also stumble into acts of *Direct Discrimination* as a result of taking a superficial approach to questions of childcare. For example:

(*a*)   Similarly, where employers provide financial assistance for childcare, or crèches, or *Career Breaks*, male employees with childcare responsibilities must be given the same access as their female colleagues to all these facilities.

(*b*)   In selecting job applicants for employment or employees for promotion or training, employers must not act on assumptions about the childcare and other family responsibilities of women. It would, for example, be a clear case of direct sex discrimination, if an employer were to refuse to appoint a woman to a post involving travel, simply because he assumes, without investigation, that her childcare responsibilities will prevent her from undertaking that travel.

The introduction of the right to request *Flexible Working* has assisted those with childcare commitments and the regime was extended in April 2007 to cover those who care for adults.

32   Chivalry

It would be surprising if the law were to penalise the display of chivalrous attitudes and good manners in dealings between the sexes. If a male manager holds a door open for a junior female employee, or allows her to precede him into the lift, it is likely that an employment tribunal would give short shrift to a complaint by a male employee that he had been denied similar benefits. It is more likely that a complaint would be presented by the female employee herself, objecting to being singled out in either of the above respects, but her complaint could not be expected to succeed either.

The reason why findings of discrimination are implausible in the above examples is that the circumstances are so trivial that neither employee has been subjected to a detriment in any real sense. It is a very different matter, however, if notions of chivalry are allowed to influence employment decisions, for example in appointments to a particular post or in allocation of work. There is almost certain to be unlawful direct discrimination if employers decide these matters on the assumption that women are unsuitable for, or should be protected from, dangerous or unpleasant work (see *Detriment*). Suggestions to the contrary in an early Court of Appeal decision, *Peake v Automotive Products [1978] 1 All ER 106*, should be disregarded.

In that case, a man complained unsuccessfully about a rule under which women were allowed to leave work five minutes early so that they would not be trampled in the rush through the factory gates. It was said to be relevant that the rule had been introduced for reasons of chivalry and the claim failed under the principle that the law does not concern itself with trivial matters. It is most unlikely that any similar case would be decided in the same way, in the light of the guidance given by the Court of Appeal in *Jeremiah v Ministry of Defence [1979] IRLR 436* (see *Detriment*). The question to be considered in any similar case now would be not the reason for the rule, or the degree of triviality, but whether a man subjected to the rule (or indeed one of the women ostensibly benefiting from the rule) would or might reasonably object to the difference in treatment.

33   Civil Partnerships

33.1   INTRODUCTION

Same-sex couples may encounter two forms of discrimination, i.e.:

(*a*)   less favourable treatment by comparison to married couples; and

(*b*)   less favourable treatment by comparison to unmarried opposite-sex couples.

Grant v South-West Trains Ltd [1998] IRLR 188 – see *Contractual Equal Opportunities Policies* – is an example of the latter form of unequal treatment. It seems clear that discrimination against unmarried same-sex couples by comparison to unmarried opposite-sex couples is direct discrimination contrary to the *SOR 2003*.

The Government's solution to discrimination against same-sex couples by comparison to married couples is to be found in the *Civil Partnership Act 2004 (CPA 2004)*. The *CPA 2004* establishes the civil partnership as an institution that runs parallel to marriage. *Section 1* establishes civil partnership as a legal relationship between two people of the same sex. It may be formed in either of two ways. The first is when two people register as civil partners with each other. The second is where the couple register an 'overseas' relationship which is treated as a civil partnership. A civil partnership only ends on death, dissolution or annulment.

33.2   AMENDMENTS TO EMPLOYMENT LAW

The *CPA 2004* amends the *SDA 1975* so as to prohibit direct and indirect discrimination against a person on the ground that he or she is either married or a civil partner. Interesting questions arise as to the choice of comparator in civil partner cases. If, for instance, free health insurance is provided to spouses of employees, but not to civil partners, seemingly the comparison, for the purpose of establishing discrimination, should be between those who are civil partners and those who are not. Yet, of those who are not civil partners, married people receive the insurance benefit, whilst unmarried people do not. It may be that case law will clarify the position.

The comparator issue is more straightforward in relation to the *SOR 2003*. A civil partner treated less favourably than a married partner is able to bring a claim of discrimination on the ground of sexual orientation.

Finally, although much recent employment legislation has been drafted so as to encompass unmarried and same-sex partners, a range of specific statutory amendments have also been made by the *CPA 2004*. The overall result is that civil partners have been placed on a level playing field, in terms of employment rights, with married partners.

34   Civil Service

Civil servants are not employees in the conventional sense, but the provisions of the *Discrimination Laws* are expressly applied to servants of the Crown as if they were in private employment (subject to specific provisions relating to the *Armed Forces* and statutory officers – but see *Office-holders*).

Accordingly, a civil servant may present a complaint under the *EPA 1970* or a complaint of sex discrimination, racial discrimination, disability discrimination, age discrimination or discrimination relating to *Religion or Belief* or *Sexual Orientation*.

Complaints of discrimination may also be made in relation to arrangements for and applications for appointment to the Civil Service. The effect of the provisions in the *RRA 1976* in relation to acts done under *Statutory Authority*, however, is that rules made by a Minister of the Crown may lawfully restrict employment in the service of the Crown (or by some public bodies) on grounds of nationality, descent or residence (but not colour).

35 Claimants

Most claimants (known as 'applicants' until October 2004) who bring claims to tribunal are employees or job applicants. So far as employees are concerned, the wide definition of *Employment* should be noted.

Claims can also be presented by *Contract Workers* and partners or candidates for *Partnerships*.

Workers, whether or not currently in employment, or applying for a specific job, can present claims against:

(*a*)   *Trade Unions*;

(*b*)   *Qualifying Bodies*;

(*c*)   *Employment Agencies*; and

(*d*)   *Training Bodies*.

Employers themselves can be claimants as well as the respondent, for example in claims against:

(*a*)   *Employers Associations*;

(*b*)   *Trade Associations*;

(*c*)   *Professional Bodies*;

(*d*)   *Qualifying Bodies*; and

(*e*)   *Employment Agencies*.

36 Claims to Tribunal

36.1 RULES OF PROCEDURE

A complaint of discrimination (including victimisation) in the employment field or a claim under the *EPA 1970* is instituted by making a claim to an employment tribunal. There are rules of procedure for employment tribunals. The rules cover not only the procedure at the hearing but also all preliminary matters, including the requirements for presenting an application. The rules which apply in England and Wales are the *Employment Tribunals (Constitution and Rules of Procedure) Regulations 2004 (SI 2004 No 1861)*. There are similar rules for Scotland. Detailed consideration of the Rules of Procedure goes beyond the scope of this book.

There are *Time Limits* in all cases and the rules – relatively straightforward in the early years of the tribunals – have become increasingly complicated, especially following the introduction in October 2004 of statutory disciplinary and dismissal procedures, and statutory grievance procedures. The aim of those procedures was to promote the resolution of disputes in-house without recourse to the tribunal, but early experience suggests that the regime is overly bureaucratic. The safe approach is to make sure that a claim or response is submitted well before the expiry of any time limit. The tactical advantages of delay in some cases tend, generally speaking, to be over-estimated. The tactical disadvantage of allowing an opposing party the chance to argue, even if unsuccessfully, that a time limit has been missed is considerable.

A prospective claimant should at all times keep in mind the need to comply with the appropriate time limit. If a claim to tribunal is not presented in time, the right to pursue the complaint could be lost.

36.2 PRELIMINARY MATTERS

So long as the time limit is not overlooked, consideration should be given at the outset to the following preliminary matters:

(*a*)   the possibility of applying for *Assistance* or seeking advice, particularly from the appropriate Commission; and

(*b*)   using the statutory *Questionnaire* procedure.

It is not necessary for the application to tribunal to contain a detailed statement running into many pages. The application should contain sufficient information to make it clear what the complaint is about. All possible heads of claim should be listed, bearing in mind that the same facts or events (such as the termination of the claimant's employment) may give rise to more than one head of complaint, such as unfair dismissal and sex discrimination. In many cases relating to discrimination as between men and women it is unclear whether the complaint falls under the *EPA 1970* or the *SDA 1975*. Both Acts should be referred to. It is better for a claim to have too many labels attached to it than too few.

36.3 NAMING OF RESPONDENT

In most cases there is no difficulty in identifying the person to be named in the claim as the respondent against whom relief is sought. It will usually be the claimant's employer, former employer or prospective employer. The following points should, however, be noted:

(a)   Consideration should be given to the possibility of naming one or more additional respondents, particularly, in a complaint of *Harassment*, the fellow employee(s) responsible for the harassment. The reason is that the employer may be successful in making out the defence that all *Reasonably Practicable Steps* to prevent the discrimination have been taken, leaving the individual harasser(s) as the only person(s) against whom relief may be claimed.

(b)   Where, after a complaint has arisen, there is a change in the identity of the claimant's employer, because of a transfer, the claim should normally be presented against the new employer, not the old employer. In cases of doubt, both the new employer and the old employer should be named as respondents. The position can be clarified later.

37 Codes of Practice

A valuable and important function of the Commission for Racial Equality, the Disability Rights Commission and the Equal Opportunities Commission has been that of issuing guidance to employees and employers on the practical application of equal opportunities law and, in particular, of issuing Codes of Practice. Codes of Practice do not create binding legal obligations, but a tribunal should take their provisions into account where relevant. This function is amongst those that the Commissions mentioned above will transfer to the new Commission for Equality and Human Rights.

The following Codes of Practice are included as Appendices to this Handbook

- Code of Practice for the Elimination of Discrimination on the Grounds of Sex and Marriage and the Promotion of Equality of Opportunity in Employment (Appendix 2).

- Code of Practice on Equal Pay (Appendix 3).

- Code of Practice on Racial Equality in Employment (Appendix 4).

- Code of Practice on the Duty to Promote Racial Equality (Appendix 5).

- Disability Rights Commission Code of Practice: Employment and Occupation (Appendix 6).

- Disability Rights Commission Code of Practice: Trade Organisations and Qualification Bodies (Appendix 7)

38   Collective Bargaining

38.1   EQUAL PAY

The employers in an *Equal Pay* case may claim, as a *Material Factor* defence, that the pay or other contract terms of the complainant and the comparator have been negotiated through different collective bargaining arrangements, particularly where the two jobs are covered by different recognition agreements, involving different unions, and there are different negotiating committees.

This defence may be successful, in a case where there is no considerable difference in the proportions of men and women in the groups of employees to which the complainant and the comparator respectively belong, and where there is no other element of sex discrimination.

The fact of the separate and distinct collective bargaining processes is not sufficient defence, however, in a case where there is a considerable disparity in the relevant percentages of men and women. In the leading case of *Enderby v Frenchay Health Authority and Secretary of State for Health [1993] IRLR 591*, speech therapists, who were almost exclusively women, claimed the same rate of pay as pharmacists and clinical psychologists, who were almost exclusively men. The defence of separate collective bargaining was rejected by the ECJ.

In *Home Office v Bailey [2004] IRLR 921*, the EAT ruled that, in considering whether a disparity of pay which has arisen between two work groups by reason of a history of different arrangements for collective bargaining evidences sex discrimination, a prima facie case will be established if the advantaged group is predominantly male and the disadvantaged group is predominantly female. Where, however, the disadvantaged group is neutral in gender, then the situation may not be fair, but it is not prima facie discriminatory on the grounds of sex. This accords with the decision of the European Court of Justice in *Enderby v Frenchay Health Authority [1995] IRLR 591*, which the EAT preferred to that in *R v Secretary of State for Employment, ex p Seymour-Smith [1999] IRLR 253*. According to the EAT, the approach in the *Seymour-Smith* case would result in turning the Equal Pay Act into a Fair Wages Act. However, the Court of Appeal allowed an appeal, holding that although the EAT was right to hold that no requirement or condition applicable to the comparator grades have been identified, the employment tribunal had not erred in finding, on the statistics of the proportions of women and men in the lower-paid group as a ratio of each other, that there was a prima facie case of pay discrimination against women, so that the employer had to show that there was a genuine material factor which was not the difference of sex and which justified that disparity.

Where there is one group of employees which contains a significant number, even though not a clear majority, of female workers whose work is evaluated as equal to that of another group of employees who are predominantly male and who receive greater pay, an employment tribunal is not precluded by the presence in the disadvantaged group of a significant number of men from holding that the disparity in favour of men requires justification by the employer.

Provided that a tribunal is satisfied as to the validity of the statistics and the appropriateness of their use, it is free to use the statistical approach applied in the *Seymour-Smith* case in order to determine whether there has been prima facie discrimination in a case where there is no condition or requirement but there is a pay disparity between the two occupational groups. There is nothing in the *Enderby* decision that precludes such an approach. *Enderby* did not purport to be defining exhaustively the only circumstances in which a prima facie case of discrimination can be established.

In this case, the Court of Appeal considered that the EAT's attempt to identify a clear and sensible difference between a conditional requirement case and cases where no such condition or requirement is identified was unpersuasive. In each case, the tribunal is concerned to determine whether what on its face is a good gender-neutral practice may be disguising the fact that female employees are being disadvantaged as compared with male employees to an extent that signifies that the disparity is prima facie attributable to a difference of sex. A common approach to the two types of case has the merit of ensuring that the equal pay laws apply consistently to all forms of indirect discrimination.

38.2   DISCRIMINATION

Access to collective bargaining may also be regarded as a benefit or facility for the purposes of the other *Discrimination Laws.*

A complaint could arise, for example, if a predominantly male group of workers is covered by collective bargaining arrangements but there is no recognition agreement in respect of a group of predominantly female workers. There could also be complaints if the groups who are not covered are predominantly ethnic or religious minority employees or contain a significant number of disabled employees.

There could also be a complaint about inequality in the operation of collective bargaining arrangements. In the following example, both the employer and the union could be liable:

(*a*)   a factory has approximately equal numbers of male and female employees, each performing a wide range of duties;

(*b*)   under the collective agreement, there are five elected shop stewards for the men, reflecting the range of duties;

(*c*)   under the same agreement, all the women are lumped together, with one shop steward; and

(*d*)   on the factory negotiating committee, each steward has one vote.

Under arrangements such as this (which are certainly not unknown in practice), the women are placed at a significant disadvantage in negotiations relating to pay, other contract terms and working conditions, wherever their interests are not identical to those of the men.

38.3   AMENDING COLLECTIVE AGREEMENTS

The *Discrimination Laws* contain provisions under which an employee or job applicant may apply to an employment tribunal for an order declaring that a term in a collective agreement is void where:

(*a*)   the inclusion of that term makes the agreement unlawful;

(*b*)   the term is included in furtherance of an unlawful act; or

(*c*)   the term provides for the doing of an unlawful act.

If, for example, a collective agreement provides for unlawful discrimination against women, who are affected employees (and therefore interested in the agreement), one of those women could apply to an employment tribunal for an order to remove or modify the offending term.

39 Colour

There is direct racial discrimination when less favourable treatment is on *Racial Grounds*. Colour is only one of those grounds, but it is perhaps the crudest and most offensive.

Colour is also one of the factors by which a *Racial Group* can be defined for purposes of indirect racial discrimination, but it is more usual for a racial group to be defined by reference to ethnic or national origins.

The definition of direct racial discrimination includes discrimination against white employees and job applicants and such cases do occur (normally as part of misconceived attempts to redress perceived imbalances or achieve targets).

40   Commission for Equality and Human Rights

The Commission for Equality and Human Rights (CEHR) was established by the *Equality Act 2006*. The CEHR will, with effect from October 2007, take over the functions of the Equal Opportunities Commission, the Commission for Racial Equality and the Disability Rights Commission. In addition, it will have responsibility in respect of discrimination on grounds of religion or belief, sexual orientation and age, as well as being responsible for the promotion of human rights.

The CEHR must publish a strategic plan setting out its planned activities, a timetable and its priorities, to be reviewed at least once every three years.

41   Commission for Racial Equality

The Commission for Racial Equality, or CRE, is the statutory body which was set up under the *RRA 1976*.

The CRE has powers and responsibilities relating to the enforcement of the *RRA 1976*. In particular, under the *RRA 1976*, it is only the CRE which can:

(*a*)   carry out *Formal Investigations*;

(*b*)   issue *Non-discrimination Notices*; and

(*c*)   take steps to prevent *Persistent Discrimination*.

It is also only the CRE which can present a complaint to an employment tribunal on the ground that there has been a breach of the provisions of the *RRA 1976* relating to:

(*a*)   *Discriminatory Practices*;

(*b*)   discriminatory *Advertisements*;

(*c*)   *Instructions to Discriminate*; or

(*d*)   *Pressure to Discriminate*.

The CRE also has more general duties:

(*a*)   to work towards the elimination of racial discrimination;

(*b*)   to promote equality of opportunity and good race relations; and

(*c*)   to keep the working of the *RRA 1976* under review and submit proposals to amend it.

One of the important functions of the CRE is to draw up, issue and consult on a *Code of Practice*. The revised Code of Practice on racial equality in employment came into force on 6 April 2006. It is a much more substantial document than the previous Code, which first appeared in 1984. Amongst other matters, it contains useful guidance on training staff in interviewing techniques. The Code is set out in *Appendix 5*.

Another, particularly important, function of the CRE is to give *Assistance* to actual or prospective complainants. There is no power to give assistance to respondents.

The CRE's responsibilities will transfer to the *Commission for Equality and Human Rights* in October 2007.

42   Common Terms and Conditions

The *EPA 1970* states that a claimant and comparator must be in the *Same Employment*. It is not essential, however, for them to be employed at the same establishment, provided that they are employed at different establishments in Great Britain at which common terms and conditions of employment are observed either generally or for employees of the relevant classes.

The test for common terms and conditions is a broad test which is easily satisfied. The leading authority is the House of Lords decision in *Leverton v Clwyd County Council [1989] IRLR 28*. In that case a nursery nurse claimed the same rate of pay as male clerical staff employed by the council at different establishments. The employees at the relevant establishments were covered by the same collective agreement, set out in a document known as the 'purple book'. The nursery nurse worked 32 1/2 hours per week and had 70 days' annual holiday; the male comparators worked 37 hours a week and had 20 days' annual holiday.

It was ruled that the claimant and the comparators were in the *Same Employment*. It was immaterial for this purpose that the comparators worked longer hours than the claimant did and had less holiday. Lord Bridge said:

> 'The concept of common terms and conditions of employment observed generally at different establishments necessarily contemplates terms and conditions applicable to a wide range of employees whose individual terms vary greatly.'

This finding did not mean that the equal pay claim was upheld. The employees in the case were salaried employees. The nursery nurse was claiming the same annual salary as the male clerical workers. Their longer hours and shorter holidays were not relevant to the 'same employment' issue, but they were relevant in terms of explaining the difference in salary. Accordingly, a *Material Factor* defence was upheld.

43   Communal Accommodation

The *SDA 1975* contains (in *section 46*) a general provision, which in certain circumstances authorises sex discrimination in the admission of persons to communal accommodation.

Communal accommodation is defined as residential accommodation:

(*a*)   which includes dormitories or other shared sleeping accommodation which for reasons of privacy or decency should be used only by men (or only by women); or

(*b*)   all or part of which should be used only by men, or only by women, because of the nature of the sanitary facilities serving the accommodation.

Sex discrimination in the admission of persons to communal accommodation is permitted if the accommodation is managed in a way which, given the exigencies of the situation, comes as near as may be to fair and equitable treatment of men and women.

There are three specific questions to be considered:

(*a*)   Is it reasonable to expect the accommodation to be altered or extended?

(*b*)   Is it reasonable to expect that further, alternative accommodation should be provided?

(*c*)   How frequently do men as compared with women demand or need to use the accommodation?

Where this exception applies, there can be discrimination in relation either to:

(*a*)   the use of the accommodation; or

(*b*)   any benefit, facility or service which cannot properly and effectively be provided except for those using communal accommodation.

The general exception relating to communal accommodation applies both in the field of employment and in other areas covered by the *SDA 1975*. Some employers provide free or subsidised accommodation for employees (for example in hostels), but in most such cases there should be a reasonable expectation that suitable accommodation for both sexes can be provided. Another possible case is that of residential training, where the sleeping quarters consist of one dormitory and nothing more.

Where an employer relies on the communal accommodation exception, such arrangements as are reasonably practicable must be made to compensate for the detriment caused by the discrimination. For example, if an employee is refused training because he or she cannot be admitted to the residential accommodation in which the training is to be provided, then the employer must provide the training in some other way if it is reasonably practicable to do so.

44   Company Cars

Many employees are provided by their employers with the use of a company car and sometimes also with free petrol, either:

(a)   to enable them to carry out the travelling which is required for the performance of their duties; or

(b)   as a perk.

In the latter case, the company car and free petrol are benefits in kind which are increasingly under attack from the Inland Revenue.

Sometimes the arrangements are contractual and sometimes they are discretionary. In either case, there must be no discrimination under the *SDA 1975*, the *RRA 1976*, the *DDA 1995*, the *RBR 2003*, the *SOR 2003* or the *AR 2006*. Any complaint relating to sex discrimination in the provision of company cars would normally be brought under the *EPA 1970* if the benefit is contractual and if a *Comparator* in the *Same Employment* can be identified; in other cases the complaint will be brought under the *SDA 1975*. It is good practice to make alternative claims by referring to both Acts.

Where a female employee has a contractual right to a company car before going on *Maternity Leave*, she will be entitled to retain that benefit during her ordinary maternity leave period.

Employers should consider *Reasonable Adjustments* for disabled employees who would normally be provided with a company car but whose disability prevents them from driving.

45   Company Directors

The *Discrimination Laws* do not contain express provision relating to company directors.

An executive director, who carries out work for the company under a contract of employment (written or unwritten) and receives payment for that work would normally fall within the definition of employee and have the same rights as any other employee.

A director who is a non-executive director and whose role is limited to attendance at board meetings would not normally be regarded as an employee. *Employment*, as defined in each of the discrimination laws, requires that there should be a contract (written or unwritten) with the individual concerned, whether a contract of service or apprenticeship or a contract to execute any work or labour personally. The statutory and other responsibilities of a non-executive director arise from his or her status as a director and not necessarily from any contract.

A company could nevertheless incur liability for any unlawful discrimination by a non-executive director if he or she was acting as an agent for the company with the authority (whether express or implied and whether precedent or subsequent) of the company – see *Principals and Agents*.

46   Comparators

Making comparisons is a key feature of discrimination law. The strongest cases of direct discrimination are those where the complainant can point to an individual, whether a fellow employee or another job applicant, who has been treated more favourably than the complainant, apparently for no better reason than his or her gender, marital status, sexual orientation, race or religion.

It is only in equal pay cases, however, that there is an explicit requirement to name a comparator of the opposite sex. As the law currently stands, it is impossible for a woman to complain that she receives or has received too little pay, if her predecessor and (if she has left) her successor were both female and she cannot point to any man in the *Same Employment* who is employed on *Like Work*, work of *Equal Value* or work rated as equivalent to her work.

There is no corresponding requirement in the other discrimination laws to identify a named comparator. A complaint of direct discrimination can be based on a hypothetical comparator. A woman, for example, can complain that she has been treated less favourably than a man has been or *would have been treated* in similar circumstances. It is even possible for a woman to present a complaint of direct sex discrimination when the only person to have been treated more favourably is another woman (the two having the same marital status and there being no question of gender reassignment). The following case would be an example:

The best qualified candidate for a job is a pregnant woman. Because of her pregnancy, she is not appointed. Instead the job goes to the second best qualified candidate, another woman. This would be a clear case of direct sex discrimination. If a man, with the same qualifications as the pregnant woman, had applied for the post, then he would have been appointed. The best qualified candidate has been turned down because of her pregnancy, which is a gender-related criterion.

Guidance on relevant evidence in cases based on the treatment of a hypothetical comparator has been given by the EAT in the case of *Chief Constable of West Yorkshire v Vento [2001] IRLR 124* – see *Evidence of Discrimination.*

It was held by the Court of Appeal in *Balamoody v United Kingdom Central Council for Nursing, Midwifery and Health Visiting [2002] IRLR 288* that it is an error of law, where there is no named comparator or the named comparators are found not to be true comparators, for the tribunal not to go on to consider the possibility of a hypothetical comparator. In this case, a tribunal chairman had dismissed a complaint at the preliminary stage because the named comparators were not true comparators, their circumstances being quite different from those of the applicant. Ward LJ said that 'it was incumbent on the chairman to construct a hypothetical comparator and test the case against that benchmark.'

Where actual comparators are named, it is important for the tribunal to consider carefully the relevant circumstances of both the complainant and the comparators. This need is well illustrated by the leading case of *Shamoon v Chief Constable of the Royal Ulster Constabulary [2003] IRLR 285*. In this case, a chief inspector had the right to carry out appraisals taken away from her. She complained of direct sex discrimination and named as comparators two male chief inspectors in her division who still had the right to carry out appraisals. Her complaint was upheld by the employment tribunal, but it was held on appeal, first by the Northern Ireland Court of Appeal and then by the House of Lords, that the two male chief inspectors were not true comparators. The relevant circumstances were different. The circumstances in which the right to carry out appraisals had been taken away from the applicant were that complaints had been made about her performance in appraising constables and representations had been made by the Police Federation. Accordingly, it was held by the House of Lords, she could have succeeded only if there had been evidence that the treatment which she had received was less favourable than the treatment which would have been received by a hypothetical male comparator whose relevant circumstances were the same as hers, i.e. a male comparator about whom similar complaints had been made.

An equal pay claimant is entitled to name her own comparator. However, the case of *Cheshire and Wirral Partnership NHS Trust v Abbott and others [2006] IRLR 546,* indicates that different considerations apply where the issue is not one of establishing 'like work' or work of equal value, but instead concerns whether there is indirect discrimination in pay arrangements. Here female domestic workers sought to compare themselves with male hospital porters who, unlike them, received an incentive bonus. The Court of Appeal held that, although in a case of indirect sex discrimination pay, it is for the employee to identify a comparator group and to produce statistical evidence to show an appreciable difference in pay for jobs of equal value, the employee is not entitled to identify an artificial or arbitrary group. In principle, the comparison should be between the disadvantaged group and the advantaged group. As a matter of statistics, a more reliable result is likely to be forthcoming if one takes as large a group as possible, so long as that group shares the relevant characteristics and can be seen as doing work of equal value. On the facts, however, an even wider comparator group was still predominantly male, so the claimants had made out a prima facie case of discrimination.

Complaints of disability discrimination, also, may be – but need not be – based on the treatment of a named comparator. Care is needed in identifying an actual comparator or defining a hypothetical comparator, because of the way in which disability discrimination itself is defined. If, for example, an employee is dismissed for an absence which is caused wholly or partly by a disability, the first question to be considered is whether the dismissal would have taken place if the part of the absence caused by the disability had been discounted. It is well established that the appropriate comparator is *not* an employee who has had a similar absence but for reasons unrelated to any disability. Where the absence has been caused wholly by the disability, the proper comparison is with an actual or hypothetical employee who has not been absent at all. If part of the absence is unrelated to the disability, then the comparator is an actual or hypothetical employee who has been off for a period corresponding with that part of the absence.

47 Compensation

47.1 GENERAL PRINCIPLES

Compensation under the *EPA 1970* is considered under *Back Pay*.

The *Discrimination Laws* provide that where a tribunal finds that a complaint of discrimination (or now a complaint of *Harassment*) is well-founded, the tribunal shall make such of the following 'as it considers just and equitable':

(*a*)   an order declaring the rights of the parties;

(*b*)   an order requiring the payment of compensation corresponding to any damages which could have been awarded by a county court or (in Scotland) a sheriff court if that court had had jurisdiction;

(*c*)   a *Recommendation*.

There is no limit on the amount of compensation which can be ordered. The heads under which compensation may be awarded are:

(*a*)   financial losses, up to the date of the hearing, and future financial losses;

(*b*)   injury to feelings;

(*c*)   damages for personal injuries, including psychiatric injury;

(*d*)   aggravated damages or exemplary damages in an appropriate case.

The case law on compensation is important for providing guidance on how the statutory rules are applied in practice, and is examined at some length below.

The *Industrial Tribunals (Interest on Awards in Discrimination Cases) Regulations 1996 (SI 1996 No 2083)* provide that an employment tribunal may award interest (and must consider whether to do so) when making an award under the *Discrimination Laws*. The main rules regarding the calculation of interest are outlined below.

47.2 FINANCIAL LOSSES

The fact that compensation is unlimited does not mean that a figure can simply be plucked from the air. When assessing compensation for actual and prospective loss of earnings, employment tribunals must adopt the usual approach of:

(*a*)   calculating the losses up to the date of the hearing;

(*b*)   deciding on an appropriate and realistic period for future losses;

(*c*)   in relation to both past and future losses, considering whether the applicant has or could have mitigated his or her losses.

In the early 1990s, there were many cases in which women who had been required to leave the armed forces, when they became pregnant, were awarded compensation for loss of earnings on the assumption that, but for their dismissal, they would have enjoyed long and successful careers. The EAT struck a cautionary note in *Ministry of Defence v Cannock [1994] IRLR 509*. Morison J gave guidance which was particularly relevant to pregnancy dismissal cases but which is applicable to any discrimination case where there is a need to address the hypothetical state of affairs which would have existed if the discrimination which has been found by the tribunal (particularly a discriminatory dismissal) had not taken place.

Morison J pointed out that, when calculating future losses, the tribunal should not decide on a balance of probabilities what would have happened but for the discrimination against the complainant. Instead, the tribunal should consider on a percentage basis the possibility that (in the context of the pregnancy dismissal cases) the complainant would have returned to work, remained in the service for a number of years and been promoted. The tribunal needs:

> 'to keep a sense of due proportion when assessing compensation. Because the policy of our law is to treat absence due to pregnancy as an event which does no more than involve a relatively short period of time away from the workplace, a tribunal should not make an award of a size which is more appropriate to compensate a person who has some kind of long-term disability. A woman who has been unlawfully dismissed whilst pregnant is not incapacitated from alternative work or from pursuing an alternative career.'

In the important case of *Vento v Chief Constable of West Yorkshire Police (No 2) [2003] IRLR 102*, Mummery LJ stated that it 'was common ground that the correct approach to compensation for future loss of earnings was that described by Morison J' (in the above-mentioned judgment): 'The question is: what were the chances, if Ms Vento had not been discriminated against and dismissed, of her remaining in the police force until the age of retirement at 55.'

In this case, Ms Vento was dismissed from the police force at the age of 30. Her complaint of sex discrimination was upheld. She had three children. At the time of her dismissal she was separated from her husband. They were subsequently divorced.

The award of compensation to her included £165,829 for loss of future earnings, calculated on the basis that there was a 75% chance that if not dismissed she would have worked in the police force for the rest of her career. This award was challenged on the ground that the adoption of the 75% chance was irrational and unsustainable. The statistical evidence had indicated that only 9% of women police officers had served more than 18 years. Ms Vento had served less than two years as a probationer and had been off sick during part of that period. The EAT concluded that the tribunal had fallen seriously into error and that the compensation should be reassessed by a freshly constituted tribunal.

The Court of Appeal, however, allowed an appeal by Ms Vento and restored the tribunal's figure for financial loss. Mummery LJ said that:

> '[The] employment tribunal was entitled to place considerable weight on the view it had formed of Ms Vento's determination to pursue her career and of the way she had dealt with the problems confronting her in her probationary period, as well as having to cope with the break-up of her marriage and the demands on a single parent with three children. These matters weighed heavily with the tribunal in estimating her chances of achieving a full period of service down to retirement.'

Furthermore (at paragraph 42):

> 'the employment tribunal was entitled to approach the statistics with circumspection. The tribunal had relevant evidence that the future situation in the police force would be different from the social and working conditions prevailing in the decade covered by the statistics. Recent and continuing social changes affecting women in society and in the workplace are reflected in the adjustments now being made to working conditions in the police force. The introduction of 'family friendly policies' is aimed at retaining more women officers in the future.'

Having regard to these factors, the 75% figure, although on the high side, was 'an option reasonably open to the employment tribunal'.

47.2 Compensation

A recent illustration of the application of the *Cannock* principles is *Visa International Service Association v Paul [2004] IRLR 42*. In that case, an employee who was on maternity leave resigned, complaining that she had not been notified of a vacancy which had arisen during her maternity leave. Her complaints of sex discrimination and victimisation were upheld.

The tribunal found that there was an 80% chance that she would have returned to part-time work after her maternity leave and would have remained at work until she started a second period of maternity leave. The tribunal then assessed the period of that further maternity leave. The tribunal then found that there was a 50% chance that she would have returned to work after her second maternity leave and would have remained at work for a further 12 months. It was also necessary to take into account that Mrs Paul would have incurred childcare costs which would have been only partly covered by a contribution from her employers. Compensation was assessed accordingly.

A further illustration, in a different context, is *Abbey National plc v Formoso [1999] IRLR 222*. In that case the applicant was dismissed for misconduct after having indicated that she would be unable to attend a disciplinary hearing because she was pregnant. It was necessary to consider how likely it was, in percentage terms, that she would have been dismissed if a fair disciplinary hearing had been held.

In the case of *O'Donoghue v Redcar and Cleveland Borough Council [2001] IRLR 615*, the employment tribunal took a rather different approach. The applicant's complaints of victimisation and unfair dismissal were upheld, but the tribunal found that, because of her divisive and antagonistic approach to her colleagues, the applicant would inevitably have been dismissed within six months and that such dismissal would have been fair and would not have been an act of victimisation. Compensation was assessed accordingly. The Court of Appeal held that this was an approach which was open to the tribunal in the exceptional circumstances, save that the tribunal were in error in discounting the award for injury to feelings by reason of the notional dismissal within six months.

Where compensation includes future loss of earnings for a lengthy period, a deduction must be made for the accelerated receipt of the money, as lump sum compensation as opposed to the pay which would have been received over the period. This is the converse of the rule that interest is payable in respect of losses up to the date of the hearing.

In the case of *Bentwood Bros (Manchester) Ltd v Shepherd [2003] IRLR 364*, the tribunal upheld a complaint of sex discrimination and unfair dismissal, finding that Mrs Shepherd had been selected for redundancy because she was pregnant. Her basic salary was just over £44,000. The tribunal awarded compensation of nearly £191,000 and interest of just over £7,000. The compensation included the sum of just over £100,000 for two and a half years' future loss of earnings and a sum of nearly £63,000 for ten years' future pension loss. The reason for the difference between the two periods was that the tribunal believed that any future employment which Mrs Shepherd found was unlikely to be pensionable.

In the Court of Appeal, Peter Gibson LJ, whilst expressing surprise at the tribunal's extraordinary finding that Mrs Shepherd (whose age was 35) would never obtain pensionable employment again said that there was some evidence before the tribunal from which they were able properly to reach that conclusion and accordingly he could not go so far as to say that the tribunal's decision on pension loss was perverse.

The tribunal had applied a total deduction of 5% to the figures for future loss of salary and pension. It was held that this was an error of law. Peter Gibson LJ said that what the tribunal had done was 'a wholly incorrect way of applying a conventional investment rate which is reflected in the discount because it fails to recognise that that rate was intended to be an annual rate'. He also indicated that he would not expect the annual rate to be as high as 5%. The appropriate rate would be one 'designed to reflect ... the annual yield that would be obtainable on investment of the sum paid'. Accordingly, it was necessary for the question of the discount for accelerated receipt of the two and a half years' earnings and ten years' pension payments to be remitted to the tribunal, so that the appropriate discount could be assessed having regard to the proper rate and the periods over which the salary and pension payments would have been received.

A further interesting aspect of the remedies in this case (and one which was not criticised by the Court of Appeal, except in relation to one particular aspect, mentioned at 47.6 below) is that the compensation for future losses reflected gross salary, but on the basis that tax and national insurance would be deducted from the compensation. As a general rule, both in discrimination cases and in unfair dismissal cases, compensation for loss of earnings has in the past been based on net pay. In most cases it has been just and equitable that this should be so, because in most cases compensation payments have been below the level (currently £30,000) at which tax on payments on termination of employment generally becomes payable. Where, however, compensation payments are significantly greater than £30,000, as is happening increasingly frequently in discrimination cases and sometimes in unfair dismissal cases, it would not be just and equitable for successful complainants to receive compensation based on net pay if part of that compensation were then to be taxable. In such circumstances, the net amount which they received would not be sufficient to compensate them for their losses. It would seem, therefore, that the approach adopted by the tribunal in the above case has much to commend it.

In *Orthet Ltd v Vince-Cain [2004] IRLR 857,* the EAT held that the tribunal did not err in awarding compensation to the claimant for loss of earnings during a four-year period when she was, or was to be, a university student retraining. Nor did it err in finding that she had not failed to mitigate her loss. It was entitled to find that her decision to change careers was a reasonable step, in circumstances in which the employers were unable to prove that there was suitable work which she could and should have taken and the tribunal found that if such work became available, she would abandon her course.

However, the tribunal was wrong to award a sum in respect of loss of pension rights covering a period of four and a half years on the basis that the employers were about to introduce a pension scheme at the time of her dismissal. The tribunal erred in failing to investigate the nature of any pension scheme that would be available to her in new employment when she had retrained, and the effect that would have on the pension loss which she would have suffered. It also erred in failing to take account of the fact that the payment of compensation to the claimant ought to reflect early receipt.

In the case where the period of loss is likely to be more than two years, the correct method of calculating future pension loss is the 'substantial loss approach' suggested in the guidelines to employment tribunal chairmen on *Compensation for Loss of Pension Right.*

47.3   INJURY TO FEELINGS

There is an express statutory power in the *SDA 1975,* the *RRA 1976,* the *DDA 1995,* the *RBR 2003,* the *SOR 2003* and the *AR 2006* to award compensation for injury to feelings whether or not compensation is awarded under any other head. Such an award is made in nearly all cases where the complaint is upheld.

In *Vento v Chief Constable of West Yorkshire Police (No 2) [2003] IRLR 102,* Mummery LJ, referred to the judgment of Smith J in *Prison Service v Johnson [1997] IRLR 162.* He adopted her summary of the general principles which, on the authorities, apply to compensation for non-pecuniary loss. He said that employment 'tribunals should have it in mind when carrying out this challenging exercise'. This summary was in the following terms:

'(i)   Awards for injury to feelings are compensatory. They should be just to both parties. They should compensate fully without punishing the tortfeasor. Feelings of indignation at the tortfeasor's conduct should not be allowed to inflate the award.

(ii)   Awards should not be too low, as that would diminish respect for the policy of the anti-discrimination legislation. Society has condemned discrimination and awards must ensure that it is seen to be wrong. On the other hand, awards should be restrained, as excessive awards could, to use the phrase of Sir Thomas Bingham MR, be seen as a way to 'untaxed riches.'

(iii)   Awards should bear some broad general similarity to the range of awards in personal injury cases. We do not think that this should be done by reference to any particular type of personal injury award, rather to the whole range of such awards.

(iv)   In exercising their discretion in assessing a sum, tribunals should remind themselves of the value in everyday life of the sum they have in mind. This may be done by reference to purchasing power or by reference to earnings.

(v)   Finally, tribunals should bear in mind Sir Thomas Bingham's reference to the need for public respect for the level of awards made.'

Mummery LJ then said that the three following cases in the EAT provided useful illustrations of the range of awards of compensation for damages for injury to feelings:

(a)   In *Gbaja-Bianila v DHL International (UK) Ltd [2000] ICR 730,* the sum of £3,750 had been awarded for injury to feelings. The EAT dismissed an appeal by the applicant, who contended that the award was too low.

(b)   In *ICTS (UK) Ltd v Tchoula [2000] IRLR 643,* the employment tribunal had awarded £22,000 for injury to feelings and £5,000 for aggravated damages. The EAT considered that the total sum awarded was so excessive as to be an error of law. The sum awarded was reduced to an overall sum of £10,000.

(c)   *HM Prison Service v Salmon [2001] IRLR 425* was a serious case of sex discrimination, in which the applicant complained of humiliating and degrading conduct which was so severe that she had suffered psychiatric harm. She was awarded £20,000 for injury to feelings, including £5,000 aggravated damages, and £11,250 for the psychiatric harm. The EAT held that these awards were not so excessive as to constitute an error of law and that there had been no double counting in respect of the three different heads of the award.

Mummery LJ stated that tribunals and practitioners 'might find it helpful if this court were to identify three broad bands of compensation for injury to feelings, as distinct from compensation for psychiatric or similar personal injury.' The three bands were as follows:

'(i)   The top band should normally be between £15,000 and £25,000. Sums in this range should be awarded in the most serious cases, such as where there has been a lengthy campaign of discriminatory harassment on the ground of sex or race [and presumably also on the ground of disability and, now, on the ground of religion or sexual orientation]. Only in the most exceptional case should an award of compensation for injury to feelings exceed £25,000.

(ii)   The middle band of between £5,000 and £15,000 should be used for serious cases, which do not merit an award in the highest band.

(iii)   Awards of between £500 and £5,000 are appropriate for less serious cases, such as where the act of discrimination is an isolated or one-off occurrence. In general, awards of less than £500 are to be avoided altogether, as they risk being regarded as so low as not to be a proper recognition of injury to feelings.'

Mummery LJ also said that common sense:

'requires that regard should also be had to the overall magnitude of the sum total of the award of compensation for non-pecuniary loss made under the various headings of injury to feelings, psychiatric damage and aggravated damage. In particular, double recovery should be avoided by taking appropriate account of the overlap between the individual heads of damage. The extent of overlap will depend on the facts of each particular case.'

In the *Vento* case itself, the sum awarded for injury to feelings, which had been assessed by the tribunal at £65,000, including £15,000 aggravated damages, was reduced to £18,000 for injury to feelings and a further £5,000 for aggravated damages.

In the *Orthet* case, the EAT upheld an award of compensation for injury to feelings for sex discrimination made without regard to the tax implications of the award, and without grossing-up the award. According to the EAT, there is no authority which holds that tax is payable on an award for injury to feelings.

In *Scott v Commissioners of Inland Revenue [2004] IRLR 713,* a male employee was accused by a female colleague of sexual harassment. He contended that the complaint was vindictive and the employer refused to investigate it objectively. He alleged that they ignored his denials and that the accusation was found proven on evidence which could not possibly justify it. He was disciplined and transferred. The employer then settled a claim brought against it by the female colleague, and publicised this fact amongst its staff, even though the male accused of harassment was going through an internal appeal process. He suffered increasing distress and clinical depression. The employers then decided to retire him on medical grounds and he was dismissed. A tribunal found that he had been unfairly and wrongfully dismissed, discriminated against on the ground of both sex and disability, and had been victimised. The tribunal said of the accusations against him:

'Without detailed explanation and elaboration and investigation we cannot for a moment believe that any reasonable person viewing matters objectively could or would view the allegations as serious. Some may have been worthy of censure; many were trivial in the extreme and relied almost totally on [the female colleague's] perception. Either those involved in giving equal opportunities advice to the Revenue were motivated by misplaced zeal or were keen to create as much discomfort for Mr Scott as they could.'

71

47.4   Compensation

The tribunal concluded that a woman accused of sexual harassment would not have been treated like this and he was awarded compensation of just below £100,000.

The Court of Appeal ruled that the tribunal did not err in making separate awards of injury to feelings for unlawful discrimination and aggravated damages. Aggravated damages are intended to deal with cases where the injury was inflicted by conduct which was high-handed, malicious, insulting or oppressive. Aggravated damages, therefore, should not be aggregated with and treated as part of the damages for injury to feelings. Nevertheless, in the present case, although a markedly higher award for injury to feelings would have been unappealable, the award of £15,000 was not untenably low.

However, the employment tribunal erred in awarding only £15,000 for the psychiatric harm done to the claimant on the basis that there was a good chance that the majority of his symptoms of depression would disappear within twelve months. This premise did not accurately represent what the expert witness had said. The Judicial Studies Board guidelines place 'moderately severe' psychiatric damage in a bracket between £10,000 and £28,000). The case was remitted for the tribunal to reappraise the award for psychiatric damage at a higher figure.

The Court of Appeal observed:

'Sexual harassment is a serious matter in the workplace and needs always to be addressed where there is a complaint about it, but it does not have to become the subject of a state trial at the time it arises. Incidents trivial in themselves can acquire a measure of seriousness, or perceived seriousness, if they appear to be recurrent. That is one reason why they should not be considered in isolate. The complaint against the applicant in the present case was one which it would have been wrong for management to trivialise or to ignore. Nevertheless, it was the type of complaint which, if sensitively addressed, can be straightforwardly resolved. It is quite common to find that the man about whom the complaint is made does not appreciate that his habits or mannerisms are making a female colleague embarrassed or uncomfortable, and that once it is explained to him he will take care not to let it happen again. It is also not uncommon to find that the man is aware of the effect his behaviour is having but thinks it acceptable. Frequently, nonetheless, a careful explanation coupled with a warning is enough.

To the extent that the employment tribunal in the present case chose to amplify their critique of the way the employers handled the inquiry by pouring scorn on the complaint of harassment, the court strongly disagreed with them. This is exactly the kind of situation which, if management ignores or trivialises it, can make the workplace a source of tension and unhappiness and escalate into formal disputes. The problem was that, the disciplinary wheels having been sent prematurely and unnecessarily in motion against the applicant, nobody seemed willing or able to halt them.'

47.4   PERSONAL INJURY

Where the discrimination complained of has caused the applicant to suffer personal injury (whether physical, mental or psychiatric), that injury should be pleaded and compensation should be claimed.

In *Sheriff v Klyne Tugs (Lowestoft) Limited [1999] IRLR 481,* the Court of Appeal considered the question of damages for personal injury arising from racial discrimination. Mr Sheriff had brought a claim of racial harassment which had been settled with no admission of liability. He subsequently brought a claim in the county court for damages for personal injury, alleging the abusive and detrimental treatment which he had complained of in the racial discrimination case. His action was struck out as an abuse of process and he appealed.

The appeal was dismissed by the Court of Appeal on two grounds. The first ground, which is one of considerable general importance, was that the employment tribunal had 'jurisdiction to award damages for the tort of racial discrimination, including damages for personal injury caused by the tort'. It followed that his present claim fell within the terms of the earlier settlement. The principle, that damages can be awarded for personal injuries caused by the discrimination, will presumably apply also to all complaints of unlawful discrimination.

The second ground of the Court of Appeal's decision was that it is contrary to a well-established public policy principle for claims that have been or could have been litigated in one tribunal to be allowed to be litigated in another. The same factual issues lay at the heart of both the earlier employment tribunal proceedings and the later county court action and Mr Sheriff 'could have brought forward his whole claim for compensation in the tribunal'.

In *Vento*, the case referred to above, the sum of £9,000 was awarded for psychiatric injury and that part of the award was upheld by the Court of Appeal.

In *Essa v Laing Ltd [2003] IRLR 346*, the complainant was Welsh and black. At the relevant time he was a successful amateur boxer, supporting himself by working as a labourer and construction worker. He later became a professional boxer. A foreman made a racist remark, in front of a gang of 15 men, and this caused immense distress to Mr Essa. He complained to the respondent, but felt that his complaint was not taken seriously. Thereafter, he was taunted by other employees. He left and presented a complaint of discrimination.

His complaint was upheld. His case was that the racist remark which had been made had so upset him that it had affected his health. He had been treated for depression and his boxing had been affected. The tribunal awarded compensation of £5,000 for injury to feelings. They refused to award compensation for psychiatric injury because that injury was not foreseeable.

The EAT allowed an appeal by Mr Essa. It was held that compensation is payable for harm which is 'caused directly', whether or not the harm is also 'reasonably foreseeable'. Judge Serota QC said:

> 'We are of the opinion that psychological injury was a type of harm the statute was intended to protect against. Indeed in cases of discrimination on the grounds of race psychological harm is a far more likely consequence than any other form of physical injury.'

The decision of the EAT was upheld on appeal by the Court of Appeal.

47.5   **AGGRAVATED DAMAGES**

Even in a serious case, an award of aggravated damages is not automatic and indeed is comparatively rare.

In *Alexander v Home Office [1988] IRLR 190*, the Court of Appeal stated that aggravated damages may be awarded where the respondent has behaved in a high-handed, malicious, insulting or oppressive manner.

47.6 Compensation

In *ITCS (UK) Ltd v Tchoula [2000] IRLR 643* a black security officer made various complaints of race discrimination. Subsequently, a manager burst into a room and claimed to have found him getting up from a prone position; this led to him being dismissed for being asleep on duty. A tribunal dismissed the race discrimination complaint but upheld Mr Tchoula's claim that he had been victimised. The tribunal accepted that, as a result of the allegations of race discrimination, the manager had hoped to find Mr Tchoula in dereliction of duty; the dismissal itself and a previous warning were also acts of victimisation. The award of compensation included £5,000 for aggravated damages.

In this case, the EAT considered that the employment tribunal had been entitled to make a separate award of aggravated damages, in addition to an award for injury to feelings. If the facts disclose the essential requirements for an award of aggravated damages, whether the award is expressed separately or whether an element of aggravated damages is included in the award for injury to feelings, is a matter of form rather than substance. On the facts, senior management was consciously motivated by Mr Tchoula's claims of racial discrimination when they tried to find him in dereliction of his duty and in carrying out a disciplinary procedure which was seriously flawed. The tribunal was entitled to regard this as amounting to high-handed, insulting or oppressive behaviour towards Mr Tchoula and to make an award of aggravated damages. The amount of the award of aggravated damages was, however, reduced to £2,500.

As already mentioned, in the *Vento* case, the Court of Appeal reduced to £5,000 the sum of £15,000 which had been awarded for aggravated damages.

In *Zaiwalla & Co v Walia [2002] IRLR 697,* aggravated damages of £7,500 were awarded, partly because of the oppressive way in which the respondent had defended the tribunal proceedings.

In *British Telecommunications plc v Reid [2004] IRLR 327*, the Court of Appeal ruled that an employer's treatment of an alleged harasser can be regarded as aggravating the injury to feelings suffered by the claimant – thus affecting the compensation awarded. There was a long internal investigation of the claimant's grievance that he had been subjected to a racially abusive remark, and the grievance was not upheld. During that time, the accused harasser was promoted. A tribunal found that the remark was made and was racially abusive and awarded £2,000 aggravated damages in addition to compensation for injury to feelings.

Ward LJ said:

> 'I am far from laying down any principle that an employer cannot promote an employee whilst disciplinary proceedings are hanging over his or her head, but it can, in the particular facts and circumstances of a particular case, be a material factor demonstrating the high-handedness of the employer.'

47.6 INTEREST

Interest may be, and normally is, awarded on all compensation except that relating to future losses. It is expressly provided in the 1996 Regulations that no interest shall be included in respect of any compensation awarded for a loss or matter which will occur after the day of calculation or in respect of any time before the contravention of the *EPA 1970* or the act of discrimination complained of.

The day of calculation is defined as the day on which the amount of interest is calculated by the tribunal. The relevant period is the period which starts on the date of the act of discrimination complained of (or, in the case of a complaint under the *EPA 1970*, the date of the contravention of that Act); and ends on the day of calculation.

The Regulations state that interest on the compensation for injury to feelings shall be for the whole of that period. Interest on arrears of remuneration, and on any other compensation awarded in respect of the period up to the date of calculation, is awarded for half the period. The Regulations state that this must be done by awarding interest from the 'mid-point date' of the period, i.e. the day which falls halfway through the period.

The Regulations provide for an adjustment where a payment has been made to the complainant, by or on behalf of the respondent, in respect of the subject matter of the award and that payment has been made before the day of calculation. In that event, the total period in respect of that part of the award ends not on the day of calculation but on the day of payment, the mid-point date being midway between the date of the act of discrimination and the date of payment.

The tribunal is given a residual power to calculate interest on the whole or part of the award for a different period than that specified in the Regulations if it considers that otherwise serious injustice would be caused.

The rate of interest, in England and Wales, is that from time to time prescribed for the Special Investment Account under *rule 27(1)* of the *Court Funds Rules 1987 (SI 1987 No 821)*. Where this rate of interest is varied during a period for which interest is to be calculated, the tribunal may in the interests of simplicity apply the median or average of the rates, whichever seems to the tribunal to be appropriate. Interest is to be calculated as simple interest accruing from day to day, not compound interest.

In *Bentwood Bros (Manchester) v Shepherd* (see 47.2 above), the tribunal had awarded compensation based on the gross loss of salary, on the understanding that tax and national insurance would be deducted from the relevant parts of the award. The tribunal, when calculating interest on the award for loss of salary up to the calculation date, did so on the gross amount of the relevant award, not the net sum after deduction of tax and national insurance. It was held by a majority of the Court of Appeal that this was an error of law and that interest should have been on the net sum after the deductions. Peter Gibson LJ said that Mrs Shepherd 'would not have received the gross sums, and for my part I can see no logical basis why interest should be awarded on what Mrs Shepherd would never have received'.

48 Conciliation

Once a complaint has been presented to an employment tribunal (and sometimes earlier), the services of an ACAS conciliation officer are made available, so that the parties can negotiate confidentially with a view to reaching a binding settlement, usually on ACAS Form COT3.

Where the complainant is being assisted by the EOC or the CRE, it is commonly a term of any settlement that the respondent should take agreed measures to prevent further acts of discrimination. Such measures can of course be in the interest of the respondent, as well as in the public interest, if future discrimination and hence future complaints are successfully prevented.

Where the services of ACAS are not used, a binding settlement can be entered into only through a consent order of the tribunal or by entering into a valid compromise agreement – see *Agreements*.

The EAT made it clear in *Clarke v Redcar and Cleveland Borough Council [2006] IRLR 324* that an ACAS officer is under no duty to advise on the merits of a case before an employee enters into a binding agreement.

49   Conditions

The word 'conditions' can be used in several different senses, as follows:

(a)   terms and conditions of employment are relevant to rights under the *Discrimination Laws* – see *Terms of Employment*;

(b)   terms and conditions of employment are also relevant to the definition of *Same Employment* under the *EPA 1970* – see *Common Terms and Conditions*;

(c)   *Working Conditions* can be the subject of complaints about *Detriment*;

(d)   *Working Conditions* can also be relevant in equal pay cases, as one of the demand factors in relation to *Equal Value* and also in relation to the *Material Factor* defence.

50 Conduct Dismissals

It is very important that employers should be consistent in disciplinary decisions, particularly decisions to dismiss an employee for misconduct. Differences in the treatment of different cases, for instance where the employees concerned belong to different *Racial Groups* or are of different sexes, are likely to lead to findings of direct discrimination, if no credible and non-discriminatory reason can be given.

The danger of subjective and potentially discriminatory decisions is particularly great during the qualifying period of one year for full unfair dismissal rights, especially where any right to a formal disciplinary procedure has been excluded for the whole or part of that year. Ideally employers should follow a formal procedure even where there is no statutory or contractual obligation to do so, in order to ensure that decisions are made consistently and objectively and that explanations can be given for any apparent difference in treatment. As a minimum, the facts of any case should be considered by a senior person and by a member of the HR department (if there is one).

There may also be a need for *Reasonable Adjustment* where a disability has contributed to a disciplinary offence, for example if a mental impairment has caused an employee to react violently to provocation; see also *Disability Discrimination* and *Unfair Dismissal*.

51   Consistency

One of the most important qualities which employers and managers need, in order to comply with the discrimination laws, is consistency. Dealing with similar cases in different ways leaves an employer wide open to tribunal complaints, if the employees concerned are, for example, of different gender or colour – see *Direct Discrimination*. The *Discrimination laws* focus heavily on comparative treatment.

The importance of consistency is emphasised in the *Codes of Practice* under both the *SDA 1975* and the *RRA 1976*.

52   Constructive Dismissal

A constructive dismissal occurs where the employer's conduct is likely to destroy or seriously damage the trust and confidence which the employee is entitled to have in the employer. The employee is entitled to treat himself as having been dismissed, and may thus resign. A constructive dismissal may give rise to a discrimination claim as well as, typically, an unfair dismissal claim.

A constructive dismissal may arise from a serious breach by the employer of an express or implied term of the employment contract, such as the implied duty of mutual trust and confidence.

The following are examples of cases where inaction or ineffective action by management could lead to a resignation and a finding of constructive dismissal:

(*a*)   The management are aware of evidence which points towards discrimination or harassment but fail to investigate.

(*b*)   The employer refuses to listen to a complaint of discrimination or harassment.

(*c*)   The employer receives a grievance but fails to take it seriously or investigate it thoroughly.

(*d*)   Allegations are made to senior management in confidence but that confidence is broken and the workforce are made aware that the employee has complained.

In all these cases there could be a finding of discriminatory dismissal as well as unfair dismissal. This can be important where the employee has not yet completed the qualifying period of employment for complaints of unfair dismissal. The case of *Reed and Bull Information Systems Ltd v Stedman [1999] IRLR 299* (referred to under *Harassment*) is an example of such a case.

In *Nottinghamshire County Council v Meikle [2004] IRLR 703*, the Court of Appeal held that an employment tribunal erred in finding that a disabled teacher was not constructively dismissed because her resignation after the local authority failed to agree to the adjustments she requested in order to be able to return to work after sickness absence was not a response to fundamental breach of contract. The EAT had correctly held that the local authority had been in fundamental breach of contract as a result of its continuing failure to deal with disability discrimination against the teacher and that she had resigned in response to that breach. Once a repudiation of the contract by the employer has been established, the proper approach is to ask whether the employee has accepted that repudiation by treating the contract of employment as at an end. It must be in response to the repudiation, but the fact that the employee also objected to the other actions or inactions of the employer, not amounting to breach of contract, would not vitiate the acceptance of the repudiation. It is enough that the employee resigned in response, at least in part, to a fundamental breach of contract by the employer. In this case, the persistent failure of the local authority to carry out *Reasonable Adjustments* amounted to a fundamental breach of the obligation of trust and confidence.

The *Meikle* case also addressed the issue of *Time Limits* in discrimination cases. The Court of Appeal confirmed that a constructive dismissal could properly be regarded as being in itself a discriminatory act. In arriving at that view, the Court of Appeal disagreed with the view expressed by Auld LJ in *Cast v Croydon College [1998] IRLR 318*, that in a sex discrimination case, where there has been a constructive dismissal, time runs from the date of the employer's breach and not from the date of the employee's resignation. According to the Court of Appeal, the act complained of in a case of constructive dismissal is the unlawful dismissal which is constituted by the termination of the employee's employment when she accepts the repudiation by her employer.

53   Continuing Discrimination

The *Discrimination Laws* are important in relation to *Time Limits* because time starts to run at the end of the period of continuing discrimination.

There is a discriminatory act extending over a period where a discriminatory rule, policy or regime is operated pursuant to which decisions may be taken from time to time. In *Cast v Croydon College [1998] IRLR 318*, the complainant was an information centre manager who worked full time. She became pregnant. Both before and after taking maternity leave, she asked if she could work part-time or job share when she returned to work. Each time her request was refused. She presented a complaint of indirect sex discrimination within three months after the last refusal, but it was held by the employment tribunal and the EAT that she was too late, because time ran from the date of the refusal of the request which she had made before going on maternity leave. She successfully appealed to the Court of Appeal. It was held that the tribunal's findings of fact clearly indicated the existence of a discriminatory policy in relation to her post, so that this was a case of an act of discrimination extending over a period.

It is frequently necessary for employment tribunals to consider in *Harassment* cases whether a series of separate incidents constitute separate acts of discrimination (in which case the complaint could be out of time in relation to the earlier acts) or a single act extending over a period. This is a question which can be decided only by looking closely at the circumstances of any particular case. If the acts complained of have occurred with some regularity, a tribunal would be likely to find that there has been a campaign of harassment, constituting a single act extending over a period. A different finding would be likely if there have been two or more unconnected acts with a long interval or intervals between them.

In *Robertson v Bexley Community Centre t/a Leisure Link [2003] IRLR 434,* the applicant argued that two separate incidents of racial abuse by a fellow employee amounted to continuing racial discrimination. One of these incidents occurred some six months earlier and had been dealt with by the employers at that time, who had disciplined the fellow employee. The applicant had apparently concurred with the steps taken. The second incident occurred the day after the applicant had presented his complaint to the tribunal and led to the fellow employee's resignation (to avoid dismissal). The employment tribunal held that the complaint was out of time. The applicant successfully appealed to the EAT, but the Court of Appeal allowed an appeal by the respondent and restored the decision of the tribunal. It was held by the Court of Appeal that the EAT had not been entitled to take the second incident into account in order to decide whether there had been a continuing act, because that second incident had taken place after the date of the application to the tribunal.

It should be noted, however, that, once jurisdiction has been established, incidents which occur after the date of the claim to tribunal can be relevant as *Evidence of Discrimination.*

54   Contract Compliance

In early 2007, a Government-commissioned report, *Developing Positive Action Policies: Learning from the Experiences of Europe and North America*, supported the use of 'contract compliance', i.e. the setting of objectives and timetables for increasing the employment of minority groups as a condition of entering into contracts with Government organisations. Positive action of this kind, although going further than the forms of action currently permitted by law, would not constitute full-blown positive discrimination of the kind experienced in the USA where policies favouring job applicants purely on the ground of their race has led to resentment and legal challenge. As a result, there has been a move in the US away from numerical quotas and towards contract compliance mechanisms. Yet even some of those who are both vociferous and effective in promoting equal opportunities at the workplace have reservations about the merits of contract compliance. It may be argued that such a form of legitimised positive discrimination would reduce the ability of employers to recruit the best person for the job. There may be a risk that a formulaic approach to contract compliance would result in personal merit being regarded as less important than fitting in with a tick-box. Nevertheless, it is likely that this subject will continue to engender debate, and strong opinions, for years to come.

55   Contractual Equal Opportunities Policies

55.1   SIGNIFICANCE OF CONTRACTUAL STATUS

Employers are increasingly issuing a wide variety of employment-related policies, including *Equal Opportunities Policies*. As policies proliferate, it is foreseeable that questions are more and more likely to arise as to the precise legal status, if any, of such policies. This is an important issue, because quite apart from any other consideration, if an equal opportunities policy forms part of an employee's terms and conditions of employment, then a breach by the employer of its own policy may mean that the employee has a legal right of redress in respect of breach of contract. Detailed discussion of the law of contract falls outside the scope of this handbook but briefly, a claim in respect of an alleged breach of an employment contract traditionally had to be brought in the civil courts. This is no longer the case; such a claim may now, subject to certain conditions (most importantly, that the employment has ended), be brought in the employment tribunal, which currently has the power to award compensation of up to £25,000, (a limit which means that contractual disputes involving highly paid senior executives are still likely to be litigated in the civil courts).

55.2   IDEALISTIC POLICY STATEMENTS

Equal opportunities policies may cover matters which are not dealt with by legislation. If an employee's contract of employment includes a binding legal obligation upon the employer to comply with such a policy, then the employee's entitlements may be extensive. But there are limits, as the decision of the High Court in *Grant v South West Trains Ltd [1998] IRLR 188*, shows. The employer's equal opportunities policy proclaimed that it was 'committed to ensuring that all individuals are treated fairly and are valued irrespective of . . . sexual preference . . . No one is to receive less favourable treatment on any of the above grounds or is to be disadvantaged by requirements or conditions which cannot be shown to be justifiable. Our aim is to eliminate unfair discrimination'. The employee was contractually entitled to travel concessions which extended to a partner of the opposite sex. She was refused a travel pass for her female partner, with whom she had been living in a stable relationship. She brought civil proceedings, claiming that the policy was incorporated into her contract and that, on that basis, she was entitled to require her employer to extend the contractual travel concessions to her partner. The High Court rejected her application. Crucially, the judge found that the policy had not been incorporated into her contract: 'It is a statement of policy and not of contractual obligation. The policy is in very general, even idealistic, terms. It also covers such matters as "health and social class" which would be alien to employment contractual law.' The judge also considered that, on the facts, the way in which the policy was brought into being was indicative that no contractual rights were in the mind of the employer or the employees' representatives. No obligations were put by the policy upon the employer and the obligation on the employee was 'of the vaguest kind', i.e. to act 'in the spirit of the policy'. There was no evidence of any contractual intention on the part of the employer or employee, either from the documents or by inference from the whole of the evidence. There was no legal basis for implying the contractual terms on the basis of the policy. Further, since the contract specifically provided that concessions were granted for a partner of the 'opposite' sex, the policy could not be incorporated into the contractual terms so as to override that express provision. The employee's argument, the judge considered, effectively entailed that the incorporation of the policy into the contract had the effect of binding the employer to increase the employee's emoluments. The judge thought that could not be right.

55.3   LEGALLY BINDING POLICIES

In *Secretary of State for Scotland v Taylor [2000] IRLR 502*, the employers issued a circular setting out an equal opportunities policy which included an undertaking 'to offer opportunities on an equal basis to all staff regardless of gender, race, religion, sexual preference, disability or age'. The employers introduced changes to their retirement policy, under which the normal retiring age was set at 55 in order to achieve a younger workforce. When the employee reached that age, he was given notice of dismissal. He claimed that this amounted to discrimination on the grounds of age, in breach of the equal opportunities provisions in his contract. The tribunal upheld his claim, having satisfied itself that the equal opportunities policy was incorporated into his contract. Changes to contracts were notified by circulars such as that setting out the policy; the change in the retirement policy had been notified in the same way. Ultimately, the House of Lords ruled that there was no evidence that the employee had been singled out on the ground of age. Given the implementation of the *Framework Directive* in relation to such matters as *Age Discrimination*, *Sexual Orientation* and *Religion or Belief*, it may be that disputes of the type seen in *Taylor* and *Grant* will become rare. Nevertheless, the cases are a reminder that the wording of policy statements needs to be as carefully conceived as it is well-intentioned.

55.4   INFERENCES FROM NON-COMPLIANCE

In *Anya v University of Oxford and another [2001] IRLR 377*, the Court of Appeal held that an employer's failure to follow its own equal opportunities policies (or other relevant policies and procedures) may, unless there is a credible alternative explanation, contribute to an inference of discrimination. This possibility of an adverse inference can arise whether the policy is contractual or non-contractual.

56   Contract Workers

56.1   TRIANGULAR CONTRACT RELATIONSHIPS

Where a person (who may be in business on his own account and performing work personally on a self-employed basis) is provided by one contracting party to perform duties for the other contracting party, a triangular relationship arises between:

(*a*)   worker;

(*b*)   labour-supplier; and

(*c*)   labour-user.

Typically, the labour-supplier is an employment agency. The labour-supplier must observe applicable parts of the *Discrimination Laws* , but on traditional principles the labour-user might fall outside the net of liability and thus there are specific provisions to address this issue.

56.2   LIABILITY OF PRINCIPALS

It is unlawful for a principal, in relation to contract work, to discriminate against a person:

(*a*)   in the terms on which he allows that person to do that work;

(*b*)   by not allowing that person to do it or continue to do it;

(*c*)   in the way he affords that person access to any benefits or by refusing or deliberately omitting to afford him access to them; or

(*d*)   by subjecting that person to any other detriment.

For these purposes:

(*a*)   'principal' means a person ('A') who makes work available for doing by individuals who are employed by another person who supplies them under a contract made with A;

(*b*)   'contract work' means work so made available; and

(*c*)   'contract worker' means any individual who is supplied to the principal under such a contract.

A principal is placed under obligations akin to those of an employer and so the duty to make *Reasonable Adjustments* applies, although what is 'reasonable' in the case of a principal will presumably in practice often reflect the fact that the relationship between the principal and the contract worker may be short-term only.

56.3   PURPOSIVE INTERPRETATION

These provisions were considered by the EAT in *MHC Consulting Services Ltd v Tansell [1999] IRLR 677*. The EAT ruled that, where there is an unbroken chain of contracts between an individual and the end-user, the latter is the 'principal'. This interpretation gives effect, the EAT said, 'to the general principle which applies in social legislation of this kind, namely that the statute should be construed purposively, and with a bias towards conferring statutory protection rather than excluding it.' The case concerned a disabled person who was on the books of an employment agency which arranged for him to be interviewed by a company interested in his services. That company rejected his services (which he was to provide via his own company) because he was disabled. A tribunal had taken the view the disabled person was a contract worker for the agency, but not for the end-user. However, that was a misunderstanding . The end user's appeal to the Court of Appeal failed: *Abbey Life Assurance Co Ltd v Tansell [2000] IRLR 387.* In accordance with the assumed intention of Parliament to confer rather than deny protection to contract workers the statutory language was reasonably capable of applying not only where a principal made work available for an individual employed by an agency, but also where an extra contract was inserted, so that there was no direct contract between the principal and the employer of the worker.

The Court of Appeal also gave a purposive interpretation to the definition of 'contract worker' in *Harrods Ltd v Remick and others [1997] IRLR 583.* Certain departments at Harrods were occupied by licensees who employed their own sales staff, but each member of the sales force had to be approved by Harrods and observe the Harrods' rules regarding dress and other matters. Employees of two of the licensees complained of racial discrimination by Harrods in withdrawing approval of them. A third complaint related to alleged discrimination in withholding approval for employment by a licensee. It was held by the Court of Appeal that the three complainants were contract workers within the meaning of *section 7* of the *RRA 1976,* even though when doing their work they were not under the managerial power or control of Harrods. The court should 'give a construction to the statutory language that is not only consistent with the actual words used but also would achieve the statutory purpose of providing a remedy to victims of discrimination who would otherwise be without one.'

The Court of Appeal held in *Allonby v Accrington & Rossendale College and others [2001] IRLR 365* that a contract worker complaining of sex discrimination may point not only to the treatment which has been or would have been received by a male contract worker but also to that which has been or would have been received by a male employee of the principal. This decision is of assistance to contract workers complaining that the principal treats them less favourably than it treats or would treat its own employees in relation to non-contractual benefits, working conditions, detriments and dismissals. Ward LJ suggested in *Allonby* that a contract worker may even present a complaint against the principal in relation to contractual terms, if the principal, when setting the terms of its own contractual arrangements with the agency, will not allow her to do the work on the terms enjoyed by the principal's own employees. Although *Allonby* is a case under the *SDA 1975*, it is also an authority for cases under other *Discrimination Laws.*

In *Patefield v Belfast City Council [2000] IRLR 664*, a woman went on maternity leave after having spent more than three years doing clerical work for the Council as a contract worker. The Council replaced her with a permanent employee, even though it was known that she wished to return to work after the birth of her baby. When she returned she was offered an alternative post, with conditions which she considered to be materially inferior. The Northern Ireland Court of Appeal held that when it replaced the contract worker with a permanent employee, on the commencement of her maternity leave, the Council was subjecting her to a detriment on grounds of sex.

57   Contracts of Employment

There is a fairly common misunderstanding that acts of discrimination can be legitimised if they are pursuant to a contract of employment which the complainant has freely entered into. The discrimination laws are about difference in treatment (or *Disparate Impact* in cases of indirect discrimination). If an act of discrimination, as defined by the relevant legislation, has taken place, it is no defence to any complaint to show that the act is authorised by the contract of employment.

Indeed, the express purpose of the *EPA 1970* is to modify contractual terms which have been agreed by the operation of the equality clause.

58   Costs

58.1   INTRODUCTION

Awards of legal costs by employment tribunals in favour of successful parties have traditionally been rare, but in recent years they have become a little more common. The reason why costs were, in the past, seldom a relevant issue in tribunal proceedings is historical. Allowing tribunals a general power to award costs would have run counter to the concept underpinning the regime. But as employment rights have proliferated, and in many respects become increasingly complex, it has become apparent that it is logical for costs to be awarded more readily in some circumstances than in the past. Furthermore, the cost of running the employment tribunal system has become a significant burden upon the Exchequer. As well as encouraging the in-house resolution of workplace disputes, therefore, the Government has eased the restrictions upon the power of tribunals to make costs awards.

It is still the case that costs do not 'follow the event' in tribunal proceedings to the extent that occurs in the civil courts, but the *Employment Tribunals (Constitution and Rules of Procedure) Regulations 2004 (SI 2004 No 1816)* permit three types of costs order to be made by a tribunal:

(*a*)   a costs order;

(*b*)   a preparation time order;

(*c*)   a wasted costs order.

58.2   COSTS ORDERS

A tribunal chairman may order one party to make a payment in respect of the costs incurred by another party. (It is also possible for an order to be made to the Secretary of State of any attendance allowance of any attendance allowance that has been paid by him to a party or witness.) A costs order may only be made if the receiving party has been legally represented at the hearing or, if there has been no hearing, at the date of determination of the case. A party who has not been legally represented will not be entitled to a costs order, although he may be entitled to a preparation time order. Legal representation for these purposes includes the employment of a legally qualified person. An application for a costs order may be made by a party at any time during the proceedings, but a written application received more than 28 days from the issuing of the judgment determining the claim will not be accepted unless a general tribunal considers it in the interests of justice to do so. Before any order is made, the proposed paying party must be given the opportunity to give reasons why the order should not be made. Costs orders may be made either on a general discretionary basis, in relation to the bringing or conduct of the proceedings, or in relation to specific matters, e.g. postponement or adjournment. Where a tribunal or a chairman has decided to make a costs order, it may take one of the following forms:

(*a*)   an order for a specified sum not exceeding £10,000;

(*b*)   an order for a specified sum agreed by the parties; or

(*c*)   an order that the whole or a specified part of the costs to be determined by way of a detailed assessment in a county court in accordance with the Civil Procedure Rules.

When considering either whether to make an order, or its amount, the tribunal may have regard to the paying party's ability to pay. Under the previous Rules of Procedure, there was no discretion to take means into account.

58.3   PREPARATION TIME ORDERS

A tribunal chairman may order one party to make a payment in respect of the preparation time incurred by another party. 'Preparation time' is time spent by the receiving party or his employees carrying out preparatory work directly relating to the proceedings and the receiving party's legal or other advisors relating to the conduct of the proceedings, up to but not including any time spent at the hearing. A preparation time order may only be made where the receiving party has not been legally represented at a hearing or at the date of determination of the case if there was no hearing. In calculating a preparation time order, the tribunal must first assess the number of hours spent on preparation time, based on information provided by the receiving party, and on the tribunal's own assessment of what is a reasonable and proportionate amount of time to spend on the preparatory work, having regard to such matters as the complexity of the case, the number of witnesses and documentation required. The tribunal must then multiply the number of hours by an hourly rate of £25 (a figure that will increase annually by £1 from 6 April 2006). There is a cap of £10,000 on the amount that can be awarded. As with a costs order, the paying party's ability to pay may be taken into account.

58.4   GROUNDS FOR MAKING COSTS AND PREPARATION TIME ORDERS

Where a tribunal or chairman is of the opinion that any of the below grounds applies, there is a duty to consider making a costs order or a preparation time order, as the case may be, against the paying party and, following consideration, a discretion to make an order if it is considered appropriate to do so. The grounds are that:

(a)   the paying party has in bringing the proceedings, or he or his representative has in conducting the proceedings, acted vexatiously, abusively, disruptively or otherwise unreasonably; or

(b)   the bringing or conduct of the proceedings by the paying party has been misconceived.

Where a settlement offer is refused by a party, costs can be awarded if the tribunal considers that the refusal was unreasonable. In *Kopel v Safeway Stores plc [2003] IRLR 753*, the EAT upheld an award of £5,000 costs against a claimant where she had failed in unfair dismissal and sex discrimination claims, and had not only turned down a 'generous' settlement offer, but had persisted in alleging breaches of the provisions of the *European Convention on Human Rights* prohibiting torture and slavery which the tribunal categorised as 'frankly ludicrous' and 'seriously misconceived'.

Specific provisions apply to costs awards and preparation time orders where a party has been ordered to pay a deposit at a pre-hearing review. The *2004 Rules* introduced a power on the part of a tribunal or chairman to make a costs order or preparation time order against a party who has not complied with an order or practice direction.

Costs awards are intended to compensate the party in whose favour the award is made, not to penalise the party ordered to make payment.

58.5 **WASTED COSTS ORDERS**

A tribunal chairman has power to make a wasted costs order against the party's representative. 'Wasted costs' are any costs incurred by a party as a result of any improper, unreasonable or negligent act or omission on the part of any representative, or which, in the light of any such act or omission occurring after they were incurred, the tribunal considers it unreasonable to expect that party to pay. Pay 'representative' for these purposes excludes a representative who is not acting in pursuit of profit in the proceedings (although a person acting under a conditional fee arrangement is regarded as acting in pursuit of profit). A wasted costs order may be made in favour of a party whether or not he is legally represented, and an order may also be made in favour of a representative's own client. However, an order may not be made against a representative who is the employee of a party. Before making a wasted costs order, the tribunal chairman must give the representative a reasonable opportunity to make representations as to why an order should not be made and, when considering the making of an order or its amount, the tribunal may have regard to the representative's ability to pay. In employment tribunal cases, the concept of a wasted costs order is relatively new, but general guidance may be found in the decision of the Court of Appeal in *Ridehalgh v Horsefield [1994] Ch 205.*

59   Cronyism

Not all jobs are filled by way of competitive examination or an objective assessment of the merits of rival candidates.

The disparaging term 'cronyism' is applicable for instance where a person is offered a job because he or she is a friend, or relative of a friend, of the person making the offer, or because they went to the same school or belong to the same club. No other candidate is considered; the job offer is made either as a favour or because it is believed that the social relationship will be a sound foundation for mutual trust in the working relationship.

Nepotism is closely related to cronyism. A son, daughter or other close relative is brought into the family business, sometimes for good reasons but sometimes because judgment has been clouded by partiality.

Similarly focused, but generally less objectionable, methods of recruitment to a post are networking and headhunting. Networkers make themselves known to potential employers, or other useful contacts, even though there may be no current job vacancy, in the hope that they will be remembered when a vacancy does arise. Headhunting is rather different. A particular individual is targeted as being the person with the outstanding credentials for the post which is to be filled. Sometimes the target is a key employee of a competitor, so that recruiting him or her serves a dual purpose.

Headhunting at an exalted level featured in the case of *Lord Chancellor and Lord Chancellor's Department v Coker and Osamor [2002] IRLR 80*. Garry Hart, a partner in a leading City firm of solicitors was appointed as Special Adviser to the then Lord Chancellor, Lord Irvine of Lairg. The post was never advertised. Lord Irvine decided that Mr Hart had all the necessary qualities for the post and obtained the Prime Minister's approval for the post to be offered to him.

Ms Coker, a solicitor, and Ms Osamor, an adviser in a law centre, both submitted complaints of direct and indirect sex discrimination; Ms Osamor also complained of direct and indirect racial discrimination. Neither of them had been aware of the vacancy before Mr Hart was appointed; both of them contended that they would have applied if the post had been advertised.

Lord Phillips MR said:

'The test of indirect discrimination focuses on the effect that the requirement objected to has on the pool of candidates. It can only have a discriminatory effect within the two statutes if a significant proportion of the pool are able to satisfy the requirement. Only in that situation will it be possible for the requirement to have a disproportionate effect on the men and the women, or the racial groups, which form the pool. Where the requirement excludes almost the entirety of the pool it cannot constitute indirect discrimination within the statutes.

For this reason, making an appointment from within a circle of family, friends and personal acquaintances is seldom likely to constitute indirect discrimination. Those known to the employer are likely to represent a minute proportion of those who would otherwise be qualified to fill the post. The requirement of personal knowledge will exclude the vast proportion of the pool, be they men, women, white or another racial group.'

Lord Phillips also said that because of the conclusion that the appointment of Mr

Hart was not discriminatory, it was not necessary to apply the test of justifiability to the appointment. He did, however, make the following statement of general principle on justifiability:

'The consideration of the question whether a requirement that is discriminatory is justifiable involves a test of proportionality. An objective balance has to be struck between the discriminatory effect of the requirement and the reasonable needs of the party who imposes it – see *Hampson v Department of Education and Science [1989] IRLR 69* at 75 per Balcombe LJ approved by the House of Lords in *Webb v EMO Air Cargo (UK) Ltd [1993] IRLR 27.*'

The decision of the Court of Appeal in *Coker* and *Osamor* is authority for the proposition that a subjective decision to appoint a particular individual to a post, to the exclusion of all other potential candidates, for reasons which have nothing to do with sex, marital status, race, disability, religion or sexual orientation, would not normally lead to a finding of indirect discrimination. It is immaterial whether the individual is singled out for reasons of cronyism or nepotism or as the result of networking or headhunting.

There are the following important cautionary notes to be struck:

(a) Since the decision in *Coker* and *Osamor,* the statutory definition of indirect sex discrimination has changed and the test for *Disparate Impact* is more flexible – see *Indirect Discrimination.*

(b) If appointing the chosen individual means overlooking a particular person who would have been a suitable appointee (for example a potential internal candidate), and if that person is not of the same sex, marital status, race, religion or sexual orientation as the appointee, or has a disability, then the *Burden of Proof* may be on the employer to show that the subjective reason given for the appointment is a genuine one and that the appointment had nothing to do with sex or race etc.

(c) The decision in the case is not concerned with the practice of *Word of Mouth Recruitment.* Lord Phillips referred to the Codes of Practice issued by the *Equal Opportunities Commission* and the *Commission for Racial Equality* and then said:

'It is possible that a recruitment exercise conducted by word of mouth, by personal recommendation or by other informal recruitment method will constitute indirect discrimination within the meaning of section 1(1)(b) of the statutes. If the arrangements made for the purpose of determining who should be offered employment or promotion involve the application of a requirement or condition to an applicant that he or she should be personally recommended by a member of the existing workforce that may, depending of course on all the facts, have the specified disproportionately adverse impact on one sex or on a particular ethnic group and so infringe section 1(1)(b).'

The above references to *section 1(1)(b)* of the statutes is to the original wording of the *SDA 1975* and the *RRA 1976,* when the test was whether a requirement or condition had been applied; not the present wording, where the test is whether a provision, criterion or practice has been applied – see *Indirect Discrimination.*

60   Crown Employment

Servants of the Crown are treated as employees for the purposes of the *EPA 1970* and the other discrimination laws, subject to very limited exceptions.

Exceptions relating to statutory officers have largely been nullified by the combined effect of the *Equal Treatment Directive* and the statutory provisions relating to *Office-holders*. Exceptions in the *DDA 1995* and the *AR 2006* relate to members of the *Armed Forces*.

61   Dangerous Work

The fact that work is dangerous is not a legal justification for discrimination against women in *Recruitment* or *Selection* for the work. There must also be no sex discrimination against existing employees in deciding who should be required to do such work – see *Detriment*.

Dangerous working conditions may require *Reasonable Adjustment* where the person who is or will be expected to do the work is disabled. The fact that working conditions are dangerous can also be relevant in an *Equal Pay* case – see *Working Conditions* – and, of course, to *Health and Safety*.

62   Defamation of Character

It is fundamental to equal opportunities in employment that a person making a complaint about (for example) a breach by a colleague or a superior of good practice should not suffer because of the making of that allegation. The legislation on sex, race and disability discrimination and discrimination relating to religion or belief and sexual orientation prohibits *Victimisation*, and for good reason. Moreover, even where (as is often the case) those against whom the allegation is made protest their innocence and seek to take legal steps to restore the damage that may have been done to their reputation, their options are apt to be limited. This is because, usually, it will not be possible to sue the person who has made the allegations for libel or slander since the allegation is likely to be protected by 'qualified privilege' under defamation law. However, it is possible for an accused person to sue for defamation if he or she can prove that the person making the allegation was motivated by malice. It is rarely easy to prove malice, but it is not always impossible. In an exceptional case that was widely reported in the press in 2000, a pharmacist was ordered to pay £400,000 in damages for defamation plus substantial legal costs to her former supervisor, after she had falsely complained to management that he had sexually assaulted and then raped her at work. Because the facts were extreme, the jury seems to have accepted the supervisor's argument that there was no scope to conclude that the accusation had arisen from a misunderstanding. Once it was found that the accusations were false, it was a short step to conclude that they were malicious. The position of the individual falsely accused of harassment is thus, whilst unenviable, not always legally hopeless.

63   Default Retirement Age

Regulation 30 of the *AR 2006* provides for a 'default retirement age' of 65 for people employed under a contract of employment, those in Crown employment and members of Parliamentary staff. The default retirement age does not apply to people who work under a contract to provide personal services, apprentices, office holders (including those in the police), barristers, advocates and partners. The effect of the default retirement age is that where an employee is compulsorily retired at 65 or above, the employer does not need to justify the retirement and there can be no claim of age discrimination. However, such a compulsory retirement may still be an unfair dismissal: see *Retirement and dismissal.*

The default retirement age was introduced because the Government decided that it would:

(*a*)   address the concerns of employers as regards workforce planning;

(*b*)   avoid adverse impact on providing work-related benefits, including pension;

(*c*)   represent a milestone for career planning purposes;

(*d*)   avoid limiting the availability of jobs for younger people;

(*e*)   motivate employees to save and provide for retirement.

The concept of a default retirement age has, however, attracted criticism. Whilst it may not be difficult, in the case of a particular employer, to provide objective justi- fication for compulsory retirement at 65, it is arguably unnecessary to enable all employers, whatever the particular circumstances, to rely upon a default retirement age of 65. It may also be said that the existence of a default retirement age is apt to discourage employers from allowing employees to work beyond 65, because it may be easier to retire an employee at 65 rather than him or her to continue for, say, a couple of years, when it may be open to argument that dismissal at a later age is for a reason other than retirement. However, the government has said that it will review the default retirement age in 2011, i.e. once the age discrimination regime has been in force for five years. The question then will be whether the default retirement age remains appropriate and necessary to assist workforce planning and to avoid adverse effects on pension and employment benefits.

64   Demotions

Demoting an employee could give rise to a complaint of wrongful or unfair dismissal, where the employee resigns and claims to have been constructively dismissed. Even if the employee has not yet completed the qualifying period for complaints of unfair dismissal and/or the demotion is authorised by a contractual term, the demotion will be a *Detriment* for the purpose of a complaint under the *Discrimination Laws*.

Furthermore, whenever a disabled employee is demoted, or subjected to any other detriment, because the performance of his or her work has been unsatisfactory, there will normally be a breach of the *DDA 1995* if the unsatisfactory job performance is for a reason wholly or partly related to the disability and the employer has not as a first step considered the question of *Reasonable Adjustment* to the job duties or working conditions.

65 Dependants, Benefits for

Some employers provide contractual or discretionary benefits for the dependants of their employees as well as the employees themselves. Such benefits can include:

(a)   life insurance;

(b)   private medical cover;

(c)   free or concessionary travel (where the employer is in the travel or passenger transport business); or

(d)   use of social or sports club facilities.

There must be no discrimination under any of the discrimination laws in relation to any such benefits or facilities. It would, for example, be a clear case of direct sex discrimination if benefits were provided for the dependants of male employees but not for those of female employees.

So far as benefits or facilities for ex-employees or their dependants are concerned, see *Post-employment Discrimination*.

66   Detriment

66.1   LEGAL PRINCIPLES

The *Discrimination Laws* prohibit discrimination against employees by dismissing them or subjecting them to any other detriment. *Dismissal* is considered separately.

The meaning of 'detriment' was considered by the Court of Appeal in *Jeremiah v Ministry of Defence [1979] IRLR 436*. In that case, male inspectors at an ordnance factory were required to carry out particularly unpleasant work, inspecting colour bursting shells. Female inspectors objected to doing the work, and were excused. One factor was that having to take a shower afterwards was a greater inconvenience for women, with their long hair, than for men. The work carried a slightly higher rate than other work in the factory.

This bare recitation of the facts indicates that the case was one of the early discrimination cases, decided more than two decades ago. It would be difficult (one hopes) to find a case with similar facts today.

The case established the following principles:

(*a*)   subjecting an employee to a detriment means no more than putting the employee under a disadvantage;

(*b*)   the test is objective – would or might a reasonable employee take the view that he or she had been put under a disadvantage?

(c)   all the circumstances must be taken into account;

(*d*)   subjecting an employee to a detriment cannot generally be excused on grounds of *Chivalry* or administrative convenience;

(*e*)   an employer cannot buy a right to discriminate by making an extra payment to an employee who is subjected to a detriment.

This approach was approved by the House of Lords in *Chief Constable of West Yorkshire Police v Khan [2001] IRLR 830* and in *Shamoon v Chief Constable of the Royal Ulster Constabulary [2003] IRLR 285*. A detriment does not necessarily involve some physical or economic consequence. For example, in *Khan*, the refusal to provide a reference amounted to a detriment, even though as matters turned out this did not cause the complainant any financial loss. In *Shamoon* the complaint was that the complainant's right to carry out appraisals had been removed from her. This step had no financial consequences, but, as Lord Hope of Craighead pointed out:

'Once it was known, as it was bound to be, that she had had this part of her normal duties taken away from her following a complaint to the Police Federation, the effect was likely to be to reduce her standing amongst her colleagues. A reasonable employee in her position might well feel that she was being demeaned in the eyes of those over whom she was in a position of authority.'

66.2   EXAMPLES OF DETRIMENT

Subjecting an employee or job applicant to a detriment can occur, for example, in the context of:

(*a*)   allocation of work;

(b)   searches;

(c)   segregation from other workers;

(d)   disciplinary matters;

(e)   demotions;

(f)   unfavourable appraisals;

(g)   overtime requirements;

(h)   mobility requirements; and

(i)   interview arrangements.

Mobility, *Demotions* and *Job Interviews* are dealt with elsewhere, as is *Post-employment Discrimination*.

66.3   ALLOCATION OF WORK

Jeremiah v Ministry of Defence [1979] IRLR 436 was a case of discrimination in requiring an employee to carry out dirty and unpleasant work. Another example would be discrimination in requiring an employee to carry out *Dangerous Work*. In this context, a difference in the treatment of two employees may amount to unlawful discrimination against both of them. Where both men and women are employed on police, security or similar work, employers, superior officers or managers sometimes make well-meaning attempts to shield the women by allocating the more dangerous duties to the men. In such circumstances, the latter could claim that they have been subjected to a detriment, having been required on grounds of sex to undertake the more dangerous work. The women could also complain, on the ground that protecting and sidelining them is effectively reducing their status and holding back their career development.

66.4   SEARCHES

In the context of race relations, where particular sensitivity is required, a detriment can take an intangible form. In *BL Cars Ltd v Brown [1985] IRLR 193*, a series of thefts had occurred and there was evidence that the offender was black. A written instruction was issued, under which black employees (but not white employees) were to be searched on entering their place of work. It was held that the issue of the instruction (which had not yet been implemented) was to subject the employees to a detriment on racial grounds. There would be a similar need for sensitivity, and for even-handed treatment, in dealing with any issue likely to have implications for workers having, for instance, a particular *Religion or Belief*.

66.5   SEGREGATION

In the *RRA 1976* the definition of racial discrimination expressly includes *Segregation* on racial grounds. It is likely that any employee segregated on racial grounds would be able to satisfy a tribunal that he or she had been subjected to a detriment, even if there was a good practical reason for the segregation, for example where a workforce includes two groups of workers whose countries of origin are at war.

Segregation from other workers is not expressly included in the definition of direct discrimination in the other laws prohibiting discrimination but there are circumstances in which a segregated employee could be said to have been subjected to a detriment. An example under the *DDA 1995* would be that of an employee who is HIV positive and who is required to sit at a separate table in the factory canteen. The detriment would consist of the sense of isolation and embarrassment caused to the employee.

66.6 **DISCIPLINARY MATTERS**

Employers also need to take care to be consistent in their approach to disciplinary action, even where the action falls short of dismissal. If, for example, an employee is given a written warning, and an employee of a different gender or ethnic origin has been given only an oral warning for the same offence, then the employer will need to be able to give an explanation for the difference in treatment which is unrelated to the difference in gender or ethnic origin.

The same principle applies in relation to suspensions, even where the suspension is to enable an investigation to be carried out, is on full pay and is not a disciplinary action. An employee who has been suspended may reasonably take the view that he or she has thereby been placed at a disadvantage, even though no pay has been lost, and the employer will be at risk of a finding of unlawful discrimination if a consistent approach cannot be demonstrated.

The same principle also applies in relation to investigations. In *Garry v London Borough of Ealing [2001] IRLR 681*, it was held by the tribunal that the nature of a disciplinary investigation which was carried out was influenced by the applicant's ethnic origin (Nigerian). Because of her ethnic origin, the investigation continued well beyond the point where it should have been concluded, even though the applicant was unaware that it was continuing. The employment tribunal found that the applicant had been subjected to a detriment on racial grounds and upheld her complaint of racial discrimination. The EAT allowed an appeal on the ground that there had been no detriment, but the applicant successfully appealed to the Court of Appeal, which restored the decision of the employment tribunal. Pill LJ stated:

> 'The present investigation was known to officers of the council whose attitude to the appellant and her work was important in the context of her present and future employment with the council. The detriment appears to me to be obvious . . .'

The requirement to be even-handed does not, however, mean that, when considering the background to an alleged offence, an employer must disregard all aspects relating to the employee's race, gender or disability. On the contrary, if an offence, such as an assault, is a response to sexual harassment, harassment on the ground of sexual orientation, racial or religious abuse or insulting remarks about the offender's disability, that mitigating factor must be taken into account. Otherwise, if an unjustified warning is given, the employee could resign and claim to have been constructively and unfairly dismissed. The case of *Sidhu v Aerospace Composite Technology Ltd [2000] IRLR 683* is dealt with under *Dismissal*, but the principle established by that case applies equally where disciplinary action short of dismissal is contemplated.

66.7 **UNFAVOURABLE APPRAISALS**

Many employers require their managers to carry out annual *Appraisals* of the employees for whom they are responsible. Even though appraisals are designed mainly to motivate employees or identify areas for improvement, they can also be taken into account when selecting employees for promotion or redundancy or when awarding pay increases.

There would clearly be grounds for a complaint of direct discrimination or victimisation in any of the following circumstances:

(*a*)   An appraisal is adversely influenced by the gender, sexual orientation, religion or ethnic origin of the employee who is being appraised.

(*b*)   A manager gives a hostile appraisal because the employee has brought a complaint of discrimination or an equal pay claim.

Where the performance of a disabled employee has been detrimentally affected by the disability, but the appraiser does not record this fact, then consideration must be given to the amendment of the appraisal as a *Reasonable Adjustment*. This is particularly the case where the poor performance was atypical, either because the consequences of the disability were unusually severe in the year in question or because a reasonable adjustment to job duties or working conditions has subsequently mitigated the adverse effect of the disability.

66.8   OVERTIME REQUIREMENTS

Access to overtime can be an important *Benefit*. Overtime pay forms an important part of the income of many employees.

There are some employees, however, who are under a contractual obligation to work overtime when required, but who dislike having to work unsocial hours. Singling out an employee for excessive overtime, or requiring the employee to work at particularly unpopular times, could lead to a tribunal complaint if a selection is influenced by discriminatory considerations.

67 Direct Discrimination

67.1 GENERAL PRINCIPLES

In essence, discrimination is direct where it is overt. Where discrimination is not explicit, it is said to be indirect. Distinguishing between the two forms of unlawful discrimination is very important, since in general direct discrimination is not capable of being justified (although, exceptionally, the *AR 2006* permit the justification of direct discrimination), whereas indirect discrimination may be justifiable.

The implications of this general principle were illustrated by the case of *Moyhing v Barts & London NHS Trust [2006] IRLR 860*. The EAT ruled that a male student nurse was subjected to a detriment within the meaning of the *SDA 1975* when, in accordance with a hospital's policy, he was not permitted, without a chaperone, to carry out an ECG on a female patient in circumstances in which a female student nurse did not have to be chaperoned when carrying out such a procedure on a male patient. Direct discrimination cannot be justified. The fact that there may be good and sound reasons for distinguishing between men and women is no defence. There is no legal basis for treating male and female student nurses differently. In particular, it would be wrong and contrary to Parliament's intentions to restrict the concept of detriment so as to make good the limited scope of the present defence of justification. However, the EAT said that given that the discrimination was not personally directed at the claimant, did not involve a personal slur on his reputation or character, and that he was only marginally inconvenienced by it, the award of compensation should be very much at the lower end of the scale. Harbouring a legitimate and principle sense of grievance is not to be confused with suffering an injury to feelings. Thus compensation of £750 was appropriate.

Where a claimant has been treated less favourably than a person of a different race, sex, etc (as the case may be), then the respondent will be expected to give an explanation for the difference in treatment – see *Evidence of Discrimination* and *Burden of Proof.*

Cases where there is no actual comparator are less straightforward. It was suggested by the EAT in *Chief Constable of West Yorkshire v Vento [2001] IRLR 124* that it is permissible for a tribunal to look at 'unidentical but not wholly dissimilar cases' to that of the complainant in order to decide how a hypothetical comparator would have been treated.

The possibility of adopting this approach was recognised by Lord Scott in his judgment in *Shamoon v Chief Constable of the Royal Ulster Constabulary [2003] IRLR 285*. He said, that:

> 'the comparator required for the purpose of the statutory definition of discrimination must be a comparator in the same position in all material respects as the victim save only that he, or she, is not a member of the protected class. But the comparators that can be of evidential value, sometimes determinative of the case, are not so circumscribed. Their evidential value, will, however, be variable and will inevitably be weakened by material differences between the different circumstances relating to them and the circumstances of the victim.'

In that same case, Lord Nicholls referred to the two-step approach which employment tribunals normally adopt in direct discrimination (and victimisation) cases. First, did the complainant receive 'less favourable treatment than the appropriate comparator (the "less favourable treatment" issue)?'. Secondly, was the less favourable treatment 'on the relevant proscribed ground (the "reason why" issue)?'. He said that there are no doubt 'cases where it is convenient and helpful to adopt this two-step approach to what is essentially a single question: did the complainant, on the proscribed ground, receive less favourable treatment than others?'. He added that, however, 'especially where the identity of the relevant comparator is a matter of dispute, this sequential analysis may give rise to needless problems. Sometimes the less favourable treatment issue cannot be resolved without, at the same time, deciding the reason-why issue. The two issues are intertwined'.

Then Lord Nicholls gave advice which is particularly important in cases where no actual comparator has been identified but which may also be helpful if there is an actual comparator. He said 'that employment tribunals may sometimes be able to avoid arid and confusing disputes about the identification of the appropriate comparator by concentrating primarily on why the claimant was treated as she was. Was it on the proscribed ground which is the foundation of the application? That will call for an examination of all the facts of the case. Or was it for some other reason? If the latter, the application fails. If the former, there will usually be no difficulty, in deciding whether the treatment, afforded to the claimant on the proscribed ground, was less favourable than was or would have been afforded to others.'

67.2   THE REASON FOR THE TREATMENT

It can be very difficult to prove the reason for a particular act or omission. It is important to note that a finding can be based on *Inferences* and that the *Burden of Proof* can shift from the claimant to the respondent.

It should also be noted that, for example, a difference in race need not be the only reason for the difference in treatment. It suffices if it is a significant or important reason. The authority for this proposition is the decision of the House of Lords in *Nagarajan v London Regional Transport [1999] IRLR 572.* That case is considered in more detail in relation to *Victimisation.*

This principle is illustrated by the case of *O'Donoghue v Redcar and Cleveland Borough Council [2001] IRLR 615.* The applicant complained of sex discrimination in not appointing her to a new post of senior solicitor. The employment tribunal upheld her complaint, having found that the decision not to appoint her was partly because of advice that she was not an easy person to work with or good with staff but partly because she had freely expressed strong feminist views over a period of years. The council appealed successfully to the EAT against this decision, but an appeal by the applicant was allowed by the Court of Appeal which restored the decision of the tribunal.

67.3   UNREASONABLE OR UNFAIR TREATMENT

It should be noted that the treatment in respect of which a complaint can be made is 'less favourable treatment' than the treatment which another person has received or would have received; not unreasonable or unfair treatment. Direct discrimination is not about unfairness. It is about differences in treatment which are for unacceptable reasons.

This point was emphasised by the House of Lords in the case of *Zafar v Glasgow City Council [1998] IRLR 36.* This was a case in which an Asian employee had been dismissed on the ground that he had sexually harassed both fellow employees and clients of the social welfare department. The tribunal held that for various reasons his dismissal had been unfair and they compared the treatment which he had received with that which he would have received from a reasonable employer. That was the wrong comparison. A finding that an employer has fallen short of the objective standards of the reasonable employer, and that the employer's reaction to particular circumstances is outside the range of reasonable responses to those circumstances, is a key finding in a complaint of unfair dismissal; such a finding does not, however, inevitably lead to a finding of direct discrimination. The proper comparison is not between the way in which the respondent employer has acted and the way in which some other employer has or might have acted, but between the way in which the respondent employer has treated the complainant and the way in which the respondent employer has treated or would have treated other persons. Lord Browne-Wilkinson quoted with approval the following passage from the judgment of Lord Morison in the Court of Session:

> 'The requirement necessary to establish less favourable treatment which is laid down by section 1(1) of the 1976 Act is not one of less favourable treatment than that which would have been accorded by a reasonable employer in the same circumstances, but of less favourable treatment which had been or would have been accorded by the same employer in the same circumstances.'

The importance of the above principle was reaffirmed in *Shamoon*, Lord Rodger, in rejecting the interpretation placed by the Northern Ireland Court of Appeal on the relevant statutory provision, said that their 'interpretation must be wrong because it reintroduces into the law of discrimination the figure of the reasonable employer whom the House was at pains to expel in *Zafar*'. This does not mean that a respondent employer who is found to have behaved badly towards, say, a black employee, will automatically escape liability by making a glib assertion that he would have behaved equally badly towards a white employee. If there is no actual *Comparator* in such a case, the employment tribunal will look at all the available evidence in order to decide how a hypothetical white *Comparator* would have been treated. A variety of matters, such as an open display of hostility by the employer towards the complainant, or unreasonable failure to reply to a *Questionnaire*, could give rise to an inference that the hypothetical white *Comparator* would have been treated more favourably.

This point was made by the Court of Appeal in *Anya v University of Oxford and another [2001] IRLR 377*. Hostility towards a black employee may justify an inference of racial bias if there is nothing else to explain it. A tribunal finding that the employer might very well behave in a similar fashion to a white employee 'will depend not on a theoretical possibility that the employer behaves equally badly to employees of all races, but on evidence that he does.'

In *Law Society and others v Bahl [2003] IRLR 640*, Elias J pointed out, that 'demonstrating the similar treatment of others of a different race or sex is clearly not the only way in which an employer who has acted unreasonably can rebut the finding of discrimination. Were it so, the employer could never do so where the situation he was dealing with was a novel one, as in this case. The inference may also be rebutted – and indeed this will, we suspect, be far more common, by the employer leading evidence of a genuine reason which is not discriminatory and which was the ground of his conduct. Employers will often have unjustified, albeit genuine, reasons for acting as they have. If these are accepted and show no discrimination, there is generally no basis for the inference of unlawful discrimination to be made. Even if they are not accepted, the tribunal's own finding of fact may identify an obvious reason for the treatment in issue, other than a discriminatory reason.'

In this case, the EAT allowed an appeal against the findings of racial and sex discrimination which had been made by the employment tribunal. Elias J said that the tribunal had 'failed to take account of the obvious explanation for any detrimental treatment ... in addition, the tribunal has made findings of discrimination where no proper evidential basis for it exists; and it has inferred in some cases that unfair and unreasonable treatment alone is evidence of discrimination.'

On this last point, Elias J said:

> 'Employers often act unreasonably, as the volume of unfair dismissal cases demonstrates. Indeed, it is the human condition that we all at times act foolishly, inconsiderately, unsympathetically and selfishly and in other ways which we regret in hindsight. It is, however, a wholly unacceptable leap to conclude that whenever the victim of such conduct is black or a woman then it is legitimate to infer that our unreasonable treatment was because the person was black or a woman. All unlawful discriminatory treatment is unreasonable, but not all unreasonable treatment is discriminatory, and it is not shown to be so merely because the victim is either a woman or of a minority race or colour. In order to establish unlawful discrimination, it is necessary to show that the particular employer's reason for acting was one of the proscribed grounds.'

67.4 THE 'DISCRIMINATORY MOTIVE'

A formula which was at one time commonly used, was that there was direct discrimination where the less favourable treatment complained of was for a *Discriminatory Motive*. That is a dangerous and misleading formula.

A discriminatory motive is not a necessary ingredient of direct discrimination. Once it has been established that, for example, a difference in race is the reason why the respondent has treated the complainant less favourably than another person has or would have been treated, then the respondent's motive for acting on the basis of the difference in race is immaterial. What matters is the reason for the difference in treatment; it does not matter whether the respondent personally has a racial bias or whether the respondent has acted in response to pressure from others.

Furthermore, a reason for a difference in treatment can be one which is not expressly formulated but which is subconscious or unconscious. This important principle was clearly stated by the House of Lords in the *Victimisation* case of *Nagarajan.*

68   Directives

Under *European Law*, a Council Directive requires Member States to legislate by a specified date in compliance with the Directive.

Probably the most important *Directives* in the context of discrimination law are the *Equal Treatment Directive,* the *Framework Directive,* the *Race Directive (2000/43/EC)* and the *Pregnant Workers Directive (92/85/EEC).* Other important Directives are those on:

(*a*)   equal pay;

(*b*)   posted workers;

(*c*)   the burden of proof in sex discrimination cases; and

(*d*)   part-time work.

The laws on discrimination relating to religion or belief, sexual orientation and age were brought in by regulations (the *RBR 2003,* the *SOR 2003* and the *AR 2006*), not by a new Act of Parliament. The changes to the *DDA 1995* which took effect on 1 October 2004 were also introduced by regulation. This is because all these measures were required in order to comply with the *Framework Directive* and could therefore be introduced by regulations under the *European Communities Act 1972.*

The ECJ has jurisdiction to rule on questions whether a Member State has duly introduced the required legislation or in any way acted in breach of the requirements of the Directive.

There are two important principles in cases where an employment tribunal is applying domestic law in circumstances which are also covered by a Directive:

(*a*)   the domestic legislation should if possible be construed in conformity with the Directive;

(*b*)   the Directive can have direct effect (if the terms of it are sufficiently precise) as against a *Public Sector* employer.

Both these principles have had an important effect in cases covered by the *Equal Treatment Directive.* For example, in *Webb v EMO Air Cargo (UK) Ltd (No 2) [1995] IRLR 645,* the House of Lords construed the definition of direct discrimination under the *SDA 1975* in conformity with the Directive in order to find that a dismissal of a woman recruited for an indefinite period, because her pregnancy would make her unavailable during a critical period, fell within the definition.

As an example of an important public sector case, the case of *Marshall v South-West Hampshire Area Health Authority* came before the ECJ twice. In the first case (*[1986] IRLR 140*) it was held that a policy of different compulsory retirement ages on grounds of sex (which was then lawful under domestic legislation) was contrary to the Directive. In the second case (*[1993] IRLR 445*) the limit on compensation which applied at that time under the *SDA 1975* was set aside as being contrary to the Directive.

69   Disability

69.1   DEFINITIONS

The *DDA 1995* gives rights to every 'disabled person'. A disabled person is defined as 'a person who has a disability.'

Section 1(1) of the *DDA 1995* provides that a person has a disability 'if he has a physical or mental impairment which has a substantial and long-term adverse effect on his ability to carry out normal day-to-day activities.'

In many cases under the *DDA 1995*, the respondent admits that the claimant has a disability. In other cases, however, it is denied that the claimant is a disabled person and this question is then generally tried as a preliminary issue.

Under *section 2* of the *DDA 1995*, the relevant provisions of the Act do not apply only to a person who currently has a disability; they also apply, with necessary modifications, to a person who has had a disability in the past. It could happen, for example, that a job applicant declares a past disability which has been cured, or which at least has ceased to have a substantial adverse effect, but the employer refuses to employ him or her, either through ignorance and prejudice or because of a concern, which may or may not be well-founded, that the condition and its substantial adverse effect could recur. In such circumstances, the job applicant would be able to present a complaint of disability discrimination in the same way as if the rejection had been for a reason relating to a current disability.

To assist tribunals in applying the definition of disability to specific cases, *section 3* of the *DDA 1995* provides for the Secretary of State to issue guidance about the matters to be taken into account. This statutory Guidance is almost invariably consulted by tribunals and practitioners in all but straightforward cases, and is set out at *Appendix 10*.

69.2   OBJECTIVE

In devising the definition of 'disability', the legislature intended to cover the vast majority of disabled persons in Britain. In committee, the then Minister for Social Security and Disabled People stated that the aim was to achieve a common-sense definition which fitted the generally accepted perception of what a disability is.

69.3   INTERPRETING THE DEFINITION

Early experience of cases brought under the *DDA 1995* showed that tribunals often struggled to come to terms with the unfamiliar legal concepts which it had introduced. Moreover, the facts of specific cases are often difficult to judge. With this in mind, the EAT offered general guidance in *Goodwin v The Patent Office [1999] IRLR 4*:

(a)   when faced with the disability issue, the tribunal should look carefully at what the parties have said in their originating application and response (the IT1 and IT3). The parties may not have identified the real questions at issue, and, generally, it will be unsatisfactory for the disability issue to remain unclear and unspecific until the hearing itself. In many, if not most, disability discrimination cases, it will be good practice either to make standard directions designed to clarify issues or to arrange a directions hearing. It may well be the parties will wish to present expert evidence to assist the tribunal, and it would be undesirable for any such evidence to be given without proper advance notice to the other party and the early provision of a copy of any expert report to be referred to;

(*b*) the role of the tribunal contains an inquisitorial element. The interventionist role which tribunals have in relation to equal value claims might be thought a suitable model for disability cases. According to the EAT, there is 'a risk of a genuine "catch 22" situation'. Some disabled persons may be unable or unwilling to accept that they suffer from any disability; indeed it may be symptomatic of their condition that they deny it. Without the direct assistance of the tribunal, there may be some cases where the claim has been drafted with outside assistance but which the applicant, for some reason related to his disability, is unwilling to support;

(*c*) the tribunal should bear in mind that with social legislation of this kind, a purposive approach to construction should be adopted. The language should be construed in a way which gives effect to the stated or presumed intention of Parliament, but with due regard to the ordinary and natural meaning of the words in question;

(*d*) at least during the early period of the *DDA 1995*'s operation, the tribunal should always make explicit reference to any relevant provision of the Guidance or Code of Practice which has been taken into account in arriving at its decision;

(*e*) in many cases, the question whether the person has a disability under the *DDA 1995* admits of only one answer. In such clear cases, it would be wrong to search the Guidance and use what it says as some kind of extra hurdle over which the applicant must jump;

(*f*) the Code of Practice gives practical guidance and will be found helpful and informative in almost every case under the *DDA 1995*;

(*g*) the definition of 'disability' requires a tribunal to look at the evidence by reference to four different conditions:

(i) The impairment condition.

Does the applicant have an impairment which is either mental or physical?

(ii) The adverse effect of the condition.

Does the impairment affect the applicant's ability to carry out normal day-to-day activities in one of the respects set out in *paragraph 4(1)* of *Schedule 1* to the Act and does it have an adverse effect?

(iii) The substantial condition.

Is the adverse effect upon the applicant's ability substantial?

(iv) The long-term condition.

Is the adverse effect upon the applicant's ability long-term?

Frequently, there will be a 'complete overlap' between conditions (iii) and (iv), but the EAT said that 'it will be as well to bear all four of them in mind. Tribunals may find it helpful to address each of the questions but at the same time beware of the risk that desegregation should not take one's eye off the whole picture'.

For ease of reference, in this handbook, the four main components of the definition are each considered in distinct sections, but their interrelationship must always be kept in mind. The four questions which arise in each case are:

(*a*)   Did the complainant have, at the material time, a *Physical or Mental Impairment?*

(*b*)   If so, did that impairment affect the complainant's ability to carry out *Normal Day-to-Day Activities?*

(*c*)   If so, was that effect a *Substantial Adverse Effect?*

(*d*)   If so, was that effect also a *Long-Term Adverse Effect?*

69.4   SPECIAL CASES

Schedule 1, paragraph 3 of the *DDA 1995*, provides that an impairment which consists of a severe disfigurement is to be treated as having a substantial adverse effect on the person's ability to carry out normal day-to-day activities. There is no need to demonstrate such an effect. However, severe disfigurements resulting from tattoos and body-piercing are excluded by the *Disability Discrimination (Meaning of Disability) Regulations 1996 (SI 1996 No 1455)* (although disfigurements resulting from the removal of such self-inflicted disfigurements appear not to be excluded). Disfigurements include: scars, birthmarks, limb or postural deformation or diseases of the skin. Assessing severity is mainly a matter of degree, although it may be necessary to take account of whereabouts on the body the disfigurement is (e.g. on the face as opposed to the back). Where the severe disfigurement is not permanent, it will be necessary to consider whether it is long-term as defined by the *DDA 1995* (as to which see *Long-Term Adverse Effect*).

With effect from 6 December 2005, pursuant to *paragraph 6A* of *Schedule 1* to the *DDA 1995* (as inserted by the *DDA 2005*) a person is treated as a disabled person if diagnosed with HIV, cancer or multiple sclerosis whether or not the condition is already having an adverse effect on that person's ability to carry out normal day-to-day activities. Previously, these conditions were treated as progressive conditions (see *Substantial Adverse Effects*).

Under *paragraph 7* of *Schedule 1* to the *DDA 1995*, a person is deemed to have had a disability if he or she was on the register of disabled persons maintained under *section 6* of the *Disabled Persons (Employment) Act 1944* on both 12 January 1995 and 2 December 1996.

70   Disability Discrimination

70.1   **THE KEY ISSUES**

The *DDA 1995* gives rights to employees, job applicants and others and imposes corresponding duties on employers and others.

The duties imposed on employers and others are:

(*a*)   a duty in certain circumstances to make *Reasonable Adjustments* for the benefit of a disabled person;

(*b*)   a duty not to discriminate, within the meaning of the *DDA 1995*, against a disabled person;

(*c*)   a duty not to victimise any person, whether or not disabled, within the meaning of the *DDA 1995*;

(*d*)   a duty not to harass employees, job applicants and others.

The following preliminary questions may need to be decided in any complaint under the Act:

(*a*)   Is the claimant a person to whom the respondent owes a duty under the *DDA 1995*? In most cases the answer to this question is obvious, because the claimant is an employee or job applicant and the respondent is an employer or potential employer. There are, however, other persons in the employment field who have rights under the Act and other persons and organisations who have duties.

(*b*)   Does the Act cover the particular matter or matters complained of? Again, in most cases, the answer will be obvious, for example where an employee is complaining of dismissal contrary to the Act or where a job applicant is complaining about a refusal to employ him or her contrary to the Act. The matters in relation to which employers must not discriminate against or victimise employees or job applicants are comprehensively specified.

(*c*)   At the material time, was the complainant a person who had or had had a *Disability*, within the meaning of the Act? This question must always be decided, if not admitted, where the complaint is about a failure to make a *Reasonable Adjustment*, discrimination or *Harassment*. It does not necessarily arise where the complaint is one of *Victimisation* as defined by the Act, because the right not to be victimised is enjoyed by disabled persons and others, for example where an employee who is not disabled gives evidence in support of a complaint of disability discrimination presented by a disabled fellow employee.

70.2   The original definition of disability discrimination is now contained in *section 3A(1)* (formerly *section 5(1)*) of the *DDA 1995*. An employer discriminates against a disabled person if –

(*a*)   for a reason which relates to the disabled person's disability, he treats him less favourably than he treats or would treat others to whom that reason does not or would not apply; and

(*b*)   he cannot show that the treatment in question is justified.'

Under *section 3A(3)* (formerly *section 5(3)*), 'treatment is justified if, but only if, the reason for it is both material to the circumstances of the particular case and substantial.'

It is important to note that the statutory comparison is *not* between the disabled claimant and a fellow employee who is not disabled. The focus is on the reason for the less favourable treatment, not on the fact of the disability. The point is illustrated by the leading case of *Clark v TDG Ltd t/a Novacold [1999] IRLR 318.* An employee who suffered a back injury was dismissed after an absence of about four months after his GP indicated that he was unlikely to be fit to return in the near future and an orthopaedic consultant said that, while the injury should improve over a period of a year, it was not possible to specify when the employee could resume his duties. A tribunal and the EAT considered that the employee had not suffered discrimination because he was treated no differently than a person who was off work for the same amount of time, but for a reason other than disability, would have been treated. The Court of Appeal said that this was the wrong approach. The test of less favourable treatment is based on the reason for the less favourable treatment of the disabled person and not on the fact of his disability. It does not turn on a like-for-like comparison of the disabled person and others in similar circumstances. The proper comparison was between the claimant and employees who had not been absent from work for about four months, because it was the absence from work, not the fact of the disability, which was the reason for the dismissal.

However, *Royal Liverpool Children's NHS Trust v Dunsby [2006] IRLR 351*, indicates that the DDA does not automatically penalise an employer who takes disability-related absences into account when operating an absence procedure.

The EAT overruled a decision by a tribunal that a decision to dismiss the claimant on grounds of her sickness absence was not for a reason which was material and substantial within the meaning of the *DDA 1995* because, but for the disability-related absences, the claimant would not have been at risk of dismissal. The *DDA 1995* does not impose an absolute obligation on an employer to refrain from dismissing an employee who is absent wholly or in part on the grounds of ill health due to disability. An employer may take into account disability-related absences in operating a sickness absence procedure. It is rare for a sickness absence procedure to require disability-related absences to be disregarded. Whether by taking disability-related absences into account, the employer acts unlawfully, will generally depend on whether or not the employer is justified. In this case, the tribunal failed to consider the question of *Justification*. A tribunal does not answer the question of whether a dismissal is justified merely by saying that it was because the employee was absent on grounds of disability. That is the starting point for an enquiry into justification, not its conclusion. The tribunal was also wrong to find that the dismissal was unfair on grounds that the employers acted unreasonably in including absences which related to disability in the 'totting-up' process. There is no absolute rule that a employer operating a sickness absence procedure acts unreasonably in taking into account disability-related absences as part of a totting-up review process or as part of a reason for dismissal on grounds of repeated short-term absences.

Taylor v OCS Group Ltd [2006] IRLR 613 also indicates a significant limit on the scope of the *DDA 1995*. The question for the Court of Appeal in this case was whether an employee had been dismissed for a reason 'which related' to his disability within the meaning of the *DDA 1995*, in that the decision to dismiss was partly based on his failure to give an adequate explanation for his conduct, and he was unable to do this because he was profoundly deaf. A tribunal focused on the reason for dismissal which was present in the employer's mind (misconduct) and found that this was not related to the claimant's disability. The EAT allowed an appeal, on the basis that it was not necessary to show that the disability-related reason was present in the employer's mind in order to demonstrate that the reason 'related to' disability. However, the Court of Appeal restored the original decision, considering that the EAT's reasoning was faulty.

Discrimination requires that the employer should have a certain state of mind. Thus the disability-related reason must be present in the employer's mind. Where there is more than one reason for treating the disabled employee differently, if the disability-related reason had a significant influence on the decision, that would be enough to conclude that the decision was for a reason related to the disability. Moreover, it is open to a tribunal to find that the decision had been effected by the disability-related reason even though the employer had not consciously allowed that reason to affect his thinking. What is important is that the disability-related reason must affect the employer's mind – whether consciously or subconsciously. At the time of writing, it was understood that leave to appeal to the House of Lords has been applied for.

Where less favourable treatment is established, there remains the possibility of justifying that treatment. For consideration generally of justification see *Justification and Disability Discrimination*. The relationship between justification and *Reasonable Adjustments* is considered below.

Since 1 October 2004, there has also been an important definition of discrimination, under *section 3A(1)*, in the following terms:

> 'A person directly discriminates against a disabled person if, on the ground of the disabled person's disability, he treats the disabled person less favourably than he treats or would treat a person not having that particular disability whose relevant circumstances, including his abilities, are the same as, or not materially different from, those of the disabled person.'

Where there is direct discrimination within the above definition, there will be no defence of justification (*section 3A(5)*). There will be direct discrimination within the above definition, if a disabled person is treated less favourably than a non-disabled person not because the disability does in fact have any material effect on his or her ability to do any particular work but because of a mistaken perception that it will or may do so. There are many workers who are disabled persons within the meaning of the *DDA 1995* but whose disability, even without *Reasonable Adjustments,* has no effect whatsoever on their ability to do any particular work.

70.3   REASONABLE ADJUSTMENTS

The statutory provisions and case law relating to *Reasonable Adjustments* are considered separately, but it is necessary to touch on the subject in this section also because of the relationship with the definition of disability discrimination. That relationship arises in two ways, as illustrated by the following example:

Suppose that an employee has an accident and becomes disabled, within the statutory definition of *Disability*. His job description involves mainly light work, but he has one particular duty which, because of his disability, is now physically beyond him. It would be fairly easy for the employer to rearrange his duties so that in future he is required to do only light work. Instead, the employer dismisses him on the ground that he is no longer capable of doing the whole of the job for which he is employed.

There would be grounds for a finding that the employer has failed to comply with the duty in relation to *Reasonable Adjustments*. The requirement to carry out the full range of duties, including the physically demanding duty, placed the disabled employee at a substantial disadvantage in comparison with employees who were not disabled. In these circumstances, it was the duty of the employer to take such steps as it was reasonable for the employer to have to take in order to remove that disadvantage. The employer has failed to comply with that duty. This failure has two consequences.

First, a failure to comply with the duty contained in *section 4A* (formerly *section 6)* of the *DDA 1995*, in relation to *Reasonable Adjustments,* is in itself treated as an act of discrimination. That is the effect of *section 3A(2))* of the *DDA 1995*. With effect from 1 October 2004 it has not been possible for an employer or any other respondent to justify a failure to comply with the duty in relation to *Reasonable Adjustments.*

70.4   **CIRCUMSTANCES IN WHICH DISCRIMINATION IS UNLAWFUL**

Section 4(1) of the *DDA 1995* renders it unlawful for an employer to discriminate against a disabled person:

(*a*)   in the arrangements which he makes for the purpose of determining to whom he should offer employment;

(*b*)   in the terms on which he offers that person employment; or

(*c*)   by refusing to offer, or deliberately not offering, him employment.

Section 4(2) renders it unlawful for an employer to discriminate against a disabled person whom he employs:

(*a*)   in the terms of employment which he affords him;

(*b*)   in the opportunities which he affords him for promotion, a transfer, training or receiving any other benefits;

(*c*)   by refusing to afford him, or deliberately not affording him, any such opportunity; or

(*d*)   by dismissing him, or subjecting him to any other detriment.

Section 4(2) does not apply to benefits of any description if the employer is concerned with the provision of benefits of that description to the public, or to a section of the public which includes the employee in question, unless:

(*a*)   that provision differs in a material respect from the provision of the benefits by the employer to his employee; or

(*b*)   the provision of the benefits to the employee in question is regulated by his contract of employment; or

(*c*)   the benefits relate to training.

'Benefits' for these purposes include facilities and services.

In *section 4*, the term 'discriminate' includes all the definitions of discrimination contained in the *DDA 1995*, including *Victimisation.*

Under *subsection 4(3),* it has since 1 October 2004 been 'unlawful for an employer, in relation to employment by him, to subject to *Harassment*:

(*a*)   a disabled person whom he employs, or

(*b*)   a disabled person who has applied to him for employment.'

71   Disability Discrimination and Unfair Dismissal

An employer may, in dismissing a disabled employed, be guilty of discrimination contrary to the *DDA 1995*. If the employee is eligible for the right not to be unfairly dismissed, he or she may well bring a claim of unfair dismissal in addition to a claim of disability discrimination. Typically, the dismissal will be unfair if the reason for it was discriminatory contrary to the *DDA 1995*, but that is not necessarily the case. In *H J Heinz Co Ltd v Kenrick [2000] IRLR 144*, for example, an employee with chronic fatigue syndrome was dismissed because of his lengthy sickness absence. The EAT upheld a tribunal's decision that the employer was in breach of the *DDA 1995* and had failed to justify the discrimination on the ground of disability. However, the tribunal's finding that the dismissal was unfair was set aside. The tribunal seemed to have proceeded on the basis that a disability-related dismissal which is not justified under the *DDA 1995* is *automatically* unfair. However, the EAT emphasised that that is not the case. There should have been separate consideration of the matters relevant to fairness which usually fall for consideration under *section 98(4)* of the *Employment Rights Act 1996*. Parliament has not provided that a dismissal that is discriminatory contrary to the *DDA 1995* is automatically unfair, in the way that, for example, certain other dismissals are deemed to be automatically unfair, e.g. because of failure to comply with the statutory dismissal procedure.

72   Disability Discrimination Legislation

72.1   THE LEGISLATION AND OTHER PROVISIONS

The principal legislation is the *DDA 1995*, which is supplemented by various regulations including the *Disability Discrimination Act 1995 (Amendment) Regulations 2003 (SI 2003 No 1673)*, which made substantial amendments as from 1 October 2004. In particular:

(*a*)   The definition of *Disability Discrimination* was amended, introducing for the first time the concept of direct discrimination for which there is no justification defence, where the less favourable treatment is on the ground of the disability itself, rather than for a reason relating to the disability.

(*b*)   The defence of justification in cases of a failure to comply with the duty in relation to *Reasonable Adjustments* was removed.

(c)   Various changes were made bringing the legislation more closely into line with other *Discrimination Laws*.

Further amendments were made by the *DDA 2005*, which extends the definition of disability to persons who have been diagnosed with HIV, cancer or multiple sclerosis, whether or not the condition has started to affect their ability to carry out normal day-to-day activities.

Pursuant to the *DDA 1995*, the Secretary of State has issued a *Code of Practice* which addresses the elimination of discrimination in the field of employment. The Code does not purport to set out a definitive statement of the detailed law, but offers general and practical guidance and is admissible in evidence in proceedings under the *DDA 1995*. If a provision of the Code itself (but not the Annexes to it, which contain information on associated matters) appears to be relevant, it must be taken into account by a tribunal. There is also a Code of Practice on the Duties of Trade Organisations to their Disabled Members and Applicants.

The Secretary of State has also exercised his power under the *DDA 1995* to issue Guidance concerning matters to be taken into account in determining whether an impairment has a substantial adverse effect on a person's ability to carry out normal day-to-day activities, or whether such an impairment has a long-term effect. The Guidance has similar status to that of the Code of Practice. For the importance of this Guidance, and some of the provisions, see *Disability*.

The *Disability Rights Commission*, established by the *Disability Rights Commission Act 1999*, came into operation in April 2000 and has a role similar to those of the *Equal Opportunities Commission* and *Commission for Racial Equality*. It will merge with the other statutory Commissions in October 2007 to form the *Commission for Equality and Human Rights*.

72.2   SCOPE OF THE DDA 1995

Part I and *Schedules 1–2* to the *DDA 1995* address the crucial definitions of 'disability' and 'disabled person'. *Part II* covers discrimination in employment and by *Trade Organisations*. The Act extends to discrimination in fields other than employment and which are *not* covered by this handbook, i.e. discrimination in relation to goods, facilities and services; the disposal and management of premises; and education and transport.

72.3 Disability Discrimination Legislation

In the employment field, the *DDA 1995* granted rights to employees, job applicants, *Contract Workers* and members of (and persons seeking to join) *Trade Unions* and other trade organisations (see *Trade Organisations and Discrimination*). Various classes of persons are excluded from protection by the *DDA 1995*:

(a)   members of the armed forces, prison officers and fire fighters;

(b)   certain overseas employees;

(c)   employees who work on board ships, aircraft or hovercraft;

(d)   members of certain special police forces and certain other police officers; and

(e)   holders of a statutory office.

72.3   OTHER PROVISIONS

The provisions in the *DDA 1995* relating to *Liability for Employees and Agents, Time Limits, Continuing Discrimination, Questionnaires, Agreements* and *Conciliation* are the same as those familiar from sex and race discrimination law.

72.4   CHARITIES

The *DDA 1995* contains special provisions relating to *Charities* for disabled people which in effect permit a limited form of *Positive Discrimination*. Nothing in *Part II* affects any charitable instrument conferring benefits on categories of persons determined by reference to any physical or mental capacity or makes unlawful any act done by a charity in pursuance of its charitable purposes, so far as these purposes are connected to such persons. Employers who provide 'supported employment' for the disabled are permitted to treat members of a particular group of disabled persons more favourably than other persons in providing such supported employment.

72.5   REMEDIES

If a complaint made under the *DDA 1995* succeeds, the tribunal must grant one or more of the following remedies:

(a)   a declaration as to the rights of the complainant and the respondent in relation to the matters to which the complaint relates;

(b)   an order that the respondent pays compensation to the complainant;

(c)   a recommendation that the respondent take, within a specified period, action which appears to the tribunal to be reasonable in all the circumstances of the case, for the purpose of obviating or reducing the adverse effect on the complainant of any matters to which the complaint relates.

Crucially, there is no limit on the amount of *Compensation* that a tribunal may award. It is almost inevitable that, in cases where discrimination results in the loss of a job, the typical award for compensation to a disabled person will tend to be higher than in most other discrimination cases, simply because of the difficulties that many disabled persons encounter in seeking to obtain work. Compensation running into six figures was awarded even in one of the earliest cases brought under the *DDA 1995*: *British Sugar plc v Kirker [1998] IRLR 624*.

The need for care in making an award of compensation for disability discrimination was highlighted by the EAT in *Buxton v Equinox Design Ltd [1999] IRLR 158*, which concerned the dismissal of a craftsman who had been diagnosed as having multiple sclerosis. The tribunal awarded compensation, including £500 for injury to feelings, on the basis that the period of future loss should be limited to one year from the date of the letter from a doctor advising on the employee's condition. The tribunal made its award without having heard oral evidence from any doctor called by either party.

The EAT ruled that the tribunal was wrong to limit the period of future loss to one year without a sufficient evidential basis. More generally, the EAT said that the remedies hearing in a case of discrimination requires careful judicial management. In a case where compensation is unlimited, the relatively brief and informal hearing on remedy that has conventionally been regarded as appropriate in unfair dismissal cases may not be appropriate. It will often be the case that the remedies hearing should involve the parties in careful pre-preparation under the management of the tribunal. For this purpose, directions may be required involving an exchange of statements of case and any witness statements. Without proper directions by the tribunal, 'there is a real probability of trial by ambush leading to significant awards'. In disability cases, a medical expert may be required if the parties have been unable to agree the evidence. Where necessary, special consideration should be given to fixing the hearing to accommodate a busy professional witness.

On the facts of the case, the crucial issue had been for the tribunal to decide, on a balance of probabilities and an assessment of the chances, what would have been the outcome of the risk assessment in relation to the employee if one had been carried out. The tribunal's finding that the period of loss should be one year could not be made on the evidence before it, since it involved making a finding as to the outcome of a risk assessment in the context of a disease which has variable effects. Without medical evidence, the tribunal was not in a position to say what the outcome would be. The case was therefore remitted back to the tribunal for further consideration.

73   Disability Policies

73.1   **IS A SEPARATE DISABILITY POLICY NECESSARY?**

Disability may be addressed in an organisation's general equal opportunities policy statement. This may help to avoid a proliferation of *Equal Opportunities Policies* as well as, from a presentational and perhaps substantive perspective, treating disabled people inappropriately as some form of 'special case'. There is, moreover, merit in having a single over-arching statement of policy in respect of equal opportunities. However, there may be attractions, perhaps especially in organisations which may not have addressed disability issues in detail previously, in having a separate disability policy statement, even if only as an interim measure while a comprehensive integrated policy is developed. It may for example be advantageous to have a separate policy on disability so as to raise awareness within the organisation of the key issues.

73.2   **REVIEWING CURRENT PRACTICE**

Whether there is to be a separate disability policy, or disability is covered by the organisation's general equal opportunities policy, it is sensible to assess current practice before drawing up the disability policy statement. The review process, sometimes called a 'disability audit', may range widely. Examples of subjects which may be considered include:

(*a*)   Is there any current policy statement or associated documentation?

(*b*)   If there is a current policy, who is responsible for implementing it?

(*c*)   How are the needs of disabled employees in respect of matters such as premises and equipment met?

(*d*)   How is disability dealt with in the recruitment process?

(*e*)   Are any steps taken to help people with disabilities to develop their careers?

(*f*)   How are *Employees Who Become Disabled* treated?

(*g*)   How are the training needs of disabled people met?

(*h*)   Does the organisation monitor its performance in respect of treating disabled employees equally?

73.3   **IMPLEMENTATION**

Because the *DDA 1995* is a much more recent enactment than either the *SDA 1975* or *RRA 1976* managers in an organisation may sometimes be slow to recognise both the importance and the implications of treating disabled people equally. The key elements of implementing an effective disability policy typically include:

(*a*)   obtaining the commitment of the top managers to the policy;

(*b*)   training staff responsible for recruitment, selection and promotion decisions to appreciate the impact of the *DDA 1995, Guidance and Code of Practice*;

(*c*)   identifying the issues which need to be covered by the disability policy;

(*d*)   drawing up the disability policy, consulting where appropriate with staff and with trade union representatives;

(*e*)   keeping the policy up to date.

73.4   CONTENTS OF THE POLICY

The specific matters that may be covered in a disability policy are likely to vary from organisation to organisation. The following is a list of examples which is far from exhaustive:

(*a*)   does recruitment literature and advertising welcome disabled people?

(*b*)   are job advertisements placed in alternative media such as teletext?

(*c*)   are questions asked at job interviews relating to disability concerned solely with the requirements of the job?

(*d*)   are any particular needs that a disabled person may have as regards access to premises or equipment discussed with the individuals?

(*e*)   are training courses accessible to disabled delegates?

(*f*)   are disabled employees encouraged to give feedback on their particular needs?

73.5   STAFF TRAINING

Lack of familiarity with disability issues is still a widespread phenomenon. Managers dealing with disabled job applicants and employees, and front-line staff dealing with disabled customers, are obvious examples of staff who are likely to need appropriate training. There may also be a case for making training available to the whole workforce. Training may tackle both general awareness of disability issues and also more specific training implications of the legislation. It is often helpful for training to cover disability etiquette, i.e. courtesies with disabled people which may not be obvious to those who have had limited contact with people who have disabilities. For example:

(*a*)   disabled adults (e.g. those with learning disabilities) should not be treated as if they are children;

(*b*)   negative or intrusive questions should be avoided;

(*c*)   jokes exploiting disabilities are unacceptable;

(*d*)   if a disabled person appears to need assistance, one should offer it, but wait for the offer to be accepted before acting and not be offended if the offer is rejected;

(*e*)   a wheelchair is part of the wheelchair user's body space and so one should not lean on it inappropriately;

(*f*)   one should not shout at deaf people;

(*g*)   one should talk directly to a deaf person rather than his or her interpreter;

(*h*)   when a blind person enters an unfamiliar room, one should offer a brief explanation of the room, identifying possible hazards;

(*i*)   one should tell a blind person when one is leaving the room;

(*j*)   one should avoid language which may be perceived as belittling. Views on terminology vary, but commonly the following words and terms are regarded as inappropriate:

(i)   'handicapped';

(ii)   'the disabled';

(iii) 'wheelchair bound' or 'confined to a wheelchair';

(iv)   'spastic';

(k)   one should avoid referring to a person simply by reference to their condition. For example, to refer to a 'person with epilepsy' is appropriate; an 'epileptic' is not.

74   Disability Rights Commission

When the *Disability Discrimination Act 1995* was introduced, there was no provision for a rights agency along the same lines as the *Commission for Racial Equality* (CRE) or the *Equal Opportunities Commission* (EOC) to which individual complaints of discrimination might be submitted. Rather, the then government established the National Disability Council (NDC) an advisory body with a limited remit and no enforcement powers. It soon became apparent that, given the complexity of many aspects of the *Disability Discrimination Legislation*, it would be desirable for there to be a Disability Rights Commission, which could make a more effective contribution than the NDC to the clarification of areas of difficulty. The *Disability Rights Commission Act 1999* established the Disability Rights Commission (DRC) which became operational in April 2000. The DRC replaces the NDC and comprises up to 15 members, the majority of them disabled.

The role and functions of the DRC include the following:

(*a*)   working towards the elimination of discrimination against disabled people;

(*b*)   promoting the equalisation of opportunities for disabled people with those of non-disabled people;

(*c*)   advising government on the law about discrimination against disabled people;

(*d*)   assisting disabled people by offering information, advice and support in taking cases forward;

(*e*)   providing information and advice to business and other stakeholders;

(*f*)   investigating where the DRC has reason to believe that discrimination is taking place and to secure compliance with the law;

(*g*)   preparing codes of practice and promoting good practice (see *Appendices 6 and 7*);

(*h*)   enforcement powers in relation to unlawful *Advertisements, Instructions to Discriminate* and *Pressure to Discriminate.*

Thus the powers of the DRC are similar to those of the CRE and EOC.

With effect from October 2007, the DRC's functions will transfer to the *Commission for Equality and Human Rights.*

75 Disciplinary Rules and Grievance Procedures

Employers should have regard to equal opportunities considerations when operating disciplinary and grievance procedures. The *ACAS Code of Practice on Disciplinary and Grievance Procedures* makes various recommendations:

(*a*) If a letter is sent to a worker to inform him or her of an apparent disciplinary problem, the content of the letter should be explained if the worker has difficulty reading or English is not their first language.

(*b*) When managing absence, employers should also bear in mind that the law expects them to be more tolerant of workers who are absent because of a disability.

(*c*) Setting out a grievance in writing is not easy, especially for employees whose first language is not English. In such circumstances, the employee should be encouraged to seek help from a work colleague, an employee representative or the Citizens Advice Bureau.

(*d*) Whilst most employers are under no legal duty to provide their workers with car parking facilities, and a grievance about such facilities would carry no right to be accompanied at a grievance hearing by a companion, if the worker were disabled and needed a car to get to and from work, there probably would be a right to have a companion at a grievance hearing, as an issue might arise as to whether the employer was meeting its obligations under the *DDA 1995*.

The statutory disciplinary and dismissal procedures introduced in October 2004 are similar to the grievance procedures discussed in the contract of *Grievances* and were also introduced by the Dispute Resolution Regulations which were roundly criticised by the Gibbons Review in March 2007, but still in force at the time of writing,

124

76   Disciplining and Dismissing Disabled Employees

76.1   **LACK OF CAPABILITY**

A reason relating to an employee's capability may constitute a potentially fair ground for dismissal. Lack of capability may take either of two forms: sub-standard performance or unsatisfactory attendance. Employers need to appreciate that a disability may lie behind both poor performance and poor attendance and take care to ensure that their procedures for dealing with such problems are not discriminatory.

The Court of Appeal's decision in *Clark v TDG Ltd t/a Novacold [1999] IRLR 318* is instructive. An employee who suffered a back injury was dismissed after an absence of about four months after his GP indicated that he was unlikely to be fit to return in the near future and an orthopaedic consultant said that, while the injury should improve over a period of a year, it was not possible to specify when the employee could resume his duties. A tribunal and the EAT considered that the employee had not suffered discrimination because he was treated no differently than a person who was off work for the same amount of time, but for a reason other than disability, would have been treated. The Court of Appeal said that this was the wrong approach. The applicant should have been compared with an employee who was not off work at all. The test of less favourable treatment is based on the reason for the less favourable treatment of the disabled person and not on the fact of his disability. It does not turn on a like-for-like comparison of the disabled person and others in similar circumstances. So it is not appropriate to make a comparison of the cases in the same way as under the *SDA 1975* or *RRA 1976*. The statutory focus in the *DDA 1995* is narrower and the emphasis is on whether the less favourable treatment of the employee is shown to be justified.

The Court of Appeal also held that the tribunal had gone wrong in another respect. The tribunal had said that if there was less favourable treatment then it would not have been justified. The Court of Appeal held that it was wrong to take that view without having regard to the relevant provisions of the *Code of Practice* relating to termination of employment.

In particular, the Code states that:

> 'It would be justifiable to terminate the employment of an employee where disability makes it impossible for him any longer to perform the main functions of his job, if an adjustment such as a move to a vacant post elsewhere in the business is not practicable or otherwise not reasonable for the employer to make.'

The Court of Appeal noted that 'the critical question . . . is that of justification of the treatment. This will also probably be the case with many other complaints under the 1995 Act'. It follows that employers should pay particular heed to the matter of whether they can justify their actions in cases of lack of capacity.

The Court of Appeal also gave guidance on a further matter which was not directly relevant to the issues in the case. Mr Clark had not pleaded that there had been an unjustified failure by the employer to comply with its duty to make reasonable adjustments. The employment tribunal found in any event that the section 6 duty does not apply to decisions to dismiss. In the Court of Appeal, Mummery LJ pointed out that, however, the duty arises in the pre-dismissal situation. He said that there may well be cases 'where a person who has been dismissed complains of both discrimination by unjustified dismissal and also discrimination by pre-dismissal breaches of duties to make reasonable adjustments while he was still in employment. There is no reason why an employee should not be able to pursue both claims: they are separate acts of discrimination and the fact that the employee has been dismissed does not deprive him of the right to complain of a wrong committed against him while he was still employed, in the employer failing to comply with the duty to make reasonable adjustments to arrangements and to premises.

In *Royal Liverpool Children's NHS Trust v Dunsby [2006] IRLR 351*, the EAT over-ruled a decision by a tribunal that a decision to dismiss the claimant on grounds of her sickness absence was not for a reason which was material and substantial within the meaning of the *DDA 1995* because, but for the disability-related absences, the claimant would not have been at risk of dismissal. The *DDA 1995* does not impose an absolute obligation on an employer to refrain from dismissing an employee who is absent wholly or in part on the grounds of ill health due to disability. An employer may take into account disability-related absences in operating a sickness absence procedure. It is rare for a sickness absence procedure to require disability-related absences to be disregarded. Whether by taking disability-related absences into account, the employer acts unlawfully, will generally depend on whether or not the employer is justified. In this case, the tribunal failed to consider the question of *Justification*. A tribunal does not answer the question of whether a dismissal is justi-fied merely by saying that it was because the employee was absent on grounds of disability. That is the starting point for an enquiry into justification, not its conclu-sion.

The tribunal was also wrong to find that the dismissal was unfair on grounds that the employers acted unreasonably in including absences which related to disability in the 'totting-up' process. There is no absolute rule that an employer operating a sick-ness absence procedure acts unreasonably in taking into account disability-related absences as part of a totting-up review process or as part of a reason for dismissal on grounds of repeated short-term absences.

76.2   **REDUNDANCY**

Most employers now realise that, even where a genuine 'redundancy situation' (to use a non-legalistic term) exists, a decision to make an employee redundant must nevertheless be handled in a fair and reasonable manner. Typically, this involves ensuring that selection is fair and reasonable and based on objective and relevant criteria; undertaking meaningful consultation before a decision to dismiss is taken; and considering properly alternatives to redundancy, which for example may include short-time working, seeking volunteers, redeployment and revising employment terms.

By virtue of the *DDA 1995*, it is discriminatory to select for redundancy on the basis of disability. It is also necessary to ensure that the way in which the redundancy process is handled is non-discriminatory. This may give rise to tricky challenges for employers, especially if their method of selecting for redundancy involves the appli-cation of criteria such as attendance, productivity or (a common but often unsatis-factory catch-all) 'flexibility'. Attendance records, for instance, may appear to constitute a sound and objective factor to take into account when considering which employees to retain within a shrinking workforce. But what if poor attendance results from a disability? In the light of the *DDA 1995*, a disability-related criterion will only be legitimate if the criterion has a demonstrably substantial and material effect on the organisation and it is not possible to make a reasonable adjustment to redress that effect.

An illustration of the general principles arose in *Morse v Wiltshire County Council [1999] IRLR 352*. Following an accident, a road worker was left with a disability involving restrictions on movement and a susceptibility to blackouts. When a redundancy situation arose, management took the view that it was essential to retain only the most flexible workers, especially in order to ensure that a proper winter road surface was maintained. But it was necessary for many of the workers to be fully qualified drivers. The disabled employee's lack of driving ability (because of the blackouts) and the limitations on what he could do led to his selection for redundancy. There was no consultation directly with him as to his current state of health. At the time of his dismissal, he had been employed by the county council for nearly 34 years and he had been working for more than 10 years since the accident which caused his disability.

A tribunal rejected his complaint of discrimination, even though it was undisputed that he had been dismissed for a reason relating to his disability. The tribunal concluded that the employers had shown that no reasonable adjustment to the working conditions or job description would have avoided the dismissal and the reason for his treatment was substantial and material within *section 5* of the *DDA 1995*.

The EAT allowed the employee's appeal. The tribunal had failed to take the correct steps in considering the question of discrimination. It had not made any real enquiry into the steps which the employer might have taken to enable the employee to be kept on, or into the additional expense, if any, which was likely to be caused by any steps to enable his retention.

76.3   **REDEPLOYMENT AND REDUNDANCY PROCEDURES**

The fact that the duty to make reasonable adjustments serves as a form of *Positive Discrimination* in favour of disabled employees is illustrated by *Kent County Council v Mingo [2000] IRLR 90*. A cook injured his back and received medical advice that it was almost inevitable that the back problem would recur if he returned to his cooking job, but that he would be fit for work that did not include heavy duties or lifting. He was found work as a supernumerary helper and, following a recommendation that he be redeployed, he was classified as a 'category B redeployee' under the employer's procedures. Category B covered staff to be redeployed on grounds of 'incapability/ill health'. In contrast, those at risk, or under notice of, redundancy were classified as category A employees and given priority consideration for suitable alternative employment. Following the introduction of the *DDA 1995*, the employers introduced a new category to cover staff with a disability where a reasonable adjustment could not be made to their present post to accommodate the disability. However, category A staff continued to be placed at a higher level. The disabled employee was turned down for an internal post for which he had applied and had been graded appointable. He was told that he would have been appointed if he had been a category A redeployee. He expressed interest in other vacancies but was told that they were reserved for category A redeployees. After his supernumerary post came to an end, he was dismissed.

The EAT upheld a tribunal's decision that the employee had been unfairly dismissed and discriminated against unlawfully. The employer's redeployment procedures did not adequately reflect the requirements of the *DDA 1995*, since the policy of giving preferential treatment to redundant or potentially redundant employees meant that people with disabilities were relatively disadvantaged in the system of redeployment. Had the employer permitted the employee to be treated as a category A redeployee, he would have been redeployed and not dismissed. This justified a finding of disability discrimination.

76.4   **MISCONDUCT**

A disabled employee may be dismissed for gross misconduct, or an instance of less serious misconduct following appropriate earlier warnings, in circumstances where another employee would have been dismissed. But, on occasion, for example in the case of an employee with a learning disability, an instance of apparent misconduct such as aggressive behaviour may be explicable by reference to the disability. In such a case, the employer may need to consider making a reasonable adjustment in terms (for instance) of establishing working conditions sufficiently flexible as to accommodate the behaviour of the employee in question without undue disruption to the business or to colleagues.

In *Taylor v OCS Group Ltd [2006] IRLR 613*, the question for the Court of Appeal was whether an employee had been dismissed for a reason 'which related' to his disability within the meaning of the *DDA 1995*, in that the decision to dismiss was partly based on his failure to give an adequate explanation for his conduct, and he was unable to do this because he was profoundly deaf. A tribunal focused on the reason for dismissal which was present in the employer's mind (misconduct) and found that this was not related to the claimant's disability. The EAT allowed an appeal, on the basis that it was not necessary to show that the disability-related reason was present in the employer's mind in order to demonstrate that the reason 'related to' disability. However, the Court of Appeal restored the original decision, considering that the EAT's reasoning was faulty.

Discrimination requires that the employer should have a certain state of mind. Thus the disability-related reason must be present in the employer's mind. Where there is more than one reason for treating the disabled employee differently, if the disability-related reason had a significant influence on the decision, that would be enough to conclude that the decision was for a reason related to the disability. Moreover, it is open to a tribunal to find that the decision had been effected by the disability-related reason even though the employer had not consciously allowed that reason to affect his thinking. What is important is that the disability-related reason must affect the employer's mind – whether consciously or subconsciously.

76.5   **SHORT-SERVING EMPLOYEES**

Even where a disabled employee lacks the necessary qualifying service to claim unfair dismissal, considerable care needs to be taken if dismissal is contemplated. An illustration of the issues that may arise is provided by *High Quality Lifestyles Ltd v Watts [2006] IRLR 850,* where an employee was dismissed after disclosing that he was HIV positive. The employers took the view that the risk of onward transmission in the residential home where he worked was too late because there had been incidents when staff were bitten. An employment tribunal found that this was direct disability discrimination, but the EAT disagreed. There was no less favourable treatment because the circumstances were not, as the tribunal found, that the comparator should have a communicable disease. The comparator had to have some attribute, whether caused by a medical condition or otherwise, which was not HIV positive. The attribute must carry the same risk of causing to others illness or injury of the same gravity. If the comparator would have been dismissed, then the claimant was not less favourably treated. In order to have shifted the burden of proof to the employers, the claimant needed to prove some evidential basis upon which it could be said by the tribunal that the comparator will not have been dismissed. This was not done.

However, the employers had failed to justify discriminating against the claimant for a disability-related reason. There had been a failure to carry out a proper investigation or adequate risk assessment of the situation caused by the claimant's condition. Further, the employers had failed to carry out *Reasonable Adjustments*. The employer's requirement that a support worker should not pose a risk of transmitting a serious medical condition such as HIV placed the claimant at a substantial disadvantage in comparison with a person who is not HIV positive. That invoked the duty to take reasonable steps, and the tribunal is entitled to find that the employer had not properly considered all relevant adjustments.

77   Discrimination Laws

The main discrimination laws referred to in this Handbbook are:

(a)   The *SDA 1975* (together with, in cases of gender-related pay discrimination, the *EPA 1970*).

(b)   The *RRA 1976*.

(c)   The *DDA 1995*.

(d)   The *RBR 2003*.

(e)   The *SOR 2003*.

(f)   The *AR 2006*.

The reason why it was possible to introduce the laws on Age Discrimination, *Religion and Belief* and on *Sexual Orientation* by regulation, rather than by means of a new Act of Parliament, is that these laws could be introduced under the *European Communities Act 1972*, because they were necessary for the implementation of a Directive (the *Framework Directive*).

It is also important to note that some provisions of *European Law* have direct effect. Workers in the *Public Sector* can take proceedings to enforce rights which are given to them by a *Directive* but not by domestic legislation. Both private sector and public sector employees have been able to claim and enforce extended rights under the *EPA 1970* and the *SDA 1975*, because of the direct effect of *Article 141* (formerly *Article 119*) of the European Treaty – see *Equal Pay* and *Pensions*.

78   Discriminatory Motive

The definition of *Direct Discrimination* requires the consideration of three questions:

(*a*)   Has a person been treated less favourably than another person has or would have been treated?

(*b*)   If so, was this treatment for the reason specified in the legislation, e.g. on racial grounds or because she was a woman?

(*c*)   Are the relevant circumstances of the two cases the same or not materially different?

In some of the early authorities, this second question was sometimes expressed in terms of a discriminatory motive. Was there such a motive for the treatment complained of?

The expression 'discriminatory motive' should, however, no longer be used. A line of House of Lords authorities, ending with the case of *Nagarajan v London Regional Transport [1999] IRLR 572*, has clearly established that there can be direct discrimination or victimisation without a discriminatory motive or desire to victimise the complainant. The focus must be on the reason or reasons for the treatment complained of and not on any motive underlying those reasons. Proof of a discriminatory motive is not necessary, although it may be helpful in terms of indicating the probable reason for the treatment complained of.

79   Dismissal

79.1   PREGNANCY-RELATED DISMISSALS

The House of Lords made it clear in *Webb v EMO Air Cargo (UK) Ltd (No 2) [1995] IRLR 645* that pregnancy is a gender-based criterion. Accordingly, dismissing a woman because she is pregnant is direct sex discrimination. Furthermore, where a woman has been engaged for an indefinite period, she cannot lawfully be dismissed if her pregnancy makes her unavailable at the time when her services are particularly required.

It is also direct discrimination to dismiss a woman because of her long absence from work or poor attendance record, in a case where the absence from work during pregnancy has been caused by a pregnancy-related illness. This principle was established by the ECJ in *Brown v Rentokil Ltd [1998] IRLR 445*.

There is no defence of justification in these cases. Justification is not available as a defence to direct discrimination.

79.2   DISABILITY

The dismissal of an employee for absences which are wholly or partly caused by a disability could lead to a complaint of disability discrimination. The employer must consider the following questions before dismissing or even giving a warning:

(*a*)   Is this a case where the employee has or could have a disability?

(*b*)   If the position is unclear, has it been thoroughly investigated by my medical adviser?

(*c*)   Is it possible that at least part of the absence or absence record which I am reviewing is caused by the disability?

(*d*)   If so, are there steps which I reasonably could and should have taken, under *section 6* of the *DDA 1995*, to enable the employee to improve his or her attendance?

(*e*)   If not, can I justify a dismissal (or a warning if that is what I propose), for example by showing that the absence of the postholder is hitting profits or adversely affecting customer service?

It is particularly important that the issue of reasonable adjustments is fully explored before any decision to dismiss or give a warning is taken.

79.3   SELECTION FOR REDUNDANCY

If attendance is one of the selection criteria, no absence caused by pregnancy or a pregnancy-related illness must be taken into account. Otherwise the employee concerned will have a claim of direct sex discrimination.

There are several selection criteria, including timekeeping and job performance as well as attendance, under which an employee's score could be adversely affected by a disability. In such cases, the employer must ask the following questions:

(*a*)   Could this employee's attendance, timekeeping or job performance have been improved if I had made a reasonable adjustment at the time?

(b)   If so, what adjustments would it now be reasonable for me to make to the employee's scores under each of the criteria?

(c)   Could I justify, within the meaning of the *DDA 1995*, relying on the adjusted scores to select the employee for redundancy?

One aspect of selection for alternative employment is considered under *Mobility*. There are also the following considerations:

(a)   there is an express statutory obligation, under the *Employment Rights Act 1996*, to give priority to a woman returning from maternity leave;

(b)   subject thereto, *section 6* of the *DDA 1995* may require that priority should be given to any disabled employee whose job is at risk;

(c)   this duty to give priority to a disabled employee may arise where he or she is facing redundancy;

(d)   it may also arise where there is a need for redeployment because a disability prevents the employee from continuing in his or her existing post.

This issue of redeployment for disabled employees is considered in the case of *Kent County Council v Mingo [2000] IRLR 90* (see *Disciplining and Dismissing Disabled Employees*).

Employers must also, of course, apply redundancy selection criteria fairly and consistently in order to have a defence to complaints of direct discrimination. The days are, one hopes, long gone when employers could believe that it is legitimate to select women rather than men for redundancy because in most households the man is the main breadwinner.

Employers must also avoid selecting part-time workers for redundancy in priority to full-time workers, or using selection criteria which are loaded against part-time workers, unless the case is an exceptional one where this approach could be objectively justified. Otherwise, the employer could face complaints of:

(a)   breach of the *Part-Time Workers (Prevention of Less Favourable Treatment) Regulations 2000 (SI 2000 No 1551)*;

(b)   indirect sex discrimination;

(c)   indirect marriage discrimination;

(d)   unfair dismissal.

The issue of indirect discrimination was considered in the case of *Clarke v Eley (IMI) Kynoch Ltd [1982] IRLR 482*. A complaint of indirect discrimination under the *SDA 1975* succeeded in the following circumstances:

(a)   part-timers were selected for redundancy in priority to full-timers;

(b)   a high proportion of the female employees and a very low proportion of the male employees worked part-time;

(c)   there was no objective justification.

79.4   CONDUCT AND CAPABILITY DISMISSALS

Some employers have a cavalier attitude towards dismissals for misconduct or poor attendance or performance, where the employee has not served the unfair dismissal qualifying period of one year. This is particularly so where employees are expressly excluded from the usual disciplinary procedures during that year. Whatever the length of service, however, employers must act consistently. Otherwise they will be vulnerable to complaints of discrimination.

The need to act consistently towards employees of different racial groups does not, however, mean that employers should ignore the context in which an offence takes place. An employer who has a rigid policy of treating all similar offences alike, disregarding racial provocation or any other mitigating circumstances, is likely to lose unfair dismissal cases.

This was one of the issues in the case of *Sidhu v Aerospace Composite Technology Ltd (2000) IRLR 602*. The employers had organised a family day out, during which Mr Sidhu and his wife were subjected to violence and racial insults by another employee, who was white. Mr Sidhu received a cut head and broken glasses. During the incident, he picked up a plastic chair, which some witnesses said he had wielded in an aggressive manner, but he did not make contact with anyone. Both Mr Sidhu and the white employee were dismissed for gross misconduct, consisting of violent behaviour towards a fellow-employee (wielding the chair in Mr Sidhu's case) and using abusive language. The employer's disciplinary and appeal committees took a deliberate decision to exclude from the decision-making process the fact that the assault on Mr Sidhu was a 'racial assault'.

The employment tribunal found that Mr Sidhu's dismissal was unfair, but not racially discriminatory. The EAT allowed an appeal and substituted a finding of racial discrimination, on the ground that the decision to disregard the racial provocation was a 'race-specific' decision. The Court of Appeal reversed this decision and restored the decision of the employment tribunal. Treating racial provocation like any other provocation was not race-specific and was not an act of racial discrimination. It should be noted, however, that the employment tribunal's finding of unfair dismissal was not challenged. It would be difficult to convince any employment tribunal that an employer had acted reasonably if, when considering whether to dismiss an employee for violence and abusive language, he deliberately disregards the fact that this conduct was provoked by serious acts of racial harassment.

79.5 VICTIMISATION

The dismissal of an employee for having made allegations of discrimination, or done some other protected act, is generally unlawful under the relevant statutes. It will also generally be an unfair dismissal.

It is immaterial if the protected act is a discrimination or equal pay claim which has failed, so long as the claim was made in good faith. It would, for example, be unlawful for an employer to dismiss a female employee for having made an equal pay claim in the genuine but misplaced belief that a named male comparator was paid more than the complainant.

There is no victimisation, within the terms of the relevant legislation, if an employee is dismissed for having made a false allegation, if that allegation was not made in good faith. Where, for example, an employee has falsely accused a colleague of sexual harassment, it may be open to the employer to dismiss the complainant, after a thorough investigation and a fair disciplinary hearing, for gross misconduct. To have a good defence to a victimisation complaint, however, the employer would need to be able to show that the dismissed employee acted in bad faith in making a false and malicious allegation.

79.6 CONSTRUCTIVE DISMISSAL

The fact that an employee has been subjected to unlawful discrimination does not necessarily entitle the employee to resign and treat himself or herself as constructively dismissed. This principle is illustrated by the case of *Driskel v Peninsula Business Services Ltd and others [2000] IRLR 151*. In that case, Mrs Driskel complained of a number of remarks made to her by the head of her department. The final remark, the day before he was to interview her for promotion, was his suggestion that she should attend the interview in a short skirt and see-through blouse, showing plenty of cleavage. Mrs Driskel made a formal complaint of sexual harassment, which was rejected after a thorough and genuine internal investigation. She was dismissed after refusing to return to her job unless the manager against whom she had complained was moved elsewhere.

The employment tribunal dismissed Mrs Driskel's complaint of sexual harassment and also her complaint that her dismissal was both unfair and an act of victimisation. Mrs Driskel appealed successfully against the dismissal of her complaint of sexual harassment. The EAT rejected, however, the appeal against the dismissal of the unfair dismissal and victimisation claims. The employers had taken seriously her complaint of sexual harassment and had carried out a genuine investigation. She had not been dismissed for making that complaint. The employers had genuinely tried to accommodate her with acceptable employment, but she placed them in the position of having to dismiss the complainant or the manager about whom she had complained. There would have been no justification for the latter step, on the basis of the investigation which had been carried out.

The case of *Reed and Bull Information Systems Ltd v Stedman [1999] IRLR 299* is one in which there was a finding of a constructive and discriminatory dismissal. The employment tribunal found that Ms Stedman had been subjected to sexual harassment by her manager. The tribunal also found that, although she had made no formal complaint, the personnel department were aware of her deteriorating health and that she had made complaints to other members of staff. By failing to investigate the matter, the employer had failed to deal with the issue of sexual harassment adequately and was in breach of the duty of trust and confidence. Ms Stedman, who had resigned, was entitled to treat herself as constructively dismissed. That dismissal was an act of discrimination, contrary to *section 6(2)* of the *SDA 1975*.

79.7 DISCRIMINATORY DISMISSALS AND UNFAIR DISMISSALS

The above-mentioned case of *Sidhu* is an example of a case with a racial background where a dismissal was unfair but not discriminatory. Conversely, a discriminatory dismissal is not automatically unfair – *H J Heinz Co Ltd v Kenrick [2000] IRLR 144*. Discriminatory dismissals will, however, commonly also be unfair dismissals and both complaints should be pleaded.

A claim of dismissal under the discrimination legislation has the following advantages from the claimant's point of view:

(a) there is no qualifying period (it was because the then qualifying period had not been completed that there was no unfair dismissal complaint in the above-mentioned case of *Reed and Bull Information Systems Ltd v Stedman*);

(b) complaints can be presented by an employee who is above normal retiring age;

(*c*)   the definition of 'employment' in each of the discrimination laws is broader than that contained in the *Employment Rights Act 1996* for unfair dismissal purposes;

(*d*)   there is no limit on the amount of compensation;

(*e*)   compensation for injury to feelings can be claimed.

The advantages of claiming of unfair dismissal as well as discriminatory dismissal are:

(*a*)   the former may succeed while the latter fails, as in *Sidhu*;

(*b*)   the compensation for unfair dismissal will include the basic award.

80   Disparate Impact

The expression 'disparate impact' is not used in any of the discrimination laws but the concept is fundamental to *Indirect Discrimination*.

It is not sufficient for B under, for example, the *RBR 2003* to show that he or she is disadvantaged by a provision, criterion or practice which A has applied to B. It is necessary also to show that the provision criterion or practice puts or would put persons of the same religion or belief as B at a particular disadvantage when compared with other persons.

In some cases the disparate impact is obvious. For example, if a Muslim woman complains about not being allowed to wear trousers at work, it should not be difficult to persuade a tribunal that this rule puts or would put other Muslim employees at a particular disadvantage when compared with other persons.

In other, cases, however, statistical evidence will be required to show the proportion of persons of the same religion or belief as B who are actually or potentially disadvantaged by the provision, criterion or practice; and the proportion of persons not of that religion or belief who are actually or potentially so disadvantaged.

81   Diversity

A statement that diversity is valued is now included in many well developed equal opportunity policies in both the public and private sectors. The recent equal opportunities agreement in the *National Health Service* is a good example.

An effective equal opportunity policy will normally lead to a workforce which is diverse in a number of different ways, with:

(*a*)   employees throughout the organisation from a variety of racial, cultural and religious backgrounds;

(*b*)   men and women well represented at all levels;

(*c*)   career opportunities for young and old;

(*d*)   encouragement and practical support to enable employees to make an important contribution notwithstanding a wide range of disabilities;

(*e*)   a culture in which a worker's sexual orientation is irrelevant to his or her career development.

The importance of making a policy statement that diversity is valued is that successful policies are more likely to result from a positive commitment of this kind than from a bland acceptance of the need to comply with the law.

Making senior management feel good about the policy is not (or should not) be the main benefit of valuing diversity. There can also be real commercial advantages. If managers and other employees come from the whole spectrum of personal, domestic, cultural and career backgrounds:

(*a*)   the quality of decision making should be improved;

(*b*)   new ideas and new and improved ways of working are more likely to be suggested;

(*c*)   morale will be enhanced if all employees know that both they and their colleagues have been appointed or promoted on merit;

(*d*)   the banishment of irrelevant factors such as race and sex encourages employees to focus on the needs of the team or organisation to which they belong.

Diversity comes at a price. Organisations need to:

(*a*)   become adaptable in accepting the need for *Flexible Working*;

(*b*)   accept the need for change and the management of change;

(*c*)   invest substantially in *Training* and in the development of *Equal Opportunity Policies* and related practices and procedures.

82 Diversity Strategies

'Diversity' in the employment context can be defined in a variety of ways. The common element is the acknowledgement that people are different and have differing expectations and needs of organisations, both as employers and as service providers. Organisations that are to succeed in attracting different people as employees and customers will benefit from addressing the diverse requirements of different people.

The key to success in establishing a suitable diversity strategy is a co-ordinated approach. This is more likely to achieve benefits to the organisation (and those benefits themselves may be diverse, e.g. financial and reputational) than a string of ad hoc initiatives that treat employment issues and customers issues separately. By way of illustration, if women are under-represented in middle and senior management, then there will be differing reasons for that under-representation in different organisations. For example, one organisation may be perceived by women as 'traditional' and inflexible, while another may be perceived as an environment of unequal pay. To tackle the problem effectively by way of a suitable diversity solution, the reason for the problem of under-representation needs to be correctly identified at the outset. Relying on statistics, e.g. in relation to monitoring, is not in itself enough; the organisation needs to be able to interpret the available evidence.

83   Documents, Disclosure of

When preparing for an employment tribunal hearing, the parties should each disclose to the other any documents on which they wish to rely and any other documents which are relevant to the proceedings. It is good practice (and it is often expressly ordered by tribunals) for the parties to prepare a single bundle of documents (or, in Scotland, inventory of productions) for use at the hearing.

If one party (usually the claimant) asks for disclosure, or discovery, of documents which the other party (usually the respondent) is unwilling to give, then application can be made to the tribunal for an order. Sometimes disclosure is resisted on the ground of confidentiality. For example, in a complaint about discrimination in access to promotion, the claimant may ask for appraisals and other documents in relation to colleagues who have been promoted. The principles to be applied in such cases were established by the House of Lords in the case of *Science Research Council v Nassé [1979] IRLR 465*, as follows:

(*a*)   An order should not be made automatically for the disclosure of a confidential document, simply because it is or could be relevant to the case.

(*b*)   Disclosure should be ordered if it is necessary to dispose fairly of the proceedings or to save costs – these considerations override any confidentiality.

(*c*)   The tribunal chairman should read the relevant documents in order to decide whether disclosure is necessary.

Disclosure is particularly important in recruitment cases, where the complainant has no information about other candidates for the post and comparisons can be made only if documents relating to successful or shortlisted candidates are produced.

Even if there is no issue of confidentiality, a request for disclosure of documents can be resisted on the ground that the request is oppressive because of the large number of documents involved. In *British Railways Board v Nagarajan [1979] IRLR 45*, an employee complained of racial discrimination in an assessment of his performance and potential. He requested disclosure of the weekly work diaries and progress report sheets of himself and six colleagues for the whole of the year to which the complaint related. He also requested disclosure of the annual appraisals and assessment sheets relating to himself and these six colleagues for the whole of that year and for the three previous years. The EAT held that the documents were of doubtful relevance. Disclosure was ordered only of:

(*a*)   the work diaries and progress report sheets for the four weeks prior to the date of the assessment complained of;

(*b*)   the annual appraisals and assessments only for that year – not the previous three years.

84   Domestic Employment

Under the *RRA 1976*, there is an exception for employment for the purposes of a private household, unless the complaint is one of *Victimisation*.

There was formerly a similar exception in the *SDA 1975*, but that general exception was removed by the *Sex Discrimination Act 1986*. The position now is that being a man (or being a woman) can be a *Genuine Occupational Qualification* (GOQ) in certain circumstances if the job is likely to involve the jobholder doing his work or living in a private home. Even where this GOQ exception applies in relation to recruitment and selection for the post, the *SDA 1975* applies once an appointment has been made. A domestic employee can complain of, for example, sexual harassment or sex discrimination in dismissing him or her.

85   Dress and Personal Appearance

85.1   THE ISSUES

Employers often seek to impose regulations relating to the personal appearance of their employees. This is especially the case in organisations where personal appearance or dress may have implications for hygiene or safety or where employees' duties bring them into regular contact with members of the public. In some organisations, recent years have seen a relaxation of appearance rules, notably with the prevalence of 'dress down Fridays'. By contrast, an increasing number of organisations perceive the appearance of members of staff as reflecting the corporate brand and attempts to impose strict rules on appearance have led to some concerns about the 'objectification' of employees for marketing purposes.

A variety of questions arise: see, for example, *Beards, Obesity, Turbans and Veils.* Although employers have a considerable discretion in imposing regulations on dress and personal appearance, that discretion is by no means unfettered. Dismissal for a failure to comply with rules on appearance which are based on no more than an employer's own taste or preferences is likely to be unfair. However, in *Boychuk v H J Symons Holdings Ltd [1977] IRLR 395*, employers who tolerated an employee wearing badges at work proclaiming her lesbian preferences drew the line at one emblazoned with the legend 'Lesbian Ignite' and the EAT ruled that it was within managerial discretion to prohibit badges which could cause offence to fellow employees and customers. If a case such as *Boychuk* arose today, issues of sex discrimination and perhaps also human rights would be likely to be considered.

85.2   SEX DISCRIMINATION

In *Smith v Safeway plc [1996] IRLR 456,* an assistant in a supermarket was dismissed because he was not prepared to comply with a code which required male employees to have tidy hair not below shirt-collar length. The decision of the Court of Appeal established the following principles:

(*a*)   where an employer adopts rules concerning appearance, those rules must be considered as a whole, not garment by garment or item by item;

(*b*)   the rules will not be discriminatory because their content is different for men and for women, if taken as a whole they enforce a common principle of smartness or conventionality and neither gender is treated less favourably in enforcing that principle;

(*c*)   the principle is the same, whether the code relates to dress or to more permanent characteristics, such as hairstyle.

In one case, the EAT applied the ruling in *Smith* in holding that a male transvestite was not unlawfully discriminated against when forbidden to wear women's clothes into work. Both male and female employees were required to attend for work 'appropriately dressed'. There was no less favourable treatment, since women were not permitted to attend work dressed as men.

Any disadvantage can constitute a 'detriment' for the purposes of the *SDA 1975.* However, in one unreported case, a tribunal said that a rule requiring female employees at a casino to wear nail polish did not amount to a detriment, and even if it did, the detriment was too trivial to justify the complaint.

142

In 2003, an office worker at a job centre successfully claimed that he had been discriminated against on the ground of sex because he was required to wear a collar and tie when female staff were allowed to wear T-shirts. The tribunal's decision attracted rather more publicity than the ruling of the EAT that the case should be reconsidered: *Department for Work and Pensions v Thompson [2004] IRLR 348*. The crucial question was not whether the man suffered discrimination because he was told what he had to wear while female colleagues were not, but rather whether the employer could only achieve an equivalent level of smartness between male and female colleagues by requiring men to wear a collar and tie. The EAT suggested that if appropriate smartness could be achieved by men without a collar and tie, the lack of flexibility in the dress code would suggest that men were being treated less favourably than women.

What about aesthetics and good looks? In theory, there is nothing in the *SDA 1975* to prevent employers from turning job applicants away on the ground that they are fat or ugly. The reality is different, unless the same standards are applied to applicants of both sexes. The following would be a clear case of direct sex discrimination:

(a)   two women apply for a secretarial post;

(b)   one of them is superior in all relevant respects, such as qualifications and experience;

(c)   the other is selected because she is younger and prettier and the employer finds her more attractive;

(d)   the employer would not have taken age or beauty or physical attraction into account if he had been considering two male candidates.

The unsuccessful female candidate has been treated less favourably than a male candidate would have been. *Her* age and appearance have been taken into account to her detriment; those factors would not have stood in the way of *his* appointment.

It may be thought unlikely that there would be sufficient evidence to prove direct discrimination in such a case. It is not unknown, however, for interviewers to write personal comments about candidates on the interview notes and for those comments to come to light as a result of the *Questionnaire* or disclosure of *Documents*. Furthermore, the employer would find it difficult in such a case to give a convincing and satisfactory explanation for his failure to appoint the better qualified candidate – see *Evidence of Discrimination*.

85.3   **RACE DISCRIMINATION**

It is not uncommon for ethnic groups to be bound by strict religious or cultural rules with regard to their dress and personal appearance. Orthodox Sikh men have to wear *Beards* and *Turbans*. A dress code which conflicts with such requirements may be discriminatory contrary to the *RRA 1976*.

Rules about uniforms may have contrasting outcomes, depending on the facts. In *Kingston and Richmond Area Health Authority v Kaur [1981] ICR 631*, a health authority withdrew an offer to a Sikh who said she would have to wear trousers with her uniform. The EAT took the view that it was desirable for nurses to have uniforms because it boosted morale, reassured patients and guarded against intruders. As the then statutory regulations did not permit trousers as part of the uniform for female nurses, the employers were justified in complying with those rules. But in another case, a tribunal rejected the argument that 'corporate image' meant that all females employed in a shop should wear a uniform of an overall over a skirt. The severe detriment to the Muslim applicant far outweighed any commercial imperative.

85.4   **DISCRIMINATION ON GROUNDS OF RELIGION OR BELIEF**

The *RRA 1976* did not, however, provide adequate protection from dress codes that discriminate on the grounds of *Religion or Belief*. The position has been addressed by the *RBR 2003*.

85.5   **DISABILITY DISCRIMINATION**

The definition of *Disability* for the purpose of the *DDA 1995* expressly includes an impairment consisting of a severe disfigurement (other than one which has been deliberately acquired as a result of tattoos or non-medical body piercing). Accordingly, rejecting a candidate for a job because he or she has a severe disfigurement would be an act of disability discrimination unless the decision could be justified.

Suppose that an employer turns down a job applicant with a severe facial disfigurement on the ground that the job involves regular contact with members of the public who would suffer embarrassment. It is most unlikely that justification could be established in a case such as this. It is a fundamental principle of discrimination law that employers and others cannot use the real or assumed prejudice of customers or others as an excuse for discrimination. Once that principle is compromised, the next step could be to argue that employers are justified in rejecting candidates with severe disfigurement because fellow employees could be embarrassed.

85.6   **HUMAN RIGHTS**

Articles 8 and *10* of *Schedule 1* to the *HRA 1998* may be prayed in aid by employees concerned about regulations regarding dress or personal appearance. The right to freedom of expression extends to self-expression by way of dress and adornments such jewellery. But in *Kara v United Kingdom (1999) EHRLR 232*, a bisexual male transvestite failed in his challenge to the employer's requirement that he should wear 'appropriate clothing'. The requirement accorded with law and was proportionate.

85.7   **PRACTICAL GUIDANCE**

Where an employer considers it appropriate to introduce a dress code, the following matters are usually worth taking into account:

(*a*)   The policy should be based on reasons relevant to the organisation or business and those reasons should be clearly communicated to employees. Typical business reasons prompting the introduction of a dress code include the maintenance of a particular public image or the promotion of a productive work environment.

(*b*)   Employees should be required to have an appropriate and well-groomed appearance. Casual dress codes should specify clothing that is considered appropriate and any special requirements for workers who are required to deal with members of the public.

(*c*)   The policy must be clearly communicated to staff and any proposed penalties for non-compliance should be appropriate and made known to the workforce.

(*d*)   In general, the dress code should apply consistently to all workers, although compliance with the law may necessitate exceptions.

(*e*)   Reasonable adjustments to the code should be made where appropriate, e.g. to accommodate disabilities or religious practices.

(*f*)   Breaches of a dress code should be dealt with in a consistent manner.

86   Duty to Consider

86.1   INTRODUCTION

Although the *AR 2006* introduce a *Default Retirement Age* which, arguably, discourages employers from retaining employees over the age of 65, *Schedule 6* to the *AR 2006* impose a brand new duty upon employers, i.e. to consider a request from an employee to continue working after the expected retirement date.

86.2   WHO IS COVERED?

The 'duty to consider' procedure applies to 'employees' within the meaning of *Regulation 30*, i.e. those working under a contract of employment, Crown employees and members of Parliamentary staff. No qualifying period of employment is required to be eligible for the duty to consider, although, in order to claim unfair dismissal an employee will still require one year's continuous employment.

86.3   DUTY TO NOTIFY

An employer who intends to retire an employee has a duty to notify the employee in writing of the employee's right to make a request not to retire on the intended date of retirement and the date on which he intends the employee to retire. Notification must be given not more than one and not less than six months before that intended date.

The duty to notify applies regardless of:

(*a*)   whether there is any term in the employee's contract of employment indicating when his retirement is expected to take place;

(*b*)   any other notification of, or information about, the employee's date of retirement given to him by the employer at any time; and

(*c*)   any other information about the employee's right to make a request given to him by the employer at any time.

Where the employer fails to comply with the duty to notify within the period of six to twelve months, he has a continuing duty to notify the employee in writing of the matters in question until the fourteenth day before the 'operative date of termination'. That date is defined as the date upon which notice given by the employer expires or, if no notice is given, the date upon which termination of the contract takes effect. In other words, the employer must comply with the duty to notify between six and twelve months before the intended date of retirement and, if he fails to do so, he should nevertheless notify no later than the fourteenth day before dismissal. Failure to comply with the duty to notify exposes the employer to a claim for up to eight weeks' pay. Failure to notify in any event no later than the fourteenth day before dismissal renders the dismissal automatically unfair.

86.4   THE RIGHT TO REQUEST NOT TO RETIRE

In making a request to his employer not to retire on the intended date of retirement, the employee must propose that his employment should continue, following the intended date of retirement either indefinitely; for a stated period; or until a stated date.

146

If the request is made at a time when it is no longer possible for the employer to comply with the duty to notify and the employer has not yet given a later notification before the fourteenth day prior to dismissal, the employee must identify the date on which he believes that the employer intends to retire him. The request must be made in writing and state that it is made under *paragraph 5* of *Schedule 6* to the *AR 2006*. At the time of writing, it was not established whether a failure to quote precisely the paragraph and schedule numbers would nullify the request; this seems unlikely, but a prudent employee will comply scrupulously with the statutory provisions.

The request must be made, in a case where the employer complied with the duty to notify, between three and six months before the intended date of retirement. Where the employer has not complied with the duty to notify, the request must be made not more than six months before the intended date of retirement.

An employee may only make one request in relation to any one intended date of retirement.

86.5   MEETING TO CONSIDER THE REQUEST

An employer to whom a request has been made is under a duty to consider it by holding a meeting to discuss the request with the employee 'within a reasonable period after receiving it'. Both employer and employee must take all reasonable steps to attend the meeting. There is no need to hold a meeting if, before the end of a reasonable period, employer and employee agree that the employment will continue indefinitely and the employer gives notice to the employee to that effect, or if it is agreed that the employment will continue for an agreed period and notice of that period is given by the employer.

The duty to hold a meeting does not apply if it is not practicable to hold a meeting within a reasonable period and the employer considers the request, having regard to any representations made by the employee.

The employer has to give the employee notice of his decision on the request as soon as it is reasonably practicable after the date of the meeting (or, in those exceptional cases where it was not necessary to hold a meeting) his consideration of the request.

If the decision is to accept the request, the notice of decision must state this and state either that the decision is that the employment will continue indefinitely, or that it will continue for a further period, and specify the length of that period or the date on which it will end. Where the decision is to refuse the request, the notice must confirm that the employer wishes to retire the employee and the date on which the dismissal is to take effect.

Where the request has not been accepted in full, the notice must inform the employee of his right to appeal.

All notices given with regard to meetings must be in writing and dated.

The employee has a right to be accompanied at the meeting (or at an appeal meeting) by a worker employed by the same employer. The companion should be permitted to address the meeting, but not to answer questions on behalf of the employee. The companion must also be allowed to confer with the employee during the meeting. If the chosen companion is not available at the time proposed for the meeting, and a convenient alternative meeting within the next seven days is proposed by the employee, the employer must defer that meeting to the proposed time.

Transitional provisions apply to dismissals due to occur after 1 October 2006 but before 1 April 2007.

87   Employees – Liability for

87.1   GENERAL PRINCIPLES

In most large organisations (and many medium-sized and small organisations) whether in the public sector or the private sector, day-to-day decisions affecting employees are made by managers and other fellow employees. It also tends to be managers, interviewers and other employees who make decisions affecting job applicants. A key issue, therefore, is whether employers can be held accountable for acts of discrimination by their employees and, if so, in what circumstances.

The general principle in the *Discrimination Laws* is that anything done by a person in the course of that person's employment shall be treated for the purposes of the relevant law as also done by that person's employer.

There is an exception for offences. An employer can be liable for any act of discrimination (including victimisation) done by an employee, but criminal liability for the handful of offences created by each law rests with the person directly responsible for the offence, whether that person is an employer or an employee.

These provisions which make employers responsible for acts of discrimination by their employees are fundamental to the effective operation of the discrimination laws. The main employment provisions of the legislation make it unlawful for employers to discriminate in relation to offers of employment at any establishment in Great Britain or against existing employees at any such establishment. It is only employers, not their managers or other employees, who have this primary liability. If matters were left there, the discrimination laws would be of little effect. This consequence is avoided by treating the act of the manager or other employee as being also the act of the employer.

An employer cannot escape liability by showing that he did not and would not have authorised the act of discrimination complained of or even that the act was done without his knowledge. The act of the employee is treated as the act of the employer whether or not it was done with the employer's knowledge or approval. The employer does, however, have a defence if it can be shown that the employer took such steps as were reasonably practicable to prevent the employee from doing the particular act or doing acts of that description in the course of his employment.

There are three questions to be considered in any particular case:

(*a*)   Was the act complained of done by a person in the course of his employment?

(*b*)   Can the employer show that all reasonably practicable steps were taken so as to establish the above-mentioned defence?

(*c*)   Does any liability attach to the individual employee who did the act complained of?

87.2   COURSE OF EMPLOYMENT

There are two questions to be considered. The first is whether there is an employment relationship, within the meaning of the relevant law, between the person who has done the act of discrimination complained of and the respondent who has been named by the complainant.

For the purposes of discrimination law, there is a wide definition of *Employment*. That definition includes not only conventional employment contracts and apprenticeships but also employment under any other contract to do any work personally. This definition is relevant for the purpose of defining the employees who have rights and it is also relevant for the purpose of defining the 'employees' for whose acts of discrimination the employer can be held liable.

The second key step, once the employment relationship has been established, is to show whether the act complained of was done in the course of that employment. The case law on course of employment, which is considered under *Harassment*, has established that the expression is a very broad one.

87.3   **REASONABLY PRACTICABLE STEPS**

The question whether reasonably practicable steps have been taken to prevent the particular act of discrimination, or acts of that description, is one of fact in each case. It can be confidently stated, however, as a general principle, that no employer can expect to make out the defence if the only step taken has been the adoption of an equal opportunity policy, without effective measures to implement the policy. *Training* for managers, supervisors and interviewers is particularly important. For general guidance, see *Equal Opportunities Policies*. For guidance on specific subjects see *Recruitment, Selection* and *Harassment*.

The acts by an employee which can also be treated as the acts of the employer are not limited to acts of unlawful discrimination. For example, when considering whether an employer has established the defence of having taken all reasonably practicable steps to prevent an act of discrimination, an employment tribunal can take into account, and impute to the employer, the failure of an employee to take appropriate action to prevent discrimination of which he has become aware. In particular, if a manager is aware that a fellow employee is being subjected to sexual and racial harassment, and does nothing about it, that omission is treated as an omission by the employer, and is likely to defeat any attempt to raise the statutory defence. This principle was referred to by the EAT in the case of *Canniffe v East Riding of Yorkshire Council [2000] IRLR 555*. The only way in which the employer could avoid being held responsible for the manager's omissions would be if the employer had taken all reasonably practicable steps to prevent such omissions.

In *Caspersz v Ministry of Defence [2006] All ER (D) 02 (Apr)* the EAT ruled that a tribunal was entitled to find that a defence of reasonably practicable steps had been made out where it was found that the employer had a good policy, which was not just paid lip service to but was observed, so that the employer had taken such reasonably practicable steps to prevent sexual comments being made by a manager to his junior. This was so even though the manager in question himself had responsibility for reviewing and publishing on a regular basis the employer's policy in respect of dignity at work. The tribunal concluded that the employer was entitled to expect that the manager was familiar with, and would observe and ensure respect for, that policy. The EAT referred to the decision of *Canniffe* and the Court of Appeal's decision in *Croft v Royal Mail Group [2003] IRLR 592*. The Court of Appeal approved the two-stage approach in *Canniffe*, i.e:

(*a*)   to identify whether the respondent took any steps at all to prevent the employee from doing the acts or acts complained of; and

(*b*)   having identified those steps, what steps if any they took to consider whether there were any further acts that they could have taken which were reasonably practicable.

It was made plain in *Croft* that, in considering what steps were reasonable in the circumstances, it is legitimate to consider the effect they are likely to have. Measures are to be judged as to their reasonable practicability, not by whether they have in fact been effective; by definition, that will not have occurred, because otherwise there would be no acts of discrimination causing for defence. What must be assessed is whether, putting oneself into the shoes of the employers prior to the acts complained about, and looking from that perspective at the possibility such acts might subsequently occur, the steps are reasonably practicable. None of this, however, means that an employer has *carte blanche* simply to adopt a policy and do no more. Everything depends upon the particular facts of a particular case.

87.4   THE EMPLOYEE'S LIABILITY

If an employee commits an act of discrimination outside the course of his employment, then both employer and employee escape liability for that act.

Where the act of discrimination is in the course of his employment, then the employee is deemed to have 'aided' the employer to do the relevant act. Accordingly, the law attaches liability to the employer by treating the employee's act as also the act of the employer; although liability then also falls on the employee himself because of what he has done, the law achieves this result by treating the employee as having aided the deemed act of discrimination by the employer.

The principle that an employee can be made liable for an unlawful act of discrimination against a fellow employee (or job applicant) is an elementary one, but it was affirmed in the case of *AM v WC and SPV [1999] IRLR 410*, a case under the *SDA 1975*.

Where the employer makes out the defence that all reasonably practicable steps were taken, that defence does not assist the individual employee who did the act complained of. It is expressly provided in each of the three Acts that the employee is treated as having knowingly aided the employer to do an unlawful act, even though the employer himself is regarded as not having acted unlawfully because the reasonably practicable steps defence has been established.

The extent of an employee's potential liability is dramatically illustrated by the case of *Yeboah v Crofton [2002] IRLR 634*. The applicant and the respondent were both employed by a local authority in senior positions. The applicant was the Assistant Chief Executive (Human Resources). The respondent, Mr Crofton, was the Director of Housing.

Mr Yeboah succeeded in complaints of racial discrimination against Mr Crofton as well as against the local authority. Mr Crofton was personally ordered to pay compensation of £45,000 to Mr Yeboah, including £10,000 aggravated damages.

It is also possible for the employer to be liable for an unlawful act and for the employee who did the act not to be so liable. The employee has a defence if:

(*a*)   he has acted in reliance on a statement by the employer that he would not be acting unlawfully because of some provision in the relevant Act; and

(*b*)   it was reasonable for him to rely on the statement.

For example, this defence could be available to an employee involved in recruiting staff if his employer gives him false information which suggests that being a man is a *Genuine Occupational Qualification* for a particular job. If the employee, reasonably believing that information, discriminates against a female candidate for the post, then the employer but not the employee would be liable for that act of discrimination.

The employer who knowingly or recklessly makes a statement which is false or misleading in a material respect is guilty of an offence.

88 Employees Who Become Disabled

88.1 DOES THE EMPLOYER NEED TO KNOW?

The *Health and Safety at Work etc. Act 1974* requires employees to take reasonable care for their health and safety and that of others who may be affected by their acts or omissions at work. If an employee's failure to disclose a disability jeopardises health and safety, the employee may be in breach of his or her statutory obligation.

There is, however, no general obligation to disclose a disability to an employer or a prospective employer and the *DDA 1995* is silent on the point. Views differ among disabled people as to whether disclosure is generally desirable. There is sometimes an understandable apprehension, perhaps based on past experience, that disclosure will lead to discrimination and that it is better to say nothing. The temptation to keep quiet may be stronger in cases where the disability is not readily apparent. The counter-argument is that employers need to have *Knowledge of Disability* in order to be able to comply with their legal obligations in respect of health and safety and the *DDA 1995*. However, it seems clear that the test of knowledge is objective.

88.2 THE EMPLOYER'S RESPONSE

Often, the employer will be well aware of the disability. It may have arisen, for example, from an accident. Typically, it will be appropriate to allow the employee a reasonable period of time for treatment and rehabilitation. The disabled person may need specific training, e.g. in the use of appropriate technology. The duty to make *Reasonable Adjustments* may involve either short-term or transitional steps, to enable the disabled employee to adapt to new circumstances, or long-term or permanent changes, such as changes in job duties or working hours.

The *DDA 1995* provides examples of types of *Reasonable Adjustments* which may be appropriate, such as:

(*a*)   making adjustments to the premises;

(*b*)   allocating some of the disabled employee's tasks elsewhere;

(*c*)   transferring the disabled employee to another job;

(*d*)   agreeing a change to the disabled employee's hours of work;

(*e*)   agreeing that the disabled employee can work at a different location;

(*f*)   allowing the disabled employee time off for treatment and rehabilitation;

(*g*)   acquiring or modifying equipment such as a Braille keyboard or a hearing loop;

(*h*)   modifying instructions or reference manuals;

(*i*)   providing a reader or interpreter;

(*j*)   providing extra supervision.

But these are only illustrations of some possibilities and are not in any way exhaustive. That said, the employer is only required to do what is reasonable. Deciding what is and what is not reasonable is a matter for judgement, taking into account the *DDA 1995* and the *Code of Practice* and viewing the matter objectively.

In addition to discussing the position with the disabled employee, the employer may need to seek advice from outside. Disability Employment Advisers and Disability

88.3 Employees Who Become Disabled

Service Teams run by the Employment Service are contactable via job centres. The guidance they may offer covers such matters as:

(*a*)   assessment of suitability of workstations for disabled employees and recommendations as to how to make necessary improvements;

(*b*)   guidance on the availability, cost and value of special equipment;

(*c*)   assistance with funding;

(*d*)   sources of further advice.

88.3   MEDICAL EXAMINATIONS

Medical advice is often essential. The more expert that advice is, the better. In some cases, typically including, but by no means limited to, cases of relatively uncommon disabilities, it will not be enough merely to consult a GP. The views of an occupational health doctor may be of considerable benefit. Usually, the employee will co-operate with a reasonable request to undergo a medical examination. In exceptional cases where the employee refuses to agree to be medically examined, he or she may be liable to disciplinary action, e.g. if the contract of employment records an employee's agreement to undergo such an examination and the request that it take place is legitimate and reasonable in the circumstances. Even where there is no contractual provision with regard to undergoing medical examinations, an employee who refuses to co-operate for no good reason runs the risk that the employer will take decisions based on inadequate and perhaps incorrect information.

In order to be able to provide a valuable opinion, the medical adviser should be given all relevant information including:

(*a*)   a clear and accurate explanation of the employee's duties;

(*b*)   an explanation of the reason why the report is required;

(*c*)   a request for advice as to any difficulties that the employee will have in carrying out his or her job duties, together with a request for a prognosis concerning prospects for improvement and any further investigations that should be undertaken.

The employee's signed consent to the examination should be provided to the adviser. Where the medical adviser has been involved in the clinical care of the employee, then it will be necessary to comply with the *Access to Medical Reports Act 1988*, which provides amongst other matters that the employer must inform the employee that he or she has:

(*a*)   the right to withhold consent to the employer seeking the report from the medical adviser;

(*b*)   the right to state that he or she wishes to have access to the report;

(*c*)   rights concerning access to the report before or after it is supplied;

(*d*)   the right to withhold consent to the report being supplied to the employer;

(*e*)   the right to request amendments to the report.

Where an employee expresses a wish to see the report, the employer must let the medical adviser know this when applying for the report and at the same time let the employee know that the report has been requested.

89 Employers

In most discrimination cases (and all equal pay cases), the respondent is an employer. Complaints of discrimination are brought against employers by employees, job applicants and contract workers. The extended definition of *Employment* (and all related terms, such as employer and employee) should be noted.

Complaints can also be brought by persons who are themselves employers, against *Qualifying Bodies* or *Employers' Associations*.

90   Employers' Associations

Section 12 of the *SDA 1975* and *section 11* of the *RRA 1976* impose obligations not only on trade unions, but also on any organisation of employers and also professional and trade organisations.

It is unlawful for any such organisation to discriminate against a non-member:

(*a*)   in the terms on which it is prepared to admit him to membership; or

(*b*)   by refusing, or deliberately omitting to accept, his application for membership.

It is also unlawful for any such organisation to discriminate against a member:

(*a*)   in the way it affords him access to any benefits, facilities or services, or refusing or deliberately omitting to afford him access to them;

(*b*)   by depriving him of membership, or varying the terms on which he is a member; or

(*c*)   by subjecting him to any other detriment.

There are similar provisions in *section 15* of the *DDA 1995, Regulation 15* of the *RBR 2003, Regulation 15* of the *SOR 2003* and *Regulation* 18 of the *AR 2006* in relation to any 'trade organisation'. The definition includes employers' associations and trade and professional associations as well as trade unions.

Section 15 of the *DDA 1995* also imposes on trade organisations the duty to make reasonable adjustments, corresponding to the section 6 duty placed on employees. There is also under the *DDA 1995* a specific *Code of Practice* on the duties of trade organisations to their disabled members and their applicants.

For the right to apply to an employment tribunal to have a rule made by an employers' association declared void in certain circumstances, see *Trade Organisations and Discrimination*.

91 Employment

The *Discrimination Laws* contain an extended definition of employment (and of related expressions such as employer and employee) to cover not only employment under a contract of service or apprenticeship, but also employment under a contract personally to execute any work or labour. This extended definition is relevant not only to the rights given to employees but also to the liability of employers for acts done by employees in the course of their employment (see *Employees – Liability for*).

In *Quinnen v Hovells [1984] IRLR 227*, it was held that a self-employed assistant taken on to sell fancy goods on commission over the Christmas season was covered by the extended definition. On the other hand, in *Mirror Group Newspapers Ltd v Gunning [1986] IRLR 27*, a contract for the distribution of newspapers, employing staff for the purpose, was not covered. It was said that the extended definition contemplates 'a contract the dominant purpose of which is the execution of personal work or labour'. In *Sheehan v Post Office Counters Ltd [1999] ICR 734*, it was said to be 'a rather brave argument' that what mattered was whether the work was in fact done personally rather than whether there was a contractual obligation to do it personally. In *Mingeley v Pennock & Ivory t/a Amber Cars [2004] IRLR 373*, the Court of Appeal ruled that a taxi driver was not protected under the *RRA 1976* because, under his contractual arrangements, there was no mutual obligation to offer or accept work.

In *South East Sheffield Citizens Advice Bureau v Grayson [2004] IRLR 353*, volunteer advisers working for a Citizens Advice Bureau were not 'employees' within the meaning of *section 68(1)* of the *Disability Discrimination Act 1995*. In order for a volunteer to be found to be an 'employee', it is necessary to be able to identify an arrangement under which, in exchange for valuable consideration, the volunteer is contractually obliged to render services to or work personally for the employer. In this case, volunteers were not obliged to work the 'usual minimum weekly commitment' of six hours per week. The crucial question was not whether any benefits flowed from the CAB to the volunteer in consideration of any work actually done by the volunteer. The mere fact that, if the volunteer did work, the CAB would reimburse them for expenses incurred and indemnify them against negligence claimed by disgruntled clients did not impose any obligation on the volunteer actually to do any work for the CAB.

Questions concerning possible employment rights often arise in respect of ministers and others associated with various churches: see *Ministers of Religion*.

92   Employment Agencies

The *Discrimination Laws* make it unlawful for an employment agency to discriminate:

(a)   in the terms on which it offers to provide any of its services;

(b)   by refusing or deliberately omitting to provide any of its services; or

(c)   in the way it provides any of its services.

An employment agency is defined as a person who, for profit or not, provides services for the purpose of finding employment for workers or supplying employers with workers. Furthermore, the services in respect of which an employment agency must not discriminate include guidance on careers and any other services related to employment (no doubt including such matters as *Psychometric Testing*).

It is not unlawful for an employment agency to discriminate against a person by refusing or deliberately omitting to offer employment which the employer could lawfully refuse to offer the person in question. An obvious example is where the employment is covered by a *Genuine Occupational Qualification* exception.

An employment agency can be liable jointly with an employer for discrimination when acting as an agent with the express or implied authority of the employer.

93 Equal Opportunities Commission

The Equal Opportunities Commission (the EOC) is the statutory body which has been set up under the *SDA 1975*. It has powers and responsibilities in relation to both the *EPA 1970* and the *SDA 1975*.

Those powers and responsibilities are similar to those given by the *RRA 1976* to the *Commission for Racial Equality*. They include the power to give *Assistance* to complainants and prospective complainants, whether under the *SDA 1975* or the *EPA 1970*.

The EOC's work has included not only publishing a Code of Practice on Equal Pay (see *Appendix 4*) but also producing various tools designed to help close the gender pay gap.

With effect from October 2007, the EOC's functions will transfer to the *Commission for Equality and Human Rights*.

94   Equal Opportunities Policies

94.1   GENERAL PRINCIPLES

Employers are under no legal obligation to adopt equal opportunities policies, but organisations are unlikely to meet the standard which the law requires unless they have adopted suitable policies and carried out those policies successfully.

A clear policy statement is only a first step. A policy which is adopted and then left to gather dust is simply a monument to failure.

A well thought out and effectively implemented policy is an essential defensive mechanism. Many acts of discrimination, particularly *Harassment*, are committed without the knowledge of employers and senior management who would not have authorised those acts if they had known about them. Nevertheless, an employer cannot avoid legal liability for such acts unless all *Reasonably Practicable Steps* have been taken to prevent them.

An equal opportunities policy should not, however, be adopted only for negative reasons. It is good employment practice, which can make a positive contribution to the success of the organisation. Useful and practical guidance is to be found in the *Codes of Practice*.

94.2   KEY STEPS

The key steps towards the adoption and implementation of an effective policy are:

(*a*)   formulate the policy and adopt it;

(*b*)   allocate overall responsibility for implementing it;

(*c*)   tell people about it and put it into effect; and

(*d*)   monitor it and review it.

94.3   POLICY FORMULATION AND ADOPTION

A policy is more likely to be supported by the workforce if employee representatives have contributed to it than if it has simply been imposed by management. Where appropriate the policy may be included in a collective agreement. Employers need to be aware, however, of the implications of adopting policies which have contractual effect – see *Contractual Equal Opportunities Policies*.

It is also necessary to consider whether there should be a single policy or separate policies on different aspects of equal opportunities. A strong argument in favour of a single, concerted policy is that the adoption of and insistence on best employment practice, such as the use of consistent and objective criteria for employment decisions, is the most effective way to eliminate unlawful discrimination and promote equality of opportunity.

On the other hand, there are particular issues, such as *Harassment*, which may need to be specifically addressed in a separate policy. Furthermore, the Code of Practice on the elimination of discrimination against disabled persons reminds employers that treating people equally will not always avoid a breach of the *DDA 1995*. An employer may be under a duty to make a *Reasonable Adjustment*. The implication of this advice is that a separate policy on disability may be appropriate.

Probably the best approach is to have an overall policy on equal opportunities, supported by additional, often more detailed, policies on specific issues, such as harassment and disability.

In summary, the questions to be considered at the outset include:

(*a*)   Who should be involved in drawing up the policy?

(*b*)   Should the policy be contractual?

(*c*)   Should there be a single policy or a whole series of policy documents?

(*d*)   Should the policy be comprehensive, going further than the bare minimum required to achieve compliance with the law?

94.4   OVERALL RESPONSIBILITY

An important requirement, at the time when the policy is being drawn up, is to decide who should have overall responsibility for ensuring that it is properly carried out. The person or persons responsible for the policy need to be senior enough to ensure that it is taken seriously. At the same time, there is a risk that the implementation of the equal opportunities policy will not be given a sufficiently high priority if it is simply one of many responsibilities piled on to senior management. It is important, particularly in a large organisation, that any senior manager(s) with overall responsibility should receive all necessary support from individuals who have both the time and the expertise to make the policy work.

There is also no reason why employee involvement should end at the point when the policy has been drawn up and adopted. The appointment of a joint management and union or staff committee, to meet regularly and discuss the policy, could help to ensure both that the policy receives the necessary attention and that employee involvement and support are maintained.

94.5   COMMUNICATING AND IMPLEMENTING THE POLICY

It is obviously necessary that the employees and job applicants who are the potential beneficiaries of a policy should be told about the policy. All employees should be told about the procedure for complaining about discrimination or a failure to comply with the policy. They should also be reminded that they have obligations as well as rights under the policy. The disciplinary code should be amended where necessary to make it clear that discrimination is a disciplinary offence (amounting, in the most serious cases, to gross misconduct).

Perhaps the most important, and one of the most neglected, steps to be taken to eliminate discrimination is to give appropriate *Training* to employees, particularly managers and supervisors. The policy should also make it clear that senior management should take steps at regular intervals to ensure that they themselves are complying with the policy. For example senior management should look regularly at standard advertisements, application forms and various practices and procedures to ensure that they comply with the law and the policy.

94.6   MONITORING AND REVIEW

The importance of effective monitoring and analysis is to identify areas where the policy is not or may not be working, so that corrective action can then be taken. For example, if women, or racial minorities, are not being recruited for or promoted to particular jobs, or in particular departments, the possible explanations could be:

(*a*)   The manager concerned is discriminating against them.

(*b*)   Indirectly discriminatory requirements or practices are operating as a barrier.

(*c*)   They are simply not coming forward.

Once a problem has been identified and analysed, then corrective action can be considered. For example, in the case where women or racial minorities are not applying for particular posts, then steps to encourage applications can be considered – this being one of the limited measures of *Positive Discrimination* which the law permits.

94.7   **NON-COMPLIANCE WITH POLICIES**

It is possible for an equal opportunities policy to become contractual and to create binding legal obligations – see *Contractual Equal Opportunities Policies.*

It was also held by the Court of Appeal in *Anya v University of Oxford and another [2001] IRLR 377* that an employer's failure to follow its own equal opportunities policy (whether contractual or not) may, unless there is a credible alternative explanation, contribute to an inference of discrimination.

95   Equal Pay

95.1   **REQUIREMENTS FOR A CLAIM**

In a typical claim under the *EPA 1970*:

(*a*)   The claim is made by a woman.

(*b*)   She names one or more male workers – the *Comparator*(s).

(*c*)   She claims the same pay, or rate of pay, as the *Comparator*(s).

(*d*)   The woman and any male comparator work for the same employer and at the same establishment.

(*e*)   The grounds of the claim are that the woman's work and a male comparator's work are the same or broadly similar – *Like Work*.

Claims under the *EPA 1970* may, however, vary in each of the above respects, as follows:

(*a*)   A claim under the *EPA 1970* may be made by a man.

(*b*)   If the claimant is a man, then it follows that the comparator(s) must be female.

(*c*)   An equal pay claim may be presented not only in order to come up to the comparator's level in terms of pay (which is very broadly defined) but also to obtain equality in relation to any other contract term in respect of which the comparator enjoys an advantage.

(*d*)   A claimant and a comparator may be in the *Same Employment* for the purposes of a claim under the *EPA 1970* even if they have different employers and work at different establishments.

(*e*)   The work which the claimant and the comparator do need not be the same or broadly similar; it suffices if it is work of *Equal Value* or work which has been rated as equivalent under a job evaluation study.

The way in which the *EPA 1970* operates is to introduce an equality clause into every contract under which a man or woman is employed at an establishment in Great Britain. The effect of an equality clause is that in certain circumstances an employee may rely on it in order to raise his or her pay or other contractual benefits up to the level enjoyed by a worker of the opposite sex. For example, where it is a woman who relies on an equality clause and who names a male comparator:

(*a*)   If any term of her contract (whether concerned with pay or not) is less favourable to her than the corresponding term in the man's contract, then that term in her contract must be modified so that it ceases to be less favourable.

(*b*)   If his contract includes a beneficial term which is not to be found in her contract, then that term must become part of her contract also.

Before an equality clause can operate in this way, it must first of all be shown that the woman and the man are in the *Same Employment*. This does not necessarily mean that an equal pay comparison can be made wherever a claimant and a comparator of a different sex are employed by the same employer. This was made clear in *Robertson and others v DEFRA [2005] IRLR 363*, having a common employer is not necessarily the same as being 'in the same employment' or having pay and conditions attributed to a 'single source' as laid down by the European Court of Justice in *Lawrence v Nugent Office Care Ltd [2002] IRLR 822*. The 'single source' test is an approach of general application, indicating that something more than just the bare fact of common employment is required for comparability purposes. The critical question is whether there is a single body responsible for the discriminatory pay differences of which complaint is made. This is not resolved by only addressing the formal legal question of the identity of the employer. If that were not the case, every civil servant would be entitled to compare herself or himself with any other civil servant of the opposite sex, subject only to objective justification by the employer of differences in pay. Pay and conditions of civil servants are no longer negotiated or agreed centrally on a civil service-wide basis. Each individual department has delegated to it responsibility for negotiating and agreeing the pay of civil servants employed inter-department, subject to overall budgetary control by the Treasury. Individual departments are free to negotiate and agree upon most terms and conditions of employment. On the facts of the present case, therefore, there were two sources of the difference in pay. DEFRA was the single source responsible for the claimants' pay and conditions, while the Department of the Environment, Transportation and the Regions (DETR) was the single source responsible for the comparators' pay and conditions. The simple fact of common employment by the Crown was not sufficient to attribute the terms and conditions to the Crown as the single source responsible for determining levels of pay in both DEFRA and DETR.

Once it has been established that the woman and the man are in the same employment, it is then necessary to compare the two jobs. Up to three questions need to be asked, in the following order:

(*a*)   Have the two jobs been given the same rating under a *Job Evaluation* study?

(*b*)   If not, are they *Like Work*?

(*c*)   If not, are they of *Equal Value*?

Most equal pay cases are either like work or equal value claims. Both these expressions are considered below.

A case is not concluded by a finding that the complainant's job and the comparator's job are like work or of equal value. A claim can be defeated, and the equality clause can be prevented from operating, if the employer can prove that the variation between the two contracts is genuinely due to a material factor which is not the difference of sex: *section 1(3)* of the *EPA 1970*.

95.2   **LIKE WORK**

A claimant is employed on like work with the comparator if:

(*a*)   their work is the same or of a broadly similar nature; and

(*b*)   any differences between the things they do are not of practical importance in relation to terms and conditions of employment.

The Act expressly states that it is relevant to have regard to the frequency or otherwise with which any differences occur in practice as well as to the nature and extent of the differences.

The Court of Appeal decision in the early case of *Shields v E Coomes (Holdings) Ltd [1978] IRLR 263* emphasised the following points:

(*a*)   The focus is on the work which the woman and the man actually do in practice, not the work which they may theoretically be required to do.

(b)   The fact that the two employees work at different times or for longer hours does not prevent the work from being like work. Night work or work for longer hours is to be dealt with by paying a night shift premium or overtime rate.

95.3   **EQUAL VALUE**

To ascertain whether two jobs are of equal value, it is necessary to measure the demands which each of the jobs makes on the person holding the job under various headings, such as effort, skill and decision making. For two jobs to be of equal value, there need be no similarity whatsoever between them in terms of the nature of the work being carried out. There are well established systems and processes for analysing jobs, allocating points under various headings and totting up the points in order to arrive at a value for the job.

There are two important differences between a like work claim and an equal value claim. The first is that any equal value claim must be dismissed by the tribunal if it is shown that the two jobs have been given different ratings under a *Job Evaluation* study, provided that the evaluation has been properly carried out on an analytical basis without any element of sex discrimination. Many employers commission job evaluation studies (even after an equal pay claim has been presented) with a view to having their pay structures reviewed objectively and comprehensively and under their own control, as opposed to having change forced on them as a result of successful equal value claims.

Secondly, there are special rules of procedure in equal value cases. In like work cases, as in other cases which come before employment tribunals, questions of fact are decided by the tribunal itself. In an equal value case, however, the tribunal may appoint an independent expert to consider whether the jobs are of equal value and to report back to the tribunal. However,even where the question is referred to an independent expert, the tribunal is not obliged to accept the expert's report. Either party may, on giving reasonable notice to the tribunal and the other party, call one witness to give expert evidence supporting or challenging the independent expert's report.

Procedural changes introduced with effect from 1 October 2004 gave employment tribunals additional powers in respect of case management. They require a series of hearings to be held in equal value cases, and regulate how the independent expert's task should be performed, and the evidence that the tribunal is to hear.

In summary, an equal value claim will usually go through three stages if an independent expert has been appointed, i.e:

Stage 1:   An equal value hearing. If it emerges that there is a job evaluation scheme rating the job in question as unequal, the claim will be struck out, unless it appears that the scheme is flawed. Otherwise, the tribunal will decide whether or not to refer the case to an independent expert.

Stage 2:   Disputed facts will be resolved at a second hearing so that the expert can proceed to evaluate the jobs.

Stage 3:   A hearing to determine whether the jobs are of equal value. The first question will be whether or not to admit the expert's report in evidence. The tribunal will consider any 'material factor' defence and consider remedy if appropriate.

Stage 2 will be omitted if no independent expert is appointed.

95.4   **THE MATERIAL FACTOR DEFENCE**

The *Material Factor* defence is relied on in many equal pay cases. It should be raised at the outset, in the employer's response to the claim.

A wide variety of factors may be relied on by employers to defend a claim under the *EPA 1970*. They include the following:

(*a*)   the comparator's better qualifications, better experience or longer service;

(*b*)   differences in grade under a genuine and non-discriminatory grading system;

(*c*)   a desire to 'protect' the pay of a comparator who has been, for example, transferred to lighter work because of ill health (the 'red circle' or 'red ringing' cases);

(*d*)   the comparator's unpleasant working conditions.

So far as this last example is concerned, it seems illogical that a factor such as unpleasant working conditions, which is one of the demand factors which are relevant to the evaluation of the two jobs, can also be relied on as a material factor defence. It was, however, held by the EAT in the case of *Davies v McCartneys [1989] IRLR 439* that there is no limitation on the matters which may be relied upon. If an employer genuinely, and without any intention to discriminate on grounds of sex, places particular weight on one particular demand of the job, then the material factor defence can be made out.

Where the difference in pay or in some other contract term involves direct discrimination against the complainant, so that the material factor relied upon is the difference of sex, the defence cannot succeed. In *Ratcliffe v North Yorkshire County Council [1995] IRLR 439*, the dinner ladies employed by the council enjoyed the same rates of pay as male manual workers, the jobs having been given equal ratings under a job evaluation study. The rates for dinner ladies in the private sector were significantly lower because the work was done (as the colloquial job title suggests) by women. The council reduced the pay of its dinner ladies in order to be able to compete effectively with private sector employers in a compulsory competitive tendering exercise. The material factor defence failed. Although the council's only objective was to win the contract (and to continue employing the complainants), the pay of the complainants had been reduced because they were women, doing work traditionally regarded as women's work. This was direct discrimination and the material factor defence could not succeed.

A second category of case is where there is indirect discrimination because the proportion of women receiving, for example, lower pay is significantly greater than the proportion of men receiving lower pay. This was the issue in *Enderby v Frenchay Health Authority and Secretary of State for Health [1993] IRLR 591*. This was a case in which speech therapists, most of whom were women, claimed the same rate of pay as pharmacists and clinical psychologists, most of whom were men. It was held by the ECJ that because of this indirect sex discrimination the difference in pay required objective justification. The fact that the different pay structures were negotiated as a result of separate and distinct bargaining processes was not sufficient justification.

Where objective justification is required, the standard required is the same as that for justification in cases of *Indirect Discrimination*. In the leading case of *Bilka-Kaufhaus GmbH v Weber von Hartz [1986] IRLR 317*, the European Court of Justice held that there is objective justification where:

'The means chosen for achieving that objective correspond to a real need on the part of the undertaking, are appropriate with a view to achieving the objective in question and are necessary to that end'

The House of Lords held in *Rainey v Greater Glasgow Health Board [1987] IRLR 26* that this same standard should be applied in equal pay cases where objective justification is required, whether the case is under *Article 141* or under the *EPA 1970*.

Is objective justification required if there is no evidence, either direct or indirect, sex discrimination? In *Strathclyde Regional Council v Wallace [1998] IRLR 146*, there was a difference in pay as between teachers and principal teachers. There were men and women in both groups and no significant disparity in the proportions. The teachers and principal teachers were employed on like work. There were genuine reasons for the difference in pay but the tribunal held that these reasons did not amount to objective justification. It was held by the House of Lords that there was no need for objective justification in the absence of any direct or indirect sex discrimination. Similar guidance was given by the House of Lords in *Glasgow City Council v Marshall [2000] IRLR 272*.

In *Parliamentary Commissioner for Administration and another v Fernandez [2004] IRLR 22*, it was argued that objective justification is required in all cases, even where there is neither direct nor indirect sex discrimination. This argument was based on the decision of the ECJ in the case of *Brunnhofer [2001] IRLR 571*. The EAT, by a majority, rejected that argument.

However, in *Sharp v Caledonia Group Services Ltd [2006] IRLR 4*, the EAT ruled that a tribunal was wrong to conclude that the difference between the claimant's pay and that of her comparator was due to a genuine material factor which was not the difference in sex. The EAT considered that the tribunal erred in not following the European approach, which required that the difference in pay has to be objectively justified, and instead followed the approach laid down by the domestic line of authorities, which simply requires the employer to be able to account for the difference by reference to a factor which is material, but is not the sex of the employee unless the fact relied upon by the employer is one which may itself indirectly discriminate against female employees, in which case the factor has to be objectively justified. According to the EAT, the *Brunnhofer* case gives a clear direction as to the need for objective justification in all cases. Once light work, or work rated as equivalent, or work of equal value has been established, a prima facie case of discrimination exists. In so far as there is a conflict between *Brunnhofer* and the UK decisions, the European decision must be followed.

Nevertheless, in *Villalba v Merrill Lynch & Co Inc [2006] IRLR 437*, in contrast to the decision in *Sharp*, the EAT endorsed the 'orthodox' view that there is no requirement of objective justification for differences in pay and circumstances where the employer has satisfactorily rebutted direct sex discrimination and there is no independent evidence of any kind to show that sex had any influence on the difference in pay. According to the EAT, this was not altered by the decision in *Brunnhofer*.

A similar approach was taken earlier by the Court of Appeal in *Armstrong v Newcastle upon Tyne NHS Hospital Trust [2006] IRLR 124*. The Court of Appeal held that a tribunal erred in finding that the employers had failed to prove that differences in the bonus arrangements between the claimants and their male comparators were not due to material factors within the meaning of *section 1(3)* of the *EPA 1970* because the tendering process which led to the removal of the bonus from the female workers was tainted with sex discrimination. There were no adequate grounds for the conclusion that disparate adverse impact existed. Once disparate adverse impact has been established, the burden passes to the employer in respect of two issues. First, that the difference between the man's and the woman's contract is not discriminatory, in the sense of being attributable to a difference of gender. The burden of establishing an arguable case of discrimination is borne by the claimant, even though the employers bear the burden of persuasion. Second, if the employer cannot show that the difference in treatment was not attributable to a difference in gender, he must then demonstrate that there is nonetheless an objective justification for the difference between the woman's and the man's contract.

In considering *section 1(3)* of the *EPA 1970*, according to the EAT in *Ministry of Defence v Armstrong [2004] IRLR 672*, 'the fundamental question is whether there is a causative link between the applicant's sex and the fact that she is paid less than the true value of her job as reflected in the pay of her named comparator.' If the material cause of the pay difference between the applicant and her comparator is tainted by sex-related factors, then the defence fails. The link may be established in various different ways, depending on the facts. The EAT made the point that: 'Pay discrimination is frequently systemic in character, arising as a result of gender job segregation or from discrimination in pay structures and grading systems, rather than from the terms of individuals' contracts of employment.' An employment tribunal should focus on 'substance', rather than form and on the result, rather than the route taken to arrive at it.

95.5   ARTICLE 141

It is impossible to explain the law on equal pay without reference to *Article 141* (formerly *Article 119*) of the EU Treaty. The *EPA 1970* is detailed and technical; in contrast, *Article 141* states the following principle:

'Each Member State shall ensure that the principle of equal pay for male and female workers for equal work or work of equal value is applied.'

The word 'pay' is broadly defined, to include any 'consideration whether in cash or in kind, which the worker receives directly or indirectly, in respect of his employment, from his employer'.

Council Directive 75/117/EEC, the *Equal Pay Directive*, puts a little flesh on the bones, without in any way detracting from the above statement of principle. For example:

(*a*)   Any job classification system which is used for determining pay must be based on the same criteria for both men and women and be so drawn up as to exclude any discrimination on grounds of sex.

(*b*)   There must be no provisions which are contrary to the principle of equal pay in legislation, administrative rules, collective agreements, wage scales or individual contracts of employment.

(*c*)   Employees must be protected against victimisation for taking steps aimed at enforcing compliance with the principle of equal pay.

The fundamental importance of *Article 141* arises from the following features of it:

(*a*)   It prevails over any conflicting provision or omission in domestic legislation.

(*b*)   Unlike Council Directives, it has direct effect, in the private sector as well as in the public sector.

Employment tribunals have jurisdiction to hear cases of the various kinds which have been assigned to them by Parliament. They have statutory jurisdiction to hear complaints under the *EPA 1970*, but not complaints under *Article 141*. This does not matter. It was held by the Court of Appeal in *Barber v Staffordshire County Council [1996] IRLR 209* that the effect of *Article 141* is to modify conflicting provisions in domestic legislation, for example by removing (or disapplying) from the *EPA 1970* (or the *SDA 1975*) exceptions which are incompatible with Community Law.

In the *EPA 1970* as originally enacted, there was an exception for provisions in relation to death or retirement. This meant that, for example, there could be no claim relating to pensions or redundancy payments. This exception was found to be incompatible with *Article 141* in the landmark pension case of *Barber v Guardian Royal Exchange Assurance Group [1990] IRLR 240*. With effect from 1 January 1996, the *EPA 1970* and the *SDA 1975* were both amended to reflect the decision in *Barber*, but because of the direct effect of *Article 141* successful claims in relation to pensions and redundancy payments could be and were brought during the intervening period. A claim relating to a contractual redundancy or severance payment falls under the *EPA 1970*; the claim is probably under the *SDA 1975* if the payment is discretionary.

95.6   CONTINGENT CLAIMS (OR LEAPFROGGING)

In *South Ayrshire Council v Milligan [2003] IRLR 153,* a female primary school headteacher had brought an equal pay claim, naming two male secondary school headteachers as comparators.

Mr Milligan was also a primary school headteacher and, like the female complainant in the earlier case, he was paid less than the secondary school headteachers. He could not, however, bring an equal pay claim naming a secondary school headteacher as a comparator, because they were all male.

Accordingly, he made a claim naming as the comparator the female complainant in the earlier case. He did so on a contingent basis, so that if she was successful in her claim, and obtained a higher rate of pay, then he would be able to claim that same rate of pay in his case. He wanted to have his case stayed until her case had been decided.

It was held by the Court of Session that this was an appropriate course of action. It was said that if 'a contingent claim made in circumstances such as these were to be excluded as a matter of law, that would make it impossible for the claimant to achieve true equality of pay.'

95.7   THE CODE OF PRACTICE

The *Code of Practice* issued under the *EPA 1970* has considerable value and significance. For example, it proved to be an important factor in the case of *Barton v Investec Henderson Crosthwaite Securities Ltd [2003] IRLR 332*, where the EAT took into account the provisions of the then code of practice relating to transparency in pay systems and the lack of transparency in the respondent's pay arrangements.

95.8   QUESTIONNAIRES

Until 6 April 2003, there was a *Questionnaire* procedure under the *SDA 1975* but not under the *EPA 1970*. With effect from that date there has been a questionnaire procedure under the *EPA 1970* as well. The employment tribunal may draw an appropriate *Inference* if the respondent fails to reply within the prescribed period of eight weeks or gives a reply which is evasive or equivocal. Serving a question-naire does not, however, count as raising a grievance under the statutory *Grievance Procedures.*

In *Holc-Gale v Makers UK Ltd [2006] IRLR 178,* the EAT confirmed that a claimant could not rely on statements made in a questionnaire served on the employers under the *EPA 1970* as constituting a statement of grievance under 'step 1' of the statutory grievance procedure. The *Dispute Resolution Regulations 2004* exclude the statu-tory anti-discrimination questionnaire procedure altogether from the statutory defi-nition of 'grievance'.

95.9   TRANSFERS OF UNDERTAKINGS

In *Powerhouse Retail Ltd and others v Burroughs and others (*formerly called *Preston and others v Wolverhampton Healthcare NHS Trust and others (No 3)) [2004] IRLR 979,* the Court of Appeal ruled that, where there had been a transfer of an undertaking, time begins to run under *section 2(4)* of the *EPA 1970,* for the purposes of an equal pay claim against a transferor, from the date of the relevant transfer. The EAT was wrong to hold that time does not begin to run until the end of an employee's employment with the transferee. The House of Lords rejected an appeal, confirming that time runs from the date of the TUPE transfer rather than from the end of the employee's employment with the transferee: *[2006] IRLR 381.*

95.10   REMEDIES

When an equal pay claim is successful, the claimant is entitled to an order declaring the rights of the claimant and the employee. The effect of an order in favour of the claimant is that (as the case may be):

(*a*)   her (or his) pay is increased to the level of the comparator's pay; or

(*b*)   her (or his) contract terms are improved to match those of the comparator.

Once the order has been made, the claimant has a contractual right to the increased pay or improved contractual terms, even if the comparator subsequently ceases to be employed by the employer. When the tribunal is considering the question of remedy, is it open to the employer to argue that the contracts of the claimant and the comparator should each be looked at as a complete package, so that no order should be made if contract terms which are more favourable to the comparator are matched by other terms which are more favourable to the complainant? This issue arose in the case of *Hayward v Cammell Laird Shipbuilders Ltd [1988] IRLR 257.* This was an equal value case in which a canteen cook succeeded in claiming the same rate of pay as male welders and other craftsmen in the shipyard. It was argued by the employers, at the remedy stage, that although she had a lower rate of pay than her comparators did, she also enjoyed several benefits, such as paid meal breaks, which they did not. This argument was rejected by the House of Lords. It was held to be necessary to compare individual terms, such as the rate of pay, and not the employment package as a whole.

An order declaring the rights of the parties for the future is not the only remedy which may be claimed by a complainant. The tribunal may also award compensa-tion, consisting of:

(*a*)   arrears of remuneration, or *Back Pay*, if the complaint is about pay; or

(*b*)   damages if the complaint is about some other contract term.

The *EPA 1970* originally provided that no payment by way of arrears of remuneration or damages may be awarded in respect of a time earlier than two years before the date on which the proceedings were instituted. As a result of a decision of the ECJ, and subsequent consideration of the matter by the EAT, this period was increased to six years in 2003 (see *Back Pay*) in order to bring the *EPA 1970* into line with *Article 141*.

In *Newcastle upon Tyne City Council v Allan [2005] IRLR 504*, the Court of Appeal ruled that an award for injury to feelings cannot be made in the claim brought under the *EPA 1970*. Nor can award of aggravated or exemplary damages. Compensation for non-economic loss is not recoverable in an equal pay claim.

95.11   LIMITATIONS OF THE EPA 1970

The *EPA 1970* is about equal pay, not about fair pay. The point is illustrated by *Home Office v Bailey [2004] IRLR 921*. The EAT ruled that, in considering whether a disparity of pay which has arisen between two work groups by reason of a history of different arrangements for collective bargaining evidences sex discrimination, a prima facie case will be established if the advantaged group is predominantly male and the disadvantaged group is predominantly female. Where, however, the disadvantaged group is neutral in gender, then the situation may not be fair, but it is not prima facie discriminatory on the grounds of sex. This accords with the decision of the European Court of Justice in *Enderby v Frenchay Health Authority [1995] IRLR 591*, which would be preferred to that in *R v Secretary of State for Employment, ex p Seymour-Smith [1999] IRLR 253*. The approach in the *Seymour-Smith* case would result in turning the *Equal Pay Act* into a *Fair Wages Act*. A limitation on the scope of the *EPA 1970* is that no claim can succeed unless a suitable comparator of the opposite sex can be identified. It is not possible, for example, for a woman to claim the increased pay which she *would have* received if she had been a man. An actual male comparator is required. If her work is being done and has always been done only by women, and there are no men in the *Same Employment* who are employed on work of equal value, then she has no remedy.

Arguably, the principle of equal pay for work of equal value is not being fully implemented if claims on the basis of a hypothetical male comparator are ruled out. In practical terms, however, equal pay claims, particularly equal value cases, are already difficult and complicated for the parties to present and the tribunal to decide. There would be new difficulties if it became possible to base complaints on hypothetical comparisons.

A second limitation on the *EPA 1970* is that it is somewhat crude in its operation. All that can be achieved is to bring the claimant's contractual terms up to the level of those of the comparator. There is no provision for a more sophisticated remedy, in order to reflect precisely any differences in value between the two jobs. The following examples illustrate the point:

(*a*)   The evaluation of the two jobs in an equal value claim indicates that the value of the claimant's job is 95 per cent that of the value of the comparator's job, even though her pay is only half the comparator's pay. There is no provision for increasing her pay up to 95 per cent of the comparator's pay.

(*b*)   A woman who is already paid as much as her comparator cannot bring an equal pay claim on the ground that she should be paid far more than he is because her work is of far greater value.

The *EPA 1970* offers workers a (frequently long and difficult) route to equality in pay and other contract terms as between men and women, where they are in the *Same Employment*, but it does not provide for fair differentials in pay as between men and women.

96   Equal Treatment Directive

Article 2 of the *Equal Treatment Directive (76/207/EEC)* begins with the uncompromising statement that 'the principle of equal treatment shall mean that there shall be no discrimination whatsoever on grounds of sex either directly or indirectly by reference in particular to marital or family status'. The Article (in its amended form – see below) contains definitions of direct and indirect discrimination, harassment and sexual harassment. It also allows for exceptions in, for example, the following cases:

(*a*)   occupational activities and related training where, by reason of the nature or context of the activities, the sex of the worker constitutes a genuine and determining occupational requirement, provided that the objective is legitimate and the requirement is proportionate;

(*b*)   provisions concerning the protection of women, particularly as regards pregnancy and maternity.

Later Articles require Member States to take the necessary steps to enable persons who consider themselves wronged to pursue their claims by judicial process and also measures to protect employees against victimisation.

The Directive was amended in 2002 by *Directive 2002/73/EC*. In order for the UK to comply with this new Directive, it was necessary for the *SDA 1975* to be amended, in particular by adopting new definitions of *Indirect Discrimination, Harassment* and the *Genuine Occupational Requirement,* similar to those contained in the *RBR 2003* and the *SOR 2003*. There have over the years been several occasions when the *Equal Treatment Directive* has been successfully relied on in complaints of *Public Sector* employers and when amendments to the *SDA 1975* have been required – see *Directives*.

97 Equal Value

Proving that the work done by a claimant and that done by a comparator in the same employment are of equal value is one of the three ways of establishing the basis for an *Equal Pay* claim. The two jobs can be totally different provided that they are of equal value in terms of the demands made by them under various headings, such as the skill and effort required and the degree of responsibility and decision making involved. In one of the earliest successful cases, a canteen cook successfully compared her job with those of craftsmen in the same shipyard.

An equal pay claim will not necessarily succeed, however, even if the two jobs are of equal value. The employer can defeat the claim by showing that the difference in pay or other contract terms to which the claim relates is genuinely due to a *Material Factor* which is not the difference in sex between the claimant and the comparators. It may be necessary to submit a material factor defence to very close scrutiny; see, for example, *Market Forces.*

98   Equality Duties

98.1   THE RACE EQUALITY DUTY

Bodies in the *Public Sector* have a duty to promote race equality. They must have due regard to the need to:

(*a*)   eliminate unlawful racial discrimination;

(*b*)   promote equality of opportunity; and

(*c*)   promote good relations between people of different racial groups.

The key principles are relevance and proportionality. 'Relevance' concerns the extent to which a function affects people as members of the public, or as employees of the body. The weight given to race equality should be proportionate to its relevance to a particular function. This may, for instance, mean giving greater consideration and resource to functions or policies that have most effect on the public, or on the body's employees.

A public body must publish a race equality scheme which:

(*a*)   lists functions likely to affect people differently, depending on their ethnic group;

(*b*)   says how it will assess any new policies it is proposing to introduce, and how it will consult people, including staff, about them;

(*c*)   says how it plans to monitor all its policies and makes sure they are not disadvantaging people from certain ethnic groups;

(*d*)   publishes the results of its consultations, assessments and monitoring;

(*e*)   makes sure that everyone can obtain information about its activities and services;

(*f*)   trains its staff in their responsibilities;

(*g*)   reviews the scheme at least every three years.

98.2   THE DISABILITY EQUALITY DUTY

Since 4 December 2006, public bodies have been required to have due regard to the need to:

(*a*)   eliminate discrimination that is unlawful under the *DDA 1995*;

(*b*)   eliminate harassment of disabled people that is related to their disability;

(*c*)   promote equality of opportunity between the disabled people and others;

(*d*)   take steps to take account of disabled peoples' disabilities;

(*e*)   promote positive attitudes towards disabled people; and

(*f*)   encourage disabled people to participate in public life.

As with the race equality duty, there are specific requirements, including a requirement to publish a disability equality scheme.

98.3 Equality Duties

98.3   **GENDER EQUALITY DUTY**

At the time of writing, it is anticipated that the *Equality Act 2006* will come into force in April 2007, and that from that time public bodies will also be subject to a gender equality duty, requiring them to have due regard to the need to:

(*a*)   eliminate unlawful discrimination;

(*b*)   promote equality of opportunity between men and women;

(*c*)   tackle occupational segregation.

Public bodies will also be required to publish a gender equality plan and gender impact assessment.

98.4   **IMPLICATIONS**

At the time of writing, it seemed as though it would take time for many public bodies to comply effectively with their equality duties. A Healthcare Commission audit undertaken into NHS Trusts' implementation of the statutory race equality duty in 2006 indicated various shortcomings in compliance. It is foreseeable that public bodies facing discrimination claims brought by individuals may find such claims even more difficult to defend if they fail to comply with their obligations under the equality duties.

99   Equality Mainstreaming

'Mainstreaming' is a concept of developing significance in the field of equal opportunities. It reflects a move away from a focus on individual rights and disadvantages towards the systems and structures that give rise to such disadvantages. There is a parallel with increasing focus upon the concept of *Institutional Discrimination*. Similarly, there is room for debate as to what 'equality mainstreaming' actually means in practice. Put simply, mainstreaming is a long-term strategy designed to make sure that equal opportunity principles and practices are integrated into every aspect of an organisation, rather than being seen as an 'add-on' to the 'core' or 'everyday' functions of that organisation. Mainstreaming provides a framework to facilitate and complement the legislation on equal opportunities and other equality measures, e.g. positive action. In the past, the main emphasis of equality mainstreaming was in the public sector, but it has gained increasing recognition in the private sector as well. The mainstreaming concept is relevant to *Diversity Strategies*. It is sometimes said that private sector companies that adopt a mainstreaming approach may gain a competitive advantage in the marketplace. Presumably, however, the more companies adopt such an approach, the less such an advantage is likely to be. Almost inevitably, therefore, the perceived value of equality mainstreaming is unlikely to reside in the arguments about the business case for it.

100   Estoppel

The old-established legal principle of estoppel operates – put simply – to prevent the same issue being re-litigated. Public policy requires finality in litigation, but if care is not taken, the unduly stringent operation of this principle can lead to hardship. Courts and tribunals therefore need to tread with care, as *Air Canada v Basra [2000] IRLR 683* shows. An applicant brought a claim of race discrimination. During the tribunal hearing, she sought to add a claim of victimisation. This was based on the employer's evidence which, she argued, suggested that she had been penalised for bringing an earlier sex discrimination complaint against the company. The tribunal did not allow the new claim to be added, so the applicant had to bring a fresh complaint of victimisation. The employer argued that the tribunal's rejection of the application to amend the discrimination claim meant that the claim had already been determined by the tribunal. Thus the principle of estoppel operated to bar new proceedings. The EAT disagreed. A victimisation claim represents a different cause of action from a claim of direct racial discrimination, since the elements of proof differ. In a direct discrimination case, the applicant must show less favourable treatment on the ground of sex or race etc. In a victimisation case, the reason for less favourable treatment must be that the applicant has done a protected act. In these proceedings, there had been no consideration of the merits of the complaint of victimisation. Thus neither 'issue estoppel' nor 'cause of action estoppel' were applicable. The fresh proceedings could be brought.

In *British Airways plc v Boyce [2001] IRLR 157*, an employee initially brought a complaint on the ground that he was discriminated against by reason of his English ethnic origins. When that was rejected because the English are not an 'ethnic group' for the purposes of *RRA 1976*, he sought to bring a new claim, identical in all respects except that the alleged discrimination was said to be on the grounds of his English 'national origins'. The EAT decided that this claim was barred. In the absence of special circumstances, all legal arguments relative to a complaint of racial discrimination should be raised in a single application to the tribunal. Parties are not permitted to bring fresh litigation because of new views they may entertain of the law of the case.

101   Ethnic Origins

The term 'ethnic origins' is relevant for the purposes of both direct and indirect racial discrimination. It is direct discrimination if on grounds of ethnic origins a person is treated less favourably than another person is or would be treated. A group of persons defined by reference to ethnic origins is also a *Racial Group* for the purposes of *Indirect Discrimination*.

Guidance on the meaning of 'ethnic origins' was given by the House of Lords in the non-employment case of *Mandla v Dowell Lee [1983] IRLR 209*. This was the case of the Sikh boy who was refused a place at a school because of his insistence on wearing a turban.

Lord Fraser said that there were two essential characteristics of an ethnic group:

(*a*)   a long shared history, of which the group is conscious as distinguishing it from other groups;

(*b*)   a cultural tradition of its own, including family and social customs and manners.

The essential cultural tradition is often but not necessarily associated with religious observance.

Lord Fraser also referred to other characteristics which are relevant but not essential:

(*a*)   a common geographical origin or descent from a small number of common ancestors;

(*b*)   a common language (not necessarily peculiar to the group);

(*c*)   a common literature peculiar to the group;

(*d*)   a common religion different from that of neighbouring groups or from the surrounding community;

(*e*)   being a minority within a larger community.

An ethnic group can include converts, including those who marry into the group.

In the above case, it was held that *Sikhs* are an ethnic group for the purpose of the *RRA 1976*. It has also been held that *Gypsies* can be an ethnic group.

It should be noted, however, that the fact that a particular group can constitute an ethnic group does not necessarily mean that a particular complainant will be held to be a member of that group. The question is one of fact in each case, particularly in relation to groups such as gypsies, where by no means all those who have adopted a travelling way of life can thereby be regarded as being members of the relevant ethnic group.

In another case, it was held that Rastafarians were not an ethnic group. One reason was that they had insufficient shared history – *Crown Suppliers (PSA) Ltd v Dawkins [1993] ICR 517.*

102 European Law

European law prevails in any conflict with domestic legislation. Several of the original provisions of the *EPA 1970* and the *SDA 1975* have been removed or amended in the light of relevant decisions by the ECJ.

Furthermore *Article 141* has direct effect. This is the Article of the European Treaty (formerly *Article 119*) which lays down the principle of equal pay for equal work or work of equal value. Because it is part of the Treaty itself, rather than a Directive, it has direct effect on employment in both the private sector and the public sector. Employees have been able to rely on its provisions in order to overcome some of the limitations of the domestic legislation on *Equal Pay*.

That direct effect is achieved by extending the relevant domestic legislation and disapplying provisions in that legislation which are inconsistent with *Article 141*. In Great Britain, the relevant domestic legislation is the *EPA 1970* in relation to contractual terms relating to pay and the *SDA 1975* in relation to non-contractual arrangements for pay. In each case, 'pay' is given a wide meaning – see *Equal Pay*.

Directives also have direct effect in the *Public Sector* so that individual complainants can rely on them even before the relevant domestic legislation has been amended. See *Directives* for examples. The *Framework Directive* has proved especially significant in influencing the development of UK law, since it resulted in the introduction of the *RBR 2003*, the *SOR 2003* and the *AR 2006*.

103   Evidence of Discrimination

103.1   DIRECT EVIDENCE RARELY AVAILABLE

The definitions of *Direct Discrimination* and *Victimisation* in employment were clarified, by the House of Lords in *Nagarajan v London Regional Transport [1999] IRLR 572*. There are three questions to be answered in each case. For example, if the complainant is a woman who alleges direct sex discrimination:

(a)   Has she been treated less favourably than a man has been or would have been treated?

(b)   Are the relevant circumstances in her case the same as those in his case or at least not materially different?

(c)   If so, is her gender the reason or (if there is more than one reason) a significant or important reason for the less favourable treatment?

The questions are clear, but answering them is more difficult, particularly in *Recruitment, Promotion* and *Redundancy* cases. The main difficulty is usually presented by the third question, about the reason for the less favourable treatment. It is frequently no easy matter for a complainant in such a case to demonstrate that race or gender was the reason for the treatment complained of, or for the tribunal to decide this issue. The difficulty was explained in the following words in the leading case of *King v The Great Britain-China Centre [1991] IRLR 513* (a case which will be considered in more detail below):

'It is important to bear in mind that it is unusual to find direct evidence of racial discrimination. Few employers will be prepared to admit such discrimination even to themselves. In some cases the discrimination will not be ill-intentioned but merely based on an assumption that "he or she would not have fitted in"?'.

The above comment that it is unusual to find direct evidence of racial discrimination also applies to complaints of direct discrimination under the *SDA 1975*, the *RBR 2003,* the *SOR 2003* and the *AR 2006* to complaints of *Victimisation* or *Harassment.*

These evidential difficulties do not usually arise in cases of *Indirect Discrimination.* Generally, the provision etc. complained of will have been openly stated, for example in an advertisement or job description. The main issues in cases of indirect discrimination are usually *Disparate Impact* and *Justification.*

Identifying the reason for the treatment complained of can be the main issue in cases of disability discrimination, particularly in *Recruitment* cases. It is more usual, however, for the main disputes of fact in cases under the *DDA 1995* to be whether the complainant is disabled, whether the treatment complained of has been justified or whether *Reasonable Adjustments* have been made.

103.2   INFERENCES AND THE BURDEN OF PROOF

The above difficulties do not mean that every complaint of direct discrimination, *Victimisation* or *Harassment* is doomed to fail, unless it is one of the rare cases where there is direct evidence of discrimination. The *European Burden of Proof Directive (1997/801/EC)* required changes to UK law which have subsequently been implemented. See *Burden of Proof.*

103.3 **EVIDENCE**

Even where there is a relevant difference in treatment, with no adequate and satisfactory explanation, it is desirable to have other evidence to support the resulting inference of discrimination.

Other evidence of discrimination could relate to:

(*a*)   the treatment of other individuals;

(*b*)   revealing questions or statements;

(*c*)   unsatisfactory replies to a questionnaire;

(*d*)   false reasons for the treatment complained of;

(*e*)   previous or subsequent incidents;

(*f*)   failure to comply with equal opportunity or other policies;

(*g*)   statistical evidence;

(*h*)   admissions of discrimination.

103.4 **QUESTIONNAIRES AND CODES OF PRACTICE**

Inferences may be drawn from false or evasive replies to a *Questionnaire* or delay in replying; or from a failure to comply with a relevant recommendation in a *Code of Practice*. *Inferences* were drawn, and the *Burden of Proof* did shift, because of such matters, in *Barton v Investec Henderson Crosthwaite Securities Ltd [2003] IRLR 332*.

The following would be examples of evasive or equivocal (or false) replies to a questionnaire which could lead to an inference of unlawful discrimination or victimisation:

(*a*)   A woman who has applied unsuccessfully for a post is told in the reply to the questionnaire that the successful male candidate had obtained a particular qualification which was relevant to the post. When the relevant documents, including the successful candidate's CV are disclosed, it turns out that he has not yet obtained that qualification.

(*b*)   A candidate who was born overseas is interviewed for a post but not appointed. The reason given in the reply to the questionnaire was his inability to communicate effectively in English. Having heard him give his evidence, the tribunal find that the interviewers could not have genuinely believed that he had any difficulty in communicating.

(*c*)   The reply to a questionnaire submitted by an unsuccessful disabled candidate for a post states that the manager who made the decision was not even aware of the disability. The tribunal, however, accept the complainant's evidence that the disability was mentioned by that manager at the interview.

(*d*)   A questionnaire is submitted by an unsuccessful female candidate for promotion, who had previously complained of sexual harassment. The reply to the questionnaire states that the complaint of harassment was never even mentioned or considered. There is, however, a reference to the complaint in the interview notes which are disclosed.

103.5   **FALSE REASONS**

There have been several cases along the following lines:

(*a*)   A black worker applies for an advertised post.

(*b*)   He or she is told that the vacancy has been filled.

(*c*)   The employer continues to advertise the post.

(*d*)   The black worker arranges for a white friend to enquire about the same post.

(*e*)   The white friend is told that the post is still available and is invited for interview.

There could be a defence in such cases if the respondent gives credible and detailed evidence that a person who had been offered the job gave back word during the interval between the two enquiries. In the absence of a credible explanation of that kind, however, there have been findings of racial discrimination in such cases.

There can be no reasonable objection to the element of subterfuge in such cases. Asking a white friend to enquire about the same job is the obvious method for the unsuccessful candidate to test whether the reason given to him is a genuine one and it is surely a legitimate method for him to use.

There are, however, grounds for some reservations about those cases, of which several have been reported in the press, in which a candidate who submits a written application for a post also submits an identical application under a false name, purporting to be that of a candidate of the opposite sex or a different racial group. Sometimes the false application is submitted only after the candidate's genuine application has been rejected, but there have been cases where both applications have been submitted at the same time. If the candidate's own application is rejected but the false application leads to the offer of an interview then a complaint of direct discrimination is presented.

In such a case, if, for example, the complainant is black and the false application purported to be from a white candidate, the complaint is not that the complainant has been treated less favourably than a white candidate *has been* treated. That cannot be the basis of the complaint, because the white candidate mentioned in the false application did not exist. The complaint is instead that the complainant has been treated less favourably than a white candidate with the same relevant qualifications and experience *would have been* treated.

In principle, no doubt, where the false application is submitted only after the complainant's own application has been rejected, there is no distinction between that tactic and that of the tactic mentioned above of asking a friend to ring up to ask if an advertised post is still available. It is a different matter, however, if the genuine application and the false application are submitted at the same time. The complainant is starting off from the standpoint that discrimination is likely to occur. Before making any finding of discrimination, the tribunal would wish to be satisfied that he was genuinely seeking employment in the post and not simply trying to make a point or obtain an award of compensation.

103.6   **PREVIOUS OR SUBSEQUENT ACTS**

There are *Time Limits* of three months for discrimination claims. Unrelated things done or words spoken more than three months before the presentation of the complaint can, however, help to identify the reason for the treatment now complained of. So can things said or done after the presentation of the complaint but before the hearing.

This principle was affirmed by the EAT in the case of *Chattopadhyay v Headmaster of Holloway School [1981] IRLR 487*. The issue in that case was whether it was relevant that a person involved in the act complained of had subsequently treated the complainant with hostility. It was held that such evidence was admissible but not conclusive. The relevant principles may be summarised as follows:

(*a*)   An inference of racial discrimination may be drawn if a decision which is adverse to the complainant has been made by a person who is hostile to the complainant on racial grounds.

(*b*)   If that person and the complainant are of different racial groups and his words or actions demonstrate hostility to the complainant, then that hostility calls for explanation.

(*c*)   There may be a wholly non-racial explanation for the hostility, but in the absence of such explanation an inference of racial hostility may be drawn.

(*d*)   It does not matter in principle whether the hostile words or actions are before or after the treatment about which the complaint is made.

The same principles would apply not only to a complaint of racial discrimination but also to other complaints of discrimination. For example:

(*a*)   A woman has applied unsuccessfully for promotion. A year or so earlier, the manager who has turned down her application conducted an appraisal in which he scoffed at her ambitions. He told her during the appraisal interview that she should put her career on hold until her children are grown up.

(*b*)   After a disabled employee had applied unsuccessfully for promotion, the manager who turned him down was heard to say to a colleague that with his disability he should think himself lucky to be employed at all.

In both the above examples, evidence about the remarks made before or after the treatment complained of would be relevant evidence about the reason for that decision.

The above case was decided many years ago, but the approach is strikingly similar to that adopted by the Court of Appeal in the recent case of *Anya v University of Oxford and another [2001] IRLR 377*. The Court of Appeal referred to the need, in many cases, to investigate 'the surrounding circumstances and the previous history' in order to identify whether a decision has been influenced by racial factors.

103.7   **EQUAL OPPORTUNITIES AND OTHER POLICIES**

It appears from the decision of the Court of Appeal in *Anya* that an employer's failure to follow its own *Equal Opportunities Policies* (or other relevant policies and procedures) may, unless there is a credible alternative explanation, contribute to an inference of discrimination. In *Anya*, the Court of Appeal criticised the employment tribunal for its failure to record inferences or conclusions from:

'two things of potential significance. One is that, in breach of the university's own equal opportunities policy, no person specification had been drawn up until minutes before the interview. As any such tribunal will be aware, a person specification is an important aid to ensuring that candidates are considered on a basis of parity and without criteria which have an unjustifiably discriminatory effect. We do not know what the industrial tribunal made of the consequent inability of both the candidates and the panel to have adequate notice of the person specification. The second is that, in breach of university policy, no references had been taken up on the candidates'.

In relation to a respondent's explanation for a difference in treatment, where there is a difference of race (or sex):

'In the allocation of jobs by any sensibly-run institution, the explanation will be straightforward: the candidates were interviewed by an unbiased panel on an equal footing, using common criteria which contained no obvious or latent elements capable of favouring one racial group over another; and the best one was chosen. By parity of reasoning, evidence that one or more members of the panel were not unbiased, or that equal opportunities procedures were not used when they should have been, may point to the possibility of conscious or unconscious racial bias having entered into the process. It will always be a matter for the tribunal's conscientious judgment'.

103.8   STATISTICAL EVIDENCE

Statistics showing the racial composition of a workforce, or the proportion of women managers or the number of disabled employees cannot in themselves prove racial, sex or disability discrimination in recruitment. There could be wholly innocent explanations for an apparent 'under-representation' of, for example, black workers, women or disabled workers. Statistical evidence can be relevant, however, particularly where the organisation is large enough for the statistics to be significant.

The principle that statistical evidence can be relevant was established by the decision of the Court of Appeal in *West Midlands Passenger Transport Executive v Singh [1988] IRLR 186.* This was a complaint of racial discrimination in the rejection of an application by an inspector for promotion to senior inspector. The issue was whether the employers should be required to produce details of the ethnic origins of successful and unsuccessful candidates for comparable posts over a two-year period. It was held by the Court of Appeal that the information should be provided.

Lord Justice Balcombe said:

'Statistical evidence may establish a discernible pattern in the treatment of a particular group; if that pattern demonstrates a regular failure of members of the group to obtain promotion to particular jobs and of under-representation in such jobs, it may give rise to an inference of discrimination against the group'.

He went on to say:

'If a practice is being operated against a group then, in the absence of a satisfactory explanation in a particular case, it is reasonable to infer that the complainant, as a member of the group, has himself been treated less favourably on grounds of race. Indeed, evidence of discriminatory treatment against the group in relation to promotion may be more persuasive of discrimination in the particular case than previous treatment of the applicant, which may be indicative of personal factors peculiar to the applicant and not necessarily racially motivated'.

This was an important judgment, but it is necessary to handle statistics with great care and to bear in mind that they may lead only to an inference, not a presumption, of discrimination. Whatever the statistics may indicate, a complaint of direct racial discrimination will fail if the employer gives, and the tribunal believes, evidence that race was not the reason or one of the reasons for the treatment complained of and that, for example, the complainant was turned down for the post because it was genuinely believed that he did not have the qualities required for the post.

The need for caution was underlined by the EAT in the case of *Carrington v Helix Lighting Ltd [1990] IRLR 6*. This was a case in which the complainant was seeking an order requiring the employer to provide a schedule containing details of the ethnic composition of the workforce. It was held that the statistical evidence required could be relevant but 'on its own is unlikely to be sufficient'.

103.9   **ADMISSIONS OF DISCRIMINATION**

There are occasionally cases where discrimination is openly admitted. The most common examples are cases where the employer believes, rightly or wrongly, that an *Exception*, such as the *Genuine Occupational Qualification* exception, applies. The issue in such cases is not whether discrimination has occurred but whether the case is in fact covered by the exception relied upon.

There may also be cases where admissions or comments to third parties may be evidence of discrimination. The evidence could come, for example, from:

(*a*)   a newspaper which has refused to take a discriminatory advertisement;

(*b*)   a recruitment agency which has refused to comply with instructions to discriminate;

(*c*)   an employee (or former employee) who has been party to or overheard a conversation in which unlawful discrimination was admitted;

(*d*)   a former employee who has been dismissed because of a refusal to comply with an instruction to discriminate.

In the last of these examples the dismissed employee would also be able to complain of an act of *Victimisation* and also (if the instruction was to discriminate on *Racial Grounds*) of direct discrimination.

103.10   **ADVICE FOR CLAIMANTS**

It is evident from the above account of matters which can constitute relevant evidence that there are key steps which claimants should take in order to prepare a case for a tribunal hearing, as follows:

(*a*)   Use the *Questionnaire* procedure. Information about your particular case, and also statistical information, can be relevant. Furthermore a failure by the respondent to reply to the questionnaire, or a response which is evasive or equivocal, could lead to an inference of unlawful discrimination.

(*b*)   Ask for production of all relevant *Documents*. Ideally the request should be made at the questionnaire stage. In any event, the documents should be requested well in advance of the hearing and if necessary the tribunal should be asked to make an order. If you have not been shortlisted, the relevant documents will include the application forms and CVs of all the shortlisted candidates. If you have been shortlisted, they will include at least the application form and the CV of the successful candidate. If you have been interviewed, then the interview notes could be important documents.

(*c*)   Evidence of what has been said to you, for example, when enquiring about the post or during an interview, can be relevant. A detailed note of any such discussion should be made as soon as possible after it has taken place. These notes should be included with any other relevant documents in the bundle of documents for the hearing.

(*d*)   Witnesses whose evidence could be helpful should be asked to attend the hearing and if necessary a witness order should be obtained. Such witnesses could include, for example, a former employee who has witnessed a display of hostility or to whom an admission of discrimination has been made. The witness should be closely cross-questioned before the hearing, however, particularly where, as in the case of a dismissed former employee, there is a risk that the witness could be motivated by a desire to harm the employer.

(*e*)   Information should be obtained, using the Questionnaire procedure, about the respondent's *Equal Opportunities Policies* and other relevant policies and procedures and an apparent failure to comply with any of them should be brought to the tribunal's attention.

(*f*)   Earlier or subsequent incidents, even if they are not part of the complaint, should be clearly identified as part of the complainant's case, and evidence about them should be given, if they suggest the possibility of bias by relevant decision-makers or a pattern of discrimination or *Institutional Discrimination*.

103.11   **ADVICE FOR RESPONDENTS**

There are also key steps which employers and others should take in order to avoid unlawful discrimination and demonstrate that they have done so. In particular:

(*a*)   The starting point is not to entrust decisions affecting employees or job applicants to managers or other employees who have shown that they cannot be relied upon to make decisions objectively and consistently. For example, managers who display racist or sexist attitudes or who disparage the abilities of disabled workers should not be allowed to take decisions relating to recruitment, promotion or dismissal.

(*b*)   Even when these obviously unreliable managers have been excluded, it is unsafe to rely simply on the good faith and good sense of managers, supervisors, interviewers and others who are called upon to make decisions about employees and job applicants. *Training* is essential.

(*c*)   The reasons for shortlisting and selection decisions must be recorded, so that those decisions can if necessary be explained.

(*d*)   Statistics should be monitored, so that any apparent patterns of discrimination can be addressed and corrected internally before they become part of the material for a tribunal hearing.

(*e*)   It is essential that a *Questionnaire*, whether or not the statutory forms are used, should be answered promptly, carefully and accurately.

(*f*)   It is important that *Equal Opportunities Policies* and other relevant policies and procedures should be strictly complied with, in view of the risk that otherwise, in the absence of a credible explanation, an adverse inference could be drawn.

(*g*)   Allegations about earlier incidents, which are out of time, or subsequent incidents, should not simply be disregarded. The tribunal's findings of fact about such incidents could, in the absence of a credible alternative explanation, lead the tribunal to draw an inference of unlawful discrimination.

104 Exceptions

The circumstances in which discrimination is not unlawful fall broadly into two categories:

(a) cases which fall entirely outside the ambit of one or more of the discrimination laws; and

(b) cases which are within the area which is broadly covered but which are subject to exceptions in particular circumstances.

The pattern has been for the ambit of the discrimination laws to be extended. For example, the *DDA 1995* was extended from 1 October 2004 to remove the exceptions relating to employment:

(a) on a *Ship*;

(b) on an *Aircraft* or *Hovercraft*;

(c) in a *Small Business* (with fewer than 15 employees);

(d) as a *Prison Officer*;

(e) as a *Police* officer;

(f) as a member of a fire brigade who is or may be required by the terms of service to engage in firefighting (there is a similar provision relating to posts in the service of the Crown where firefighting may be involved).

The employment provisions of the *RRA 1976* (except in relation to *Advertisements* and *Victimisation*) do not apply to employment for the purposes of a private household. The latter exclusion was at the time also contained in the *SDA 1975*. There is now no blanket exclusion under the *SDA 1975* for employment in a private household, but such employment can in certain circumstances be covered by one of the *Genuine Occupational Qualification* (GOQ) exceptions.

The *SDA 1975* excludes, for instance, employment as a *Minister of Religion* or any other employment for the purposes of an organised religion (where the employment is limited to one sex or to persons who are not undergoing and have not undergone *Gender Reassignment*), where that limitation is imposed so as to comply with the doctrines of the religion or to avoid offending the religious susceptibilities of a significant number of its followers. This means that, for example, a woman could not complain under the *SDA 1975* about the refusal of the Roman Catholic Church to consider her for ordination as a priest.

Examples of other exceptions commonly found in the *Discrimination Laws* are relating to:

(a) acts done under *Statutory Authority*;

(b) acts done for the purpose of safeguarding *National Security*.

105   Extended Leave

Employees may request extended leave from time to time in order to visit relations in their countries of origin or relations who have emigrated to other countries. Employers should take care to apply consistently and without unlawful discrimination any policies under which:

(*a*)   annual leave entitlement can be accumulated; or

(*b*)   extra unpaid leave can be taken.

106   Fair Employment

None of the discrimination laws contains an express requirement for employers or others to act fairly. The *DDA 1995* comes closest to such a requirement, with the obligation to make *Reasonable Adjustments*.

Employers and others who do not adopt fair employment practices, however, will find it difficult to comply with their statutory obligations. It is in practice a very difficult exercise to avoid disability discrimination or direct or indirect racial or sex discrimination or discrimination relating to religion or belief or sexual orientation, and at the same time to be unfair, subjective and erratic in other respects. The organisations which are the most likely to comply with the law are those which have comprehensive *Equal Opportunities Policies* promising their employees and job applicants fair employment practices and which take effective measures to implement those policies.

107   Fertility Treatment

Infertility is understood to affect one couple in seven. Yet despite this, there is relatively little authoritative guidance for employers and employees as to how to deal with employment issues arising when an employee wishes to undergo a course of fertility treatment. An employee does not have a statutory right to take time off for fertility treatment, such as in vitro fertilisation (IVF). It is, however, possible that if a woman is treated less favourably for a reason related to her undergoing fertility treatment, she may complain of sex discrimination. But since men as well as women may undergo fertility treatment, a claim of direct discrimination will not necessarily succeed.

Employers should be wary of taking action based on inappropriate assumptions – eg that the employee undergoing IVF treatment will take more time off if she becomes pregnant. This potentially amounts to direct discrimination. However, in *Greenwich London Borough Council v Robinson (1994) EAT 754/94*, the Employment Appeal Tribunal concluded that time taken off work to undergo IVF treatment concerned *not* being pregnant and thus, unlike maternity leave, was apt to be taken into account when assessing an employee's absence record in the context of a redundancy selection exercise.

108   Fixed-Term Contracts and Discrimination

108.1   INTRODUCTION

A fixed-term employment contract involves an agreement that the job will last for a specified period of time, although often provisions are included to enable the contract to be renewed if so desired. Termination during the currency of the fixed term is also a possibility. Although fixed terms allow for the job to end through a 'natural break', the expiry of the fixed period of employment still counts as a dismissal for various legal purposes, such as the right to claim unfair dismissal or redundancy pay. A notable attraction of fixed terms from an employer's point of view used to be that they offered a possible means of cutting out the statutory rights to claim unfair dismissal or a statutory redundancy payment, subject to certain conditions. This is, however, no longer possible.

The attractions of such contracts to employers have further diminished as a result of the *Fixed-term Employees (Prevention of Less Favourable Treatment) Regulations 2002 (SI 2002 No 2034)*, which came into force on 1 October 2002 and which aim to eliminate improper discrimination against fixed-term workers and say that they should be treated no less favourably than permanent workers, unless different treatment is objectively justified.

108.2   THE REGULATIONS

The Regulations include the following provisions for the benefit of fixed-term workers:

(*a*)   The right not to be treated less favourably than a comparable permanent employee, if that treatment is on the ground of the fixed-term status and is not objectively justified.

(*b*)   The right to be informed of available vacancies in the establishment.

(*c*)   The right to become a permanent employee after having been continuously employed under successive fixed-term contracts and after their continuous employment has lasted for four years since 10 July 2002 (unless the current contract was entered into before that date and has not been renewed since that date).

There is an exception to (*c*) where, on the last renewal, the use of a fixed-term contract was justified on objective grounds.

108.3   MATERNITY LEAVE

The expiry of a fixed-term contract without its being renewed constitutes a dismissal for the purposes of unfair dismissal law. This means that if the employer opts not to renew a fixed-term contract which has expired either during or shortly before or after a period of maternity leave or extended maternity leave and the decision is for a reason connected with pregnancy or childbirth, the dismissal will *automatically* be unfair regardless of the length of the contract.

108.4   DIRECT OR INDIRECT SEX DISCRIMINATION

The decision of the EAT in *Caruana v Manchester Airport plc [1996] IRLR 378*, made it clear that a decision not to offer a new fixed-term contract may also constitute sex discrimination. A self-employed researcher (who was not, by virtue of her self-employed status, eligible to claim unfair dismissal) gave notice that she would commence maternity leave shortly before the expiry of her fixed-term contract. She was then told that her current contract would not be renewed for a further period because she would not be available for work at its commencement. The company argued that the rulings in the *Webb* litigation – see *Pregnancy* – did not apply to fixed-term contacts. That argument was rejected. The EAT declined to offer 'a positive encouragement to employers to offer or to impose, not a continuous and stable employment relationship, but a series of short-term contracts, with the object or collateral advantage of avoiding the impact of the discrimination laws'.

In any circumstances where workers on fixed-term contracts are predominantly female (or predominantly male) there may be grounds for arguing indirect sex discrimination as well as a breach of the Regulations.

In *Whiffen v Millham Ford Girls School [2001] IRLR 468*, a case heard before the Regulations came into force, teachers on fixed-term contracts were selected for redundancy before permanent teachers were considered. The teachers on fixed-term contracts were predominantly female and there was a finding of indirect sex discrimination.

108.5   NON-RENEWAL OF FIXED-TERM CONTRACT

In *Department for Work and Pensions v Webley [2005] IRLR 288*, the Court of Appeal upheld a ruling that the claimant had not been treated less favourably than a permanent employee within the meaning of *Regulation 3(1)(b)* of the *Fixed-Term Employees (Prevention of Less Favourable Treatment) Regulations 2002*, when her temporary fixed-term contract of employment was not renewed in accordance with the policy that temporary employees had their employment terminated after 51 weeks' service. The EAT had been wrong to allow an appeal on the ground that non-renewal of a fixed-term contract, amounting to dismissal, was capable of amounting to less favourable treatment of a fixed-term employee. Where the only matter of which the claimant complains is that her employer has refused to review or extend her fixed-term contract, that is not capable of involving less favourable treatment within *Regulation 3(1)*.

109   Flexible Working

109.1   INTRODUCTION

A rigid adherence to particular employment requirements and methods of working can make employers vulnerable to complaints of *Indirect Discrimination*. For example, indirect sex discrimination is likely to occur if an employer:

(a)   automatically says no every time a full-time employee asks to go part-time because of her childcare commitments;

(b)   rejects out of hand all job share requests;

(c)   is unwilling to consider modifying start and finish times for employees who cannot work unsocial hours;

(d)   insists that all employees should be prepared to relocate, even when the need hardly ever arises.

Furthermore, an organisation which is wedded to established practices and working arrangements and is resistant to change will have difficulty in making the *Reasonable Adjustments* which are required under the *DDA 1995*.

Conversely, employers are more likely to comply with the law if they adopt working arrangements which are as flexible as the need of the business or organisation permits. Furthermore, employees are more likely to be loyal and enthusiastic if they can see that real efforts are being made to accommodate their personal and domestic circumstances.

109.2   TYPES OF FLEXIBLE WORKING

Common forms of flexible working include:

(a)   *Annualised hours*, i.e. working time organised on the basis of the number of hours to be worked over a year, rather than during the course of a week. Typically, an annualised hours arrangement is intended to smooth out the peaks and troughs of workload. Pay is linked to the hours worked in the relevant pay period.

(b)   *Compressed hours*, whereby a person works for a total number of agreed hours over a shorter period, e.g. working the total weekly hours over four instead of five days. Under such an arrangement, the worker would be paid as if 'full-time', but would not be entitled to overtime pay for the agreed extra hours worked in any single day.

(c)   *Flexitime*, i.e. giving the worker a degree of discretion as to the precise working hours undertaken, usually outside specified core hours. Pay is for the number of hours worked.

(d)   *Home working*; see *Teleworking*.

(e)   *Job-sharing*, i.e. where, for example, two people work on a part-time basis, combining to cover a full-time job. Each will be paid for the hours actually worked.

(f)   *Shift working*, i.e. where the organisation operates for longer periods than the typical eight-hour day.

(*g*)   *Staggered hours*, i.e. permitting workers to start and finish at different times of the day, e.g. in retail businesses, where a high concentration of staffing is typically required at lunchtimes rather than at the start and end of the typical working day. Pay is linked to total hours worked rather than when they are worked.

(*h*)   *Term-time Working.*

(*i*)   *V-time working*, i.e. a voluntary arrangement by which an employer reduces the number of hours worked for an agreed period, on the basis that full-time employment will be guaranteed after the end of the period.

109.3   THE RIGHT TO REQUEST FLEXIBLE WORKING

The *Employment Act 2002* introduced a new right for an employee to request a change in terms and conditions of employment to allow flexible working. The detailed rules are set out in the *Flexible Working (Eligibility, Complaints and Remedies) Regulations 2002 (SI 2002 No 3236)* and the *Flexible Working (Procedural Requirements) Regulations 2002 (SI 2002 No 3207)*, which came into force on 6 April 2003. The thinking behind the new regime was to introduce a family friendly policy that promoted a 'work-family balance', rather than going so far as to promote a better work-life balance for all employees, regardless of childcare obligations.

To qualify for the right to make a request, a male or female employee must meet the conditions set out in *section 80F(1)* of the *Employment Rights Act 1996*, i.e. he must:

(*a*)   be an employee;

(*b*)   have a child under six, or under 18 in the case of a disabled child;

(*c*)   have worked continuously with the employer for 26 weeks at the time the application is made;

(*d*)   make the application before the child's sixth birthday or eighteenth birthday in the case of a disabled child;

(*e*)   have or expect to have responsibility for the child's upbringing and have a specified relationship to the child (i.e, biological parents, legal guardian, adoptive or foster parent or spouse of these, including same-sex partners who have parental responsibility to the child);

(*f*)   not be an agency worker;

(*g*)   not be a member of the armed forces;

(*h*)   not have made such a request during the previous 12 months;

(*i*)   have, as the reason for applying for flexible working, the object of being enabled to care for someone who is, at the time of the application, a child in respect of whom he has childcare obligations.

An employee may request the following types of flexibility:

(*a*)   a change to working hours;

(*b*)   a change to the times when he is required to work;

(*c*)   the ability to work from home.

The request must be made in writing (including email or fax) and must state if and when a previous application has been made, as well as being signed and dated.

The employer is only permitted to refuse a duly made request on the grounds specified in *section 80G(1)(a)* of the *Employment Rights Act 1996*, in the following situations where there is:

(*a*)   burden of additional costs;

(*b*)   detrimental effect on ability to meet customer or client demand;

(*c*)   inability to reorganise work among existing staff;

(*d*)   inability to recruit additional staff;

(*e*)   detrimental impact on quality or performance;

(*f*)   lack of work during the periods that employee proposes to work;

(*g*)   planned structural changes;

(*h*)   such other grounds as may be specified in regulations.

The mere fact that a request is refused on one of the above grounds does not preclude the possibility that the refusal may constitute an act of discrimination on the ground of sex, race or disability.

Within 28 days of the request being made, the employer must arrange to meet with the employee. The purpose of the meeting is for the parties to discuss the desired work pattern and how it might best be accommodated, as well as any available alternative working patterns should that requested be unavailable. The employee may be accompanied at the meeting and the companion has limited representational rights, i.e. he may address the meeting and confer with the employee, but may not answer questions on the employee's behalf.

Within 14 days of the meeting, the employer must write to the employee, either to agree to a new work pattern and date of commencement, or to provide a clear business ground, or grounds, as to why the request is to be refused, and the reason why the ground or grounds are applicable. An employee has the right to appeal against the employer's decision within 14 days of its being notified.

Where the parties do not agree, one possibility is for them to attempt to resolve the issue with the assistance of an external third party mediator or conciliator. This might be an ACAS officer, a trade union representative or another person with appropriate expertise; the DTI guidance suggests that such an expert might be identified through the local Business Link organisation and explains that the objective of conciliation or mediation should be to achieve an informal solution as opposed to addressing the problem formally through the ACAS arbitration scheme or by way of a complaint to an employment tribunal.

An employee who considers that the employer has failed to comply with the statutory duties, or whose rejection of the request is based on incorrect facts, may make a complaint to an employment tribunal. Before doing so, however, the employee must first have exhausted any internal appeal process. A complaint must be made within three months of either the date when the appeal decision was notified or the date on which the alleged breach of duty occurred, although these time limits may be extended in certain circumstances. A tribunal that upholds such complaint must make a declaration to that effect and may award compensation. However, the sum awarded may not exceed a maximum of eight weeks' pay and the tribunal has no power to order the employer to comply with the request. An employee who exercises or purports to exercise the right to seek a flexible working arrangement is protected from victimisation. To subject an employee to a detriment or dismissal in such circumstances is automatically unfair.

When a request for a flexible working arrangement is accepted, the change thereby effected to the employee's terms and conditions of employment is treated as permanent. Accordingly, the employee has no statutory right to revert to the status quo should, for instance, his domestic circumstances change. But a mutually agreed variation of the contractual terms of employment would be possible.

109.4 **FLEXIBLE WORKING AND CARING FOR ADULTS**

The *Work and Families Act 2006* extends the right to request flexible working to employees with caring responsibilities for adults. The new right, which takes effect from 6 April 2007, is implemented by the *Flexible Working (Eligibility, Complaints and Remedies) (Amendment) Regulations 2006 (SI 2006 No 3314)*. To qualify for the right to request flexible working, an employee must have 20 weeks' qualifying service and be, or expect to be, caring for a person aged 18 or over who:

(*a*)   is married to, or is the partner or civil partner of the employee; or

(*b*)   is a near relative of the employee; or

(*c*)   falls into neither of the above categories but lives at the same address as the employee.

'Care' for these purposes is not expressly defined. The definition of 'near relative' includes parents, parents-in-law, adult children, adopted adult children, siblings (including those who are in-laws), uncles, aunts, grandparents and step-relatives.

110   Framework Directive

Council Directive 2000/78/EC, otherwise known as the EU *Employment Framework Directive*, is a highly important measure. It establishes a general framework for equal treatment in employment and requires the prohibition of age discrimination in employment and discrimination on grounds of sexual orientation. It also covers discrimination on grounds of religion or belief and disability discrimination.

Member states were required to implement the provisions on sexual orientation and religious discrimination by 2 December 2003. That is why the *SOR 2003* and the *RBR 2003* came into effect on that date. Regulations were already being adopted to amend the *DDA 1995* with effect from 1 October 2004 – see *Disability Discrimination Legislation*. Further, the *AR 2006* came into force on 1 October 2006, shortly before the deadline of 2 December 2006 specified in the Framework Directive.

111   Freedom of Information

The *Freedom of Information Act 2000* and the *Environmental Information Regulations 2004 (SI 2004 No 3391) (EIR)* came into force from January 2005. They make it possible to request information held by public authorities in England, Wales and Northern Ireland. A 'public authority' for these purposes includes:

(*a*)   central government and government departments;

(*b*)   local authorities;

(*c*)   hospitals, doctors' surgeries, dentists, pharmacist and opticians;

(*d*)   state schools, colleges and universities;

(*e*)   police forces;

(*f*)   prison services.

This 'right to know' is enforced by the Information Commissioner who has responsibility for ensuring that information is disclosed promptly and that exemptions from disclosure are applied lawfully.

The Act provides for 23 exemptions, some of which are 'absolute' and some 'qualified'. There are 12 'qualified' exceptions from disclosure in the EIR. Where information falls under an 'absolute' exemption, the harm to the public interest that would result from its disclosure is already established, e.g. in relation to personal information, or if disclosure would result in an actionable breach of confidence. If a public authority believes that the information is covered by a 'qualified' exemption or exception, it must apply the 'public interest test'. This favours disclosure.

Information may be withheld, but only if the public authority considers that the public interest in withholding the information is greater than the public interest in disclosing it. If a public authority decides not to disclose the information requested, it must give reasons for its decision.

The potential afforded by the Act for, amongst others, people claiming equal pay to seek information relevant to their case, is becoming widely recognised.

Employers receiving such requests need to consider them promptly and with the utmost care. The Act does not require them to create new information, but it may require them to collate and summarise existing information. In certain circumstances, an employer may be able to rely on an exemption because the cost of compliance is excessive, but there is a duty to provide guidance as to how to refine the request so as to bring it within the prescribed level of cost (at the time of writing £450).

At the time of writing, the government was proposing to introduce modifications to the Act which, speaking very broadly, would make it a little easier to decline to respond to certain attempts to exercise the 'right to know'.

112   Gender-Based Criteria

There are two clear cases where a particular act can be said to be one of *Direct Discrimination* by reason of the application of a gender-related criterion.

The first case is where the reason for the act complained of is a factor or state of affairs which itself arises as a result of an act of direct discrimination, as in *James v Eastleigh Borough Council [1990] IRLR 288*. In that case, the difference in treatment was based on a difference in State retirement age which itself was discriminatory as between men and women.

The second case is where a woman is treated less favourably because of her pregnancy, which is a condition unique to women. It was said by Lord Keith of Kinkel in *Webb v EMO Air Cargo (UK) Ltd [1993] IRLR 27* that:

> 'There can be no doubt that in general to dismiss a woman because she is pregnant or to refuse to employ a woman of childbearing age because she may become pregnant is unlawful direct discrimination. Childbearing and the capacity for childbearing are characteristics of the female sex. So to apply these characteristics as the criterion for dismissal or refusal to employ is to apply a gender-based criterion . . .'

Case law does not, however, support the extension of the principle of gender-based criteria to other cases where a person is treated less favourably because of a particular physical characteristic or medical condition, even if that characteristic or condition is unique either to men or to women. The case of *Webb v EMO Air Cargo (UK) Ltd* was referred to the ECJ, *[1994] IRLR 482*. The judgment referred to the earlier case of *Handels [1991] IRLR 31*, in which 'the Court drew a clear distinction between pregnancy and illness, even where the illness is attributable to pregnancy but manifests itself after the maternity leave . . . there is no reason to distinguish such an illness from any other illness'.

This principle was further developed by the ECJ in *Brown v Rentokil Ltd [1998] IRLR 445*. On the one hand, if a woman is treated less favourably because of absences during her pregnancy, caused by the pregnancy itself or a pregnancy-related illness, then that is an act of direct sex discrimination; on the other hand, if she is ill after her return from maternity leave, and even if that illness is attributable to her pregnancy (and accordingly results from a condition which is unique to women), that absence through illness is to be treated in the same way as any other absence through illness.

113   Gender Reassignment

The *SDA 1975* was amended with effect from 1 May 1999 by the *Sex Discrimination (Gender Reassignment) Regulations 1999 (SI 1999 No 1102)*. Under the new *section 2A*, the definition of discrimination was extended to include direct discrimination (but not indirect discrimination) in relation to gender reassignment. There is discrimination for the purposes of the *SDA 1975* if a person is treated less favourably than other persons are or would be treated on the ground that he or she:

(*a*)   intends to undergo gender reassignment;

(*b*)   is undergoing gender reassignment; or

(*c*)   has undergone gender reassignment.

For these and other issues in relation to gender reassignment see *Transsexuals* and *Genuine Occupational Qualifications*.

114   Genetic Testing

114.1   WHAT IS GENETIC TESTING?

Advances in science bring challenges as well as benefits. The availability of genetic tests of individuals raises a variety of employment questions, including equal opportunities concerns. Genetic tests take several different forms, but commonly involve an examination designed to find out if there is an otherwise undetectable disease-related 'genotype' which may indicate an increased chance of an individual developing a specific disease in the future. Genetic testing has been the subject of a report issued in 1999 by the Human Genetics Advisory Commission (HGAC) and a *Code of Practice*, revised in 1999 and issued by the Association of British Insurers in connection with the use by insurers of results from genetic tests in deciding whether, and on what terms, to make insurance cover available. The worldwide publicity given to the Human Genome Project illustrates that ethical debates about issues raised by advances in genetic science are here to stay. Some of those debates impact on employment.

114.2   REASONS FOR GENETIC TESTING

Genetic testing offers a variety of possible benefits:

(*a*)   diagnosis and treatment of a condition;

(*b*)   provision of information about a person's future risk of contracting certain specific inherited diseases;

(*c*)   ascertaining whether the person carries a gene for an inherited disorder;

(*d*)   ascertaining whether the person may be susceptible to a condition (such as heart disease) which is technically described as 'multi-factorial', i.e. where the gene is not the only cause of the disorder but may, together with other factors such as living conditions and behaviour, lead to the person having the condition.

Employers and, perhaps especially, their insurers, see a variety of benefits from genetic testing. For instance, it may permit the identification of job applicants whose genetic make-up might render them a danger to themselves or other (e.g. drivers or pilots susceptible to heart attacks). Testing may also enable screening of individuals who might have a genetic sensitivity to a particular feature of the working environment (such as chemicals necessarily used in that environment). But opponents of genetic testing question its accuracy and its value. Testing also carries with it the potential for discriminatory treatment.

114.3   LEGAL IMPLICATIONS

In the UK, unlike certain other jurisdictions including France and Austria, there is no legislation which specifically addresses the issue of genetic testing in the workplace. It is, arguably, a curiosity (and perhaps a weakness in the drafting) of the *DDA 1995* that it does not protect an individual who is not disabled, but who is identified, as a result of a genetic test, as being at risk of having a disability at a future date.

In cases where the condition identified by genetic testing is gender or race-specific, the *SDA 1975* or *RRA 1976* may afford at least some safeguards. Haemophilia, for

200

instance, is a condition found in men but not women. Thus to refuse to offer employment to a person because genetic testing reveals that he has haemophilia might constitute indirect discrimination on the ground of sex, although the employer might in an appropriate case be able to demonstrate an objective justification for the requirement that the employee should not have haemophilia. It may even be arguable that the requirement is *Gender-Based*, so as to amount to *Direct Discrimination* and be incapable of justification. Members of ethnic groups which are particularly susceptible to certain medical conditions (an example might be the relatively high incidence of sickle cell disorder in Afro-Caribbean people in comparison to white people) may be able to complain under the *RRA 1976* if discriminated against in the context of genetic testing.

The *Data Protection Act 1998* may assist employees. The results of genetic testing would almost inevitably fall within the ambit of *section 2(e)* of the Act as 'sensitive personal data', i.e. personal data relating to the individual's 'physical or mental health or condition'. To comply with the regime established by the data protection law, a data controller must observe various conditions, such as obtaining express consent from the individual.

Human rights issues may also be relevant. Requiring an applicant or employee to take a genetic test might constitute a breach of the right to privacy and family life and, in appropriate circumstances, an individual might be able to make a complaint under the *Human Rights Act 1998* or the European Convention on Human Rights. Similar issues have already arisen in respect of an AIDS screening test. In *X v Commission of the European Community [1995] IRLR 320*, the European Court ruled that *Article 8* of the *European Convention* includes in particular a person's right to keep his state of health secret, and although pre-recruitment medical examinations served a legitimate interest of the employer (the European Commission itself) that did not justify the carrying-out of a test against the will of the person concerned. This was so even though, if the individual concerned, after being properly informed, withholds his consent to a test which the medical officer appropriately considers necessary in order to evaluate the person's suitability for the post in question, the employer cannot be obliged to take the risk of recruiting him.

115   Genuine Occupational Qualifications (GOQs)

115.1   GENERAL PRINCIPLES

The law recognises that there are exceptional circumstances in which a person's gender or racial group is a genuine qualification for a particular job. Where this GOQ exception applies, the law permits discrimination in relation to:

(*a*)   recruitment or selection;

(*b*)   promoting or transferring an employee to the job;

(*c*)   training an employee for the work involved;

(*d*)   not allowing a *Contract Worker* to do the work or continue to do it.

Discrimination is also permitted in relation to the offer of a *Partnership* or the appointment of an *Office-holder,* where one of the GOQ exceptions would apply if employment were being offered. Where a job is covered by the GOQ exception, the *SDA 1975* contains additional provisions relating to persons who intend to undergo, are undergoing or have undergone *Gender Reassignment*. Where, because of gender reassignment, the person is or will not be of the gender required, the Act permits discrimination not only in the respects mentioned above but also in dismissing the person from the relevant post.

The *RBR 2003*, and the *SOR 2003* and the *AR 2006* refer not to GOQs, but to genuine occupational requirements. Whereas the approach adopted in the *SDA 1975* and the *RRA 1976* was to refer to the various circumstances in which the GOQ exception would apply, the exception is expressed in much more general terms in the *RBR 2003* and the *SOR 2003*.

115.2   THE RBR 2003, SOR 2003 AND THE AR 2006

The *RBR 2003*, the *SOR 2003* and the *AR 2006* contain general provisions under which the exception applies if, having regard to the nature of the employment or the context in which it is carried out, the following questions could all be answered yes:

(*a*)   Is being of a particular religion or belief (or a particular sexual orientation or possessing a characterstic related to age) a genuine and determining occupational requirement?

(*b*)   Is it proportionate to apply that requirement in a particular case?

(*c*)   Does the person to whom the requirement is applied fail to meet it; alternatively, is the employer (or otherwise as the case may be) not satisfied that that person meets the requirement, and in all the circumstances is it reasonable for the employer not to be satisfied?

The *RBR 2003* also contains a further provision under which the above questions must be considered having regard to an ethos which the employer has based on religion or belief as well as having regard to the nature of the employment or the context in which it is carried out.

The *SOR 2003* also contains a provision to cover cases where the employment or contract work is for purposes of an organised religion and the employer applies a requirement related to sexual orientation:

(*a*)   so as to comply with the doctrines of the religion; or

(*b*)   so as to avoid (because of the nature of the employment and the context in which it is carried out) conflicting with the strongly held religious convictions of a significant number of the religion's followers.

115.3   THE SDA 1975 AND THE RRA 1976

It remains the position under the *SDA 1975* that the GOQ exception can apply in one of several specified circumstances.

The position under the *RRA 1976* is more complicated. The Act continues to specify particular circumstances (much more limited than in the *SDA 1975*) in which the GOQ exception applies. In addition, however, there is now a more general provision, which applies only when the discrimination to be permitted is on grounds of race or ethnic or national origins (but not colour or nationality).

There are very few instances in which a job will qualify for a GOQ on the ground of sex. There are even fewer jobs where the original GOQ exception under the *RRA 1976* applies. It is not safe for an employer to act on the assumption that a job of a particular kind is always covered by the exception. It is necessary to look closely at the circumstances of each individual case.

The GOQ exception in the *SDA 1975* and the original GOQ exception in the *RRA 1976* can apply where only some of the duties of the job call for (as the case may be) a man or woman or member of a particular racial group. The employer must consider, however, whether there are existing employees of the required gender or racial group:

(*a*)   who are capable of carrying out the relevant duties;

(*b*)   whom it would be reasonable to employ on those duties; and

(*c*)   whose numbers are sufficient to meet the employer's likely requirements in respect of those duties without undue inconvenience.

115.4   THE RRA 1976 – PERSONAL SERVICES

The most important GOQ exception in the *RRA 1976* is that relating to social and welfare work. The exception applies if:

(*a*)   the holder of the job provides persons of a particular racial group with personal services promoting their welfare; and

(*b*)   those services can most effectively be provided by a person of that same racial group.

The case of *Tottenham Green Under-Fives' v Marshall [1989] IRLR 147* is an example of a case where the exception can apply. The centre ran a nursery for children aged between two and five, of whom 84 per cent were of Afro-Caribbean origin. When a nursery worker of Afro-Caribbean origin left, the advertisement for her replacement stipulated an Afro-Caribbean worker. The duties of the post included reading books in Afro-Caribbean dialect and talking to the children in the dialect. This was a genuine duty. It was a personal service which could most effectively be provided by a worker of Afro-Caribbean origin.

On the other hand, in *London Borough of Lambeth v CRE [1990] IRLR 230*, the Council advertised for Afro-Caribbean or Asian applicants for the post of assistant head and group manager in the housing benefits department. These racial groups were stipulated because over half of the tenants were of Afro-Caribbean or Asian ethnic origin. It was held by the Court of Appeal that the GOQ exception did not cover these jobs. For the exception to apply, there must generally be direct contact between the holder of the job and the person to whom personal services are to be given; in this case, the posts were management jobs involving minimal contact with the public.

115.5   THE RRA 1976 – AUTHENTICITY

The *RRA 1976* also states that the GOQ exception can apply if a person of a particular racial group is required for reasons of authenticity in a job involving:

(*a*)   participation in a dramatic performance or other entertainment;

(*b*)   specified work of various kinds as an artist's or photographic model; or

(*c*)   working in a place where food or drink is provided and consumed (the need for authenticity being because of the particular setting).

115.6   THE SDA 1975 – PERSONAL SERVICES

The *SDA 1975* contains a similar but slightly broader exception to that contained in the *RRA 1976*, for jobs where personal services are to be provided.

There is a supplementary GOQ exception which applies where the job involves providing vulnerable individuals with personal services promoting their welfare or similar personal services. The GOQ exception applies if in the reasonable view of the employer the services cannot effectively be provided by a person whilst that person is undergoing gender reassignment. This exception permits discrimination, however, only against a person who intends to undergo or is undergoing gender reassignment; not one who has already undergone gender reassignment.

115.7   THE SDA 1975 – AUTHENTICITY

There are two cases under the *SDA 1975* where being of a particular gender can be a GOQ because the essential nature of the job calls for a person of that gender, so that the essential nature of the job would be materially different if carried out by a person not of that gender. The requirement can be:

(*a*)   for reasons of physiology (excluding physical strength or stamina) – an obvious example would be certain modelling jobs; or

(*b*)   for reasons of authenticity, in dramatic performances or other entertainment.

115.8   THE SDA 1975 – DECENCY OR PRIVACY

Of the remaining GOQ exceptions under the *SDA* 1975, the one which has given rise to most litigation is where a job needs to be held by (for example) a man to preserve decency or privacy because:

(*a*)   it is likely to involve physical contact with men in circumstances where they might reasonably object to its being carried out by a woman; or

(*b*)   the job holder is likely to do his work in circumstances where men might reasonably object to the presence of a woman because they are in a state of undress or are using sanitary facilities.

In *Lasertop Ltd v Webster [1997] IRLR 498*, a salesperson's duties involved taking prospective members on a tour of a health club which was for women only. The duties included taking the prospective members into the changing room, sauna area, sunbed room and toilet. Women using these facilities would be likely to object if it was a man who came into these areas with the prospective members. The business was a new business, which had not yet recruited many female employees. The GOQ exception applied because the duties which involved going into the changing room and other areas could not be allocated to existing female employees without undue inconvenience.

There is a supplementary exception relating to gender reassignment where a job holder may be liable to be called upon to perform intimate physical searches pursuant to statutory powers. This exception permits discrimination against a person who intends to undergo, is undergoing or has undergone gender reassignment.

In *A v Chief Constable of the West Yorkshire Police and another [2003] IRLR 32,* a male to female post operative transsexual applied to become a police constable. Her application was refused on the ground that candidates would not be appointed unless they were capable of performing the full duties of a constable. Legislation (the *Police and Criminal Evidence Act 1984*) affected the carrying out by transsexuals of searches of persons in custody. The question which then arose was whether the above GOQ exception applied.

It was held by the Court of Appeal that, having regard to *Article 8* of the *Human Rights Act 1998* (the *HRA*), the exception did not apply. Buxton LJ said that in any case to which the *HRA* applies 'it will in future be necessary to consider whether a failure or refusal to treat a post-operative transsexual as being of the reassigned gender involves a breach of *Article 8*. Since the application of *Article 8* is case-specific and does not confer absolute rights, the courts will have to consider in every case whether the subject's interest in achieving respect and recognition for her gender reassignment is outweighed by countervailing considerations of the public interest.'

In the particular case, once the court had been informed that the complainant had no objection to the disclosure of her transsexuality 'that destroyed the Chief Constable's defence of genuine occupational qualification based on the difficulties of complying with *section 54(9)* of *PACE* if an undisclosed transsexual was a member of the force'.

115.9 THE DDA 1995

The *DDA 1995* does not contain any provision for GOQs. It does not need to, because of the provisions relating to *Justification and Disability Discrimination.*

116   Grading

For the purposes of the *EPA 1970*, the fact that the complainant and the comparator have different grades under a grading scheme can be a *Material Factor* defence, even though the two employees are employed on:

(*a*)   *Like Work*;

(*b*)   work of *Equal Value*; or

(*c*)   work rated as equivalent under a *Job Evaluation* Scheme.

This principle was recognised by the Court of Appeal in the case of *National Vulcan Engineering Insurance Group Ltd v Wade [1978] IRLR 225*. It was said in that case that a grading system according to skill, ability and experience is an integral part of good business management. A defence based on the different grades of the complainant and the comparator will not be upheld, however, if the way in which the grading scheme is applied includes any direct or indirect sex discrimination.

An employee can present a complaint under the other *Discrimination Laws* if there is discrimination in relation to a grading decision. If because of the discrimination the employee has been given a lower grade than another person has or would have been given he or she can complain of having been subjected to a detriment or denied access to a benefit or facility.

117   Grievances

117.1   INTRODUCTION

Schedule 2 to the *Employment Act 2002*, which came into force on 1 October 2004, contains two statutory grievance procedures; a three-stage 'standard' procedure and a two-stage 'modified' procedure. The circumstances in which they apply are set out in the *Employment Act 2002 (Dispute Resolution) Regulations 2004 (SI 2004 No 752)*. The purpose of the procedures is to ensure that workplace concerns are raised, discussed and in many cases resolved without the need to have resource to proceedings in the employment tribunal. The procedures provide for a minimum legal standard and it is entirely possible for an employer to operate more comprehensive procedures, provided that they include all the steps contained in the statutory procedures and fulfil their general requirements.

Importantly, *section 32* of the *Employment Act 2002* provides that, where a statutory grievance procedure applies in respect of an employee's workplace concern, and where the employee presents an employment tribunal claim arising from that concern, the tribunal claim will be inadmissible unless the employee has first sent a written statement of grievance to the employer in compliance with Step 1 of the applicable procedure. Once a statutory procedure has been initiated, both parties should comply with its requirements. Moreover, where an applicable procedure has not been completed owing to the fault of either party, the tribunal award made to the employee in the event of a successful claim will generally be adjusted under *section 31* of the *Employment Act 2002*.

117.2   STANDARD GRIEVANCE PROCEDURE

In Step 1 of the standard procedure, the employee must set out the grievance in writing and send a statement, or a copy of it, to the employer.

Step 2 requires that:

(*a*)   the employer must invite the employee to attend a meeting to discuss the grievance;

(*b*)   the meeting must not take place unless –

(i)   the employee has informed the employer what the basis for the grievance was when he or she made the statement under Step 1 above; and

(ii)   the employer has had a reasonable opportunity to consider his response to that information;

(*c*)   the employee must take all reasonable steps to attend the meeting;

(*d*)   after meeting, the employer must inform the employee of his decision as to his response to the grievance and notify the employee of the right to appeal against the decision if the employee is not satisfied with it.

Under Step 3:

(*a*)   if the employee does wish to appeal, he or she must inform the employer;

(*b*)   the employee informs the employer of his or her wish to appeal, the employer must invite the employee to attend a further meeting;

(*c*)   the employee must take all reasonable steps to attend the meeting;

(d)   after the appeal meeting, the employer must inform the employee of his final decision.

If a statutory regime applies, the standard grievance procedure applies as a default procedure. The modified grievance procedure can only apply where the employee in question has left employment and the parties have agreed not to follow the standard grievance procedure.

Regulation 14 of the *2004 Regulations* provides that, where an employee serves a discrimination questionnaire under the appropriate statutory provisions, this will not amount to the sending of Step 1 statement of grievance and, accordingly, will not initiate the statutory procedures. Thus an employer is not obliged to follow the requirements of the statutory procedures merely because of receipt of a discrimination questionnaire. The rules do not, however, prevent an employee from raising a grievance at the same time as submitting a questionnaire.

117.3   MODIFIED GRIEVANCE PROCEDURE

Step 1 of the modified procedure provides that the employee must set out in writing both the grievance and the basis for it and send the statement or a copy of it to the employer. Step 2 provides that the employer must set out his response in writing and send the statement or a copy of it to the employee.

The modified grievance procedure only applies where the employment has ended and the standard grievance procedure has not already been completed in relation to the grievance. A former employee may follow the standard grievance procedure if he or she so wishes. If he or she prefers not to meet the former employer, it is open to him or her to seek to agree to the operation of the modified grievance procedure.

117.4   APPLYING THE PROCEDURES

In *Mark Warner Ltd v Aspland [2006] IRLR 87*, the question was whether a solicitor's letter on behalf of an employee concerned at her employer's treatment of her would fulfil the statutory requirement with regard to raising a grievance. The EAT held that it did. The action complained of was the employer's alleged breach of the implied duty of mutual trust and confidence, and victimisation arising out of the claimant's earlier protected act (a previous complaint to an employment tribunal). Accordingly, given that she had raised a grievance, she was allowed to proceed with her complaint of unfair constructive dismissal and victimisation contrary to the *SDA 1975*.

The point that a grievance does not have to be raised in any 'unduly legalistic or technical manner' was reiterated by the EAT in *Canary Wharf Management Ltd v Edebi [2006] IRLR 416*. The President of the EAT acknowledged that the Dispute Resolution Regulations 'are complex and are not happily structured'. He agreed with the view previously expressed in *Galaxy Showers Ltd v Wilson [2006] IRLR 83*, that a complaint about an act can also include a failure to act: 'For example, in the context of a disability claim, the complaint may be that an employer has failed to make reasonable adjustment. In my view, that would constitute a matter in respect of which there should be a grievance raised under the statute before the tribunal can exercise jurisdiction.' On the facts, the EAT overruled a tribunal chairman's decision that the claimant's letter to his employers detailing various complaints about working conditions and to the effect that they had on his health and that of his colleagues amounted to the raising of a grievance under the *DDA 1995*. The chairman had been justified in focusing solely on the claimant's final letter to his employers. Although the claimant pointed out in that letter that he raised issues relating to his health going back some nine months, the timescale was extensive and no specific reference was made to the detail of earlier complaints. However, the tribunal chairman had erred in concluding that the final letter raised a complaint of disability discrimination. The references to the claimant's health problems could not be said to have fairly raised, even in a non-technical and unsophisticated way, an issue which the employer could reasonably understand had arisen under the *DDA 1995*. The claimant did not identify any failure specifically to make adjustments, nor did he allege that he was treated less favourably than his colleagues. This was a generalised complaint about the adverse consequences to health, both generally and to the claimant in particular, of the conduct of the employer. It did not raise an issue of disability discrimination.

It follows from these early decisions on the Dispute Resolution Regulations that:

(*a*)   prudent employers will treat most if not all written complaints from employees or their representatives as potential grievances; but also that

(*b*)   prudent employees will also take care to express their grievances clearly, even if not in a technical fashion.

In short, the unsatisfactory wording of the Dispute Resolution Regulations may, ironically, in itself in some instances give rise to, rather than resolve, disputes between employers and employees. Unsurprisingly, there is growing pressure for the rules to be amended. In March 2007, the Gibbons Review into the working of the regime was severely critical of it and significant changes seem likely to be made. It is to be hoped that such changes will simplify, not further complicate, the practical handling of workplace disputes.

117.5   GRIEVANCES AND CONSTRUCTIVE DISMISSAL

In *Abbey National plc v Fairbrother [2007] IRLR 320*, a tribunal held that an employee with obsessive compulsive disorder who was bullied by colleagues was entitled to claim constructive unfair dismissal because the employers failed to deal properly with the grievance, and that she suffered disability discrimination. But the EAT upheld the employers' appeal on both issues, saying that 'it is necessary to ask whether the employer's conduct of the grievance procedure was within the band of reasonable responses to the grievance'. The decision has been questioned by the editor of the IRLR.

118 Gypsies

In the non-employment case of *Commission for Racial Equality v Dutton [1989] IRLR 8*, it was held by the Court of Appeal that gypsies could constitute a *Racial Group* for the purposes of the *RRA 1976* because they have a common race or *Ethnic Origin*.

If a gypsy were to apply for a job and be turned down for lack of a permanent address, that requirement could amount to indirect discrimination against him or her, unless the employer could show it to be justifiable in the particular circumstances. Turning a gypsy down because he or she is a gypsy would be direct discrimination, being less favourable treatment on racial grounds.

A person does not, however, become a member of a racial group, for the purposes of the *RRA 1976*, simply by adopting a travelling way of life. Far more than that is required – see *Ethnic Origin*.

Relations between members of the public, and gypsies and Irish travellers, have been an issue of concern to the *Commission for Racial Equality*, which has published various recommendations on how to improve those relations, often in areas (such as the provision of sites) falling outside the employment sphere.

119   Harassment

119.1   GENERAL PRINCIPLES

The law prohibiting discrimination by way of harassment has evolved in a rather piecemeal and messy way. Gradual implementation of the *Equal Treatment Directive* has, however, resulted in increasing consistency of approach in the various *Discrimination Laws*.

In essence, A subjects B to harassment where, on grounds of disability, religion or belief, sexual orientation or age A engages in unwanted conduct which has the purpose or effect of:

(*a*)   violating B's dignity; or

(*b*)   creating an intimidating, hostile, degrading, humiliating or offensive environment for B.

Conduct will be regarded as having such an effect only if, having regard to all the circumstances, including in particular the perception of B, it should reasonably be considered as having that effect.

The modern statutory definitions of harassment differ from conventional definitions of *Direct Discrimination*, in that there is no need for a finding that the claimant has been treated less favourably than an actual or hypothetical *Comparator*.

119.2   PROVING THE ACTS COMPLAINED OF

Harassment, particularly sexual harassment, frequently takes place in the absence of witnesses. In many cases, the employment tribunal has only the evidence of the claimant and the alleged harasser(s).

Sometimes, in a case of sexual or racial harassment or harassment of a disabled person, the claimant may allege that several fellow employees have ganged up on him or her and participated in the alleged acts. At first sight, the claimant in such a case may appear to be at a serious disadvantage, because it will be one person's evidence, that of the claimant, against the evidence of the alleged harassers. It is, however, by no means unknown for the evidence of the one person to be believed, if that evidence carries credibility, particularly if the evidence of the alleged harassers contains inconsistencies and contradictions.

It is difficult for an alleged harasser to respond to, and for an employment tribunal to form a view on, allegations of harassment which are expressed in general terms. Before the hearing takes place, the claimant should state exactly what has been said or done to her (or him) and where and when each incident took place. If sufficient details are not given in the application to the tribunal, then further particulars should be requested and given.

It is also desirable to establish before the hearing whether there were witnesses to any of the alleged incidents. If there is a fellow employee who witnessed one or more incidents, but is unwilling to give evidence, and the claimant does not wish to take the risk of asking for a witness order to compel an unwilling witness to attend, the name of the fellow employee should nevertheless be disclosed to the respondent(s) so that the latter can then consider whether the witness should be called.

119.3 Harassment

Employees who are being subjected to harassment are frequently advised to keep a diary, giving the date and details of each incident. Such a record can be relevant evidence in support of a complaint. Keeping the diary is also, however, an indication that the claimant is aware of the potential legal implications of the harassment and underlines the need for the claimant to be able to explain any failure to try to get the harassment stopped by making an internal complaint at the time.

Whether or not a written record is kept, a failure to speak up at the time is often relied on by respondents to challenge the credibility of the claimant. If the claimant did speak about the harassment at the time, even to someone outside the workplace, such as a family member or close friend, the evidence of that person can be relevant at the hearing.

There may be circumstances in which the employment tribunal can draw an *Inference*, so that the *Burden of Proof* shifts from the claimant to the respondent. This could happen, for example, if a failure to comply with a recommendation in a *Code of Practice* or an evasive reply to a *Questionnaire* suggests that the respondent has tried to cover up the matter complained of.

From the employer's point of view, once a complaint of harassment has been received and particularised, it is important to carry out a rigorous internal investigation without delay. If harassment has in fact taken place, it is better to find out at the outset, discipline the offender(s) and offer redress to the claimant rather than to incur the odium and unwelcome publicity of fighting a complaint which is well founded.

119.3   CASE LAW GUIDANCE

Useful guidance was given to tribunals by the EAT in the case of *Reed and Bull Information Systems Ltd v Stedman [1999] IRLR 299,* a case which arose prior to the insertion, in 2005, into the *SDA 1975* of a statutory definition of harassment. The claimant was employed as a secretary for just over a year. She made a number of allegations against the manager to whom she reported. She alleged that he made remarks to her which had sexual connotations; that on one occasion he made an attempt to look up her skirt and laughed when she angrily left the room; that he frequently stood behind her when telling other colleagues dirty jokes (but ceased to do so after she complained). Her allegations were upheld by the tribunal, which also found that she had made complaints to her mother and to colleagues at work, but not to her own manager (apart from the complaint about the dirty jokes) or to other managers. There was also a finding that colleagues in the personnel department were aware of the claimant's deteriorating health, although not of the harassment which was causing that deterioration. Eventually she left because of the harassment and because of the effect of it on her health.

The tribunal found that the respondent had discriminated against the claimant, contrary to the *SDA 1975*, in subjecting her to a detriment and dismissing her. The finding of dismissal was because there had been a failure to investigate the cause of her illness and because the complaints which she had made to other members of staff (albeit not managers) had been dismissed by those members of staff. The employer was responsible for these omissions by its employees in the personnel department and elsewhere. There had been a breach of the implied term of trust and confidence and the claimant had been entitled to treat herself as constructively dismissed. Even though she had not completed the qualifying period for a complaint of unfair dismissal, she was entitled to be compensated for her dismissal under the *SDA 1975*.

The EAT dismissed an appeal against the findings and gave guidance which included the following matters:

(a)   A characteristic of sexual harassment is that it undermines the victim's dignity at work. It creates an 'offensive' or 'hostile' environment for the victim and an arbitrary barrier to sexual equality in the workplace.

(b)   The essential characteristic of sexual harassment is that it is words or conduct which are unwelcome to the recipient; it is for recipients to decide for themselves what is acceptable to them and what they regard as offensive.

(c)   It is particularly important in cases of alleged sexual harassment that the fact-finding tribunal should not carve up the case into a series of specific incidents and try and measure the harm or detriment in relation to each.

The EAT illustrated this last point by reference to the facts of the case. A blatant act of a sexual nature, such as deliberately looking up the complainant's skirt, may well make other incidents, such as asking to be shown personal photographs which she was looking at, take on a different colour and significance. Once unwelcome sexual interest has been shown by a man in a female employee, she may well feel bothered about attentions which, in a different context, would appear quite unobjectionable.

Once the tribunal has assembled the totality of the matters complained of, and looked at the complaint as a whole, the tribunal must then decide whether the complainant was thereby subjected to a detriment. The EAT recognised that there may well be difficult factual issues to resolve in order to decide whether the conduct now complained of was unwelcome. The following guidance was given:

(a)   Some conduct, if not expressly invited, could properly be described as unwelcome; a woman does not, for example, have to make it clear in advance that she does not want to be touched in a sexual manner.

(b)   If the conduct about which a complainant now complains to the tribunal would normally be regarded as unexceptionable behaviour, the question is whether by words or conduct the complainant had made it clear that she found such conduct unwelcome.

(c)   It is not necessary for a woman to make a public fuss to indicate her disapproval; walking out of the room might be sufficient. Tribunals will be sensitive to the problems that a victim may face in dealing with a man, perhaps in a senior position to herself, whose defence may be that she was being over-sensitive.

(d)   Provided that any reasonable person would understand her to be rejecting the conduct of which she was complaining, continuation of that conduct would, generally, be regarded as harassment.

The need to look at the totality of relevant incidents, and at the context in which each incident occurs, was underlined by the decision of the EAT in the case of *Driskel v Peninsula Business Services Ltd and others [2000] IRLR 151*. In that case, Mrs Driskel complained of a number of remarks made to her by the head of her department. The final remark, the day before he was to interview her for promotion, was his suggestion that she should attend the interview in a short skirt and see-through blouse, showing plenty of cleavage. Mrs Driskel made a formal complaint of sexual harassment, which was rejected after a thorough and genuine internal investigation. She was dismissed after refusing to return to her job unless the manager against whom she had complained was moved elsewhere.

The employment tribunal dismissed Mrs Driskel's complaint of sexual harassment and also her complaint that her dismissal was both unfair and an act of victimisation. In relation to the complaint of sexual harassment, the tribunal carefully examined each incident complained of, accepted Mrs Driskel's evidence but, nevertheless, dismissed her complaint. The EAT upheld the tribunal's decision regarding her dismissal, in view of the genuine investigation which had been carried out by the employers – see *Dismissal*. The EAT upheld, however, Mrs Driskel's appeal in relation to the sexual harassment, finding that the tribunal had fallen into error in the following respects:

(*a*)   The tribunal failed to give due weight to the fact that the remarks complained of on the final occasion were made the day before Mrs Driskel was to be interviewed by her manager for promotion. In those 'circumstances she was in receipt of remarks that in an appalling fashion sought to exploit the situation by reference to the sex of, respectively, interviewee and interviewer? . . . that which was complained of was objectively prima facie discriminatory and it would need some exceptional findings to negate that inference . . .'

(*b*)   The tribunal looked at the incident in isolation and failed to put it in context 'as the latest in a line of incidents'.

(*c*)   The tribunal placed excessive weight on Mrs Driskel's failure to complain immediately, disregarding the obvious risk that an immediate complaint would have damaged her chances of the promotion which she was seeking.

The EAT in *Reed and Bull Information Systems Ltd v Stedman* also stated that a one-off act may be sufficient to damage a woman's working environment and constitute a barrier to sexual equality in the workplace, which would constitute a detriment. This principle was illustrated in the earlier case of *Bracebridge Engineering Ltd v Darby [1990] IRLR 3*, in which the employee resigned after a serious assault by two managers. It is also illustrated by *InSitu Cleaning Co Ltd v Heads [1995] IRLR 4*, which is an example of a case where the nature of the remark which was made indicated strongly that it was being made on the ground of the sex of the victim. This was a case in which a manager, the son of two directors of the company, addressed an employee twice his age using the expression 'Hiya, big tits'. It was held by the EAT that this single remark was sufficiently serious to constitute a detriment and that the nature of the remark was such that it was clearly on the ground of her sex that the complainant was being treated less favourably than a man would have been treated. For a manager to make a remark of this kind was a form of bullying which was not acceptable in the workplace in any circumstances. The conduct of the manager who made the remark was conduct likely to create an intimidating, hostile and humiliating work environment for the victim.

In *Moonsar v Fiveways Express Transport Ltd [2005] IRLR 9*, the EAT overruled a tribunal's decision that a woman was not discriminated against on the ground of sex when on three occasions male colleagues in the same room downloaded pornographic images onto a computer. Viewed objectively, this behaviour clearly had the potential effect of causing an affront to a female employee working in a close environment, and as such would be regarded as degrading or offensive to an employee as a woman. It was clearly potentially less favourable treatment and a detriment clearly followed from the nature of the behaviour. There was evidence that the claimant found the behaviour unacceptable. The fact that she did not complain at the time did not afford a defence where the behaviour was so obvious, as in the present case. The burden then shifted to the employers to show that there was not less favourable treatment – for instance, that the claimant was a party to, or enjoyed, what was going on.

119.4   **THE EMPLOYER'S LIABILITY**

It should first of all be noted that the interpretation section in the various *Discrimination Laws*, contains an extended definition of *Employment*. An employer can be liable for acts of harassment, and other acts of discrimination, not only by conventional employees but also by persons who are for the purposes of the relevant Act deemed to be employees under this extended definition. Furthermore, an employer is also liable to his employees for acts of discrimination against them by the employer's 'agent' if the employer has authorised the acts of discrimination, whether expressly or by implication; see also *Employees – Liability For.*

The employer, but not the employee who has done the act complained of, has a defence if the employer has taken *Reasonably Practicable Steps* to prevent the employee from doing the act complained of, or acts of that description.

Accordingly, the position can be summarised as follows:

(a)   if an employee does an act of harassment or discrimination outside the course of his employment, then neither that employee nor his employer is liable for that act;

(b)   if the act of harassment or other discrimination is in the course of the employee's employment, then the employee is liable for aiding an act of discrimination;

(c)   in those circumstances the employer is also liable, unless he has taken all reasonably practicable steps to prevent the act of discrimination or acts of that description.

At one time a person complaining of particularly serious acts of racial or sexual harassment faced the argument that such acts were outside the course of employment, because the common law test of *Vicarious Liability* should be applied. In particular, under that test, indecent or other serious assaults could not be regarded as improper ways of doing what the employer had authorised; they fell entirely outside the course of the employment.

That approach was rejected by the Court of Appeal in *Jones v Tower Boot Co Ltd [1997] IRLR 168.* In that case, a 16-year-old boy started work at a shoe factory. He was of mixed ethnic parentage. The workforce which he joined had never previously included anyone of ethnic minority origin. From the outset he was called by racially offensive names such as 'chimp' and 'monkey'. Two employees whipped him on the legs with a piece of welt and threw metal bolts at his head and one of them burned his arm with a hot screwdriver. The same two employees later tried to put his arm in a machine, causing the burn to bleed again. Understandably unable to endure this treatment, the boy left the job after four weeks. He complained of racial discrimination. His complaint was upheld by an employment tribunal which awarded him compensation of £5,000, but the EAT, by a majority, allowed the employer's appeal, on the ground that what had been done was not done in the course of the harassers' employment. The Court of Appeal restored the decision of the employment tribunal. The judgment of Lord Justice Waite contained the following important passages:

(a)   'The legislation now represented by the *Race* and *Sex Discrimination Acts* currently in force broke new ground in seeking to work upon the minds of men and women and thus affect their attitude to the social consequences of difference between the sexes or distinction of skin colour. Its general thrust was educative, persuasive and (where necessary) coercive? ... consistently with the broad front on which it operates, the legislation has traditionally been given a wide interpretation ...'

(b)   'A purposive construction accordingly requires *section 32* of the *Race Relations Act* (and the corresponding *section 41* of the *Sex Discrimination*

Act) to be given a broad interpretation. It would be inconsistent with that requirement to allow the notion of the 'course of employment' to be construed in any sense more limited than the natural meaning of those everyday words would allow'.

(c) 'It would be particularly wrong to allow racial harassment on the scale that was suffered by the complainant in this case at the hands of his workmates – treatment that was wounding both emotionally and physically – to slip through the net of employer responsibility by applying to it a common-law principle evolved in another area of the law to deal with vicarious responsibility for wrongdoing of a wholly different kind. To do so would seriously undermine the statutory scheme of the Discrimination Acts and flout the purposes which they were passed to achieve'.

Lord Justice Waite said that he would 'reject … entirely' a submission that 'the more heinous the act of discrimination, the less likely it will be that the employer would be liable'. He said that that submission:

'cuts across the whole legislative scheme and underlying policy of *section 32* (and its counterpart in sex discrimination), which is to deter racial and sexual harassment in the workplace through a widening of the net of responsibility beyond the guilty employees themselves, by making all employers additionally liable for such harassment, and then supplying them with the reasonable steps defence under *section 32(3)* which will exonerate the conscientious employer who has used his best endeavours to prevent such harassment, and would encourage all employers who have not yet undertaken such endeavours to take the steps necessary to make the same defence available in their own workplace.'

There can also be liability for acts outside the workplace. In the case of *Chief Constable of the Lincolnshire Police v Stubbs [1999] IRLR 81*, the complainant was seconded to a Regional Crime Squad. She complained of sexual harassment by a detective sergeant. One incident was at a pub, when she met the detective sergeant and other officers. The other involved an offensive remark at a leaving party for a colleague. On each occasion the complainant and the detective sergeant were off duty.

The EAT held that the chief constable was liable for the acts complained of. Although these acts took place at social functions away from the police station, those social functions were work-related. There was an extension of the employment of the two officers.

On this basis, it is clearly open to employment tribunals to hold employers liable for acts of harassment which take place at (or in the aftermath of) office parties, sales and other conferences and away days. Employers must take the necessary steps to ensure that the appropriate standards of behaviour are maintained at such events. It could be difficult for an employer to make out the reasonably practicable steps defence in relation to an event which is awash with alcohol.

A discrimination claim is not the only risk facing employers in cases of harassment. In *Waters v Commissioner of Police of the Metropolis [2000] IRLR 720*, a woman police constable alleged that a colleague subjected her to a serious sexual assault. She reported this to superiors, but following an internal enquiry, no action was taken against the colleague. She alleged that from that time on, she was subjected to harassment, unfair treatment and victimisation by other police officers, which led to ill health, including mental illness and post-traumatic stress disorder. She brought two sets of proceedings, i.e. a complaint of sex discrimination and a negligence claim. The former claim was dismissed on the ground that the alleged perpetrator was not acting in the course of his employment: *[1997] IRLR 589*. The negligence claim was struck out by the High Court on grounds that it disclosed no reasonable cause of action. The case ultimately reached the House of Lords, which allowed the appeal. The negligence claim should not have been struck out. It was not plain and obvious that no duty of care could be owed to the woman constable by the Commissioner on the facts as alleged or that, if there was such a duty, the facts could not amount to a breach. If an employer knows that acts being done by employees during their employment may cause physical or mental harm to a particular colleague, and does nothing to supervise or prevent such acts when it is within his power to do so, it is clearly arguable that he may be in breach of his duty to the victim. He may also be in breach if he can foresee that such acts may happen and if they do, that physical or mental harm may be caused to an individual. If sexual assault by a colleague is alleged and a complaint pursued, it is arguable that it can be foreseen that retaliatory steps may be taken against the complainant and that she may suffer harm as a result. Even if this is not necessarily foreseeable at the beginning, it may become foreseeable to those in charge that there is a risk of harm and that some protective steps should be taken. Lord Hutton acknowledged that it might be that, on full investigation at the trial, the allegations would be shown to be groundless or exaggerated. But assuming they were true, he considered that this was not a case in which the claim should have been struck out as disclosing no reasonable cause of action or as being frivolous or vexatious or an abuse of the process of the courts. He acknowledged, however, that 'it is not every course of victimisation or bullying by fellow employees which would give rise to a cause of action against the employer, and the employee may have to accept some degree of unpleasantness from fellow workers. Moreover, the employer will not be liable unless he knows or ought to know that the harassment is taking place and fails to take reasonable steps to prevent it'. But the allegations in this case were serious and known to senior officers in the chain of command leading to the Commissioner.

Can an employer be held accountable where the person who does an act of harassment (or some other discrimination) is neither an employee, in the extended sense, nor an agent? This question arose in the case of *Burton v De Vere Hotels [1996] IRLR 596*. This is the case in which two black waitresses at a hotel were subjected to racially offensive remarks by a well-known comedian who was the guest speaker at a social function. The speaker was not in any sense an employee or agent of the hotel. Nevertheless, the EAT held that the hotel company were directly liable for subjecting the two employees to racial harassment.

In *Pearce v Governing Body of Mayfield Secondary School [2003] IRLR 512* it was held by the House of Lords that *Burton* was wrongly decided. It is good employment practice for employers to take reasonable steps to protect employees from racial or sexual abuse by third parties; but a failure to do so is not racial or sex discrimination, where that failure has nothing to do with the sex or race of the employees.

In the case which was under consideration by the House of Lords, Ms Pearce was a teacher who was subjected by pupils at the school to a sustained campaign of verbal abuse on the ground that she was as lesbian. She claimed that the school was in breach of the *SDA 1975* by failing to prevent the harassment. (the *SOR 2003* was not in force at the time). Her complaint was unsuccessful and she appealed unsuccessfully to the EAT, then the Court of Appeal and then the House of Lords.

In the House of Lords, it was pointed out that there were two reasons why Ms Pearce could not succeed in her claim. The first was that she had not been treated less favourably than a man would have been treated in comparable circumstances. She had accepted that the pupils would have pursued a comparable campaign of harassment against a homosexual man.

119.5 Harassment

In *Equal Opportunities Commission v Secretary of State for Trade and Industry* [2007] IRLR 327, the High Court ruled that the *Employment Equality (Sex Discrimination) Regulations 2005* failed adequately to amend the *SDA 1975* in line with the revised *Equal Treatment Directive*. The decision in *Pearce* is incompatible with EU law. A key practical effect of the High Court's ruling is that employers will have to set up systems to deal with their employees' claims of harassment by third parties. This logic will, it seems, apply also to forms of discriminatory harassment on grounds other than sex.

119.5 REASONABLY PRACTICABLE STEPS

Where an employee harasses a fellow employee, the employer has a defence if he can show that he took all reasonably practicable steps to prevent the act complained of or acts of that description. It was held in the case of *Canniffe v East Riding of Yorkshire Council [2000] IRLR 555* that a respondent cannot make out the above defence simply by persuading the tribunal that there was nothing they could have done to prevent the act complained of. This was a very serious complaint of sexual harassment, involving assaults or threats of assaults by a fellow employee on a woman who was also disabled, being profoundly deaf. The tribunal found that there was only one incident in respect of which a complaint had been made in time, but that incident was a particularly serious one. There was evidence that a personal harassment policy had been drawn to the attention of employees in a newsletter and at team meetings and the complainant herself gave evidence that the harasser had told her that he knew that he could lose his job as a result of what he was doing. The employment tribunal held that in these circumstances the employer had made out the defence under *section 41(3)* of the *SDA 1975* that all reasonably practicable steps to prevent acts of the type complained of had been taken. It was said by the tribunal that they failed to see that any better implementation of the adopted policies would have had any effect in relation to the criminal behaviour complained of.

It was held by the EAT that this was the wrong approach and that the case should be sent back to a freshly constituted tribunal. It is not appropriate for a tribunal to uphold the defence on the ground that nothing could have been done. The proper approach is:

(*a*)   to identify whether the respondents took any steps at all;

(*b*)   to consider whether there were any further steps which they could have taken and which were reasonably practicable.

The EAT added that:

(*a*)   the question whether taking these further steps would have been successful in preventing the acts of discrimination may be worth addressing but is not determinative either way;

(*b*)   the employer will not be exonerated if it has not taken reasonably practicable steps simply because those reasonable steps would not have led anywhere or achieved anything or prevented anything from occurring.

In the particular case, there was evidence that the complainant had spoken, albeit in confidence and without making a formal complaint, to three colleagues at work about the earlier incidents. One of these colleagues was also the harasser's line manager. It was held by the EAT that the employment tribunal had failed to consider whether there were steps which these three colleagues, for whose acts and omissions the employer was responsible, could have taken. The EAT also referred to the need to apply a purposive construction to the legislation, following the guidance given in the case of *Jones v Tower Boot Co Ltd [1997] IRLR 168* which has already been referred to.

The above guidance must now however be considered in the light of the decision of the Court of Appeal in *Croft v Royal Mail Group plc [2003] IRLR 592*. One of the issues in that case was whether the complainant, who was a pre-operative trans-sexual, had been subjected to harassment and, if so, whether the respondent employer was liable for that harassment. It was held by the employment tribunal that the statutory defence had been made out. The managers had, for example, stressed the harassment policy to the workforce on a number of occasions and had taken successful action on the one occasion when the applicant named individuals who had been harassing her.

It was contended on appeal that the tribunal had accepted that there were two further steps which could have been taken and that the tribunal had gone wrong in law in stating that the defence had nevertheless been made out because those steps would have had at most a marginal effect. The Court of Appeal rejected that argument.

Pill LJ said:

'I agree that a consideration of the likely effect, or lack of effect, of any action it is submitted the employer should have taken is not the sole criterion by which that action is to be judged in this context. In considering whether an action is reasonably practicable, within the meaning of the sub-section, it is however permissible to take into account the extent of the difference, if any, which the action is likely to make. The concept of reasonable practicability is well-known to the law and it does entitle the employer in this context to consider whether the time, effort and expense of the suggested measures are disproportionate to the result likely to be achieved.'

He added that steps 'which require time, trouble and expense, and which may be counterproductive given an agreed low-key approach, may not be reasonable steps if, on an assessment, they are likely to achieve little or nothing.' If Burton J was adopting a different approach in *Canniffe*, then Pill J respectfully disagreed.

In *Caspersz v Ministry of Defence [2006] All ER (D) 02 (Apr)*, the EAT ruled that a tribunal was entitled to find that reasonably practicable steps had been taken by the employer to prevent sexual comments being made by a manager to his junior where the employer had a good policy, which was not merely paid lip service to, but observed.

119.6   THE EUROPEAN UNION CODE OF PRACTICE

Important guidance is given to employers in the 1991 European Union Recommendation and Code of Practice on the Protection of the Dignity of Women and Men at Work. The Code is frequently referred to by tribunals and it was held by the ECJ in *Grimaldi v Fonds des Maladies Professionelles [1990] IRLR 400* that recommendations of the kind under which the Code was adopted must be taken into consideration by national courts and tribunals.

The Code refers to the responsibilities of trade unions and individual employees as well as those of employers, but the main guidance is given to employers. The Code states that dealing with complaints is only one component of a strategy to deal with the problem. The prime objective should be to change behaviour and attitudes, to seek to ensure the prevention of sexual harassment. The key steps for employers are to:

(a)   put the appropriate policies in place;

(b)   communicate those policies to staff and job applicants;

(c)   adopt and publicise mechanisms for assisting victims of harassment and enabling them to complain;

(d)   provide training for managers and supervisors;

(e)   monitor and review complaints of sexual harassment and how they have been resolved.

The *policy statement* should expressly state that:

(a)   all employees have a right to be treated with dignity;

(b)   sexual harassment at work will not be permitted or condoned;

(c)   employees have a right to complain about it should it occur;

(d)   allegations of sexual harassment will be dealt with seriously, expeditiously and confidentially;

(e)   employees will be protected against victimisation or retaliation for bringing a complaint;

(f)   appropriate disciplinary measures will be taken against employees found guilty of sexual harassment.

The policy statement should make clear what is considered inappropriate behaviour at work and explain that such behaviour may in certain circumstances be unlawful.

Disciplinary rules should also be amended where necessary to make it clear that both harassment itself and victimisation will be disciplinary offences. Indeed many employers have now adopted disciplinary rules under which sexual harassment or victimisation are treated as gross misconduct for which summary dismissal will be the normal penalty.

Effective *communication* of the policy is important. It is recommended in the code that managers should explain the policy to their staff and take steps to promote the policy positively. Effective communication of the policy will highlight management's commitment to eliminating sexual harassment, thus encouraging a climate in which it will not occur.

It is particularly important to tell employees where they can turn for assistance and to whom they can complain if they are subjected to sexual harassment. Many serious cases of harassment over a long period of time occur because the victim does not know where to turn or how to complain. The code recommends that employers should:

(a)   designate a person or persons, such as confidential counsellors, to provide advice and assistance to employees;

(b)   advise employees that if possible in the first instance they should attempt to resolve the problem informally;

(c)   make employees aware that if this is too difficult or embarrassing then they may seek support from or ask for an initial approach to be made by a sympathetic friend or confidential counsellor;

(d)   provide a formal procedure, in which employees can have confidence, for resolving complaints in those cases where informal resolution is inappropriate or unsuccessful.

The Code suggests that it may be helpful if confidential counsellors are designated with the agreement of the trade unions or employees, as this is likely to enhance their acceptability. They may be selected from, for example:

(*a*)   the personnel department;

(*b*)   the equal opportunities department;

(*c*)   a trade union;

(*d*)   women's support groups.

They must be given adequate resources to carry out their function and protection against victimisation for assisting any recipient of sexual harassment.

The complaints procedure should cater for the case where the normal grievance procedure is unsuitable, for example, because the alleged harasser is the employee's line manager. The code suggests that employees should also be able in the first instance to bring a complaint to someone of their own sex, should they so choose.

Training is a key step. Training should be given to managers and supervisors and any other employees with relevant responsibilities, such as the above-mentioned confidential counsellors and also those playing an official role in any formal complaints procedure. The training should cover:

(*a*)   the factors which contribute to a working environment free of sexual harassment;

(*b*)   the detail of the organisation's policy and procedures;

(*c*)   knowledge and awareness of common signs that sexual harassment is occurring or has occurred (although the Code does not specifically mention this);

(*d*)   the responsibilities under the policy of each of the individuals receiving training;

(*e*)   how to deal with any problems they are likely to encounter.

It is necessary to *monitor* and review complaints of sexual harassment, and how they have been resolved, in order to ensure that the policy and procedures are working effectively. If several complaints are received, following the adoption and publication of the policy, this may be an indication that victims of harassment now have the confidence to complain; it could also mean, however, that the policy is not yet being successfully implemented and that attitudes are not being changed.

A defence that all reasonably practicable steps to prevent harassment have been taken could be undermined if it is shown that complaints have not been properly investigated and dealt with. The Code of Practice gives the following advice:

(*a*)   internal investigations of any complaints must be handled with sensitivity and with due respect for the rights of both the complainant and the alleged harasser;

(*b*)   the investigation should be seen to be independent and objective;

(*c*)   those carrying out the investigation should not be connected with the allegation in any way;

(*d*)   every effort should be made to resolve complaints speedily;

(*e*)   the investigation should focus on the facts of the complaint;

(*f*)   a complete record should be kept of all meetings and investigations.

The Code recommends that where a complaint is upheld and it is determined that it is necessary to relocate or transfer one party, consideration should be given, wherever practicable, to allowing the complainant to choose whether he or she wishes to remain in post or be transferred to another location. If anything, this advice in the Code is insufficiently forceful. There are often commercial objections to transferring the harasser to other work, particularly if he or she is in a senior position, but there may be no legally acceptable alternative, if the complainant finds it intolerable to continue working with the harasser.

The Code of Practice adds that:

(*a*)   no element of penalty should be seen to attach to a complainant whose complaint is upheld;

(*b*)   where a complaint is upheld, the employer should monitor the situation to ensure that the harassment has stopped;

(*c*)   even where a complaint is not upheld, consideration should be given to transferring or re-scheduling the work of one of the employees concerned.

So far as the last of the above points is concerned, care must be taken not to victimise, for example by way of a compulsory transfer, an employee who has made a complaint which has not been upheld but which cannot be shown to have been made falsely and in bad faith.

The Code of Practice applies only to sexual harassment, but similar principles apply to racial and religious harassment, harassment on grounds of sexual orientation and the harassment of disabled employees. In particular:

(*a*)   there should either be a single policy on harassment or dignity at work, or a separate policy on each form of harassment;

(*b*)   there should be assistance for employees and informal and formal complaints procedures to deal with all kinds of harassment;

(*c*)   all forms of harassment should be disciplinary offences;

(*d*)   training, particularly for managers and supervisors, is essential;

(*e*)   complaints should be monitored and reviewed.

119.7   **THE PROTECTION FROM HARASSMENT ACT**

Rather unexpectedly, imaginative use of remedies provided by the *Protection from Harassment Act 1997* has assisted those complaining of harassment in the workplace. The primary objective of the Act was to address the problem of *Stalking* but the House of Lords confirmed in *Majrowski v Guy's & St Thomas' NHS Trust [2006] IRLR 695* that an employer can be liable under the Act for harassment committed by employees in the cause of employment.

120   Health and Safety at Work

120.1   THE SCOPE OF HEALTH AND SAFETY LAW

Health and safety law is a subject of rapidly increasing importance. The detail of the extensive rules in this area lies outside the scope of this handbook, but briefly, an employer is under a common law duty to have regard to the safety of his employees. In addition, statutory obligations have been imposed upon employers in various circumstances e.g. by the *Health and Safety at Work etc. Act 1974*, and many regulations made pursuant to the legislation. The *Employment Rights Act 1996* protects employees from dismissal or victimisation by the employer in health and safety cases. An employer who breaks his common law duties in respect of health and safety may also face a claim of constructive unfair dismissal if the employee resigns because of an alleged breach of the employer's obligations. The rules are significant generally in respect of all employers and employees; some of them also have particular significance where equal opportunities issues arise.

120.2   THE LONG HOURS CULTURE

There has been growing recognition that the 'long hours culture' associated with many sectors of employment in the UK has implications not only for health and safety but also in respect of equal opportunities. The *Working Time Regulations 1998 (SI 1998 No 1833)* implement in the UK the provisions of the European Directive on Working Time, which was introduced through qualified majority voting (so that the then UK government could not veto it) because it was classed as a health and safety measure. Hours of work have long been regarded as primarily a matter of concern, in the equal opportunities context, in relation to women, because of issues surrounding *Part-time Work*. But it is now more widely recognised that the 'long hours culture' is apt to disadvantage men and result in discrimination against them. The debate about the proper 'work-life balance' is relevant, if sometimes in different ways, to both men and women. The *Working Time Regulations 1998* provide some protection, despite being complicated and selective in their coverage.

120.3   AIDS AND HIV

Acquired Immunity Deficiency Syndrome (AIDS) is caused by the HIV virus. Where an individual is HIV-positive, he or she may not develop an AIDS-related illness or the full-blown condition of AIDS for many years, if at all. Even those suffering from the full-blown condition may be able to work normally between periods of sickness. Medical screening of job applicants or existing employees for the HIV virus requires their specific consent to the test and also to disclosure of the result to the employer. The virus is apt to be transmitted when bodily fluids mix. This means that, in many jobs, the risk of contracting the disease from another person is minimal. Consequently, the employer will not be in breach of his duty of care to other employees if he allows an employee who is HIV positive or suffering from AIDS to continue to report for work. It may be unfair to dismiss a sufferer, even if the sufferer's colleagues, or the employer's clients, do not wish to work with him or her: the test of fairness to be applied is that set out in *section 98* of the *Employment Rights Act 1996*. For an employer to disclose that an employee is HIV-positive or suffering from AIDS would be likely to amount to a breach of the implied duty of mutual trust and confidence in the contract of employment, entitling the employee to resign and claim constructive unfair dismissal. The *DDA 1995* classes HIV infection as a progressive condition. Accordingly, employers are under a duty to make reasonable adjustments to meet the needs of employees with that condition.

120.4 STRESS AT WORK

An employee who suffers from stress-related illness may contend that it was caused by conditions at work. This is a developing area of the law, but despite the publicity accorded to a few hefty settlements and compensation awards, proving cause and effect so as to justify a claim for compensation for personal injury is often difficult in practice. But where an employer exposes an employee to a reasonably foreseeable risk of illness as a result of work-induced stress, there may be a breach of the duty of care and liability for damages. The Court of Appeal set out detailed guidance on the operation of the law in *Sutherland v Hatton [2002] IRLR 263*.

Where a risk of stress is a feature of a particular job, a risk assessment ought to be made pursuant to the *Management of Health and Safety at Work Regulations 1999 (SI 1999 No 3242)*. An employee who is subjected to excessive stress at work may also be able to establish that the employer has broken the implied contractual obligation of mutual trust and confidence, entitling the employee to resign and claim to have been constructively unfairly dismissed. This may arise in the case of *Harassment* by fellow employees, customers or others. In extreme cases, the criminal law, e.g. the *Protection from Harassment Act 1997*, may become relevant in addition to the above principles. In practice, therefore, a prudent employer will investigate promptly and thoroughly any allegation from an employee that he or she is suffering from stress, whether as a result of discrimination or otherwise. Failure to take appropriate action will expose the employer to legal proceedings.

120.5 RISK ASSESSMENT AND PREGNANT WORKERS

Every employer, as well as each self-employed person, has to make a risk assessment relating to the premises, so as to identify the measures he must take to comply with the regulations applicable to him in respect of health and safety and fire precautions. The requirements are laid down by the *Management of Health and Safety at Work Regulations 1999* (which revoked the original 1992 Regulations *(SI 1992 No 2051)* of the same name). A risk assessment must be reviewed when necessary and (where there are more than five employees) recorded. Every employer must also make, and give effect to, adequate health and safety arrangements, including effective planning, organisation, control, monitoring and review of the measures to be taken. The employer must make sure that his employees are provided with appropriate health surveillance and appoint one or more competent people to assist him in implementing the measures to be taken. Specifically, each employer must, amongst other matters, establish (and where necessary give effect to) procedures to be followed in the event of serious and imminent danger to people working in his undertaking and nominate sufficient competent people to implement such procedures as regards the evacuation of the premises.

An assessment must be made of workplace risks to new and expectant mothers and measures taken to avoid any risk by altering working conditions or hours of work. Where it is not practicable to take those steps, the woman should be suspended from work on full pay (although she has the right to an offer of suitable alternative work, if the employer has it available, in accordance with *section 67* of the *Employment Rights Act 1996*). Where it is necessary for her health and safety, a new or expectant mother must be removed from night work.

The decision of the *EAT in Day v T Pickles Farms Ltd [1999] IRLR 217*, shows that the employment of a woman of child-bearing age in itself suffices to trigger the need for risk assessment. That case concerned a sandwich shop assistant who became pregnant and told her manager that the smell of food made her feel nauseous. She became unfit for work and received statutory sick pay until a point when (mistakenly) the employers thought that her entitlement to it ceased. She claimed, amongst other matters, unfair constructive dismissal and sex discrimination. She argued that the employers were in breach of their obligations under the *Management of Health and Safety at Work Regulations 1992* (now revoked and replaced) to have carried out a risk assessment and that this would have led to her suspension on full pay. She also claimed to have suffered a detriment by not being allowed time off for antenatal care. The EAT upheld a tribunal's ruling that she had not been constructively dismissed by reason of a failure to carry out the risk assessment when she was pregnant. This was because she had not given the employers an unequivocal communication that she was accepting some form of repudiation on the employer's part and treating the contract of employment as at an end. However, the tribunal had misdirected itself in finding that she had not suffered a detriment. The tribunal erred in finding that the obligation to carry out a risk assessment only applies when an employer has a pregnant employee. The employer should have carried out the assessment at the start of the employee's employment before she became pregnant. When the case returned to the tribunal, however, the tribunal concluded on the evidence that, despite its failure to carry out a risk assessment, the employer did not default in its obligations under *Regulation 13A(2)* or *(3)* of the Regulations. The tribunal took into account the EAT's observation that 'the employer ... cannot be expected to have in mind the most particular kind of conditions or objections or disabilities that some women might suffer from, for example being nauseous at handling fish or hard boiled eggs or something very much applicable only to the particular individual'.

In *Hardman v Mallon [2002] IRLR 516*, the EAT allowed an appeal against a tribunal's decision that a care assistant was not discriminated against on grounds of sex when her employer failed to carry out a risk assessment when she was pregnant. The tribunal was wrong to reason that the woman was not treated less favourably than the employer treated or would treat a man, since the employer had not produced risk assessments in respect of any of its employees regardless of their sex. A failure to carry out a risk assessment in respect of a pregnant woman is sex discrimination. Carrying out a risk assessment, the EAT pointed out, is one way in which a woman's biological condition during and after pregnancy is given special protection. It is not necessary for the treatment of a pregnant woman to be compared with the employer's treatment of a comparable male employee, or a non-pregnant female employee. If the basis of the treatment is pregnancy, it is unlawful irrespective of the comparable treatment of men.

In *Madarassy v Nomura International plc* [2007] IRLR 246, the employer did not carry out a risk assessment in respect of a senior banker when she became pregnant. However (and perhaps surprisingly), the Court of Appeal ruled that there was no finding that the banker's work involved potential risks to health and safety so as to trigger the duty to carry out a risk assessment.

In *New Southern Railway Ltd v Quinn [2006] IRLR 266*, the EAT upheld a finding that an employee was not suspended from work on 'maternity' grounds within the meaning of *section 66* of the *Employment Rights Act 1996* when, after she became pregnant, she was removed from her trial post as a duty manager and returned to her former post as a personal assistant on a lower rate of pay. The tribunal was entitled to find that the management had jumped to the conclusion that she could not continue in her position because of their personal feelings and had simply attached to that conclusion a label of health and safety concern. In any event, an employer is only entitled to suspend a woman from work on maternity grounds where a risk cannot be 'avoided'. Here, the employers failed to show that the risk could not be avoided. The term 'avoid the risk' in *Regulation 16* of the *Management of Health and Safety at Work Regulations 1999* cannot mean the complete avoidance of all risks, but means reduced to their lowest acceptable level. There needs to be a balancing exercise. It is for the employer to show that it is necessary for health and safety reasons in effect to discriminate. The requirement of proportionality requires that, the greater the discriminatory act, the greater the necessity must be.

120.6   **MIGRANT WORKERS**

The Morecambe Bay tragedy, where 23 Chinese cocklers lost their lives when trapped by the rising tide, has highlighted the potential vulnerability, in the context of health and safety at work, of migrant workers.

Employers carrying out risk assessments should consider the position of migrant workers. For example, poor language and literacy skills might be a factor compromising safety. Methods of training may need to be adapted to different groups of workers, with a focus on the need to check that migrant workers understand guidance relevant to safeguarding their health and safety.

121 Health-Related Benefits and Disability

121.1 TIME OFF FOR MEDICAL APPOINTMENTS AND TREATMENT

As a general principle, the effect of the *DDA 1995* is that an employer must allow disabled employees the same rights to time off for medical appointments as other employees. This is a matter which should be addressed in the contractual terms of employment. On occasion, *Reasonable Adjustments* may include agreement by the employer to allow the disabled employee extra time off for treatment. The cost and practicability of this may be relevant in deciding what is reasonable, e.g. in cases where extensive absence from work would create unacceptable difficulties for other members of the workforce and it is not cost-effective to engage others to cover the absences.

121.2 SICK PAY

In addition to Statutory Sick Pay, many employers operate schemes for occupational sick pay. This is a matter which ought to be covered in any adequately drafted contract of employment. To state the obvious, the effect of the *DDA 1995* is that employers should not discriminate in the matter of occupational sick pay between disabled employees and those who are not disabled. Some organisations even provide more generous terms to disabled employees than to other members of the workforce and this form of *Positive Discrimination* is not outlawed by the *DDA 1995*.

It may be unfair to dismiss an employee at a time when the employee's ongoing entitlement to sickness pay has not been exhausted, but this is not *automatically* the case. Once the contractual right to occupational sick pay has expired, an employee may be eligible for benefits under a permanent health insurance scheme. Failing that, the employer may be prepared to continue to make payments of sick pay (either in whole or in part) on a discretionary basis for a period of time, but it may be imprudent or inappropriate to offer an open-ended commitment at the outset. Allowing a period of unpaid leave is another possibility, especially if the duties of the absent employee can be adequately covered either by members of the existing workforce or by temporary replacements.

121.3 INSURED BENEFITS

While the *DDA 1995* applies generally to insurance schemes for employees, it permits insurers to discriminate in respect of disabled employees where actuarial or statistical data, or other evidence, indicate a higher risk. An employer can treat a disabled person less favourably than colleagues who are not disabled if there is medical evidence relating to the employee or general actuarial data, and providing the cover would entail substantial additional costs. What is 'substantial' would be a matter for judgment in each case.

Notwithstanding the *DDA 1995*, medical insurance cover for an employee with a disability may, if available at all, be restricted to cover in respect of conditions unrelated to the disability. If comprehensive cover is available, a higher premium may be required. Similarly, in the case of permanent health insurance, cover may be linked to long-term ill health not related to the disability. Increased premiums may again be justifiable.

121.4 Health-Related Benefits and Disability

Permanent Health Insurance ('PHI') is a valuable benefit offered by a significant number of employers. Typically, the insurance provides ongoing financial benefit (typically linked, on a proportionate basis, to the employee's salary) if the employee is unable to work due to ill health. The benefit will usually continue to be provided until death, retirement or a return to work.

In practice, most employees who become eligible for PHI benefits will be disabled within the meaning of the *DDA 1995*. This will be so even if the definition of 'disability' to be found in the small print of the policy differs from that in the legislation. In particular cases, the employer's duty to make *Reasonable Adjustments* might include a duty to help the employee to make a claim for PHI benefits. A failure to ensure that the employee is provided with PHI benefits due within a reasonable period of time may constitute a breach of the duty to make *Reasonable Adjustments*.

The *AR 2006* may also provide rights of redress in certain circumstances. To restrict access to PHI schemes, e.g. by operating a maximum age for membership of the scheme, is potentially discriminatory, although there may be circumstances in which the discrimination is capable of *Justification*.

121.4 PENSION BENEFITS

The *DDA 1995* and regulations address discrimination in the context of occupational pension schemes. The rules apply to the following benefits, where they are provided by way of an occupational pension scheme:

(*a*)   benefits arising in the event of accident, sickness, injury or invalidity;

(*b*)   benefits arising on termination of employment;

(*c*)   benefits arising on retirement, old age or death.

An unjustifiable act or omission by an employer or the trustees of the pension scheme is deemed to be contrary to the rules of the scheme. The employer and the trustees may, however, take into account an existing medical condition that increases the likelihood of a claim or of an earlier pension, provided so doing is based appropriately, on actuarial data. Where the cost of providing benefits is likely to be substantially greater by reason of the disability, it may be justifiable to revise the terms of membership of the scheme and contribution rate to be paid by the disabled scheme member. If all members pay the same rate, a disabled member who is excluded from certain benefits may nevertheless be obliged to pay at the standard rate of contribution.

122   Hours of Work

It can be difficult for employees with childcare or other family responsibilities to work long or unsocial hours. A requirement that a female or married employee should work unsocial hours (or a refusal to agree to part-time working) could amount to *Indirect Discrimination* unless the requirement (or refusal) can be objectively justified. As with other discrimination cases, it is no defence to a complaint that the employee has freely entered into a contract containing the requirement about which she now complains.

A reduction in the number of hours worked can also in certain circumstances be one of the *DDA 1995 section 6 Reasonable Adjustments* which must be considered in relation to a disabled employee.

The number of hours worked can also be relevant as a *Material Factor* defence in an *Equal Pay* case, where the comparison which the complainant seeks to make is between the salaries (rather than the hourly rates) of the complainant and the comparator. The time at which work is done is not, however, a relevant factor. The fact that the complainant's work is done by day and the comparator's work is done by night does not prevent the jobs being like work or work of equal value and cannot be relied on as a material factor in relation to a difference in basic pay. The proper way to compensate an employee for working at night or at some other unsocial time is to pay a shift premium of a reasonable amount – *National Coal Board v Sherwin [1978] IRLR 122*.

Working hours may also raise questions relating to *Health and Safety at Work*.

123   Human Rights

123.1   BACKGROUND

The European Convention on Human Rights is a treaty of the Council of Europe adopted in 1950 and ratified by the UK in 1951. It was designed to give binding effect to the guarantee of various rights and freedoms in the United Nations Declaration on Human Rights, adopted in 1948. The immediate aim of the Convention was to protect Europe against totalitarianism and a repeat of the atrocities of the Second World War. However, its general purpose has been described as to protect human rights and fundamental freedoms and to maintain and promote the ideals and values of a democratic society. It is therefore not only of continuing relevance in the 21st century, but also capable of far-reaching interpretation, unforeseen at the time of original adoption.

While the Convention has had particular significance in the UK since 1966, when the government recognised the jurisdiction of the European Court of Human Rights and accepted the right of the individual in the UK to petition the Court, the Convention's impact on domestic employment law was for many years negligible. The landscape has been transformed by the *Human Rights Act 1998*. This came fully into force on 2 October 2000 and requires that the courts interpret UK law in accordance with the Convention.

123.2   EUROPEAN CONVENTION '

The Convention sets out, in broad terms, various fundamental rights and freedoms. It also established the European Commission of Human Rights and the European Court of Human Rights, both of which are based in Strasbourg. The Convention and its institutions should not be confused with the law and institutions of the European Union. The subscribing states are the Members of the Council of Europe. The Convention provides a right of direct complaint by an individual affected by an alleged breach of the Convention. A limiting factor in practice is that the aggrieved person must pursue every remedy available under domestic law. Only when these are exhausted without the complaint having been resolved to his satisfaction may he present a petition to the Commission. The Commission will then investigate and if it decides that there is, or may be, a breach of the Convention and that the complaint is admissible, it will endeavour to obtain a settlement between the parties. If no settlement can be achieved, the Commission will refer the case, together with its report, to the Court, which will decide on the complaint.

A leading case which had a direct connection with the law of equal opportunities was *Halford v United Kingdom [1997] IRLR 471*. The applicant was a senior police officer who was pursuing a complaint of sex discrimination against her employer. The employer recorded her telephone conversations with a view to gathering material to be used in defence of the claim. The court ruled that such recording, without her knowledge, was a breach of her right to privacy under *Article 8* of the Convention and she was awarded compensation of £10,000.

Even before its incorporation into domestic law, the Convention had an influence on European Community law, as in a *Sexual Orientation* case, *Smith and Grady v United Kingdom [1999] IRLR 734*, where the European Court of Justice took the Convention into account.

123.3   HUMAN RIGHTS ACT 1998

The *Human Rights Act 1998* (the *HRA 1998*) is one of the UK's most significant constitutional measures. Its immediate effect is to allow people to claim their rights under the Convention in UK courts and tribunals, instead of having to go to Strasbourg.

The *HRA 1998*:

(*a*)   makes it unlawful for a public authority to act incompatibly with Convention rights, although an authority will not have acted unlawfully if as the result of primary legislation it could not have acted otherwise;

(*b*)   requires all legislation to be interpreted and given effect so far as possible compatibly with Convention rights.

Article 14 of the Convention requires that its rights and freedoms shall be enjoyed 'without discrimination on any grounds such as sex, race, colour, language, religion, political or other opinion, national or social origin, association with a minority, property, birth or other status'. The application of this principle involves more than simply deciding whether a person has been discriminated against in the enjoyment of a Convention right. The question would also arise as to whether there is an objective and reasonable justification for treating different categories of people in a different way, and whether any such differential treatment was proportionate to the matter being pursued. It is not possible to pursue a case on *Article 14* grounds alone; there must be another Convention right at issue to which a claim of discrimination can be attached.

Perhaps the Convention rights which are most likely to impact on UK employment law are:

(*a*)   the prohibition of slavery and forced labour (*Article 4*);

(*b*)   the right to a fair trial (*Article 6*);

(*c*)   the right to respect for private and family life (*Article 8*);

(*d*)   the right to freedom of religion (*Article 9*);

(*e*)   the right to freedom of expression (*Article 10*);

(*f*)   the right to freedom of assembly and association (*Article 11*).

'Proportionality' is a crucial concept. Any interference with a Convention right must be proportionate to the intended objective. This means that even if a particular policy or action which interferes with a Convention right is aimed at a legitimate goal (for example, preventing crime), this will not justify the interference if the means used to achieve the aim are excessive in the circumstances. Interference with a Convention right must be appropriate, and neither arbitrary nor unfair. In any event, interference may be unjustified if the impact on an individual or group is too severe.

Only a person considered to be a victim can bring proceedings against a public authority under the Act. A victim is someone who is directly affected by the conduct in question. Victims can include companies as well as individuals and may also be relatives of the victim where a complaint is made about his death. A victim may also be a person who is at risk of being directly affected by a measure.

In relation to some Convention rights (particularly those requiring a balance to be struck between competing considerations), the European Court of Human Rights allows a 'margin of appreciation' to the domestic authorities, meaning that it is reluctant to substitute its own view of the merits of the case for those of the national authorities. It remains to be seen whether UK courts and tribunals will develop a doctrine analogous to that of 'the margin of appreciation'.

123.4   PRACTICAL IMPLICATIONS

Remedies are available under the *HRA 1998* only against employers which are public authorities. The *HRA 1998* does not provide an exhaustive definition of 'public authorities' and borderline cases will need to be resolved by the courts. There is scope for the category of employers which carry out some functions of a 'public nature' to be defined quite broadly. That said, a Parliamentary report published in 2004 expressed concern that the combined effects of restrictive judicial interpretation and the changing nature of private and voluntary sector involvement in public services had limited the protection afforded by the *HRA*.

In any event, incorporation of the Convention into domestic law will have a significant effect on private, as well as public, employment. For example, courts and tribunals, which are themselves public authorities, must act compatibly with Convention rights. Because of this, it may be expected that common law will develop in private employment disputes in a manner which gives effect to Convention rights. It may be argued, for instance, that the implied contractual duty of mutual trust and confidence embodies a duty to respect the Convention rights.

Codes relating to *Dress and Personal Appearance* imposed by employers may give rise to issues under the *HRA 1998*.

In *Parry v Lancashire Probation Service [2004] IRLR 129*, a probation officer complained that he had been unfairly dismissed and that his employers had breached his rights under *Articles 8* and *10*. Most of his clients on probation were sex offenders. Independently of his job with a probation service, the employee was also a director of a company that, through its website, marketed products connected with bondage, domination and sado-masochism. This came to the attention of the probation service and, on investigation, the employee admitted his involvement in the company and that he performed shows in clubs that specialised in hedonism and fetishism. Links on the website led to another site where photographs of him were available. The probation service considered that his activities were incompatible with his role as a probation officer, to whom sex offenders in particular look for guidance, and also with the role of the probation service. The employers also considered that public knowledge of the employee's activities would damage its reputation and thus he was dismissed. The tribunal held that the dismissal was fair. As regards *Article 8*, the activities were not private in the requisite sense because they were carried out in the public domain. *Article 10* was engaged, but the tribunal found that the activities were such as to damage the probation officer's reputation. Dismissal was a proportionate response in pursuit of the probation service's legitimate aim to protect its reputation and demonstrate the integrity of its officers. The EAT upheld the tribunal's decision. The case illustrates the distinction between activities which are truly private and those which, although conducted away from work, have a 'public' element.

The conflicting issues that gave rise to practical difficulties in implementing human rights are illustrated by the case of *XXX v YYY [2004] IRLR 471*. The question was whether a covert video recording should be admitted in evidence before an employment tribunal considering a nanny's claims of constructive unfair dismissal and sex discrimination. She worked as a nanny for a couple with a young son. She claimed that the child's father had made unwelcome and improper sexual advances towards her. Her employers, however, claimed that there had been a consensual relationship between her and the father and that the allegations were made following the break-down of this relationship. In support of her case, that nanny sought to submit a video recording that she had made secretly one morning in the kitchen of the family home. The recording shows the father making sexual advances to her in the presence of the child. An employment tribunal concluded that she had infringed the father and son's right to privacy under *Article 8*, but that this infringement was justified because the family home was also her place of work. The tribunal suggested that it would need to view the recording in order to protect the nanny's right under *Article 6* to a fair hearing in public. Her employers appealed against the tribunal's decision that the nanny could adduce the video recording in evidence. The EAT referred the matter back to the same tribunal to consider whether the tribunal's Convention rights affected the admissibility of the video material. At the remitted hearing, the tribunal viewed the video recording in private. The parties conceded that showing the recording in a public hearing would infringe the child's right to respect for his private life. The tribunal concluded, however, that on balance the interference was justified and that it would be lawful for the video recording to be shown. The employers argued that this could not be the case where there had been a breach of confidence. The tribunal reasoned that the child's confidence was not breached by a video recording in which he happened to feature as an 'incidental' character. The tribunal concluded, however, that the recording did not advance the nanny's case, as it was wholly consistent with the contention that the sexual relationship in issue was consensual. The matter returned to the EAT which took the view that it was impossible to conclude that the video recorded did not advance her case without seeing it in the context of the remaining evidence. But the Court of Appeal ruled that the EAT was not entitled to conclude that the tribunal's decision that the video had no probative value was irrational. Evidence is only admissible if it is relevant to an issue between the parties. On the dispute as pleaded, the video was irrelevant.

124   Illegality

Can a complaint of discrimination be defeated on the ground that the contract under which the complainant was employed was tainted with illegality?

This question arose in the case of *Hall v Woolston Hall Leisure Ltd [2000] IRLR 578*. The complainant was employed as the head chef at a golf club. She was told that she was being dismissed on grounds of redundancy and incapability. She complained of sex discrimination and the employment tribunal found that she would not have been dismissed had she not been pregnant. The tribunal awarded her compensation for injury to feelings, but held that she was not entitled to compensation for loss of earnings. The reason was that her weekly pay was understated on her payslips. She had negotiated a pay rise on her promotion, asking for and being granted £250 per week net of deductions. The payslips, however, falsely showed £250 as her gross pay, not her net pay. When she queried this, she was told: 'It's the way we do business.' It was held by the employment tribunal that the contract of employment was tainted with illegality. The complainant knew that her employers were defrauding the Inland Revenue and turned a blind eye. She appealed unsuccessfully to the EAT against the decision not to award her any compensation for loss of earnings.

There was then a further appeal to the Court of Appeal, which allowed the appeal. In considering the relevant law, Lord Justice Peter Gibson started with the *Equal Treatment Directive*. He pointed out that although the complainant could not rely on it directly (the employer was a private sector employer), the tribunal must interpret the national law in the light of the wording and purpose of the Directive and, so far as possible, give effect to the Directive. He pointed out the Directive requires the United Kingdom to give real and effective judicial protection to victims of sex discrimination at work and to provide a sanction with a real deterrent effect on the employer. He said that a person in the complainant's position was clearly within the ambit of the Directive. Her dismissal because of her pregnancy contravened the purpose of the Directive, which also supported her not being denied an effective remedy under the *SDA 1975*.

It was also important to note that the complainant did not base her complaint on the terms of her contract. She had to establish that she was employed and was dismissed from her employment; to that extent reliance was placed on the contract of employment. She was, however, complaining not about breach of contract but about the statutory tort of sex discrimination. At most, she had acquiesced in her employer's conduct; that acquiescence was in no way causally linked with her sex discrimination claim. Accordingly her claim should be allowed.

The Court of Appeal also approved the decision of the EAT in the earlier case of *Leighton v Michael [1996] IRLR 67*. In that case the employee worked in a fish and chip shop. After a change of ownership, her new employers, despite her complaint, refused to make proper deductions of tax and national insurance contributions. She presented complaints of sexual harassment and victimisation in dismissing her. The tribunal dismissed her complaint because the carrying out of her contract of employment involved a fraud on the Inland Revenue and she was a party to that illegality. Her appeal was allowed by the EAT.

In approving the decision of the EAT, Lord Justice Peter Gibson in *Hall* said that it was the sex discrimination that was the core of the complaint. In upholding that complaint, the court would not be seen to be condoning unlawful conduct by the employee. The complaint of sex discrimination was not based on the contract of employment. It was still less the case that the complaint of sex discrimination and the complainant's acquiescence in her employer's unlawful failure to make proper deductions were closely connected or inextricably linked.

If the claim had been based on the contract of employment, then illegality would have defeated the contract in any of the following circumstances:

(*a*)   if the contract had been entered into for an illegal purpose;

(*b*)   if the contract had been prohibited by statute;

(*c*)   if the complainant had actively participated in the illegal performance of the contract.

These principles relating to claims based on contract would be relevant in *Equal Pay* cases. An employee would almost certainly not be permitted to pursue a claim under the *EPA 1970* if he or she had actively participated in a scheme for his or her pay to be under-declared so as to defraud the Inland Revenue. In such a case, the complaint would be based on the contract of employment and the illegality would go to the heart of the matter in respect of which a remedy was being claimed.

125   Immigration

Immigration is a sensitive social and political issue with significant equal opportunities implications. The control of immigration necessarily involves direct and indirect racial discrimination, because persons are admitted to the UK subject to conditions which prevent them from taking employment, or which restrict the work they can do, and those conditions are imposed on grounds of nationality or by reference to residential factors. Such discrimination is, however, authorised by *section 41* of the *RRA 1976* – see *Statutory Authority*.

The *Asylum and Immigration Act 1996* made it a criminal offence to employ a person aged 16 or over who is subject to immigration control unless that person either:

(*a*)   has current and valid permission to be in the UK and that permission does not prevent him or her from taking the job in question; or

(*b*)   comes into a category specified by the Home Secretary where such employment is allowed.

There is a statutory defence where the employer does not know that the person was not entitled to do the work, and saw one of several specified documents before the person started work.

The *Immigration, Asylum and Nationality Act 2006* received Royal Assent in March 2006. The Act introduces new provisions to tackle illegal working, including:

(*a*)   a new civil penalty scheme for employers who employ illegal workers;

(*b*)   fixed penalty fines for employers in breach of the rules;

(*c*)   custodial sentences for employers who take on an individual 'knowing that the employee is an adult subject to immigration control'.

At the time of writing, the Act was not fully in force. The new regime is controversial, not least because it introduces a new system for determining eligibility to enter the UK, by way of a 'points-based tier system'. The rules are discussed further under *Immigration Control.*

The *Immigration (European Economic Area) Regulations 2006 (SI 2006 No 1003)*, which came into force on 30 April 2006, cover free movement of EEA nationals and family members both into and within the EEA. The rules provide for an initial three-month right of residence for all EU citizens (including family members irrespective of nationality) irrespective of purpose. As compared to previous regulations, there are increased rights of residence for family members in the event of breakdown of the family relationship and increased permanent rights of residence after five years' legal residence.

The difficulty for employers is that of assuring that they comply with the restrictions on recruiting immigrant workers whilst avoiding discrimination on racial or religious grounds in the way in which they carry out checks. Guidance is provided by a *Code of Practice*: see *Appendix 4.*

126   Immigration Control

In essence, the *Immigration, Asylum and Nationality Act 2006* provides that overseas nationals (other than those from within the European Economic Area) will only be allowed to come to work in the UK if they fall within one of five tiers, each of which carries a different number of points and will permit those who achieve the requisite points to enter the UK for varying lengths of time. The tiers are:

(1)   highly skilled individuals to contribute to growth and productivity;

(2)   skilled workers with a job offer, and workers to meet specific requirements;

(3)   workers to fill low skills shortages;

(4)   overseas students;

(5)   other temporary categories of entrant, including visiting workers, selected development schemes, working holidaymakers and cultural exchanges.

Scientists or entrepreneurs will typically fall within Tier 1; nurses, teachers and engineers within Tier 2; and construction workers for a particular project within Tier 3.

The government announced in April 2007 that Tier 3 would be launched at the beginning of 2008; Tiers 2 and 5 in the third quarter of 2008; and Tier 4 at the beginning of 2009.

Points will bee awarded to individuals to reflect aptitude, experience, age and also the level of need in any given sector 'to allow the UK to respond flexibly to changes in the labour market'.

The government also intends to set up a Migrants Advisory Committee to advise on where migration might sensibly fill gaps in the labour market, and a Migration Impacts Forum to provide information on the wider impacts of migration on local communities.

127   Independent Expert

Until 31 July 1996, no *Equal Value* claim could succeed unless the employment tribunal had appointed an independent expert to consider and report on the jobs of the claimant and the comparator(s). This did not mean that an independent expert was appointed in all cases. There are many *Equal Pay* cases which fail before the stage of appointing an independent expert is reached, for example because at some earlier stage the tribunal considers and upholds a *Material Factor* defence.

Now the position is that the tribunal may appoint an independent expert but is not obliged to do so. Where no independent expert is appointed, the usual practice is for the applicant and the respondent each to call their own expert witness. The tribunal then makes a decision after considering the expert and other evidence which it has heard.

Even where a report by an independent expert is commissioned and received by the tribunal, that report may be challenged and each party may, on giving reasonable notice to the tribunal and to the other party, call one expert witness. The directions made by the tribunal normally provide for the parties to exchange the reports of any expert witnesses before the hearing.

128   Indirect Discrimination

128.1   GENERAL PRINCIPLES

To strike at employment decisions and practices which, while applied equally to all employees or job applicants, have a disproportionately adverse effect, or *Disparate Impact*, on members of a relevant group (such as women or ethnic or religious minority workers), the legislation, outlawing discrimination generally (but not always) utilises the concept of indirect discrimination.

A possible approach would have been to define indirect discrimination in general and flexible terms, leaving it to the employment tribunals to apply the definition to particular cases in the light of the relevant circumstances and the practical experience of the Members. That is the European approach. The *Council Directive 76/207/EEC*, the *Equal Treatment Directive*, states in *Article 2(1)*:

> 'For the purposes of the following provisions, the principle of equal treatment shall mean that there shall be no discrimination whatsoever on grounds of sex either directly or indirectly by reference in particular to marital or family status.'

That one word, 'indirectly', is the Directive's only reference to indirect discrimination. It was left to national courts and, on receipt of a reference from a national court, the ECJ, to develop the principle.

The *SDA 1975* and the *RRA 1976* were until relatively recently based on a very different approach. Each of them contained a detailed definition or definitions of indirect discrimination. In some respects those definitions were inflexible and restrictive. Both Acts have now been amended. Unfortunately, however, the adoption of a common approach in these two Acts and in the *RBR 2003* and the *SOR 2003* is not yet complete. Furthermore, there is no separate definition of indirect discrimination in the *DDA 1995*.

128.2   THE STATUTORY DEFINITIONS

The definition of indirect discrimination in the *RBR 2003* provides that there is discrimination by A against B if:

> 'A applies to B a provision, criterion or practice which he applies or would apply equally to persons not of the same religion or belief as B, but:

> (i)   which puts or would put persons of the same religion or belief as B at a particular disadvantage when compared with other persons,

> (ii)   which puts B at that disadvantage, and

> (iii) which A cannot show to be a proportionate means of achieving a legitimate aim.'

The *SOR 2003* contains an identical definition, with the substitution of 'sexual orientation' for 'religion or belief' in the two places where those words appear.

The definitions of indirect discrimination in the *SDA 1975*, the *RRA 1976* and the *AR 2006* address a provision, criterion or practice which puts persons of B's 'age group' at a particular disadvantage.

128.3 Indirect Discrimination

128.3 PROVISION, CRITERION OR PRACTICE

The reference to a 'provision, criterion or practice' is clearly more flexible than the original reference in the *SDA* 1975 and the *RRA* 1976 to a 'requirement or condition'.

In *Allonby v Accrington & Rossendale College [2001] IRLR 365*, the Court of Appeal, considering a case where the requirement or condition applied to the complainant could be defined in more than one way, held that:

> 'It is for the applicant to identify the requirement or condition which she seeks to impugn. These words are not terms of art; they are overlapping concepts and are not to be narrowly construed (*Clarke v Eley (IMI) Kynoch [1982] IRLR 482, 485*). If the applicant can realistically identify a requirement or condition capable of supporting her case ... it is nothing to the point that her employer can with equal cogency derive from the facts a different and unobjectionable requirement or condition. The employment tribunal's focus moves directly to the question of unequal impact'.

The same principle will presumably apply in relation to any provision, criterion or practice. It will be for the claimant to identify the provision, criterion or practice about which he or she wishes to complain.

In a sex discrimination case, the *Employment Equality (Sex Discrimination) Regulations 2005 (SI 2005 No 2467)*, which update the definition of indirect discrimination in the *SDA 1975*, do not limit a claimant to using 'pools' for comparative purposes, such an approach is legitimate.

Statistical evidence may be required, in cases where the answer is not obvious without that evidence.

128.4 THE POOL

The definition of the pool is a question of fact according to the circumstances of the case. There are at least five possible definitions:

(*a*)   all the workers at a particular establishment;

(*b*)   the whole workforce of a particular employer;

(*c*)   all having a particular qualification;

(*d*)   all economically active men and women in Great Britain;

(*e*)   all workers in the catchment area of a particular factory.

The first or second of these cases will commonly apply when the complaint is made by an existing employee, as in the redundancy case of *Clarke v Eley (IMI) Kynoch Ltd [1982] IRLR 482*. This was a case where part-timers were selected for redundancy before full-timers were considered and a complaint of indirect sex discrimination was upheld. One of the other cases would normally apply in relation to a complaint made by a job applicant. For example, in *Jones v University of Manchester [1993] IRLR 218*, the complaint of indirect sex discrimination was about an upper age limit. An unchallenged requirement for the post was possession of a degree. It was held by the Court of Appeal that the pool consisted of the whole graduate population.

128.5   **STATISTICAL EVIDENCE**

Relevant statistics are most likely to be available in the two extreme cases, that of a pool which covers all economically active men and women and that of a pool which is limited to the workers in a particular factory. National statistics relating to the former pool are published at regular intervals; even where the employer has not kept statistics, it is usually possible to count the men and women at a particular factory and (perhaps with more difficulty) the members of a particular ethnic group working at the factory.

Finding statistical evidence is likely to be more of a problem where the pool consists, for example, of all those with a particular qualification or of all the workers in an ill-defined catchment area. In such a case, an employment tribunal is likely to take a practical approach by, for example, using the statistics which relate to a larger group or by basing decisions on the knowledge and experience possessed by the members of the tribunal acting as an industrial jury. For example, it would not normally be difficult to persuade a tribunal that a considerably smaller percentage of women than of men can comply with a requirement of full-time working.

If statistics are available and are to be used, then once the pool has been defined the following calculations must be carried out:

(*a*)   How many members does the pool contain of the relevant group (e.g. women) to which the complainant belongs?

(*b*)   What percentage of them are qualifiers (i.e. those who can comply with the requirement or condition complained of)?

(*c*)   How many non-members (e.g. men) are there in the pool?

(*d*)   What percentage of them are qualifiers?

It is then necessary to compare the two percentages. There is disproportionate impact (and, it is suggested, particular disadvantage) if the percentage of qualifiers in the complainant's group (e.g. women) is considerably smaller than the percentage of qualifiers amongst the non-members of that group (e.g. men).

In cases under the *SDA 1975*, it has been held that there is no simple arithmetical test to show whether any particular percentage difference is considerable. The exercise is not one of pure mathematics.

In *London Underground Ltd v Edwards (No 2) [1998] IRLR 364*, a female train operator was unable to comply with new rostering arrangements. This was because she was a single parent with a young child. The pool consisted of all the train operators to whom the new rostering arrangements applied. There were only 21 women in that pool and 20 of them (or 95.2 per cent) could comply with the new arrangements. There were more than 2,000 men in the pool and all of them could comply with the new roster.

In terms of the bare statistics, 95.2 per cent (the female qualifiers) may not seem considerably smaller than 100 per cent (the male qualifiers). The difference is only 4.8 per cent, but a finding by the tribunal that 95.2 per cent was considerably smaller than 100 per cent was upheld by the Court of Appeal. Potter LJ accepted that a percentage difference of no more than 5 per cent or thereabouts is inherently likely to lead a tribunal to the conclusion that the case has not been made out, but he was not prepared to say that the conclusion must inevitably follow in every case (including this one). He made the following general observations:

128.5 Indirect Discrimination

(a) An employer should be required to justify a requirement or condition only if there is a substantial, and not merely marginal, discriminatory effect (or disparate impact) as between men and women.

(b) That disparate impact should be inherent in the application of the requirement or condition and not simply the product of unreliable statistics or fortuitous circumstance.

(c) There is an infinite number of employment situations and there is a need for an area of flexibility (or margin of appreciation).

In the present case, the tribunal were entitled to look behind the bare percentages. Even though the pool was a restricted one, the tribunal were entitled to take into account the fact, based on their own knowledge and experience, that nationally about 10 female single parents for every male single parent have care of a child. This fact helped to show that the percentage difference in the present case was not fortuitous.

The tribunal was also entitled to have regard to the large discrepancy in numbers. Not one male operator out of more than 2,000 was able to comply with the rostering arrangements. If there had been one male non-qualifier, the percentage of male qualifiers would have been hardly at all affected; on the other hand, if there had been one extra woman who could not comply, then the percentage of female qualifiers would have been reduced by nearly 5 per cent.

Further guidance was given by both the ECJ and the House of Lords in *R v Secretary of State for the Employment, ex p Seymour Smith and Perez*. This case concerned the qualifying period for most complaints of unfair dismissal, which in 1985 was increased to two years and remained at two years until 1999. The question was whether the two-year qualifying period was contrary to the *Equal Treatment Directive* because of an indirectly discriminatory effect on women.

The statistics showed that in 1985, when the qualifying period was increased, the percentage of men who had the two years' service was 77.4, as against 68.9 of women. The gap narrowed in most subsequent years, although with some fluctuations. The respective percentages were 74.5 and 67.4 in 1991, the year in which the applicants were dismissed, and 78.4 and 74.1 two years later.

The ECJ (*[1999] IRLR 253*) expressed the view that the 1985 statistics did not appear on the face of it to show that the percentage of women who could comply was considerably smaller than the percentage of men who could. In the House of Lords, *R v Secretary of State for the Employment, ex p Seymour Smith and Perez (No 2) [2000] IRLR 263*, Lord Nicholls pointed out that the relevant statistics were those for 1991, when the applicants were dismissed. The percentage difference was smaller than it had been in 1985, but that was not the end of the matter. The ECJ had observed that 'statistical evidence revealing a lesser but persistent and relatively constant disparity over a long period could also be evidence of apparent sex discrimination'.

Lord Nicholls pointed out that over the period of seven years from 1985 up to and including 1991 the ratio of men and women who qualified was roughly 10:9. He said that these figures were 'in borderline country', but he found himself 'driven to the conclusion that a persistent and constant disparity of the order just mentioned in respect of the entire male and female labour forces of the country over a period of seven years cannot be brushed aside and dismissed as insignificant or inconsiderable. I think these figures are adequate to demonstrate that the extension of the qualifying period had a considerably greater adverse impact on women than men'.

Lord Nicholls also suggested, in relation to disparate impact, that it may be appropriate to look at the respective percentages of non-qualifiers as well as those of qualifiers.

He referred to several ECJ decisions where this had been done, but left the question open for another occasion. In *Barry v Midland Bank plc [1999] IRLR 581* he had taken a step further and suggested that a better guide will often be found in expressing the proportions of men and women in the disadvantaged group as a ratio of each other.

The following principles can be extracted from the above authorities:

(*a*)   the starting point is to look at the percentage difference;

(*b*)   a small percentage difference may be magnified somewhat if it is constant over a long period;

(*c*)   the actual numbers of (if the case is one of indirect sex discrimination) women and men can also be relevant, if there is a big disparity;

(*d*)   evidence which indicates that a disparity which is (on the one hand) fortuitous or (on the other hand) linked to the difference in sex can also be relevant.

In *Allonby v Accrington and Rossendale College and others [2001] IRLR 365*, the relevant percentages were 38 per cent of men who could comply with the condition complained of and 21 per cent of women who could comply. There was no express finding by the employment tribunal that the proportion of women able to comply was considerably smaller than the proportion of men who could comply. It had already been decided that the case should be remitted to the tribunal on the issue of justifiability and it was decided by the Court of Appeal that this issue should be sent back also.

128.6   **DETRIMENT OR DISADVANTAGE**

There appears to be no practical difference between the expressions 'detriment' and 'disadvantage'. It is well established that the term 'detriment' must be given a wide meaning. In *Ministry of Defence v Jeremiah [1979] IRLR 436*, Brightman LJ said that 'a detriment exists if a reasonable worker would or might take the view that the [treatment] was in all the circumstances to his detriment.' The above passage was quoted with approval by Lord Hoffmann in *Chief Constable of West Yorkshire Police v Khan [2001] IRLR 830*, and by Lord Hope of Craighead in *Shamoon v Chief Constable of The Royal Ulster Constabulary [2003] IRLR 285*. A detriment does not necessarily involve any financial loss and the expression must be given its broad, ordinary meaning.

This means that, for example, a person who is denied the opportunity to be interviewed for a job, because of an indirectly discriminatory, provision, criterion or practice, may suffer a detriment or disadvantage on that account, even if he or she would have had little chance of being appointed if an interview had been granted.

128.7   **PROPORTIONATE MEANS AND LEGITIMATE AIMS**

Most of the significant decisions to date have been on the 'old' question whether the respondent has shown a requirement or condition to be 'justifiable', rather than the 'new' question of whether the respondent has shown a provision, criterion or practice to be a proportionate means of achieving a legitimate aim. The leading cases have, however, referred to the need for proportionality, or a proper balance between the discriminatory effect and the objectives to be achieved; and also to necessity, or reasonable necessity, which would appear to be at least as strict a test as legitimacy.

Hampson v Department of Education and Science [1989] IRLR 69, concerned a refusal to recognise a teaching qualification obtained in Hong Kong, because the initial training course there was only two years, as opposed to the three years in England. The Department of Education did not regard it as sufficient that Mrs Hampson had completed a further teaching course, lasting a full year, some years after the initial two years. The case went to the House of Lords, but the meaning of 'justifiable' was dealt with by the Court of Appeal (*[1989] IRLR 69*). An odd feature of the case was that Balcombe LJ gave a dissenting judgment, but the other members of the Court endorsed the guidance which he gave on the issue of justification. His judgment included the following key features:

(*a*)   the test is objective;

(*b*)   the standard is the reasonable need of the undertaking;

(*c*)   that reasonable need may be, but is not confined to, economic or administrative efficiency;

(*d*)   the tribunal considering the matter must strike an objective balance between the discriminatory effect of the condition and the reasonable need of the undertaking.

This guidance was approved by the House of Lords, some years later, in *Webb v EMO Air Cargo (UK) Ltd [1993] IRLR 27.*

The above authorities were also referred to by the Court of Appeal in *Coker and Osamor v Lord Chancellor and Lord Chancellor's Department [2002] IRLR 80.* Lord Phillips MR commented:

'The consideration of the question of whether a requirement that is discriminatory is justifiable involves a test of proportionality. An objective balance has to be struck between the discriminatory effect of the requirement and the reasonable needs of the party who imposes it – see *Hampson v Department of Education and Science [1989] IRLR 69 at 75,* per Balcombe LJ, approved by the House of Lords in *Webb v EMO Air Cargo Ltd [1993] IRLR 27.*'

Allonby v Accrington and Rossendale College and others [2001] IRLR 365, concerned a complaint of indirect sex discrimination in relation to steps taken by the college to terminate or not renew the employment contracts of part-time lecturers and instead retain their services (on less beneficial terms) as subcontractors. The Court of Appeal held that the case should be remitted to the employment tribunal on the issue of justification and gave the following guidance:

'Once a finding of a condition having a disparate and adverse impact on women had been made, what was required was at the minimum a critical evaluation of whether the college's reasons demonstrated a real need to dismiss the applicant; if there was such a need, consideration of the seriousness of the disparate impact of the dismissal on women including the applicant; and an evaluation of whether the former were sufficient to outweigh the latter.'

Moreover the dismissal could not be justified if its purpose was, as had been contended, 'to deny part-time workers, a predominantly female group, benefits which Parliament had legislated to give them'.

In *Hardys & Hansons plc v Lax [2005] IRLR 726,* a tribunal found that an employer's refusal to consider allowing the claimant to job share on her return from maternity leave was not shown to be justifiable within *section 1(2)(b)(i)* of the *SDA*

1975. The EAT ruled that the tribunal did not err by failing to grant to the employers a margin of discretion in deciding whether to permit a job share. The employer has to show that the proposal is justified objectively, notwithstanding its discriminatory effect. The principle of proportionality requires the tribunal to take into account the reasonable needs of the business, but it had to make its own judgment, upon a fair and detailed analysis of the working practices and the business considerations involved, as to whether the proposal is reasonably necessary. On the facts, the tribunal was entitled to conclude the employers had insufficiently explored the possibilities for job sharing and that their objections to it were overstated.

In *Cross v British Airways plc [2005] IRLR 423*, the EAT ruled that a tribunal was entitled to include as a justification for indirectly discriminatory provisions (in respect of normal retiring age) the costs to the employer of changing its terms and conditions relating to retirement. The tribunal did not misdirect itself in holding that cost grounds can properly be held a factor justifying indirect discrimination, provided that they are combined with other reasons.

128.8   **COMPENSATION**

Compensation is usually awarded when a tribunal has made a finding of indirect discrimination, but an award of compensation is not inevitable. There is no limit in the amount of compensation that may be awarded.

129   Inferences

There is rarely an admission or other direct evidence of *Direct Discrimination* or *Victimisation*. Findings of discrimination or victimisation are usually based on the inferences to be drawn by the tribunal from, in particular:

(*a*)   a difference in treatment;

(*b*)   false or evasive answers to a *Questionnaire*;

(*c*)   failure to comply with guidance in a relevant *Code of Practice*.

There are now statutory provisions under which, where an inference can properly be drawn from the primary facts, the burden of disproving discrimination, victimisation or harassment shifts from the claimant to the respondent.

130   Injury to Feelings

An award of compensation under the *Discrimination Laws* (other than in respect of an equal pay claim) may include compensation for injury to feelings. This power is similar to the power of a court to award general damages in personal injury cases.

It is almost inevitable that an act of unlawful discrimination will cause distress, humiliation or some other hurt to the victim. Compensation for injury to feelings is normally awarded. See *Compensation*.

131   Institutional Discrimination

The concept of institutional discrimination came into public prominence as a result of the Macpherson Inquiry into matters arising from the death of Stephen Lawrence. The Macpherson Report defined institutional racism as:

> 'The collective failure of an organisation to provide an appropriate and professional service to people because of their colour, culture or ethnic origin [which] can be seen or detected in processes, attitudes and behaviour which amount to discrimination through unwitting prejudice, ignorance, thoughtlessness and racist stereotyping which disadvantage minority ethnic people.'

Increasing awareness of the concept of institutional discrimination throws into sharp focus matters concerning *Evidence of Discrimination*. Courts and tribunals need to apply the law to the facts of particular cases with sensitivity and must not lean too far in one particular direction.

In *Commissioners of Inland Revenue and another v Morgan [2002] IRLR 776*, an employment tribunal upheld a claim of racial discrimination brought by a barrister employed in the legal department of the Inland Revenue. In its conclusion, the tribunal said: 'There appears to be "institutionalised" racism in the Department. The Department, run mainly by white old-established university educated persons had a practice based on values which did not embrace wholly ethnic minority lawyers.' The EAT said that the tribunal had not erred in law in finding that the applicant had been discriminated against on grounds of her race; its conclusion that the employers' explanations were not satisfactory or adequate was not 'a mere intuitive hunch'. However, the EAT said of the conclusion in respect of 'institutionalised' racism: 'It is difficult to exaggerate how unsatisfactory that conclusion is.' The EAT pointed out that there is no statutory or other offence consisting of a body being institutionally racist. Moreover, the applicant had not even identified 'institutional racism' as an issue, formally or informally in the proceedings. There was no suggestion that the tribunal had the definition of the Macpherson Report in mind (it was not put to them) and, even if they had, as that definition concerned attitude in an official body – there, the police – to members of the public with whom it dealt, the EAT said it would have been inappropriate to apply it in this case, which was concerned with attitude of an official body to its own members. The EAT concluded:

> 'Tribunals have quite enough to do in race cases determining whether the requirements of a statute are met or not without their venturing, as this tribunal did, into serious and wounding conclusions based on charges not advanced and unknown to the law.

> We are not saying that something reasonably describable as institutional racism can never be required to be examined into by a tribunal. It would be possible to imagine a body whose habitual rules or practice was such that one could fairly say of the body that as an institution it was racist. Forms of indirect discrimination would, perhaps, be the more likely to bring about some such case. But the charge would be relevant only as a step in the reasoning toward a conclusion that the body was or was not guilty of some unlawful discrimination that fell within the Act.'

132   Internal Investigations

Employers and other respondents should carry out a thorough internal investigation into any allegation of harassment or other unlawful discrimination, whether the allegation is made before or after a complaint to tribunal is presented. Where an allegation is well founded, it is in the employer's interest to establish that fact and to take appropriate action without delay.

An issue which frequently arises where allegations of *Harassment* have been made is whether the alleged harasser should be suspended. In particular, what action should be taken where the complainant states that she (or occasionally he) would find it impossible to continue working with the alleged harasser?

The following general guidelines may be helpful:

(*a*)   The law does not require the *automatic* suspension of any employee against whom an allegation of harassment is made. Although suspension on pay need not be a disciplinary action, it can be detrimental to the employee concerned (and indeed to the employer if that employee has an important role in the organisation).

(*b*)   It may be necessary to suspend the alleged harasser on full pay in order to carry out a thorough investigation.

(*c*)   If the complainant objects strongly to continuing to work with the harasser, possible options, during the investigation, are to move the alleged harasser to other work (if this can be done within the terms of his or her contract), a voluntary transfer for either party or voluntary paid leave for either party.

(*d*)   Compulsory transfer or suspension of the complainant is not an option – see *Victimisation*.

(*e*)   If it proves to be unavoidable for the complainant and alleged harasser to continue to work together, appropriate safeguards, including instructions to managers and supervisors, should be given to prevent any (further) harassment and give reassurance to the complainant.

133   Job Applications

Many complaints of discrimination relate to the handling of job applications, whether made by external candidates or by employees seeking promotion or transfer. For guidance on the avoidance of discrimination see *Recruitment, Promotion, Selection* and *Job Interviews*.

Job applications and all related documents should be kept until at least six months after the job has been filled (longer if practicable). The time limit for a complaint of discrimination is three months, but the time limit can be extended. If a suitably qualified but unsuccessful candidate complains of discrimination, and the employer has destroyed the job applications and other relevant documents, the employment tribunal could draw an adverse inference.

It is also necessary to record information about job applications, and the reasons for shortlisting and selection decisions, as part of the *Monitoring* which should be carried out in order to ensure that an *Equal Opportunities Policy* is operating successfully.

134   Job Descriptions

Job descriptions should be prepared for all posts, whether they are to be filled externally or internally – see *Recruitment*, *Promotion* and *Selection*.

Without a job description (and also a person specification, showing the qualities required in the light of the job description) it is difficult to show that shortlisting and selection decisions have been made objectively, without any unlawful discrimination.

135   Job Duties

Whatever flexibility the contract of employment may give to the employer, in terms of the duties which employees can be required to carry out, there must be no unlawful discrimination in the way in which job duties are allocated – see *Benefits* and *Detriment*.

In considering whether a complainant's job and a comparator's job are *Like Work* or work of *Equal Value* for the purposes of a claim under the *EPA 1970*, it is necessary to focus on the duties which are actually performed in practice (and how frequently they are performed) and not on theoretical requirements.

Employers can be obliged to change or modify the job duties of disabled employees in order to comply with the duty to make *Reasonable Adjustments*.

136   Job Evaluation

Job evaluation is the science (or art) of evaluating a job in terms of the demands made on the person doing that job under various headings. The process requires considerable expertise. It involves:

(*a*)   identifying various demand factors, such as the skill, physical effort, mental effort, decision making and level of responsibility which a job demands;

(*b*)   giving appropriate weightings to these factors, having regard to the nature of the particular job;

(*c*)   allocating points under each heading.

This is a simplified account of a complicated process.

Job evaluation can be relevant in three respects in relation to *Equal Pay* cases, as follows:

(*a*)   If the complainant's job and the comparator's job have been rated as equivalent under a job evaluation study, then the equal pay claim must succeed (assuming that the two workers are in the *Same Employment*), unless the *Material Factor* defence can be made out. A claim can be based on a job evaluation study which has been carried out, even if for some reason the study has not then been implemented – *O'Brien v Sim-Chem Ltd [1980] IRLR 373*.

(*b*)   In an *Equal Value* case, any experts appointed by the parties (and also the *Independent Expert* if the tribunal decide that one should be appointed) will carry out a job evaluation limited to the jobs of the complainant and the comparator(s).

(*c*)   Under *section 2A* of the *EPA 1970* an *Equal Value* claim must fail if a job evaluation study has been carried out and has given a greater value to the work of the comparator (or all the comparators if there is more than one) than to the work of the complainant, so long as the study was a proper analytical study and did not involve any sex discrimination.

137 Job Interviews

Many employers still use the generally unscientific (and in some cases almost random) method of job interviews to make the final decision on the appointment of internal or external candidates to job vacancies. Many successful complaints of racial or sex discrimination in not appointing the complainant (or not offering the complainant a second interview) have been based on:

(*a*)   questions or remarks which reveal discriminatory attitudes; or

(*b*)   detailed and negative questioning about personal matters which are irrelevant to the job for which the candidate has applied.

In the case of *Simon v Brimham Associates [1987] IRLR 307*, Lord Justice Balcombe said that he was prepared to accept, as a proposition of law, that:

'in appropriate circumstances, words or acts of discouragement can amount to treatment of the person discouraged less favourable than that given to other persons.'

For general guidance on avoiding discrimination in filling job vacancies – see *Recruitment* and *Selection*.

Interviewers should prepare in advance for the interview by:

(*a*)   agreeing the selection criteria and the scoring system, in the light of the job description and any person specification;

(*b*)   deciding on standard questions, including situational questions relating to the particular job, and agreeing which interviewer should ask which questions;

(*c*)   reading the candidates' application forms and CVs;

(*d*)   ascertaining and meeting the special needs of any candidates who are known to be disabled (including, where necessary, allowing extra time).

During the interview itself, the focus should be on the requirements of the particular job for which the candidate has applied. For example:

(*a*)   questions should relate to the requirements of the job – where personal circumstances may affect job performance (for example because the job involves unsocial hours or extensive travel) the issues should be discussed objectively, without detailed questioning based on assumptions about marital status, childcare or domestic obligations;

(*b*)   questions about marriage plans or family intentions should not be asked, if they could be construed as showing bias against women;

(*c*)   interviewers should be aware of the possible misunderstandings that can occur in interviews between persons of different cultural backgrounds.

If a candidate has a disability which could be relevant to the job, the issue should be discussed frankly but positively, with particular reference to any *Reasonable Adjustments* which may be required.

When making notes, interviewers should avoid flippant or derogatory comments, since the notes will be relevant and disclosable documents for the purpose of any tribunal proceedings. Scores, comments and reasons for decisions should be recorded and preserved.

138   Job Offers

Although most complaints of discrimination in *Recruitment* or *Promotion* are made by unsuccessful candidates, it should be noted that a complaint can also be made if there is discrimination in relation to the terms on which employment is offered. For example it is unlawful for an employer to offer a job to a disabled candidate but at a rate of pay which is lower than the rate which would have been offered if he had not been disabled, unless offering that pay can be justified – see *Justification and Disability Discrimination*.

Where a person wishes to complain under the *SDA 1975* about the salary which is offered or any other proposed contractual term for the payment of money, she can do so only if, on taking up the employment, she would have had a claim under the *EPA 1970* – see *Recruitment*.

139   Job Share

Many full-time employees who have childcare responsibilities need to reduce their working hours. This issue is frequently (but not exclusively) raised when a woman returns or is about to return from maternity leave.

A request for a jobshare may be relevant to a request for *Flexible Working*. But the scope of the right to request *Flexible Working* introduced in 2003 is somewhat limited. Where there is an unjustifiable refusal of a request by a woman to go part-time because of her childcare responsibilities, she may need to have recourse to her right to complain of *Indirect Discrimination*. An employer who rejects job sharing out of hand as a possible alternative to part-time working will be at risk. Job share is not an easy option, because of the compatibility and commitment which it requires from the job sharers, but it is one which must be explored as an alternative to the outright rejection of a request to work part-time.

Job share is not a facility which can lawfully be made available only for female employees. It would be direct sex discrimination to reject a request by a male employee to job share if a request by a female employee (the relevant circumstances being the same or not materially different) would have been accepted.

Job share should also be considered as a *Reasonable Adjustment* where a disabled employee seeks reduced working hours.

140   Joint Respondents

Most acts of discrimination are committed by managers and other employees acting in the course of their employment. In theory, in any such case, the employee responsible for the discrimination could be named as a joint respondent. In practice, it is usually in cases where the complaint is one of harassment that the complainant names the alleged harassers as additional respondents. The importance of doing so, from the complainant's point of view, is that a finding can be made against the harassers, and they can be ordered to pay compensation, even if the employer establishes the defence that all *Reasonably Practicable Steps* to prevent the discrimination were taken.

Where a complaint is upheld against more than one respondent, then the tribunal decides how much compensation each respondent should be ordered to pay. The tribunal may make a separate award against each respondent, or order payment of a sum for which each respondent is jointly and severally liable.

In *Gilbank v Miles [2006] IRLR 538*, an employee brought a sex discrimination claim, alleging that after she became pregnant, there was no attempt to adjust her working practices, or to undertake a risk assessment, or to help in arranging breaks for meals or rest. She was not able to keep antenatal appointments and was told 'she was not ill'. The tribunal accepted that Ms Miles, a director of the company, had treated her in this way. It also found that the claimant was subjected to unsympathetic remarks from other staff and to detrimental treatment by other manager. The tribunal concluded that Ms Miles consciously fostered and encouraged a discriminatory culture to grow up which targeted the claimant. An award for injury to feelings of £25,000 was made. The award was made jointly and severally against Ms Miles and the company on grounds that Ms Miles had aided the employer's unlawful discrimination within the meaning of *section 42* of the *SDA 1975*. The company was dissolved and struck off the register and therefore could not pay compensation. Ms Miles appealed to the EAT on grounds that the award should not have been joint and several where some of the acts of discrimination were carried out by managers other than herself. She also submitted that the award for injury to feelings was excessive. The EAT dismissed the appeal, as did the Court of Appeal. Furthermore, there were no grounds for interfering with the tribunal's award of £25,000 for injury to feelings, even though this was at the top of the range indicated by *Chief Constable of West Yorkshire Police v Vento (No 2) [2003] IRLR 102*, as appropriate in the most serious cases. The tribunal was entitled to take the view that this was a most serious case, which should attract an award at the upper limit. The award was not manifestly excessive.

Further, the tribunal was entitled to find that Ms Miles was jointly and severally liable to pay compensation for acts of pregnancy discrimination against the claimant, even though some of those acts were carried out by others, in circumstances in which she could be regarded as having unlawfully aided discriminatory acts within the meaning of *section 42* of the *SDA 1975* by consciously discouraging the discrimination.

Sedley LJ said:

> 'It would be remarkable if legislation which takes such pains to outlaw not only the commission of acts of sex discrimination but instructions, inducement and assistance to commit such acts, had inadvertently left out the encouragement or promotion of them, particularly in the context of common employment.'

In this case, by encouraging and fostering discriminatory treatment of the claimant by her other staff, Ms Miles could be regarded as having subjected the claimant to a detriment.

141 Jokes

The world would be a very bleak place without humour. However, crass attempts at humour, whether verbal or physical (sometimes inadequately described as 'banter' or 'horseplay') can be very upsetting to the person who is the recipient, or butt, of that supposed humour. In such cases, and in cases where the humour takes the form of acts which may even constitute criminal assaults, the rights of employees to equal opportunities in employment are likely to be infringed.

Misguided jokes may constitute *Harassment* or *Victimisation* and may, for instance, discriminate on the ground of race, sex, disability, *Religion or Belief* or *Sexual Orientation*. An individual's *Human Rights* may also be infringed.

A typical example of a 'joke' constituting sexual harassment occurred in *Driskel v Peninsula Business Services Ltd and others [2000] IRLR 151*. A manager suggested that a female subordinate should attend a promotion interview in a short skirt and see-through blouse, showing plenty of cleavage. Strangely enough, both the harasser and his victim worked for a consultancy in the employment law field.

In *Majrowski v Guy's and St Thomas's NHS Trust [2006] IRLR 695*, discussed in the context of *Stalking*, Baroness Hale said: 'It is easy to see why the definition of harassment was left deliberately wide and open-ended ... It includes alarming a person or causing her distress ... But conduct might be harassment even if no alarm or distress were in fact caused. A great deal is left to the wisdom of the courts to draw sensible lines between the ordinary banter and badinage of life and genuinely offensive and unacceptable behaviour.' It is almost inevitable that the courts should be given a wide discretion in these matters. But this does mean, in practice, that calm and logical judgment is required to determine which jokes form part of 'the ordinary banter and badinage of life' and which constitute unlawful harassment.

142   Justification

Complaints which would otherwise have succeeded can be defeated in the following cases:

(a)   where a criterion etc. having an indirectly discriminatory effect under the *SDA 1975*, the *RRA 1976,* the *RBR 2003* or the *SOR 2003* is objectively justified by the respondent – see *Indirect Discrimination*;

(b)   where less favourable treatment of a disabled person, for a reason relating to the disability, is justified – see *Justification and Disability Discrimination*;

(c)   where a difference in pay or some other contract term as between a complainant and comparator involves indirect discrimination but that difference can be objectively justified – see *Equal Pay* and *Material Factor*.

There are no circumstances in which direct discrimination under the *SDA 1975*, the *RRA 1976,* the *RBR 2003,* the *SOR 2003* or the *AR 2006* can be justified, unless the case falls within one of the express exceptions (such as the *Genuine Occupational Qualification* exception).

143   Justification and Disability Discrimination

143.1   KEY PRINCIPLES

A finding of less favourable treatment, for a reason relating to the disabled person's disability, does not necessarily lead to a finding of disability discrimination. The issue of justification must then be addressed. The employer must show that the reason for the less favourable treatment of the disabled person is:

(*a*)   material to the circumstances of the particular case; and

(*b*)   substantial.

This defence of justification in relation to less favourable treatment of a disabled person is contained in *section 3A(1)(b)* and *(3)* of the *DDA 1995* as amended.

With effect from 1 October 2006 justification for less favourable treatment has no longer been permitted if the less favourable treatment is direct discrimination on the grounds of the disability itself, as opposed to less favourable treatment for some reason relating to the disability (such as absence from work or inability to do particular work). Nor is it now possible (as was originally the case) to mount a defence of justification in a case of failure to comply with the duty to make *Reasonable Adjustments*.

The *Code of Practice* for the elimination of discrimination in the field of employment against disabled persons or persons who have had a disability provides useful examples of what will, and what will not, be justified treatment.

In *Clark v TDG Ltd t/a Novacold [1999] IRLR 318*, the Court of Appeal ruled that whether treatment has been shown to be justified is a question of fact to be determined by an employment tribunal and on a proper self-direction on the relevant law. This includes taking into account those parts of the Code which a reasonable tribunal would regard as relevant to the determination of that question. In *Clark*, the tribunal had failed to have regard to relevant provisions in the Code relating to termination of employment. The question of justification of the dismissal therefore had to be remitted to the tribunal for re-hearing.

Although a tribunal should always have regard to relevant provisions in the *Code of Practice*, it is necessary to look to appeal decisions for the interpretation of the statutory test of justification. The leading authority is the Court of Appeal decision in *Jones v Post Office [2001] IRLR 384*. A mail delivery driver, operating in a mainly rural area, was for many years treated by diet and then by tablets for mature onset diabetes and continued with his driving duties throughout this period. He then had a heart attack, following which insulin treatment was prescribed. His employers decided, on medical advice, to take a number of precautionary steps, which included the restriction of his driving duties to two hours in any 24-hour period. The employee objected to this restriction.

The employment tribunal heard medical witnesses, decided that the medical advice given to the employers was wrong and on that basis upheld the complaint of disability discrimination, rejecting the defence of justification. The EAT and then the Court of Appeal both held that this approach was wrong in law and that the case should be re-heard by a differently constituted tribunal.

Giving the leading judgment in the Court of Appeal, Pill LJ said:

'The 1995 Act is plainly intended to create rights for the disabled and to protect their position as employees, but those intentions must be considered in the context of the employer's duties to employees generally and to the general public. I cannot accept, in a case such as the present, involving an assessment of risk, that Parliament intended in the wording adopted to confer on employment tribunals a general power and duty to decide whether the employer's assessment risk is correct. The issue is a different one from whether a person has a disability, within the meaning of section 1 of the Act, which is to be determined by the employment tribunal (*Goodwin v Patent Office [1999] IRLR 4*).

Upon a consideration of the wording of *section 5(3)* in context, I conclude that the employment tribunal are confined to considering whether the reason given for the less favourable treatment can properly be described as both material to the circumstances of the particular case and substantial.'

He went on to say:

'In order to rely on *section 5(3)* it is not enough for the employer to assert that his conduct was reasonable in a general way; he has to establish that the reason given satisfies the statutory criteria. The respondent asserts in this case that the risk arising from the presence of diabetes is material to the circumstances of the particular case and is substantial. Where a properly conducted risk assessment provides a reason which is on its face both material and substantial, and is not irrational, the tribunal cannot substitute its own appraisal. The employment tribunal must consider whether the reason meets the statutory criteria; it does not have the more general power to make its own appraisal of the medical evidence and conclude that the evidence from admittedly competent medical witnesses was incorrect or make its own risk assessment.

The present problem will typically arise when a risk assessment is involved. I am not doubting that the employment tribunal is permitted to investigate facts, for example as to the time-keeping record of the disabled person or as to his rate of productivity, matters which would arise upon some of the illustrations given in the Code of Practice. Consideration of the statutory criteria may also involve an assessment of the employer's decision to the extent of considering whether there was evidence on the basis of which a decision could properly be taken. Thus if no risk assessment was made or a decision was taken otherwise than on the basis of appropriate medical evidence, or was an irrational decision as being beyond the range of responses open to a reasonable decision-maker . . . the employment tribunal could hold the reason insufficient and the treatment unjustified.

The tribunal cannot, however, in my judgment, conclude that the reason is not material or substantial because the suitably qualified and competently expressed medical opinion, on the basis of which the employer's decision was made, was thought by them to be inferior to a different medical opinion expressed to them. Moreover, a reason may be material and substantial within the meaning of the section even if the employment tribunal would have come to a different decision as to the extent of the risk. An investigation of the facts by the tribunal will often be required, but it cannot go to the extent of disagreeing with a risk assessment which is properly conducted, based on the properly formed opinion of suitably qualified doctors and produces an answer which is not irrational. This constraint limits the power of tribunals to provide relief to disabled employees, but in my view it follows from the wording of the section, which requires consideration of the reason given by the employer, and recognises the importance of the employer's responsibility for working practices.'

Giving a concurring judgment, LJ gave valuable guidance on the interpretation of both 'material' and 'substantial'. She said that:

'the expression 'material' denotes the quality of the connection which must exist between, on the one hand, the employer's reason for discriminating against the employee and, on the other hand, the circumstances of the particular case. The circumstances of the particular case may include those of both the employer and employee (*Baynton v Saurus Ltd [1999] IRLR 604*) ... The use of the word "material" rather than "relevant" or "applicable" indicates to me that there must be a reasonably strong connection between the employer's reason and the circumstances of the individual case.'

Turning to the term 'substantial', she said that:

'[the] reason which the employer adopted as his ground for discrimination must carry real weight and thus be of substance. However, the word 'substantial' does not mean that the employer must necessarily have reached the best conclusion that could be reached in the light of all known medical science. Employers are not obliged to search for the Holy Grail. It is sufficient if their conclusion is one which on a critical examination is found to have substance.'

Arden LJ also said that 'the standard by which the employer's reason is to be reviewed is an objective one, and not a subjective one' and that the test represents one of many intermediate points on a scale which ranges from 'complete re-trial of the issue which the employer had to decide at one end of the scale ... to absolute deference to the employer's decision provided he acts in good faith, at the other end of the scale'.

In *Williams v J Walter Thompson Group Ltd [2005] IRLR 376*, the Court of Appeal confirmed the approach taken in *Jones*, that the function of the tribunal, in adjudicating on the employer's defence of justification, is to apply an objective test to the reason relied on by the employer and to the known facts The approach is similar to the 'band or range of reasonable responses test' applied in unfair dismissal cases. It is for the tribunal to decide whether the reason advanced by the employer for the treatment of the disabled employee was within the range of what a reasonable employer would have relied on as a material and substantial reason for less favourable treatment.

143.2   MEDICAL EVIDENCE

The decision in *Jones v Post Office* does not mean that the employment tribunal cannot question the medical evidence or the use which the employer makes of that evidence. In the passage quoted above from the judgment of Pill LJ, the risk assessment with which a tribunal cannot disagree is one 'which is properly conducted, based on the properly formed opinion of suitably qualified doctors' and one which 'produces an answer which is not irrational'.

In *Paul v National Probation Service [2004] IRLR 190* the applicant, who had a chronic depressive illness, was offered a job as a part-time community service supervisor, subject to a satisfactory occupational health report. The offer was withdrawn because of an adverse report by an occupational health adviser, who in turn had relied on a form completed by the job applicant and a report from the applicant's GP, who did not know the applicant well. She did not act upon a suggestion by the applicant that she should obtain a report from the applicant's consultant.

The employment tribunal dismissed the complaint, holding that they were not entitled to decide the case on the basis of their own appraisal of the medical evidence. The EAT allowed an appeal.

143.2 Justification and Disability Discrimination

Mrs Justice Cox said that 'the tribunal's reliance on the case of *Post Office v Jones* in this context seems to us to be misplaced. That authority decides that a tribunal is not permitted to make up its own mind on justification on the basis of its own appraisal of an employer's medical evidence, when there has been a properly conducted risk assessment by reference to competent and suitably qualified medical opinion. The nature and qualities of the GP's evidence in this case was plainly in issue before the tribunal, as it had been when the matter was being considered by the respondents, since the GP had never treated Mr Paul for his condition, did not know him well and said nothing in his report about his fitness for the post or his ability to cope with stress. No approach was ever made to Mr Paul's treating consultant, who could have provided an assessment of the kind required.'

Furthermore, medical evidence which was not available at the time of the alleged discrimination can be relevant to the question whether there had been a properly conducted risk assessment and in particular as to whether there was material at that time on which a decision could properly be made. In *Surrey Police v Marshall [2002] IRLR 843*, the applicant had applied for a job as a fingerprint recognition officer. She disclosed that she had bipolar affective disorder (or manic depression). She was offered the post subject to medical clearance, but when her application was considered by a highly qualified force medical officer she was rejected on medical grounds. The medical officer's decision was based on information provided by the applicant herself and a letter from the applicant's GP. The medical officer had not asked for a report from the applicant's consultant (which the applicant had requested should be done).

At the tribunal hearing, there was evidence on behalf of the respondent from an eminent consultant psychiatrist. Part of his evidence was that it would have been unacceptably risky for the respondent to employ the applicant and, moreover, that there was material in the information provided by the applicant and in the GP's report on which the above opinion could properly have been formed.

The employment tribunal held that it could not take account of this evidence because the employers did not have the evidence when they decided to withdraw the offer of employment. Allowing an appeal, the EAT held that this decision was wrong in law. Lindsay J said:

'there is, in our judgment, nothing in *Jones* which barred the tribunal in our case from making findings of fact on some of the medical evidence obtained after Miss Marshall's rejection. Parts of the evidence were material, not as to whether Dr Cahill's assessment of risk was right or wrong in the light of further post-rejection medical inquiry or of other material not before the employer at the time (which we could accept to be inadmissible), but as to whether there was material in Dr Cahill's hands by the point of decision on which a decision such as she made could properly have been made and as to whether it was a decision open to a reasonable decision-maker on the material before her.'

144   Keeping In Touch Days

The *Maternity and Parental Leave etc and the Paternity and Adoption Leave (Amendment) Regulations 2006 (SI 2006 No 2014)*, discussed generally under *Maternity*, introduced the concept of 'keeping in touch' (KIT) days. The new rules permit an employee to undertake up to ten days' work for his or her employer during statutory maternity or adoption leave without losing statutory payments for that week, or bringing the leave to an end. For these purposes, 'work' means any work done under the contract of employment, which may include training or any activity undertaken to keep the employee in touch with the workplace. Any days of work carried out on this basis do not have the effect of extending the total duration of the statutory maternity or adoption leave period. Such work can be carried out at any time during the statutory leave period, except during the two-week compulsory leave period immediately following childbirth. KIT days are intended to encourage women and adopters to make contact during the statutory leave period. Previously, even if they undertook a single day's leave, they would be barred from receiving statutory maternity or adoption pay for that entire week. There are clear policy reasons to facilitate communication between employers and employees during the statutory leave period, so as to facilitate the employee's return to work.

Any work undertaken must be agreed between the parties. The employer cannot compel the employee to carry out work during the statutory leave period. Equally, the employee does not have a right to do work during that period. It is for the parties to decide whether KIT days should be taken as a single block or separately. At the time or writing, It was further proposed to introduce KIT days for fathers who take up additional paternity leave.

145   Knowledge of Disability

145.1   THE STATUTORY POSITION

It is expressly provided, in *section 4A(3)* of the *DDA 1995*, that the duty to make *Reasonable Adjustments* does not apply if the employer does not know, and could not reasonably be expected to know:

(*a*)   [in relation to a job application] that the disabled person is or may be an applicant for the employment; or

(*b*)   [in any case] that the disabled person has a disability and is therefore likely to be placed at a substantial disadvantage in comparison with persons who are not disabled.

It should be noted, however, that actual knowledge of the disability (or that the disabled person is or may be applying for a job) is not required. The employer is liable if he could reasonably be expected to have known. Accordingly employers must not shut their eyes to the obvious or avoid making usual and proper enquiries.

There are no corresponding provisions in relation to complaints of discrimination contrary to *section 3A(1)* being complaints of less favourable treatment for a reason relating to the disability.

145.2   COMPLAINTS OF LESS FAVOURABLE TREATMENT

The law took a wrong turning in the early case of *O'Neill v Symm & Co Ltd [1998] IRLR 233*. An employee who had previously suffered from viral pneumonia was dismissed during an absence from work (having had previous absences). Unknown to the employer, she had had several hospital appointments which had led to a diagnosis of chronic fatigue syndrome (CFS). A tribunal found that the employer understandably attributed the employee's hospital visits to viral illness and had not been put on notice that she had been diagnosed as having CFS. The EAT upheld that decision, ruling that knowledge of the disability, or at least the material features of it as set out in *Schedule 1* to the *DDA 1995*, was relevant as to whether the reason for the employer's action relates to the disabled person's disability.

In a later case, again involving CFS, a different division of the EAT disagreed with the decision in *O'Neill*. In *H J Heinz Co Ltd v Kenrick [2000] IRLR 144*, an employee who had a lengthy absence from work told the employer's medical adviser that he thought that he was suffering from CFS. He was later dismissed because he was unfit to work, although he had asked the employer to wait until he had seen an immunologist before acting. After the dismissal, a diagnosis of CFS was confirmed. The EAT upheld a tribunal's view that, on the facts, the employer, through the medical adviser, knew that the employee was suffering from a disability. More importantly, the EAT held that there is nothing in the statutory language that requires that the relationship between the disability and the treatment should be judged subjectively through the eyes of the employer. The correct test is the objective one of whether the relationship exists, not whether the employer knew about it. This requires employers to pause to consider whether the reason for a dismissal that they have in mind might relate to disability and, if it might, to reflect on the *DDA 1995* and the Code of Practice before dismissing. The EAT pointed out that, unless the test is objective, there will be difficulties with credible and honest yet ignorant or obtuse employers who fail to recognise or acknowledge the obvious. In *London Borough of Hammersmith and Fulham v Farnsworth [2000] IRLR 691*, there was deemed on the facts of the case to be actual knowledge of the disability. It was also held, however, that knowledge of the disability is irrelevant to the question whether the employer has treated the disabled person less favourably than he treats or would treat others and has done so for a reason which relates to the disability. It was expressly stated that the contrary view expressed in *O'Neill* 'is no longer good law.'

145.3   IGNORANCE AND JUSTIFICATION

In *H J Heinz Co Ltd v Kenrick*, however, the EAT held that an employer's unawareness of the disability may be highly material justification and in *London Borough of Hammersmith and Fulham v Farnsworth [2000] IRLR 691* it was stated that neither knowledge nor lack of knowledge is a necessary ingredient of justification.

In the case of *British Gas Services Ltd v McCaull [2001] IRLR 60*, a service engineer, whose job involved driving a van, blacked out as a result of an epileptic fit and collided with a post, leaving the van a write-off. His driving licence was withdrawn by the DVLA. His manager was told by the occupational health service that he should work only subject to certain restrictions, including no driving. This meant that he could no longer do his existing job. He rejected an offer of redeployment to clerical work. There was no suitable alternative employment available and he was dismissed.

The tribunal found as a fact that the employer never considered the applicant to be a disabled person, never considered the *DDA 1995* and never considered whether it was under a section 6 duty to the applicant. In these circumstances, the tribunal found that the employer had failed to comply with the *section 6* duty and that this failure was not justified.

The EAT allowed an appeal. Keane J said that the tribunal seemed to be saying that an employer must consciously consider what steps it should take in the context of its duty. There is no automatic breach because an employer is unaware of that duty: the question is not one of such awareness but of what steps the employer took and did not take. A benevolent and conscientious employer with a disabled employee might well take all reasonable steps while remaining entirely ignorant of the statutory duty itself.

A similar approach was adopted by the Court of Session in *Quinn v Schwarzkorpf Ltd [2002] IRLR 602*. The employers dismissed an employee after a sick leave lasting more than five years but did not know that he was disabled. The case appears to have proceeded on the basis that the employer should have been aware of the disability – understandably in view of the length of the absence. The employment tribunal found that there was no possible reasonable adjustment and dismissed the complaint. The Court of Session allowed an appeal by the employer and restored the decision of the employment tribunal.

Lord Coulsfield referred to the finding by the EAT 'that the issue of justification could not arise at all and that the legislation could not be held to contemplate attempts by employers to justify an act later held to be discriminatory on a hypothetical and ex post facto basis.' He went on to say that when the case came before the Court of Session, Counsel for Mr Quinn conceded that the EAT had misdirected themselves on this point, in the light of the relevant authorities. These were the above-mentioned case of *London Borough of Hammersmith and Fulham v Farnsworth* and *Clark v TDG Ltd t/a Novacold [1999] IRLR 318*.

A later decision of the EAT, however, suggests that there will always be a breach of the duty in relation to *Reasonable Adjustments* if the duty arises (because the employer should have known about the disability) but the employer, through ignorance or otherwise, fails to give active consideration to the question of what steps should be taken.

In *Mid-Staffordshire General Hospitals NHS Trust v Cambridge [2003] IRLR 566*, the applicant was a team leader who was dismissed on grounds of incapacity due to ill-health. She was suffering from a bowing of the vocal chords and tracheitis at the time of her dismissal. She had been off work, or working reduced hours, for more than a year. It was held by the employment tribunal that the Trust had failed to seek or obtain a full and proper assessment of her position at any relevant time. The tribunal concluded that her loss should be assessed by reference to what the chances would be of establishing that steps could easily have been taken to enable her to return to her former post or be redeployed to an appropriate alternative post.

The decision was criticised on appeal on the ground that an assessment of what is required is not one of the steps which an employer must take to comply with the duty in relation to *Reasonable Adjustments*. No substantive steps which could and should have been taken had been identified. The EAT rejected this criticism and the appeal. Keith J said:

'There must be many cases in which the disabled person has been placed at a substantial disadvantage in the workplace, but in which the employer does not know what it ought to do to ameliorate that disadvantage without making enquiries. A proper assessment of what is required to eliminate the disabled person's disadvantage is therefore a necessary part of the duty.'

Keith J also said that the tribunal's approach of assessing loss on a percentage chance basis could not properly be criticised. He said that it 'is true that the law only recognises the assessment of loss by reference to the loss of a chance when liability has been established, but that principle has not been infringed here.'

On the face of it, it is hard to reconcile this decision with the decisions in the earlier cases mentioned above, since an employer who is unaware of a disability will not normally make a proper assessment of what is required to eliminate the disadvantage at which the disabled person is placed. There may, however, be cases in which even an employer who is unaware of the disability will nevertheless give proper and detailed assessment to all the alternatives to dismissal as part of the consultation and decision-making process which should precede a dismissal on the ground of capability.

146   Language Requirements

Adopting excessive or otherwise unjustifiable language requirements gives rise to complaints of *Indirect Discrimination*. Where English is not the first language of a job applicant from a racial group defined by reference to nationality or national origin, it could be unlawful for an employer to insist on a standard of written or spoken English which is higher than that needed for the safe and effective performance of the job.

In particular, employers should not disqualify job applicants because they are unable to complete an application form unassisted, unless the requirement to complete the form personally is a valid test of the standard of English required for safe and effective performance of the particular job. There are also circumstances in which special arrangements in relation to application forms, and modification of language requirements generally, may be required as a *Reasonable Adjustment* for disabled job applicants.

The responsibilities of individual employees should not be overlooked. Employees from the racial minorities should recognise that in many occupations advancement is dependent on an appropriate standard of English.

It is lawful under *section 35* of the *RRA 1976* for employers and others to afford persons of a particular racial group access to facilities or services to meet their special needs in regard to education, training or welfare. This provision would cover special arrangements to provide language tuition.

147   Lawful Discrimination

An act of discrimination may be lawful in one of the following respects:

(*a*)   if the discrimination is of a kind which has not yet been made unlawful, such as age discrimination;

(*b*)   if the act complained of is outside the scope of the legislation, for example where work has been refused or withdrawn, but the complainant is not an employee even within the extended definition of *Employment*;

(*c*)   where the case is covered by a specific exception, such as the *Genuine Occupational Qualification* exceptions.

It should never be assumed too readily, however, that a particular act can have no implications under discrimination legislation. For example:

(*a*)   the scope of the legislation can be extended in reliance on Articles of the *EC Treaty* (such as *Article 39* on the free movement of labour) or, in the public sector, in reliance on Directives;

(*b*)   an Article of the Treaty or, in the public sector, a Directive can also require a provision containing an exception to be disapplied.

148   Legal Aid

The general principle that legal aid is not available for representation before an employment tribunal stems from the philosophy which lay behind the creation of the original industrial tribunal system. The aim was for a straightforward and easily accessible regime in which legalism was discouraged. For example, costs were rarely to be awarded against an unsuccessful party. But times have changed, and although the fight against legalism continues, no-one can seriously deny that at least a proportion of tribunal cases unavoidably involve complex matters of law. The availability of free advice from trade unions, Citizens' Advice Bureaux, pro bono advisers and consultants and solicitors who offer so-called, 'no win, no fee' schemes has not been enough to ensure that all employees who in truth need competent representation receive it. For example, the quality of many 'no win, no fee' services is seriously open to question.

From the political perspective, making legal aid for representation before a tribunal widely available would carry a significant financial cost. However, the Scottish Executive introduced in 2001 a limited entitlement to legal aid in employment tribunal cases with a view to pre-empting claims that the absence of legal aid breaches the right to a fair trial under the *Human Rights Act 1998*. This assistance is known as ABWOR, i.e. Assistance by Way of Representation: see *Advice and Assistance (Assistance by Way of Representation) (Scotland) Regulations 2003 (SI 2003 No 179)*.

149   Less Favourable Treatment

Less favourable treatment is an important element in *Direct Discrimination*.

The *Discrimination Laws* do not prohibit unreasonable or unfair treatment (although most discriminatory treatment also satisfies both those descriptions). The essence of the definition is that the complainant has been treated less favourably than an actual or hypothetical *Comparator.*

The definition of direct sex discrimination under *section 1(1)(a)* of the *SDA 1975* refers to the actual or hypothetical comparator in the singular. There is direct sex discrimination against a woman if on the ground of her sex a person treats her less favourably than he treats or would treat a man.

The new statutory definitions of *Harassment* do not require a comparison between the treatment received by the complainant and that received by an actual or hypothetical *Comparator.*

150   Liability for Aiding Discrimination

The *Discrimination Laws* each provide that a person who knowingly aids another person to do an unlawful act must be treated as himself doing an unlawful act of the like description. Liability for aiding discrimination arises most frequently in the context of complaints against agents or fellow-employees, because of the provisions under which they are deemed to have 'aided' discrimination by principals or employers – see *Employees – Liability For*.

In the case of *Anyanwu and another v South Bank Students' Union and another [2000] IRLR 36*, two students, both of black African origin, who had been elected as paid officers of the students' union, were expelled from the university on the basis of serious allegations against them. Their expulsion meant that it was inevitable that their contracts of employment with the students' union would be terminated. They had not been employed by the university and the issue in the case was whether the university had knowingly aided their dismissal by the students' union, so as to bring the case within *section 33* of the *RRA 1976*. The Court of Appeal held by a majority that the university could not be said to have done so.

This decision was reversed by the House of Lords: *[2001] IRLR 305*. Lord Bingham of Cornhill said:

'The expression "aids" in *section 33(1)* is a familiar word in everyday use and it bears no technical or special meaning in this context. A person aids another if he helps or assists him. He does so whether his help is substantial and productive or whether it is not, provided the help is not so insignificant as to be negligible. While any gloss on the clear statutory language is better avoided, the subsection points towards a relationship of co-operation or collaboration; it does not matter who instigates or initiates the relationship.'

151   Liability for Employees and Agents

The circumstances in which discrimination by an employee is treated as discrimination by the employer are considered in relation to *Employees – Liability For*.

There is a distinction between the liability for an employee and that for an agent. An employer is liable for discrimination by an employee in the course of his or her employment, whether or not that discrimination was authorised by the employer, subject only to the defence that the employer has taken all *Reasonably Practicable Steps* to prevent the act of discrimination or acts of that description. A principal is responsible for anything done by a person as his agent only if it was done with the principal's authority (whether express or implied and whether precedent or subsequent). The distinction is, however, of limited importance in practice – see *Principals and Agents*.

152   Like Work

In an *Equal Pay* case, if the claimant's job and the comparator's job have not been given the same value in a *Job Evaluation* study, the next question to be considered is whether the claimant's work and the comparator's work are like work. There are two questions:

(*a*)   is the work of the same or a broadly similar nature;

(*b*)   are the differences (if any) between the things the claimant does and the things the comparator does not of practical importance in relation to terms and conditions of employment?

The *EPA 1970* expressly states that in comparing the work regard shall be had to the frequency or otherwise with which any differences occur in practice, as well as to the nature and extent of the differences.

The case of *Capper Pass Ltd v Lawton [1976] IRLR 366* illustrates that quite considerable differences between two jobs may nevertheless not be of practical importance in relation to terms and conditions of employment. In that case the claimant worked as a cook for the directors of a company, providing lunch for between 10 and 20 persons per day. The two male comparators were assistant chefs who provided 350 meals a day for six sittings in the factory canteen. It was held that the claimant and the comparators were employed on like work, so that she was entitled to the higher hourly rate which they enjoyed.

153   Local Authorities

Local authorities are major employers. They are also *Public Sector* employers, so that the *Equal Treatment Directive* and other *Directives* have direct effect and can be relied on in any proceedings if the relevant provisions are sufficiently precise. They are subject to the *Equality Duties*, as are other public bodies, as well as the *Freedom of Information* regime.

154   Long-term Adverse Effect

154.1   THE 12-MONTH DURATION

Section 1(1) of the *DDA 1995* provides that, for there to be a 'disability', the effect which a physical or mental impairment has on a person's ability to carry out normal day-to-day activities must be 'a substantial and long-term adverse effect'.

Paragraph 2 of *Schedule 1* to the *DDA 1995* states that the effect of an impairment is a long-term effect if:

(*a*)   it has lasted at least 12 months;

(*b*)   the period for which it lasts is likely to be at least 12 months; or

(*c*)   it is likely to last for the rest of the life of the person affected.

It is not necessary for the effect to be the same throughout the relevant period. The main adverse effect might disappear permanently or temporarily while one or other effects on ability to carry out normal day-to-day activities continue or develop. Provided the impairment continues to have, or is likely to have, such an effect throughout the period, there is a long-term effect.

154.2   RECURRING EFFECTS

It is also stated, in *paragraph 2(2)* of *Schedule 1 to* the *DDA 1995*, that, where an impairment ceases to have a substantial adverse effect on a person's ability to carry out normal day-to-day activities, it is to be treated as continuing to have that effect if that effect is likely to recur. It is noted in the statutory Guidance that conditions which recur only sporadically or for short periods (e.g. epilepsy) can still qualify. The *1996 Regulations (SI 1996 No 1455)*, however, specifically exclude seasonal allergic rhinitis (e.g. hayfever) from this category, except where it aggravates the effects of an existing condition. The Guidance also gives the example of a condition such as rheumatoid arthritis. A person with this condition may experience effects for a few weeks and then have a period of remission. If the effects are likely to recur beyond 12 months after the first occurrence, they are to be treated as long-term.

The Guidance states that the likelihood of recurrence should be considered, taking all the circumstances into account. But the possibility that 'coping strategies' may legitimately break down should be taken into account, if relevant, when assessing the likelihood of a recurrence.

The Guidance states that an event is likely to happen if it is more probable than not that it will happen. In assessing the likelihood of an effect lasting for any period, account should be taken of the total period for which the effect exists. This includes any time before the point when the discriminatory behaviour occurred as well as time afterwards. Account should also be taken of the typical length of such an effect on an individual, and any relevant factors specific to the individual in question, such as the general state of health and age.

The Guidance also refers to the question of medical or other treatment. If the treatment is likely to cure an impairment, this should be taken into consideration. If, however, the treatment simply delays or prevents a recurrence, and a recurrence would be likely if the treatment stopped, then the treatment is to be ignored and the effect is to be regarded as likely to recur.

154.3   **DATE OF ASSESSMENT**

It was held in the case of *Cruickshank v VAW Motorcast Ltd [2002] IRLR 24* that the material time at which to assess the disability is the time of the alleged discriminatory act.

This does not mean, however, that a tribunal considering whether an impairment was, at the relevant date, likely to continue or recur must (or even may) disregard evidence of what has actually happened in practice since the relevant date. The need to take into account the continuation or recurrence of the impairment beyond the relevant date was stated by the EAT in *Greenwood v British Airways plc [1999] IRLR 600*. Reference was made to paragraph B8 of the Guidance, which states that 'account should be taken of the total period for which the effect exists. This includes any time before the point when the discriminatory behaviour occurred as well as time afterwards'. This cannot mean that the fact that an adverse effect has continued for a period after the alleged act of discrimination is conclusive evidence that the effect was likely to continue for that period; it is, however, relevant evidence in assessing what the likelihood was at the date of the alleged act of discrimination.

154.4   **PAST DISABILITY**

A person who has had a disability within the statutory definition is protected from discrimination (i.e. less favourable and unjustified treatment for a reason which relates to that past disability) even if he or she has since recovered or the effects have become less substantial. In deciding whether a past condition was a disability, its effects count as long-term if they lasted 12 months or more after the first occurrence, or if a recurrence happened more than 12 months after the first occurrence or continued until the end of that 12-month period.

In *Greenwood v British Airways plc*, one of the reasons why the EAT upheld the appeal was that, on the facts, the applicant had a past disability. He had some years previously had an impairment which had had a substantial adverse effect on his ability to carry out normal day-to-day activities and that substantial adverse effect had recurred more than 12 months after the date of the first recurrence.

155   Market Forces

It was held by the House of Lords in *Rainey v Greater Glasgow Health Board [1987] IRLR 26* that a *Material Factor* defence in an *Equal Pay* case does not necessarily fail because it involves market forces. That, however, was a case where it was necessary to pay higher wages in order to recruit skilled persons from the private sector and there were significant numbers of both men and women in the existing employees on lower pay and the new employees on higher pay. Any material factor defence which involves reliance on market forces will be very carefully examined to ensure that it is genuinely unrelated to the sex of the employees concerned. For instance, a 'market forces' argument based on a 'need to compete' which depends on the historically low-paid work done mainly by women in, say, the catering industry, is not genuinely due to a material difference other than the difference of sex, as appears from the later House of Lords decision in *Ratcliffe v North Yorkshire County Council [1995] IRLR 439.*

156   Marriage Discrimination

The definition of discrimination under the *SDA 1975* includes discrimination against a married person of either sex, but only for the purposes of Part II of the Act, which is the part relating to discrimination in the employment field.

Most complaints of marriage discrimination are of indirect discrimination, for example where requirements to work full-time or relocate or attend residential courses have a *Disparate Impact* on married women compared with unmarried women. In most such cases, however, there is also disparate impact on women compared with men.

157   Married Couples

Under the *SDA 1975*, the *Genuine Occupational Qualification (GOQ)* exception applies where a job is one of two to be held by a married couple. This means that, for example, if two employees are required to manage a club or public house, the employer can discriminate in favour of a married couple and against two men or two women who wish to live and work together.

Regulation 24 of the *SOR 2003* states that nothing in *Part II* or *III* of the Regulations 'shall render unlawful anything which prevents or restricts access to a benefit by reference to marital status'. This rules out the possibility of claiming that restricting benefits to married persons can be indirect discrimination for the purposes of the *SOR 2003*.

158   Material Factor

Many *Equal Pay* cases fail, even though the complainant can establish that the complainant's work and the comparator's work are *Like Work* or work of *Equal Value*.

The reason is that an *Equality Clause* does not operate in relation to any difference in pay or other contract terms if the employer can show that that difference is genuinely due to a material factor which is not the difference of sex – see *Equal Pay*.

In a *Like Work* case, or one based on a *Job Evaluation*, the material factor to be relied on must be a material difference between the complainant's case and the comparator's case. In an *Equal Value* case, the material factor may be of a more general nature and need not be a material difference between the two individual cases.

A material factor defence should always be raised by a respondent at the outset, in the response (or by way of a prompt application to amend if it does not come to light until later). In equal value cases, a material factor defence is generally considered before the tribunal decides whether the two jobs are of equal value (and before an *Independent Expert* is appointed to report on that question).

159   Maternity

The rights to maternity leave are contained in *sections 71–75* of the *Employment Rights Act 1996* and in *Part II* of the *Maternity and Parental Leave etc. Regulations 1999 (SI 1999 No 3312* as amended). The provisions relating to statutory maternity pay are contained in *sections 164–171* of the *Social Security Contributions and Benefits Act 1992*. With the coming into force of the *Work and Families Act 2006*, the rules have been significantly revised in relation to women whose expected week of childbirth is on or after 1 April 2007.

The main provisions of the statutory scheme for maternity leave for those who did not benefit from the changes in 2007 could be summarised as follows:

(*a*)   ordinary maternity leave is for 26 weeks, during which the employee continues to be entitled to contractual benefits (other than relating to remuneration);

(*b*)   an employee is entitled to additional maternity leave of 26 weeks if she has been continuously employed for at least 26 weeks ending with the 15th week before the expected week of childbirth;

(*c*)   certain contractual terms remain in force during additional maternity leave, including the employee's right to compensation in the event of redundancy and her implied obligation of good faith, but she is not entitled to contractual benefits (such as provision of a car) during this period unless the employer has expressly agreed to provide them (note, however, the decision of the High Court in *Equal Opportunities Commission v Secretary of State for Trade and Industry [2007] IRLR 327*, that the rules on the distinction between ordinary and additional maternity leave need to be 'recast');

(*d*)   failure to return to work at the end of the additional maternity leave period does not lead to the automatic termination of the employment.

Regulation 10 of the 1999 Regulations gives a woman on maternity leave an important right where she is at risk of dismissal on the ground of redundancy. If there is a suitable available vacancy, she must be offered that vacancy (on terms and conditions which are not substantially less favourable than those of her existing contract) in priority to any employee who is not on maternity leave.

There have been several cases in which it has been unsuccessfully argued that the terms of the statutory maternity scheme infringe the principles of Community law (particularly *Article 141*), for example because a woman on maternity leave is treated less favourably than a man on sick leave.

The main reason why such challenges have been unsuccessful was stated by the ECJ in the case of *Gillespie and others v Northern Health and Social Services Board and others [1996] IRLR 214*, a case in which the ECJ rejected a claim that women should continue to receive full pay during maternity leave. The judgment contained the following passage:

'It is well-settled that discrimination involves the application of different rules to comparable situations or the application of the same rule to different situations ... The present case is concerned with women taking maternity leave provided for by national legislation. They are in a special position which requires them to be afforded special protection, but which is not comparable either with that of a man or with that of a woman actually at work.'

It was, however, held in the above case that, insofar as maternity pay is based on the employee's average pay when she is at work, she must benefit from any relevant pay rise, even if backdated.

In the case of *Boyle v Equal Opportunities Commission [1998] IRLR 717*, the ECJ considered, amongst other things, a contractual term under which annual holiday entitlement accrued only during what is now the ordinary maternity leave period, not the additional maternity leave period. It was held that this term is not incompatible with Community law. Statutory leave may accrue under the *Working Time Regulations 1998*.

It is, however, contrary to the *Equal Treatment Directive* for a woman to be disadvantaged in her working conditions, on her return to work, by reason of having taken maternity leave. It was held in *CNAVTS v Thibault [1998] IRLR 399* that it was contrary to the Directive for a woman on maternity leave to be deprived of her right to an annual assessment of her performance and therefore of the opportunity to qualify for promotion to a higher pay grade.

The *Maternity and Parental Leave etc and the Paternity and Adoption Leave (Amendment) Regulations 2006 (SI 2006 No 2014)* amend the 1999 Regulations in various respects for employees whose expected week of childbirth is on or after 1 April 2007.

Importantly, the qualifying period of length of service required for the right to additional maternity leave is removed. Thus a woman whose expected week of confinement is on or after 1 April 2007 will be entitled to a maximum of 52 weeks' maternity leave – regardless of length of service. The distinction between the different types of leave endures, however, so as to cater for different contractual rights between the first and second six-month periods, as well as the slightly different rights on returning to work after ordinary and additional maternity leave respectively.

The length of notice an employee intending to return before the end of maternity leave must give is doubled from 28 days to eight weeks, so as to give employers more time to plan their staffing needs. The length of time by which an employer can postpone an employee's early return to work where the requisite notice has not been given is also extended to eight weeks, although it cannot be postponed to a date after the end of the relevant maternity leave period. Furthermore, where an employee who has previously notified an employer of intention to return early from maternity leave has a change of mind about the return date, and decides to return even sooner, there is a requirement to give eight weeks' notice of the date of intended return. Where the proposed new return date is later than the original return date, the employee must give at least eight weeks' notice ending with the original return date, to give the employer the full benefit of the notice period.

The new regime also introduces the concept of 'keeping in touch' (KIT) days. An employee can add up to ten days' work for the employer during statutory maternity leave without losing statutory payments for that week, or bringing the leave to an end. 'Work' for these purposes means any work done under the contract of employment, and may include training or any activity undertaken for the purpose of the employee keeping in touch with the workplace. Further, any days of work carried out under the relevant provisions do not have the effect of extending the total duration of the statutory maternity leave period. Such work can be carried out at any time during the statutory leave period, except during the compulsory two-week period immediately following childbirth.

The objective is to avoid discouraging women from making contact during the statutory leave period, recognising the desirability for both employees and employers of adequate communication during the leave period for the purpose of facilitating a return to work. Going into work for 'appraisals' or 'team meetings' are amongst the possibilities that were mentioned by Ministers during the parliamentary debate.

Any work done on this basis must be agreed between the parties. The employer has no right to require an employee to carry out work during the statutory maternity leave period. Nor does the employee have a right to do work during such a period. It is a matter for the parties to agree whether KIT days should be taken as a single unit or separately. An employee who undertakes, considered undertaking, or refused to undertake KIT days is entitled to protection against detriment pursuant to *section 47C* of the *Employment Rights Act 1996*. To dismiss an employee for undertaking, considering undertaking, or refusing to undertake KIT days is automatically unfair. It is also made clear that reasonable contact is permitted during the statutory leave period, with either party being entitled to make contact from time to time without the leave period being brought to an end.

The maternity pay period is extended from 26 weeks to a potential maximum of 52 weeks. The 1992 Act as amended provides that the period for paying maternity allowance is to be the same as that for statutory maternity pay, but for the time being, the maternity pay period will be restricted to 39 weeks. The government intends the maternity pay period to be increased to the full 52 weeks by the end of this Parliament, so as to harmonise periods of maternity leave and maternity pay. Until then, three months maternity leave will remain unpaid, unless maternity pay is supplemented by contractual benefits.

With effect from 1 April 2007, the previous exemption for small employers, with five or fewer employees, is removed.

160   Medical Advice and Evidence

160.1   RELEVANT CIRCUMSTANCES

Any prudent employer will seek medical advice before dismissing an employee because of a long-term and continuing absence. Otherwise the dismissal will almost certainly be unfair and may also involve disability discrimination.

Medical advice should also be sought in other cases. For example:

(a)   An employee has had frequent short sickness absences, to the extent that dismissal is being considered. Could these absences be linked to an underlying medical condition, amounting to a disability?

(b)   An employee has a serious illness or accident. Has he or she become disabled, so that the employer must consider *Reasonable Adjustments* under the *DDA 1995*?

(c)   A pool of employees for redundancy selection includes one who is or may be disabled and who scores badly on one or more of the selection criteria. Is the employee disabled and if so has the disability adversely affected the employee's score?

(d)   An offer of employment is made conditionally on a satisfactory reference from a previous employer. That reference reveals a poor attendance record. Could that poor record be caused by a disability?

Furthermore, medical reports and evidence will be part of the material placed before the employment tribunal in almost every disability discrimination case where the respondent does not concede that the complainant is disabled.

160.2   IMPORTANCE OF MEDICAL EVIDENCE

Useful guidance as to the role of a medical expert in cases concerning the question of whether there is a disability was provided in *Abadeh v British Telecommunication plc [2001] IRLR 23*. The EAT said:

'It is not the task of the medical expert to tell the tribunal whether the impairments were or were not substantial. That is the question which the tribunal itself has to answer. The medical reports should deal with the doctor's diagnosis of the impairments, the doctor's observation of the applicant carrying out day-to-day activities and the ease with which he was able to perform those functions, together with any relevant opinion as to prognosis and the effect of medication. (*Vicary v British Telecommunications plc [1999] IRLR 680*).'

In *Kapadia v London Borough of Lambeth [2000] IRLR 699*, Pill LJ pointed out that there will be cases in which a tribunal is not obliged to accept medical evidence, even where that evidence is uncontested. The evidence on the basis of which a doctor has formed an opinion may be rejected, or it may be clear that the medical witness misunderstood the evidence which he was invited to consider in expressing his opinion. That was not the position in *Kapadia*. There was uncontested medical evidence that the employee's anxiety, neurosis and depression would have had a substantial adverse effect on his normal day-to-day activities, but for the fact that he had received medical treatment. Indeed, the evidence was that without the medical treatment, which took the form of counselling sessions by a consultant clinical psychologist, there would have been a very strong likelihood of a total mental breakdown. There was no contrary expert medical evidence or challenge to the factual bases of the opinions expressed by two medical experts. The employment tribunal had been wrong to substitute, for the opinions of the two experts, their own impressions of the employee formed in the course of a tribunal hearing which took place a year at least after the relevant date at which his medical state had to be considered.

160.3 **THE LIMITS OF MEDICAL EVIDENCE**

Although guidance was given about the matters which *should* be covered by the medical expert, the actual issue in both *Vicary* and *Abadeh* was whether the tribunal had relied too heavily on the evidence of the medical expert. These two cases establish that it is for the tribunal, not for the medical expert, to decide:

(*a*)   if a particular activity is a normal day-to-day activity;

(*b*)   if the overall adverse effect of an impairment is substantial;

(*c*)   if, having regard to these and other relevant matters, the complainant is disabled.

This guidance is also relevant to employers faced with management decisions in circumstances such as those outlined at the beginning of this chapter. An employer cannot safely delegate to a medical expert the task of deciding whether a particular employee or job applicant is or is not disabled. Clearly, as part of the assessment, the employer must:

(*a*)   seek medical advice;

(*b*)   put the relevant questions to the medical expert (in accordance with the guidance in *Abadeh*);

(*c*)   try to ensure that the medical expert has all the information needed to answer those questions.

Having obtained the report, however, the employer must then carry out the same careful assessment as that which would be carried out by an employment tribunal considering the question whether the individual is disabled. In carrying out the assessment, the employer should assume that there is a disability in any borderline or doubtful case, bearing in mind that:

(*a*)   further information may come to light which was not available to the employer or the medical adviser;

(*b*)   the medical adviser's opinion may well be challenged by medical evidence on the other side if the case goes to a tribunal hearing;

(*c*)   an employer and a tribunal, both carrying out an assessment objectively and conscientiously, may reach different conclusions, especially in a borderline case.

160.4 **CONFIDENTIALITY**

In *London Borough of Hammersmith and Fulham v Farnsworth [2000] IRLR 691*, the employers withdrew a job offer after receiving an adverse report from their occupational health physician. The adverse report was based on the candidate's medical history, even though her health had been good for the last year. If the employers had made further enquiries into the medical history, they would have found that there

287

was no good reason for not employing the candidate. They failed to make those enquiries. It was their practice not to enquire into any candidate's medical history, because of the issue of confidentiality.

Although the occupational health physician was not employed by the employers, she was their agent. By their practice of denying themselves information as to the medical history upon which the occupational health physician made her report, the employers constituted the physician a relevant decision-maker as to whether the candidate should be employed. It was decided by the EAT that their self-denying practice of not making further enquiries as to the candidate's medical history after receiving the report was not justified by any supposed duty of confidence owed by the employers to the candidate.

On the contrary, the position was as follows:

(*a*)   The occupational health physician was acting on behalf of the employers.

(*b*)   The candidate was aware of this.

(*c*)   The consent which she had given for medical information to be provided was for it to be provided to the employers (not simply to the physician).

(*d*)   The purpose of the medical examination and the purpose for which the candidate gave consent for information to be given to the employers was to enable them to reach a decision as to whether or not she would be employed by them.

The medical information which was provided was and remained confidential information, but it should have been made available to those making the decision on the candidate's employment and not only to the physician. Both the decision-makers and the physician were then under a duty not to use or disclose the information for any other purpose, except with the candidate's prior consent. It was suggested also that if she had been employed then the information could (pursuant to the consent already given by the candidate) have been used for legitimate purposes relating to her employment (for example in relation to the duty to make *Reasonable Adjustments*).

A different issue of confidentiality was considered by the Court of Appeal in *Kapadia*. The medical evidence given on behalf of the complainant in that case had gone unchallenged. There was a suggestion that this was because an independent doctor nominated by the employers had refused to provide a report to them without first obtaining the complainant's consent. It was stated by Lord Justice Pill that the report should have been disclosed. He said:

> 'By consenting to being examined on behalf of the employers the claimant was consenting to the disclosure to the employers of a report resulting from that examination. A practice under which a person has agreed to be examined in circumstances such as these, but then claims a veto upon disclosure of the report to those who obtained it is not, in my view, a good practice. Indeed it is an impediment to the fair and expeditious conduct of litigation.'

161   Men – Discrimination Against

The *SDA 1975* covers discrimination against men as well as discrimination against women. The definitions of direct and indirect discrimination in *section 1* refer to discrimination against a woman, but *section 2* then states that *section 1*, and other provisions relating to sex discrimination against women, are to be read as applying equally to the treatment of men. The only proviso is that special treatment afforded to women in connection with pregnancy or childbirth is not treated as discrimination against men.

Although most complaints under the *EPA 1970* and the *SDA 1975* have been presented by women, there have also been many equal pay and sex discrimination complaints by men. For example, there are still employers who discriminate against men when recruiting for secretarial work. There has also traditionally been discrimination against men in relation to *Pensions*, as in the leading case of *Barber v Guardian Royal Exchange Assurance Group [1990] IRLR 240*.

The *EPA 1970* adopts a similar approach to that in the *SDA 1975*. The *EPA 1970* refers to the operation of equality clauses in favour of women and to complaints by women, but *section 1(13)* states that provisions framed with reference to women and their treatment relative to men are to be read as applying equally in a converse case to men and their treatment relative to women.

162   Ministers of Religion

Questions often arise as to whether a member of the clergy has employment rights. Members of the clergy may be regarded as holding an office and it is sometimes suggested that the spiritual nature of their duties are incompatible with the existence of a contract of employment. Even if that is the case, however, they may be protected by the wider definition of *Employment* and have rights under the *Discrimination Law*. This point emerged clearly from the decision of the House of Lords in *Percy v Church of Scotland Board of National Mission [2006] IRLR 195,* where the House of Lords ruled that an associate minister's relationship with the Church of Scotland constituted 'employment' within the meaning of *section 82(1)* of the *SDA 1975* even though she was not an employee in the conventional sense and did not have the right to claim unfair dismissal. She was employed under a contract 'personally to execute' work and was entitled to bring her claim of sex discrimination against the Church in an employment tribunal. Her agreement with the Church had all the ingredients that would be needed for it to be treated by the courts as intended to create legal obligations as between the parties. The fact that her status might readily be described as an ecclesiastical office 'led nowhere'. Holding an office and being in 'employment' were not inconsistent. Lady Hale made the point that the fact that the worker has very considerable freedom and independence in how she performs the duty of her office does not take her outside the definition of 'employment'. Lord Nicholls added that it was time to recognise that employment arrangements between a church and its ministers should not lightly be taken as intended to have no legal effect and, in consequence, its ministers denied protection.

In *New Testament Church of God v Stewart [2007] IRLR 178*, the EAT went further, holding that a pastor with an American church operating in England could bring an unfair dismissal claim and it expressed the view that:

> 'the House of Lords in *Percy* ... have reversed the traditional thinking on the issue as to whether the parties to the contract as a minister of religion did intend to be legally bound in two very important respects. Firstly, that they have cast considerable doubt upon, if not reversed, the old presumption that a minister and a church do not intend to enter into legal relations; and secondly that an individual can be an employee as well as office holder and thus the task is to determine whether a contract existed at all and if so whether it was a contract of employment, disregarding any presumption against an intention to enter into legal relations.'

In short, there is no general rule of law and that a church minister is an employee, but equally there is no presumption that he or she is not. Everything depends upon the facts of a particular case.

Section 19 of the *SDA 1975* authorises discrimination in relation to employment (and also any authorisation or qualification by a *Qualifying Body*) for purposes of an authorised religion by limiting the employment (or the authorisation or qualification) to:

(*a*)   men;

(*b*)   women; or

(*c*)   persons who are not undergoing and have not undergone *Gender Reassignment*.

The discrimination in these cases is permitted if the limitation is imposed so as to:

(*a*)   comply with the doctrines of the religion; or

(*b*)   avoid offending the religious susceptibilities of a significant number of its followers.

The appointment of a person as a minister of religion would no doubt be covered by the general *Genuine Occupational Qualification* provision in *Regulation 7* of the *RBR 2003* and the specific one in *Regulation 7(1)* and *7(3)* of the *SOR 2003* (where the employment is for purposes of an organised religion).

163 Mobility

163.1 MOBILITY REQUIREMENTS AND ASSUMPTIONS

The issue of mobility can arise in several contexts. For example:

(*a*) there is a business need to move an employee to a different establishment;

(*b*) alternative employment on redundancy involves relocation;

(*c*) a move is a condition of a promotion;

(*d*) a job involves considerable travel and overnight stays;

(*e*) contracts of employment contain a standard mobility clause;

(*f*) assumptions about mobility are made when selecting staff.

Sometimes it is the employee himself who wishes to move and is denied the opportunity. That issue is considered in *Transfers*. This chapter is concerned with mobility requirements as a *Detriment* and also in the context of *Recruitment* and also with assumptions about mobility in the context of *Selection*.

163.2 MOBILITY CLAUSES

If a contract of employment gives the employer the right to require the employee to change working locations, either generally or on promotion, that contract term can be challenged if it has a discriminatory effect under the *Discrimination Laws*. The fact that the employee has willingly signed the contract does not bar a complaint about a term which is unlawful under the discrimination legislation. Furthermore, the employee does not have to wait until he or she is required to move.

The latter point was considered by the Court of Appeal in the case of *Meade-Hill and National Union of Civil and Public Servants v British Council [1995] IRLR 478*. This case concerned a mobility clause under which Officers at and above a specified grade were required to 'serve in such parts of the United Kingdom . . . as the Council may in its discretion require'. Mrs Meade-Hill, having agreed to the clause a year or two earlier, was faced with the prospect of a compulsory move to Manchester. That move would have caused difficulties because her husband, who earned substantially more than she did, would also have had to move. Accordingly she and her union issued proceedings in the County Court (which was the appropriate procedure at the time) under section 77 of the SDA 1975.

The application was dismissed in the County Court on the ground that it was impossible to say in the abstract whether the mobility clause did discriminate; it would be necessary for Mrs Meade-Hill to wait until she was required to move and then consider that concrete factual situation.

The Court of Appeal, by a majority, allowed her appeal. The key elements of the decision were:

(*a*) The contract term itself could be challenged – it was not necessary to wait until the mobility requirement was implemented.

(*b*) The matter was to be judged as at the date when the contract was made.

(*c*)   The proportion of women who were primary wage earners was considerably smaller than the proportion of men in that category.

(*d*)   It followed that the clause was unlawful unless the British Council could justify it.

The case was remitted to the County Court to consider the question of justification. Millett LJ suggested that it was likely that justification could be proved. The British Council had only to show a need to be in a position if circumstances so required at any time in the future to direct an employee of the relevant grade to work elsewhere in the United Kingdom. Furthermore, even if the clause could not be justified in its present form, relatively minor adjustments could remove the questionable aspects of the clause.

Employers may also be required to consider *Reasonable Adjustments* to mobility clauses. If an employee who has signed a contract containing a mobility clause is or becomes subject to a disability which would prevent him or her from complying with the clause if so required, the employer must consider whether it is reasonably practicable to remove or modify the clause.

163.3   RECRUITMENT, SELECTION AND PROMOTION

The issues of indirect discrimination and reasonable adjustments can also arise before the contract is entered into, at the stage when the employer is advertising the post, preparing a job description or making a job offer. These issues can also arise when existing employees are being considered for promotion.

A woman may be able to make out a case of indirect sex discrimination if her inability, because of her domestic circumstances, to sign a mobility clause prevents her from:

(*a*)   applying for a particular post;

(*b*)   accepting an offer of a post;

(*c*)   accepting a promotion.

She would, of course, need to be able to show that the requirement to sign a mobility clause has a disproportionate impact on women. Employers who are taking steps to fill a job vacancy, whether internally or externally, must also have regard to the impact of the clause on disabled employees or applicants. Consideration must always be given to the possibility of removing or modifying the clause where it operates as a bar to a disabled worker.

The question of reasonable adjustment must also be considered where the duties of the post involve travel and overnight stays. The *DDA 1995* requires the employer to consider modifying the job description (particularly where the duties in question form only a small part of the job), in order to make the job available to a worker whose disability would limit his or her ability to travel or stay away overnight.

Direct Discrimination is most likely to arise where the employer makes selection or promotion decisions on the basis of unwarranted assumptions. It would be a clear case of direct discrimination if an employer assumed, without enquiry, that a female candidate would be less capable than a male candidate of complying with a mobility clause; a disabled candidate would have an unanswerable claim of disability discrimination if turned down for a post because the employer simply assumed that he would not be able to undertake job duties involving travel and overnight stays.

163.4   **REDUNDANCY SELECTION**

Where redundancies have been declared, but there are alternative jobs available, the employer has an absolute obligation, under *Regulation 10* of the *Maternity and Parental Leave etc. Regulations 1999 (SI 1999 No 3312)*, to give priority, in relation to any suitable vacancy, to a woman returning from maternity leave.

The employer must then have regard to the duties not to discriminate unlawfully and to make adjustments under the *DDA 1995*. Suppose, for example, that a disabled employee is facing dismissal, whether for redundancy or inability to continue in his or her present post, and there are two vacancies, one of which involves a mobility requirement. If, because of the disability, the employee cannot comply with that requirement, then the section 6 duty may require the employer to give the disabled employee priority in relation to the other vacant post, provided that he or she is a suitable candidate.

163.5   **COMPULSORY MOVES**

When an employer implements a mobility clause, and requires an employee to move (or be dismissed for refusing to do so), the fact that the employer is acting in pursuance of a contractual provision is not a defence to a complaint under the discrimination legislation. It is a common feature of discrimination claims that the employer has taken a step which he is contractually at liberty to take but which involves unlawful discrimination.

164   Monitoring

Monitoring is an important part of any *Equal Opportunities Policy*, to ensure that the policy is working effectively. The way in which monitoring should be carried out depends on the size and nature of the organisation and (so far as the prevention of racial discrimination is concerned) the racial composition of the workforce and of the area(s) from which employees are recruited. General guidance is given in the *Codes of Practice* under the *SDA 1975* and the *RRA 1976*.

Regular analysis of the information obtained may indicate a need for investigation and possible corrective action if, for example, women, racial minorities or disabled workers:

(*a*)   are not applying for particular posts;

(*b*)   have a high failure rate when they do apply;

(*c*)   are not well represented in senior positions; or

(*d*)   are concentrated in certain jobs, shifts, sections or departments.

165   National Health Service

The National Health Service is part of the *Public Sector*, so that the *Equal Treatment Directive* and other *Directives* have direct effect. The leading case of *Marshall v Southampton and South-West Hampshire Area Health Authority [1986] IRLR 140* involved employment in the National Health Service.

There is the possibility of *Equal Pay* claims by employees of one NHS body being made in relation to comparators in another NHS body, on the basis that employees in the two bodies are employed in the same service – see *Same Employment*.

Employment at different units run by the same NHS Trust does not necessarily amount to *Same Employment* for the purposes of making a claim under the *EPA 1970*: *Armstrong v Newcastle upon Tyne NHS Hospital Trust [2006] IRLR 124*.

At the time of writing, in excess of 10,000 *Equal Pay* claims were being pursued against NHS employers. The claims are, put simply, for *Back Pay* arising out of the introduction of 'Agenda for Change', which is a *Job Evaluation* scheme jointly established by NHS employers, the Department of Health and trade unions.

Like other *Public Sector* employers, NHS bodies are subject to the *Equality Duties* and the *Freedom of Information* regime.

166   National Origin

There is a distinction between national origin and *Nationality*. In particular:

(*a*)   persons who and whose parents were born in England, Scotland, Wales and Northern Ireland could have four different national origins but the same British nationality;

(*b*)   the great majority of men and women working in Great Britain are British citizens, sharing the same nationality, but racial minority workers have a wide variety of national origins because they (or more commonly their parents or remoter ancestors) were born overseas.

Under the earlier race relations legislation, the distinction between national origin and nationality was important; discrimination on grounds of national origin was covered but discrimination on grounds of nationality was not. Now, however:

(*a*)   discrimination on grounds of nationality or national origin is discrimination on *Racial Grounds* and is, therefore, direct discrimination;

(*b*)   a group of persons defined by reference to nationality or national origin is a *Racial Group* for the purposes of complaints of indirect racial discrimination.

In *BBC Scotland v Souter [2001] IRLR 150*, an English journalist complained of racial discrimination in relation to the non-renewal of his contract as a sports presenter and the appointment of a Scottish woman. He alleged that his national origin was a major factor in the decision. The tribunal considered as a preliminary point whether the English and the Scots are distinct *Racial Groups* by reference to national origin. The case went to the Court of Session, where it was held that the English and the Scots are separate racial groups defined by reference to national origins (although not by reference to ethnic origins).

167   National Security

The *Discrimination Laws* provide that an act done for the purpose of safeguarding national security is not unlawful, provided it is justified.

168   Nationality

Reference has already been made to the distinction between nationality and *National Origin*. Discrimination against a person on grounds of nationality is discrimination on *Racial Grounds* and is, therefore, direct racial discrimination; a group of persons defined by reference to nationality is a *Racial Group* for the purposes of a complaint of indirect racial discrimination.

There is statutory discrimination on grounds of nationality – see *Immigration* and *Work Permits*. No employer (or other person or organisation having a duty not to discriminate) may discriminate on grounds of nationality unless there is a statutory requirement to do so.

169   Night Work

Where an employer requires certain work to be carried out at night, for example on a night shift in a factory, complaints of discrimination could arise in the following circumstances:

(*a*)   an unjustifiable refusal to allow a woman to transfer to the day shift, because of her childcare commitments, could be indirect sex and marriage discrimination;

(*b*)   There may be a need to make *Reasonable Adjustments* (for example by a transfer to the day shift) if an employee has a disability which puts him at a substantial disadvantage when working at night.

The fact that one job is done at night and another by day does not prevent two jobs from being *Like Work* for the purposes of an *Equal Pay* claim. The appropriate way to compensate an employee for working at night is by paying a night shift premium of a reasonable amount.

170   Non-Discrimination Notices

A non-discrimination notice may be served by the EOC under *section 67* of the *SDA 1975* as a result of a *Formal Investigation* by one of the relevant Statutory Commissions.

The person (or organisation) on whom the notice is or is to be served:

(*a*)   must be given notice of the grounds on which the Commission proposes to issue the notice and must be given at least 28 days to make oral or written representations; and

(*b*)   has a right of appeal to an employment tribunal.

A non-discrimination notice may include requirements to change relevant practices or arrangements and provide information, as well as a requirement not to commit any further unlawful acts. The sanction for failure to comply with a non-discrimination notice is an application by the Commission for an injunction (or interdict in Scotland).

The power to issue non-discrimination notices will transfer in October 2007 to the *Commission for Equality and Human Rights*.

171   Normal Day-To-Day Activities

The *DDA 1995* provides that an impairment affects the ability of the person concerned to carry out normal day-to-day activities only if it affects one of the following:

(*a*)   mobility;

(*b*)   manual dexterity;

(*c*)   physical co-ordination;

(*d*)   continence;

(*e*)   ability to lift, carry or otherwise move everyday objects;

(*f*)   speech, hearing or eyesight;

(*g*)   memory or ability to concentrate, learn or understand; or

(*h*)   perception of the risk of physical danger.

The statutory Guidance states that the term 'is not intended to include activities which are normal only for a particular person or group of people. Therefore in deciding whether an activity is a 'normal day-to-day activity' account should be taken of how far it is normal for most people and carried out by most people on a daily or frequent and fairly regular basis.'

The guidance goes on to state, in paragraph C3, that the term:

'does not, for example, include work of any particular form, because no particular form of work is "normal" for most people. In any individual case, the activities carried out might be highly specialised. The same is true of playing a particular game, taking part in a particular hobby, playing a musical instrument, playing sport or performing a highly skilled task. Impairments which affect only such an activity and have no effect on "normal day-to-day activities" are not covered.'

Later paragraphs of the Guidance where adverse effects which would be regarded as substantial are contrasted with adverse effects which would not be so regarded, give various examples of normal day-to-day activities, such as walking short distances, travelling on public transport, lifting everyday objects, holding a normal conversation, reading a newspaper, writing a cheque and crossing the road. An illustration of misunderstandings that may arise is provided by *Vicary v British Telecommunications plc [1999] IRLR 680*. An employment tribunal, having made extensive reference to the Guidance, concluded that 'DIY tasks, filing of nails, tonging hair, ironing, shaking quilts, grooming animals, polishing furniture, knitting, sewing and cutting with scissors' were not 'normal day-to-day activities'. The EAT strongly disagreed: 'These are all activities which most people do on a frequent or fairly regular basis.'

In that case, the EAT stated that it is not for the medical expert to tell the tribunal what is or is not a normal day-to-day activity. That is a question of fact for the tribunal. It is also stated in this case that the statutory Guidance will only be of assistance in marginal cases.

It is an error of law for an employment tribunal to conclude that a particular activity is not a normal day-to-day activity because it is not done by the majority of the population. It was held by the EAT in *Ekpe v Commissioner of Police of the Metropolis*

[2001] IRLR 605 that the tribunal had been wrong to conclude that putting rollers in one's hair and applying makeup are not normal day-to-day activities because they are carried out almost exclusively by women.

In the case of *Abadeh v British Telecommunications plc [2001] IRLR 23*, the tribunal had found that travelling by Underground was not a day-to-day activity for the complainant, because he did not live or work in London, and nor was flying, because his work did not involve having to travel by aeroplane. This was a wrong approach in two respects.

First of all, the EAT pointed out (referring to the Guidance) that 'the question of what is a normal day-to-day activity must be addressed without regard to whether it is normal to the particular applicant.' This would mean, for example, that if a complainant has to do exceptionally heavy lifting at work, and that activity is the only one to be impaired, then he or she is not disabled.

Secondly, the tribunal 'erred in law in finding that travelling by Underground or aeroplane was not a normal day-to-day activity within the meaning of the Act'. This was because 'the matter should be considered not by reference to individual forms of transport but by looking at transport as a whole. Travelling by car or public transport is a normal day-to-day activity for most people and carried out by them on a daily or frequent and fairly regular basis.'

172   Obesity

Statistics suggest that recent years have seen a significant increase in the number of people in England and Wales who are obese. The trend has prompted a debate about whether individuals have remedies under equal opportunities law if they suffer discrimination on the ground of their obesity. Although there is no distinct legal regime outlawing discrimination on grounds of obesity, obese individuals who suffer discrimination at work may nevertheless have certain rights of redress.

Obesity is not (unlike alcoholism) expressly excluded from the scope of the *DDA 1995*. Where obesity is caused by an underlying medical condition that meets the statutory definition of *Disability*, discrimination may be contrary to the *DDA 1995*. In December 2006, the *DDA 2005* removed the requirement that mental impairments must be 'clinically well recognised' in order to be classed as disabilities. Thus, obesity may amount to a disability in law if it is caused by, or causes, mental impairment – examples might include depression or an eating disorder that has a substantial and long-term effect on the employee's day-to-day activities.

Guidance on the *DDA 1995* indicates that a tribunal should take into account how far a person can modify their own behaviour to improve their condition when considering whether that condition amounts to a 'disability'. In the case of obesity, if reasonable exercise, health eating and lifestyle changes – for example – might affect the condition, a tribunal might conclude that the individual did not have a disability.

173   Office-holders

Office-holders, as well as employees, contract workers and partners, are afforded protection against discrimination and harassment. In the *AR 2006*, the *Default Retirement Age* of 65 does not apply to office-holders.

174   Oil and Gas Platforms

The employment provisions of the *Discrimination Laws* cover employment at establishments not only in Great Britain and British territorial waters but also (for the purposes of employment in connection with oil or gas exploration) at establishments in parts of the continental shelf which are designated by order for that purpose.

175   Omissions

The general interpretation section in each of the *Discrimination Laws* provides that any reference to an act includes a deliberate omission. There is, for example, direct racial discrimination when on racial grounds an employer either gives a negative reply to a job application or deliberately omits to reply at all. For the purposes of *Time Limits* a deliberate omission is treated as done when it is decided upon. A person is taken to decide upon an omission:

(*a*)   when he does an act inconsistent with doing the omitted act; or

(*b*)   if he does no such inconsistent act, when the period expires within which he might reasonably have been expected to do the omitted act if it was to be done.

176   Overseas Qualifications

The Code of Practice under the *RRA 1976* recommends that overseas degrees, diplomas and other qualifications which are comparable with UK qualifications should be accepted as equivalents, and not simply be assumed to be of an inferior quality.

Where a job application is made by a foreign national, or a person of overseas national origin, the unjustifiable rejection or downgrading of any overseas qualifications obtained by that person would be an act of indirect racial discrimination.

177   Overseas Work

Under the *SDA 1975*, the *RRA 1976* and the *AR 2006*, employment is to be regarded as being at an establishment in Great Britain unless the employee does his work wholly outside Great Britain.

Under the *RBR 2003* and the *SOR 2003*, employment which is wholly outside Great Britain is covered if:

(*a*)   the employer has a place of business at an establishment in Great Britain;

(*b*)   the work in question is for the purposes of the business carried on at that establishment; and

(*c*)   the employee is ordinarily resident in Great Britain, either at the time when he applies for or is offered the employment or at any time during the course of the employment.

The *DDA 1995* has contained a similar provision since 1 October 2004 and the *RRA 1976* contains a similar provision for cases of alleged discrimination or harassment on grounds of race or ethnic or national origins.

Furthermore, racial discrimination in relation to wholly overseas employment could offend against *Article 39* (formerly *Article 48*) of the *EC Treaty*. This is the Article which relates to the free movement of workers. In *Bossa v Nordstress Ltd [1998] IRLR 284*, the complainant saw an advertisement in the national press for cabin crew to be based in Italy. He was interviewed and asked to produce his passport, which was Italian. He was told that he could not be interviewed because the Italian authorities would not allow the airline to take employees of Italian nationality back to Italy. A tribunal held that it did not have jurisdiction to hear a complaint of direct discrimination on the ground of nationality, because the employment would have been wholly or mainly outside Great Britain and accordingly was not deemed to be at an establishment in Great Britain.

An appeal was allowed by the EAT. The free movement of workers included the right for Mr Bossa to work anywhere within the EC. *Section 8(1)* of the *RRA 1976* prevented him from enforcing that right and had, therefore, to be disapplied.

178 Overtime

The law does not permit sex, racial or disability discrimination, or discrimination in relation to religion or belief, sexual orientation or age in either the allocation of voluntary overtime (see *Benefits*) or in a requirement to work compulsory overtime (see *Detriment*). Payment of standard overtime rates during working hours which are additional to the normal full-time working week does not infringe the principle of *Equal Pay*. Furthermore, there is no requirement to pay overtime rates for *Part-Time Work* where the hours worked exceed the employee's normal part-time hours but fall short of the normal hours of full-time employees.

179 Parental Leave

179.1   The right to take unpaid parental leave is given to both men and women by the *Maternity and Parental Leave etc. Regulations 1999 (SI 1999 No 3312)*.

If an employer decides to give additional parental leave, or to pay employees for the whole or part of their parental leave, then in principle male or female employees should be treated the same. Otherwise there could be a claim under the *SDA 1975* (or the *EPA 1970* if the arrangements are contractual) in respect of the additional leave and under the *EPA 1970* in respect of the pay.

The conditions which must be satisfied before the employee can take statutory parental leave are:

(*a*)   the employee must (subject to transitional provisions) have been continuously employed in the employment for at least a year;

(*b*)   the employee must have or expect to have responsibility for a child.

Unless otherwise agreed (or unless the child is entitled to a disability living allowance) the leave must be taken in segments of one or more weeks, and not in shorter segments. In *Rodway v South Central Trains Ltd [2005] IRLR 583*, the Court of Appeal confirmed that a tribunal was wrong to hold that the legislation accorded parental leave to be taken for one day only. Where all the conditions are satisfied, an employee is entitled to 13 weeks' leave in respect of any individual child (18 weeks if the child is entitled to a disability living allowance). Not more than four weeks' leave may be taken in any one year. For the purpose of the Regulations, a year runs from the date of the birth of the child (or adoption or placement for adoption) or, if later, the date of completion of the qualifying period of one year's continuous employment.

Parental leave must be taken:

(*a*)   by the date of the child's fifth birthday;

(*b*)   in adoption cases, by whichever is the earlier of the child's 18th birthday and the fifth anniversary of the date on which the placement for adoption began; or

(*c*)   if the child is entitled to a disability living allowance, by the child's eighteenth birthday.

There are notice requirements and provisions enabling employers to postpone the date on which leave must be taken, but subject to the special provisions for expectant fathers (see *Paternity Leave*) and similar provisions at the time of a placement for adoption. Apart from these special cases, and unless otherwise agreed, the employee must give at leave 21 days' advance notice before taking any parental leave, specifying the dates on which the period of leave is to begin and end. The employer may, however, postpone the commencement of the period of parental leave for up to six months, subject to the following conditions:

(*a*)   if the employer considers that the operation of his business would be unduly disrupted if the employee were to take the leave during the period identified in the employee's notice;

(*b*)   the employer must consult the employee about the date to which the commencement of the period of leave is to be postponed;

(c)   the employer's notice must be in writing;

(d)   that notice must state the reason for the postponement and must also state the date to which the commencement of the period of leave is to be postponed; and

(e)   the employer's notice must be given to the employee not more than seven days after the employee's notice was given to the employer.

There is an automatic extension if the effect of a written notice of postponement by the employer is to take the period of leave beyond the date by which it would normally have to be taken (e.g. beyond the child's fifth birthday).

179.2   **ADOPTION LEAVE**

The *Paternity and Adoption Leave Regulations 2002 (SI 2002 No 2788)* came into force on 8 December 2002. They apply in relation to children placed for adoption on or after 6 April 2003 or matched with a person who is notified as having been matched on or after that date.

The principle is that where two people have been jointly matched with a child for adoption, they agree which of them should be the adopter for the purpose of the right to adoption leave.

There is a qualifying period of 26 weeks' continuous employment ending with the week in which the adopter was notified as having been matched with the child. There are various other conditions and notice requirements.

Ordinary adoption leave is for 26 weeks. It may be followed by additional adoption leave of a further 26 weeks. The person taking adoption leave has the right to statutory adoption pay at the currently prevailing rate for up to 26 weeks. The other provisions relating to ordinary and additional adoption leave are very similar to those relating to ordinary and additional *Maternity* leave. These provisions include the right, as an alternative to redundancy, to be offered alternative employment where there is a suitable available vacancy.

Following the introduction of the *Work and Families Act 2006*, the rules in respect of adoption leave have been amended in relation to adopters whose children are expected to be placed with them for adoption on or after 1 April 2007 (the date on which the child is *actually* placed for adoption is immaterial). Again, the changes are similar to those made in relation to *Maternity* leave and pay. The concept of 'keeping in touch' (KIT) days has also been introduced in relation to adoption leave.

180   Partnerships

Rights under discrimination law are given not only to employees, but also to partners and those who wish to become partners. Exceptionally, the provisions in the *RRA 1976* apply only to firms consisting of six or more partners. Since 19 July 2003, however, the force of that exemption has been much reduced. The special concession for partnerships with fewer than six partners no longer applies in relation to discrimination on grounds of race or ethnic or national origins. It only applies to situations where the discrimination is on grounds of colour or nationality. In addition, the application of discrimination protection to where a partner is expelled from a position as partner has been extended, where the discrimination is on grounds of race or ethnic or national origins, to termination of a partnership without renewal on the same terms, and to where the partnership is terminated by act of the partner in circumstances where he is entitled to terminate it without notice by reason of the conduct of the other.

In *Dave v Robinska [2003] ICR 1248*, the EAT confirmed that the *SDA 1975* applies to a two-partner firm, so that one partner can bring a claim of sex discrimination against the sole remaining partner, in that partner's own name.

The rights given to partners and potential partners are similar to those given to employees and job applicants.

So far as a person who has not yet become a partner is concerned, it is unlawful for a firm to discriminate (within the definition contained in either Act):

(*a*)   in the arrangements made for the purpose of determining who should be offered a position as a partner;

(*b*)   in the terms on which a position is offered; or

(*c*)   by refusing or deliberately omitting to offer a position as a partner.

It is unlawful for a firm to discriminate against an existing partner:

(*a*)   in the way he or she is afforded access to any benefits, facilities or services;

(*b*)   by a refusal or deliberate omission to afford him or her access to any of the above;

(*c*)   by expelling him or her from the partnership; and

(*d*)   by subjecting him or her to any other detriment.

In the *AR 2006*, the *Default Retirement Age* of 65 does not apply to partners; nor does the *Duty to Consider*.

181   Part-Time Work

181.1   INTRODUCTION

An employer's refusal on racial grounds or grounds of gender of an employee's request to transfer to (or from) part-time work would be discrimination in the way the employee is afforded access to opportunities for transfer, contrary to such complaints are not unknown. It would, for example, be direct sex discrimination to grant requests for part-time working when those requests are made by female employees but to refuse a request when made by a male employee, if:

(*a*)   the relevant circumstances of the women's case and the man's case are the same or not materially different; and

(*b*)   the refusal of the man's request is on the ground of his sex.

In practice, however, most complaints are of indirect sex discrimination in refusing a request by a female employee to transfer to part-time working. Such requests are commonly but not exclusively made when the employee returns or is about to return from maternity leave. It is usually not difficult to prove *Disparate Impact* because significantly more women than men have exclusive or primary responsibility for childcare – see *Indirect Discrimination*.

Complaints of indirect sex discrimination may also be made if part-timers are excluded from opportunities for *Promotion*, *Training* or other *Benefits* or if a redundancy procedure is weighted against part-timers.

Differences in the pay and other contractual terms of part-time or full-time workers can also give rise to complaints of *Equal Pay*, so long as the part-timer can identify a suitable full-time *Comparator* of the opposite sex. The mere fact that the complainant's work is done on a part-time basis cannot be relied on as a *Material Factor* to explain or justify the difference in pay or other contract terms. Objective justification is required. The effect of the ECJ decision in the leading case of *Bilka-Kaufhaus GmbH v Weber von Hartz [1986] IRLR 317* is that the employer must be able to show that the measures taken are appropriate for the achievement of a necessary objective on the part of the undertaking.

This was a case on *Article 141* (formerly *Article 119*) of the European Treaty, which has direct effect. Any provisions in the *EPA 1970* which are inconsistent with *Article 141* must be disapplied. This principle has proved to be particularly important in relation to *Pensions*.

181.2   THE DDA 1995

A transfer from full-time work to part-time work must be looked at as a possible *Reasonable Adjustment* in cases where a disability places a disabled worker at a substantial disadvantage if he or she is required to work full-time. If a disabled employee is transferred to part-time work for a reason relating to a disability, it could then be *Disability Discrimination* to treat that employee less favourably than full-time employees in any respect by reason of his or her part-time status.

181.3   THE PART-TIME WORKERS REGULATIONS 2000

The *Part-time Workers (Prevention of Less Favourable Treatment) Regulations 2000 (SI 2000 No 1551)* came into force on 1 July 2000.

The Regulations give rights to part-time workers not to be treated less favourably than comparable full-time workers if:

(*a*)   the treatment is on the ground that the worker is a part-time worker; and

(*b*)   the treatment is not justified on objective grounds.

A complaint may be presented about less favourable treatment relating to:

(*a*)   pay or other contract terms; or

(*b*)   subjection to any other detriment (whether caused by an act or a deliberate omission on the part of the employer).

It is clear, from the official guidance on the Regulations, that the above reference to 'detriment' is intended to include denial of a benefit, such as promotion, training and fringe benefits, as well as detriment in the conventional sense. A successful complainant under the Regulations may be awarded such amount of compensation as the employment tribunal deems to be just and equitable, with no limit on the amount. The compensation may not, however, include compensation for injury to feelings.

To a large extent the rights given by the Regulations overlap with existing rights under the *EPA 1970* and the *SDA 1975*, but they break new ground in the following respects:

(*a*)   the full-time comparator can be of the same sex as the part-time complainant; and

(*b*)   they give a right for the first time to men who suffer detriment (not relating to contract terms) by reason of their status as part-time workers.

The rights under the Regulations do not, however, replace existing rights under the *EPA 1970* and *SDA 1975*. Where there is an overlap, complaints will normally be presented under the *EPA 1970* or *SDA 1975* as well as under the Regulations.

In *Matthews and others v Kent and Medway Towns Fire Authority and others [2006] IRLR 367*, the House of Lords broadened the scope for bringing claims under the Regulations. Decisions of lower courts held that retained and full-time firefighters do not do the 'same or broadly similar work' because full-timers carry out additional duties. By a majority, the House of Lords decided that the focus should be on the similarities in work, not the differences, since some differences are almost inevitable. Baroness Hale said that particular weight should be given to the extent to which their work is exactly the same, and to the importance of that work to the enterprise as a whole.

181.4   **OVERTIME**

The Regulations contain an important provision to bring them into line with case law on *Article 141*. It is not a breach of either the Regulations or *Article 141* or the *EPA 1970* for a part-time worker to be denied overtime rates until he or she has worked the number of hours above which overtime is paid to full-time workers. For example, it would not be unlawful to deny a part-time worker overtime pay (assuming that there is no contractual provision requiring overtime to be paid) in the following circumstances:

(*a*)   the normal working week for full-timers in the organisation is 35 hours and they are paid overtime for any additional hours worked each week;

(*b*)   a part-time worker normally works 15 hours per week; and

(*c*)   in one particular week the part-timer works 30 hours.

182 Past Discrimination

There is a *Time Limit* of three months for presenting a complaint under the employment provisions of the *SDA 1975*, the *RRA 1976*, the *DDA 1995*, the *RBR 2003*, the *SOR 2003* or the *AR 2006*. Broadly speaking, time limits are extended only in exceptional circumstances.

In *BUPA Care Homes (BNH) Ltd v Cann [2006] IRLR 248*, although *section 32(4)* of the *Employment Act 2002* prevents an employee from presenting a complaint to a tribunal where Step 1 of the statutory grievance procedure was not complied with until 'more than one month after the end of the original time limit for making the complaint', the EAT held that this does not have the effect of displacing the tribunal's discretion to extend time in discrimination cases on 'just and equitable grounds'.

Acts of discrimination which have occurred more than three months before the presentation of a complaint can, however, be relevant in one of the following ways:

(a)   The case could be one of discrimination extending over a period – *Continuing Discrimination*.

(b)   The earlier act or acts of discrimination could be relied on as *Evidence* that the more recent treatment now complained of was, for example, on racial grounds.

Allegations of or other steps in relation to earlier acts of discrimination are 'protected acts' for the purpose of a complaint of victimisation.

183   Paternity Leave

There is a statutory right, under the *Paternity and Adoption Leave Regulations 2002 (SI 2002 No 2788)*, to qualify for two weeks' paid paternity leave.

The conditions for this right are that the employee:

(*a*)   has been continuously employed for a period of at least 26 weeks ending with the 15th week before the expected week of the child's birth;

(*b*)   is either the father of the child or married to or the partner of the child's mother;

(*c*)   has or expects to have responsibility (or the main responsibility apart from that of the mother) for the upbringing of the child.

There are further provisions for various special cases and there are notice and evidential requirements.

The employee must take the paternity leave during a period which starts when the child is born and ends either:

(*a*)   56 days after that date; or

(*b*)   56 days after the first day of the expected week of the child's birth (where the child is born before that expected week).

There are separate regulations regarding statutory paternity pay.

The *Work and Families Act 2006* introduces a new right for an employed father or partner of a mother or an adopter to be absent from work for a maximum of 26 weeks to care for a child. This leave, known as additional paternity leave, must be taken before the child's first birthday; it is a right over and above current entitlement to paternity leave. The aim is to allow the mother to return to work after six months and the father (or partner) to take a more active role in childcare responsibilities in the first year of the child's life. Although additional paternity leave is unpaid, a father will be entitled to additional paternity pay if the mother or adopter has not used up all of her entitlements to statutory maternity pay, maternity allowance or statutory adoption pay when she returns to work. At the time of writing, the detail of the new scheme had not been published. The scheme is intended to come into operation by the end of the present Parliament.

184 Pay

184.1 THE MEANING OF PAY

There are many contractual and non-contractual arrangements which affect the pay received by employees.

The terms which are normally contractual include:

(*a*)   hourly rates of pay;

(*b*)   salary, whether paid weekly or monthly;

(*c*)   overtime rates;

(*d*)   shift premia;

(*e*)   commission on sales; and

(*f*)   holiday pay.

The matters which may be either contractual or discretionary include:

(*a*)   bonus arrangements;

(*b*)   access to overtime; and

(*c*)   sick pay (over and above SSP).

Redundancy payments are also treated as pay, whether they are statutory, contractual or discretionary.

Pensions are a form of deferred pay.

184.2 PAY AND DISCRIMINATION

There is direct discrimination whenever an employee is, on one of the proscribed grounds, paid less than another employee is or would be paid. The relevant principles are illustrated by the Court of Appeal decision in *Wakeman and others v Quick Corporation and another [1999] IRLR 424*. Three English managers employed at the London office of a Japanese company complained of direct racial discrimination. Their complaint was that they were paid substantially less than Japanese employees who had originally been employed in Japan and had been temporarily seconded to London. The picture was a complicated one. The company pointed out that they also had Japanese employees who had been hired in London and that these employees were paid on the same scale as non-Japanese employees who had been hired in London. It was argued by the claimants, however, that the locally hired Japanese employees were junior to them.

The claims were rejected by the Employment Tribunal. This decision was upheld on appeal by both the EAT and the Court of Appeal. It was held by the Court of Appeal that the claimants could not claim the same pay as the managers who had been seconded from Japan, even if their work was identical or of equal value to that of the Japanese secondees. This was because the relevant circumstances of the complainants were materially different from those of the Japanese comparators. The latter were secondees and this was an important factor in the difference of pay. The complainants were not secondees; they had been recruited locally.

The locally recruited Japanese employees were not appropriate comparators either. This was because they were junior to the complainants in terms of the work which they carried out.

Accordingly, since there were no actual comparators, the tribunal had to consider how the employer would have treated Japanese employees whose relevant circumstances were the same as those of the claimants or at least not materially different from those of the claimants. This meant that the comparators had to be Japanese employees who were doing similar work, or work of equal value, to the work of the complainants and who were not secondees. There were no actual employees who fitted this description. The tribunal found that there was no evidence that hypothetical Japanese comparators fitting this description would have been paid more than the claimants.

The complaint was one of direct discrimination in relation to rates of pay and it was decided on the basis of a hypothetical comparison. There can be no similar case under the *SDA 1975*.

If an employee has a complaint about rates of pay on grounds of gender, that complaint relates to *Equal Pay* under the *EPA 1970* and it is necessary for the claimant to identify an appropriate comparator of the opposite sex. No complaint about rates of pay, or any other contractual term for the payment of money, may be brought under the *SDA 1975* and no complaint may be based on a hypothetical comparison.

184.3   **THE DDA 1995**

An employee would have a case for disability discrimination if his or her rate of pay were to be reduced, because of an assumption that job performance would be adversely affected by the disability.

Where a disability does in fact cause an employee to work more slowly or less efficiently, the starting point is the employer's duty to make *Reasonable Adjustments*. It may be possible, through the provision or adaptation of equipment, or by making other adjustments, to improve the employee's performance.

Once the duty to make *Reasonable Adjustments* has been fully complied with, there would probably be a defence of justification to any complaint of disability discrimination in relation to the pay received. That defence is likely to be available in whatever way the slow or inefficient work affects the pay received, whether in relation to:

(*a*)   the amount of weekly pay;

(*b*)   the amount of a productivity bonus; or

(*c*)   the payment to the employee for piecework or measured work.

184.4   **CONTRACTUAL OR DISCRETIONARY PAYMENTS**

Many employers prefer to adopt discretionary rather than contractual arrangements in relation to such matters as sick pay (over and above SSP), bonus arrangements and extra redundancy payments, because of the flexibility which it gives them.

There is, however, a risk of a successful complaint of discrimination if the arrangements for these benefits are not:

(*a*)   transparent;

    (*b*)   consistent; and

    (*c*)   objective.

184.5   **EQUAL PAY – NOT FAIR PAY**

The *EPA 1970* and the *Discrimination Laws* do not give employees the right to a fair day's pay for a fair day's work. The law is about equality, not about fairness. If an employer pays no more than the minimum wage, for work which is worth far more, an employee receiving that wage has a remedy only if a suitable comparator can be identified under the *EPA 1970* or if racial or disability or other discrimination can be proved.

184.6   **SERVICE-RELATED PAY**

Service-related pay scales give rise to particular complications, as is clear from *Cadman v Health & Safety Executive [2006] IRLR 969*; see further *Seniority*.

185   Penalties

None of the discrimination laws provide for an employer or any other respondent to be fined or subjected to any other penalty for unlawful discrimination. Such discrimination can be costly to employers and others, but that is because the individual complainant can be awarded unlimited amounts of compensation. There are offences under the *SDA 1975*, the *RRA 1976*, the *DDA 1995*, the *RBR 2003*, the *SOR 2003* and the *AR 2006* but they do not include unlawful discrimination.

The statutory Commissions have enforcement powers, but the ultimate step is for the Commission to apply to a county court (or sheriff court in Scotland) for an injunction (or interdict in Scotland). No application may be made for an injunction or interdict to prevent any unlawful act in the employment field until after:

(*a*)   an employment tribunal has made a finding of unlawful discrimination;

(*b*)   an employment tribunal has made a finding (on an application by the relevant Commission) of an unlawful act relating to discriminatory *Advertisements, Instructions to Discriminate* or *Pressure to Discriminate*; or

(*c*)   a *Non-Discrimination Notice* has been served by the relevant Commission.

Furthermore, in each case, the application for an injunction or interdict cannot be made until the employment tribunal finding or non-discrimination notice has become final (i.e. an appeal has been unsuccessful or has been withdrawn or the time for appealing has expired).

186 Pensions

186.1 THE EPA 1970 AND THE SDA 1975 – ORIGINAL PROVISIONS

The *EPA 1970* and the *SDA 1975*, in their original form, permitted discrimination in access to occupational pension schemes and in benefits under such schemes, as well as other acts of discrimination in relation to death or retirement (including discrimination in relation to *Redundancy* payments). The most widespread forms of discrimination were:

(*a*)   discrimination against women in relation to access to pension schemes (including the exclusion of most part-time workers);

(*b*)   discrimination against female employees in relation to benefits for surviving spouses; and

(*c*)   discrimination against men in relation to the age from which pensions could become payable.

The discriminatory structure of most occupational pension schemes began to collapse in 1990, with the decision of the ECJ in *Barber v Guardian Royal Exchange Assurance Group [1990] IRLR 240*, the case in which it was found to be incompatible with *Article 141* (then *Article 119*) to require a man to wait for his pension for five years longer than his female colleagues.

Following a series of further decisions of the ECJ, our domestic law was amended as mentioned below.

186.2 THE CURRENT LAW

The *Pensions Act 1995* and the *Occupational Pension Schemes (Equal Treatment) Regulations 1995 (SI 1995 No 3183)* both came into effect on 1 January 1996. With effect from that date, every occupational pension scheme is to be treated as including an equal treatment rule. This rule has the same effect in relation to pensions as an equality clause has in relation to other terms of employment. It applies to the right to join a scheme, the terms of membership and the terms on which members are treated.

A special feature of discrimination in relation to benefits under a pension scheme is that discriminatory provisions which exist during a complainant's employment do not directly impinge on the complainant until he or she retires and becomes entitled to a lump sum payment and a pension. Accordingly, the *1995 Regulations* provide that it is only pensioner members who can be awarded arrears of benefits or damages. The remedy for an employee member is a declaration. In either case, although the proceedings have been brought against the trustees of the scheme, the employer can be ordered to provide additional resources and accordingly is treated as a party and is entitled to appear.

186.3 RETROSPECTIVE CLAIMS

A major issue is that of retrospective claims. Many pensioners and would-be pensioners spent most of their working lives under the discriminatory regimes which were permitted by domestic legislation until 1 January 1996.

The ECJ ruled in *Barber* that claims of discrimination in relation to pension benefits (apart from those already in the pipeline) could be based only on pensionable service after 17 May 1990 (the date of the decision in *Barber*). The position is different in relation to access to pension schemes. In *Preston and others v Wolverhampton Healthcare NHS Trust and others [2000] IRLR 506*, the ECJ considered a number of questions referred to it by the House of Lords. These were 22 test cases which were representative of some 60,000 claims by workers who had been excluded, because they were part-timers, from membership of various public and private sector occupational pension schemes. One of the questions referred to the ECJ was whether the respondents could rely on the provision in the *EPA 1970* under which no arrears of remuneration or damages could be awarded in respect of any time earlier than two years before the commencement of proceedings (see also *Back Pay*). It was held by the ECJ that this provision in the *EPA 1970* was precluded by Community law. The ECJ did not specify the period of service by reference to which claims for compensation can be based, but the logic of the decision is that compensation claims can be calculated by reference to any period of exclusion since 8 April 1976. This was the date of the decision of the ECJ in *Defrenne v Sabena [1976] ECR 455*, the first case in which the ECJ held that *Article 119* had direct effect. It was, however, pointed out by the ECJ in *Preston*, citing the case of *Fisscher [1994] IRLR 662*, an earlier decision of the ECJ, that the fact that a worker can claim retroactively to join an occupational pension scheme does not allow him or her to avoid paying the contributions relating to the period of membership concerned.

In *Preston and others v Wolverhampton Healthcare NHS Trust and others (No 3) [2004] IRLR 96*, it was held by the EAT that there is a breach of the *EPA 1970* where pension scheme membership is compulsory for full-time staff but part-time staff are excluded. It was also held that part-time staff cannot complain of a breach of the *EPA 1970* where pension scheme membership is optional for them but compulsory for full-time staff.

186.4   AGE DISCRIMINATION

The *AR 2006* introduced measures to combat age discrimination in pension schemes with effect from 1 December 2006; see *Age Regulations*.

187 Performance of Job Duties

The way in which an employee performs his or her job duties may lead either to a benefit, such as *Promotion*, or a *Detriment*, such as a warning (or ultimately *Dismissal*) for unsatisfactory performance.

It is important that all decisions based on an employee's performance at work, whether beneficial or detrimental, should be made objectively and consistently. Complaints of direct discrimination arise when double standards are applied.

Even a strictly objective and consistent approach will not always be sufficient. There could be complaints of *Indirect Discrimination* or *Disability Discrimination* in the following examples:

(*a*)   where a manual worker's performance or the assessment of that performance is adversely affected by language difficulties which the employer has made no attempt to resolve;

(*b*)   where the consideration of a female employee's performance by reference to output or sales ignores the fact that she has been on *Maternity* leave for part of the relevant period; or

(*c*)   where a disabled employee's job performance is substantially affected by the *Disability* and no *Reasonable Adjustment* has been considered.

188   Permanent Health Insurance

Permanent Health Insurance ('PHI') is a valuable benefit offered by a significant number of employers. Typically, the insurance provides ongoing financial benefit (typically linked, on a proportionate basis, to the employee's salary) if the employee is unable to work due to ill health. The benefit will usually continue to be provided until death, retirement or a return to work.

In practice, most employees who become eligible for PHI benefits will be disabled within the meaning of the *DDA 1995*. This will be so even if the definition of 'disability' to be found in the small print of the policy differs from that in the legislation. In particular cases, the employer's duty to make *Reasonable Adjustments* might include a duty to help the employee to make a claim for PHI benefits. A failure to ensure that the employee is provided with PHI benefits due within a reasonable period of time may constitute a breach of the duty to make *Reasonable Adjustments'*.

The *AR 2006* may also provide rights of redress in certain circumstances. To restrict access to PHI schemes, e.g. by operating a maximum age for membership of the scheme, is potentially discriminatory, although there may be circumstances in which the discrimination is capable of *Justification*.

189 Persistent Discrimination

The relevant Commission may apply for an injunction (or interdict in Scotland) to prevent a person (or organisation) from discriminating unlawfully within five years after either of the following becoming final:

(*a*)   a *Non-Discrimination Notice* served on that person; or

(*b*)   a finding by an employment tribunal, on an individual complaint, of unlawful discrimination or breach of a contractual term modified or included by virtue of an equality clause.

All references to a person include any organisation.

190   Person Specifications

A person specification aims to match the right person to a vacant post. Properly used, it helps to reduce subjectivity and bias in the selection process. Typically, it will identify the criteria that a candidate *must* meet to be considered for the job. It will usually reflect the terms of the *Job Description*. If an employer's *Equal Opportunities Policies* provides – as it often will – that a person specification should be drawn up as part of a process of *Recruitment,* then failure to draw up such a specification in a particular case may give rise to an *Inference* of *Indirect Discrimination* (or possibly *Direct Discrimination*).

Checklist 17 sets out key issues for consideration in drawing up a person specification.

191   Physical or Mental Impairment

191.1   MEANING

The term 'impairment' is fundamental to the definition of 'disability' in the *DDA 1995*. However, the *DDA 1995* does not contain a comprehensive definition of 'impairment'. The World Health Organization has defined it as 'any loss, or abnormality of psychological, physiological, or anatomical structure or function'. It is worth noting that:

(*a*)   often, there will be no dispute as to whether a person has an 'impairment'. A dispute is more likely to arise as to whether the effects of the impairment are sufficient to fall within the scope of the *DDA 1995*;

(*b*)   sensory impairments, such as those affecting sight or hearing, are included;

(*c*)   'mental impairment' includes a wide range of impairments, such as learning disabilities, prior to 5 December 2005, any impairment resulting from or consisting of a mental illness was excluded unless that illness is clinically well-recognised, i.e. by a respected body of medical opinion – but the additional hurdle of showing a clinically well-recognised mental illness has now been removed;

(*d*)   mental illness does not have the special meaning attributed to it in other legislation.

In *McNicol v Balfour Beatty Rail Maintenance Ltd [2002] IRLR 711*. Mummery LJ highlighted 'the crucial importance (a) of applicants making clear the nature of the impairment on which the claim of discrimination is advanced and (b) of both parties obtaining relevant medical evidence on the issue of impairment'. He also pointed out that the statutory guidance states that it is not necessary to consider how an impairment was caused. He said that the 'essential question in each case is whether, on sensible interpretation of the relevant evidence, including the expert medical evidence and reasonable inferences which can be made from all the evidence, the applicant can fairly be described as having a physical or mental impairment.'

191.2   PHYSICAL IMPAIRMENTS

In *McNicol*, the claimant complained that he was suffering from back pain, as a result of an injury, and that this pain severely affected his ability to carry out normal day-to-day activities. The medical evidence, however, indicated that the pain was not caused by any physical impairment. There was no evidence before the tribunal of any functional overlay or of any clinically well-recognised mental illness. The tribunal rejected a submission that a mental condition which causes pain is, by reason of that, a physical impairment. Appeals by the applicant were rejected by the EAT and by the Court of Appeal.

In the case of *College of Ripon & York St John v Hobbs [2002] IRLR 185*, the medical evidence was that the applicant had muscle weakness, creating difficulty in mobility, and also other symptoms. The medical expert had, however, been unable to identify the medical cause of the symptoms. The employment tribunal held that the applicant had a physical impairment and this decision was upheld on appeal.

Giving judgment in the EAT, Lindsay J approved a comment by the tribunal that in simple terms the expression 'physical impairment' means 'that there is something wrong with the body as opposed to the mind'.

In *Millar v Inland Revenue Commissioners [2006] IRLR 112*, the Court of Session noted that it seems to be that physical impairment can be established without reference to its cause, and in particular without reference to any form of 'illness'. Many forms of physical impairment result from conditions that cannot be described as 'illness'. An amputee, for example, does not have an 'illness' but it would be sufficient to point to the physical condition as establishing an impairment. The implication of this case is that a claimant now will have to show by evidence that they have a physical or mental impairment (and that it has the requisite characteristics to satisfy the other limbs of the statutory definition of disability), but that they will not have to show *why* they have that particular impairment, such as they have a particular illness.

In *Cosgrove v Northern Ireland Ambulance Service [2007] IRLR 397*, the disability protected was the severe disfigurement aspect of the claimant's psoriatic condition. On the facts, the differential treatment of him had not arisen as a result of his disfigurement.

191.3   **MENTAL IMPAIRMENTS**

Important guidance was given by the then President of the EAT, Lindsay, J, in *Morgan v Staffordshire University [2002] IRLR 190*. In this case, the applicant claimed to be suffering from a mental impairment which was variously described as anxiety, stress, nervous debility and depression. The applicant gave evidence and copies of many of her medical notes were produced, but no medical evidence was called by either party. It was held that she had not made out her case that she had a mental impairment within the *DDA 1995* and her appeal was unsuccessful.

The President referred to the available routes to establishing the existence of mental impairment within the *DDA 1995*. The ways in which is could be proved that a particular mental illness was a clinically well-recognised illness included specific mention in the World Health Organization's International Classification of Diseases or in some other classification of very wide professional acceptance; or proof by other means that the condition was recognised as a mental illness by a respected body of medical opinion. The President pointed out that the WHO classification was specifically mentioned in the statutory guidance.

The President also referred to a further possibility which exists as a matter of construction of the legislation, but which may not exist in medical terms. The guidance expressly states that physical or mental impairment includes sensory impairments, such as those affecting sight or hearing, and that mental impairment includes a wide range of impairments which are often known as learning disabilities. The wording of the Act suggests the possibility that, quite apart from these cases, there may exist a state recognisable as mental impairment which neither results from nor consists of a mental illness. The President said that this category is likely to be rarely if ever invoked and could be expected to require substantial and very specific medical evidence to support its existence.

The President made some important general observations. Tribunals and practitioners should familiarise themselves with the full text of those observations. The following are some of the key points:

191.4   Physical or Mental Impairment

(*a*)   Claimants should identify in good time before the hearing exactly what is the impairment they say is relevant; respondents should indicate whether impairment is an issue and why it is. Tribunals should insist that both sides should do so. Otherwise, the parties cannot be clear as to what has to be proved or rebutted, in medical terms, at the hearing.

(*b*)   Loose descriptions such as anxiety, stress or depression will not suffice, without credible and informed evidence that in the particular circumstances the loose description identifies a clinically well-recognised illness. What is required is a clear diagnosis by name of either an illness specified in the WHO classification or some other clinically well-recognised mental illness. In the latter case, the medical report should give the grounds for asserting that the condition is to be accepted as a clinically well-recognised mental illness. Where the WHO classification is relied on, the medical report should refer to the presence or absence of the symptoms identified in the diagnostic guidelines contained in the classification.

(c)   '... the existence or not of a mental impairment is very much a matter for qualified and informed medical opinion... The dangers of the tribunal forming a view on 'mental impairment' from the way the claimant gives evidence on the day cannot be overstated.'

The guidance given by the President was expressly approved by the Court of Appeal in *McNicol v Balfour Beatty Rail Maintenance Ltd.*

In *Hewett v Motorola Ltd [2004] IRLR 545*, the claimant was diagnosed as having autism, in the form of Asperger's Syndrome. He contended that, without medication or medical treatment, this affected his ability to understand. A tribunal dismissed his complaint on the grounds that although his disorder had an 'adverse effect', particularly 'on his ability to participate in human interaction, social relationships and communication', this did not fall within the statutory definition. The EAT allowed his appeal, taking the view that a broad approach to the concept of 'understanding' should be taken. Ability to 'understand' for the purposes of *paragraph 4(1)(g) of Schedule 1* to the *DDA 1995* is not limited simply to an ability to understand information, knowledge or instructions. There was clear evidence before the tribunal regarding the claimant's difficulties in understanding the more subtle aspects of human interaction. The case was remitted to determine whether the adverse effect of the claimant's impairment was substantial.

191.4   EXCLUDED CONDITIONS

Certain conditions are not regarded as impairments. They are excluded by the *Disability Discrimination (Meaning of Disability) Regulations 1996 (SI 1996 No 1455)*, as mentioned in paragraph 8 of the guidance, as follows:

(*a*)   addiction to or dependency on alcohol, nicotine, or any other substance (other than in consequence of the substance being medically prescribed);

(*b*)   hay fever, except where it aggravates the effect of another condition;

(*c*)   pyromania, kleptomania, exhibitionism, and voyeurism: or

(*d*)   the tendency to physical or sexual abuse of others.

There is an important distinction between an excluded condition, such as an addiction to drugs or alcohol, and a physical or mental impairment caused by that addiction. The latter must be assessed on its merits, without reference to the addiction which has caused it.

This principle was affirmed by the EAT in *Power v Panasonic UK Ltd [2003] IRLR 151*. In this case, there was evidence of both alcohol abuse and depression. The employment tribunal approached the case on the basis that the core issue was whether the applicant had become clinically depressed and turned to drink or whether her depression was caused by alcohol addiction.

Allowing an appeal by the applicant, the EAT stated that this approach was mistaken. It was not material to consider how the impairment from which the applicant was suffering was caused. If she had a mental impairment within the meaning of the Act, it was immaterial that this impairment may have been caused by alcohol addiction.

Attention was also drawn in the decision to paragraph 11 of the statutory guidance, as follows:

> 'It is not necessary to consider how an impairment was caused, even if the cause is a consequence of a condition which is excluded. For example, liver disease as a result of alcohol dependency would count as an impairment.'

In *Edmund Nuttall Ltd v Butterfield [2005] IRLR 751*, the EAT overruled a tribunal's decision that the claimant was discriminated against on grounds of disability when he was dismissed after being convicted of offences of indecent exposure. The tribunal was wrong to reason that, although 'exhibitionism' is an excluded condition under the *Disability Discrimination (Meaning of Disability) Regulations 1996*, in the claimant's case it was a manifestation of a mental impairment, depression, and had the claimant not had a mental illness, he would not have committed the criminal offences. The concept set out by the EAT in *Murray v Newham Citizens Advice Bureau [2003] IRLR 340*, that the exclusion in the Regulations refer to only 'free-standing conditions' and not to those that are the direct consequence of a physical or mental impairment, was not helpful. The claimant may have both a legitimate impairment and an excluded condition. The critical question is one of causation – what was the reason for less favourable treatment? If the reason was the legitimate impairment, then that is prima facie discrimination. If the reason was the excluded condition and not the legitimate impairment, then the claim fails. Where the excluded condition is the reason for the less favourable treatment, the fact that there is an underlying legitimate impairment does not mean that disability is a reason for the less favourable treatment. That would render the effect of the Regulations nugatory. On the facts, the sole reason for dismissal related to the excluded condition, not to the legitimate impairment.

192   Physical Requirements

192.1   HEAVY WORK

There are physically demanding jobs both in construction and other industries and also in some jobs involving the care of the elderly and others.

The following principles apply in recruitment for such jobs:

(a)   It must never be assumed that a man is qualified and a woman is disqualified for such work on account of their respective genders. The assumption is unsound and acting on it would be a clear case of sex discrimination.

(b)   It would also be an act of direct discrimination in the arrangements for recruitment for the job to require female candidates but not male candidates to undertake a test of strength or stamina.

(c)   Direct discrimination can be avoided by asking candidates of both sexes to undergo the same tests, but there could be indirect discrimination against female candidates if the test requirements are excessive in relation to the demands of the job. There are many jobs which at first glance require considerable physical strength but which can be adapted by using equipment or skilled techniques.

192.2   MANUAL DEXTERITY

Similar principles apply to the many jobs for which employers regard female candidates as being generally more suitable. Many of these jobs require some degree of manual dexterity. They include traditional jobs operating machines, typing letters or assembling parts and also jobs in modern industries for which keyboard skills are required.

192.3   HEIGHT REQUIREMENTS

A requirement that candidates for the post should have at least a specified minimum height is indirectly discriminatory against women (and perhaps also candidates from some ethnic groups) unless it can be objectively justified; subject to that same proviso, a requirement that candidates should be below a specified height is indirectly discriminatory against men (and perhaps candidates from other ethnic groups).

It is difficult to envisage many circumstances in which requirements of either kind could be objectively justified. In particular, the notion that an imposing physical presence is a necessary (let alone sufficient) attribute for law enforcement or private security work is a somewhat unfashionable one.

The adoption of different height requirements for men and women (or candidates or employees of different racial groups) would be direct discrimination. There are statutory exceptions for *Prison Officers* and *Police* officers.

193   Physical Strength

The demands which different jobs make in terms of the physical effort required, is one of the relevant demand factors in evaluating the jobs for the purposes of an *Equal Value* claim.

In cases of *Selection* for jobs involving physical strength:

(*a*)   there is direct sex discrimination if a decision is based on an untested assumption that a man is more suitable than a woman for such a job;

(*b*)   there is also direct sex discrimination if a woman is required to demonstrate that she has the necessary strength and the man is not; and

(*c*)   there is indirect sex discrimination if the physical strength required is excessive in relation to the needs of the job.

Under *section 7* of the *SDA 1975*, one of the cases where being a man can be a *Genuine Occupational Qualification* for a job is where the essential nature of the job calls for a man for reasons of physiology. It is expressly stated, however, that the reference to physiology excludes physical strength or stamina.

194 Police

Police officers are not employees in the conventional sense, but they are protected by the *Discrimination Laws*. It is, however, expressly stated, in the *SDA 1975*, the *RRA 1976*, the *RBR 2003* and the *SOR 2003* that the holding of the office of constable (which includes any rank) shall be treated as employment by:

(*a*)   the chief officer of police as respects any act done by him; or

(*b*)   by the police authority as respects any act done by them.

The *SDA 1975* provides that regulations under what is now the *Police Act 1996* may not treat men and women differently except in relation to:

(*a*)   height requirements;

(*b*)   uniform or equipment requirements or allowances;

(*c*)   special treatment of women in connection with pregnancy or childbirth; or

(*d*)   pensions to or in respect of special constables or police cadets.

The last-mentioned exception is subject to the principle of equal pay under *Article 141* and the *Equal Pay Directive*. Police work falls within the *Public Sector* so that directives can have direct effect.

However, in *Heath v Commissioner of Police for the Metropolis [2005] IRLR 270*, the Court of Appeal confirmed that there was no jurisdiction to hear a complaint under the *SDA 1975* that a civilian police worker had been discriminated against in the course of a disciplinary hearing under the *Police (Discipline) Regulations 1985 (SI 1985 No 518)* into allegations she had made of sexual assault by a police inspector. The rule of absolute immunity from suit that attaches to judicial or quasi-judicial proceedings excludes complaints about unlawful discriminatory conduct in the course of such proceedings to other judicial bodies, including employment tribunals. The rationale is to protect the integrity of the judicial process and hence the public interest.

In *Husan v Commissioner of Police of the Metropolis (unreported)*, the EAT ruled that a police commissioner's decision, pursuant to regulation 13 of the Police Regulations 2003, relating to the discharge of a probationary police officer was not subject to the doctrine of 'absolute immunity from suit'. The probationer was, therefore, able to bring claims under the *RRA 1976* and the *RBR 2003*.

195   Political Opinions

UK law does not expressly protect those who hold specific political opinions. But political opinions may have implications in respect of both *Human Rights* and the *Discrimination Laws*.

The Department of Trade and Industry has expressed a view that the *RBR 2003* do not 'generally' apply to support for a political party. But the right to respect for private and family life established by *Article 8* of the *European Convention on Human Rights* may offer some protection to those who hold controversial political opinions. That protection may, however, to an extent be counter-balanced by the application of the *Discrimination Laws*, for example if political opinions or beliefs prompt discrimination against, say, those who subscribe to other beliefs covered by the *RBR 2003* or constitute discrimination contrary to the *SOR 2003*.

In *Redfearn v Serco Ltd t/a West Yorkshire Transport Service [2006] IRLR 623*, a bus driver was dismissed when his employer discovered that he was a candidate representing the British National Party in a local election. A tribunal accepted the employer's argument that he had been dismissed on health and safety grounds, having regard to the significant number of passengers and employees who were of Asian origin. The EAT allowed an appeal but the Court of Appeal restored the original decision. The bus driver had not been dismissed 'on racial grounds' within the meaning of *section 1(1)(a)* of the *RRA 1976*. Discrimination 'on racial grounds' is not confined to less favourable treatment on the ground of the colour or race of the claimant. The racial characteristic of C, rather than that of B, the victim of the less favourable treatment, may be a racial ground of less favourable treatment of B by A, and therefore direct discrimination by A against D. The reasoning in *Showboat Entertainment Centre v Owens [1984] IRLR 7* is not confined to cases of an employer implementing a policy of race discrimination by giving a racially discriminatory instruction to an employee, who is then treated less favourably by being dismissed for not carrying it out. White persons would also be treated less favourably than other white persons on the ground of colour in the case of a white employer who dismisses a white employee for marrying a black person, or a white publican who refuses to admit or serve a white customer on the ground that he is accompanied by a black person. The basis of the decision in *Showboat*, however, is that the racially discriminatory employer is liable 'on racial grounds' for the less favourable treatment of those who refuse to implement his policy or are affected by his policy or are affected by his policy. It does not support the proposition that the expression 'on racial grounds' covers any case in which the discriminator's less favourable act was significantly influenced by racial considerations, even if the race was that of a third party. That proposition was far too wide, wrong in principle, inconsistent with the purposes of the legislation and unsupported by authority. Taken to its logical conclusion, it would mean that it could be an act of direct discrimination for an employer, who is trying to improve race relations in the workplace, to dismiss an employee, whom he discovered had committed an act of race discrimination, such as racial abuse, against a fellow employee or customer. This claimant was no more dismissed 'on racial grounds' than an employee who is dismissed for racially abusing his employer, a fellow employee or valued customer. Nor could it be held that the employers adopted race-based criteria for dismissing the claimant on grounds of his membership of the BNP, because the BNP is confined to white people. The BNP cannot make a non-racial criterion (party membership) a racial one by the terms of its constitutional limiting membership to white people.

196   Positive Discrimination or Affirmative Action

Most *Discrimination Laws* permit only very limited measures of positive sex discrimination by employers, *Training Bodies*, *Trade Unions* and other organisations. Subject to these exceptions, positive discrimination – however well-intentioned – is unlawful.

An employer, for example, is permitted under the *SDA 1975* to take certain measures to discriminate in favour of women if, during the previous 12 months, there were no women doing some particular work or the number of women doing that work was comparatively small. The permitted measures are:

(*a*)   encouraging women to take advantage of opportunities for doing that work; or

(*b*)   affording only his female employees access to facilities for training which would help to fit them for that work.

Similar measures of positive action in favour of men are permitted where it is men who have not been doing the work or doing it only in comparatively small numbers.

In either case, however, there must be no discrimination at the point of *Selection*.

Similar measures of encouragement or training are permitted to trade unions and other organisations. Training bodies may discriminate in favour of persons of one sex or the other where it reasonably appears that during the previous 12 months there have been no persons of that sex, or only a comparatively small number of persons of that sex, doing the work either in Great Britain as a whole or in the particular area where the persons given training are likely to take up work.

Similar, but not identical, provisions apply in other areas of discrimination law. However, it is important to note that

there is nothing in the *DDA 1995* to prevent affirmative action or positive discrimination in favour generally of disabled employees or job applicants. It would, however, be unlawful to discriminate in favour of disabled workers with one kind of disability if this meant discriminating against workers with different kinds of disability, unless the case is covered by a specific provision in the *DDA 1995* (for example that relating to supported employment).

Increasingly, it is suggested that the law might be changed to allow more scope for positive discrimination; see *Contract Compliance*. But this remains highly controversial.

197   Post-Employment Discrimination

197.1   THE ISSUE

The issue in relation to post-employment discrimination is whether an employee, or any other person to whom rights are given by the laws against discrimination, can present a complaint about an act or omission which occurs after the employment has ended.

Until June 2003, the position was that a complaint could be presented under the *SDA 1975* about post-employment victimisation. This was because of the decision of the ECJ in the case of *Coote v Granada Hospitality Ltd [1998] IRLR 656* and the subsequent decision of the EAT in *Coote v Granada Hospitality Ltd (No 2) [1999] IRLR 452.*

As a result of the decision of the Court of Appeal in *Adekeye v Post Office (No 2) [1997] IRLR 105,* no other complaint of discrimination, about an act or omission after the end of the employment or other relationship, could be presented.

197.2   THE HOUSE OF LORDS DECISION

Parliament has now addressed this unsatisfactory state of affairs, but not before the House of Lords had resolved it, in *Rhys-Harper v Relaxion Group plc [2003] IRLR 484.* The decision was given in this case and in five other cases which were heard at the same time.

Ms Rhys-Harper's complaint was one of sexual harassment. She alleged that she had been subjected to sexual harassment during her employment, but her complaint was out of time if those allegations were looked at in isolation. She also alleged, however, that the respondent local authority had failed to carry out a proper investigation of a complaint which she made to them after her employment had been terminated. She claimed that this meant that there was continuing sex discrimination against her. If this was right, then her claim was not out of time. It was held by the EAT and then by the Court of Appeal that, because of the decision in *Adekeye,* the employment tribunal did not have jurisdiction to consider her complaint about the handling of the post-employment complaint which she had made to the respondent.

Four of the other five appeals involved complaints about victimisation under the *DDA 1995.* In three of these cases, the applicant complained that the former employer had provided references which were unsatisfactory (or refused to give one at all) and had done so because the applicant had made claims under the *DDA 1995.* One of these applicants was Mr Kirker, who had brought one of the very earliest cases under the *DDA 1995* and had been awarded compensation of more than £100,000.00. The fourth victimisation complaint under the *DDA 1995* was about delay in returning, after the applicant's dismissal, business cards which he had left in his office. The employment tribunals in all four of these cases held that there was no jurisdiction to hear the complaints.

The remaining appeal was in the case of *D'Souza v London Borough of Lambeth [2003] IRLR 484.* Mr D'Souza had brought a successful complaint of unfair dismissal, direct racial discrimination and victimisation against the council. Having decided that Mr D'Souza had been unfairly dismissed, the employment tribunal exercised its power to order the council to reinstate him. The council refused to do so and it was held by the tribunal, more than two years later, that it had not been practicable for the council to do so. In the meantime, however, Mr D'Souza had presented two further tribunal applications, complaining of racial discrimination and victimisation in the council's decision not to reinstate him. It was held by the employment tribunal, applying the decision in *Adekeye*, that it had no jurisdiction to hear these two further applications.

It was held by the House of Lords that *Adekeye* had been wrongly decided. The decision was inconsistent with that in *Coote v Granada Hospitality Ltd (No 2)* and was no longer good law.

The House of Lords held by a majority (with one dissenting opinion) that there is jurisdiction to hear complaints of discrimination or victimisation arising out of the employment relationship, whether the acts complained of take place before or after the termination of that relationship. Lord Nicolls of Birkenhead said:

> 'The preferable approach is to recognise that in each of the relevant statutory provisions the employment relationship is the feature which triggers the employer's obligation not to discriminate in the stated respects ... Once triggered, the obligation not to discriminate applies to all the incidents of the employment relationship, whenever precisely they arise. For the reasons already given, this obligation cannot sensibly be regarded as confined to the precise duration of the period of employment if there are incidents of the employment which fall to be dealt with after the employment has ended. Some benefits accrue during the period of employment, some afterwards. For the purposes of discrimination, there is no rational ground for distinguishing the one from the other. They all arise equally from the employee's employment'.

Lord Nicolls added, that the true comparison in any case 'is the way the employer treats the complainant former employee and the normal way he treats or would treat other former employees in similar circumstances.' This means that, for example, if the complaint is about a refusal to provide a reference, the question to be considered would be whether the period of time since the end of the employment, and the other circumstances, are such that a request in similar circumstances if made by another former employee would normally have been granted.

The House of Lords allowed the appeals in the following individual cases (in each case remitting the case to the employment tribunal to be decided on the merits):

(*a*) the case of Ms Rhys-Harper, about the handling of the internal complaint which she made after her dismissal;

(*b*) the three complaints under the *DDA 1995* about unsatisfactory references or, in one case, the refusal to supply a reference;

(*c*) the complaint under the *DDA 1995* about the delay in returning the business cards after the applicant's dismissal.

Mr D'Souza's appeal, however, was dismissed. This was because the benefit to a former employee of having a reinstatement order made in his favour arises not from the employment relationship but from an order of the tribunal, made in the exercise of its discretion.

197.3 THE CURRENT LEGISLATION

The principle underlying the above House of Lords decision has been given statutory effect in the *Discrimination Laws*. These statutory provisions apply not only where a complaint arises from a former employment relationship but also when it arises from any other relationship in the field of employment and training to which the relevant Act applies.

For example, *Regulation 21(2)* of the *RBR 2003* states that:

'Where a relevant relationship has come to an end, it is unlawful for A –

(*a*)   to discriminate against B by subjecting him to a detriment; or

(*b*)   to subject B to harassment,

where the discrimination or harassment arises out of and is closely connected to that relationship.'

A 'relevant relationship' is defined as one which is covered by the employment and training provisions of the Act so that it is unlawful in the course of the relationship for A to discriminate against B or subject B to harassment.

197.4   **EXAMPLES OF POST-EMPLOYMENT DISCRIMINATION**

The House of Lords appeals mentioned above involved complaints of victimisation relating to:

(*a*)   withholding or refusing a reference;

(*b*)   giving a damaging reference;

(*c*)   dealing with an internal appeal against dismissal; and

(*d*)   delay in returning property to a dismissed employee.

The following further examples were given by the EAT in *Coote*:

(*a*)   continued use of sports (or social) facilities;

(*b*)   bonuses to former staff; and

(*c*)   concessionary travel facilities.

198   Pregnancy

198.1   STATUTORY RIGHTS

A dismissal is automatically unfair if the reason or principal reason for the dismissal is a reason connected with the pregnancy of the employee or the fact that she has given birth to a child. The normal requirement that the employee must have been continuously employed for not less than one year does not apply and there is no upper age limit.

Further entitlements include the rights to paid time off for antenatal care during pregnancy and the rights under *sections 66–71* of the *ERA 1996* relating to suspensions from work on maternity grounds. A suspension is on maternity grounds if:

(*a*)   an employee is suspended from work on the ground that she is pregnant, has recently given birth or is breastfeeding a child; and

(*b*)   the suspension is in consequence of one of several statutory provisions which have been specified by regulations.

Before the suspension takes place, the woman must be offered any suitable alternative work which is available (and which can be offered on terms and conditions which are not less favourable than her existing terms and conditions). If no such work is available, then she is entitled to remuneration during the period of suspension.

198.2   PREGNANCY AND SEX DISCRIMINATION

It is an act of direct sex discrimination to dismiss a woman because she is pregnant or because of an absence from work caused by a pregnancy-related illness – see *Dismissal*.

It was, however, held by the ECJ in *Brown v Rentokil Ltd [1998] IRLR 445*, that under the *Equal Treatment Directive* there was a distinction between, on the one hand, a pregnancy-related absence during pregnancy or maternity leave and, on the other hand, absence after maternity leave. The latter may be treated like any other absence, even though it is pregnancy related and is therefore caused by a condition which is unique to women.

It is also direct sex discrimination to refuse to employ a woman because she is or may become pregnant. That principle was established by the House of Lords in *Webb v EMO Air Cargo (UK) Ltd [1993] IRLR 27*. Lord Keith said:

'There can be no doubt that in general to dismiss a woman because she is pregnant or to refuse to employ a woman of child-bearing age because she may become pregnant is unlawful direct discrimination. Child-bearing and the capacity for child-bearing are characteristics of the female sex. So to apply these characteristics as the criterion for dismissal or refusal is to apply a gender-based criterion . . .'

The claimant had not been dismissed because she was pregnant, or because of any special feature of pregnancy, such as the statutory right to return to work. She had been dismissed because she would be unavailable for work at the very time when her services were required, to provide maternity cover. The House of Lords referred to the ECJ the question whether there was a breach of the *Equal Treatment Directive* in these circumstances.

The ECJ rather fudged the question by focusing on evidence that the complainant had been recruited not simply to provide maternity cover but for an unlimited term. The ECJ ruled that the Directive precluded dismissal in these circumstances. When the case came back to the House of Lords (*[1995] IRLR 645*), it was held that the *SDA 1975* could be construed in accordance with the ruling of the ECJ and accordingly the complaint succeeded. It was expressly stated by Lord Keith, however, that the outcome would not necessarily be the same in a case where a woman 'is denied employment for a fixed period in the future through the whole of which her pregnancy would make her unavailable for work, nor in the situation where after engagement for such a period the discovery of her pregnancy leads to cancellation of the engagement'.

The ECJ has, however, given an unequivocal answer to the above question in the case of *Tele Danmark A/S v Handels OG [2001] IRLR 853*. A woman was recruited on a temporary contract for the period of six months from 1 July 1995. It was agreed that she would spend the first two months on a training course. In July she told her employers that she was pregnant and expected to give birth in early November. She was dismissed from the end of September on the ground that she had not informed her employers that she was pregnant when she was recruited.

It was held by the ECJ that dismissal in these circumstances was contrary to the *Equal Treatment Directive* and the *Pregnant Workers Directive*. The relevant provisions of these Directives were to be interpreted as precluding a worker from being dismissed on the ground of pregnancy where:

(*a*)   she was recruited for a fixed period;

(*b*)   she failed to inform the employer that she was pregnant, even though she was aware of this when the contract of employment was concluded; and

(*c*)   because of her pregnancy she was able to work during the substantial part of the term of that contract.

In *Abbey National plc v Formoso [1999] IRLR 222*, it was held that there was direct sex discrimination in dismissing an employee for misconduct, in circumstances where she was unable to attend the disciplinary hearing because of a pregnancy-related condition and the hearing went ahead in her absence.

In *Fletcher and others v Blackpool Fylde and Wyre Hospitals NHS Trust [2005] IRLR 689*, the EAT confirmed that women on maternity leave are in a special, protected position and cannot compare themselves to men and women at work. However, the decision in *Webb v EMO Air Cargo (UK) Ltd [1993] IRLR 27*, did not rule out a comparison between sickness and pregnancy and all circumstances. Whilst it is not necessary for a pregnant woman to compare her treatment with that of a sick man in order to succeed in her claim of discrimination, and whilst an employer dismissing a woman on grounds of pregnancy cannot defeat her sex discrimination claim by stating that he would have treated a sick man in the same way, the purpose of the *Webb* principle is to protect pregnant women. It is not to prevent them from comparing their treatment with more favourable treatment afforded to sick men, where appropriate, in order to demonstrate that a different rule is being applied in comparable circumstances and that discrimination has occurred.

Health and Safety at Work issues also arise in relation to pregnant workers.

199   Principals and Agents

Employers use outside agents or consultants in a wide variety of ways. The most obvious example is in relation to *Recruitment*. An employer looking for a candidate for a post may:

(*a*)   approach a private employment agency;

(*b*)   ask for the vacancy to be advertised in a Jobcentre; or

(*c*)   use 'head hunters' particularly if the post is a senior one.

Employers also use agents or consultants in order, for example, to:

(*a*)   train and instruct employees;

(*b*)   carry out medical examinations; and

(*c*)   undertake *Psychometric Testing*.

An agency worker or *Contract Worker* can also be an employer's agent, where he or she is given responsibility for supervising employees.

The general rule is that employers and others who have obligations under the *Discrimination Laws* cannot escape their responsibilities by using agents. Anything done by the agent with the authority of the principal is also deemed to be done by the principal. The latter cannot escape responsibility by giving a nod and a wink or turning a blind eye. The authority may be express or implied and may be given before or after the event. The agent is also liable, because he is treated as having aided the principal in doing an unlawful act.

Sometimes it is the employer alone, and not the agent, who is legally liable for an unlawful act. The agent has a defence if he has reasonably relied on a statement made by the principal that a particular action would not be unlawful by reason of some provision contained in the Act concerned. This defence could apply, for example, to a recruitment agency which has placed an advertisement, if the employer has falsely but convincingly told the agency that the post being advertised is covered by one of the *Genuine Occupational Qualification (GOQ)* exceptions. In such a case, the principal who knowingly or recklessly makes the false or misleading statement to the agent is guilty of an offence and is liable to a fine on summary conviction.

Employers and others who use agents to recruit or manage staff or for any other purpose should bear in mind that:

(*a*)   A principal cannot avoid liability for discrimination by acting through an agent.

(*b*)   Clear instructions should be given to the agent, to ensure compliance with the law.

(*c*)   The activities of agents should be monitored and reviewed, bearing in mind that authority for an unlawful act can be implicit and retrospective.

A principal against whom a complaint is presented should generally apply to have the agent joined in the proceedings as an additional respondent. If the case is proved, but the tribunal is satisfied that the principal took all reasonable steps to prevent the discrimination by the agent, then although that will not enable the principal to escape liability, it is a factor which the tribunal could take into account in deciding on what would be the just and equitable apportionment, as between the principal and the agent, of the liability to pay compensation.

200   Prison Officers

Discrimination and harassment in relation to service as a prison officer is covered by the *Discrimination Laws*.

There is a special provision in *section 18* of the *SDA 1975* relating to height requirements. It is lawful to specify different minimum height requirements for male and female officers. Without this special provision, it would have been direct sex discrimination against male officers to require a greater minimum height for them than for female officers.

201   Professional Bodies

A professional body (as well as being an employer in its own right) can be:

(*a*)   an *Employers' Association* for the purposes of the *SDA 1975* and the *RRA 1976*;

(*b*)   a *Qualifying Body* for the purposes of those same Acts or a qualifications body for the purposes of the *DDA 1995*, the *RBR 2003* or the *SOR 2003*;

(*c*)   a *Trade Organisation* for the purposes of the *DDA 1995*, the *RBR 2003* or the *SOR 2003*.

There are provisions in the *Discrimination Laws* under which an interested party, as defined below, can apply to an employment tribunal for an order that a rule made by any of these bodies should be declared void where:

(*a*)   the rule is included or made in furtherance of an unlawful act; or

(*b*)   the rule provides for the doing of an unlawful act.

The interested parties who can make such a complaint include, in relation to rules made by employers' associations or other trade organisations, a person who:

(*a*)   is a member; or

(*b*)   who is genuinely and actively seeking to become a member.

In relation to a qualifying body or qualifications body, an interested person is one:

(*a*)   on whom the qualifying body has conferred an authorisation or qualification; or

(*b*)   who is genuinely and actively seeking an authorisation or qualification.

202   Promotion

The *Discrimination Laws* make it unlawful for an employer to discriminate in the way he affords an employee access to opportunities for promotion or by refusing or deliberately omitting to afford an employee access to such opportunities.

It is generally good practice for job vacancies to be advertised both internally and externally; it is particularly important that all vacancies should be advertised internally, so that any qualified employee can apply. There is an increased risk of complaints of discrimination if employees are *invited* to apply for posts, or simply *appointed* without any competition. Qualified employees could be overlooked because of (perhaps unstated) assumptions or prejudices based on gender, race or disability.

The general advice on *Selection* applies to promotion as well as to external *Recruitment*. It is particularly important, when considering an internal candidate, to ensure that the sources of information about the candidate are untainted by discrimination. If decisions are to be based partly on performance appraisals, they should where practicable be checked by a senior manager. The candidate should be given the opportunity to challenge negative comments and also to suggest the names of other managers who may be able to give a more favourable or balanced view.

203   Psychometric Testing

Psychometric testing was originally conceived about a century ago, but its use in *Recruitment* has much increased over the past few years. Broadly speaking, psycho-metric tests are designed to assess either ability or personality and typically take one of the following forms:

(*a*)   tests of specific ability, e.g. numeracy and verbal and spatial perception;

(*b*)   tests of general mental ability, such as power of analytical reasoning; or

(*c*)   tests for specific personality traits.

Alternatively, either tests may permit a comparison of the results of an individual with the average score for a population or the results may be descriptive instead of being scored.

Many different tests are now on the market, including tests which purport to identify specific characteristics such as 'leadership', 'honesty' and 'commercial acumen'. Tests vary in innumerable ways, not least in terms of cost and how time-consuming they are to operate. Even tests which are acknowledged as market leaders will not be 100 per cent accurate and therefore it is, as a practical matter, unwise for an employer not to utilise in addition other ways of assessing individual applicants or existing employees.

In any event, the use of psychometric tests, like *Genetic Testing*, may raise equal opportunities concerns. Some tests, especially those which were devised several years ago, are characterised by an element of bias. For instance, a test of a woman might suggest that she was by nature aggressive. An employer who refused to offer her employment because aggression was perceived as an unsuitable characteristic of a female employee, although regarded as acceptable in a male employee, would be vulnerable to a claim of direct discrimination on the ground of sex. Similarly, if a candidate for whom English is not the first language is rejected essentially because of a poor command of English in circumstances where adequate command of the English language is unnecessary to do the job, the employer may be vulnerable to a complaint of indirect discrimination under the *RRA 1976*.

Disabled employees may face particular difficulties with psychometric testing. For instance, the Royal National Institute for the Blind has expressed concern that such testing may have a negative effect on visually impaired people. The *DDA 1995* requires employers to make *Reasonable Adjustments* to tests which may discrimi-nate against people with disabilities and particular problems unique to visually impaired people make this a complex task. A blind candidate tackling a numerical reasoning test in Braille, for instance, is said to need as much as seven times longer to complete the test comfortably as someone with no impairment. When a test takes a substantial amount of extra time, factors such as fatigue and boredom will affect performance. Similar problems occur when tests are taken in large print or on tape. Such issues make it even more essential that a thorough job analysis is carried out before a psychometric test is administered, and its contents regarded as valid. The RNIB has, in conjunction with the Employment Service, produced a guide for employers, *Psychometric Testing and Visual Impairment*, which includes useful practical tips. A companion guide for visually impaired individuals is also available.

204   Public Sector

An important distinction between public sector and private sector employment is that in the public sector a *Directive* can have direct effect, where its terms are clear and specific, so as to be relied on by an employee or job applicant. Directives are addressed to Member States and the employers on whom a Directive can have direct effect are those employers who are emanations of the State. The ECJ, in *Foster and others v British Gas plc [1990] IRLR 353* gave the following definition:

> 'a body, whatever its legal form, which has been made responsible, pursuant to a measure adopted by the State, for providing a public service under the control of the State and has for that purpose special powers beyond those which result from the normal rules applicable in relations between individuals'.

Relevant bodies include local authorities, NHS Trusts and the police.

Certain public authorities are also now subject to a duty under the extended provisions of *section 71* of the *RRA 1976* to make appropriate arrangements to ensure that their various functions are carried out with due regard to the need to:

(*a*)   eliminate unlawful racial discrimination; and

(*b*)   promote equality of opportunity and good relations between persons of different racial groups.

205 Qualifying Bodies

The *Discrimination Laws* contain provisions in almost identical terms relating to any authority or body which can confer an authorisation or qualification which is needed for, or facilitates, engagement in a particular profession or trade. These qualifying bodies (the term used in the *DDA 1995*, the *RBR 2005*, the *SDR 2005,* and the *AR 2006* is 'qualifications bodies') must not discriminate:

(*a*)   in the terms on which they are prepared to confer an authorisation or qualification;

(*b*)   by refusing or deliberately omitting to grant an application for an authorisation or qualification; or

(*c*)   by withdrawing an authorisation or qualification or varying the terms on which it is held.

The expressions 'authorisation or qualification' are broadly defined to include, for example, registration or approval; the reference to conferring an authorisation or qualification includes renewing or extending it.

In *Patterson v Legal Services Commission [2004] IRLR 153,* a case under the *RRA 1976,* it was held by the Court of Appeal that the Legal Services Commission is a qualifying body when deciding whether to grant or refuse a legal aid franchise. The case concerned a sole practitioner, but it was suggested that the position would have been the same if the complaint had been by the partners in a firm, because the application for a franchise would have been an application to confer the authorisation on the partners jointly and severally.

206 Qualifying Periods

There is no qualifying period for rights under the *Discrimination Laws*. Rights are granted from the commencement of the employment and rights are also granted to job applicants. Thus a person who lacks the necessary service to claim unfair dismissal or a redundancy payment may nevertheless be entitled to bring a claim of unlawful discrimination before an employment tribunal.

207 Questionnaire

The statutory questionnaire is an important facility which is given to complainants in discrimination cases, including equal pay cases. Persons who suspect unlawful discrimination against them, particularly job applicants, are frequently handicapped by a lack of information. The questionnaire is an important means of obtaining that information.

Questionnaire forms have been prescribed for use by persons who consider that they may have been discriminated against. The prescribed forms may be used by a claimant to question the respondent (the person suspected of unlawful discrimination) so long as the questionnaire is served:

(*a*)   before a claim has been presented to an employment tribunal and during the period of three months beginning when the act complained of was done;

(*b*)   within the period of 21 days beginning with the day on which a claim has been presented to an employment tribunal; or

(*c*)   at a later date, if the tribunal gives leave, and in accordance with any directions made by the tribunal.

The questions and any replies are admissible in evidence in any employment tribunal proceedings. The tribunal may draw any inference which it considers just and equitable to draw, including an inference that the respondent has acted unlawfully, if it appears to the tribunal that:

(*a*)   the respondent has deliberately, and without reasonable excuse, omitted to reply within eight weeks; or

(*b*)   the respondent's reply is evasive or equivocal.

Respondents should reply to the questions within the specified time. They must reply carefully, accurately and fully. The risk of an adverse inference being drawn is greatest when false or misleading information is given.

The questionnaire procedure is now of increased importance because an adverse *Inference* can cause the *Burden of Proof* to shift from the complainant to the respondent.

208   Questions at Interview

The ways in which the questions asked at interviews can constitute unlawful discrimination or, more commonly, provide evidence of discrimination (even when none was intended) are considered under *Job Interviews*. The key rules for interviewers are:

(*a*)   prepare the questions, or at least the main areas to be covered, in advance, studying the job description and any person specification in order to identify the main topics to be explored;

(*b*)   read the application forms and CVs submitted by the interviewees, to avoid asking for information which you have already been given;

(*c*)   cover broadly the same ground with all the candidates – do *not* have one set of questions for men and a different set for women;

(*d*)   do not ask candidates about private matters which are irrelevant to the job, such as plans to marry or start a family;

(*e*)   if a candidate has a disability which could affect job performance, discuss it in a positive way, with particular reference to possible *Reasonable Adjustments*; and

(*f*)   similarly, if a job involves mobility or unsocial hours, raise that issue positively with all the candidates – men as well as women.

209 Quotas

The law does not permit discrimination in appointing persons to vacancies (whether by external recruitment or by internal promotion or transfer) in order to achieve a quota of employees defined by reference to race, sex, religion or sexual orientation. There are, however, limited measures of encouragement or discrimination in the provision of training in certain circumstances – see *Positive Discrimination*. It would be lawful for an employer to discriminate in favour of disabled workers generally in order to achieve a minimum quota, but discrimination *against* disabled workers once that quota has been achieved is emphatically not permitted.

210   Racial Discrimination

Whenever the terms 'discriminate' and 'discrimination' are used in the *RRA 1976*, they are so used in the sense defined in *sections 1* and *2* of the Act.

Section 1 contains the definitions of direct and indirect racial discrimination. It also expressly incorporates, within the definition of direct discrimination, segregation on racial grounds.

Section 1A which contains a new definition of indirect racial discrimination against persons defined by race or ethnic or national origins. The original definition of indirect racial discrimination, against persons defined by reference to colour or nationality, remains.

Section 2 provides that references to discrimination include *Victimisation*, as defined in that section.

Section 3A contains a definition of *Harassment* for cases where the unwanted conduct is on grounds of race or ethnic or national origins. Harassment on grounds of colour or nationality would still be dealt with as subjection to a detriment in accordance with the substantial case law on racial and sexual harassment.

Part II of the *RRA 1976* deals with discrimination in the employment field. It is *section 4* which makes it unlawful for employers to discriminate in various respects against job applicants or employees in relation to employment at an establishment in Great Britain. *Subsection 4(2A)* makes it unlawful for an employer to subject a job applicant to harassment (as expressly defined above).

Part II also deals with discrimination and harassment by other persons in the employment field and also contains the provisions relating to the *Genuine Occupational Qualification* exception.

The matters covered by later sections of the Act include provisions relating to enforcement and *Remedies*.

There are several other respects (for example in relation to *Genuine Occupational Qualifications* and *Partnerships*) in which the *RRA 1976* has been amended only as regards discrimination by reference to race, ethnic or national origins (as opposed to colour or nationality). This is because the regulations which amended the *RRA 1976* with effect from 19 July 2003 were made pursuant to the *European Communities Act 1972* in order to implement the *Directive on equal treatment between persons irrespective of racial or ethnic origin (2000/43/EC)*. That Directive referred only to discrimination on grounds of race or national or ethnic origin and accordingly the regulations were limited in the same way.

211 Racial Grounds

There is direct racial discrimination where a person is, on racial grounds, treated less favourably than other persons are or would be treated. Treatment is on racial grounds if it is on grounds of colour, race, nationality or ethnic or national origins.

This is a much more flexible definition than that of direct sex and marriage discrimination. In particular:

(*a*)   For the purposes of direct racial discrimination (as opposed to indirect racial discrimination) it is probably unnecessary to establish whether a group to which a complainant belongs is in fact a racial group. For example, less favourable treatment would arguably be on racial grounds if a Yorkshireman, regarding Lancastrians as an ethnic group and being hostile to that group, were to turn down a job application because the candidate comes from across the Pennines, or if a Cornishman, believing that he belongs to a Cornish race, turns down a job application because it is not from a fellow Cornishman.

(*b*)   Similarly, a complaint of direct discrimination could succeed even though the discrimination is based on a mistaken belief about the relevant group to which the complainant belongs. Suppose that an English candidate for a job is married to a Frenchman and her married name is Jean Dubois. She is not shortlisted for the post, because the employer does not wish to employ a man or a French person. She could succeed in a complaint of direct racial discrimination but not in one of direct sex discrimination (unless, possibly, the job is in the *Public Sector* and she is able to base her complaint on the *Equal Treatment Directive*).

(*c*)   Under the *RRA 1976*, a complaint could succeed if the less favourable treatment is on the ground of the race of the complainant's spouse or partner. There has been at least one case in which a white woman succeeded in a complaint of racial discrimination after being turned down for a job because her husband was black.

(*d*)   It is direct racial discrimination (and also *Victimisation* in most cases) to dismiss an employee because he or she refuses to co-operate in a policy of racial discrimination. There have been several such cases, the most recent being the Court of Appeal decision in *Weathersfield Ltd v Sargent [1999] IRLR 94.*

354

212   Racial Group

Under the *RRA 1976*, a racial group is a group of persons defined by reference to colour, race, nationality or ethnic or national origins. The Act contains that definition because *Disparate Impact*, for the purpose of the definition of indirect racial discrimination, is established by comparing the adverse impact on members of the complainant's racial group with that on non-members of that group.

The statutory definition of indirect racial discrimination differs according to whether the group is defined on the one hand by reference to race or ethnic or national origins or on the other hand by reference to colour or nationality – see *Racial Discrimination* and *Indirect Discrimination*.

The terms 'racial minorities' and 'ethnic minorities' are commonly used to describe minority racial groups, even where those groups are defined by reference to one of the other factors mentioned above. A person can belong to more than one racial group, depending on how the group is defined.

213   Racial Harassment

The law relating to both sexual and racial harassment is explained under *Harassment*. The legal principles and most of the case law are common to both kinds of harassment. The European Code of Practice was drawn up specifically in relation to sexual harassment, but most of the guidance is equally applicable to racial harassment.

The most extreme forms of racial harassment involve racial abuse or assaults, but racist jokes and nicknames can also amount to racial harassment. An employee is subjected to a detriment if he is made to hear racist remarks about himself or persons of his race generally which are intrinsically offensive or which he has indicated are unwelcome to him.

Managers and supervisors must be given clear instructions on the need for vigilance to prevent racial harassment, particularly where racial minority workers are employed for the first time or are isolated or unpopular for any reason. Guidance should be given on the signs to look out for and the action to be taken when racial harassment is reported, observed or suspected.

214   Racial Segregation

The definition of *Direct Discrimination* under *section 1* of the *RRA 1976* includes segregation on racial grounds. There is no need for a complainant to prove less favourable treatment. That is deemed to have occurred by reason of the segregation.

215   Reasonable Adjustments

215.1   THE CONCEPT

The *DDA 1995* is distinct from the other discrimination laws in imposing upon employers a duty to make reasonable adjustments to work arrangements and the working environment so as to avoid discrimination. It is a concept which is fundamental to the scheme of the legislation. If employers were not required to adjust working practices and policies, and to modify physical features of premises where appropriate, disabled people would face serious disadvantages.

215.2   THE STATUTORY DUTY

Section 4A(1) of the *DDA 1995* as amended (formerly *section 6(1)*, provides that where any provision, criterion or practice applied by or on behalf of an employer, or any physical feature of premises occupied by the employer, place a disabled person at a substantial disadvantage in comparison with persons who are not disabled, the employer is under a duty to take such steps as it is reasonable, in all the circumstances, for him to have to take in order to prevent the provision, criterion or practice or feature having that effect.

Since 1 October 2004, it has not been possible to defend a failure to comply with the statutory duty on the basis of justification.

215.3   EXAMPLES OF STEPS TO BE TAKEN

The *DDA 1995* sets out examples of steps which an employer may have to take in relation to a disabled person in order to comply with the duty to make adjustments, i.e:

(*a*)   making adjustments to premises;

(*b*)   allocating some of the disabled person's duties to another person;

(*c*)   transferring him to fill an existing vacancy;

(*d*)   altering his working hours or training;

(*e*)   assigning him to a different place of work or training;

(*f*)   allowing him to be absent during working or training hours for rehabilitation, assessment or treatment;

(*g*)   giving him, or arranging for training or mentoring;

(*h*)   acquiring or modifying equipment;

(*i*)   modifying instructions or reference manuals;

(*j*)   modifying procedures for testing or assessment;

(*k*)   providing a reader or interpreter; and

(*l*)   providing supervision or other support.

The leading case is *Archibald v Fife Council [2004] IRLR 651*, in which the House of Lords ruled that employers failed to comply with the duty of reasonable adjustments when they dismissed the claimant in circumstances in which she became totally incapable of doing the job for which she was employed, but was able to do another job within the organisation. A tribunal was wrong to reject her contention that it would have been a reasonable adjustment not to require her to go through competitive interviews, if she could show that she was qualified and suitable for an existing vacancy.

The House of Lords emphasised that the *DDA 1995* is different from the *SDA 1975* and the *RRA 1976* in that employers are required to take steps to help disabled people which they are not required to take further. The *DDA 1995* does not regard the differences between disabled people and others as irrelevant. It does not expect each to be treated in the same way. The duty to make adjustments may require the employer to treat a disabled person more favourably to remove the disadvantage which is attributable to the disability. This necessarily entails a measure of positive discrimination.

The duty to make an adjustment is triggered where an employee becomes so disabled that she can no longer meet the requirements of her job description. The terms 'arrangements' made by an employer in the *DDA 1995* is undefined and applies to the job description for a post and the liability of anyone who becomes incapable of fulfilling the job description to be dismissed, as much as it applies to an employer's arrangements for deciding who gets what job or how much each is paid.

The duty to take such steps as is reasonable in all the circumstances to take could include transferring without competitive interview a disabled employee from a post she can no longer do to a post which she can do. The employer's duty may require moving the disabled person to a post at a slightly higher grade. A transfer can be upwards as well as sideways or downwards. What steps are reasonable depends on the circumstances of the particular case.

215.4   **ASSESSING REASONABLENESS**

The *DDA 1995* provides that, in determining whether it is reasonable for an employer to have to take a particular step in order to comply with the duty to make reasonable adjustments, regard shall be had in particular to:

(*a*)   the extent to which taking the step would prevent the effect in question;

(*b*)   the extent to which it is practicable for the employer to take the step;

(*c*)   the financial and other costs which would be incurred by the employer in taking the step and the extent to which taking it would disrupt any of his activities;

(*d*)   the extent of the employer's financial and other resources;

(*e*)   the availability to the employer of financial or other assistance with respect to taking the step;

(*f*)   the nature of the employer's activities and the size of his undertaking; and

(*g*)   where the step would be taken in relation to a private household, the extent to which taking it would disrupt that household or disturb any person residing there.

215.5   **TO WHOM IS THE DUTY OWED?**

Section 4(A)2 provides that, for the purposes of the duty to make reasonable adjustments, 'the disabled person concerned' means:

(a)   in the case of a provision, criterion or practice for determining to whom employment should be offered, a disabled person who is, or who has notified the employer that he may be, an applicant for that employment;

(b)   in any other case, a disabled person who is–

(i)   an applicant for the employment concerned;

(ii)   an employee of the employer concerned.

Section 4(A)3 of the Act provides that an employer is not subject to a duty to make reasonable adjustments in relation to a disabled person if the employer does not know, and could not reasonably be expected to know:

(a)   in the case of an applicant, or potential applicant, that the disabled person concerned is, or may be, an applicant for the employment;

(b)   in any case, that the person has a disability and is likely to be placed at a substantial disadvantage in comparison with persons who are not disabled.

The difficult question which arises is whether an employer can comply with the duty in relation to reasonable adjustments where the employer does not know, but could reasonably be expected to know, about the disability – see *Knowledge of Disability.*

215.6   **INTERPRETING THE DUTY**

Complying with the duty may, in certain circumstances, mean that a new job has to be created. In *Southampton City College v Randall [2006] IRLR 18*, the EAT upheld a tribunal ruling that the employer failed to comply with their statutory duty of 'reasonable adjustment' in respect of a lecturer who was no longer able to do his work because his voice had broken down. In finding that the employers had a duty 'to devise a job which would take account of the effects of the claimant's disability', the tribunal did not wrongly extend the duty of reasonable adjustment. There was a substantial reorganisation and the claimant's line manager conceded in evidenced that he had a 'blank sheet of paper' so far as the job's specification was concerned. It followed that it was possible to devise a job which would have taken account of the effects of the claimant's disability, but the employers did not consider reasonable adjustments at all.

The tribunal did not err in finding that the employers should have considered voice amplification as a reasonable adjustment, notwithstanding that there is no evidence to suggest that amplification would have been effective as an adjustment. There must be many cases in which the disabled person has been placed at a substantial disadvantage at work, but in which the employer does not know what it ought to do to ameliorate that disadvantage without making enquiries. To say that a failure to make those enquiries would not amount to a breach of the duty would render the duty of reasonable adjustment practically unworkable in many cases. That could not have been Parliament's intention.

However, according to the EAT in *Tarbuck v Sainsbury's Supermarkets Ltd [2006] IRLR 664*, there is no separate and distinct duty of reasonable adjustment on an employer to consult with a disabled employee about what adjustment might be made. In this case, a disabled employee unsuccessfully applied for internal vacancies when her job was under threat of redundancy. A tribunal found that the employers had failed to make a reasonable adjustment given that they had not consulted with the claimant in order to agree the particular steps to be taken to eliminate disadvantage in the competition for jobs. The EAT allowed an appeal, indicating that the key question is, objectively, whether the employer has complied with his obligations or not (even though it will always be good practice for the employer to consult and it will potentially jeopardise the employer's legal position if he does not do so, because the employer cannot use the lack of knowledge that would have resulted from consultation as a shield to defend a complaint that he has not made reasonable adjustments). If the employer does what is required of him, then the fact that he failed to consult about it, or did not know that the obligation existed, is irrelevant. Conversely, if he fails to do what is reasonably required, it avails him nothing that he has consulted the employee.

In *Nottinghamshire County Council v Meikle [2004] IRLR 704*, the Court of Appeal held that the persistent failure of a local authority to carry out reasonable adjustments amounted to a fundamental breach of the obligation of trust and confidence. The employee resigned in response to those fundamental breaches of contract and was thus constructively dismissed. The tribunal was wrong to hold that a constructive dismissal does not fall within the scope of the word 'dismissal' in the *DDA 1995* and was therefore not in itself a discriminatory act. The terms should be given a purposive construction.

For *Time Limit* purposes, the Court of Appeal disagreed with the obiter view of Auld LJ in *Cast v Croydon College [1998] IRLR 318*, that in a sex discrimination case, where there has been constructive dismissal, time runs from the employer's breach and not from the date of the employee's resignation. The act complained of in a case of constructive dismissal is the unlawful dismissal – and that is constituted by the termination of the employee's employment when she accepts the employer's repudiation.

Further, the tribunal here was wrong to find that the local authority did not discriminate against the claimant on the grounds of disability by reducing her sickness benefit to half pay. The proper approach would have been to ask whether the local authority had shown that if all reasonable adjustments required by *section 6* to the claimant's working conditions had been made, she would have been absent for a period such as to render her liable to a cut in sick pay under the contractual scheme. On the facts, had the requisite adjustments been made, there was no reason to believe that she would have been absent for long enough to have her sick pay reduced under the scheme.

In other words, contractual sick pay is subject to the duty to make 'reasonable adjustments'. Thus an employer's duty can extend to not reducing a disabled employee's sick pay where her entitlement to full pay under a sick pay scheme would otherwise be exhausted, if it would have been a reasonable adjustment for the employee to make. This is more likely to be the case where, as here, the employer has failed to make other reasonable adjustments which would have reduced the disabled employee's absence level.

However, *O'Hanlon v Commissioners for HM Revenue & Customs [2006] IRLR 840*, is an interesting decision of the EAT which indicates the limits of the statutory duty. An employee suffering from clinical depression was entitled under her employer's sick pay rules to full pay for a maximum of six months in any period of twelve months; and half pay for a further maximum period of six months. After that she became entitled to her equivalent pension rate of pay, or half pay, whichever was the less. She was absent for so long that she was on pension rate for further absences. After the employers rejected her grievance that absences because of depression should not be included in the overall sickness total when calculating sick pay, she claimed disability discrimination. She argued that she should have received full pay for all disability-related absences. Alternatively, she argued that she should have received full pay for all non-disability-related sickness absences. She contended that she was substantially disadvantaged by the sick pay rules and that the employers had failed to make a reasonable adjustment to counter that disadvantage.

The claim failed and the EAT dismissed the employee's appeal. It was not a reasonable adjustment to expect the employers to pay the claimant's salary in full when she was absent from work due to disability-related absence, in circumstances in which she had exhausted her entitlement to sick pay under the employer's rules. According to the EAT, it would be a very rare case where giving higher sick pay than would be payable to a non-disabled person, who in general does not suffer the same disability-related absence, would be considered necessary as a reasonable adjustment. Other than in exceptional circumstances, it would not be an appropriate adjustment, because the tribunal would have to usurp the management function of the employer by deciding whether employers were financially able to meet the costs of modifying their policies by making enhanced payments. The purpose of the legislation is to integrate the disabled into the workforce, not simply to put more money into their wage packets – which might sometimes act as a positive disincentive to return to work.

The Court of Appeal upheld the EAT's decision at *[2007] IRLR 404*. It is worth noting that Sedley LJ said: 'The Disability Discrimination Act 1995 in its amended form is not at all easy to follow. This is a particular misfortune in an Act which it ought to be possible for employers and managers to read, understand and implement without legal advice or litigation.'

216   Reasonably Practicable Steps

A key principle of discrimination law is that employers are liable for the acts and omissions of their employees in the course of their employment. There is an extended definition of *Employment* (and hence of employee).

Course of employment is also broadly defined – see *Harassment*.

The employer is given a statutory defence, however, if he has taken such steps as were reasonably practicable to prevent the act complained of or acts of that description. The question whether such steps have been taken most commonly arises in the context of *Harassment* and the matter is dealt with under that heading. It should be noted that:

(*a*)   careful consideration should be given to the guidance contained in the European Union Code of Practice.

(*b*)   the adoption of comprehensive and well-written policies is only a first step, which should be followed up by other steps, including training.

Caspersz v Ministry of Defence [2006] All ER (D) 02 (Apr) is an example of a case where an employer which had a good policy, not just paid lip service to but actually observed, was found to have taken reasonably practicable steps to prevent sexual comments being made by a manager to a subordinate. The manager in question happened to be responsible for implementation of the policy, a fact which makes the EAT's decision all the more interesting.

217   Recommendations

Where an employment tribunal finds a discrimination complaint to be well founded, it has the power to recommend that the respondent should take action appearing to the tribunal to be reasonable, in all the circumstances of the case. The purpose is to obviate or reduce the adverse effect on the complainant of any matter to which the complaint relates. The recommendation should specify the period within which the action is to be taken.

There is no power to compel the respondent to take the recommended action. If, however, the respondent does not comply with a recommendation, the complainant can then bring the matter back before the tribunal. Compensation, or increased compensation, can then be ordered by the tribunal if:

(*a*)   the respondent has failed, without reasonable justification, to comply with the recommendation; and

(*b*)   the tribunal thinks it just and equitable to order the payment.

In practice, recommendations are most likely to be necessary or desirable where there has been harassment or other discrimination against a person who continues to be employed by the respondent. If a complaint of discrimination in recruitment is upheld, a possible recommendation would be that the complainant should be guaranteed an interview if he or she makes a further application for a particular kind of post, within a specified period.

218   Recruitment

218.1   GENERAL PRINCIPLES

One of the fundamental objectives of the discrimination laws is to promote equality of opportunity in access to employment. It is a great social and economic evil if workers are unfairly denied suitable employment for reasons relating to colour etc, disability or gender or marital status, religion or belief, or sexual orientation.

The law forbids discrimination both in the arrangements for deciding who should be offered employment and in the actual selection for the post. The arrangements can involve several stages prior to the *Selection* of the successful candidate, including drawing up the job description, advertising the post, shortlisting, first interviews and second interviews.

There must be no discrimination, as defined by the legislation, at any stage of the recruitment process. An employer's obligation not to discriminate in the arrangements for deciding who should be offered employment covers both the setting up of those arrangements and their implementation. This principle was confirmed by the House of Lords in *Nagarajan v London Regional Transport [1999] IRLR 572*.

Although most complaints are by unsuccessful job applicants, a person who is actually offered a job can also bring a complaint if there is discrimination in the terms on which employment has been offered.

It is foreseeable that the introduction of the *AR 2006* will have particular significance with regard to recruitment practices.

218.2   TERMS OF THE OFFER

Complaints about the terms on which employment is offered are rare in practice, but can occur. For example:

(*a*)   Offers of employment are made both to a female candidate and a male candidate, but the woman is required to serve a longer probationary period.

(*b*)   The rate of pay offered to a black candidate is lower than the rate which would have been offered if he had been white.

(*c*)   A disabled candidate receives a job offer, but the employer is not prepared to modify the job duties by removing a small and non-essential duty which, because of his disability, would cause the candidate considerable difficulties.

A candidate who wishes to complain under the *SDA 1975* about the rate of pay which has been offered, or any other financial term, can do so only if he or she would, on taking the job, have had a claim under the *EPA 1970*. For example, a woman who wishes to complain that she has been offered lower pay than a man has been offered, will be unable to present a complaint if the previous holder of the post is also a woman and if the employer does not have any male employees employed on *Like Work*, work of *Equal Value* or work which has been given an equivalent rating under a *Job Evaluation Scheme*.

218.3   DIRECT DISCRIMINATION AND VICTIMISATION

Most complaints of direct discrimination or victimisation are presented by complainants who:

218.4 Recruitment

(*a*)   have enquired about a job, or applied informally, and been rejected at that stage, perhaps even by a receptionist;

(*b*)   have been falsely told that a vacancy no longer exists;

(*c*)   have applied for a post but not been shortlisted or offered an interview; or

(*d*)   have been interviewed but not offered the job.

In the context of the *AR 2006*, an obvious form of direct discrimination is an express age limit.

218.4   INDIRECT DISCRIMINATION AND REASONABLE ADJUSTMENTS

Employers must consider the risk of indirect discrimination and also the need to make *Reasonable Adjustments* under the *DDA 1995*, in relation to:

(*a*)   job advertisements and vacancy notices;

(*b*)   job descriptions;

(*c*)   person specifications; and

(*d*)   application forms.

Employers must also have regard to the same risk and the same need, in relation to the various methods used for whittling down the number of candidates and making an appointment, including:

(*a*)   aptitude tests;

(*b*)   psychometric testing;

(*c*)   IQ tests;

(*d*)   other tests and assessments; and

(*e*)   shortlisting and selection criteria.

Employers, when drawing up or using any of the above, should:

(*a*)   ensure that they are focused on the needs of the job;

(*b*)   avoid using language that could be seen as indicating an intention to discriminate, for example in favour of a man or against a disabled candidate;

(*c*)   carefully scrutinise any method of assessment, to ensure that it is not 'loaded', for example against members of any particular ethnic group; and

(*d*)   be prepared at all times to modify the requirements and conditions of the job, or the method of assessment, to overcome disadvantages faced by a disabled candidate.

The advice regarding shortlisting and selection criteria applies whether the criteria are written or unwritten. In one case a retailer automatically excluded job applicants from a particular district in a city. That district had a high proportion of black workers. There was indirect racial discrimination against candidates from the district, even though the requirement being applied to them was neither written down in any job advertisement nor communicated to them in any other way.

218.5   TRAWLING FOR CANDIDATES

In the majority of complaints about recruitment arrangements, the complainant has applied for the post but been unsuccessful either at the shortlisting stage or when the ultimate selection is made. There can be circumstances, however, in which a complaint is made by a person who never actually applied for the job.

This was the case in *Coker v Lord Chancellor [2002] IRLR 80*. This was the widely reported tribunal case which related to the arrangements made by the Lord Chancellor for the appointment of a special adviser. The complainants had not been invited to apply for the post. Indeed they were not aware that an appointment was being made. Their contention was that they would have been suitable candidates, and would have had a chance of being appointed, if selection had not been limited to eligible candidates who were known personally to the Lord Chancellor.

The decision of the Court of Appeal highlights the limitations of all the various definitions of *Indirect Discrimination*. There is no *Disparate Impact,* where virtually all the members and non-members of the relevant group are equally disadvantaged.

The Codes of Practice under both the *SDA 1975* and the *RRA 1976* caution employers against *Word of Mouth Recruitment.* For example, local black workers could be effectively excluded from employment at a factory with a predominantly white workforce if jobs are offered informally to relatives of existing employees. If such methods also exclude, however, all but a tiny percentage of the white workers in the locality, then this could be an answer to any complaint of indirect discrimination or enforcement proceedings for a *Discriminatory Practice.* Nevertheless, the better practice is for employers to advertise all posts both internally and externally, for reasons which include the following:

(*a*)   it may well prove possible, in future appeal decisions, for a way to be found of overcoming the above-mentioned defects in the legislation;

(*b*)   some practices may involve direct discrimination (for example offering secretarial vacancies exclusively to pupils at a local single sex school could be said to involve *Gender Based Criteria*);

(*c*)   the practice is more efficient, in terms of identifying a wide range of suitable candidates.

Whatever the general practice, the employer must also cater for the following special circumstances:

(*a*)   Where a woman returning from maternity leave cannot go back to her old job, because of redundancy, she must be offered a suitable alternative post, if one is vacant and available.

(*b*)   Where there is a need to redeploy a worker, because of his or her disability, consideration should be given to offering any suitable alternative post as a *Reasonable Adjustment.*

(*c*)   It would normally be justifiable for an employer to suspend any policy of advertising posts externally during any redundancy period, so that priority can be given to finding suitable alternative employment for the employees who are facing redundancy.

It can be a difficult exercise for employers to comply with sometimes conflicting legal obligations in a way which:

(*a*)   promotes equal opportunity;

(*b*)   gives the employer the widest possible choice;

(*c*)   encourages diversity; and

(*d*)   motivates existing staff.

218.6   **PRACTICAL ADVICE ON RECRUITMENT**

Some suggestions have been made about avoiding indirect or disability discrimination in methods of testing. Further advice is given in relation to *Advertisements*, *Job Interviews* and *Selection*. The following are guidelines on the recruitment process as a whole:

(*a*)   The general practice should be to prepare at the outset a job description and also a person specification, listing both the essential and the desirable qualities for the post. It helps to avoid both the fact and the appearance of discrimination at any stage if candidates can be measured against specified criteria.

(*b*)   The general practice should be to advertise jobs, always internally and usually externally as well. Simply picking a person out, or using other informal recruitment methods, invites complaints from potential candidates, particularly internal candidates who have been overlooked.

(*c*)   Many organisations have a large number of employees who are involved in recruitment in some way and who have the power to reject or eliminate candidates. Sometimes the employee can be quite junior, such as a receptionist or telephonist who deals with enquiries about unskilled jobs which have been advertised. Appropriate guidance and preferably *Training* should be given to all these employees.

(*d*)   It is good practice to include a short statement of the equal opportunity policy and the 'disability symbol' in all advertisements and application forms, both to encourage candidates and to help focus the minds of employees involved in selection.

Requiring, for instance, 'maturity', qualifications linked to age and experience have all become more problematic following the introduction of the *AR 2006*.

Even where guidance and training have been given, there are some decisions which should always be made at a senior level and based on specialist advice, for example from the HR department. These include decisions relating to:

(*a*)   any decision in exceptional circumstances to recruit for a post without advertising that post, even internally;

(*b*)   the adoption of criteria etc. which will exclude candidates who cannot comply with them;

(*c*)   the design and content of application forms;

(*d*)   adoption of the limited measures of *Positive Discrimination* which the law permits;

(*e*)   reliance on the *Genuine Occupational Qualification*; and

(*f*)   the use of *Psychometric Testing* or other tests.

219   Redundancy

The question of discrimination in relation to selection for redundancy is considered under *Dismissal*.

Access to voluntary redundancy is potentially a *Benefit*. There must be no unlawful discrimination when inviting or dealing with applications.

Complaints may also be made about the amount of a redundancy payment, whether the redundancy is voluntary or compulsory and whether the scheme under which the payment is made is statutory, contractual or discretionary. Where the complaint is one of sex discrimination, it should be under both the *SDA 1975* and the *EPA 1970*. A redundancy payment is pay for the purposes of *Article 141*, but the *SDA 1975* may be the appropriate Act if the scheme is discretionary.

The *AR 2006* provides that for an employer to make a redundancy payment under the statutory scheme (which, arguably, has discriminatory age-related components) is legitimate by reason of *Statutory Authority*.

The *AR 2006* also contain provisions legitimising enhanced redundancy payments based upon, but more generous than, the statutory scheme.

220 References

Great care must be taken by employers in considering applications for references by or in respect of former employees. A refusal to grant a reference, or giving an unfavourable reference, could lead to a complaint of discrimination or victimisation – see *Post Employment Discrimination.*

221 Relationships at Work

Many people marry or have long-term relationships with people whom they meet at work. But in some employments, it is potentially inappropriate and a breach of trust for certain workers to form relationships with those whom they meet through the job. This includes teachers and their pupils, social workers and their clients, foster parents and their charges, and probation officers and those on probation. The *Sexual Offences (Amendment) Act 2000* outlaws sexual activity between those caring for young people or vulnerable adults and their clients. It also includes volunteers, regardless of whether they are in the public, private or voluntary sectors.

Some employers lay down policies about forming relationships at work. These may set out, for example, what the parties should do in terms of reporting the relationship to management. In some cases, it may be appropriate for the parties to agree to appropriate redeployment, so that they are not working directly together. But it is important that any such provision should not discriminate unlawfully, e.g. on grounds of marital status contrary to the *SDA 1975*, and that there should be a clear objective justification for it.

The pitfalls are illustrated by the EAT's decision in *Chief Constable of Bedfordshire Constabulary v Graham [2002] IRLR 239*. A woman was appointed to the post of area inspector in the division of a police force of which her husband was divisional commander. The Chief Constable rescinded the appointment because he considered that:

(*a*)   she would not be a competent and compellable witness against her spouse in any criminal proceedings (and he later said in evidence that this was the major factor in his reasoning);

(*b*)   it would be difficult for officers under her supervision to make a complaint or take out a grievance against her;

(*c*)   it would be more difficult to deal with any possible problems relating to under-performance by her.

A tribunal found that a man would have been treated in the same way, so dismissed the complaint of direct sex discrimination. However, the tribunal found indirect sex discrimination and both direct and indirect marriage discrimination. The tribunal pointed out that the Chief Constable had not given any examples of the perceived problems and they regarded his concerns as speculative. The evidence was that many forces had married officers and couples working together at all ranks and some forces encouraged couples to work together. The tribunal considered that this was a case where discriminatory effect was disproportionate to the reasonable needs of the employer, as the perceived problems could readily have been overcome. The EAT upheld this decision. Since the issue of competence and compellability can only arise between people who are married to each other, the Chief Constable's action was marriage-specific and thus directly discriminatory.

Nevertheless, there may be legitimate areas of concern in respect of relationships at work. For example, other employees may have the perception that one person in the relationship may be guilty of favouritism towards the other. Such perceptions, whether justified or not, can be corrosive, as can any perceptions of nepotism or *Cronyism*.

A second danger concerns a possible increased risk of improper disclosure of confidential information. In cases where breach of confidentiality is an objectively demonstrable risk, the problem may in some cases be resolved by ensuring that the partners in the relationship work separately, although in many cases that may neither be feasible nor desirable and in any event care needs to be taken to ensure that there is no unlawful discrimination in relation to the person who is moved.

A further possible danger concerns adverse effects upon productivity, which are occasionally manifested by inappropriate or excessive uses of an internal email system. In appropriate cases, action pursuant to the employer's disciplinary procedures may become relevant.

Employers may also have a legitimate concern that if a relationship at work breaks down, then personal animosity may spill over into the workplace. For instance, if one party tries to rekindle the relationship when the other party is unwilling to do so, there may be a risk of *Harassment*.

In the United States of America, some businesses have asked employees who form personal relationships to sign legally binding agreements, by which typically they undertake not to sue the company if the relationship breaks down. These 'consensual relationship agreements' are sometimes colloquially referred to as 'love contracts'. They may range from letters countersigned by the employees, indicating that they have entered voluntarily into the relationship (and, therefore, not as a result of improper pressure, perhaps from one partner who occupies a more senior role than the other) to more formal documents setting out explicit examples of appropriate behaviour. The agreement may require the couples to use the organisation's grievance procedure if the relationship breaks down or to agree to use *Alternative Dispute Resolution* in preference to issuing court proceedings to resolve any disputes.

It seems unlikely that such agreements will find widespread favour in the UK. Quite apart from differences in workplace culture, the statutory prohibition on contracting-out of employment protection rights operates as a major constraint on the value of any such agreement. Furthermore, it may be that the *Human Rights Act 1998* will be relevant in some cases, since a public employer's attempt to control personal relationships may fall foul of the right to respect for private life.

222   Religion or Belief

222.1   INTRODUCTION

The *RBR 2003*, implementing provisions of the *Framework Directive,* came into force on 2 December 2003. Prior to that time, acts of discrimination on religious grounds were not generally prohibited in Great Britain unless they constituted acts of indirect racial discrimination. The *RBR 2003* utilised concepts familiar from other *Discrimination Laws* (and some less familiar concepts) in outlawing:

(*a*)   Direct Discrimination;

(*b*)   Indirect Discrimination;

(*c*)   Victimisation;

(*d*)   Harassment;

on grounds of 'religion or belief'.

The less familiar concepts are the definitions of indirect discrimination and harassment, taken from the *Framework Directive.*

The *RBR 2003* protect workers and cover:

(*a*)   employment;

(*b*)   contract work;

(*c*)   office-holders;

(*d*)   partners;

(*e*)   providers of vocational training;

(*f*)   employment agencies.

The *RBR 2003* were modified by the *Equality Act 2006.*

222.2   RELIGION OR BELIEF

Regulation 2(1) of the RBR 2003 originally defined 'religion or belief' as 'any religion, religious belief, or similar philosophical belief'. As a result of changes made by the *Equality Act 2006:*

(*a*)   'religion' means any religion;

(*b*)   'belief' means any religious or philosophical belief;

(*c*)   a reference to religion includes a reference to lack of religion; and

(*d*)   a reference to belief includes a reference to lack of belief.

It is no longer necessary for a philosophical belief to be 'similar' to a religious belief; and non-believers are now given specific protection.

It is for courts and tribunals to determine, in accordance with the *Framework Directive*, whether a particular religion or belief falls within this definition. The definition is in line with the right to freedom of religion prescribed by *Article 9* of the *European Convention on Human Rights.* It includes religions widely recognised in this country such as Christianity, Islam, Hinduism, Judaism, Buddhism, Sikhism and Rastafarianism. Equally, branches of sects within a religion – e.g. Protestants or Catholics within the Christian Church – can fall within the definition. The European Court of Human Rights has recognised other collective religions, which include Druidism and the Church of Scientology. For the purposes of *Article 9*, a religion must have a clear structure and belief systems, but even if a belief does not meet that test, it may constitute a 'similar philosophical belief'.

Similarly, 'religious belief' is a broad context, again in accordance with *Article 9*. It may go further than a belief about adherence to a religion or its main articles of faith. It may include other beliefs found in a religion, if they attain a certain level of cogency, seriousness, cohesion and importance, provided that the beliefs are worthy of respect in a democratic society and are not incompatible with human dignity.

References to 'religious beliefs' and 'similar philosophical belief' include reference to a person's belief structure involving the absence of particular beliefs, because as the explanatory notes state, 'these are two sides of the same coin . . . For example, if a Christian employer refuses an individual a job, because he is not Christian, regardless of whether he is a Muslin, Hindu, Atheist (etc), that would be direct discrimination on grounds of the individual's religious belief, which can be described as 'non-Christian'. It is not necessary to identify the individual as an atheist or a Hindu . . . in such circumstances if he can be identified as a 'non-Christian'. The same is true of persons who might describe themselves as 'unconcerned' by religious beliefs or 'unsure' of them'.

A 'manifestation' of, or conduct based upon or expressing a religion or belief is not covered by the definition. For instance, a person might wear certain clothing, or pray at certain times in accordance with the tenets of his religion, or may express views, and say or do other things reflecting his beliefs. It is not in itself unlawful *Direct Discrimination* under *RBR 2003* for such a person to suffer a disadvantage because he has done or said something in this way. It would only be *Direct Discrimination* if a person with different beliefs (or none) was treated more favourably in similar circumstances. However, where an employer lays down conditions about, for instance, a dress code or prayer breaks, these may constitute indirect discrimination under *RBR 2003* unless they are justified. The DTI's explanatory notes add:

> 'It has been suggested that membership of a cult or sect considered dangerous, or centred on unlawful conduct could not be considered as a religion for the purposes of [*RBR 2003*]. However, there are no cults of which a membership is unlawful in Britain. In principle, such a sect could be recognised as a religion for the purposes of [*RBR 2003*] . . . But . . . "religion or belief" does not include conduct based on those beliefs. So it would not be direct discrimination to treat an individual less favourably because he is involved in unlawful conduct. Nor would it generally be indirect discrimination, even if such treatment particularly disadvantaged members of a sect, if it could be justified by the concern about unlawful conduct.'

222.3   DIRECT DISCRIMINATION

The general principles of *Direct Discrimination* apply to the *RBR 2003*. Thus it would not, for instance, constitute direct discrimination on grounds of religion or belief for an employer to refuse to allow Muslim employees to take a prayer break at certain times, if he refused breaks for all employees at that time. (Although, if unjustified, the refusal might constitute *Indirect Discrimination*.) Discrimination based on perception of a person's religion or belief (whether the perception is or is not correct) is covered. However, direct discrimination because of the discriminator's religion or belief is not. Accordingly, an employer with strong religious views who refuses to employ a person because she is female or gay does not discriminate on grounds of religion or belief. The cause of the difference of treatment, viewed objectively, is the sex or sexual orientation of the applicant. There would, however, be grounds for a complaint under the *SOR 2003*, unless one of the specific exceptions applied.

222.4   **INDIRECT DISCRIMINATION**

Regulation 4 of the *RBR 2003* provides that *Indirect Discrimination occurs* where:

(*a*)   A applies to B a provision, criterion or practice which A applies equally to other person; and

(*b*)   that provision, criterion or practice puts persons of B's religion or belief at a particular disadvantage; and

(*c*)   B suffers that disadvantage; and

(*d*)   A cannot justify the provision, criterion or practice as a proportionate means of achieving a legitimate aim.

The test of 'group disadvantage' is relatively flexible; statistical evidence will not always be necessary in order to show that there has been a 'particular disadvantage'. This is significant, since reliable statistics in respect of certain religions or beliefs may not be readily available.

Under the *RBR 2003*, the person's relevant religion or belief group may be identified in two ways. It may be that his religion or belief is identified as being (for instance) Jewish or atheist on the one hand, or 'non-Muslim' on the other. However, he describes his beliefs, he must establish that the relevant group of people with those beliefs is put at a particular disadvantage. The DTI gives the illustration of a job advertisement for a leader of a play group for Muslim children which specifies that applicants must be familiar with the teachings of the Koran. A Jewish applicant might be disadvantaged, and to establish a 'group disadvantage', he might demonstrate that the requirement disadvantaged all Jewish applicants, or simply all non-Muslim applicants. There will be no difference in the practical outcome – although it might, of course, be that the requirement could be justified by the nature of the job.

Further, the requirement of 'individual disadvantage' means that abstract test cases cannot be brought.

A danger area for employers is where special treatment is given to avoid discriminating against certain employees. That treatment might amount to unlawful *Direct Discrimination* if it amounts to less favourable treatment of others on the grounds of their religion or belief. This could be the case if a Jewish employee was given an extra day of paid leave to mark a religious festival, because it would directly discriminate against employees who are atheist or who follow other faiths. If the Jewish employee were required to use one day of his existing holiday leave entitlement, there would be no direct discrimination against other employees.

222.5   **VICTIMISATION AND HARASSMENT**

It is not necessarily harassment contrary to *RBR 2003* for an employee who happens to be Hindu to be bullied. The religion or belief would have to be the reason for the harassment in question. To constitute harassment, the conduct must have the 'purpose or effect' of harassing the person, i.e. violating his dignity or creating an intimidating, hostile, degrading, humiliating or offensive environment for him. But if an excessively sensitive individual unreasonably took offence at a perfectly innocent comment related to his religious beliefs, that would not constitute harassment because the comment could not reasonably have been considered to have violated his dignity or created an offensive environment for him. Whether the person alleged to have committed the act of harassment was aware of the religion or belief in question may be relevant, but by no means provides an absolute defence to a complaint. Thus, if an employer tells a joke which he admits is offensive to Muslims, it would be reasonable to consider that the joke offended a Muslim employee to whom he told it.

222.6   DISCRIMINATION AGAINST EMPLOYEES

The impact of the *RBR 2003* is potentially far-reaching. For example, an employer may need to consider whether pay arrangements providing for double pay on Sundays are discriminatory. Where they disadvantage employees whose faith recognises a day of rest other than Sunday, they may constitute *Indirect Discrimination*. Often, however, the arrangements may be justifiable by reference to market forces requiring the employer to pay such rates in order to attract sufficient staff to work on Sundays.

To deal with requests for days off in a discriminatory way may cause a detriment to employees which is unlawful. For instance, an employer who refuses all requests for time off during a specific period might disadvantage employees of a particular faith requiring followers to abstain from work during that period. The employer would need to justify his conduct as a proportionate means of achieving a legitimate objective, e.g. coping with a large order crucial to the business which requires an intense work period. The refusal to grant time off would, for instance, be unlikely to be proportionate if the business needs could still be met in circumstances where only a small number of staff were taking, say, a single day off work to mark a festival.

Conversely, an employer's insistence that all employees take time off on Christmas Day would not constitute *Direct Discrimination* against employees of faiths other than Christianity, because all employees would be required not to work on that day, regardless of their faith. Such requirement might amount to *Indirect Discrimination* if unjustified. In most circumstances, however, the requirement could be justified on the basis that Christmas Day is a holiday widely recognised throughout Britain, on which few businesses are open and most employees take holiday so that it is difficult to find a sufficient number of employees to work on Christmas Day.

222.7   GENUINE OCCUPATIONAL REQUIREMENT

Regulation 7 of RBR 2003 provides an exception permitting an employer, when recruiting for a post, to treat applicants differently on grounds of religion or belief if being of a particular religion or belief is a genuine occupation requirement (GOR) for that post. The exception may also be relevant when an employer promotes, transfers or trains a person for a post, and when dismissing from a post where a GOR applies in relation to that post. A GOR cannot justify victimisation or harassment. The exception may apply where a person is dismissed because, after taking up a post to which a GOR applies, his religion or belief changes. The DTI guidance notes that 'in the vast majority of jobs, a person's religion or belief has no bearing on whether or not they can perform the functions of the job in question'. However, there are some jobs where a GOR could apply. For example, if a hospital were to employ a chaplain to minister to patients and staff, it might specify that he or she must be

Christian, because almost all the patients and staff are Christian. If the patients and staff represented a number of different faiths, the hospital might need to give consideration to whether a minister of another faith could also carry out the job, including ministering to those of faiths other than his or her own. Even in that case, the hospital could probably specify that the chaplain must be a minister of religion, rather than an atheist, for example.

In essence, a GOR must be:

(*a*)   essential;

(*b*)   determining;

(*c*)   occupational;

(*d*)   genuine.

A further exception protects employers with an ethos based on religion or belief. The employer must show that he has an ethos based on religion or belief and that the GOR has to be applied having regard to that ethos. In such circumstances, however, the GOR does not have to be a determining requirement. The DTI guidance points out that sometimes questions may arise as to the identity of the employer for the purpose of establishing if it has religious ethos. For instance, if a play group with a Jewish ethos hires a member of staff, the employer is the person or body running the group who hires the recruit. Thus it is for the employer to show that its organisation running the group has an ethos based on religion or belief.

222.8   **POSITIVE ACTION**

Regulation 25 of the *RBR 2003* permits *Positive Discrimination*, or 'positive action', in certain circumstances, and so comparable to *sections 37* and *38* of the *RRA 1976*. Positive action is allowed where it reasonably appears that it prevents or compensates for disadvantages linked to religion or belief among the relevant section of people to whom the positive action relates. For example, if an employer based in an area with a large Hindu population has only a small number of Hindu employees, when advertising for new recruits he could include a statement that 'applications from Hindus are particularly welcome'. But it would be unlawful to give preference to a Hindu job applicant over an applicant of another faith, simply because the employer wishes to have more Hindu employees.

223   Remedies

In the event of a successful discrimination claim, an employment tribunal must consider which of the following remedies it is just and equitable to grant:

(*a*)   a declaration as to the rights of the complainant and the respondent in relation to the matters to which the complaint relates;

(*b*)   an order for the respondent to pay *Compensation* to the complainant; or

(*c*)   a *Recommendation*.

There is no limit on the amount of compensation which may be awarded although an award of compensation is not automatic where the complaint is one of *Indirect Discrimination*.

Where a complaint under the *EPA 1970* is upheld, the employment tribunal makes an order declaring the rights of the parties. The employment tribunal may also award damages or arrears of remuneration. No payment by way of arrears of remuneration or damages may be awarded in respect of a time earlier than two years before the date of commencement of the proceedings. That limitation has now been disapplied because it was inconsistent with *Article 141* – see *Back Pay*.

224   Residential Requirements

The issue of residential requirements is more likely to arise outside the employment field, but *Indirect Discrimination* in employment can occur where there are requirements or conditions relating to the place of residence or length of residence in a particular area.

An obvious example is a requirement or condition relating to length of residence in the UK.

A policy of not employing workers from a particular district could also be indirect racial discrimination, if that district contains a high proportion of racial minority workers. *Hussein v Saints Complete House Furnisher [1979] IRLR 337* is an example of such a case. The owner of the business had found in the past that, when he recruited staff from the central districts of Liverpool, their unemployed friends tended to loiter outside the shop and discourage customers. Accordingly he stipulated that he would not consider job applicants from those districts. Approximately half of the population of the districts in question were black. The employment tribunal decided that the requirement was not justifiable. Accordingly, a complaint of indirect racial discrimination was upheld.

225   Respondent

The respondent to a tribunal case is the party against whom the case is brought.

Most complaints about discrimination in employment are by job applicants or employees against employers and most of the examples given in this handbook relate to such cases.

Where the alleged act of discrimination is by an agent or by a manager or other employee acting in the course of his employment, that agent or manager or other employee can also be made a respondent to the complaint – see *Joint Respondents*.

Respondents can also include:

(*a*)   Qualifying Bodies;

(*b*)   Employers', Trade and Professional Associations;

(*c*)   Trade Unions;

(*d*)   Training Bodies;

(*e*)   Employment Agencies; and

(*f*)   Partnerships.

Partnerships, like any other employer, can be respondents to complaints by job applicants and employees. In addition, they can be respondents to complaints by partners in the firm or by a person who wishes to become a partner.

226   Restricted Reporting Orders

An employment tribunal may make a restricted reporting order in two circumstances:

(*a*)   if the case involves allegations of sexual misconduct; or

(*b*)   if the complaint is under the *DDA 1995* and evidence of a personal nature is likely to be heard by the tribunal.

Either party may apply for a restricted reporting order. Alternatively the tribunal may make an order of its own motion. An order may not be made until each party has been given the opportunity to oppose the making of the order at a hearing.

Where a restricted reporting order is made, it specifies the persons who may not be identified in any report of the proceedings. The order is, however, of limited value to any party or witness who is protected by it, because it remains in force only until the promulgation of the decision (or earlier if revoked by the tribunal).

In *Chief Constable of the West Yorkshire Police v A [2000] IRLR 465*, an employment tribunal made a restricted reporting order to protect the identity of a transsexual complainant, having heard unchallenged evidence of the abuse which she was likely to suffer if her identity were to be revealed. The tribunal purported to make the order under the Rules of Procedure and also under an inherent jurisdiction deriving from the *Equal Treatment Directive*, the respondent in the case, the *Police* being an emanation of the State (see *Public Sector*). The EAT held that the case was not covered by the Rules of Procedure but there was no appeal against the making of the order under the Directive and the President of the EAT said that he was not in a position to rule the tribunal to have been wrong in law. Furthermore, the EAT exercised its own jurisdiction under the Directive to grant a restricted reporting order in perpetual terms.

In *X v Stevens [2003] IRLR 411*, a post-operative transsexual was turned down for a post with a police force. She claimed she had been discriminated against because of her gender reassignment, but the police contended that she had been turned down because she was suspected of criminal offences. Issues arose as to whether or not a restricted reporting order and/or an order for register deletion (available in a case that appears to involve allegations of the commission of a sexual offence) should be made so as to protect the transsexual's identity. A tribunal, following *Chief Constable of West Yorkshire Police v A,* concluded that there is no power to make a restricted reporting order whether there is an allegation of 'sexual misconduct'. However, the EAT said that even where there is no allegation of sexual misconduct or a sexual offence, employment tribunals and the EAT have the power to make orders analogous to a restricted reporting order and/or a register deletion order. Alternatively, they can make some provision in respect of confidentiality, so as to protect the identity of an applicant in a case where there has been a finding of fact that they would be deterred from bringing proceedings under the *SDA 1975* in the absence of such an order. According to the EAT, such a power is necessary to give effect to *Article 6* of the *Equal Treatment Directive*.

227   Retirement and Dismissal

227.1   INTRODUCTION

The coming into force of the *AR 2006* means that compulsory retirement is more susceptible to legal challenge than previously. Compulsory retirement may amount to age discrimination and/or unfair dismissal.

Regulation 7(2)(d) of the *AR 2006* provides that it is unlawful for an employer to discriminate against a person whom he employs in Great Britain by dismissing him. Since any compulsory retirement is potentially discriminatory, each would need to be justified in accordance with *Regulation 3* were it not for the rules concerning the *Default Retirement Age* of 65 prescribed in relation to employees by *Regulation 30(2)*. However, *Regulation 30* does not apply to compulsory retirement at an age below 65 and providing *Justification* for a lower compulsory retirement age may prove difficult in practice. Further, the *Duty to Consider* procedure requires the employer to consider a request by an employee to continue working after the expected retirement date.

227.2   UNFAIR DISMISSAL

The *AR 2006* abolished the upper age limit for eligibility to claim unfair dismissal. Further, 'retirement' of the employee is now a potentially fair reason for dismissal.

Establishing whether the principal reason for dismissal is retirement is important. If retirement is the reason for dismissal, the *Duty to Consider* procedure must be followed. In other cases, the statutory dismissal and disciplinary procedure must be followed. An employer who follows the wrong procedure will find it difficult to escape a finding of unfair dismissal.

The *AR 2006* presumes that retirement is the reason for dismissal where:

(*a*)   the employee has no normal retirement age (NRA), the employer gives the required notice and the dismissal takes effect on or after the employee's 65th birthday and on the intended date of retirement;

(*b*)   the employee has an NRA over 65, the employer gives the required notice and the dismissal takes effect on or after the employee has reached the NRA and on the intended date of retirement;

(*c*)   the employee has an NRA below 65 but which does not amount to unlawful discrimination, the employer has given the required notice and the dismissal takes effect on or after the employee has reached the NRA and on the intended date of retirement.

Retirement is deemed not to be the reason for dismissal where:

(*a*)   the employee has no NRA, but the dismissal takes effect before the employee attains 65;

(*b*)   the employee has no NRA, the employer gives the required notice, but the dismissal takes effect before the intended date of retirement notified to the employee;

(*c*)   the employee has an NRA but the dismissal takes effect before the employee reaches the NRA;

(*d*)   the employee has an NRA of 65 or more, the employer gives the required notice but the dismissal takes effect before the intended date of retirement;

(*e*)   the employer does not give the required notice to the employee, but does notify the employee of an intended date of retirement, where the dismissal takes effect before that intended date;

(*f*)   the dismissal takes effect before that intended date;

(*g*)   he employee has an NRA below 65, the dismissal takes effect after the NRA, but the employer has discriminated on the ground of age by failing objectively to justify that NRA;

(*h*)   the employee has an NRA below 65, that NRA is justified and the employer has given the required notice, but the dismissal takes effect before the intended retirement date.

Further, the tribunal has to consider whether retirement is the reason for dismissal or not where:

(*a*)   the employer has not given the required notification to the employee; or

(*b*)   where the employer has given the required notification, but the dismissal takes effect after the intended date of retirement.

In the former case, the tribunal must take into account, and in the latter case it may take into account, the factors set out in *section 98ZF* of the *Employment Rights Act 1996*, i.e.:

(*a*)   whether or not the employer notified the employee in accordance with *paragraph 4 of Schedule 6* to the *AR 2006*;

(*b*)   if notice was given in accordance with that paragraph, how long before the intended retirement date it was given; and

(*c*)   whether or not the employer followed, or tried to follow, the procedures in *paragraph 7* of *Schedule 6* to the *AR 2006*.

There is a special test of fairness in respect of retirement dismissals, prescribed by *section 98ZG* of the *Employment Rights Act 1996*. An employee is deemed to have been unfairly dismissed if, and only if, there has been a failure on the part of the employer to comply with an obligation imposed on him by *paragraphs 4, 6 and 7, or 8 of Schedule 6* to the *AR 2006*. In practical terms, the key question is whether the employer has correctly followed the *Duty to Consider* procedure. 'Reasonableness' is not the issue.

In the case of an unfair dismissal, a question that may arise when considering compensation is whether the sum awarded should be reduced to reflect the chance that the employer would have dismissed in any event if a fair procedure had been followed. In summary, compensation may be reduced in the event of a formal defect in the *Duty to Consider* procedure where it can be shown that the employee would have been dismissed in any event.

228   Review

As with other tribunal cases, an unsuccessful party in a discrimination case can apply for the tribunal to review its decision, for example because new evidence has become available or because the interests of justice require a review.

An application for a review must be made at the hearing or in writing, supported by full grounds, not later than 14 days after the date on which the decision is sent to the parties. Although a chairman may extend the time extensions are not lightly granted.

Where review hearings are granted, they do not always take place within 42 days after the date on which the decision is sent to the parties. In such circumstances any appeal should be lodged within the 42-day period (and withdrawn if the review is successful and there is no longer any need for the appeal).

229   Same Employment

The *EPA 1970* requires that any comparator must be in the same employment as the claimant. They must be employed at the same establishment or at two establishments, at which *Common Terms and Conditions* are observed. But 'same employment' is a developing concept and it is not synonymous with 'working for the same employer'.

It was held by the EAT in *Scullard v Knowles and Southern Regional Council for Education and Training [1996] IRLR 344* that *Article 141*, which has 'paramount force', permits a wider class of comparators. Under the wider test, a complainant may name a comparator carrying out work 'in the same establishment or service'. The EAT remitted the case to a different employment tribunal to consider whether unit managers employed by two different regional advisory councils were part of the same service for the purpose of *Article 141*.

In *Lawrence and others v Regent Office Care and others [2002] IRLR 823*, the ECJ considered whether catering assistants and school cleaners, all now employed by private contractors but some being former employees of North Yorkshire County Council, were entitled to bring an equal pay claim naming as comparators current employees of the county council whose work had been rated as of equal value to their own work. The ECJ ruled that they were not entitled to do so.

In *Allonby v Accrington & Rossendale College [2004] IRLR 224*, the college had terminated or not renewed the contracts of employment of part-time lecturers and instead obtained their services as subcontractors, through an agency. Their contracts with the agency, as self-employed workers, were less beneficial than the contracts of their former colleagues who continued to be employed by the college as full-time lecturers. The ECJ ruled that *Article 141* was not directly applicable as between on the one hand the full-time lecturers employed by the college and on the other hand the part-time lecturers who were no longer employees of the college and were self-employed contract workers.

In both the above cases, the ECJ confirmed that the application of *Article 141* is not limited to situations in which men and women work for the same employer. The Article may be relied on in particular in cases arising directly from legislative provisions or collective labour agreements, as well as in cases in which work is carried out in the same establishment or service, whether private or public. Where, however, the differences identified in the pay conditions of workers performing equal work or work of equal value cannot be attributed to a single source, there is no body which is responsible for the inequality and which could restore equal treatment. Such a situation does not come within the scope of *Article 141(1) EC*.

In *Robertson and others v DEFRA [2005] IRLR 363*, the Court of Appeal made it clear that the simple fact that a complainant and their comparator of a different sex are employed by the same employer is not in itself sufficient to allow an equal pay comparison. Having a common employer is not necessarily the same as being 'in the same employment' or having pay and conditions attributed to a 'single source' as laid down by the European Court of Justice in *Lawrence v Regent Office Care Ltd [2002] IRLR 822*. The 'single source' test is an approach of general application, indicating that something more than just the bare fact of common employment is required for comparability purposes. The critical question is whether there is a single body responsible for the discriminatory pay differences of which complaint is made. This is not resolved by only addressing the formal legal question of the identity of the employer. If that were not the case, every civil servant would be entitled to compare herself or himself with any other civil servant of the opposite sex, subject only to objective justification by the employer of differences in pay. Pay and conditions of civil servants are no longer negotiated or agreed centrally on a civil service-wide basis. Each individual department has delegated to it responsibility for negotiating and agreeing the pay of civil servants employed inter-department, subject to overall budgetary control by the Treasury. Individual departments are free to negotiate and agree upon most terms and conditions of employment. On the facts of the present case, therefore, there were two sources of the difference in pay. DEFRA was the single source responsible for the claimants' pay and conditions, while the Department of the Environment, Transportation and the Regions (DETR) was the single source responsible for the comparators' pay and conditions. The simple fact of common employment by the Crown was not sufficient to attribute the terms and conditions to the Crown as the single source responsible for determining levels of pay in both DEFRA and DETR.

In *Armstrong v Newcastle upon Tyne NHS Hospital Trust [2006] IRLR 124*, the Court of Appeal upheld a tribunal's decision that female ancillary workers employed at hospitals (other than the Royal Victoria Infirmary) run by the Trust could not use male ancillary workers at the Royal Victoria Infirmary as comparators for equal pay purposes, notwithstanding that they had the same employer. The Trust could not be regarded as a 'single source' for the purposes of *Article 141*. To constitute a single source for those purposes, it is not enough for a claimant to show that they have the same employer as the comparator. In accordance with the Court of Appeal's decision in *Robertson v DEFRA*, they must show that the employer was also the body responsible for setting the terms of both groups of employees. Whether this is the case depends on an evaluation of all the evidence. In this case, that the Trust had taken some part in negotiating terms and conditions at departmental level, and there was some evidence of the harmonisation of terms and conditions, did not mean that the tribunal could only properly conclude that the Trust had assumed responsibility for the terms and conditions of all the employees for the purposes of the *Robertson* test.

230   Schools

It is always important for an employee to be clear as to the identity of his or her employer. In some cases, identifying the employer precisely is by no means straight-forward. Examples often arise in the education sector. Is a teacher, or another employee of a school, employed by the governing body of the school or by the local education authority?

The question arose in *Murphy v Slough Borough Council [2005] IRLR 382* and the Court of Appeal made it clear that determining the appropriate respondent was not a purely formal issue. The real significance in that case related to the financial position of the employer in relation to a claim of disability discrimination by a teacher. The employer's financial resources were relevant both to the question of justification and as to whether there had been any breach of the duty to make *Reasonable Adjustments*. The financial position of the governing body was potentially very different from that of the local education authority. The Court of Appeal decided that the only proper respondent on the facts was the governing body. But the tribunal was wrong to conclude that, in accordance with *Article 3(1)(b)* of the *Education (Modifications of Enactments Relating to Employment Order 1999*, the governing body is made the employer in all cases brought by a teacher under the *Disability Discrimination Act 1995*. That was too sweeping a view of the law. The liability of the governing body as an employer when a disability discrimination claim is brought by a teacher only exists when the claim relates to the exercise by such a body of the employment powers vested in it. If complaint is being made about the exercise of an employment power retained by the local authority, the claim should cite the auth-ority as the respondent. But if the act complained of is one where the governing body is given the power, the only the governing body can be made a respondent. In this case, given that the governing body had the power to appoint, suspend and dismiss a teacher, it would be absurd if it were not to be held to have the power to grant leave to a teacher at its school and to decide whether or not such leave should be paid or unpaid – i.e. the issue in dispute.

231   Scotland

The *Discrimination Laws* all apply to Scotland as well as to England and Wales. There are some differences in terminology and in references to other legislation, but in substance the same rules apply in each part of Great Britain.

Employment Tribunals sit in Scotland as well as in England and Wales, but with their separate (albeit similar) rules of procedure – see *Tribunal Procedure*.

In England and Wales, a statutory Commission can apply to the county court for an injunction to prevent *Persistent Discrimination*. In Scotland, the application is made to the sheriff court for an interdict.

232   Search and Selection

Not all posts filled with the assistance of recruitment consultants are advertised. In some cases, particularly where the post is a senior one, potentially suitable candidates are approached and invited to apply, or even 'head-hunted' and offered the post without having to compete for it.

There is a danger that any such process, if it tends to exclude, for example, women or racial minorities, may be vulnerable to an individual complaint of *Indirect Discrimination* or to a complaint by the relevant Commission that a *Discriminatory Practice* is being operated. Such methods of recruitment may be justifiable, however, particularly in circumstances where suitable candidates who already occupy senior positions in other organisations would not be likely to answer an advertisement and would respond only to a direct approach. The decision of the Court of Appeal in *Coker v Lord Chancellor [2002] IRLR 80*, moreover, suggests that *Indirect Discrimination* is unlikely in such circumstances.

It is, of course, essential that this process should not be influenced in any way by the race, sex, sexual orientation or religion of the person who is approached or of any other potential candidate. Care must also be taken to comply with the *DDA 1995* in a case where a potential candidate has a disability.

233   Secondment

Questions may arise as to the status of *Contract Workers*, with particular reference to the case where there is a commercial relationship between the agency which supplies the workers and the organisation which needs to have the work carried out.

Arrangements for employees to do work for other organisations also commonly take the form of secondments, for example by one group company to another. In any such case, it is necessary to look closely at the circumstances in order to ascertain what obligations either or both of the organisations have under the discrimination laws. Where one group company seconds or assigns a worker to another group company, the most likely consequences are:

(*a*)   the second company becomes the employer for the duration of the secondment; or

(*b*)   the first company continues to be the employer, and has obligations in that capacity, but the worker also, as a contract worker, has rights against the second company.

The case of *Chief Constable of the Lincolnshire Police v Stubbs [1999] IRLR 81* has already been referred to under *Harassment*. In that case, both the complainant and the harasser were seconded by their own force to the Regional Crime Squad. It was held that the Chief Constable of their own force continued to be the employer and was therefore liable for the acts of harassment complained of.

234   Segregation

It is only the *RRA 1976* which expressly includes segregation (on racial grounds) within the definition of direct discrimination.

Even though segregation is not expressly referred to in the other *Discrimination Laws*, however, there are circumstances in which segregation by reference to gender or disability could be unlawful – see *Detriment*.

235   Selection

The *Discrimination Laws* render it is unlawful for an employer to discriminate:

(*a*)   against a job applicant by refusing or deliberately omitting to offer employment; and

(*b*)   against an employee, by refusing or deliberately omitting to afford the employee access to opportunities for promotion.

There are a handful of jobs covered by *Genuine Occupational Qualifications* or requirements, Guidance is given elsewhere in this book on avoiding discrimination in *Recruitment, Shortlisting* or *Job Interviews*. The following general guidance applies at all stages, from shortlisting to the selection of the candidate to be appointed:

(*a*)   An objective, structured and consistent approach will help to ensure that selection decisions are demonstrably free from the taint of discrimination or victimisation.

(*b*)   Essential requirements should be specified, so as to eliminate unqualified candidates at an early stage. At the same time, standards must not be set too high and unnecessary requirements must be avoided.

(*c*)   Training should be given to all interviewers and other persons involved in the selection process. Unlawful discrimination will not necessarily be avoided by individuals who rely only on untutored good intentions.

(*d*)   The reasons for all decisions, whether in shortlisting or at later stages, should be recorded. A person who has made a decision to reject a particular candidate could have great difficulty in explaining the decision to a tribunal many months later if the reasons were not written down at the time.

(*e*)   Wherever possible, shortlisting and interviewing should not be done by one person alone but should at least be checked at a more senior level. That is good advice. Decisions are more likely to be made objectively and consistently (albeit more slowly) if they are discussed by two or more decision-makers acting together rather than being made by one person acting alone. It is also good practice for a member of the personnel department to be a party to all decisions and to be present at all interviews.

(*f*)   Candidates should at all times be treated with courtesy and consideration, whether at interviews or in correspondence or on the telephone. If the treatment which they receive is off-hand, inconsiderate or rude, they are more likely to suspect discrimination even when none has occurred.

(*g*)   All documents, including the notes made by those involved in shortlisting and selection and interview notes, should be preserved for at least six months, and longer if possible, in case any aspect of the selection process leads to a tribunal complaint. Indeed it may be necessary to keep statistical information, and summary reasons for decisions, indefinitely, as part of the *Monitoring* of the equal opportunities policy.

236   Self-Employed Workers

Discrimination Laws give rights to workers who are not conventional employees and who may be self-employed for the purposes of tax, national insurance and/or unfair dismissal – see *Employment*.

237   Seniority

Giving preferential treatment to employees on the basis of their seniority, or length of service, may contradict some principles of equal opportunities law. For instance, in some circumstances promotion on the basis of length of service could amount to unlawful indirect discrimination, as it may unjustifiably affect more women than men. It is desirable for promotion and career development patterns to be reviewed to ensure that the traditional qualifications are justifiable requirements for the job to be done, especially following the introduction of the *AR 2006*.

Cadman v Health & Safety Executive [2006] IRLR 969, is an important and controversial European Court ruling in an *Equal Pay* case concerning service-related pay scales. Pay linked to length of service tends to discriminate indirectly against women who have less continuous service than men. However, in *Danfoss [1989] IRLR 532*, the European Court held that use of length of service as a criterion in a pay system need not be justified by the employer, even if it works to the disadvantage of women, since 'length of services goes hand in hand with experience and since experience generally enables the employee to perform duties better'. In *Cadman*, the European Court ruled that, where there is a disparity in pay between men and women employed on equal work or work of equal value, as a result of using the criterion of length of service as a determinant of pay, the employer does not have to establish specifically that recourse to that criterion is appropriate as regards a particular job in order to attain the legitimate aim of rewarding experience acquired which enables the worker to perform his duties better – unless, that is, the worker provides evidence capable of raising serious doubts in that regard. In accordance with Article 141, whenever there is evidence of discrimination, it is for the employer to prove that the practice at issue is justified by objective factors unrelated to any discrimination based on sex. The justification given must be based on a legitimate objective, and the means chosen to obtain that objective must be appropriate and necessary for that purpose. The ruling in *Danfoss* acknowledged that rewarding experience acquired which enables the worker to perform his duties better constitutes a legitimate objective of pay policy. The employer is therefore free to reward length of service, without having to establish the importance it has in the performance of specific tasks entrusted to the employee. Where, however, the worker provides evidence capable of giving rise to serious doubts as to whether recourse to the criterion of length of service is, in the circumstances, appropriate to attain the objective of rewarding experience which enables the worker to perform his duties better, then it is for the employer to justify in detail his recourse to the criterion of length of service by proving, as regards to the job in question, that length of service goes hand in hand with experience and that experience enables the worker to perform his duties better. Where pay is based on a job evaluation system, if the objective pursued by using the criterion of length of service is to recognise experience, there is no need for the employer to show that an individual worker has acquired experience during the relevant period which has enabled him to perform his duties better.

In other words, there is a presumption that greater experience leads to better performance, but it is rebuttable rather than absolute. The European Court's ruling attracted considerable publicity and was the subject of a wide range of contrasting interpretations. The question that arises from the judgment was summarised by the editor of the Industrial Relations Law Reports as:

> 'How easy it will be for claimants, especially in large-scale equal value claims, to provide evidence that longer services does not actually lead to better perfor-

mance. It is certainly arguable that the proficiency gained as a result of additional service is subject to the law of diminishing returns, but the extent to which this operates will vary according to the skills required for the particular job. This, in turn, leads to the . . . question of how the worker is to get the evidence capable of raising serious doubts. This would normally be via the statutory equal pay questionnaire, but that would seem to be tantamount to asking the employer to provide evidence justifying the length between service and performance, which the Court has said is only required once serious doubts about this have been established . . . To summarise, the . . . ruling does not prohibit long-service payments, nor does it allow service as a blanket defence to equal pay claims. It appears to be saying that service-based pay cannot be unreasonably disproportionate to the proficiency gained by experience, but, if so, why invert the ordinary rules of proof and carve out a special exception for job evaluation schemes?'

In certain circumstances, seniority-related benefits are treated as not contravening the bar on age discrimination; see *Age Regulations*.

238   Sexual Harassment

The law relating to sexual harassment is considered in some detail under *Harassment*.

There are superficial differences between, on the one hand, some of the forms which sexual harassment can take and, on the other hand, the most common examples of racial harassment and harassment of disabled workers. In the latter cases, harassment usually takes the form of openly offensive or insulting language or even violence or threats of violence. Sexual harassment, however, frequently takes the form of words or actions which are intended, or apparently intended, to be friendly – indeed too friendly.

The differences are, however, only superficial. The essential characteristic of any harassment, whether sexual, racial or otherwise, is that it is conduct which is unwelcome to the recipient. The Code of Practice issued with the European Commission's Recommendation on the protection of the dignity of women and men at work contains the following passage:

> 'The essential characteristic of sexual harassment is that it is unwanted by the recipient, that it is for each individual to determine what behaviour is acceptable to them and what they regard as offensive. Sexual attention becomes sexual harassment if it is persisted in once it has been made clear that it is regarded by the recipient as offensive, although one incident of harassment may constitute sexual harassment if sufficiently serious. It is the unwanted nature of the conduct which distinguishes sexual harassment from friendly behaviour, which is welcome and mutual.'

The Code of Practice points out that sexual harassment covers a range of behaviour, including both words and actions and including:

(*a*)   conduct which is unwanted, unreasonable and offensive to the recipient;

(*b*)   the use of a person's rejection of or submission to such conduct as a basis for a decision affecting that person's access to vocational training or to employment, continued employment, promotion, salary or any other employment decisions;

(*c*)   conduct which creates an intimidating, hostile or humiliating working environment for the recipient.

239   Sexual Orientation

239.1   UNFAIR DISMISSAL

The leading case on the fairness of an employee's dismissal on the ground of sexual orientation dates back nearly a quarter of a century: *Saunders v Scottish National Camps Association Ltd [1980] IRLR 174*. A maintenance handyman was employed to work at a children's camp. His job did not require him to be in contact with the children. However, the camp manager received complaints that the employee had been found at night in the company of boy residents, although the explanations which the employee gave were accepted. A senior manager was told that the employee was homosexual and that he 'had recently been involved in a homosexual incident'. The matter was investigated and the employee was dismissed. He claimed that his dismissal was unfair. He contended that he was able to keep his private life separate from his work, and was not, in any event, interested in young persons. A psychiatrist who gave evidence on his behalf expressed the view that the employee's sexual orientation did not create a danger to young people. However, a tribunal found that the dismissal was for a 'substantial reason' and that it was fair. The EAT sitting in Glasgow upheld that ruling. In the light of changing attitudes and experience and the introduction in 2003 of regulations specifically outlawing discrimination on grounds of sexual orientation, a tribunal nowadays might arrive at a different conclusion.

To bully someone on the ground of their sexual orientation may found a claim of constructive unfair dismissal.

239.2   DEVELOPMENT OF THE LAW

Prior to the introduction of the *Employment Equality (Sexual Orientation) Regulations 2003 (SOR 2003)*, attempts to utilise existing laws to protect victims of discrimination on grounds of sexual orientation met with mixed results. Some of the decisions in which victims of discrimination succeeded were well-intentioned, but there was a tendency to try to protect victims by stretching legal principles which had not been designed for that purpose. In the joined cases of *Macdonald v Advocate General for Scotland and Pearce v Governing Body of Mayfield Secondary School [2003] IRLR 512*, the House of Lords upheld decisions that neither a member of the Royal Air Force who was dismissed because he was a homosexual, nor a teacher who was subjected to a sustained campaign of harassment because she was a lesbian, was discriminated against on grounds of sex contrary to *section 1(1)(a)* of the *SDA 1975*. The House of Lords ruled that, in that legal context, 'sex' means 'gender' and it does not include sexual orientation. Gender and sexual orientation are distinct personal characteristics. Since the *SDA 1975* is not aimed at sexual orientation, there is no justification for interpreting the expression 'on the ground of her sex' expansively so as to include cases which, in truth, are cases of discrimination on the ground of sexual orientation.

Years earlier, the European Court had ruled in *Grant v South West Trains Ltd [1998] IRLR 206*, that discrimination based on sexual orientation is not sex discrimination prohibited by European law. The focus of gay rights campaigners therefore shifted to the law on *Human Rights*.

Smith and Grady v United Kingdom [1999] IRLR 734, concerned claims brought by men and women discharged from the UK armed forces by reason of their homo-

239.3   Sexual Orientation

sexual orientation. Under domestic law, their claims failed. They lodged complaints with the European Commission on Human Rights, which were successful. It was held that the employees' right to respect for their private lives under *Article 8* of the *European Convention on Human Rights* was violated by the investigations conducted into their homosexuality and by their discharge from the armed forces pursuant to the policy of the Ministry of Defence.

The coming into force of the *Human Rights Act 1998* extended protection against dismissal or detriment on the ground of sexual orientation to all individuals employed by 'public authorities'.

239.3   THE EMPLOYMENT EQUALITY (SEXUAL ORIENTATION) REGULATIONS 2003

The *SOR 2003*, implementing provisions of the *Framework Directive*, came into force on 1 December 2003 and utilised concepts familiar from other *Discrimination Laws* in outlawing;

(*a*)   *Direct Discrimination*;

(*b*)   *Indirect Discrimination*;

(*c*)   *Victimisation*;

(*d*)   *Harassment*.

on grounds of 'sexual orientation'.

The *SOR 2003* protect workers and cover:

(*a*)   employment;

(*b*)   contract work;

(*c*)   office-holders;

(*d*)   partners;

(*e*)   providers of vocational training;

(*f*)   employment agencies.

239.4   SEXUAL ORIENTATION

Regulation 2(1) of the *SOR 2003* defines 'sexual orientation' as an orientation towards a person of the same sex (thus covers gay men and lesbian women); the opposite sex (this covers heterosexual men and women); or both sexes (this covers bisexual men or women).

239.5   DIRECT DISCRIMINATION

The general principles of *Direct Discrimination* apply to the *SOR 2003*. Discrimination based on perception of a person's sexual orientation (whether the perception is or is not correct) is covered. However, direct discrimination because of the discriminator's sexual orientation is not.

239.6   INDIRECT DISCRIMINATION

Regulation 4 of the *SOR 2003* provides that *Indirect Discrimination* occurs where:

(*a*)   A applies to B a provision, criterion or practice which A applies equally to other persons; and

(*b*)   that provision, criterion or practice puts persons of B's sexual orientation at a particular disadvantage; and

(*c*)   B suffers that disadvantage; and

(*d*)   A cannot justify the provision, criterion or practice as a proportionate means of achieving a legitimate aim.

239.7   VICTIMISATION AND HARASSMENT

The definition of 'victimisation' essentially follows those in the *SDA 1975* and the *RRA 1976*. There were no statutory definitions of harassment before 2003. To constitute harassment, the conduct must have the 'purpose or effect' of harassing the person, i.e. violating his dignity or creating an intimidating, hostile, degrading, humiliating or offensive environment for him.

239.8   GENUINE OCCUPATIONAL REQUIREMENT

Regulation 7 of the *SOR 2003* provides an exception permitting an employer, when recruiting for a post, to treat applicants differently on grounds of sexual orientation if being of a particular sexual orientation is a genuine occupation requirement (GOR) for that post. The exception may also be relevant when an employer promotes, transfers or trains a person for a post, and when dismissing from a post where a GOR applies in relation to that post. A GOR cannot justify victimisation or harassment. The exception may apply where a person is dismissed because, after taking up a post to which a GOR applies, his sexual orientation changes.

There is also a more limited GOR for cases of employment 'for purposes of an organised religion' – see *Genuine Occupational Qualifications*.

239.9   POSITIVE ACTION

Regulation 26 of the *SOR 2003* permits *Positive Discrimination*, or 'positive action', in certain circumstances, and is comparable to *sections 37* and *38* of the *RRA 1976*. Positive action is allowed where it reasonably appears that it prevents or compensates for disadvantages linked to sexual orientation among the relevant section of people to whom the positive action relates. As with the other discrimination laws, positive action is permitted only in encouraging persons to take advantage of opportunities or providing training. Discrimination at the point of selection is not permitted.

240   Shift Work

The fact that two jobs are done at different times, one during the day and the other at night, does not prevent them from being *Like Work*. It does not, however, infringe the principle of *Equal Pay* for the employer to pay a shift premium of a reasonable amount for night shifts and weekend shifts.

There must be no direct or indirect discrimination or disability discrimination in allocating employees to different shifts, whether dealing with a request to transfer to a popular shift or in transferring an employee against his wishes.

A requirement for a woman with childcare commitments to work unsocial hours or on a rotating shift pattern could be an act of indirect sex discrimination; on the other hand, one would expect a tribunal to find such a requirement to be justifiable where there is a business need for a rotating shift pattern and there is no other suitable work available for the employee.

Consideration must be given to transferring a disabled employee away from shift work, as a *Reasonable Adjustment*, if having to work at night or on an irregular pattern places the disabled employee at a substantial disadvantage (for example because of the effect on the diet which must be followed).

241   Ships

Employment on board ship is, broadly speaking, excluded from protection by equal opportunities law, but the statutory rules provide some exceptions, for example in certain cases where the ship is registered at a British port of registry and the employee does not work wholly outside Great Britain.

242   Shortlisting

Where discrimination in not shortlisting a complainant is proved, compensation can be awarded for injury to feelings and loss of opportunity, even if the evidence shows that candidates who *were* shortlisted were better qualified than the complainant.

All the documents on the basis of which shortlisting takes place, such as application forms and CVs, must be disclosed to the tribunal hearing the complaint. Where the complainant is on paper better qualified than shortlisted candidates of a different race or gender (or non-disabled candidates in a case under the *DDA 1995*), tribunals will look closely at the credibility of any explanation which is given for this difference in treatment.

For general advice on avoiding discrimination when filling vacancies see *Recruitment* and *Selection*. In addition, it is worth noting specifically that a candidate should never be excluded from the shortlist by reason of a disability, unless it is clear beyond all possible doubt that the disability disqualifies the candidate, no matter what *Reasonable Adjustments* may be made – where a disability is not an obvious disqualification, its relevance or otherwise and possible adjustments should be discussed positively at the interview. Reasons for shortlisting or not shortlisting candidates should be recorded, if necessary simply by noting them on the application forms or CVs.

243   Sikhs

Sikhs have been held to be a *Racial Group*, defined by reference to *Ethnic Origin* – see *Indirect Discrimination*. Sikhs are also covered by the *RBR 2003*.

It is neither racial discrimination nor religious discrimination to give a Sikh a dispensation from wearing a safety helmet on a construction site. On the contrary, it is indirect racial and religious discrimination to penalise a Sikh for wearing a turban instead of a safety helmet on a construction site – see *Turbans*.

244   Small Businesses

The general principle is that small businesses have the same obligations under the *Discrimination Laws* (and are equally subject to the *EPA 1970*) as government departments, local authorities and major companies. Originally, small employees were exempted from the employment provisions of the *DDA 1995*, but the exception was removed on 1 October 2004.

245   Special Needs

Under the *RRA 1976*, it is lawful to provide facilities or services to meet the special needs of persons of a particular racial group in regard to their education, training or welfare, or any ancillary benefits.

An obvious example is language training for racial minority employees who, because they were born overseas or because their education has been disrupted, are unable to communicate effectively.

Under the *SDA 1975* it is lawful for *Training Bodies* (but not employers) to give persons access to facilities for training which would help to fit them for employment, where it reasonably appears that those persons are in special need of training by reason of the period for which they have been discharging domestic or family responsibilities to the exclusion of regular full-time employment. Further, it is lawful for a *Training Body* to discriminate in affording certain persons access to facilities for training to help fit them for employment. This discrimination is permitted where it reasonably appears to the training body that the persons in question are in special need of training, by reason of the period for which they have been discharging domestic or family responsibilities to the exclusion of full-time employment.

246 Sport

246.1 THE SDA 1975

Section 44 of the *SDA 1975* authorises sex discrimination in relation to any sport, game or other activity of a competitive nature where:

(*a*)   the discrimination is in relation to the participation of a person as a competitor in events which are confined to competitors of one sex; and

(*b*)   the activity is one where the physical strength, stamina or physique of the average woman puts her at a disadvantage to the average man.

Accordingly, where, for example, there is a football league in which all the teams are exclusively male, a football club playing in that league is permitted to discriminate against women in the recruitment of playing staff and the governing body of the sport is permitted to discriminate in refusing to permit women to play in the league.

The exception applies only to competitors, however, and not for example to administrators, referees or other officials – *British Judo Association v Petty [1981] IRLR 484.*

246.2 THE RRA 1976

Section 39 of the *RRA 1976* permits direct discrimination on the ground of nationality and indirect discrimination on the basis of residential requirements in:

(*a*)   selection to represent a country, place or area, or any related association, in any sport or game; or

(*b*)   in pursuance of the rules of any competition so far as they relate to eligibility to compete in any sport or game.

This provision is, however, subject to the requirements of European Law regarding the free movement of labour between Member States.

246.3 THE DDA 1995

There are no provisions in the *DDA 1995* expressly relating to sport, but clearly physical (and sometimes mental) fitness is a justifiable requirement for most sports professionals.

247   Stalking

In *Majrowski v Guy's & St Thomas' NHS Trust [2006] IRLR 695*, the House of Lords ruled that an employer can be vicariously liable under the *Protection From Harassment Act 1997* for acts of harassment conducted by employees in the course of employment.

The decision was striking, because the Act, which makes harassment both a criminal and civil offence, was primarily aimed at addressing the problem of stalking. When it was first introduced, its potential for rendering employers liable for workplace harassment (a matter already dealt with by the civil law and the *Discrimination Laws*) was not widely recognised.

In 1998, a hospital employee alleged that his departmental manager had harassed him at work. His employer investigated and found that harassment had occurred. In 1999 he was dismissed for reasons unconnected with his earlier allegations. In 2003 – more than four years after the original complaint – he brought a county court claim against his employer under *section 3* of the *Protection from Harassment Act 1997*, which provides that a victim of harassment may seek compensation in the civil courts. He alleged that he could bring the claim directly against his employer on the basis that it was vicariously liable for the manager's acts of harassment. A county court judge struck out the claim on the basis that Parliament had not intended to import into the Act general principles of vicarious liability. The Court of Appeal, however, found that as a general rule, an employer may be vicariously liable for a statutory tort committed by an employee, where the legislation in question does not express or impliedly exclude such liability. Further, it held by a majority that an employer could be vicariously liable for harassment contrary to the Act. The House of Lords upheld the Court of Appeal's decision, although not its precise reasoning. In interpreting the Act, their Lordships had regard to provisions covering Scotland, which differ in various respects from those applicable in England and Wales, and make it clearer that a claim could be made against an employer for workplace harassment. There was no reason to believe that Parliament intended there should be any difference in substance between the two jurisdictions. Further, the employer argued that Parliament could not have intended the Act to incorporate principles of vicarious liability, as this was inconsistent with the discrimination law regime, derived from European Directives which release the employer from liability if he can show that he took all reasonably practicable steps to prevent the employee from acting unlawfully. This argument was rejected, although Lord Nicholls noted that the contrast between the Act and the *Discrimination Laws* was 'discordant and unsatisfactory'.

A claim brought under the Act has various potential advantages for a claimant, i.e.:-

(*a*)   there is no need to show fault or foreseeability on the part of the employer. In practice, if the alleged harassment was by a manager, it will be extremely difficult to escape vicarious liability, having regard to the 'work connection' test for 'in the course of employment' established in *Lister v Hesley Hall [2001] IRLR 472*;

(*b*)   there is no statutory definition of 'harassment' in the Act and thus evidence as to fact and belief is crucial;

(*c*)   damages can be claimed for 'anxiety caused by the harassment' – there is no need to establish a defined personal injury;

(*d*)   the employer cannot rely on the defence of taking reasonably practicable steps to prevent harassment;

(*e*)   the time limit for bringing a claim in England and Wales is six years, rather than three.

The decision has understandably prompted worries that it will open the 'floodgates' to claims that may, perhaps, lack real merit. Lady Hale, however, said that courts should draw 'sensible lines between the ordinary banter and badinage of life and genuinely offensive and unacceptable behaviour'. Further, Lord Nicholls expressed the view that: 'Courts are well able to separate the wheat from the chaff at an early stage . . . They should be astute to do so. In most cases courts should have little difficulty in applying the 'close connection' test. Where the claim meets the requirement and the quality of the conduct said to constitute harassment is being examined, courts will have in mind that irritations, annoyances, even a measure of upset, arise at times in everybody's day-to-day dealings with other people. Courts are well able to recognise the boundary between conduct which is unattractive, even unreasonable, and conduct which is oppressive and unacceptable. To cross the boundary from the regrettable to the unacceptable the gravity of the misconduct must be of an order which would sustain criminal liability'.

248   Statistics

Statistics are commonly produced to employment tribunals (and in some cases are essential) to show whether there has been *Disparate Impact* in a case of *Indirect Discrimination*. There are, however, some cases where a tribunal may be prepared to make a finding without statistical evidence. For example a tribunal could take the view that it is a matter of common knowledge that because of childcare commitments a considerably smaller percentage of women than of men are able to comply with a requirement of full-time working.

In any case of *Indirect Discrimination* where relevant statistics are unavailable, or available only with considerable difficulty or at great expense, it may be appropriate for one or both of the parties to ask the tribunal for a pre-hearing discussion, so that appropriate directions can be considered.

Complainants also commonly ask for relevant statistics when submitting a *Questionnaire* (for example the numbers of men and the numbers of women at each grade in the respondent organisation). Statistics may indicate a pattern of discrimination – see *Evidence of Discrimination*.

249   Statutory Authority

There are varying exemptions from the scope of the *Discrimination Laws* in relation to acts done by virtue of statutory authority, e.g. pursuant to a statute or a statutory instrument. For instance, the *AR 2006* legitimises the making of statutory (and enhanced) redundancy payments, even though the formula for calculating them includes components (age and length of service) which are arguably discriminatory.

250   Statutory Bodies

The *Discrimination Laws* provide that service on behalf of the Crown for the purposes of a statutory body is treated in the same way as ordinary employment. Complaints may be presented to an Employment Tribunal both by persons working for statutory bodies and by persons who have applied to work for a statutory body.

251   Stereotypes

Not all acts of discrimination are committed by employers or others who have gone out of their way to discriminate – see *Unintentional Discrimination*. Many employers, managers and interviewers have mental pictures of the kind of person they expect to see or are accustomed to see in a particular occupation and reject almost automatically any candidate for *Recruitment* or *Promotion* who does not fit the stereotype. In doing so they are acting unlawfully if gender, race, religion, sexual orientation or disability (or absence of disability) is one of the factors contributing to the stereotype.

Employers have a duty to ensure that both they and their employees are properly informed, so that *Selection* and other employment decisions can be made objectively and rationally, not subjectively and instinctively.

252 Subconscious Discrimination

The judgment of Lord Nicholls of Birkenhead, in *Nagarajan v London Regional Transport [1999] IRLR 572* (see *Direct Discrimination* and *Victimisation*) contains the following important passage:

'I turn to the question of subconscious motivation. All human beings have preconceptions, beliefs, attitudes and prejudices on many subjects. It is part of our make-up. Moreover, we do not always recognise our own prejudices. Many people are unable, or unwilling, to admit even to themselves that actions of theirs may be racially motivated. An employer may genuinely believe that the reason why he rejected an applicant had nothing to do with the applicant's race. After careful and thorough investigation of a claim, members of an Employment Tribunal may decide that the proper inference to be drawn from the evidence is that, whether the employer realised it at the time or not, race was the reason why he acted as he did. It goes without saying that in order to justify such an inference the tribunal must first make findings of primary fact from which the inference may properly be drawn. Conduct of this nature by an employer, when the inference is legitimately drawn, falls squarely within the language of s 1(1)(a). The employer treated the complainant less favourably on racial grounds. Such conduct also falls within the purpose of the legislation. Members of racial groups need protection from conduct driven by unrecognised prejudice as much as from conscious and deliberate discrimination.'

Lord Nicholls added that the same approach should be adopted in relation to complaints of *Victimisation*. A complaint is made out if it is shown that the complainant was treated less favourably by reason of having done a 'protected act', even if that person 'did not consciously realise, for example, that he was prejudiced because the job applicant had previously brought claims against him under the Act'.

413

253 Subjectivity

It is not unlawful for an employer or anyone else to make *Selection* or other employment decisions which are subjective, irrational or eccentric, so long as no unlawful discrimination is involved.

Where, however, there is a difference in the treatment of persons of different race, religion, gender etc, an employment tribunal will expect to hear a genuine and non-discriminatory reason for that difference in treatment – see *Evidence of Discrimination*. Where decisions are made objectively, and reasons are recorded, the decision-maker should be able to explain to the tribunal the process of reasoning which was followed. Where no rational explanation can be given for a decision, however, a tribunal is unlikely to believe a bare assertion that no discrimination was involved.

254   Substantial Adverse Effects

254.1   RELEVANCE TO DEFINITION OF 'DISABILITY'

Section 1(1) of the *DDA 1995* provides that, for there to be a 'disability', the effect which a physical or mental impairment has on a person's ability to carry out normal day-to-day activities must be 'a substantial and long-term adverse effect'.

254.2   SUBSTANTIAL

The statutory guidance provides useful clarification of the meaning of 'substantial' in this context. As the EAT pointed out in *Goodwin v The Patent Office [1999] IRLR 4*, the word 'is potentially ambiguous' since it might mean 'very large' or 'more than minor or trivial'. The guidance shows that the word is used in the latter sense. Factors which may need to be considered include:

(*a*)   the time taken by a person with an impairment to carry out a normal day-to-day activity in comparison with the time that might be expected if the person did not have the impairment; and

(*b*)   the way in which the person with the impairment carries out a normal day-to-day activity in comparison to the way the person may be expected to carry it out if he or she did not have the impairment.

The EAT said in *Goodwin* that 'the tribunal may where the applicant still claims to be suffering from the same degree of impairment as at the time of the events complained of, take into account how the applicant appears to the tribunal to "manage", although tribunals will be slow to regard a person's capabilities in the relatively strange adversarial environment as an entirely reliable guide to the level of ability to perform normal day-to-day activities', as *Kapadia v London Borough of Lambeth [2000] IRLR 14* (below) illustrates.

The EAT also noted, in *Goodwin*, that judging what it described as 'the adverse effect condition' may be difficult to judge, and offered further general guidance:

'What the Act is concerned with is an impairment of the person's ability to carry out activities. The fact that a person can carry out such activities does not mean that his ability to carry them out has not been impaired. Thus, for example, a person may be able to cook, but only with the greatest difficulty. In order to constitute an adverse effect, it is not the doing of the acts which is the focus of attention but rather the ability to do (or not do) the act. Experience shows that disabled persons often adjust their lives and circumstances to enable them to cope for themselves. Thus a person whose capacity to communicate through normal speech was obviously impaired might well choose, more or less voluntarily, to live on their own. If one asked such a person whether they managed to carry on their daily lives without undue problems, the answer may well be "yes", yet their ability to lead a "normal" life had obviously been impaired. Such a person would be unable to communicate through speech and the ability to communicate through speech is obviously a capacity which is needed for carrying out normal day-to-day activities, whether at work or at home. If asked whether they could use the telephone, or ask for directions, or which bus to take, the answer would be "no". This might be regarded as day-to-day activities contemplated by the legislation, and that person's ability to carry them out would clearly be regarded as adversely affected.

Furthermore, disabled persons are likely, habitually, to 'play down' the effect that their disabilities have on their daily lives. If asked whether they are able to cope at home, the answer may well be 'yes', even though, on analysis, many of the ordinary day-to-day tasks were done with great difficulty due to the person's impaired ability to carry them out.

These points are illustrated by the case of *Leonard v Southern Derbyshire Chamber of Commerce [2001] IRLR 19*. In this case, the complainant's clinical depression caused her to be easily tired and clearly suggested an inability to sustain an activity over a reasonable period. It was held by the EAT that the tribunal had failed to take 'proper account of the overarching effects of tiredness' on her capacities. The employment tribunal also fell into error by carrying out a balancing exercise between the things which the complainant could do and things which she could not do. This approach was inappropriate. Her ability to catch a ball did not diminish her inability to negotiate pavement edges safely; her difficulties in using a recipe were not mitigated by her ability to write a cheque.

The EAT reminded employment tribunals that they must concentrate on what the complainant cannot do or can only do with difficulty, rather than on the things that the complainant can do. Having identified the things which the complainant cannot do, or can only do with difficulty, it is a faulty line of reasoning for the tribunal to conclude that the adverse effect cannot be substantial because there are many things which the complainant can do.

254.3   CUMULATIVE EFFECT

An impairment is to be taken to affect the ability of a person to carry out normal day-to-day activities only if it affects:

(*a*)   mobility;

(*b*)   manual dexterity;

(*c*)   physical co-ordination;

(*d*)   continence;

(*e*)   ability to lift, carry or otherwise move everyday objects;

(*f*)   speech, hearing or eyesight;

(*g*)   memory or ability to concentrate, learn or understand; or

(*h*)   perception of the risk of physical danger.

However, an impairment might not have a *substantial* adverse effect on a person in any one of these respects, but its effects in more than one of these respects taken together could result in a substantial adverse effect on the person's ability to carry out normal day-to-day activities. Moreover, a person may have more than one impairment, any one of which alone would not have a substantial effect. It is necessary to consider whether the impairments together have a substantial effect overall on the person's ability to carry out normal day-to-day activities.

254.4   EFFECTS OF BEHAVIOUR

A relevant issue is how far a person can reasonably be expected to modify behaviour to prevent or reduce the effects of an impairment on normal day-to-day activities. If a person can behave so that the impairment ceases to have a substantial adverse effect on his or her ability to carry out normal day-to-day activities, the definition of 'disability' under the *DDA 1995* would no longer be satisfied. Some people, however, have 'coping' strategies which cease to work in certain circumstances (e.g. when subjected to stress). If the management of the effects of an impairment may break down so that the effects will sometimes still occur, that must be taken into account when making the overall judgement. If a disabled person is advised by a medical practitioner to behave in a particular way so as to reduce the impact of the disability, that may count as treatment to be disregarded (see below).

254.5   **EFFECTS OF ENVIRONMENT**

Variable environmental conditions may be relevant to the question of whether adverse effects are 'substantial'. These include temperature and the hour of the day. When assessing whether adverse effects are 'substantial', the extent to which environmental factors are likely to have an impact should be taken into account.

254.6   **EFFECTS OF TREATMENT – DEDUCED EFFECTS**

In most cases where there is a finding of disability, that finding is made because of the actual effect of the impairment at the relevant time. In some cases, however, the adverse effect of the impairment is mitigated, masked or prevented altogether by medication or other medical treatment or by corrective action (such as the use of a prosthesis or other aid). In such cases, the measures which have been taken to treat or correct the impairment must be disregarded (except in the case of spectacles or contact lenses). There must be a finding as to what the effect of the impairment would have been if it had been untreated and uncorrected and the decision on whether or not the complainant was disabled must then be based on that finding. In *Kapadia v London Borough of Lambeth [2000] IRLR 699*, it was held by the Court of Appeal that counselling sessions by a consultant clinical psychologist amounted to medical treatment. There was unchallenged medical evidence of a very strong likelihood of a total mental breakdown without the counselling sessions. The EAT had accordingly been right to substitute a finding of disability for the employment tribunal's majority decision that the complainant was not disabled.

It was argued in this case that the counselling sessions did not constitute treatment, because they consisted only of talking to the patient and were directed to reducing his symptoms rather than to correcting the impairment. That argument was rejected on appeal.

A further error by the tribunal in this case was to disregard the unchallenged medical evidence in favour of a judgment made on the basis of how the applicant appeared when giving his evidence. It was held that there may be exceptional circumstances in which a tribunal may, for good reason, reject uncontradicted medical evidence; but this was not such a case.

In *Abadeh v British Telecommunications plc [2001] IRLR 23*, the EAT gave further guidance on the circumstances in which the effects of medical treatment must be disregarded. The following possibilities were considered:

(*a*)   The treatment has ceased – the effects of it must be taken into account, and a decision based on the actual effect of the impairment, because it is only continuing medical treatment which must be disregarded.

(*b*)   Treatment is continuing and it is known that removal of the treatment would result in a relapse or a worsened condition – the effect of the treatment must be disregarded, and a decision based on what the effect of the impairment would have been but for the treatment, as in *Kapadia*.

(c) The treatment is continuing and the final outcome cannot be determined – in this case also, the effect of the treatment must be disregarded.

(d) The treatment is continuing and the effect has been 'to create a permanent improvement rather than a temporary improvement' – that improvement should be taken into account, as measures to treat or correct the impairment are no longer needed once the permanent improvement has been established.

In *Abadeh*, the case was remitted to a differently constituted employment tribunal, to consider, inter alia, whether treatment which the complainant had been receiving for post-traumatic stress disorder had resulted in a permanent improvement or in one which was only temporary, so that adverse effects were likely to return once the treatment had ceased.

In *Woodrup v London Borough of Southwark [2003] IRLR 111* the applicant produced letters, a sick note and a medical certificate showing that she had had an anxiety neurosis for some years and was receiving psychotherapy. She represented herself and called no medical evidence. She said that her full symptoms would return if medical treatment were to be stopped. It was held that she was not a disabled person within the meaning of the *DDA 1995*. Her appeals to the EAT and the Court of Appeal were unsuccessful. Simon Brown LJ said:

'In any deduced effects case of this sort the claimant should be required to prove his or her alleged disability with some particularity. Those seeking to invoke this peculiarly benign doctrine under para 6 of the Schedule should not readily expect to be indulged by the tribunal of fact. Ordinarily, at least in the present class of case, one would expect clear medical evidence to be necessary.'

254.7 PROGRESSIVE CONDITIONS

A claimant may be deemed to have an impairment which has a substantial adverse effect on his ability to carry out normal day-to-day activities in the following circumstances:

(a) if the applicant has a progressive condition (such as cancer);

(b) as a result, the applicant has an impairment which has (or had) some effect, but not a substantial adverse effect, on his ability to carry out normal day-to-day activities; and

(c) the condition is likely to result in his having an impairment which does have a substantial adverse effect on his ability to carry out normal day-to-day activities.

The statutory guidance refers to progressive conditions. Where a person has a progressive condition, he or she will be treated as having an impairment which has a substantial adverse effect from the time when an impairment resulting from the condition first has some effect on ability to carry out normal day-to-day activities. The effect need not be continuous and need not be substantial. For this principle to operate, medical diagnosis of the condition is not by itself enough. The further requirements are evidence that the condition is having or has had some effect; and evidence that the effect is likely to become substantial in the future.

The *DDA 2005* has, with effect from 5 December 2005, made special provision for cases where the progressive condition is HIV, cancer or multiple sclerosis. In such cases, the date when the person is deemed to become disabled will be the date of diagnosis, not the date when the condition begins to have some adverse effect on the ability to carry out normal day-to-day activities.

255   Supported Workshops

In addition to special provisions for *Charities*, there is a provision in the *DDA 1995* under which it is lawful for a person who provides 'supported employment' to treat members of a particular group of disabled persons more favourably than other disabled persons in providing such employment.

256   Surveillance in the Workplace

Although employment protection rights have become increasingly well established in recent years, over the same period technological changes have given rise to new challenges, notably the availability of means for employers to conduct covert surveillance on employees' activities in the workplace. This trend raises a variety of general concerns, including concerns about *Human Rights* and on occasion issues connected with equal opportunities, as a leading case demonstrates. *Halford v United Kingdom [1997] IRLR 471*, concerned a senior police officer who unsuccessfully applied for promotion in her own force and others on numerous occasions. She alleged that she had been subjected to a campaign which included interception of her telephone calls at work and at home for the purpose of obtaining information to use against her in sex discrimination proceedings which she had brought. Her claim to an employment tribunal was settled, but the European Court of Human Rights ruled that interception of calls she made on her office telephone was a violation of *Article 8* of the *European Convention on Human Rights*. The UK Government argued that an employer should in principle, without the employee's prior knowledge, be able to monitor calls made to the employee on telephones provided by the employer, but the court rejected that view. Since no warning had been given to the employee that calls made on her office telephone would be liable to interception, she would have had a reasonable expectation of privacy for such calls.

The *Regulation of Investigatory Powers Act 2000*, provides for the interception of communications to be authorised with consent. Monitoring without consent may also sometimes be legitimate pursuant to the *Telecommunications (Lawful Business Practice) (Interception of Communications) Regulations 2000 (SI 2000 No 2699)*. The *Data Protection Act 1998* may also be relevant: Part 3 of the Employment Practices Data Protection Code, addresses issues raised by surveillance at work.

Although typically surveillance in the workplace is conducted by employers, exceptionally an employee may engage in some form of surveillance. A case concerning a covert video recording made by a nanny in the family home where she worked gave rise to much dispute in a case discussed in relation to the practical implication of *Human Rights*. In *Chairman and Governors of Amwell View School v Dogherty [2007] IRLR 198* the claimant clandestinely recorded the disciplinary and appeal hearings which led to her dismissal. She then sought to make use of the transcript of the proceedings for the purpose of her claim to a tribunal. A tribunal decided that the evidence should be received. The EAT distinguished between recordings of the 'open' part of the hearings, where the claimant was present, and the private deliberations of the panel when she was out of the room. It was more appropriate to admit the former than the latter. However, the EAT added that:

> 'the balance between the conflicting public interests might well have fallen differently if the claim had been framed in terms of unlawful discrimination, where . . . the inadvertent recording of private deliberations . . . produced the only evidence – and incontrovertible evidence – of discrimination.'

257   Targets

Some employers, as part of their equal opportunity policies, have set targets to be achieved over a period. The targets set commonly include one or more of the following:

(*a*)   an increased number or percentage of women at senior levels;

(*b*)   a minimum percentage of black or ethnic minority employees; and

(*c*)   a minimum percentage of disabled employees.

The third of these targets should give rise to no legal difficulty, because the *DDA 1995* does not prohibit discrimination *in favour of disabled employees generally*. It is a different matter if there is discrimination in favour of certain categories of disabled workers and against other categories (unless the case is covered by the exceptions relating to *Charities* and *Supported Workshops*).

There is, however, a need for great care in setting targets which are based on gender or on racial factors. The law does permit certain measures in relation to encouragement and training for 'under-represented' groups (see *Positive Discrimination*), but there must be no discrimination in *Selection* for any particular post. Targets are legitimate if (but only if) they are used in the following ways:

(*a*)   to discriminate in favour of disabled workers generally;

(*b*)   to identify apparent 'under-representation' of other groups, defined by reference to gender or a racial factor;

(*c*)   to underline the need for vigilance in avoiding direct or indirect discrimination against members of those groups; and

(*d*)   to take advantage of the modest measures of *Positive Discrimination* which the law permits.

258   Teleworking

Teleworking is a flexible employment arrangement which has grown enormously in popularity as a result of advances in information technology. Sometimes teleworkers are described as 'elancers', i.e. internet-enabled mobile workers, or 'virtual employees'. From an equal opportunities perspective, teleworking may offer considerable advantages to employees with childcare commitments. There is as yet no specific legislation dedicated to teleworking although *Health and Safety at Work* issues are sometimes especially significant and it may be more than usually difficult for the employer to ensure that it complies with its statutory duties in respect of the health and safety at work of the teleworker.

The European Commission Social Partners (that is, members of the umbrella organisation representing employers and employees) signed up to a framework agreement on teleworking in July 2002 which makes the following main points:

(*a*)   teleworking must be agreed to voluntarily by both parties;

(*b*)   any change to a teleworking arrangement will not affect the worker's legal status;

(*c*)   teleworkers should enjoy the same terms and conditions of employment, together with collective rights, as comparable workers at the employer's premises;

(*d*)   the employer remains responsible for ensuring the protection of data used and processed by the teleworker in connection with the business;

(*e*)   the employer remains responsible for safeguarding the health and safety of the teleworker;

(*f*)   the employer should put in place measures to reduce the risk of the teleworker becoming isolated from colleagues;

(*g*)   teleworkers should have the same access to training and career development as colleagues, although their training will be targeted at teleworking.

It is important to bear in mind the potential relevance of teleworking to *section 80F* of the *Employment Rights Act 1996*, which entitles employees to request flexible working, including a request for a change in terms and conditions that relates to 'where, as between his home and the place of business of his employer, he is required to work'.

The provisions of the *Working Time Regulations 1998* apply to teleworkers as they do to other workers and employers therefore have to meet the challenge of monitoring people working remotely from establishments. Care will also be needed to ensure compliance with the *Data Protection Act 1998*.

Checklist 14 notes issues commonly addressed in teleworking agreements.

259   Temps

The expression 'temp' is traditionally used to describe office workers who provide secretarial services, usually on a short-term basis, to clients of an agency. Usually the temp is employed by the agency but sometimes he or she is self-employed. In either case, there is usually no contractual relationship between the temp and the client, but see *Dacas v Brook Street Bureau (UK) Ltd [2004] IRLR 358*, a majority decision of the Court of Appeal, and the more orthodox subsequent decision of the EAT in *James v London Borough of Greenwich [2007] IRLR 168*.

The client is, however, under a duty not to discriminate against the temp, for example by subjecting him or her to racial or sexual harassment – see *Contract Workers*.

260   Term-Time Working

Term-time working is becoming steadily more common. It is an example of *Flexible Working*. The object is to enable a parent with children of school age to work around the school holiday programme. Quite apart from reflecting good employment practice, it offers organisations the chance to recruit and retain additional staff members at a time of labour shortages, although this benefit may need to be balanced against any complication inherent in providing cover when term-time workers are absent; the more senior the term-time worker, the more acute this problem may be. A possible disadvantage from the employee's perspective may be constraints on opportunities for promotion.

In practice, most people who seek the opportunity to work on a term-time basis are women. Refusal to grant a request for term-time working may therefore give rise to a claim of indirect sex discrimination unless the requirement to work full-time can be justified on objective commercial grounds.

261   Terms of Employment

The *RRA 1976*, the *DDA 1995*, the *RBR 2003*, the *SOR 2003* and the *AR 2006* all apply to complaints of discrimination relating to *Pay* or other *Benefits*, whether the complaint relates to a contractual term or to discretionary pay or benefits.

The position under the *EPA 1970* and the *SDA 1975* is more complicated. In summary:

(*a*)   a complaint about a contractual term for the payment of money must be brought under the *EPA 1970*;

(*b*)   a complaint about any other contractual term must be brought under the *EPA 1970* if there is an available *Comparator*, but otherwise may be brought under the *SDA 1975*;

(*c*)   a complaint about a non-contractual benefit must be brought under the *SDA 1975*.

The effect of these provisions is that a person who wishes to complain about a contractual term for the payment of money has no remedy if a suitable comparator cannot be identified, but it may be possible to rely on *Article 141* to extend the ambit of search for a comparator beyond the strict confines of the *EPA 1970* – see *Same Employment*.

262   Territorial Extent

The general rule is that the provisions relating to employment in the *Discrimination Laws* all apply to employment at an establishment in Great Britain.

Parts of the *DDA 1995* do apply, with modifications, in Northern Ireland, but it is expressly stated that the provisions making it unlawful for employers to discriminate against employees, job applicants and contract workers apply only in relation to employment or contract work at an establishment in Great Britain. The other discrimination laws do not apply at all to employment in Northern Ireland, which has its own legislation.

A key provision is that employment is deemed to be at an establishment in Great Britain unless the employee works wholly overseas. Accordingly all the discrimination laws will apply in a case where an employee spends only a few days each year working at an establishment in Great Britain and spends the rest of the time working overseas.

Indeed, under the *RBR 2003*, the *SOR 2003*, the *AR 2006* and the *DDA 1995* it is possible for an employee or contract worker to present a complaint even if he or she worked wholly outside Great Britain, provided that certain conditions are satisfied. These conditions are that:

(*a*)   the employer has a place of business at an establishment in Great Britain;

(*b*)   the work in question is for the purposes of the business carried on at that establishment; and

(*c*)   the employee or contract worker in question is ordinarily resident in Great Britain either at the time when he applies for or is offered the employment or at any time during the course of the employment.

There is a similar provision in the *RRA 1976*, but only if the case involves discrimination on grounds of race or ethnic or national origins or *Harassment*.

There are special rules relating to *Ships* and *Aircraft* (including hovercraft). It is also relevant, particularly in relation to ships, that the references to Great Britain include the UK territorial waters adjacent to Great Britain. The references to Great Britain also include, for the purposes of certain kinds of employment (such as employment concerned with oil or gas extraction) specified parts of the Continental Shelf.

263   Tests

Employers use a wide variety of tests in *Recruitment* and also in selecting candidates for *Promotion*. They include:

(*a*)   *Aptitude Tests*;

(*b*)   Intelligence Tests; and

(*c*)   *Psychometric Testing*.

Whatever kind of test is used, there is a risk of:

(*a*)   direct discrimination, if all candidates are not tested in the same way;

(*b*)   indirect discrimination, if tests are biased or 'loaded' against women (or men) or against members of particular racial groups; and

(*c*)   disability discrimination if *Reasonable Adjustments* are not made.

264   Time Limits

264.1   **THE THREE-MONTH TIME LIMIT FOR CLAIMS**

Broadly speaking, a discrimination claim (other than for equal pay) must be presented before the end of the period of three months beginning when the act complained of was done. Since the position has become complicated by a requirement in many cases under the *Employment Act 2002 (Dispute Resolution Regulations 2004) (SI 2004/752)* to submit a written grievance before a complaint can be presented and in those cases the time limit will be extended – see *Claims to Tribunal*.

The conventional starting point is to ascertain the date on which time starts to run. The question for the Employment Appeal Tribunal in *Virdi v Commissioner of Police of the Metropolis [2007] IRLR 24* was whether an allegedly discriminatory act (a decision to reject an internal appeal) was 'done' when the decision was taken or when the claimant was notified of the decision. The EAT held that an act is 'done' when it is completed, rather than when it is communicated. On the facts, therefore, the claimant's claim was one day out of time. However, the tribunal had erred in finding that it was not just and equitable to extend time for bringing the claim. It was wrong to find that the claimant had provided no explanation for the late claim when he said he had put the matter in the hands of his solicitors. According to the EAT, a claimant cannot be held responsible for the failings of his solicitors. Whatever the reason why the solicitors failed in their duty would be immaterial when assessing whether the claimant was at fault. In this case, the explanation indicated that the blame for the lateness of the claim could not be laid at the claimant's door. This was an important consideration in the exercise of discretion. The availability of a negligence claim against the solicitors was not a legitimate reason for refusing to extend time. The EAT also queried the earlier decision of *Aniagwu v London Borough of Hackney [1999] IRLR 303*, that where the act consists of refusal to accept a grievance, the employee is not subjected to a detriment until he is notified that the grievance was rejected.

The general principles are that:

(*a*)   any act extending over a period shall be treated as done at the end of that period – see *Continuing Discrimination*;

(*b*)   where the inclusion of any term in a contract renders the making of the contract an unlawful act, that act shall be treated as extending throughout the duration of the contract; and

(*c*)   a deliberate omission shall be treated as done when the person in question decided upon it.

In *HM Prison Service v Barua [2007] IRLR 4* the EAT upheld a tribunal's decision that the claimant had lodged a grievance within the normal time limits of presenting claims for unfair dismissal, breach of contract and unlawful deduction, even though the grievance was lodged before the respective time limits began to run. Therefore the three-month extension time limit provided for by *Regulation 15* of the *Dispute Resolution Regulations* applied. His claims, which were presented almost six months after his employment ended, were accordingly presented in time. Grievances can be lodged about contemplated action by the employer, so that they pre-date the accrual of the cause of action. In constructive dismissal cases in particular, there may well be a mismatch between the date of the accrual of the cause of action for unfair dismissal and the date of the employer's conduct which is said to have caused the dismissal. It follows that the extended time limit may apply in circumstances where the events complained of have occurred and the claimant has complained of them, weeks or months before time even started to run.

It is also provided that, in the absence of evidence establishing the contrary, an omission is decided upon by a person:

(*a*)   if the person does an act inconsistent with doing the omitted act, at the time of doing the inconsistent act; or

(*b*)   otherwise, when the period expires within which the person might reasonably have been expected to do the omitted act, if it was to be done at all.

The case of *Cast v Croydon College [1998] IRLR 318* has already been referred to, under *Continuing Discrimination*. It was also held in that case, where the complainant had twice asked if she could work part-time or job share, and been twice refused, that each refusal was a separate act of discrimination. This was because the matter had been reconsidered in response to the further request. The employer had not simply referred back to the earlier decision.

A discriminatory dismissal includes a *Constructive Dismissal*. The EAT held in *Reed and Bull Information Systems Ltd v Stedman [1999] IRLR 299* that time runs from the date on which the employee's resignation takes effect, not from the date of the earlier discrimination which was the effective cause of the employee's resignation. In the later case of *Commissioner of Police of the Metropolis v Harley [2001] IRLR 263*, the EAT took a different view, suggesting that *Reed* was wrongly decided on this point and was inconsistent with the decision of the Court of Appeal in *Cast v Croydon College [1998] IRLR 318.*

A tribunal may consider a complaint which is out of time if, in all the circumstances, the tribunal considers that it is just and equitable to do so. The tribunal has a very wide discretion and the changes made to the rules for presenting claims by the Dispute Resolution Regulations do not remove that discretion: *BUPA Care Homes (BNH) Ltd v Spillet [2006] IRLR 248.*

Factors which should be taken into account were identified by the EAT in *British Coal Corporation v Keeble and others [1997] IRLR 336*. Consideration must be given to the prejudice which each party would suffer as the result of the decision to be made, the respondent if the time is extended and the complainant if it is not. The relevant circumstances of the case could also include:

(*a*)   the length of and reasons for the delay;

(*b*)   the extent to which the cogency of the evidence is likely to be affected by that delay;

(*c*)   the extent to which the respondent had co-operated with any request for information;

(*d*)   the promptness with which the complainant acted once he or she knew of the facts giving rise to the action; and

(*e*)   the steps taken by the complainant to obtain appropriate professional advice once he or she knew of the possibility of taking action.

It was said by Peter Gibson LJ, in *London Borough of Southwark v Afolabi [2003] IRLR 220*, that there is no strict requirement for the tribunal 'to go through such a list in every case, provided of course that no significant factor has been left out of account by the ET in exercising its discretion.' In this case, time was extended by the tribunal to enable the applicant to proceed with a complaint of racial discrimination in not appointing him to a post as an auditor more than nine years earlier. The special factor in this case was that the applicant had presented his complaint less than three months after being allowed to inspect, for the first time, his personal file and it was information in that file which persuaded him that there had been racial discrimination in not appointing him to the auditor post some nine years earlier.

The Council appealed unsuccessfully first to the EAT and then to the Court of Appeal. Peter Gibson LJ said, however, 'that it can only be in a wholly exceptional case that the ET could properly conclude that despite a delay of a magnitude anywhere approaching nine years it was just and equitable to extend time. The policy of the Act is made clear by the brevity of the limitation period; that period of three months is in marked contrast to the limitation period in ordinary litigation. Parliament having envisaged that complaints within the jurisdiction of the ET will be determined within a short space of time after the events complained of, it will be an extremely rare case where the ET can properly decide that there can be a fair trial so long after those events.'

Prior to the introduction of the Dispute Resolution Regulations, there was no general rule of law that it is invariably just and equitable for time to be extended where the delay in commencing proceedings is connected with an internal grievance or appeal. In *Robinson v Post Office [2000] IRLR 804*, a disabled employee was dismissed on grounds of incapability, after a sickness absence of some six months. He lodged an internal appeal and the hearing took place, but a decision was deferred for a further medical report to be obtained. He then presented his complaint of disability discrimination, approximately three weeks out of time. The employment tribunal refused to extend the time and his appeal was unsuccessful. Giving the judgment of the EAT, the President, Lindsay J, said that the decision in *Aniagwu* did not establish a general proposition of law that delay to await the outcome of an internal procedure necessarily furnishes an acceptable reason for delaying the presentation of a tribunal complaint. He warned that 'as the law stands an employee who awaits the outcome of an internal appeal and delays the launching of an ET1 must realise that he is running a real danger.'

In *Robertson v Bexley Community Centre [2003] IRLR 434*, Auld LJ said:

> 'It is also of importance to note that the time limits are exercised strictly in employment and industrial cases. When tribunals consider their discretion to consider a claim out of time on just and equitable grounds there is no presumption that they should do so unless they can justify failure to exercise the discretion. Quite the reverse. A tribunal cannot hear a complaint unless the applicant convinces it that it is just and equitable to extend time. So, the exercise of discretion is the exception rather than the rule.'

264.2   **THE EPA 1970**

Under *section 2* of the *EPA 1970*, a claim must be presented either during the employment or within six months after the end of the employment.

The question of time limits was considered by the ECJ, on a reference from the House of Lords, in the case of *Preston and others v Wolverhampton Healthcare NHS Trust and others [2000] IRLR 506*. Some of the claimants in the case were teachers or lecturers who worked regularly but were employed under successive and legally separate contracts. Under one of the questions which was referred, the ECJ was asked whether it was compatible with *European Law* (and in particular with *Article*

141) if time starts to run at the end of each separate contract and not at the end of the employment relationship. If so, the employees concerned would be able to pursue their complaints only in relation to the final contract in each case, because they would have been out of time as regards the earlier contracts.

It was held by the ECJ that time should not start to run so long as there is a stable relationship resulting in a succession of short-term contracts concluded at regular intervals in respect of the same employment to which the same pension scheme applies. This ruling was adopted when the case came back to the House of Lords (*[2001] IRLR 237*), with the converse that 'Where there are intermittent contracts of service without a stable employment relationship, the period of six months runs from the end of each contract of service'.

The more general question which had been referred to the ECJ related to the time limit of six months itself. The way in which direct effect is given to equal pay claims in Great Britain is by modifying the *EPA 1970* to make it compatible with *Article 141*. Effectively, therefore, the time limit under *section 2* is a time limit for the exercise of rights under *Article 141*. The question which was referred to the ECJ was whether that time limit was compatible with the principle of Community law that national procedural rules must not make it excessively difficult or impossible in practice to exercise rights under *Article 141*.

The answer given by the ECJ was that the six-month time limit is not precluded provided that the limitation period is not less favourable for actions based on Community law than for those based on domestic law. The House of Lords, applying this ruling, compared the time limit of six months for equal pay claims with the time limit of six years for bringing a claim for breach of contract. It was pointed out that there are factors to be set against the obvious difference in the two periods. Time for equal pay claims runs only from the date of termination of the employment and the lower costs and relative informality of employment tribunal proceedings are also relevant factors. Looking at the matter as a whole, the House of Lords held that the rules of procedure for a claim under *section 2(4)* of the *EPA 1970* are not less favourable than those applying to a claim in contract.

In *National Power plc v Young [2001] IRLR 32*, the Court of Appeal considered the case of an employee who had been employed under a single employment contract but who had had more than one job during her employment. Her complaint related to the pay which she had received for a job which she had ceased to do 17 months before the termination of her employment. Her complaint was presented within six months after the termination of her employment, but it was well out of time if the relevant date was that when she ceased to be employed in the particular job to which the complaint related. It was held by the Court of Appeal that time ran from the date of termination of the employment and that accordingly there was jurisdiction to hear the complaint.

Statutory effect to the decision in *Preston* has been given by the *Equal Pay Act 1970 (Amendment) Regulations 2003 (SI 2003 No 1656)*. Provision was also made for certain special cases as mentioned below.

The general principle is that a complaint must be presented during or within six months after the end of the contract of employment or the stable employment relationship (as the case may be). Special provision is made for 'concealment cases' and 'disability cases'.

A concealment case is one in which the employer deliberately concealed a relevant fact and the complainant could not reasonably have been expected to present the complaint without knowledge of that fact. In a concealment case, the six-month period does not start to run until the date when the complainant discovered the qualifying fact or could with reasonable diligence have discovered it.

A disability case is one in which the complainant is under a disability at any time during the period of six months in which the complainant would otherwise have been obliged to present her complaint. 'Disability' is not used in the sense in which it is used in the *DDA 1995*. In this context it means that the complainant is a minor or is of unsound mind. Time does not start to run until the complainant ceases to be under the disability.

264.3   RESPONSES

The 2004 Rules of Procedure provide that a response must be presented within 28 days of the date on which the respondent 'was sent a copy of the claim'. The EAT made it clear in *Bone v Fabcon Projects Ltd [2006] IRLR 908*, that time runs from the date the claim is sent – even where it is never received by the employer. If a respondent is time-barred from defending a claim as a result, he may apply for the decision to accept its response to be reviewed under Rule 34.

265   Time Off

Employees have numerous statutory rights to take paid or unpaid time off (such as the right to have a reasonable amount of unpaid time off to take necessary action relating to dependants). In addition, employers operate a wide variety of contractual and discretionary arrangements under which employees are given time off, for example, to care for children or for study, or continue to receive full pay during sickness and other absences.

There must be no unlawful discrimination in the adoption or implementation of any such arrangements. It would be direct sex discrimination (as well as a breach of the employee's rights under the *ERA 1996* in the first example) for an employer:

(*a*)   to refuse a male employee time off to look after a child who has been sent home sick from school, on the ground that his wife should take time off from her employment; and

(*b*)   to grant a male employee time off for study, but refuse a request from his female colleague because she is pregnant and may not return after her maternity leave.

Permitting an employee to take time off, for example for medical treatment, may also be a *Reasonable Adjustment* under the *DDA 1995*.

433

266   Time Off for Dependants

The *ERA 1996* entitles every employee, regardless of length of service, to take a reasonable amount of unpaid time off work 'to take action which is necessary':

(*a*)   to help when a dependant gives birth, falls ill or is injured or assaulted;

(*b*)   to make (longer-term) arrangements for the care of a sick or injured dependant;

(*c*)   as a result of a dependant's death;

(*d*)   to cope when the arrangements for caring for a dependant unexpectedly breakdown; or

(*e*)   to deal with an unexpected incident involving a dependent child during school hours or on a school trip or in other circumstances when the school has responsibility for the child.

What action is 'necessary' is not specified. A 'dependant' of an employee means the spouse, or child or parent, of that employee, whether they live with the parent or not, or any member of the employee's household who is not his or her employee, tenant, lodger or border. The definition includes the unmarried partner of the employee, who may be of the same sex.

There is no specified limit to the amount of time that the employee can take off; the question is what was reasonable in the circumstances of the case. The right does not apply unless the employee, as soon as reasonably practicable, tells the employer why he or she is absent and, unless the employee is already back at work, for how long the absence is likely to last. An employee may bring a claim to an employment tribunal that the employer has unreasonably refused to allow him or her to take time off as required. The legislation protects employees from being victimised for exercising their right to take time off to look after dependants.

267   Trade Organisations and Discrimination

A 'trade organisation' is an organisation of workers, an organisation of employers or any other organisation whose members carry on a particular profession or trade for the purposes of which the organisation exists. The *Discrimination Laws* apply to such organisations, although the *SDA 1975* and the *RRA 1976* do not use the term 'trade organisation'.

It is unlawful for a trade organisation to discriminate against a person:

(*a*)   in the terms on which it is prepared to admit him to membership of the organisation; or

(*b*)   by refusing to accept, or deliberately not accepting, his application for membership.

It is unlawful for a trade organisation to discriminate against one of its members:

(*a*)   in the way it affords him access to any benefits or by refusing or deliberately omitting to afford him access to them;

(*b*)   by depriving him of membership, or varying the terms on which he is a member; or

(*c*)   by subjecting him to any other detriment.

268   Trade Union Activities and Sex Discrimination

The detail of the law on trade union activities falls outside the scope of this Handbook. But there can be an overlap between claims of 'discrimination' against a trade union officer and of sex discrimination. *Southwark London Borough Council v Whillier (2001) ICR 142*, is a case in point. While the employee was pursuing a grievance, she was elected branch secretary of her union, a position involving full-time release. The grievance process resulted in the employer making her an offer of promotion to a suitable post, with the increased salary for such post being paid from the point at which she took up the duties of the post. She complained that the decision that her promotion would not mean an increase in salary until she ceased her full-time union activities constituted action short of dismissal in breach of *section 146* of the *Trade Union and Labour Relations (Consolidation) Act 1992* and also sex discrimination. A tribunal upheld both claims, finding that the employer's purpose in not paying the rate for the new job until the employee took up the duties was to deter her within the meaning of *section 146* and that the treatment given to her was less favourable than that given eight years earlier to a male branch secretary. The EAT upheld the decision that the branch secretary had suffered action short of dismissal contrary to *section 146*, but allowed the employer's appeal in relation to the sex discrimination claim. Although there can be occasions on which the same conduct by an employer amount to both 'trade union discrimination' and sex discrimination, the onus in the sex discrimination claim is on the branch secretary to show some evidential connection, such as company policy, between the comparator and applicant. Where events were separated by eight years and evidence as to the earlier instance was sparse, it was difficult to make a genuine comparison. Since the tribunal's only reason for finding sex discrimination was that it was legitimate to infer it in the absence of any other explanation, that finding could not stand, since the tribunal had itself concluded that the reason for the employer's conduct was 'trade union discrimination'. In other words, a finding of 'trade union discrimination' may in some cases militate against a finding of discrimination on other grounds.

269   Trade Unions

The *Discrimination Laws* provide that trade unions should not discriminate against applicants for membership:

(*a*)   in the terms on which the organisation is prepared to admit the applicant to membership; or

(*b*)   by refusing, or deliberately omitting to accept, the application for membership.

It is unlawful for an organisation of workers to discriminate against a member:

(*a*)   in the way it affords the member access to any benefits, facilities or services, or by refusing or deliberately omitting to afford access to them;

(*b*)   by depriving the member of membership, or varying the terms of membership; or

(*c*)   by subjecting the member to any other detriment.

There are provisions under which a union member can apply to an employment tribunal for an order that a term in a collective agreement or union rule is void if, for example, that term provides for the doing of an act of unlawful discrimination, see *Collective Bargaining.*

Trade unions can play an important part in promoting equal opportunities, for example by:

(*a*)   co-operating in the introduction and implementation of *Equal Opportunity Policies*;

(*b*)   negotiating the adoption or extension of such policies; and

(*c*)   co-operating with measures to monitor the progress of such policies.

Shepherd and others v North Yorkshire County Council [2006] IRLR 190, however, illustrates that trade union members may sometimes be concerned about the relationship between their unions and their employers. This case was associated with a large group of equal pay claims brought by local authority employees against the authorities. The claimants argued that they were discriminated against by the local government unions contrary to *section 12* of the *SDA 1975* and that the employers knowingly aided the unions in their unlawful act. An employment tribunal struck out the claim as having no reasonable prospect of success. On appeal to the EAT, it was argued that there was an express or tacit agreement between the employers and the trade unions that a 'single status' agreement should not be implemented for as long as possible. However, the EAT ruled that, even making that assumption, it could not be said that the local authority thereby aided the unions in failing to represent their members adequately. Merely to agree to a particular result in collective bargaining did not mean that the employer was aiding a failure by the unions to represent their female members properly.

In *Unison v Jarvis (EAT 29/3/2006)* the EAT overruled a tribunal's decision that a trade union had discriminated against a member when deciding not to support his claims of unfair dismissal and sex and race discrimination. There was no evidence that the union would have behaved differently had the member been white or female or both.

270   Training

The *Discrimination Laws* contain provisions prohibiting discrimination against an employee in the way the employer affords him or her access to opportunities for training or by refusing or deliberately omitting to afford the employee access to such opportunities. There are also varying provisions with regard to discrimination in providing or arranging for vocational training.

It would, for example, be a clear case of *Direct Discrimination* if an employer failed to send a female employee on a suitable training course because she was pregnant and he was concerned that the cost of the course would be wasted if she failed to return to work after her maternity leave. An example of indirect sex discrimination would be an employer's refusal to consider alternative arrangements for a female employee who is unable to attend a residential training course because of her child-care commitments.

Residential training could also be an issue in relation to certain *Disabilities*. If a disabled worker is placed at a substantial disadvantage in relation to any residential or other training which is provided by the employer, then consideration must be given to providing the training in some other way, as a *Reasonable Adjustment*.

In *Treasury Solicitor's Department v Chenge [2007] IRLR 386* the EAT held that the definition of 'training' in the *RRA 1976* encompassed the government legal service's Vacation Placement Scheme, which is unpaid and lasts ten working days.

The law permits a measure of *Positive Discrimination* in favour of employees who are in a minority by reason of their gender or employees who belong to a racial group which is 'under-represented'. See also *Special Needs*.

Training is a vital component of any effective *Equal Opportunities Policy*. In a small business *Selection* and other employment decisions may be made personally by the owners, partners or directors. In many such cases, they themselves need training. In larger organisations, where decisions are made by managers, the employer has little or no prospect of persuading a tribunal that *Reasonably Practicable Steps* have been taken to prevent discrimination unless appropriate training has been given at least to managers. In many organisations, an effective policy will also require training for other employees as well as managers.

Effective training in relation to *Health and Safety at Work* is highly important. It is worth noting, for example, that migrant workers may have particular training needs in this area.

271 Transfers

A transfer may be from one place to another, from one kind of work to another or from full-time work to part-time work (or vice versa). For the latter case, please see *Indirect Discrimination* and *Part-Time Work*.

The *Discrimination Laws* contain provisions making it unlawful for an employer to discriminate in the way an employee is afforded access to opportunities for transfer or by refusing or deliberately omitting to afford an employee access to a transfer.

A compulsory transfer, for example from one job to another or from one place of work to another, will normally be a *Detriment* and accordingly any discrimination in relation to any such transfer will also be covered by the above provisions. It is immaterial, for the purposes of the discrimination laws, whether the compulsory transfer is in pursuance of an express or implied contract term.

A transfer involving a change of duties, a change of location or a reduction in hours may also be a *Reasonable Adjustment* under the *DDA 1995*.

272   Transsexuals

272.1   BACKGROUND

A small but significant minority of people, estimated at about 5,000 in the UK, is affected by transsexualism. Medical treatment to enable transsexuals to alter their bodies to match their gender identity is known as 'gender reassignment'.

The *SDA 1975* did not, on its face, cover discrimination in employment on the ground of transsexualism or gender reassignment. The picture altered as a result of a ruling of the European Court which led to an amendment of the Act. In *P v S and Cornwall County Council [1996] IRLR 347*, the European Court held that the scope of the *Equal Treatment Directive* cannot be confined simply to discrimination based on the fact that a person is of one or other sex. The Directive is the expression of the principle of equality, a fundamental principle of Community law. In view of its purpose and the fundamental nature of the rights which it seeks to safeguard, the scope of the Directive also applies to discrimination based essentially, if not exclusively, on the sex of the person concerned. Where such discrimination arises from the gender reassignment of the person concerned, he or she is treated unfavourably by comparison with persons of the sex to which he or she was deemed to belong before undergoing gender reassignment. To tolerate such discrimination would, the European Court held, be tantamount as regards such person to a failure to respect the dignity and freedom to which he or she is entitled and which the Court has a duty to safeguard. Thus dismissal of a transsexual for a reason related to a gender reassignment is contrary to *Article 5(1)* of the Directive.

Following that decision, the EAT upheld a tribunal's decision to construe the *SDA 1975* to accord with the European Court's decision: *Chessington World of Adventures Ltd v Reed [1997] IRLR 556*. The EAT held that discrimination arising from a declared intention to undergo gender reassignment is based on the person's sex. Where the reason for unfavourable treatment is sex based, in accordance with the reasoning of the House of Lords in *Webb v EMO Air Cargo (UK) Ltd [1993] IRLR 27*, there is no requirement for a male/female comparison to be made. Accordingly, the *SDA 1975* can be interpreted consistently with the purpose of the *Equal Treatment Directive* as interpreted in *P v S*. The employee in question had been subjected to concerted harassment by male colleagues following her announcement of a change of gender identity from male to female. The EAT upheld the tribunal's decision that the employers were directly liable for sex discrimination by failing to act on knowledge that the employee was being subjected to harassment, which constituted a continuing detriment.

However, this measure of legal protection is based on discrimination, which requires an appropriate comparison and worse treatment. *Bavin v NHS Trust Pensions Agency and another [1999] ICR 1192*, is a reminder of the limits of the protection. Under the NHS pension scheme, a widow or widower could benefit on a member's death, but unmarried partners of scheme members could not. The employee was in a long-term relationship with a transsexual, who had been registered as female at birth, but who had undergone gender reassignment and was accepted as a male. The employee claimed that the pension scheme was discriminatory and in breach of *Article 119*, but a tribunal found that it was not, since it applied equally to men and women and depended entirely on whether the survivor had been married in accordance with English law. The EAT upheld that ruling: the terms 'widow' and 'widower' in the pension scheme could only mean surviving spouse, so that unmarried partners of members could never obtain benefits whatever the reason for their not being married. Accordingly, the scheme discriminated between members who were married and members who were not, and the employee was not discriminated against because her partner was a transsexual, but rather because they were unmarried.

272.2   GENDER REASSIGNMENT REGULATIONS

The *Sex Discrimination (Gender Reassignment) Regulations 1999 (SI 1999 No 1102)* came into force on 1 May 1999. They extend the *SDA 1975* to cover discrimination in employment and vocational training on the ground of gender reassignment. They bring domestic law into line with the decision of the European Court in *P v S and Cornwall County Council* (above) by making discrimination on the basis of gender reassignment discrimination on the ground of sex contrary to the *SDA 1975*. The Regulations:

(*a*)   define 'gender reassignment' broadly so as provide protection against discrimination by employers at all stages of the process of gender reassignment, including the sometimes critical phase where the individual indicates an intention to embark upon gender reassignment;

(*b*)   define discrimination in terms of the comparative treatment of a transsexual and the treatment of 'other persons';

(*c*)   equate the absence allowed to a person undergoing gender reassignment with absence due to sickness or injury in order to determine whether there has been less favourable treatment; and

(*d*)   establish genuine occupational qualification exceptions to the core principle of non-discrimination.

The Regulations do not, however, define the time when sex actually changes or the time when the process of gender reassignment is deemed to be complete.

The Department for Education and Employment has published *A Guide to the Sex Discrimination (Gender Reassignment) Regulations 1999* to provide guidance and suggest good practice. But the guide is not a Code of Practice and has no special legal status. Moreover, although the recommendations it makes are likely to be found useful by tribunals as well as by employers and employees, they must be treated with some caution. For instance, the Guide suggests that it may be discriminatory to dismiss a person because of their impending gender reassignment treatment, in the same way as it is unlawful to dismiss a woman for pregnancy – but the Regulations do not give gender reassignment protected status equal to that afforded by legislation to pregnancy. The Guide recognises that medical treatment for transsexualism 'could result in a prolonged incapacity for work. If incapacity continues beyond the normal expectations for the process undergone, a transsexual employee could be retired on medical grounds in the same way as any other person who becomes unfit for duty'. It remains to be seen whether this caveat to the principle of non-discrimination survives legal challenge.

In *Croft v Royal Mail Group plc [2003] IRLR 592*, the claimant was a pre-operative transsexual who worked as a van driver. She had worked as a man for more than 10 years before informing her employers that she wished to be treated as a woman. They dealt with the case sensitively. Their position was that they would be prepared to allow her to use the female toilet facilities, but a key issue was how and when they moved to this stage. Until the time was right for her to use the female toilet facilities she was to continue using a disabled toilet facility. She resigned and complained of discrimination on the ground of gender reassignment.

It was held by the Court of Appeal that there had been no unlawful discrimination against her. The Court rejected the two extreme arguments which had been presented. For the claimant, it had been argued that it is unlawful for an employer to refuse to allow a pre-operative transsexual to the female sex, who presents with a female gender, to use the female toilets. For the employers, it was argued that a male to female transsexual changes gender for the purpose of the *SDA 1975* only when the final operation to change the physical characteristics is performed.

Pill LJ gave the following guidance:

> 'The moment at which a person in the applicant's position is entitled to use female toilets depends on all the circumstances, including her conduct and that of the employers. The employers must take into account the stage reached in treatment, including the employee's own assessment and presentation. They are entitled to take into account, though not to be governed by, the susceptibilities of other members of the workforce.'

In *EB v BA [2006] IRLR 471*, the Court of Appeal ruled that a tribunal erred in finding that the claimant was not unlawfully discriminated against in the allocation of work following her gender reassignment and was not discriminated against in being selected for redundancy. The tribunal was wrong to find that the burden of proof did not shift to the employers in respect of the period between her transition to a female role and her gender reassignment surgery, on the basis that there was no significant reduction in her 'billability' during that period, even though she was only assigned to three projects at proposal stage during that period. The tribunal should have found that the burden of proof shifted to the employers in respect of the period starting with her transition to a female role and running through to her dismissal. On the facts of this case, the employers could only discharge the burden of proof by a detailed analysis of the projects and proposals to which the claimant was not assigned. Without such an analysis, it was very difficult to see how the employers could justify the fact that the claimant was only allocated to three projects over such a long period. Employers should not be permitted to escape the provisions of *section 63A* of the *SDA 1975* by leaving it to the employee to prove her case.

273   Tribunal Procedures

273.1   BACKGROUND

Complaints of discrimination relating to employment are heard by employment tribunals. The rules of procedure are the same as those which apply in other employment tribunal cases. They are the *Employment Tribunals (Constitution and Rules of Procedure) Regulations 2004 (SI 2004 No 1861)* and the corresponding regulations for Scotland (referred to in this Handbook as the Tribunal Rules).

The usual procedure is for the claimant and the claimant's witnesses to give evidence first. It follows that in cases in England and Wales (but not in Scotland) the claimant's representative (or the claimant personally if unrepresented) will have the last word in making submissions to the tribunal.

A special feature in certain complaints under the *DDA 1995* and in cases involving allegations of sexual misconduct (usually complaints of *Sexual Harassment* under the *SDA 1975*) is the tribunal's power to make a *Restricted Reporting Order*.

Where a case appears to involve allegations that a sexual offence has been committed, the tribunal and tribunal staff must take steps to protect the identity of the person making the allegation and the person against whom it is made. This means omitting names and other identifying material from the decision and any other document which is available to the press or public. Where the persons whose identities are to be protected are parties to the proceedings, their names will be omitted from the case details which are displayed at the tribunal offices throughout each day's hearing. Allegations of sexual offences are unlikely to be made except in cases of *Sexual Harassment* (and are not a normal feature even of these cases).

The Tribunal Rules include separate rules of evidence for *Equal Value* cases. The main special feature is the power of the tribunal to appoint an *Independent Expert*.

273.2   THE 2004 TRIBUNAL RULES

The Tribunal Rules which came into force on 1 October 2004 differ in several significant respects from the previous regime. Some of the changes were necessitated by the introduction of the statutory grievance procedure, while others were intended to improve the efficiency of the system, and contribute to the effective, and preferably early, resolution of disputes.

With effect from 6 April 2005 it became necessary to use the prescribed claim form (form ET1) when making a *Claim to Tribunal*. Amongst other matters, a claimant must provide information as to compliance with the statutory grievance procedures applicable to employees and, where a grievance has not been raised, an explanation should be provided. A claim may not be accepted in certain circumstances, including (subject to limited exceptions) the case where the claimant does not use the prescribed ET1 form. A claim, or part of a claim, may be rejected where a claimant has failed to comply with applicable statutory grievance procedures. Where a claim is rejected for this reason, the claimant must be notified of any extended *Time Limit* applicable and explain the consequences of failure to comply with the procedures. The normal time period for bringing a valid claim, which usually ends three months after the act complained of, may be extended by a further three months where the claim was rejected because of non-compliance with the statutory grievance procedure. In such cases, therefore, the employee has a second 'bite of the cherry'.

273.2 Tribunal Procedures

The employer must make sure that a *Response* to the claim (previously known as a 'Notice of Appearance') reaches the tribunal office within 28 days of the date on which the employer was sent a copy of the claim (*not* the date when the employer received a copy of the claim). The rules on extensions of time for presenting a Response are now tighter than the regime under the previous Tribunal Rules. Since 6 April 2005, and subject to limited exceptions, it has been compulsory to submit the Response on the prescribed form ET3. The respondent should explain the position as regards compliance, or otherwise, with the statutory grievance procedure.

A Response will not be accepted in certain circumstances, e.g. where it is not submitted on the prescribed form ET3, where it does not include all the required information, or where it has not been presented within the applicable *Time Limit*.

The Tribunal Rules of 2004 establish a system of default judgments enabling a tribunal chairman, in certain circumstances, to determine a claim without hearing it, if such a course is considered appropriate. The determination may deal with liability only, or with both liability and remedy. A default judgment may be issued by a chairman where a respondent has failed to submit a response within a time limit, or where a response has failed to meet pre-acceptance conditions.

The chairman has the power to hold a *Case Management Discussion*, i.e. an interim hearing to deal with matters of procedure management of the case.

A chairman may order a pre-hearing review which may:

(*a*)   determine an interim or preliminary issue;

(*b*)   issue directions;

(*c*)   order payment of a deposit; or

(*d*)   consider any oral or written representations or evidence.

The Tribunal Rules also introduce a fixed period during which the parties have the opportunity to reach an ACAS-conciliated settlement. The fixed period (much criticised in many quarters) does not, however, apply in relation to claims brought under the *Discrimination Laws*.

The Tribunal Rules introduced in 2004 also provide for a substantially revised regime in respect of *Costs*.

274   Turbans

274.1   SIKHS ON CONSTRUCTION SITES

There are express provisions in relation to *Sikhs* and turbans under *sections 11* and *12* of the *Employment Act 1989*.

Normal requirements to wear a safety helmet do not apply when a Sikh:

(*a*)   is on a construction site (whether as an employee or as a contract worker or otherwise); and

(*b*)   is wearing a turban.

The Act defines:

(*a*)   'construction site' as any place where any building operations or works of engineering construction are being undertaken;

(*b*)   'safety helmets' as any form of protective headgear; and

(*c*)   'Sikh' as a follower of the Sikh religion.

This last definition distinguishes the case from the normal one in which a Sikh must be defined as a member of an ethnic group in order to bring a complaint of indirect racial discrimination, but the Act goes on to ensure that a Sikh would succeed in a complaint of indirect racial discrimination if he were to be penalised in any way for refusing to wear a safety helmet on a construction site. The Act does this by expressly providing that the requirement could not be shown to be justifiable in such circumstances. The Act also provides that a person who is not a Sikh cannot present a complaint of racial discrimination on the ground that he has been required to wear a safety helmet and denied the special treatment which is given to Sikhs on construction sites.

Similar provisions in relation to religious discrimination are contained in *Regulation 26* of the *RBR 2003*.

274.2   OTHER CASES

Away from construction sites, the normal principles in cases of *Indirect Discrimination* apply. If a Sikh (or a member of any other relevant ethnic or religious group) is unable to comply with a requirement relating to protective headgear (or a requirement not to wear a turban) then the question for consideration will be whether the requirement is 'justifiable'. It may well be justifiable if it is on safety grounds and there is no satisfactory way of reconciling the safety requirements with the needs of the individual concerned – see also *Beards*.

275   Unconscious Discrimination

As a result of the decision of the House of Lords in *Nagarajan v London Regional Transport [1999] IRLR 572*, it has been clearly established that there can be *Direct Discrimination* or *Victimisation* without conscious motivation. Lord Nicholls of Birkenhead said in that case:

'Members of racial groups need protection from conduct driven by unrecognised prejudice as much as from conscious and deliberate discrimination.'

He referred also to the comment by Lord Justice Balcombe in *West Midlands Passenger Transport Executive v Singh [1988] IRLR 186*, that a high rate of failure to achieve promotion by members of a particular racial group may indicate that 'the real reason for refusal is a conscious or unconscious racial attitude which involves stereotyped assumptions' about members of the group.

These comments apply equally to cases of discrimination on the ground of sex, disability, religion or belief, sexual orientation and age.

276   Unfair Dismissal

Where an employment tribunal makes a finding that a dismissal was unlawfully discriminatory a finding of unfair dismissal does not *automatically* follow: *H J Heinz Co Ltd v Kenrick [2000] IRLR 144*. The tribunal must give separate consideration to the question of unfair dismissal under *section 98* of the *Employment Rights Act 1996*.

Furthermore there are cases where a tribunal has jurisdiction to hear a complaint of discrimination but not a complaint of unfair dismissal, for example where:

(*a*)   the employee does not have the necessary period of continuous employment for the purpose of presenting a complaint of unfair dismissal; or

(*b*)   the complainant is an employee within the extended definition of *Employment* contained in the discrimination laws but not for the purposes of a complaint of unfair dismissal.

An employee who has been subjected to unlawful discrimination is not *necessarily* entitled to resign and treat himself or herself as constructively dismissed, so as to bring a complaint of discriminatory dismissal and/or unfair dismissal – see *Dismissal, Constructive Dismissal and Grievances*.

277   Uniforms

Under the *SDA 1975*, it is lawful for an employer to require employees to wear uniforms and to insist on different uniforms for male and female employees, so long as, looking at uniform requirements as a whole, employees of one gender are not being treated less favourably than employees of the other gender – see *Dress and Personal Appearance*.

It could be indirect racial or religious discrimination for an employer to refuse to modify a uniform which a racial or religious minority employee cannot wear because of the customs or conventions of the *Racial Group* or religion to which he or she belongs – see *Indirect Discrimination*.

If, because of a disability, a disabled employee cannot wear a particular uniform, or cannot do so without discomfort, then a *Reasonable Adjustment* may be called for.

278   Unintentional Discrimination

Nouns like 'intention' and 'motive' can be misleading when used imprecisely.

There are several questions to be considered in relation to any complaint of *Direct Discrimination* or *Victimisation*. Some of those questions are factual questions which do not involve any consideration of the intention, motivation or mental processes of the person who is alleged to be responsible for the act complained of. In particular:

(*a*)   has the complainant been treated in the way complained of;

(*b*)   is that treatment less favourable than the treatment afforded to some other relevant person or persons (such as persons of a different gender or racial group or who have not done a protected act);

(*c*)   are the relevant circumstances of the complainant's case, and of those other cases, the same or not materially different; and

(*d*)   if the relevant act has not been done by the respondent personally, has the act been done by a person (such as an employee or agent) for whose actions the respondent is responsible?

Where there is no actual comparator, it may be necessary to consider the mental processes of the person who has done the act complained of in order to ascertain how a hypothetical comparator would have been treated.

Establishing whether there has been less favourable treatment is only the first question. Lord Nicholls of Birkenhead pointed out in *Nagarajan v London Regional Transport [1999] IRLR 572* that:

'in every case it is necessary to enquire why the complainant received less favourable treatment. This is the crucial question ... save in obvious cases, answering the crucial question will call for some consideration of the mental processes of the alleged discriminator. Treatment, favourable or unfavourable, is a consequence which follows from a decision.'

If a person has treated the complainant less favourably than an actual or hypothetical comparator has been treated, it is relevant, in order to ascertain the reason for the less favourable treatment, to look at that person's state of mind or mental processes in the following respects:

(*a*)   knowledge of (or, in cases under the *RRA 1976*, belief about – see *Racial Grounds*) the complainant's race (or, as the case may be the complainant's gender or marital status or the fact that the complainant has done a protected act); it is difficult to see how a particular factor can be the reason for a particular act unless the person doing that act is aware of that factor;

(*b*)   intention – in the sense of deliberately doing the relevant act or omission; and

(*c*)   probably also intention, in the sense that less favourable treatment of the complainant than of an actual or hypothetical comparator was intended or at least foreseen.

Evidence of conscious motivation (for example the use of language which indicates an intention to treat the complainant less favourably because she is a woman) can assist a tribunal to decide the reason for the treatment complained of but such evidence is usually not available and is not essential. As Lord Nicholls of Birkenhead said in *Nagarajan*:

449

'Direct evidence of a decision to discriminate on racial grounds will seldom be forthcoming. Usually the grounds of the decision will have to be deduced, or inferred, from the surrounding circumstances.'

In deciding what the grounds of the decision were, it is not necessary to find that there was conscious motivation connected with, for example, the race or gender of the complainant. Lord Nicholls said:

'Members of racial groups need protection from conduct driven by unrecognised prejudice as much as from conscious and deliberate discrimination.'

Lord Nicholls also said that the crucial question of the reason for the treatment complained of:

'is to be distinguished sharply from a second and different question: if the discriminator treated the complainant less favourably on racial grounds, why did he do so? The latter question is strictly beside the point when deciding whether an act of racial discrimination occurred . . . racial discrimination is not negatived by the discriminator's motive or intention or reason or purpose (the words are interchangeable in this context) in treating another person less favourably on racial grounds.'

Accordingly, there are two respects in which it can be said that there are cases of unlawful discrimination which do not necessarily involve a hostile intention towards the complainants:

(*a*)   there can be a finding that, for example, the race or gender of the complainant was the reason for the treatment complained of, even though the discriminator did not articulate this reason even to himself and acted on the basis of an unconscious or subconscious prejudice; and

(*b*)   once it is established that, for example, the race or gender of the complainant was the reason, or an important reason, for the act complained of, it is irrelevant to consider why that factor played a part in the decision-making.

279   Unmarried Persons

The definition of discrimination under the *SDA 1975* includes direct and indirect discrimination against married workers; it does not include discrimination against unmarried workers.

It would, however, be *Direct Discrimination* to discriminate against, say, a man because of his single status, if there would have been no discrimination against an unmarried woman in similar circumstances. The unlawful discrimination in such a case would be treating the man, on the ground of his sex, less favourably than a woman would have been treated in similar circumstances.

280   Variation of Contracts

The *Discrimination Laws* contain provisions under which application may be made to a county court (or sheriff court in Scotland) for the removal or modification of a term which, for example, provides for the doing of an act which is unlawful under the legislation – see *Agreements*.

There is also provision for an application to an employment tribunal for the removal or modification of an offending term in a collective agreement – see *Collective Bargaining*.

281   Veils

Questions concerning the wearing of veils attracted much high profile publicity in late 2006. At the centre of much of the debate by politicians, social commentators and others was the case of *Azmi v Kirklees Metropolitan Council [2007] All ER (D) 528 (Mar)*. The claimant was a bilingual support worker, helping to teach English as a second language to children from predominantly ethnic minority backgrounds. A devout Muslim, she had since the age of 15 worn a veil covering the whole of her head and face (except for her eyes) when in the presence of unrelated adult males. However, at both interview and on an initial training day, she instead wore a head-scarf, which did not cover her face. She did not indicate that her religious beliefs required her to wear a full veil. Shortly after commencing work, however, she asked if she could wear the veil when working with male teachers, or alternatively if arrangements could be made so that she would not have to work with male teachers at all. The employers concluded that it would not be possible to isolate the claimant from male teachers and also that the veil had an adverse effect on the children's ability to learn language skills from her, as they were deprived of the visual clues that ordinarily come from the teacher's facial expression. Further, her diction was not as clear as it would have been without the veil. Advice from the local authority's Education Service supported these views, indicating that the desire to express religious identity did not outweigh the importance of optimal communications between teacher and students. The claimant was allowed to wear the veil when in communal areas, but not when working directly with children in the classroom. She declined to follow this guidance and continued to wear the veil while teaching. When instructed to comply, she refused and commenced a period of sickness absence. She presented a grievance, complaining that she had been discriminated against on the ground of her religious belief, but the grievance was never dealt with. She returned to work, but remained unwilling to comply with the instruction and was eventually suspended from work. She brought a claim under the *RBR 2003* contending that the suspension amounted to less favourable treatment on the ground of her religious belief which constituted direct discrimination under *Regulation 3(1)(a)*.

An employment tribunal rejected her complaint, finding that the appropriate hypothetical comparator was a person not of the Muslim religion who covered their face, e.g. with a balaclava. On the evidence, the tribunal accepted that such a comparator would have been extended. Since there was no less favourable treatment, there was no need to consider the related question of whether the manifestation of a belief came within the provisions on direct discrimination. Nevertheless, the tribunal indicated that the right to manifest one's religion is not absolute, and thus should be considered in the context of indirect discrimination which can be justified by a proportionate response to a legitimate aim. As regards indirect discrimination, the requirement not to wear a veil while teaching was a *Provision, criterion or practice* putting persons of the claimant's belief at a disadvantage compared with others. However, there was a legitimate aim, i.e. ensuring that the claimant could communicate fully with children. Further, the means of achieving it were proportionate. The tribunal rejected a complaint that the complainant had been harassed, finding that she had exaggerated the subjective effect of the treatment complained of. However, she succeeded in a victimisation claim. The authority's inaction with regard to the grievance could only be due to the fact of the complaint of religious discrimination. Accordingly, she was awarded compensation of £1,000 for injury to feelings, increased by 10 per cent to reflect the failure to complete an applicable statutory grievance procedure. The tribunal refused to refer the case to the European Court of Justice, but the claimant indicated an intention to appeal to the EAT.

282   Vicarious Liability

Vicarious liability is the expression commonly used in other areas of the law, particularly in relation to accidents at work, where employers are made legally responsible for the negligent actions of their employees.

The same expression is also frequently used to describe the liability of employers under the *Discrimination Laws* for acts and omissions by their employees in the course of their employment. The expression is apt to be misleading in this context, however, because of the broader and more robust approach adopted in discrimination cases following the decision of the Court of Appeal in *Jones v Tower Boot Co Ltd [1997] IRLR 168* – see *Harassment*.

283   Victimisation

283.1   THE STATUTORY PROVISIONS

Protection from victimisation is one of the most important areas of equal opportunities law. The statutory definition of discrimination includes treating a person less favourably than other persons would be treated in the same circumstances, by reason that the person victimised has done what is commonly (although not in the legislation itself) referred to as a 'protected act'. The acts covered by this term are:

(*a*)   bringing proceedings under the relevant legislation;

(*b*)   giving evidence or information in connection with any proceedings under the relevant legislation (whether the proceedings are brought by the person victimised or any other person and whether they are brought against the discriminator or against any other person);

(*c*)   doing anything else under or by reference to the relevant legislation (in relation to the discriminator or any other person); and

(*d*)   alleging that the discriminator or any other person has committed an act which would amount to a contravention of the relevant legislation (whether or not the allegation expressly states that the act committed contravenes the legislation).

There is also discrimination by way of victimisation if the discriminator:

(*a*)   knows that the person victimised intends to do any of the above things;

(*b*)   suspects that the person victimised has done any of them; or

(*c*)   suspects that the person victimised intends to do any of them.

Less favourable treatment does not, however, amount to discrimination by way of victimisation if it is by reason of an allegation which was false and not made in good faith.

The various statutes use different language in referring to the circumstances of the claimant and of the other persons whose treatment is to be compared with that of the claimant. It is, however, questionable whether the differences in wording have important practical consequences.

283.2   THE CASE LAW

In early appeal decisions relating to victimisation, the EAT and then the Court of Appeal extended the ambit of protected acts very widely, so that something was done under or by reference to the relevant legislation even where it was an unconventional and discreditable action. In *Kirby v Manpower Services Commission [1980] IRLR 229,* making a report containing allegations of discrimination was treated as a protected act even though the report was made in breach of an obligation of confidentiality. In *Aziz v Trinity Street Taxis Ltd [1988] IRLR 204,* secretly tape recording conversations with fellow taxi drivers, in order to obtain evidence of discrimination, was also treated as a protected act.

No remedy was given in these cases, however, because it was held, notably by the Court of Appeal in *Aziz,* that in making a complaint of discrimination by way of victimisation the complainant had to be able to prove that the respondent had a motive which was consciously connected with the relevant discrimination legislation. Unfortunately, this also meant that a discriminatory motive of this kind also had to be proved even where the protected act was of a wholly conventional and legitimate nature. In theory, at least, the effect of the decision in *Aziz* was that a complaint that, for example, the respondent had dismissed the complainant for bringing proceedings under the *EPA 1970* was at risk of failing if the respondent could show that he would have dismissed an employee for bringing any other proceedings (unrelated to the relevant legislation) against him.

There is no longer, however, a requirement for conscious motivation, following the decision of the House of Lords in *Nagarajan v London Regional Transport [1999] IRLR 572*. In that case, the complainant applied to the respondent for a post as a travel information assistant. He was interviewed and was subsequently told that his application had been unsuccessful. The two interviewers, and an equal opportunities adviser who was also present, were aware at the time of the interview that he was a former employee of the respondent who had previously brought racial discrimination cases against the respondent.

The tribunal upheld a complaint of victimisation. The tribunal found that the score which one of the interviewers had given to the complainant for articulacy was ridiculous and unrealistically low. The tribunal found that a view formed by the same interviewer that the complainant was very anti-management was derived from the interviewer's knowledge of his previous complaint. The tribunal reached the conclusion that the interviewers, particularly the one who had given the above score and formed the above view, were 'consciously or subconsciously influenced' by the fact that the complainant had brought the previous proceedings.

The EAT, later supported by the Court of Appeal, set aside the decision of the tribunal on two grounds, the first of which was that *section 2(1)* of the *RRA 1976* 'contemplates a motive which is consciously connected with the race relations legislation'. There was no scope for subconscious influence.

The House of Lords, by a majority, allowed a further appeal and restored the decision of the tribunal. No conscious motivation need be proved, whether the complaint is one of *Direct Discrimination* or one of *Victimisation*. In the words of Lord Nicholls: 'If racial grounds or protected acts had a significant influence on the outcome, discrimination is made out.'

The other leading case on victimisation is that of the House of Lords in *Chief Constable of West Yorkshire Police v Khan [2001] IRLR 830*. In that case a sergeant, who had applied unsuccessfully for promotion to inspector, presented an employment tribunal complaint of racial discrimination. Before the case was heard, he applied to another force for an inspector's post. The West Yorkshire Police refused to give the other force an opinion about his suitability, giving the pending tribunal case as the reason.

A complaint of victimisation was upheld by the tribunal. The complainant was awarded compensation of £1,500 for injury to feelings. That decision was upheld on appeal first by the EAT and then by the Court of Appeal, but a further appeal by the Chief Constable was unanimously allowed by the House of Lords.

Lord Nicholls of Birkenhead pointed out that the Chief Constable had refused to give a reference because of the pending tribunal case and that case was because the views of Sergeant Khan's supervising officers about his suitability for promotion 'were being challenged by Sergeant Khan as racially discriminatory'. Those views, he said, 'constituted unlawful racial discrimination. That issue remained to be decided. That being so, the Chief Constable could hardly be expected to repeat those selfsame views to another potential employer while that serious challenge against the authors of those views remained outstanding. Repetition of those views at that time could justifiably have been castigated as irresponsible behaviour by the Chief Constable, as well as possibly leading to a further allegation of direct racial discrimination . . . but, according to Sergeant Khan, that is the course the Chief Constable should have followed . . . this is a surprising proposition. To my mind it has only to be spelled out for it to be apparent that this cannot be right.'

The judgments in the House of Lords considered the following three ingredients of a complaint of victimisation:

(a)   the relevant circumstances;

(b)   less favourable treatment;

(c)   'by reason that'.

It was stated by Lord Nicholls of Birkenhead and by Lord Hoffmann, with both of whose judgments Lord Hutton agreed, that the relevant circumstances are 'circumstances in respect of which discrimination is unlawful under the Act'. In this case the Act was the *RRA 1976* and the relevant circumstances were the request for a reference and the refusal of that request. The second ingredient of the definition is straightforward. It was necessary only for Sergeant Khan to show that he had been treated less favourably than any actual or hypothetical officer who had not done the protected act, i.e. in this case brought a case of racial discrimination against the Chief Constable.

It is the third ingredient, the reason for the treatment complained of, that has caused the most practical difficulty. Two different and contrasting errors are discernible in some of the earlier approaches which had been adopted.

On the one hand, it is plainly an error of law, when considering a victimisation case, to make a simple comparison between the discrimination proceedings brought by the complainant and proceedings of another kind which might have been brought by a comparator; so that a complainant who has been dismissed for bringing discrimination proceedings would fail in his victimisation complaint if the employer could show that he would also have dismissed a person bringing any other kind of complaint. Lord Nicholls quoted with approval the decision of the Court of Appeal in *Brown v TNT Express Worldwide (UK) Ltd [2001] ICR 182*. In that case, an employee requested an afternoon off to consult his adviser about a racial discrimination claim which he had brought against his employer. Permission was refused, although requests for time off for personal reasons were normally granted. The employee left work to keep his appointment and was dismissed. His victimisation claim succeeded. The Court of Appeal rejected the employer's contention that the appropriate comparator was an employee who had brought proceedings against the employer but not under the *RRA 1976*.

On the other hand, the courts below in *Khan* had erred in law in treating the *bringing* of racial discrimination proceedings by Sergeant Khan as the effective cause of the withholding of the reference. The *But For* approach was not required by the legislation and had proved to be inappropriate in this case. Although the reference request would not have been refused but for the bringing of the proceedings, it was not Sergeant Khan's conduct in bringing the racial discrimination proceedings but the fact that those proceedings were still existing and had not yet been resolved that was the effective cause of the Chief Constable's action in withholding the reference.

The House of Lords approved the decision of the Court of Appeal in the case of *Cornelius v University College of Swansea [1987] IRLR 141*. In that case, Mrs

283.2 Victimisation

Cornelius had made a complaint of sex discrimination against the university which employed her. While the proceedings were pending she applied to transfer to another post and also asked for a grievance hearing. She was told that no action could be taken on either of these matters while the tribunal proceedings were pending. Her complaint of victimisation was unsuccessful. Bingham LJ, in a passage quoted by Lord Hoffmann in *Khan*, made a distinction between the bringing of proceedings, which had not influenced the decisions of the university; and the existence of current proceedings which plainly did influence their decision. Lord Hoffmann in *Khan*, suggested the following test:

'A test which is likely in most cases to give the right answer is to ask whether the employer would have refused the request if the litigation had been concluded, whatever the outcome. If the answer is no, it will usually follow that the reason for refusal was the existence of the proceedings and not the fact that the employee had commenced them. On the other hand, if the fact that the employee had commenced proceedings under the Act was a real reason why he received less favourable treatment, it is no answer that the employer would have behaved in the same way to an employee who had done some non-protected act, such as commencing proceedings otherwise than under the Act.'

An illustration, in a different context, of a successful complaint of victimisation is the decision of the EAT in *Visa International Service Association v Paul [2004] IRLR 42*. Mrs Paul resigned and brought proceedings complaining of, inter alia, sex discrimination, on the ground that she had not been told about, and not been considered for, a vacancy which arose during her maternity leave. The respondent brought a counterclaim for the repayment of enhanced maternity pay which Mrs Paul had received. The EAT upheld a finding that the issue of the counterclaim was an act of victimisation.

One of the most important cases on victimisation is *St Helens Metropolitan Borough Council v Derbyshire and others [2005] IRLR 801*. A large number of female catering staff brought equal pay claims. Most agreed to a compromise, but a minority did not accept the settlement and proceeded with their claims. After a tribunal hearing was scheduled, the Council wrote to all catering staff, warning that if the claims were persisted in and were successful, it could lead to closure of the school meal service. Another letter was sent directly to each claimant and warned of 'the impact that the current course of action will have on the service and everyone employed in it'. An employment tribunal found that the letters were 'intimidating', and 'caused distress' and 'odium'. Both the tribunal and the EAT held that the letters amounted to victimisation. However, the Court of Appeal (albeit only by a majority) ruled in favour of the employer. The tribunal erred in drawing a distinction from the position in *Chief Constable of West Yorkshire Police v Khan [2001] IRLR 830*, in which the House of Lords held that it was open to any employer, against whom proceedings of a protected kind were pending, to take honest and reasonable steps to protect its position in that litigation without infringing the victimisation provisions, on the basis that in the present case the employers did not merely seek to avoid prejudicing their position in the litigation, but wanted the claimants to abandon their claims. If an employer facing equal pay proceedings could not take steps to try to persuade claimants to settle without infringing the victimisation provisions, then their ability to take reasonable steps to protect themselves in litigation would be much attenuated as compared to what it would be in other, non-protected litigation. At the time of writing, a ruling from the House of Lords was awaited.

283.3   **PRACTICAL ADVICE**

Guidance and training should be given:

(*a*)   to interviewers and others involved in the selection process, where a person who has done a protected act applies for employment;

(*b*)   to managers and supervisors, where a person continues in employment after having done a protected act.

Where a complaint of harassment or discrimination has been made against an individual manager (and particularly if the complaint has been upheld), it is not good practice to give that manager responsibility for future decisions relating to the complainant, unless the employer:

(*a*)   is fully satisfied that the manager understands and will comply with the obligation not to victimise the complainant; and

(*b*)   has given appropriate reassurance to the complainant.

The following steps should also be taken (or at least considered) in all cases where an employee has done a protected act:

(*a*)   a clear explanation to that employee of the procedure for making an internal complaint if any victimisation does take place;

(*b*)   the involvement of an independent person, such as a personnel manager from another department, in all future decisions relating to the employee;

(*c*)   the appointment of a senior person to monitor any such decisions to ensure that they are made fairly and objectively;

(*d*)   appropriate disciplinary action against the persons concerned, if the allegations made by the employee have been upheld.

284   Voluntary Bodies

A voluntary body is subject to obligations under the *Discrimination Laws* in the same way as any other employer.

285   Voluntary Workers

It is unlikely that a voluntary worker would be treated as an employee for the purposes of the *Discrimination Laws*. Where a person works entirely without any payment or other reward, that work is not normally done under a contract, whether a conventional contract of service or a contract personally to execute any work or labour.

This generalisation made in earlier editions of this Handbook, is supported by the decision of the EAT in *South East Sheffield Citizens Advice Bureau v Grayson [2004] IRLR 353,* in this disability discrimination case, volunteer advisers working for a Citizens Advice Bureau were not 'employees' within the meaning of *section 68(1) DDA 1995.* In order for a volunteer to be found to be an 'employee', it is necessary to be able to identify an arrangement under which, in exchange for valuable consideration, the volunteer is contractually obliged to render services to or work personally for the employer. In this case, volunteers were not obliged to work the 'usual minimum weekly commitment' of six hours per week. The crucial question was not whether any benefits flowed from the CAB to the volunteer in consideration of any work actually done by the volunteer. The mere fact that, if the volunteer did work, the CAB would reimburse them for expenses incurred and indemnify them against negligence claimed by disgruntled clients did not impose any obligation on the volunteer actually to do any work for the CAB.

286 Wales

The *Discrimination Laws* all apply in Wales. Both the substantive law and the procedure are identical, whether the employment is at an establishment in Wales or at one in England.

287   Whistle-blowing

Detailed consideration of the Public Interest Disclosure Act 1998, which protects 'whistle-blowers' in certain circumstances, falls outside the scope of this Handbook. The Act has not conventionally been regarded as an 'equal opportunities' measure, but there are some points of similarity, as was made clear in *Woodward v Abbey National plc [2006] IRLR 677*.

In *Woodward* the Court of Appeal ruled that the statutory protection given to whistle-blowers continues to apply after the contract of employment has ended. A redundant whistle-blower claimed that she had subsequently been victimised by her former employers in respect of other job applications, and that this was due to protected disclosures that she had made during her employment. The Court of Appeal treated detrimental treatment of a whistle-blower as a type of victimisation, analogous to that under the *Discrimination Laws*. Accordingly, it applied the decision of the House of Lords in *Rhys-Harper v Relaxion Group plc [2003] IRLR 484*, i.e. that an employment tribunal has jurisdiction to consider a claim of victimisation which relates only to acts which are alleged to have taken place after the complainant's employment has ended. Ward LJ said:

> 'Although the language and the framework might be slightly different, it seems to me that the four Acts are dealing with the same concept, namely, protecting the employee from detriment being done to him in relation to his or her sex, race, disability or whistle-blowing . . . All four Acts are, therefore, dealing with victimisation in one form or another. If the common theme is victimisation, it would be odd indeed if the same sort of act could be victimisation for one person, but not for the other.'

However, in *Kuzel v Roche Products Ltd [2007] IRLS 309*, the EAT held that, although the protection afforded to whistle-blowers is protection against a form of discrimination in the sense of victimisation, it does not follow that the principles on the reversal of the *Burden of Proof* in discrimination cases are applicable.

288   Without Prejudice

Attempts to resolve employment disputes are usually made on a 'without prejudice' basis. However, not every discussion, and not every document, that is labelled as being 'without prejudice' is genuinely without prejudice and, if it is not without prejudice, then what is said may be referred to in evidence at a subsequent employment tribunal hearing.

The point is illustrated by the decision of the EAT in *BNP Paribas v Mezzotero [2004] IRLR 508*. In that case an employee had, two weeks after returning to work on maternity leave, raised a grievance relating to the way she had been treated prior to on her return from maternity leave. After invoking the grievance procedure she was asked to attend a meeting to discuss her position. At the start of the meeting the employers said that they wanted the discussions to be 'without prejudice' and then explained that it was not viable for her to return to her old job. There was no other available alternative position for her and they suggested that it would be best for the business and for her if she terminated her employment, in which case she would be paid standard redundancy package of almost £100,000. She subsequently presented an application to the employment tribunal alleging direct sex discrimination and victimisation in that the employers had attempted to terminate her employment after she had raised a grievance. The employers sought to exclude the evidence relating to the meeting on the grounds that it was without prejudice and therefore subject to legal privilege. The EAT supported the employment tribunal chairman's ruling that the evidence could be adduced since there was no extant dispute between the parties as to the termination of her employment as the act of raising a grievance did not by itself mean that the parties to the employment relationship were necessarily in dispute.

The *Paribas* decision was subsequently considered in *Vaseghi and another v Brunel University [2006] All ER (D) 163 (Oct)*, in which the EAT said:

'It seems to us that in discrimination claims the necessity of getting to the truth of what occurred and if necessary eradicating the evil of discrimination may tip the scales as against the necessity of protecting the "without prejudice" rule . . . In our view it would be a clear abuse of a privileged occasion not to allow the respondents to refer to the discussions to support their claim of victimisation.'

289   Word of Mouth Recruitment

It is generally desirable for employers to avoid the use of word of mouth or similar informal methods to recruit employees. Such methods could involve *Indirect Discrimination* where, for example, a considerably smaller proportion of women than of men or a considerably smaller proportion of black workers than of white workers are made aware of a particular vacancy.

An employer adopting such methods could face complaints of indirect discrimination by individuals or action in relation to the *Discriminatory Practice* which is being operated.

290   Workers From Overseas

The *RRA 1976* permits an employer to discriminate in favour of a person not ordinarily resident in Great Britain:

(*a*)   where the purpose of the employment is to provide that person with training in certain skills; and

(*b*)   it appears to the employer that the person intends to exercise those skills wholly outside Great Britain.

There is also a more general provision to a similar effect in *section 36* of the *RRA 1976*, under which either an employer, a training body or any other person or body can discriminate for the benefit of persons not ordinarily resident in Great Britain in affording them access to facilities for education or training or any ancillary benefits. Such discrimination is permitted where it appears to the discriminator that the persons in question do not intend to remain in Great Britain after their period of education or training there.

In practical terms, these provisions now apply only when the discrimination is on the grounds of nationality, not on the ground of race or ethnic or national origin, following amendments which were made to the *RRA 1976* with effect from July 2003.

291 Working Conditions

The fact that work is to be carried out in dangerous, difficult, dirty or otherwise unpleasant working conditions can be relevant in the following respects:

(a) There must be no direct discrimination in the allocation of such work, and in particular the person deciding who should do what work must not act on the basis that dangerous or difficult work is more suitable for men than for women – see *Detriment*.

(b) Similarly, an employer must not make recruitment or selection decisions on the basis that dangerous or unpleasant working conditions make a job 'men's work' rather than 'women's work'.

(c) An employer must consider *Reasonable Adjustments*, where the nature of the work places a disabled employee at a substantial disadvantage.

The fact that the work of a comparator named by the complainant in an *Equal Pay* case has to be done in unpleasant conditions can be relevant to the following questions:

(a) Is the comparator's work and that of the complainant *Like Work*?

(b) Are the two jobs of *Equal Value*?

(c) If a difference in pay or other contract terms is attributable to the unpleasant working conditions, has a *Material Factor* defence been made out?

Issues relating to *Health and Safety at Work* may also arise.

292   Works Rules

Most employers make rules to be obeyed by their employees and set them out in a handbook or in notices which are displayed or issued to the workforce.

The *Discrimination Laws* contain provisions under which an employee or job applicant may apply to an employment tribunal for an order declaring to be void a works rule which:

(*a*)   is made in furtherance of an unlawful act; or

(*b*)   provides for the doing of an unlawful act.

An example would be a works rule stating that a particularly hazardous machine may be operated by a woman only if she is supervised.

CHECKLISTS

INTRODUCTORY NOTE

These checklists indicate matters which commonly arise or should usually be considered. They do not purport to be comprehensive or to cover all possible eventualities.

1. ADOPTING AND IMPLEMENTING AN EQUAL OPPORTUNITY POLICY

- Involve staff and unions in policy formulation.
- Consider more detailed policies, e.g. on harassment and disability.
- Appoint a suitable person or team to take responsibility for policy implementation.
- Set up effective mechanisms for informal and formal complaints.
- Identify new disciplinary offences where necessary, both for managers and for other employees (e.g. racial, sex, religious, sexual orientation or disability discrimination as misconduct and harassment, victimisation or, for managers, condoning harassment or victimisation as gross misconduct).
- Revise other policies, procedures and practices, e.g. those on recruitment, selection and redundancy, in the light of the equal opportunity policy.
- Communicate the policy effectively to all employees and to job applicants.
- Provide effective training for managers and for other persons involved in recruitment and selection, redundancy selection and other employment decisions.

2. MONITORING AND REVIEWING EQUAL OPPORTUNITY POLICIES

- Decide on a system of classification.
- Obtain the starting information about the racial composition of the workforce and numbers of men and women and of disabled workers at various levels.
- Set up systems for recording changes to this initial information.
- Set up systems for classifying job applications at various levels and successful and unsuccessful applicants by reference to racial origin, gender and disability.
- Adopt a system for recording and classifying all complaints and how they are dealt with.
- Set up arrangements to analyse and review all the information at regular intervals.
- Consider, at each review, whether the policy needs to be changed or whether implementation needs to be improved in any respect.
- Adopt a system of regular reporting on the success or otherwise of the policy, including reports to senior management at least once a year.

3. REASONABLY PRACTICABLE STEPS TO PREVENT DISCRIMINATION

- Adopt a suitably worded policy which clearly describes the kind of conduct which is unacceptable in the organisation.

Checklists

- Ensure that the policy is communicated effectively to employees and in particular that all employees are aware that they must not discriminate unlawfully themselves and that they must report any discrimination of which they become aware.

- Provide detailed training and guidance where necessary, particularly for managers, supervisors, interviewers and any other persons responsible for dealing with, or making decisions about, job applicants or employees.

- Give any necessary instructions and guidance to recruitment and other agents used by the organisation.

- Provide further training when necessary, e.g. refresher courses and updates, training for new managers and training for new eventualities.

- Consider at regular intervals whether further measures are required.

- Investigate thoroughly and promptly any cases which come to light, whether through the complaints procedure or otherwise, and take appropriate action.

4. RECRUITMENT AND SELECTION

- Appoint a senior person or team to oversee and be responsible for the policies and procedures and their implementation.

- As a general policy, advertise all job vacancies, both internally and externally (but with special provision for cases where there is a need to redeploy, if possible, potentially redundant employees, particularly women returning from maternity leave, or disabled employees).

- Set up objective procedures, involving the use of job descriptions, person specifications, structured interviews and scoring systems.

- Scrutinise and review, in the light of legal requirements and the equal opportunity policy, all documents which are used in recruitment or selection, including job advertisements and application forms.

- Review any tests which are used, such as intelligence tests, aptitude tests or psychometric tests, to ensure that they are not indirectly discriminatory in their operation.

- Set up a system for asking all candidates invited for interview to indicate in advance whether arrangements are needed to accommodate any disability.

- Provide effective training for all selectors, interviewers and other persons involved in recruitment or selection.

- Set up a system under which the consent of a suitably qualified person is required before treating a post as one to which a GOQ or other exception applies.

- Review all procedures and standard documentation at regular intervals and consider whether any changes are needed.

- Ensure that all shortlisting and selection decisions and the reasons for them are recorded and that the records are kept.

5. COMMON EXAMPLES OF INDIRECT RACIAL DISCRIMINATION

- Many acts of religious discrimination are also examples of indirect racial discrimination.

- Inflexible rules on dress and appearance, which fail to take account of the customs or religious practices of particular ethnic groups.

470

- Refusal to give reasonable consideration to requests for short prayer breaks, for accumulation of annual leave or to take annual leave on a feast or holy day.

- Recruitment arrangements which artificially restrict the pool of candidates, with a disproportionate impact on particular racial groups.

- Failing to give due weight to qualifications or relevant experience obtained overseas.

- Requiring qualifications which are excessive in relation to the duties to be performed.

- The use of intelligence or psychometric or other tests which have the effect of disadvantaging candidates not brought up in Great Britain.

- Requiring a standard of written or spoken English which is excessive in relation to the duties to be performed (including a requirement to complete a written application form for a manual job).

Note: the three last-mentioned requirements are likely to disadvantage racial minority workers who have recently settled in Great Britain. At one time these would have been predominantly Afro-Caribbean and Asian workers; they are now increasingly members of other racial minorities.

6. COMMON EXAMPLES OF INDIRECT SEX DISCRIMINATION

- Recruitment arrangements which artificially restrict the pool of candidates to one consisting mainly of men (or women).

- Intelligence or psychometric or other tests which are biased in their operation against women (or men).

- A refusal to agree to part-time working or job sharing.

- Inflexibility in relation to starting and finishing times.

- Insistence on a rotating shift pattern.

- A requirement to attend residential training courses.

- Obligations to undertake overseas or overnight travel.

- Contractual mobility requirements or the implementation of such requirements.

Note: all but the first two of the above-mentioned criteria and practices are potentially indirectly discriminatory against women because a much greater proportion of women than of men have childcare and other family responsibilities which limit their freedom of action. These criteria and practices are, however, unlawful only if not objectively justified.

7. PRELIMINARY ACTION FOR CLAIMANTS

- Check on the time limit for presenting the claim to the tribunal – this is vital.

- Enquire about the possibility of assistance, e.g. from the relevant Commission and apply in good time.

- Comply with the statutory grievance procedure.

- Use the statutory questionnaires – taking advice if possible on the questions to be asked.

- Keep the time limits in mind throughout – if out of time, present a claim without any further delay.

471

Checklists

- Ensure that the claim to tribunal specifies all your grounds of complaint (e.g. unfair dismissal as well as discrimination).
- Consider whether you have correctly identified the respondent and whether there is any further respondent to be added (e.g. a fellow employee against whom you have made allegations of harassment).

8. PRELIMINARY ACTION FOR RESPONDENTS

- Comply with the 28-day time limit for filing the response.
- Investigate the claim as thoroughly as possible before filing the response, but subject to the time limits.
- Deal promptly and fairly with any grievance submitted by the claimant, whether before or after the commencement of proceedings.
- Respond promptly, carefully, thoroughly and accurately if a questionnaire is submitted.
- If the claimant is still employed by you, take effective measures to prevent any victimisation.
- If further information is required, ask for it promptly.
- Consider whether you can take any points on jurisdiction, such as a failure to present the claim in time, and bring any such point to the attention of the tribunal.
- In a discrimination case, consider whether to plead the defence that all reasonably practicable steps have been taken to prevent the act complained of or acts of that description.
- In an equal pay case, consider whether there is any material factor defence to be pleaded.
- Consider the possibility of trying to settle the case through ACAS.

9. PREPARING A CASE FOR HEARING

- Has the case been fully pleaded, so that all the issues have been clearly identified?
- Have the parties been correctly identified and are there any further parties to be joined in?
- Have you disclosed all relevant documents to the other party?
- Have all relevant documents been disclosed to you – or do you need to apply for an order for discovery?
- Have steps been taken to agree a joint bundle of documents for the hearing – and which party is to prepare the necessary copies for the hearing?
- Have all the witnesses whom you wish to call been interviewed and statements obtained?
- Is a witness order required?
- Is there any need to apply for a postponement (in which case an application must be made promptly, supported by full reasons)?
- Have all the legal issues in the case been fully researched?
- Has the possibility of a negotiated settlement through ACAS been fully explored?

10. INDIRECT DISCRIMINATION – KEY ISSUES

- What is the precise definition of the criterion etc. complained of?
- Has that criterion etc. been applied to the claimant?
- Was the claimant put at a disadvantage by the criterion etc?
- If so, was the inability to comply with the requirement or condition to the claimant's detriment?
- Is disparate impact admitted or self-evident (in which case it is appropriate to proceed to the final question)?
- If not, what is the relevant 'pool' of workers?
- Within that pool, what are the respective percentages (in a case of indirect sex discrimination, the percentage of women and the percentage of men) who are put at a disadvantage by the criterion etc?
- Is the difference between these percentages a significant one, having regard to the case law on how this question should be approached?
- If the indirectly discriminatory effect of the criterion etc. is established, can the respondent defeat the claim by showing it to be a proportionate means of achieving a legitimate aim?

11. EQUAL PAY – KEY ISSUES

- To what contract term(s) (e.g. rate of pay) does the claim relate?
- Has the claimant identified one or more comparators of the opposite sex?
- Are the claimant and the comparator(s) in the same employment – bearing in mind the case law on the extended definition of 'same employment'?
- Have the jobs of the claimant and one or more comparator(s) been given the same rating under a job evaluation scheme (in which case proceed to the final question)?
- If not, are they like work (in which case proceed to the final question)?
- If the claim is that the jobs of the claimant and the comparator(s) are of equal value, can the respondent defeat the claim by showing that the jobs have been given different values under a non-discriminatory and analytical job evaluation scheme?
- If not, should the question of whether the jobs are of equal value be referred to an independent expert?
- In any event, has the respondent made out the material factor defence so as to defeat the claim?

12. RECRUITING PEOPLE WITH DISABILITIES

- Ensure that staff involved in the recruitment process are familiar with the legal rules.
- Consider the post and what could be done to encourage applications from people with disabilities, e.g. by ensuring that the 'disability symbol' is displayed on all advertising outlets.
- Check that the job description is framed in a way which enables a disabled applicant to apply.

Checklists

- Check that the essential requirements in the person specification (qualifications, experience etc.) are genuinely necessary, so as not unjustifiably to exclude certain applicants, perhaps including disabled applicants.

- Check the wording of any advertisement and make any appropriate reference to the organisation's equal opportunities policy, providing a copy to the disability employment adviser.

- Where a disabled person attends for interview, ensure that the venue is accessible and any additional facilities that are provided are identified in the response to the interview invitation or subsequently in discussion.

- Consider providing an induction loop to assist hearing-aid users or where sign language interpreters might be obtained if necessary. It may also be appropriate to allow an applicant with learning disabilities to be accompanied in the interview by a friend or support worker.

- Check with the disabled applicant whether they have any special needs at the interview stage and if there are any special requirements for this interview. For example, if there is a typing aptitude test, adaptation may be required.

- Check that staff who may be escorting or directing candidates to interview are aware of any special needs and facilities and that any appropriate aids are provided.

- Make sure that, at the interview, the disability is not the main item of discussion.

- Respond in a positive and appropriate manner to any reasonable adjustments suggested by the disabled applicant.

- If a disabled person is appointed, check what reasonable adjustments, if any, need to be made.

13. CAREER BREAK SCHEMES – KEY ISSUES

- Who is eligible for a career break (e.g. in terms of length of service)?
- Is a career break only available for the care of dependent children, or in other circumstances?
- What is the permissible duration of the break?
- Is an employee entitled to have more than one career break?
- How is contact maintained with the employee during the break?
- What steps should be taken before the employee returns to work after the break?
- Does the break have the effect of breaking the period of continuous employment?
- Is the employee entitled to return to a job at the same grade as the original job after the career break?

14. TELEWORKING – KEY ISSUES

- Obligations of the employer.
- Obligations of the teleworker.
- Place of work.
- Hours of work.
- Pay and benefits.

- Provision, use and return of equipment, goods and materials.
- Health and safety.
- Employer's right to inspect the place of work.
- Insurance.
- Taxation.
- Computer security.
- Data protection.
- Duration of agreement and termination provisions.

15. JOB SHARING – KEY ISSUES

- Which posts in the organisation are suitable for job sharing?
- Which jobs, if they fall vacant, are suitable for sharing?
- What is the procedure for applying for a job share?
- Hours of work.
- Pay and benefits.
- Holidays.
- Training.
- Appraisal.
- Criteria for promotion.
- Liaison between job sharers.
- Termination arrangements

16. DRAFTING A POLICY ON HARASSMENT

- State that every worker has the right to be treated with dignity and respect.
- Describe comprehensively the conduct which is prohibited.
- Explain that the prohibition on harassment applies to – and benefits everyone in the workplace (including, for example, agents and self-employed consultants).
- Encourage those who suffer harassment to take informal action, where appropriate, to tell the harasser to stop (for example, if the harasser is unaware that his or her conduct is unwelcome) but acknowledge that a formal complaint may be the proper course in certain cases.
- Confirm that those who complain of harassment or provide relevant information (e.g. through witness statements) will be protected from victimisation.
- Confirm that, so far as is practicable, confidentiality with regard to complaints will be respected.
- Specify a clear, logical and accessible complaints procedure.
- Provide for prompt, thorough and impartial investigation.
- Provide for disciplinary action (which may include dismissal) in appropriate cases.

- Reserve the right to suspend on full pay or redeploy, where appropriate, the person accused of harassment.
- Confirm that, once investigation has been completed, the employer will take proper steps to remedy the situation.

17. PERSON SPECIFICATIONS – KEY ISSUES

- Experience and know-how essential for the job.
- Skills and abilities essential for the job.
- Behavioural attributes essential for the job.
- The contents of the person specification must be clear and the criteria unambiguous.
- The criteria must relate to the job in question.
- The criteria must be justifiable.

18. JOB DESCRIPTIONS – KEY ISSUES

Job descriptions typically cover the following:

- The main purpose and objectives of the job.
- The place of the job-holder in the organisational structure. The main tasks and responsibilities of the job-holder.
- Associated tasks.
- The relationship between the job-holder and colleagues.

19. IMPLEMENTING A DIVERSITY STRATEGY

- Research how diversity impacts upon the different parts of the organisation and its stakeholders.
- Identify the organisation's vision, aims and objectives.
- Devise an action plan.
- Communicate the contents of the action plan.
- Measure the impact of the plan, e.g. by way of benchmarks and targets.

20. TRAINING OF RECRUITERS

The training given to interviewers and others involved in the selection process should cover:

- Relevant provisions of the discrimination legislation and the costs of practice.
- Recognition and avoidance of the common prejudices and assumptions which can lead to direct discrimination.
- The preparation and use of job descriptions, person specifications and scoring systems.
- The importance of not adopting new requirements and conditions, particularly at the shortlisting stage (with a consequent risk of indirect discrimination), in order to reduce the number of candidates.

- The preparation and conduct of interviews.

- Information about the disabilities which are most likely to be encountered and the positive steps which should be taken.

- Handling applications from candidates who have previously complained of discrimination and the ways in which such candidates should be reassured that there will be no victimisation against them.

21. LEGITIMATE POSITIVE ACTION

In essence, 'positive discrimination' is unlawful, but equal opportunities legislation does permit employers to take positive action to attract employees from particular groups that are under-represented in their workforce, e.g.:

- Advertisements designed to reach members of a specific group through the use of sector-specific publications such as newspapers and magazines.

- Using the services of employment agencies and careers officers in areas where members of under-represented groups are concentrated.

- Targeted recruitment and training schemes for people leaving school.

- Encouragement and training designed to bring the best out of people's individual skills.

22. GUIDANCE TO EMPLOYERS ON AVOIDING AGE DISCRIMINATION

A sensible first step is to audit existing practices in the organisation to see whether a mixed-age workforce is being attracted and retained. Having done this, some or all of the following measures may usefully be implemented:

- Avoid using ageist language in advertisements (e.g. 'young graduates' or 'mature person'.

- Focus on the essential requirements of the job.

- Advertise in the outlets most likely to attract a mixed-age response.

- Separate personal details when sifting applications (they can be re-introduced at the end of the recruitment process).

- Select candidates on the basis of skills and abilities.

- Ask only job-related questions at interview.

- Use a mixed-age interview panel where possible.

- Avoid making assumptions, e.g. about fitness, based on age.

- Make opportunities for promotion available to all members of the workforce.

- Take business needs and the desirability of choice for individuals into account when framing a retirement policy.

- Always seek to respond positively to a request to stay on at work.

23. AVOIDING AGE DISCRIMINATION IN PARTNERSHIPS

Most partnerships are regulated by an agreement or deed that is often very detailed. Because partnership law is long-established (the Partnership Act 1890 still holds sway), the drafting of partnership terms has not developed as rapidly as the drafting of contractual terms in employment relationships. In seeking to avoid problems of age discrimination, it is worth considering in particular contractual terms relating to the following issues, which often arise in partnerships, especially the more substantial and long-established professional firms:

- Provisions relating to retirement.
- Profit-sharing provisions linked to length of service (sometimes termed 'lockstep' arrangements).
- Annuities for retiring partners.
- Provisions differentiating between 'good leavers' and 'bad leavers', e.g. clauses discriminating between people who leave the partnership by agreement or on retirement, and those who commit some form of breach of duty, or who leave to join a competitor.
- Promotion arrangements (e.g. from one category of partnership status to another).

24. BREASTFEEDING POLICY

Breastfeeding policies are currently the exception rather than the rule, but it is foreseeable that questions relating to breastfeeding will become increasingly significant and well-organised employers will wish to have in place a policy that addresses issues that commonly arise, such as:

- Explanation of the organisation's support for combining work with breastfeeding.
- Identification of the facilities provided.
- Guidelines for the safe and appropriate use of those facilities.
- Summary of permitted breaks (e.g. for expressing milk or breastfeeding).
- Guidance on the provision of facilities for visitors who wish to breastfeed on the premises.

25. RETIREMENT PROCEDURES

- Make sure that the normal retirement age for each employee is clear.
- Ensure that any retirement age below 65 is objectively justifiable.
- Keep records of employees' ages so as to identify normal retirement dates.
- Operate systems to flag up when notices of intended retirement dates should be sent.
- Identify the reason for each dismissal to ensure that retirement procedures are followed in appropriate cases.
- With retirement dismissals, follow the duty to consider procedure.
- Comply with all statutory deadlines.
- Advise employees prior to appropriate meetings of the right to have a companion present.
- Ensure that all notices are appropriately dated and, where appropriate, follow the terms of specimen letters in the ACAS guidance on age in the workplace.

26. RISK ASSESSMENTS – POINTS TO CONSIDER

- Carry out a risk assessment in all relevant cases, remembering that risks are sometimes far from obvious.

- Seek to establish what the employee considers might be a risk.

- Consider any medical advice that the employer has received from a GP or midwife.

- Discuss the findings of the risk assessment with the employee and, if there are queries about the conclusions of the risk assessment, discuss them with the employee and the assessor.

- Avoid making unilateral changes to the assessor's findings or recommendations without consulting the employee (even if the changes are intended to benefit the employee).

- Implement any appropriate changes to working conditions without delay or find suitable alternative duties without delay.

- If there is no alternative to suspension, undertake it in full consultation with the employee and keep in touch with her.

- More detailed advice is available from the Health & Safety Executive.

27. TRAINING OF RECRUITERS

The training given to interviewers and others involved in the selection process should cover:

- Relevant provisions of the discrimination legislation and the codes of practice.

- Recognition and avoidance of the common prejudices and assumptions which can lead to direct discrimination.

- The preparation and use of job descriptions, person specifications and scoring systems.

- The importance of not adopting new requirements and conditions, particularly at the shortlisting stage (with a consequent risk of indirect discrimination), in order to reduce the number of candidates.

- The preparation and conduct of interviews.

- Information about the disabilities which are most likely to be encountered and the positive steps which should be taken.

- Handling applications from candidates who have previously complained of discrimination and the ways in which such candidates should be reassured that there will be no victimisation against them.

Appendix 1

ACAS Age and the Workplace – Putting the Employment Equality (Age) Regulations 2006 into Practice

INTRODUCTION

From 1 October 2006 the Employment Equality (Age) Regulations make it unlawful to discriminate against workers, employees, job seekers and trainees because of their age. This booklet describes the regulations and gives you guidance on how to implement them.

Terms in this guide – workers and employees

Workers are covered in the regulations and in this guidance. Workers often undertake roles similar to employees but do not have contracts of employment like employees, these include office holders, police, barristers and partners in a business.

Our guidance uses the term **'employee'** throughout to cover all workers except under length of service issues, retirement, and right to request which are for a narrower range of employees.

Fairness at work and good job performance go hand in hand. Tackling discrimination helps to attract, motivate and retain staff and enhances your reputation as an employer. Eliminating discrimination helps everyone to have an equal opportunity to work and to develop their skills.

Employees who are subjected to discrimination, harassment or victimisation may:

- be unhappy, less productive and less motivated

- resign

- make a complaint to an employment tribunal.

In addition employers may find:

- their reputation as a business and as an employer may be damaged

- the cost of recruitment and training will increase because of higher employee turnover

- they may be liable to pay compensation following a claim to an employment tribunal – there is no upper limit to the amount of this compensation.

There is already legislation to protect people against discrimination on the grounds of sex, race, disability, gender reassignment, sexual orientation and religion or belief.

The new regulations should pose few difficulties in organisations where people are treated fairly and with consideration.

This guidance aims to:

- help employers and vocational training providers fulfil their obligations under the Employment Equality (Age) Regulations 2006

- make employees, job seekers and trainees aware of how they will be affected by the regulations.

WHAT THE REGULATIONS SAY – IN SUMMARY

These regulations apply to all employers, private and public sector vocational training providers, trade unions, professional organisations, employer organisations and trustees and managers of occupational pension schemes. In this context an employer is anyone who has employees or who enters into a contract with a person for them to do work. The regulations cover recruitment, terms and conditions, promotions, transfers, dismissals and training. They do not cover the provision of goods and services.

The regulations make it unlawful on the grounds of age to:

- discriminate directly against anyone – that is, to treat them less favourably than others because of their age – unless objectively justified

- discriminate indirectly against anyone – that is, to apply a criterion, provision or practice which disadvantages people of a particular age unless it can be objectively justified

- subject someone to harassment. Harassment is unwanted conduct that violates a person's dignity or creates an intimidating, hostile, degrading, humiliating or offensive environment for them having regard to all the circumstances including the perception of the victim

- victimise someone because they have made or intend to make a complaint or allegation or have given or intend to give evidence in relation to a complaint of discrimination on grounds of age

- discriminate against someone, in certain circumstances, after the working relationship has ended.

Employers could be responsible for the acts of employees who discriminate on grounds of age. This makes it important to train staff about the regulations.

Upper age limits on unfair dismissal and redundancy will be removed.

There will be a national default retirement age of 65, making compulsory retirement below 65 unlawful unless objectively justified.

Employees will have the right to request to work beyond 65 or any other retirement age set by the company. The employer has a duty to consider such requests.

There are limited circumstances when discrimination may be lawful (see section on genuine occupational requirements, objective justifications, exceptions and exemptions).

This guide does not use the precise legal terms contained within the regulations – reference needs to be made to the regulations.

GUIDANCE FOR EMPLOYERS

WHAT DO THE REGULATIONS MEAN?

A brief explanation of the regulations

Direct discrimination

Direct discrimination is less favourable treatment because of someone's age.

For example it will be unlawful on the grounds of age to:

- decide not to employ someone
- dismiss them
- refuse to provide them with training
- deny them promotion

Appendix 1

> **Example:** Whilst being interviewed, a job applicant says that she took her professional qualification 30 years ago. Although she has all the skills and competences required of the job holder, the organisation decides not to offer her the job because of her age. This is direct discrimination.
>
> **NOTE:** A job applicant can make a claim to an employment tribunal, it is not necessary for them to have been employed by the organisation to make a claim of discrimination.

- give them adverse terms and conditions
- retire an employee before the employer's usual retirement age (if there is one) or retire an employee before the default retirement age of 65 without an objective justification.

Indirect discrimination

Indirect discrimination means selection criteria, policies, benefits, employment rules or any other practices which, although they are applied to all employees, have the effect of disadvantaging people of a particular age unless the practice can be justified. Indirect discrimination is unlawful whether it is intentional or not.

Lawful discrimination

There are limited circumstances when it is lawful to treat people differently because of their age.

It is not unlawful to discriminate on the grounds of age if:

- there is an **objective justification** for treating people differently – for example, it might be necessary to fix a maximum age for the recruitment or promotion of employees (this maximum age might reflect the training requirements of the post or the need for a reasonable period of employment before retirement)
- where a person is older than, or within six months of, the employer's normal retirement age, or 65 if the employer doesn't have one, there is a specific exemption allowing employers to refuse to recruit that person
- the discrimination is covered by one of the **exceptions** or **exemptions** given in the regulations – for example pay related to the National Minimum Wage
- there is a **genuine occupational requirement** (GOR) that a person must be of a certain age – for example, if you are producing a play which has parts for older or younger characters.

For more details see the section on genuine occupational requirements, objective justifications, exceptions and exemptions [below].

Harassment

Harassment includes behaviour that is offensive, frightening or in any way distressing. It may be intentional bullying which is obvious or violent, but it can also be unintentional, subtle and insidious. It may involve nicknames, teasing, name calling or other behaviour which is not with malicious intent but which is upsetting. It may be about the individual's age or it may be about the age of those with whom the individual associates. It may not be targeted at an individual(s) but consist of a general culture which, for instance, appears to tolerate the telling of ageist jokes.

You may be held responsible for the actions of your employees – as well as the employees being individually responsible. If harassment takes place in the workplace or at a time and place associated with the workplace, for example a work-related social gathering, you may be liable. You may be ordered to pay compensation unless it can be shown that you took reasonable steps to prevent harassment. Individuals who harass may also be ordered to pay compensation.

It is good practice to protect your workers from harassment by third parties, such as service users and customers.

> **Example:** A young employee is continually told he is 'wet behind the ears' and 'straight out of the pram' which he finds humiliating and distressing. This is harassment.

> **Example:** An employee has a father working in the same workplace. People in the workplace often tell jokes about 'old fogies' and tease the employee about teaching 'old dogs new tricks'. This may be harassment on the grounds of age, even though it is not the victim's own age that is the subject of the teasing.

When you are investigating claims of harassment, consider all the circumstances before reaching a conclusion. Harassment is often subjective so think carefully about the complainant's perception of what has happened to them. Ask yourself if what has taken place could 'be reasonably considered to have caused offence?'

Victimisation

Victimisation is when an individual is treated detrimentally because they have made a complaint or intend to make a complaint about discrimination or harassment or have given evidence or intend to give evidence relating to a complaint about discrimination or harassment.

> **Example:** An employee claims discrimination against their employer on the grounds of age. A work colleague gives evidence on their behalf at the employment tribunal. When the work colleague applies for promotion her application is rejected even though she is able to show she has all the necessary skills and experience. Her manager maintains she is a 'troublemaker' because she had given evidence at the tribunal and should not be promoted. This is victimisation.

> **Example:** A manager is approached by someone from another organisation. He says that Ms 'A' has applied for a job and asks for a reference. The manager says that he cannot recommend her as she was not accepted by other staff because she was 'too young and inexperienced'. This is direct discrimination because of age.

They may become labelled 'troublemaker', denied promotion or training, or be 'sent to Coventry' by their colleagues. If this happens or if you fail to take reasonable steps to prevent it from happening, you may be ordered to pay compensation. Individuals who victimise may also be ordered to pay compensation.

Discrimination, harassment or victimisation following the end of a working relationship covers issues such as references either written or verbal.

AN EQUALITY POLICY AND ACTION PLAN

You can start to address fairness at work by writing an equality policy or updating an existing one – with an action plan to back it up. You may already have equal opportunity or diversity policies which cover age but, if not, age should now be included. It is good practice in drawing up a policy to consult with your workforce or their representatives.

Appendix 1

To make sure age discrimination is eliminated in your workforce draw up an action plan to review your policies for:

- recruitment, selection and promotion
- training
- pay, benefits and other conditions
- bullying and harassment
- retirement.

Also consider the make up of your workforce and whether positive action is required to tackle any age imbalance.

Ensure that all employees know about your equality policy and what is expected of them; a communications strategy should be a key part of your action plan.

Employees are often attracted to an organisation if it has a robust equality policy. Although not a legal necessity, such a policy makes applicants feel confident and discourages those who do not embrace equality of opportunity.

Acas can help you to draw up and implement an equality policy and to train you and your employees to use it. For further information see the Acas booklet *Tackling discrimination and promoting equality – good practice guidance for employers*.

RECRUITMENT

See comment about specific recruitment exemption [below].

Base your decisions about recruitment on the skills required to do the job. Provide training to help those making judgements to be objective and avoid stereotyping people because of their age.

Application form

Remove age/date of birth from the main application form and include it in a diversity monitoring form to be retained by HR/Personnel. In addition review your application form to ensure that you are not asking for unnecessary information about periods and dates. Asking for age-related information on an application form could allow discrimination to take place.

Monitor your decisions for any evidence of age bias, particularly after shortlisting.

Job description and person specification

A job description outlines the duties required of a particular post holder. A person specification gives the skills, knowledge and experience required to carry out these duties.

Avoid references, however oblique, to age in both the job description and the person specification. For example, avoid asking for 'so many years' experience'. This may rule out younger people who have the skills required but have not had the opportunity to demonstrate them over an extended period. A jobseeker could challenge any time requirement and you may have to justify it in objective terms.

> **Example:** Scrape and Co, a local driving school, have been advertising for instructors who must be qualified and have a minimum of 10 years' driving experience. Effectively this would prevent people under 28 applying for this job and could therefore be discriminatory. Scrape would need to justify this 10-year experience criterion if challenged by a jobseeker under 28 especially as only four years' experience is formally required to qualify as a driving instructor.

Educational and vocational qualifications have changed and developed over the years. Make sure that the qualifications you specify are not disadvantaging people at different ages.

Ask yourself:

- are the qualifications really necessary?
- are they still current?
- are there other ways of specifying the skill level you require?

If you are going to be specific about qualifications be sure you can justify their need in objective terms and make it clear you will consider equivalent or similar level alternative qualifications.

Advertising

It makes sound business sense to attract a wide field of applicants – if you rely on the friends or family of current staff you will miss the opportunity to tap into the diverse skills of your local community.

Advertise in a way that will be accessible to a large audience. For instance, avoid using a publication or employment agency that is focused on a niche market. This may limit the diversity of applicants and may constitute indirect discrimination.

> **Example:** An advertisement placed only in a magazine aimed at young people may indirectly discriminate against older people because they are less likely to subscribe to the magazine and therefore less likely to find out about the vacancy and apply.

Write your job advert using the information in the job description and person specification. Avoid using language that might imply that you would prefer someone of a certain age, such as 'mature', 'young' or 'energetic'.

> **Example:** Try to avoid stereotyping. For example, which vacancy is asking for an older person and which a younger person?
>
> 1 'We require an enthusiastic person, flexible enough to fit in with our fast moving market place, not afraid of challenging the status quo and in touch with latest thinking'.
>
> 2 'Our ideal candidate will need to manage competing demands. He or she should be reflective, and have boardroom presence and gravitas.'

Be clear about what skills you actually need for the post – and what skills are merely desirable or reflect the personal preferences of the selector. Recruit and/or promote for these essential skills and aptitudes – you can always decide not to recruit or promote someone if the applicant does not have these necessary skills or abilities.

As well as considering the language you use in adverts think also about the hidden messages that may be present in any promotional literature that you have, particularly the pictures.

Graduates

If you ask for graduates, remember that the term can be interpreted as code for someone in their early twenties. Graduates can be almost any age. Make it clear that you are interested in the qualification and not the age of the applicant.

Appendix 1

> **Example:** A local engineering company is looking for a new Personnel Officer and asks for applicants to be graduates and hold the IPD qualification. As many more people attend university today than say 25 years ago, there is a lower chance that older Personnel Officers will be university graduates even though holding the IPD qualification and having considerable practical experience. This graduate requirement might thus be indirect age discrimination if the employer is unable to justify it. Remember also that the IPD qualification was formerly the IPM qualification.

If you limit your recruitment to university 'milk rounds' only, you may find that this is indirect age discrimination as this practice would severely restrict the chances of someone over say, 25 applying for your vacancies. If challenged you would need to objectively justify this practice (see section on genuine occupational requirements, objective justifications, exceptions and exemptions).

Consider enhancing any 'milk round' programme with a broader recruitment strategy, using other avenues to capture a wider pool of applicants of differing ages.

Shortlisting

If you have removed age-related material from your application form then you will generally not know a person's age although applicants may make reference to their age on the form so this is not always the case.

Whether or not you know someone's age, it is important that those doing the shortlisting, ideally more than one person, base their decisions on skills and ability alone. They should be trained, reminded of their responsibility not to discriminate on age grounds and use the requirements of the person specification to judge applicants.

Before moving on to the next stage of the recruitment process, check that no bias, deliberate or unintentional, has influenced decisions. In all organisations this check should be carried out by someone who has not been involved in the shortlisting. In all instances, you should record your decisions and retain these records, ideally for 12 months.

Interviewing

Interviews should preferably not be carried out by one person on their own. When interviewing, try to avoid:

- Asking questions related to age, for example, "how would you feel about managing older/younger people?".

- Throwaway comments such as "you're a bit young for a post of this responsibility" or "don't you think someone like you should be looking for something with more responsibility?".

Focus on the applicant's competence and where more than one demonstrates the required competence the one who is more competent or offers the best skill mix should be appointed.

Check decisions for any bias and make sure interviewers have received training in the skills required and equal opportunities/diversity.

Again, in all instances, record your decisions and retain these records, ideally for 12 months from the date of the interviews.

Working with employment agencies

If you use a recruitment agency you need to be sure the agency acts appropriately and in accordance with your company's equality and diversity policies.

486

If you tell an employment agency to discriminate on age grounds because you consider you have objective justification for doing so, then the regulations enable the agency to rely on this justification if challenged. In such circumstances the agency should obtain this justification in writing from the employer and if at all unhappy to raise that with the employer.

Vocational training

As well as training provided by employers for their own employees, the regulations also cover organisations providing vocational education and training to the wider community. For the purpose of anti-discrimination law, all forms of vocational training including general educational provision at further, higher and other adult education institutions will be covered.

This means that vocational training providers will not be able to set age limits or age-related criteria:

- for entry to training; or

- in the terms under which they provide training, for example when offering help with costs to encourage participation among under represented groups of people.

As an employer, training provider, college or university you will need to consider the following questions:

- do you set a minimum or maximum age for entry generally or in relation to admission or access to particular courses? If so, what are the justifications for these?

- even if you do not have formal minimum or maximum ages, is age taken into account when you consider applications for admission or access, eg do you offer preferential fee discount arrangements based on age?

In either case, you need to consider:

- can you objectively justify any age-related criterion, eg what evidence have you in support of restricting such financial help to a particular age group?

- what legitimate aim does any age-related criterion help you achieve, eg have you clear evidence that demonstrates particular age groups would be excluded from your learning provision if they had to pay full fees?

- are your age-related criteria a proportionate means of achieving that aim?

- is there another way of achieving that aim without resorting to discrimination?

The EU Employment Directive allows for the setting of age requirements relating to institutions of further and higher education and in respect of access to vocational training if they can be objectively justified, for example on the grounds of vocational integration.

RETAINING GOOD STAFF

Many factors motivate employees and make them want to stay with an organisation. People are more likely to feel positive about an organisation if they are treated fairly and with consideration regardless of their age.

Promotion and training

Opportunities for promotion and training should be made known to all employees and be available to everyone on a fair and equal basis.

Where employees apply for internal transfers take care with informal and verbal references between departmental heads, supervisors, etc. These references are covered by the regulations and should be fair and non-discriminatory.

Job-related training or development opportunities should be available to all employees regardless of age – monitor the training to make sure no particular age group is missing out.

Review the style and location of training to ensure:

- there are no barriers to any particular age group participating
- it is suitable for people of all ages
- everyone is encouraged to participate.

For example, if you are using computer-based training, do not assume everyone will be fully competent using a PC.

Age discrimination awareness

However large or small an organisation, it is good practice for them to have an Equality Policy and to train all employees and update them on a regular basis. This will help to reduce the likelihood of discrimination, harassment and victimisation taking place and may help to limit liability if a complaint is made.

All employees should understand:

- what the terms 'discrimination' and 'harassment' mean
- why discrimination and harassment are hurtful, unlawful and totally unacceptable.

Tell all employees about your company policy on age discrimination and train those who make decisions that affect others. Training should apply not only to those who recruit and select but also to those involved in day-to-day decisions about work allocation, performance appraisal, etc. Supervisors and managers also need training in recognising and dealing with bullying and harassment.

Performance appraisal

Check any performance appraisal system you have to ensure that it is working fairly and without bias. Many people have preconceptions about age and these can influence the judgements we make about people. If these preconceptions appear in performance appraisals through use of inappropriate comments – such as 'does well despite their age' or 'shows remarkable maturity for their age' – they will undermine the whole basis of a fair appraisal system. Such comments could also lead to further discrimination when decisions about promotion or work allocation are being made.

A fair and transparent appraisal system will become increasingly important when the changes to the retirement age are introduced. However, young people in the early stages of their career also need to be assessed on their actual performance unclouded by any preconceptions about their age.

> **Example:** Two candidates have done equally well for the post on offer, so the selectors decide to review previous assessments to try and draw a fair distinction between them. On one they read: 'Despite his many years with the company John remains capable and enthusiastic' and 'John does very well at work considering his age'.
>
> There are no such comments on Mark's assessments.
>
> Which candidate now has a question mark against them?

Treat all employees the same when setting objectives or measuring performance. Ignoring shortfalls in performance because an employee is nearing retirement may be discriminatory – particularly if the same shortfalls are addressed in younger employees.

Redundancy selection

Check that your selection processes for redundancy are free of age discrimination. This means that practices such as last in first out (LIFO), and using length of service in any selection criteria are likely to be age discriminatory.

Policies and procedures

Review policies and procedures for age bias, including those covering:

- sick absence
- leave and holidays
- discipline and grievances
- staff transfers
- flexible working
- use of computers
- individual space requirements (ergonomic policies).

Bullying and harassment

Every individual member of staff has the right to be treated fairly and with dignity and respect. Harassment occurs when someone engages in unwanted conduct which has the purpose or effect of violating someone else's dignity or creating an intimidating, hostile, degrading, humiliating or offensive environment.

It is not the intention of the perpetrator which defines whether a particular type of conduct is harassment but the effect it has on the recipient.

Bullying is just as unacceptable as any other form of harassment.

People can become targets of harassment because of their age. Harassment could take the form of:

- inappropriate comments – for example, by suggesting someone is too old ('over the hill') or too young ('wet behind the ears')
- offensive jokes
- exclusion from informal groups such as social events.

Example: George is in his 60s and works in an office with a team of younger colleagues in their 20s and 30s. The team, including the manager, often go out socialising. They do not ask George because they feel that he wouldn't like the venues they choose for such events. However, George finds out that many workplace issues and problems are discussed and resolved during these informal meetings. George feels undervalued and disengaged by this unintended action. This is a form of harassment, even though unintended, as George is being excluded from the team. To prevent this, the manager ought to consider office-based meetings to consult more fully with all staff in decision-making to prevent George feeling excluded because of his age.

Appendix 1

Dealing with harassment

Make sure your anti-harassment policy covers age. You may have a stand alone policy or one that is part of a wider equal opportunities policy (for more detailed information see the Acas booklet *Tackling discrimination and promoting equality*).

If managers see unacceptable behaviour **whether or not a complaint is made** they need to treat the matter seriously and take action to eliminate the behaviour in question. This may involve just pointing out to someone the effect that their behaviour has on others and getting them to stop. If this informal approach fails, or in more serious cases, or where the person being harassed prefers, it will be necessary to take formal action within the normal disciplinary procedures of the company or within the guidelines laid down by a specific antiharassment policy.

For further information see the Acas leaflet *Bullying and harassment at work: a guide for managers and employers*.

RETIREMENT

> **Pension age** is when an employee can draw down their pension; for many, but not all, it is also the time when they can retire if they wish.
>
> **Retirement age** in this guidance is either the employer's normal retirement age (if there is one) or the default retirement age of 65.
>
> **Normal retirement age** means the age at which the employer requires employees in the same kind of position as the employee to retire.

The regulations set a default retirement age of 65 (to be reviewed in 2011). This means you can retire employees or set retirement ages within your company at or above 65. Retirements or retirement ages below the default retirement age will need to satisfy the test of objective justification.

However, you do not have to have a fixed retirement age. Indeed, there are many business benefits to adopting a flexible approach to the employment and work patterns of older workers. Employees will have the right to request to continue working beyond their retirement date and you have a duty to give consideration to such requests.

Think about each request on an individual basis – taking into account opportunities to vary the employee's hours or the duties they perform. You are under no obligation to agree to such requests.

Fair retirement

A fair retirement is one that:

- takes effect on or after the default retirement age (or on or after the employer's normal retirement age – if there is one) and

- where the employer has given the employee written notice of the date of their intended retirement and told them about their right to request to continue working. (See below for the timing requirements of this notice).

If the employer's normal retirement age is below the age of 65, it must be objectively justified.

For the retirement to be classed as 'fair' you need to have informed the employee in writing of their intended retirement date and of their right to make a request to work beyond retirement age at least six months in advance (but no more than 12 months before the intended date). If they do make such a request, you must have followed the correct procedure for dealing with it.

Working beyond retirement date – notification of right to request to continue working

You should notify the employee in writing of their right to request to go on working beyond their retirement date (at least six months in advance but no more than 12 months before the intended date).

When you write to the employee it is good practice to set out how you will manage the retirement process. Remind them of your obligation to give consideration to any request to work after the normal retirement age and in order not to raise the expectations of the employee, explain that you are entitled to refuse the request. You are not required to give a reason for your decision as – if you have followed the retirement procedure correctly (see Annex 5) – the reason for their dismissal will always be retirement.

However giving reasons and a more detailed explanation of your retirement policy may enable the employee to leave with dignity and respect and help you maintain good workplace relationships with other employees. This would be in line with normal good practice recommended by Acas.

If you choose to give reasons, take the time to consider what you are going to say and how you are going to say it. You must be careful not to suggest that you might be discriminating against the employee on the grounds of race, gender, disability, sexual orientation or religion or belief.

If the employee has been properly notified (as above) and wishes to continue working, they must request to do so more than three months before the intended retirement date.

If you fail to notify the employee six months in advance of retirement, you may be liable for compensation and you have an ongoing duty (up until two weeks before the retirement dismissal) to inform the employee of both the intended date and their right to request working longer. Failure to do this will make the dismissal automatically unfair.

If you fail to inform the employee of their intended retirement date and of their right to request to continue working, the employee will still be able to make a request not to retire at any stage until dismissal. If the employee does make a request the employment must continue until the day after the employer notifies the employee of their decision on the request.

Employees should be able to retire with dignity so try and use as much tact and sensitivity as possible.

Dealing with the request

If the employee requests in writing not to be retired this request must be considered before the employee is retired. Failure to do so will make the dismissal automatically unfair. You must meet the employee to discuss their request within a reasonable period of receiving it (unless agreeing to the request or it is not practicable to hold a meeting) and inform them in writing of your decision as soon as is reasonably practicable. The employee's employment continues until you have informed them of your decision on the request.

As preparation for this meeting, it would be good practice for you to reflect on the positive reasons why you should grant an extension, in particular:

● savings to the organisation in recruitment and training costs

● retaining the valuable experience and knowledge of the employee.

Try to avoid making stereotypical assumptions about the capabilities of the employee. At the meeting the employee has a right to be accompanied by a colleague. There is the same right in relation to any subsequent appeal meeting.

The individual accompanying the employee must be:

- chosen by the employee;

- a worker or trade union representative employed by the same employer as the employee;

- permitted to address the meeting but not answer questions on behalf of the employee; and

- permitted to confer with the employee during the meeting.

The employee may appeal against your decision as soon as is reasonably practicable after receiving notification of your decision. If the employee does appeal, the appeal meeting should be held as soon as is reasonable. The employee may appeal the decision if you refuse the request in its entirety or if you accept it but decide to continue employing the employee for a shorter period than the employee requested. The appeal meeting can be held after the retirement has taken effect.

This procedure must be repeated each time an individual nears an extended point for retirement.

As long as employers follow this procedure correctly they may rely on their normal retirement age (if they have one) or the default retirement age without the dismissal being regarded as unfair or age discriminatory. Where a dismissal is for reasons of retirement, the statutory dismissals procedure does not apply.

Transitional arrangements

There are transitional arrangements produced by the Department for Trade and Industry (DTI) for employees who are retiring on or shortly after 1 October 2006. These arrangements are available at the DTI website.

KNOW YOUR EMPLOYEES

You will probably have information that shows the ages of your employees. It makes sense to analyse this information (probably in age bands) to get an age profile of your workforce.

This profile will help you decide whether there is a need for any remedial action.

For example, do you need to:

- plan for a retirement peak?

- take positive action to rectify any obvious imbalance in the age bands?

You can also use this profile to check that your entire workforce is getting access to training and other facilities.

Staff attitude surveys and exit interviews can also give you valuable insights into how people view their work and you as an employer, and help you to create a positive working environment.

It is important to monitor in this way if you wish to claim an objective justification or, when reviewing service related benefits, 'conclude' a business benefit (see section on genuine occupational requirements, objective justifications, exceptions and exemptions). In considering these matters you should always use evidence in your decision-making rather than merely continuing old working practices or relying on 'gut feeling' as these may be based on unfounded assumptions.

Positive action

You can take positive action to prevent or compensate for disadvantages linked to age.

This might involve:

- giving people of a particular age access to vocational training; or
- encouraging people of a particular age to take up employment opportunities

where it reasonably appears to the person undertaking such positive action that it will prevent or compensate for disadvantages linked to age that they have or may suffer.

For example, you might place advertisements where they are more likely to be seen by people in a disadvantaged group. Or you might limit access to a computer training course to those over 60 because they may have had less exposure to such training in the past.

Positive action on age can help you to attract people from all age groups in your local community.

Example: Green and Co, a transport company, see from their internal monitoring processes that the company has a mature age profile with disproportionately few workers under 40. Not wanting to miss out on the talents of all the local community, they include a statement in their next adverts saying "We welcome applications from everyone irrespective of age but, as we are under-represented by people under 40, would especially welcome applications from these jobseekers. Appointment will be on merit alone".

OBJECTIVE JUSTIFICATIONS, EXCEPTIONS, EXEMPTIONS AND GENUINE OCCUPATIONAL REQUIREMENTS

Treating people differently because of their age will only be justifiable in the following exceptional circumstances.

Objective justification

You may treat people differently on the grounds of their age if you have an **objective justification**.

An objective justification allows employers to set requirements that are directly age discriminatory. Remember that different treatment on grounds of age will only be possible exceptionally for good reasons (see below).

You will need to provide real evidence to support any claim of objective justification. Assertion alone will not be sufficient and each case must be considered on its individual merits.

Both direct and indirect discrimination will be justified if it is:

- a proportionate means (of)
- achieving a legitimate aim.

What is proportionate?

This means:

Appendix 1

- what you are doing must actually contribute to a legitimate aim, eg if your aim is to encourage loyalty then you ought to have evidence that the provision or criterion you introduce is actually doing so

- the discriminatory effect should be significantly outweighed by the importance and benefits of the legitimate aim

- you should have no reasonable alternative to the action you are taking. If the legitimate aim can be achieved by less or non-discriminatory means then these must take precedence.

What is a legitimate aim?

A legitimate aim might include:

- economic factors such as business needs and efficiency

- the health, welfare and safety of the individual (including protection of young people or older workers)

- the particular training requirements of the job.

A legitimate aim **must** correspond with a real need of the employer – economic efficiency may be a real aim but saving money because discrimination is cheaper than non-discrimination is not legitimate. The legitimate aim cannot be related to age discrimination itself.

The test of objective justification is not an easy one and it will be necessary to provide evidence if challenged; assertions alone will not be enough.

Example: Jones and Company are unsure if they need an objective justification. To help make the decision they ask themselves:

- STOP – Why do we want to do this?

- Set out the reason clearly on paper

- Do we have evidence to support us in this reason?

- Are we certain this is real hard evidence and not just based on assumptions?

- Is there an alternative less or non-discriminatory way of achieving the same result?

The HR director seeks a second opinion from the Board and keeps all records of how the decision was made in case it is reviewed in the future.

In a smaller company, you could consult your partner or colleague.

Exceptions and exemptions

There are also **exceptions** to or **exemptions** from the age regulations in the following areas:

- pay and other employment benefits based on length of service

- pay related to the National Minimum Wage

- acts under statutory authority

- enhanced redundancy

- life assurance

- retirement

- occupational pension systems (not covered in this guidance).

Exemptions based on length of service

In many cases employers require a certain length of service before increasing or awarding a benefit such as holiday entitlement. Without the exemptions contained in the regulations this could often amount to indirect age discrimination because some age groups are more likely to have completed the length of service than others.

Any benefit earned by five years' service or less will be exempt. Employers may use pay scales that reflect growing experience or limit the provision of non-pay benefits to those who have served a qualifying period, subject to the five-year limit.

The use of length of service of more than five years for all types of employment benefits is lawful if:

- awarding or increasing the benefit is meant to reflect a higher level of experience of the employee, or to reward loyalty, or to increase or maintain the motivation of the employee;

- the employer has reasonable grounds for concluding that using length of service in this way fulfils a business need of his undertaking.

In order to meet these requirements employers would need evidence from which they can conclude there is a benefit to the organisation. This could include information the employer might have gathered through monitoring, staff attitude surveys or focus groups for example.

National Minimum Wage

Nothing in the regulations will alter the provisions of the National Minimum Wage. The exemption linked to the National Minimum Wage will allow employers using exactly the same age bands, ie 16 and 17, 18 to 21 and 22 and over, to pay at or above the national minimum rates provided those in the lower age group(s) are paid less than the adult minimum wage.

This will allow an employer to pay those aged 22 and over more than those aged under 22 as long as those under 22 are paid less than the minimum adult rate; likewise an employer may pay those aged 18 to 21 more than those under 18 as long as those under 18 are paid less than the minimum adult rate. The exemption does not allow employers to pay different rates to those in the same age category. Apprentices not entitled to the National Minimum Wage may continue to be paid at a lower rate than those that are.

Acts under statutory authority

Age criteria are widely used in legislation, notably to qualify for various licences. Where this is the case the employer must follow the criteria laid down by statute and will not be contravening the age regulations by doing so.

Enhanced redundancy payments

The statutory redundancy scheme will not substantially change (except in respect of the years worked when an employee was below 18 or over 64). Both the statutory authority exemption and this regulation make it clear that, even though statutory redundancy payments are calculated using age-related criteria, such payments are lawful.

The exemption linked to statutory redundancy payments is for an employer who wants to make more generous redundancy payments than under the statutory scheme. It allows the employer to use one of the methods specified, based on the statutory redundancy scheme, to calculate the amount of redundancy payment. An employer can use a different method of their own to calculate the amount of redundancy payment, but if it is based on length of service and if an employee brings a discrimination claim under the regulations, the employer will have to objectively justify it in so far as age discrimination arises. (This is because the exception for pay and benefits based on length of service does not apply to redundancy payments.)

The exemption allows the employer to either raise or remove the maximum amount of a week's pay so that a higher amount of pay is used in the calculation, or multiply the total amount calculated by a figure of more than one, or both. Having done this, the employer may again multiply the total by a figure of more that one.

The exemption also allows an employer to make a redundancy payment to an employee who has taken voluntary redundancy, and an employee with less than two years continuous employment. In such cases, where no statutory redundancy payment is required, an employer may make a payment equivalent to the statutory minimum payment, or if they so wish an enhanced payment as above.

Life assurance cover

Some employers provide life assurance cover for their workers. If a worker retires early due to ill health, the employer may continue to provide that life assurance cover for that worker. This exemption allows an employer to stop doing so when the worker reaches the age at which he would have retired had he not fallen ill. If there was no normal retirement age at which the worker would have retired, the employer can stop providing life assurance cover when the worker reaches 65.

Genuine occupational requirement (GOR)

In very limited circumstances, it will be lawful for an employer to treat people differently if it is a genuine occupational requirement that the job holder must be of a particular age. When deciding if this applies, it is necessary to consider the nature of the work and the context in which it is carried out. Jobs may change over time and you should review whether the requirement continues to apply, particularly when recruiting.

> **Example:** An organisation advising on and promoting rights for older people **may be able** to show that it is essential that its chief executive – who will be the public face of the organisation – is of a certain age. The age of the holder of the post may be a genuine occupational requirement.

Appendix 2

Code of Practice for the Elimination of Discrimination on the Grounds of Sex and Marriage and the Promotion of Equality of Opportunity in Employment

Editorial note: This Code of Practice was issued by the Equal Opportunities Commission under the Sex Discrimination Act 1975 and was brought into effect on 30 April 1985 by the Sex Discrimination Code of Practice Order 1985, SI 1985/387.

INTRODUCTION

1. The EOC issues this Code of Practice for the following purposes:

    (a) for the elimination of discrimination in employment;

    (b) to give guidance as to what steps it is reasonably practicable for employers to take to ensure that their employees do not in the course of their employment act unlawfully contrary to the Sex Discrimination Act (SDA);

    (c) for the promotion of equality of opportunity between men and women in employment. The SDA prohibits discrimination against men, as well as against women. It also requires that married people should not be treated less favourably than single people of the same sex. It should be noted that the provisions of the SDA – and therefore this Code – apply to the UK-based subsidiaries of foreign companies.

PURPOSE OF THE CODE

2. The Code gives guidance to employers, trade unions and employment agencies on measures which can be taken to achieve equality. The chances of success of any organisation will clearly be improved if it seeks to develop the abilities of all employees, and the Code shows the close link which exists between equal opportunity and good employment practice. In some cases, an initial cost may be involved, but this should be more than compensated for by better relationships and better use of human resources.

SMALL BUSINESSES

3. The Code has to deal in general terms and it will be necessary for employers to adapt it in a way appropriate to the size and structure of their organisations. Small businesses, for example, will require much simpler procedures than organisations with complex structures and it may not always be reasonable for them to carry out all the Code's detailed recommendations. In adapting the Code's recommendations, small firms should, however, ensure that their practices comply with the Sex Discrimination Act.

EMPLOYERS' RESPONSIBILITY

4. **The primary responsibility at law rests with each employer to ensure that there is no unlawful discrimination.** It is important, however, that measures to eliminate

discrimination or promote equality of opportunity should be understood and supported by all employees. Employers are therefore recommended to involve their employees in equal opportunity policies.

INDIVIDUAL EMPLOYEES' RESPONSIBILITY

5. While the main responsibility for eliminating discrimination and providing equal opportunity is that of the employer, individual employees at all levels have responsibilities too. They must not discriminate or knowingly aid their employer to do so.

TRADE UNION RESPONSIBILITY

6. The full commitment of trade unions is essential for the elimination of discrimination and for the successful operation of an equal opportunities policy. Much can be achieved by collective bargaining and throughout the Code it is assumed that all the normal procedures will be followed.

7. It is recommended that unions should co-operate in the introduction and implementation of equal opportunities policies where employers have decided to introduce them, and should urge that such policies be adopted where they have not yet been introduced.

8. Trade Unions have a responsibility to ensure that their representatives and members do not unlawfully discriminate on grounds of sex or marriage in the admission or treatment of members. The guidance in this Code also applies to trade unions in their role as employers.

EMPLOYMENT AGENCIES

9. Employment agencies have a responsibility as suppliers of job applicants to avoid unlawful discrimination on the grounds of sex or marriage in providing services to clients.

The guidance in this Code also applies to employment agencies in their role as employers.

DEFINITIONS

10. For case of reference, the main employment provisions of the Sex Discrimination Act, including definitions of direct and indirect sex and marriage discrimination, are provided in a Legal Annex to this Code.

PART 1: THE ROLE OF GOOD EMPLOYMENT PRACTICES IN ELIMINATING SEX AND MARRIAGE DISCRIMINATION

11. This section of the Code describes those good employment practices which will help to eliminate unlawful discrimination. It recommends the establishment and use of consistent criteria for selection, training, promotion, redundancy and dismissal which are made known to all employees. Without this consistency, decisions can be subjective and leave the way open for unlawful discrimination to occur.

RECRUITMENT

12. It is unlawful: UNLESS THE JOB IS COVERED BY AN EXCEPTION*: TO DISCRIMINATE DIRECTLY OR INDIRECTLY ON THE GROUNDS OF SEX OR MARRIAGE – IN THE ARRANGEMENTS MADE FOR DECIDING WHO SHOULD BE OFFERED A JOB – IN ANY TERMS OF EMPLOYMENT – BY REFUSING OR OMITTING TO OFFER A PERSON EMPLOYMENT. [*Section 6(1)(a); 6(1)(b); 6(1)(c)*]†

* There are a number of exceptions to the requirements of the SDA, that employers must not discriminate against their employees or against potential employees.

† For the full text of section 6 or other sections of the Sex Discrimination Act referred to in this code, readers are advised to consult a copy of the Act which is available from Her Majesty's Stationery Office.

13. It is therefore recommended that:

    (a) each individual should be assessed according to his or her personal capability to carry out a given job. It should not be assumed that men only or women only will be able to perform certain kinds of work;

    (b) any qualifications or requirements applied to a job which effectively inhibit applications from one sex or from married people should be retained only if they are justifiable in terms of the job to be done; [*Section 6(1)(a), together with section 1 (1)(b) or 3(1)(b)*]

    (c) any age limits should be retained only if they are necessary for the job. An unjustifiable age limit could constitute unlawful indirect discrimination, for example, against women who have taken time out of employment for child-rearing;

    (d) where trade unions uphold such qualifications or requirements as union policy, they should amend that policy in the light of any potentially unlawful effect.

GENUINE OCCUPATIONAL QUALIFICATIONS (GOQS)

14. It is unlawful: EXCEPT FOR CERTAIN JOBS WHEN A PERSON'S SEX IS A GENUINE OCCUPATIONAL QUALIFICATION (GOQ) FOR THAT JOB to select candidates on the ground of sex. [*Section 7(2); 7(3) and 7(4)*]

15. There are very few instances in which a job will qualify for a GOQ on the ground of sex. However, exceptions may arise, for example, where considerations of privacy and decency or authenticity are involved. The SDA expressly states that the need of the job for strength and stamina does not justify restricting it to men.

    When a GOQ exists for a job, it applies also to promotion, transfer, or training for that job, but cannot be used to justify a dismissal.

16. In some instances, the GOQ will apply to some of the duties only. A GOQ will not be valid, however, where members of the appropriate sex are already employed in sufficient numbers to meet the employer's likely requirements without undue inconvenience. For example, in a job where sales assistants may be required to undertake changing room duties, it might not be lawful to claim a GOQ in respect of all the assistants on the grounds that any of them might be required to undertake changing room duties from time to time.

17. It is therefore recommended that:

Appendix 2

– A job for which a GOQ was used in the past should be re-examined if the post falls vacant to see whether the GOQ still applies. Circumstances may well have changed, rendering the GOQ inapplicable.

SOURCES OF RECRUITMENT

18. It is unlawful: UNLESS THE JOB IS COVERED BY AN EXCEPTION:

– TO DISCRIMINATE ON GROUNDS OF SEX OR MARRIAGE IN THE ARRANGEMENTS MADE FOR DETERMINING WHO SHOULD BE OFFERED EMPLOYMENT WHETHER RECRUITING BY ADVERTISEMENTS, THROUGH EMPLOYMENT AGENCIES, JOB CENTRES, OR CAREER OFFICES.

– TO IMPLY THAT APPLICATIONS FROM ONE SEX OR FROM MARRIED PEOPLE WILL NOT BE CONSIDERED. [*Section 6(1)(a)*)]

– TO INSTRUCT OR PUT PRESSURE ON OTHERS TO OMIT TO REFER FOR EMPLOYMENT PEOPLE OF ONE SEX OR MARRIED PEOPLE UNLESS THE JOB IS COVERED BY AN EXCEPTION. [*Sections 39 and 40*]

It is also unlawful WHEN ADVERTISING JOB VACANCIES,

– TO PUBLISH OR CAUSE TO BE PUBLISHED AN ADVERTISEMENT WHICH INDICATES OR MIGHT REASONABLY BE UNDERSTOOD AS INDICATING AN INTENTION TO DISCRIMINATE UNLAWFULLY ON GROUNDS OF SEX OR MARRIAGE. [*Section 38*]

19. It is therefore recommended that:

Advertising

(a) job advertising should be carried out in such a way as to encourage applications from suitable candidates of both sexes. This can be achieved both by wording of the advertisements and, for example, by placing advertisements in publications likely to reach both sexes. All advertising material and accompanying literature relating to employment or training issues should be reviewed to ensure that it avoids presenting men and women in stereotyped roles. Such stereotyping tends to perpetuate sex segregation in jobs and can also lead people of the opposite sex to believe that they would be unsuccessful in applying for particular jobs;

(b) where vacancies are filled by promotion or transfer, they should be published to all eligible employees in such a way that they do not restrict applications from either sex;

(c) recruitment solely or primarily by word of mouth may unnecessarily restrict the choice of applicants available. The method should be avoided in a workforce predominantly of one sex, if in practice it prevents members of the opposite sex from applying;

(d) where applicants are supplied through trade unions and members of one sex only come forward, this should be discussed with the unions and an alternative approach adopted.

Careers Service Schools

20.   When notifying vacancies to the Careers Service, employers should specify that these are open to both boys and girls. This is especially important when a job has traditionally been done exclusively or mainly by one sex. If dealing with single sex schools, they should ensure, where possible, that both boys' and girls' schools are approached: it is also a good idea to remind mixed schools that jobs are open to boys and girls.

SELECTION METHODS

Tests

21.

(a)   If selection tests are used, they should be specifically related to job and or career requirements and should measure an individual's actual or inherent ability to do or train for the work or career;

(b)   Tests should be reviewed regularly to ensure that they remain relevant and free from any unjustifiable bias, either in content or in scoring mechanism.

Applications and Interviewing

22.   It is unlawful: UNLESS THE JOB IS COVERED BY AN EXCEPTION: TO DISCRIMINATE ON GROUNDS OF SEX OR MARRIAGE BY REFUSING OR DELIBERATELY OMITTING TO OFFER EMPLOYMENT. [*Section 6(1)(c)*]

23.   It is therefore recommended that:

(a)   employers should ensure that personnel staff line managers and all other employees who may come into contact with job applicants, should be trained in the provisions of the SDA, including the fact that it is unlawful to instruct or put pressure on others to discriminate;

(b)   applications from men and women should he processed in exactly the same way. For example, there should not be separate lists of male and female or married and single applicants. All those handling applications and conducting interviews should be trained in the avoidance of unlawful discrimination and records of interviews kept where practicable, showing why applicants were or were not appointed;

(c)   questions should relate to the requirements of the job. Where it is necessary to assess whether personal circumstances will affect performance of the job (for example, where it involves unsocial hours or extensive travel) this should be discussed objectively without detailed questions based on assumptions about marital status, children and domestic obligations. Questions about marriage plans or family intentions should not be asked, as they could be construed as showing bias against women. Information necessary for personnel records can be collected after a job offer has been made.

PROMOTION, TRANSFER AND TRAINING

24.   It is unlawful: UNLESS THE JOB IS COVERED BY AN EXCEPTION, FOR EMPLOYERS TO DISCRIMINATE DIRECTLY OR INDIRECTLY ON THE

Appendix 2

GROUNDS OF SEX OR MARRIAGE IN THE WAY THEY AFFORD ACCESS TO OPPORTUNITIES FOR PROMOTION, TRANSFER OR TRAINING. [*Section 6(2)(a)*].

25. It is therefore recommended that:

(a) where an appraisal system is in operation, the assessment criteria should be examined to ensure that they are not unlawfully discriminatory and the scheme monitored to assess how it is working in practice;

(b) when a group of workers predominantly of one sex is excluded from an appraisal scheme, access to promotion, transfer and training and to other benefits should be reviewed, to ensure that there is no unlawful indirect discrimination;

(c) promotion and career development patterns are reviewed to ensure that the traditional qualifications are justifiable requirements for the job to be done. In some circumstances, for example, promotion on the basis of length of service could amount to unlawful indirect discrimination, as it may unjustifiably affect more women than men;

(d) when general ability and personal qualifies are the main requirements for promotion to a post, care should be taken to consider favourably candidates of both sexes with differing career patterns and general experience;

(e) rules which restrict or preclude transfer between certain jobs should be questioned and changed if they are found to be unlawfully discriminatory. Employees of one sex may be concentrated in sections from which transfers are traditionally restricted without real justification;

(f) policies and practices regarding selection for training, day release and personal development should be examined for unlawful direct and indirect discrimination. Where there is found to be an imbalance in training as between sexes, the cause should be identified to ensure that it is not discriminatory;

(g) age limits for access to training and promotion should be questioned.

HEALTH AND SAFETY LEGISLATION

26. Equal treatment of men and women may be limited by statutory provisions which require men and women to be treated differently. For example, the Factories Act 1961 places restrictions on the hours of work of female manual employees, although the Health and Safety Executive can exempt employers from these restrictions, subject to certain conditions. The Mines and Quarries Act 1954 imposes limitations on women's work and there are restrictions where there is special concern for the unborn child (e.g. lead and ionising radiation). However the broad duties placed on employers by the Health and Safety at Work, etc. Act 1974 makes no distinctions between men and women. Section 2(1) requires employers to ensure, so far as is reasonably practicable, the health and safety and welfare at work of all employees. SPECIFIC HEALTH AND SAFETY REQUIREMENTS UNDER EARLIER LEGISLATION ARE UNAFFECTED BY THE ACT. It is therefore recommended that: company policy should be reviewed and serious consideration given to any significant differences in treatment between men and women, and there should be well-founded reasons if such differences are maintained or introduced.

Note. Some statutory restrictions placed on adult women's hours of work were repealed in February 1987 and others in February 1988.

They now no longer apply. Paragraph 26 of the code is still relevant, however, to other health and safety legislation which requires men and women to be treated differently, and which has not been repealed.

TERMS OF EMPLOYMENT, BENEFITS, FACILITIES AND SERVICES

27. It is unlawful: UNLESS THE JOB IS COVERED BY AN EXCEPTION: TO DISCRIMINATE ON THE GROUNDS OF SEX OR MARRIAGE, DIRECTLY OR INDIRECTLY, IN THE TERMS ON WHICH EMPLOYMENT IS OFFERED OR IN AFFORDING ACCESS TO ANY BENEFITS*, FACILITIES OR SERVICES. [*Sections 6(1)(b); 6(2)(a);29*].

* Certain provisions relating to death and retirement are exempt from the Act.

28. It is therefore recommended that:

    (a) all terms of employment, benefits, facilities and services are reviewed to ensure that there is no unlawful discrimination on grounds of sex or marriage. For example, part-time work, domestic leave, company cars and benefits for dependants should be available to both male and female employees in the same or not materially different circumstances.

29. In an establishment where part-timers are solely or mainly women, unlawful indirect discrimination may arise if, as a group, they are treated less favourably than other employees without justification. It is therefore recommended that:

    (b) where part-time workers do not enjoy pro-rata pay or benefits with full-time workers, the arrangements should be reviewed to ensure that they are justified without regard to sex.

GRIEVANCES, DISCIPLINARY PROCEDURES AND VICTIMISATION

30. It is unlawful: TO VICTIMISE AN INDIVIDUAL FOR A COMPLAINT MADE IN GOOD FAITH ABOUT SEX OR MARRIAGE DISCRIMINATION OR FOR GIVING EVIDENCE ABOUT SUCH A COMPLAINT. [*Section 4(1); 4(2): and 4(3)*].

31. It is therefore recommended that:

    (a) particular care is taken to ensure that an employee who has in good faith taken action under the Sex Discrimination Act or the Equal Pay Act does not receive less favourable treatment than other employees, for example by being disciplined or dismissed;

    (b) employees should be advised to use the internal procedures, where appropriate, but this is without prejudice to the individual's right to apply to an employment tribunal within the statutory time limit i.e. before the end of the period of three months beginning when the act complained of was done. (There is no time limit if the victimisation is continuing);

    (c) particular care is taken to deal effectively with all complaints of discrimination, victimisation or harassment. It should not be assumed that they are made by those who are over-sensitive.

Appendix 2

DISMISSALS, REDUNDANCIES AND OTHER UNFAVOURABLE TREATMENT OF EMPLOYEES

32. It is unlawful: TO DISCRIMINATE DIRECTLY OR INDIRECTLY ON GROUNDS OF SEX OR MARRIAGE IN DISMISSALS OR BY TREATING AN EMPLOYEE UNFAVOURABLY IN ANY OTHER WAY. [*Section 6(2)(b)*]. It is therefore recommended that:

  (a) care is taken that members of one sex are not disciplined or dismissed for performance or behaviour which would be overlooked or condoned in the other sex;

  (b) redundancy procedures affecting a group of employees predominantly of one sex should be reviewed, so as to remove any effects which could be disproportionate and unjustifiable;

  (c) conditions of access to voluntary redundancy benefit* should be made available on equal terms to male and female employees in the same or not materially different circumstances;

* Certain provisions relating to death and retirement are exempt from the Act.

  (d) where there is down-grading or short-time working (for example, owing to a change in the nature or volume of an employer's business) the arrangements should not unlawfully discriminate on the ground of sex;

  (e) all reasonably practical steps should be taken to ensure that a standard of conduct or behaviour is observed which prevents members of either sex from being intimidated, harassed or otherwise subjected to unfavourable treatment on the ground of their sex.

PART 2: THE ROLE OF GOOD EMPLOYMENT PRACTICES IN PROMOTING EQUALITY OF OPPORTUNITY

33. This section of the Code describes those employment practices which help to promote equality of opportunity. It gives information about the formulation and implementation of equal opportunities policies. While such policies are not required by law, their value has been recognised by a number of employers who have voluntarily adopted them. Others may wish to follow this example.

FORMULATING AN EQUAL OPPORTUNITIES POLICY

34. An equal opportunities policy will ensure the effective use of human resources in the best interests of both the organisation and its employees. It is a commitment by an employer to the development and use of employment procedures and practices which do not discriminate on grounds of sex or marriage and which provide genuine equality of opportunity for all employees. The detail of the policy will vary according to size of the organisation.

IMPLEMENTING THE POLICY

35. An equal opportunities policy must be seen to have the active support of management at the highest level. To ensure that the policy is fully effective, the following procedure is recommended:

(a)   the policy should be clearly stated and where appropriate, included in a collective agreement;

(b)   overall responsibility for implementing the policy should rest with senior management;

(c)   the policy should be made known to all employees and, where reasonably practicable, to all job applicants.

36.   Trade unions have a very important part to play in implementing genuine equality of opportunity and they will obviously be involved in the review of established procedures to ensure that these are consistent with the law.

MONITORING

37.   It is recommended that the policy is monitored regularly to ensure that it is working in practice. Consideration could be given to setting up a joint Management/Trade Union Review Committee.

38.   In a small firm with a simple structure it may be quite adequate to assess the distribution and payment of employees from personal knowledge.

39.   In a large and complex organisation a more formal analysis will be necessary, for example, by sex, grade and payment in each unit. This may need to be introduced by stages as resources permit. Any formal analysis should be regularly updated and available to Management and Trade Unions to enable any necessary action to be taken.

40.   Sensible monitoring will show, for example, whether members of one sex:

(a)   do not apply for employment or promotion, or that fewer apply than might be expected;

(b)   are not recruited, promoted or selected for training and development or are appointed/selected in a significantly lower proportion than their rate of application;

(c)   are concentrated in certain jobs, sections or departments.

POSITIVE ACTION

Recruitment, Training and Promotion

41.   Selection for recruitment or promotion must be on merit irrespective of sex. However, the Sex Discrimination Act does allow certain steps to redress the effects of previous unequal opportunities. Where there have been few or no members of one sex in particular work in their employment for the previous 12 months, the Act allows employers to give special encouragement to, and provide specific training for, the minority sex. Such measures are usually described as Positive Action. [*Section 48*].

42.   Employers may wish to consider positive measures such as:

(a)   training their own employees (male or female) for work which is traditionally the preserve of the other sex, for example, training women for skilled manual or technical work;*

* *Note.* Section 47 of the SDA 1975 allowed training bodies to run single-sex courses. Since November 1986, this has applied also to other persons including employers. Single-sex training

505

need therefore no longer be confined to an organisation's own employees, as indicated in paragraph 42(a) of the Code, but may be extended to other groups – for example, job applicants or school leavers. Positive Action in recruitment for employment however, is still not allowed.

(b)   positive encouragement to women to apply for management posts – special courses may be needed;

(c)   advertisements which encourage applications from the minority sex, but make it clear that selection will be on merit without reference to sex;

(d)   notifying job agencies, as part of a Positive Action Programme that they wish to encourage members of one sex to apply for vacancies, where few or no members of that sex are doing the work in question.

In these circumstances, job agencies should tell both men and women about the posts and, in addition, let the under-represented sex know that applications from them are particularly welcome. Withholding information from one sex in an attempt to encourage applications from the opposite sex would be unlawful.

Other Working Arrangements

43.   There are other forms of action which could assist both employer and employee by helping to provide continuity of employment to working parents, many of whom will have valuable experience or skills. Employers may wish to consider with their employees whether:

(a)   certain jobs can be carried out on a part-time or flexi-time basis;

(b)   personal leave arrangements are adequate and available to both sexes. It should not be assumed that men may not need to undertake domestic responsibilities on occasion, especially at the time of childbirth;

(c)   child-care facilities are available locally or whether it would be feasible to establish nursery facilities on the premises or combine with other employers to provide them;

(d)   residential training could be facilitated for employees with young children. For example, where this type of training is necessary, by informing staff who are selected well in advance to enable them to make childcare and other personal arrangements; employers with their own residential training centres could also consider whether childcare facilities might he provided;

(e)   the statutory maternity leave provisions could be enhanced, for example, by reducing the qualifying service period, extending the leave period, or giving access to part-time arrangements on return.

These arrangements, and others, are helpful to both sexes but are of particular benefit to women in helping them to remain in gainful employment during the years of child-rearing.

Appendix 3

Code of Practice on Equal Pay

Editorial note: This Code is a reissue, significantly expanded and rewritten, of the Equal Opportunities Commission's 1997 Code of Practice on Equal Pay. It came into effect on 1 December 2003 (see SI 2003 No 2865) and has the usual legal status of employment-related Codes in accordance with section 56A of the Sex Discrimination Act 1975. Amongst the significant changes in the Code is a section on the extent of an employer's obligation to disclose details of other employees' remuneration in response to Equal Pay Questionnaires, and the reconciliation between transparency in pay schemes and duties of confidentiality under the Data Protection Act 1998.

INTRODUCTION

1   The Equal Pay Act gives women (or men) a right to equal pay for equal work. An employer can only pay a man more than a woman for doing equal work if there is a genuine and material reason for doing so which is not related to sex. The Equal Opportunities Commission (EOC) has issued this revised Code of Practice on Equal Pay in order to provide practical guidance on how to ensure pay is determined without sex discrimination. The revised Code (the Code) is aimed at employers, but employees and their representatives or advisers – for example, from a trade union, or Citizens Advice Bureau, may also find it useful[1].

2   The Act applies to both men and women but to avoid repetition the Code is written as though the claimant is a woman comparing her work and pay with those of a man. The Equal Pay Act specifically deals with the pay of women compared to men, (or vice versa), and not to comparisons between people of the same sex.

3   The Code is admissible in evidence in any proceedings under the Sex Discrimination Act 1975 or the Equal Pay Act 1970 (each as amended), before the Employment Tribunal. This means that, while the Code is not binding, the Employment Tribunal may take into account an employer's failure to act on its provisions.

4   Despite the fact that it is over 30 years since the Equal Pay Act became law, women working full-time earn on average 81 per cent of the hourly earnings of male full-time employees.[2] Part-time working further accentuates the gender pay gap with women working part-time earning on average only 41% of the hourly earnings of male full-time employees. Both the Government and the EOC regard this as unacceptable. By helping employers to check the pay gap in their organisation and by encouraging good equal pay practice, this Code reinforces the Government's commitment to closing the gap between men's and women's pay.

5   Depending on the particular circumstances a number of other pieces of legislation can give rise to claims related to pay discrimination. They include the Race Relations Act, the Disability Discrimination Act, the Pensions Act 1995, the Part-Time Workers (Prevention of Less Favourable Treatment) Regulations 2000 and the Fixed-Term Employees (Prevention of Less Favourable Treatment) Regulations 2002. A female part-time cleaner, for example, could claim equal pay under the Equal Pay Act with a male part-time cleaner, but she could also claim

507

under the Part-Time Workers Regulations, that she was being treated less favourably than a female full-time cleaner. These other pieces of legislation are dealt with in Annex A, but employers should be aware of the need to pay particular attention to the situation in respect of part-time, black and minority ethnic employees and employees with a disability.

6   It is in everyone's interest to avoid litigation, and the Code recommends equal pay reviews as the best means of ensuring that a pay system delivers equal pay. Employers can avoid equal pay claims by regularly reviewing and monitoring their pay practices, in consultation with their workforce. Consultation is likely to increase understanding and acceptance of any changes required. Involving recognised trade unions or other employee representatives also helps to ensure that pay systems meet the legal requirement for transparency.

7   The Code includes, as good equal pay practice, a summary of EOC guidance on how to carry out an equal pay review. The full guidance is in the EOC's Equal Pay Review Kit.[3] The EOC has also produced a separate kit for smaller organisations without specialist personnel expertise.[4] Both are available on the EOC website www.eoc.org.uk or from the EOC Helpline 0845 601 5901.

8   Whilst every effort has been made to ensure that the explanations given in the Code are accurate, only the Courts or Tribunals can give authoritative interpretations of the law.

[1]   For ease of communication the word 'employee' is used throughout this document, but it is not used as a legal term. 'Employee' should be read as referring to all people who work in your organisation.

[2]   *New Earnings Survey 2002*, Office for National Statistics.

[3]   The EOC Equal Pay Review Kit.

[4]   EOC Equal Pay, Fair Pay: a guide to effective pay practices in small businesses.

SECTION ONE: EQUAL PAY LEGISLATION

THE TREATY OF ROME AND THE EQUAL PAY DIRECTIVE

9   The principle that a woman is entitled to equal pay for equal work is set out in European Union and British legislation[5]. The British Courts take into account the decisions of the European Court of Justice in interpreting the Equal Pay Act and the Sex Discrimination Act. A woman bringing an equal pay claim will usually do so under the domestic British legislation, but in some circumstances she can claim under European law.

10   Article 141 of the Treaty of Amsterdam (previously Article 119 of the Treaty of Rome) requires Member States to ensure that the principle of equal pay for male and female workers for equal work or work of equal value is applied. The Equal Pay Directive[6] explains the practical application of the principle of equal pay, namely the elimination of sex discrimination in pay systems. European law defines pay as:

'The ordinary basic or minimum wage or salary and any other consideration, whether in cash or kind, which the worker receives directly or indirectly, in respect of his employer or employment.'

Pensions are treated as pay.

⁵   This Code applies to Great Britain. Northern Ireland has its own equivalent equal pay and sex discrimination legislation and Equality Commission. 6 European Council Directive 75/117/EEC.

⁶   European Council Directive 75/117/EEC.

THE EQUAL PAY ACT 1970

11   The Equal Pay Act 1970, as amended, entitles a woman doing equal work with a man in the same employment to equality in pay and terms and conditions. The meaning of 'same employment' is considered in paragraph 21. The Act does so by giving her the right to equality in the terms of her contract of employment. The man with whom she is claiming equal pay is known as her comparator. Equal work is work that is the same or broadly similar, work that has been rated as equivalent, or work that is of equal value (see paragraphs 27–32).

12   Claims for equal pay are taken through the Employment Tribunal. If a woman succeeds in a claim:

   • Her pay, including any occupational pension rights, must be raised to that of her male comparator

   • Any beneficial term in the man's contract but not in hers must be inserted into her contract

   • Any term in her contract that is less favourable than the same term in the man's contract must be made as good as it is in his

   • Compensation consisting of arrears of pay (if the claim is about pay) and/or damages (if the complaint is about some other contractual term).

13   The woman can compare any term in her contract with the equivalent term in her comparator's contract. This means that each element of the pay package has to be considered separately and it is not sufficient to compare total pay. For example, a woman can claim equal pay with a male comparator who earns a higher rate of basic pay than she does, even if other elements of her pay package are more favourable than his.

14   Once a woman establishes that she and her comparator are doing equal work it is up to her employer to show that the explanation for the pay difference is genuinely due to a 'material factor' that is not tainted by sex discrimination. This defence is known as the 'genuine material factor' defence. In practice, an employer may identify more than one factor. For example, an employer may argue that the man is paid more because he is better qualified than the woman *and* because it is difficult to recruit people with his particular skills.

THE SEX DISCRIMINATION ACT 1975

15   The Equal Pay Act applies to pay or benefits provided under the contract of employment. The Sex Discrimination Act 1975, as amended, complements the Equal Pay Act. It covers non-contractual issues such as recruitment, training, promotion, dismissal and the allocation of benefits, for example, flexible working arrangements or access to a workplace nursery.

16   The Sex Discrimination Act also covers non-contractual pay matters, such as promotion and discretionary bonuses. Decisions about performance markings in a performance-related pay scheme are aspects of treatment which could be challenged under the Sex Discrimination Act if discriminatory. By contrast, where

those decisions result in different levels of pay, that difference and the terms of the scheme could be challenged under the Equal Pay Act. This means that if a woman wishes to make a claim in respect of non-contractual or discretionary payments her claim will be made under the Sex Discrimination Act[7].If there is any doubt as to which Act a payment falls under, legal advice should be sought.

[7]   Also, if a woman considers that a term in a collective agreement, or an employer's rule, provides for the doing of an unlawful discriminatory act, and that the term or rule may at some time have effect in relation to her, she can challenge that term or rule under the Sex Discrimination Act 1986 as amended by section 32 of the Trade Union Reform and Employment Rights Act 1993.

PROTECTION AGAINST VICTIMISATION

17   The Sex Discrimination Act also protects employees from being victimised for making a complaint (unless this is both untrue and made in bad faith) about equal pay or sex discrimination, or for giving evidence about such a complaint. Victimisation because a woman intends to bring a claim is also unlawful. The 'complaint' does not have to be by way of filing a claim with the Employment Tribunal, but includes any discussion or correspondence about the matter between the woman and her employer. The protection against victimisation also includes not only the woman bringing the claim, but also anyone who assists her, for example, her comparator and any trade union or employee representatives.

THE SCOPE OF THE EQUAL PAY ACT

Employers

18   The Equal Pay Act applies to all employers irrespective of their size and whether they are in the public or the private sector.

Employees

19   The Equal Pay Act applies to:

- All employees (including apprentices and those working from home), whether on full-time, part-time, casual or temporary contracts, regardless of length of service

- Other workers (eg self employed) whose contracts require personal performance of the work

- Employment carried out for a British employer unless the employee works wholly outside Great Britain[8]

- Employment carried out on British registered ships or UK registered aircraft operated by someone based in Great Britain unless the employee works wholly outside Great Britain.

20   The Equal Pay Act also applies to Armed Services personnel, but there is a requirement to first make a complaint to an officer under the relevant service redress procedures and submit a complaint to the Defence Council under those procedures before presenting a claim to the Employment Tribunal[9].

[8]   Great Britain includes such of the territorial waters of the UK as are adjacent to Great Britain and certain areas designated in relation to employment in the offshore oil and gas industry.

[9]   Section 7A (5) of the Equal Pay Act read with the Service Redress Procedures.

Same employment

21 A woman can claim equal pay with a man working:

- For the same employer at the same workplace

- For the same employer but at a different workplace where common terms and conditions apply, for example at another branch of a store

- For an associated employer; for example, at her employer's parent company

- European law also allows a comparison to be made between employees who do not work for the same employer, but who are *'in the same establishment or service'*. As there is no clear definition of *'in the same establishment or service'* this is an area of law on which specific legal advice should be sought. However, European law as it currently stands suggests a comparison can only be made where the differences in pay are attributable to a 'common source' and there is a single body, responsible for and capable of remedying the pay inequality, for example where pay differences arise from a sector-wide collective agreement or from legislation.

The pay package

22 The Equal Pay Act covers all aspects of the pay and benefits package, including:

- Basic pay

- Non-discretionary bonuses

- Overtime rates and allowances

- Performance related benefits

- Severance and redundancy pay

- Access to pension schemes

- Benefits under pension schemes

- Hours of work

- Company cars

- Sick pay

- Fringe benefits such as travel allowances.

Comparators

23 A woman can claim equal pay for equal work with a man, or men, in the same employment. It is for the woman to select the man or men with whom she wishes to be compared, and her employer cannot interfere with her choice of comparator(s). She can claim equal pay with more than one comparator, but to avoid repetition the Code (and the law) is written as though there is only one comparator.

24 The comparator can be:

- Someone with whom she is working at the present time, subject to the usual time limits (see paragraphs 47–48)

- Her predecessor, however long ago he did the job, or her successor.

25   The comparator does not have to give his consent to being named. If the woman's equal pay claim is successful, the result will be that her pay is raised to the same level as his. There will not be any reduction in the comparator's pay and benefits.

26   There are a number of ways in which a woman may be able to select a comparator. These include:

- Her own knowledge and experience

- The internal grievance procedure (see paragraph 36)

- The Equal Pay Questionnaire (see paragraph 37)

- Discovery (asking for documents through the Employment Tribunal). Once a woman has filed her claim with the Employment Tribunal, provided that she has shown that her contractual terms are less favourable than those of male colleagues, she can apply for discovery to enable her to name appropriate comparators.

Equal pay for equal work

27   The comparator may be doing the *same* job as the woman, or he may be doing a *different* job. She can claim equal pay for equal work with a comparator doing work that is:

- The *same*, or broadly similar (known as **like work**)

- *Different*, but which is rated under the same job evaluation scheme as equivalent to hers known as **work rated as equivalent)**

- *Different*, but of equal value in terms of demands such as effort, skill and decision-making (known as **work of equal value**).

Like work

28   Like work means the woman and her comparator are doing the same or broadly similar work. Job titles could be different, yet the work being done could be broadly similar – the nature of the work actually being done needs to be considered. Where differences exist the Employment Tribunal will look at the nature and extent of the differences, how frequently they occur, and whether they are of practical importance in relation to the terms and conditions of the job.

Like work comparisons that have succeeded, in the particular circumstances of the case, include:

- Male and female cleaners doing 'wet' and 'dry' cleaning in different locations on the same site

- A woman cook preparing lunches for directors and a male chef cooking breakfast, lunch and tea for employees.

Work rated as equivalent

29   Work rated as equivalent means that the jobs being done by the woman and her comparator have been assessed under the same job evaluation scheme as being equivalent, that is, they have been assessed as having the same number of points, or as falling within the same job evaluation grade.

Work rated as equivalent comparisons that have succeeded in the particular circumstances of the case, include: ➡

- Where a woman and a man had been placed in the same job evaluation grade, but the employer had refused to pay the woman (who had been evaluated as having fewer points) the rate for the grade.

Work of equal value

30 Work of equal value means that the jobs done by the woman and her comparator are different, but can be regarded as being of equal value or worth. This can be measured by comparing the jobs under headings such as effort, skill and decision-making.

31 Comparing jobs on the basis of equal value means jobs that are entirely different in their nature can be used as the basis for equal pay claims. Job comparisons can be made both within a particular pay/grading structure and between different structures or departments, for example, in a printing firm, between a bindery and a press room. Equal value is likely to be relevant where men and women are in the same employment but do different types of work.

Equal value comparisons that have succeeded in the particular circumstances of the case, include:

- Cooks and carpenters

- Speech therapists and clinical psychologists

- Kitchen assistants and refuse workers.

32 A woman can claim equal pay under more than one heading. For example, a woman working as an administrator in a garage could claim 'like work' with a male administrator working alongside her and 'equal value' with a mechanic.

Pregnant women and women on maternity leave

33 During the period of Ordinary Maternity Leave a woman's contract remains in place and all of her contractual terms and conditions must continue, with the exception of her normal pay (ie wages or salary)[10].The position with regard to bonuses, occupational pension rights, and the provision of maternity benefits over and above those required by the statutory scheme is unclear, and specific legal advice will be needed.

34 When a woman is on Additional Maternity Leave[11], even though her contract remains in place, her contractual terms cease to apply, except for some limited exceptions not relevant to pay. However, her entitlement to paid leave under the Working Time Regulations continues to accrue, and in some circumstances it may be unlawful under either the Equal Pay Act or the Sex Discrimination Act to treat a woman on maternity leave differently from other workers, eg by failing to pay her a bonus. The situation will vary according to the facts and again, this is an area where detailed legal advice should be sought.

35 Pay increases continue to accrue while a woman is on maternity leave and she is entitled to the benefit of any pay increases that she would have received had she been at work[12].

[10] Under the Employment Rights Act 1996, and the Maternity and Parental Leave Regulations 1999, as amended by the Maternity and Parental Leave (Amendment) Regulations 2002, Ordinary Maternity Leave is 26 weeks for all mothers whose expected week of childbirth is after 6 April 2003.

[11] Under the Employment Rights Act 1996, as amended by the Employment Relations Act 1999, women who have at least 26 weeks service at the beginning of the 14th week before the expected week of childbirth are entitled to 26 weeks Additional Maternity Leave starting after their Ordinary Maternity Leave.

[12] *Gillespie v Northern Health and Social Services Board C-342/93 [1996]; IRLR 214, [1996]; ICR 498, ECJ.*

RAISING THE MATTER WITH THE EMPLOYER

Using the grievance procedure

36   Before making a complaint to the Employment Tribunal, a woman should try to resolve the issue of equal pay by mutual agreement with her employer, perhaps through the employer's own grievance procedure. Employers and employees can also seek advice from an Acas conciliator. Acas can be contacted at www.acas.org.uk. However, the time limit for making a complaint to the Employment Tribunal will still apply and will not be extended to take account of the time taken to complete the grievance procedure[13]. Although there is no legal requirement to do so it is good practice for the employer, the employee, and/or her union representative, to keep records of any meetings.

[13] A woman will be obliged to use the grievance procedure once the relevant provisions of the Employment Act 2002 have come into effect in October 2004. Time limits will be amended to allow the grievance procedure to be used.

The Equal Pay Questionnaire

37   A woman is entitled to write to her employer asking for information that will help her establish whether she has received equal pay and if not, what the reasons for the pay difference are. There is a standard questionnaire form which can be used to do this. The focus of the questionnaire is on establishing whether she is receiving less favourable pay and contractual terms and conditions than a colleague or colleagues of the opposite sex, and whether the employer agrees that she and her comparator are doing 'equal work'. The woman can send the questionnaire to her employer either before she files her claim with the Employment Tribunal or within 21 days of doing so. Copies of the questionnaire can be obtained from the Women and Equality Unit website www.womenandequalityunit.gov.uk.

38   If the woman takes a case to the Employment Tribunal, the information provided by her employer should enable her to present her claim in the most effective way and the proceedings should be simpler because the key facts will have been identified in advance. If her employer fails, without reasonable excuse, to reply within 8 weeks, or responds with an evasive or equivocal reply, the Employment Tribunal may take this into account at the hearing. The Employment Tribunal may then draw an inference unfavourable to the employer, for example, that the employer has no genuine reason for the difference in pay.

RESPONDING TO REQUESTS FROM AN EMPLOYEE FOR INFORMATION

Transparency

39   The European Court of Justice has held that pay systems must be transparent. Transparency means that pay and benefit systems should be capable of being

understood by everyone (employers, employees and their trade unions). Employees should be able to understand how each element of their pay packet contributes to total earnings in a pay period. Where the pay structure is not transparent, and a woman is able to show some indication of sex discrimination, the burden of proof switches to the employer who then has to demonstrate that the pay system does not discriminate.

40   It is advisable for an employer to keep records that will allow him or her to explain why he or she did something, showing clearly what factors he or she relied on at the time that the decision on pay was made. Employers should be aware that employees may bring complaints or make enquiries about pay decisions which were taken many years previously, since when the person who took the decision may have left the organisation. For this reason it is advisable for employers to keep records that may, in the future, help them to explain why pay decisions were made.

41   Bearing in mind the guidance given in the preceding paragraphs, when responding either to a grievance or to the questionnaire employers need to:

●   Decide whether or not they agree that the woman is doing equal work

●   Consider the reasons for any difference in pay

●   If they do not agree that the woman's work is equal to that of her comparator, they should explain in what way the work is not equal

●   Explain the reasons for any difference in pay.

Further guidance is given in the notes accompanying the questionnaire.

Confidentiality

42   The principle of transparency set out above does not mean that an individual has the automatic right to know what another individual earns. The principle of transparency means that a woman has the right to know how the calculations are made, not the content of the calculation. It is necessary to balance the ideal of transparency with the rights of individual privacy. The equal pay questionnaire cannot be used to require an employer to disclose confidential information, unless the Employment Tribunal orders the employer to do so. A woman can use the questionnaire to request key information and it is likely that in many cases an employer will be able to answer detailed questions in general terms, while still preserving the anonymity and confidentiality of employees.

The Data Protection Act

43   Much of the information requested will not be confidential but some information, such as the exact details of a comparator's pay package, may be confidential to that person. Personal data is protected by the Data Protection Act 1998 and can only be disclosed in accordance with data protection principles. Pay records will usually be personal data covered by the Data Protection Act. Moreover, other issues such as ethnic origin and medical details are sensitive personal data to which particular safeguards apply. The disclosure of confidential information in the employment context is also protected by the implied duty of trust and confidence owed by an employer to an employee.

44   The EOC has produced a guidance note that explains an employer's legal obligations when responding to an equal pay questionnaire or to a request for information during the course of tribunal proceedings[14]. However, this is a

developing area of law and, if in doubt, an employer should seek specific advice from the Information Commissioner www.informationcommissioner.gov.uk and/or take legal advice.

[14] EOC practical tips: responding to an equal pay questionnaire and requests for information during tribunal proceedings in accordance with Data Protection Act principles.

Disclosure of information to trade unions or employee representatives

45   Under the Trade Union and Labour Relations (Consolidation) Act 1992 an employer is under a duty, on request, to disclose to a recognised trade union, information to enable constructive collective bargaining. Information about pay and terms and conditions of employment usually comes within the duty to disclose, but it is important to note that the duty applies only to information for collective bargaining.

46   It also represents good practice for employers who do not recognise trade unions to communicate regularly with their workforce and, where appropriate, their representatives.

BRINGING AN EQUAL PAY CLAIM

The time limits for applying to an Employment Tribunal

47   If a woman wishes to lodge a claim with the Employment Tribunal she must do so within the prescribed time limits. **It is her responsibility to ensure that she does so.** The woman bringing the claim and her representatives should be alert to the importance of lodging the equal pay claim with the Employment Tribunal within the time limits. Using the internal grievance procedure does not extend the time limits set for lodging a claim, nor does serving the questionnaire[15].

[15] See footnote 13.

48   The Equal Pay Act and the Sex Discrimination Act have different time limits.

   - Claims under the Equal Pay Act can be taken at any time up to six months after leaving the employment with the employer (as opposed to leaving the particular post about which the equal pay claim is made, but remaining in the same employment). This time limit also applies to equal pay claims taken where a stable relationship with an employer has come to an end. The time limit can be extended only where the employer deliberately conceals the existence of pay inequality from the complainant, or the complainant is a minor or of unsound mind[16]

   - In contracting out situations the time limit runs from the date of the contracting out in respect of periods of service up to that date

   - Claims under the Sex Discrimination Act can be taken within three months of the alleged act of discrimination, subject to the tribunal's discretion to extend the time limit where it is just and equitable to do so

   - Because of the requirement on Armed Services personnel to use the relevant Service Redress Procedure referred to in paragraph 20 different rules apply. In the case of the Equal Pay Act, the time limit is nine months from the end of the period of service, and in the case of the Sex Discrimination Act, the time limit is six months from the date of the act complained of. The time limits can be extended only as described above.

[16] The Equal Pay Act 1970 (Amendment) Regulations 2003 (SI 2003 No 1656).

The burden of proof

49   The woman bringing an equal pay claim has to show the Employment Tribunal
       that on the face of it she is receiving less pay than a man in the same employment
       who is doing equal work. Her employer must then either accept her claim or prove
       to the Employment Tribunal that the difference in pay was for a genuine and
       material reason, which was not the difference of sex.

The Employment Tribunal procedure

50   The fact that a woman is paid less than a man doing equal work does not
       necessarily mean that she is suffering sex discrimination in pay. In making a
       decision about a case the Employment Tribunal has to assess the evidence about:

       •   The work done by the woman and her comparator

       •   The value placed on the work (sometimes with the advice of an Independ-
             ent Expert), in terms of the demands of the jobs

       •   The pay of the woman and her comparator and how it is arrived at

       •   The reasons for the difference in pay.

51   In *like work* and *work rated as equivalent* claims the procedure is the same as in
       any other employment case. There are special tribunal procedures for *work of
       equal value* claims[17].

[17] These are to be found in the Employment Tribunals (Constitution and Rules of Procedure)
     Regulations 2001 (SI 2001 No 1171) and the Employment Tribunals (Constitution and Rules of
     Procedure) (Scotland) Regulations 2001 (SI 2001 No 1170) and section 2A of the Equal Pay Act
     itself.

Assessing equal value

52   The concept of equal pay for work of equal value means that a woman can claim
       equal pay with a man doing a completely different job. In comparing such jobs
       the Employment Tribunal will apply techniques akin to analytical job evaluation,
       whereby the demands on the jobholders and the skills required of them are
       assessed using objective criteria. The Employment Tribunal may also appoint an
       Independent Expert to assess the value of the jobs. The Employment Tribunal-
       appointed Independent Expert may make a detailed study of an employer's pay
       system and the employer would be expected to co-operate with any such exercise.

53   Employers should be aware that they, and the woman bringing the claim, might
       also appoint someone with equal pay expertise to act as an expert on their behalf.
       It is important when dealing with experts to be clear who is the Independent
       Expert appointed by the Employment Tribunal and who is acting for the parties
       to the claim.

The employer's defence

54   The possible defences against an equal pay claim are as follows:

       •   The woman and the man are not doing equal work

       •   For equal value claims only – the jobs being done by the woman and the
             man have been evaluated and rated differently under an analytical job
             evaluation scheme that is free of sex bias. An analytical job evaluation
             scheme evaluates jobs according to the demands made on the jobholders. **A
             non-analytical job evaluation scheme does not provide a defence to a claim**

       •   The difference in pay is genuinely due to a material factor, which is not the
             difference of sex.

Appendix 3

The job evaluation defence

55 Where employers use analytical job evaluation schemes they need to check that the scheme has been designed and implemented in such a way that it does not discriminate on grounds of sex. An analytical evaluation discriminates on the grounds of sex where values have been attributed to the different demands against which it has measured the jobs, and these values cannot be justified irrespective of the sex of the person on whom these demands are made.

56 A job evaluation scheme will be discriminatory if it fails to include, or properly take into account, a factor, or job demand, that is an important element in the woman's job (eg caring demands in a job involving looking after elderly people), or if it gives an unjustifiably heavy weighting to factors that are more typical of the man's job (eg the physical demands of being employed as a gardener).

57 A woman may also challenge a job evaluation scheme on the basis that instead of a factor, say, 'mental concentration' (in her job) being awarded fewer points than 'physical effort' (in her comparator's job), it should have received the same or more points. Similarly, she may argue that 'physical effort' (in his job) has been overrated compared with the skill her job requires for 'manual dexterity'. Even where she has received the same or more points than a man for a particular factor, she may still argue that the demands of her job under this factor have been underrated, that is, that the difference in points under the factor should have been bigger.

58 Employers also need to check the outcomes of the job evaluation for sex bias. This means checking what impact the scheme has had on women and men, that is, how many women and how many men have moved up or down the grades? Any ensuing pay protection (red-circling) should also be free of sex bias and should be phased out as soon as is practicable[18].

59 The EOC has produced a guidance note recommending that matters, such as the following, should be considered as a matter of good practice[19]. In order to check that a scheme is non-discriminatory, an employer needs to look at matters such as:

- Whether statistics recorded on pay are broken down by gender

- Whether the scheme is appropriate to the jobs it will cover

- If a proprietary scheme is used does the supplier have equal opportunities guidelines?

- If any groups of workers are excluded from the scheme, are there clear and justifiable reasons for their exclusion?

- Is the composition of the job evaluation panel/steering committee representative of the jobs covered by the scheme and are the members trained in job evaluation and avoiding sex bias?

- Are the job descriptions written to an agreed format and assessed to a common standard? Are trained job analysts used and have the jobholders been involved in writing their own job descriptions?

- Where the scheme uses generic/bench mark jobs are these free from sex bias?

- Are the factor definitions and levels exact and are detailed descriptions provided for each factor? Do the factors cover **all** the important job demands?

518

If a job evaluation scheme is to remain free of sex bias it should be monitored. The employer (and not the job evaluation supplier or consultant) will need to show that the scheme is non-discriminatory.

[18] The EOC Equal Pay Review Kit Guidance Note 4: Job Evaluation Schemes Free of Sex Bias.
[19] The EOC Equal Pay Review Kit Guidance Note 4: Job Evaluation Schemes Free of Sex Bias.

The 'genuine material factor defence' – testing for sex discrimination

60 The Employment Tribunal tests for sex discrimination by first establishing a difference in pay or terms between the woman bringing the claim and a man doing equal work, and then asking whether the difference is due to discrimination or some other factor that does not amount to sex discrimination. This means that an employer can pay a man more than a woman for doing equal work, but only if the reason for doing so – the factor which the employer regards as the reason for the difference in pay – is not related to the sex of the jobholders.

61 The employer will have to show that the factor, or factors, on which he or she relies is free from both direct and indirect sex discrimination:

- Direct sex discrimination occurs when the difference in pay or terms is directly related to the difference of sex

- Indirect sex discrimination arises when the pay difference is due to a provision, criterion or practice which:

  — Applies to both men and women, but

  — Adversely affects a considerably larger proportion of women than men, and

  — Is not objectively justified irrespective of the sex of the jobholders.

62 Whether a defence succeeds or fails will always depend on the circumstances of the case and there is no such thing as an automatic or blanket defence. The defences that are likely to succeed include allowances such as London weighting and night-shift payments. Factors such as different market rates of pay for different specialisms or different levels of skills and experience have been successful in some cases but not in others.

63 The factor put forward to explain the difference in pay has to be significant; it has to be the real reason for the difference and it must not be connected with the sex of the people doing the job. For example, if the employer considers that the reason for paying the comparator more than the woman bringing the claim is that people will not do the work for the lower rate of pay, then the employer would have to bring evidence of actual difficulties in recruiting and retaining people to do the job being done by the male comparator.

64 Where a woman is claiming equal pay on the basis that the two jobs are work of equal value, indirect discrimination may arise where one of the jobs is done by a much higher proportion of women than the other job. The onus lies on the employee to provide evidence of significant disparate impact[20].

[20] The advice given here is based on *Nelson v Carillion Services Ltd [2003] EWCA Civ 544; [2003] IRLR 428; [2003] ICR 1256*. Specific legal advice should be sought.

65 In such a case, if the Employment Tribunal accepts that the jobs are of equal value, the employer will need to provide objective justification for the pay difference between the two kinds of job. This is a higher standard of justification than that of the material factor defence.

Appendix 3

66   The employer must show that:

- The purpose of the provision or practice is to meet a real business need

- The provision or practice is appropriate and necessary as a means of meeting that need.

An example of objective justification is:

- A pay system that makes an additional payment to employees working unsocial hours, in which most of the employees getting the bonus are men. Here the employer would have to show that:

    — There is a real business need to create a system to encourage a particular group of employees to work unsociable hours, and

    — The additional payments meet that need, and

    — The payments are an effective way of meeting that need, and do not go beyond what is necessary to achieve it (ie without the payment, the extra work would not be done, and the payment is only made when the workers actually do the work).

Awards of equal pay

67   If the woman succeeds in her claim she is entitled to:

- An order from the Employment Tribunal declaring her rights

- Equalisation of contractual terms for the future (if she is still in employment)

- Compensation consisting of arrears of pay (if the claim is about pay) and/or damages (if the complaint is about some other contractual term).

Back pay can be awarded up to a maximum of six years (five years in Scotland) from the date that proceedings were filed with the Employment Tribunal.[21] In addition, the Employment Tribunal may award interest on the award of compensation. With up to six year's worth of back pay being awarded, the interest element of any award is likely to be considerable.

[21] Special rules apply where the woman is under a disability or the employer has concealed a breach of the Equal Pay Act.

SECTION TWO: GOOD EQUAL PAY PRACTICE

INTRODUCTION

68   The loss to women arising out of the gender pay gap is well documented, but organisations also lose out by failing to properly reward the range of skills and experience that women bring to the workforce. The most commonly recognised risk of failing to ensure that pay is determined without sex discrimination is equal pay cases being taken against the organisation. The direct costs of a claim can include not only any eventual equal pay award to the woman bringing the claim (see paragraph 67) but also the costs of time spent at a hearing, and the costs of legal representation. The indirect costs are harder to quantify, but include lower productivity on the part of those employees who consider that they are not getting equal pay and on the part of managers whose time is taken up in dealing with the claim.

69   Tackling the gender pay gap reduces the risk of litigation. It can also increase efficiency by attracting the best employees, reducing staff turnover, increasing commitment, and reducing absenteeism. Pay is one of the key factors affecting motivation and relationships at work. It is therefore important to develop pay arrangements that are right for the organisation and that reward employees fairly. Providing equal pay for equal work is central to the concept of rewarding people fairly for what they do.

THE ESSENTIAL FEATURES OF AN EQUAL PAY REVIEW

70   Employers are responsible for providing equal pay and for ensuring that pay systems are transparent. Pay arrangements are frequently complicated and the features that can give rise to sex discrimination are not always obvious. A structured pay system is more likely to provide equal pay and is easier to check than a system that relies primarily on managerial discretion. Acas, the employment relations' experts, provide basic advice on the various different types of pay systems and on job evaluation.

71   The advice given in paragraphs 39–46 on striking a balance between transparency and confidentiality are also relevant to equal pay reviews. The EOC has produced a guidance note that explains an employer's legal obligations when carrying out an equal pay review[22].

72   While employers are not required, by law, to carry out an equal pay review, this Code recommends equal pay reviews as the most appropriate method of ensuring that a pay system delivers equal pay free from sex bias. Whatever kind of equal pay review process is used, it should include:

●   Comparing the pay of men and women doing equal work. Here employers need to check for one or more of the following: like work; work rated as equivalent; work of equal value. *These checks are the foundation of an equal pay review*

●   Identifying any equal pay gaps

●   Eliminating those pay gaps that cannot satisfactorily be explained on grounds other than sex.

These features are the same whatever the size of the organisation and they are essential. **A pay review process that does not include these features cannot claim to be an equal pay review.** Moreover, an equal pay review is not simply a data collection exercise. It entails a commitment to put right any sex based pay inequalities and this means that the review must have the involvement and support of managers with the authority to deliver the necessary changes.

73   The validity of the review and success of subsequent action taken will be enhanced if the pay system is understood and accepted by the managers who operate the system, by the employees and by their unions. Employers should therefore aim to secure the involvement of employees and, where possible, trade union representatives, when carrying out an equal pay review.

[22]   EOC practical tips: conducting an equal pay review in accordance with Data Protection Act principles.

Appendix 3

VOLUNTARY EQUAL PAY REVIEWS

A model for carrying out an equal pay review

74   The EOC recommends a five-step equal pay review model:

STEP 1: Deciding the scope of the review and identifying the data required

STEP 2: Determining where men and women are doing equal work

STEP 3: Collecting pay data to identify equal pay gaps

STEP 4: Establishing the causes of any significant pay gaps and assessing the reasons for these

STEP 5: Developing an equal pay action plan and/or reviewing and monitoring.

The EOC Equal Pay Review Kit sets out the detail of the model recommended here and provides supporting guidance notes.

STEP 1: Deciding the scope of the review and identifying the data required

75   In scoping the review employers need to decide:

- Which employees are going to be included? It is advisable to include all employees who are deemed to be in the same establishment or service (see paragraph 21)

- What information will be needed? Employers will need to collect and compare broad types of information about:

  — All the various elements of pay, including pensions and other benefits

  — The personal characteristics of each employee, that is, gender; full-time or part-time; qualifications relevant to the job; hours worked and when and where they work these; length of service; role and time in grade and performance related pay ratings[23]

  — It is particularly important to ensure that information is collected about part-time employees.

The information will vary depending upon the type of organisation, its pay policies and practices and the scope of the review.

- Who should be involved in carrying out the review? An equal pay review requires different types of input from people with different perspectives. There will be a need for knowledge and understanding of the pay and grading arrangements; of any job evaluation schemes; and of the payroll and human resource systems. It can also be helpful to have someone with an understanding of equality issues, particularly the effects of indirect discrimination in pay systems

- When to involve the workforce? Employers need to consider when to involve the trade unions or other employee representatives

- Whether expert advice is needed? Employers may also wish to consider whether to bring in outside expertise. Acas can provide practical, independent and impartial advice on the employee relations aspects of equal pay reviews.

[23] The EOC Equal Pay Review Kit Guidance Note 2: Data collection provides detailed guidance on the information required to carry out an equal pay review.

The scope of the Equal Pay Review[24]

In nearly three quarters of organisations, the review applied (or applies) to the whole workforce. In over half of all the cases it involved an examination of a job evaluation system to ensure that it was free of sex bias. Moreover, just under half of organisations had extended the review beyond pay and gender, to include other processes such as recruitment and selection; two-fifths had covered pay differences by ethnicity; more than a third had covered age and nearly a third had covered disability.

The scope of the Equal Pay Review

	Percentage of organisations covering
Whole workforce	73
Examination of job evaluation system	55
Other HR processes	49
Pay differences by ethnic origin	40
Pay differences by age	36
Pay differences by disability	31
N = number of organisations	67

---

[24] Case study taken from *Monitoring Progress Towards Pay Equality*, Neathey, Dench & Thomson, Institute for Employment Studies, EOC 2003.

Include ethnicity and disability in the review

76   This Code is concerned with an important, but narrow, aspect of sex discrimination in employment – the pay of women compared to men doing equal work, (or vice versa). It does not deal with comparisons on the grounds of ethnicity or disability. However, as a matter of good practice employers may also want to look at ethnicity and disability, or age. Before deciding to do so it may be helpful to consider the quality of the information available to the employer, and whether it is adequate for the purposes of carrying out a wider review. To ensure the relevant provisions of race and disability legislation are taken into account, it would be appropriate to seek advice from the Commission for Racial Equality and/or the Disability Rights Commission.

77   Public Sector organisations obliged by the Race Relations (Amendment) Act 2000 to adopt an Equality Scheme should ensure that their pay review deals with any pay gaps between workers from different ethnic groups as well as the gaps between men's and women's pay. Here too, advice can be obtained from the Commission for Racial Equality.

STEP 2: Determining where men and women are doing equal work

78   In Step 2 employers need to do one or more of the following checks:

- Like work

- Work rated as equivalent

- Work of equal value.

These checks determine where men and women are doing equal work. They are the foundation of an equal pay review.

523

Appendix 3

Example[25] – determining where men and women are doing equal work

Human Resources and the unions met to agree which areas to examine. According to the HR manager, 'we already had an idea of where the discrepancies were'. Data collection was on the basis of figures from: the personnel database, the pay database, the performance pay database and the starters and leavers database. A small local consultancy had helped to introduce a new job evaluation scheme; however, the basis for making equal work comparisons was predominantly by existing grade. The organisation looked at global differences, differences by grade and differences by components of pay (basic pay, overtime and allowances).

---

[25] Case study taken from *Monitoring Progress Towards Pay Equality*, Neathey, Dench & Thomson, Institute for Employment Studies, EOC 2003.

79 Employers who do not have analytical job evaluation schemes designed with equal value in mind will need to find an alternative means of estimating whether men and women are doing equal work. The EOC Equal Pay Review Kit includes suggestions as to how this can be done[26]. Employers who do use analytical job evaluation schemes need to check that their scheme has been designed and implemented in such a way and at all times so as not to discriminate on grounds of sex.[27]

[26] The EOC Equal Pay Review Kit Guidance Note 5: Assessing Equal Value.

[27] The EOC Equal Pay Review Kit Guidance Note 4: Job Evaluation Schemes Free of Sex Bias.

STEP 3: Collecting pay data to identify equal pay gaps

80 In Step 3 employers need to collect and compare pay information for men and women doing equal work by:

- Calculating average basic pay and total earnings

- Comparing access to and amounts received of each element of the pay package.

   To ensure comparisons are consistent, when calculating average basic pay and average total earnings for men and women separately, employers should do this either on an hourly basis or on a full-time salary basis (grossing up or down for those who work fewer, or more, hours—excluding overtime—per week than the norm).

81 Employers then need to review the pay comparisons to identify any gender pay gaps and decide if any are significant enough to warrant further investigation. It is advisable to record all the significant or patterned pay gaps that have been identified.

Example[28] – data collection and analysis

The organisation had a well-established process for undertaking equal pay audits. Data were brought together and presented in tabular form by the data analysis section of the human resources department. The data were then reviewed, analysed and commented on by the head of employee relations, who shared the data with trade union representatives. Union and management worked together to develop action points arising from the data.

---

[28] Case study taken from *Monitoring Progress Towards Pay Equality*, Neathey, Dench & Thomson, Institute for Employment Studies, EOC 2003.

524

STEP 4: Establishing the causes of any significant pay gaps and assessing the reasons for these

82   In Step 4 employers need to:

- Find out if there is a genuine and material reason for the difference in pay that has nothing to do with the sex of the jobholders

- Examine their pay systems to find out which pay policies and practices are contributing to any gender pay gaps.

Example[29] – finding out which policies and practices are contributing to the gender pay gap

The review showed a 23 per cent gap in the average basic pay of men and women across the organisation. In grades with a large enough number of staff to make a comparison, 50 per cent had variances of five per cent or greater in favour of either men or women. Starting pay was not found to be an issue, nor was performance pay. The key factor in grade inequalities was identified as long pay ranges and the impact of past restructuring. There was a body of staff (largely male), who had reached the upper quartile of their current pay range prior to the most recent restructuring. However, new appointees, who were increasingly female, and those who had taken career breaks, had little chance of progressing to this level.

The other area of concern identified by the review was premium payments for working unsocial hours. These were paid at the rate of 20 per cent of basic salary to some grades. However, in 1998 these payments were restricted to existing staff. The period since 1998 had seen an increase in the number of female recruits into what were traditionally male areas. Due to the change in the rules they were not eligible for the premium payments. The result was that overall in the eligible grades, men received on average two and a half times the amount of earnings from premium pay that women received.

---

[29] Case study taken from *Monitoring Progress Towards Pay Equality*, Neathey, Dench & Thomson, Institute for Employment Studies, EOC 2003.

83   Pay systems vary considerably. Pay systems that group jobs into pay grades or bands have traditionally treated jobs in the same grade or band as being of broadly equal value, either because they have been evaluated with similar scores under a job evaluation scheme, or because they are simply regarded as equivalent. However, recent years have seen a trend towards structures with fewer, broader grades or bands and greater use of performance pay and market factors. A single broad band or grade may contain jobs or roles of significantly different value because it encompasses a wide range of job evaluation scores. This, coupled with a wider use of other determinants of pay and more complex methods of pay progression, means that it is important for employers to check all aspects of the pay system from a variety of standpoints: design, implementation, and impact on men and women[30].

[30] The EOC Equal Pay Review Kit Guidance Note 6: Reviewing your payment systems, policies and practices.

STEP 5: Developing an equal pay action plan and/or reviewing and monitoring

84   Where the reason for the pay difference is connected with sex, employers will need to provide equal pay for current and future employees.

Appendix 3

85   Employers who find no gaps between men's and women's pay, or who find gaps for which there are genuinely non-discriminatory reasons, should nevertheless keep their pay systems under review by introducing regular monitoring undertaken jointly with trade unions. This will ensure that the pay system remains free of sex bias.

Example[31] – developing an action plan

Following the review, an Action Plan looking at internal processes was developed. This is ongoing and is reviewed through partnership processes. The aim is to integrate equal pay issues into employee relations' work.

Early action has been in relation to internal recruitment processes. This included looking at whether people were encouraged (or not) to apply for particular jobs. This lack of recognition of potential opportunities was closing off progression routes to some groups, and impacting on the organisational gender pay gap. The organisation also found that it had a body of staff (mainly women) that did not seek promotion. A challenge for the organisation was to encourage more women to aim for promotion, especially once they had fewer family responsibilities.

The remuneration manager anticipated that the gender pay gap in the main staff would fall from the 13 per cent identified in the pay review to under five per cent over the following five years. A recent repeat of the review had already shown a fall, however, the decline in the gap might not always be maintained. This is because the company's pay system is highly market sensitive and a tightening of the labour market in areas in which men are in the majority (such as Information Technology) would have a negative impact on the downward trend.

---

[31] Case study taken from *Monitoring Progress Towards Pay Equality*, Neathey, Dench & Thomson, Institute for Employment Studies, EOC 2003.

SECTION THREE: AN EQUAL PAY POLICY

THE ORGANISATION'S INTENTIONS IN RESPECT OF EQUAL PAY

86   It is good equal pay practice to provide employees with a clear statement of the organisation's intentions in respect of equal pay. Evidence of an equal pay policy may assist an employer's defence against an equal pay claim

87   It is recommended that an equal pay policy should:

- Commit the organisation to carry out an equal pay review and to monitor pay regularly in partnership with trade union/employee representatives
- Set objectives
- Identify the action to be taken
- Implement that action in a planned programme in partnership with the workforce
- Assign responsibility and accountability for the policy to a senior manager
- Commit the organisation to set aside the resources necessary to achieve equal pay.

88   Everyone involved in setting the pay of staff should be committed to and, if possible, trained in the identification of sex discrimination in the pay process.

We are committed to the principle of equal pay for all our employees. We aim to eliminate any sex bias in our pay systems.

We understand that equal pay between men and women is a legal right under both domestic and European law.

It is in the interest of the organisation to ensure that we have a fair and just pay system. It is important that employees have confidence in the process of eliminating sex bias and we are therefore committed to working in partnership with the recognised trade unions. As good business practice we are committed to working with trade union/employee representatives to take action to ensure that we provide equal pay.

We believe that in eliminating sex bias in our pay system we are sending a positive message to our staff and customers. It makes good business sense to have a fair, transparent reward system and it helps us to control costs. We recognise that avoiding unfair discrimination will improve morale and enhance efficiency.

Our objectives are to:

- Eliminate any unfair, unjust or unlawful practices that impact on pay
- Take appropriate remedial action.

We will:

- Implement an equal pay review in line with EOC guidance for all current staff and starting pay for new staff (including those on maternity leave, career breaks, or non-standard contracts)
- Plan and implement actions in partnership with trade union/employee representatives
- Provide training and guidance for those involved in determining pay
- Inform employees of how these practices work and how their own pay is determined
- Respond to grievances on equal pay as a priority
- In conjunction with trade union/employee representatives, monitor pay statistics annually.

[Annex A (Other legislation that may impact on pay), Annex B (Useful Addresses)] *Omitted for reasons of space*

Appendix 4

Code of Practice on Racial Equality in Employment

1 INTRODUCTION

1.1   This code replaces the statutory Code of Practice for the Elimination of Racial Discrimination and the Promotion of Equality of Opportunity in Employment, issued by the Commission for Racial Equality (CRE) in 1984 under the Race Relations Act 1976 (RRA).

1.2   References in this code to the RRA include all subsequent amending legislation.

1.3   The RRA gives the CRE a legal duty to:

   a.   work towards the elimination of racial discrimination and harassment;

   b.   promote equality of opportunity and good relations between people from different racial groups; and

   c.   keep under review the way the RRA is working, and, if necessary, make proposals to the secretary of state for amending it.

1.4   Section 47 of the RRA gives the CRE the power to issue codes of practice in the field of employment, and to give such practical guidance as it sees fit.

Purpose of the code

1.5   The purpose of this code is to:

   a.   give employers and principals (referred to in this code as 'employers') practical guidance on how to prevent unlawful racial discrimination, and achieve equality of opportunity in the field of employment;

   b.   help employers and others who have duties under the employment provisions of the RRA to understand their responsibilities and rights;

   c.   help lawyers and other advisers to advise their clients;

   d.   give employment tribunals and courts clear guidelines on good equal opportunities practice in employment; and

   e.   make sure anyone who is considering bringing legal proceedings under the RRA, or attempting to negotiate in the workplace, understands the legislation and is aware of good practice in the field of employment.

Status of the code

1.6   This code is a statutory code. This means it has been approved by the Secretary of State and laid before parliament. The code does not impose any legal obligations.

   Nor is it an authoritative statement of the law; only the courts and employment tribunals can provide this. However, the code can be used in evidence in legal proceedings brought under the RRA. Courts and tribunals must take account of any part of the code that might be relevant to a question arising during those proceedings.

1.7   Employers are liable for acts of unlawful racial discrimination or harassment by their workers. However, employers should be able to defend themselves better in any case of alleged racial discrimination brought against the organisation, if they can show they have taken the steps recommended in this code.

Application of the code

1.8 The RRA and this code apply to:

a. all employers in England, Scotland and Wales, whatever their size, resources or number of workers; Northern Ireland is covered by separate legislation;

b. certain organisations, such as employment and recruitment agencies (including online agencies), trade unions, professional associations, partnerships, accrediting bodies and vocational training organisations, in relation to their role as providers of services specifically covered by the RRA; and

c. applicants for employment, workers and former workers.

Public authorities

1.9 While the RRA applies to all employers, section 71(1) gives public authorities additional statutory duties (see paras 2.28–2.29). The aim is to make the promotion of racial equality central to their work. However, it should be emphasised that much of the guidance and good practice associated with these duties is relevant to all employers.

Smaller organisations

1.10 Some employers in smaller organisations may not need detailed procedures, such as some of those recommended in this code; for example, in the arrangements they make to monitor workers and applicants by racial group. The guidance may therefore need to be adapted, occasionally, to suit an organisation's individual circumstances. However, smaller organisations should note that employment tribunals have dismissed the argument that they should make allowance for the size or nature of a business in considering its liability for acts of unlawful racial discrimination or harassment by its workers. It is recommended that smaller organisations make sure their policies and practices are consistent with the RRA, and that they follow the general spirit and intentions of this code.

1.11 The CRE has produced a practical guide for this sector: Racial Equality and the Smaller Business: A practical guide. This guide recognises the heavy demands on the time and resources of smaller organisations, and suggests simple but effective procedures that should help ensure that everyone is treated fairly and equally.

Benefits of the code

1.12 This code should help employers to:

a. understand and meet their legal obligations;

b. adopt and put into practice effective policies, designed to prevent unlawful racial discrimination or harassment, and ensure equality of opportunity for all;

c. draw on the talents, skills, experience, networks and different cultural perspectives of a diverse workforce;

d. create a working environment where people feel they are respected and valued;

e. reduce the risks of legal liability, costly and time-consuming grievances and damage to productivity, staff morale and the organisation's reputation; and

f. foster good race relations in the workplace.

1.13 The code should also help workers and their representatives understand their rights under the RRA, and what constitutes good practice in the field of employment.

Appendix 4

Other areas of equality

1.14 This code is restricted by the terms of the RRA to matters concerning racial discrimination, and equality of opportunity in employment, between people from different racial groups. However, the principles of good practice may also be useful when promoting equality of opportunity generally, though the statutory requirements differ in other areas of equality.

1.15 Discrimination in employment on grounds of religion or belief is unlawful under the Employment Equality (Religion or Belief) Regulations 2003. However, if people affected by religious discrimination are from a particular racial group, the discrimination might also amount to indirect racial discrimination (see para 2.9).

How to use the code

1.16 The code has six chapters and seven appendices, as described below.

    a.   Following this introduction, Chapter 2 looks at the legal context and explains briefly the basic legal concepts used in the RRA.

    b.   Chapter 3 recommends a framework for action, based on drawing up an equal opportunities policy, and putting it into practice. The chapter concludes with advice for employers on promoting equality of opportunity in their roles as purchasers and suppliers of goods, facilities and services.

    c.   Chapter 4 makes recommendations on good employment practice in the main areas of employment, from recruitment to employers' responsibilities to former workers.

    d.   Chapter 5 considers the additional responsibilities that certain organisations, including trade unions, professional associations, employment and recruitment agencies, partnerships, accrediting bodies and vocational training organisations, have under the RRA in relation to the services they provide for their members, and for the public.

    e.   Chapter 6 is aimed at workers and draws together the corresponding rights and responsibilities they have under the RRA.

1.17 The seven appendices contain:

    a.   more detailed explanation of positive action and genuine occupational requirements and qualifications;

    b.   a sample policy on equal opportunities in employment;

    c.   a sample anti-harassment policy;

    d.   guidelines on job application forms;

    e.   a list of relevant organisations and websites;

    f.   a list of CRE publications; and

    g.   a glossary.

1.18 The examples in text boxes refer to cases that have been heard in employment tribunals or courts. The cases have been chosen because they illustrate a point, not because they have been won or lost. Other examples illustrate how a concept or policy is likely to be applied in practice, and should not be treated as complete or authoritative statements of the law.

1.19 Each chapter of the code forms part of an overall explanation of the RRA's provisions on employment. It is therefore important to read the code as a whole, in order to understand the law properly. The code should not be read too narrowly or literally. It is intended to explain the principles of the law, to illustrate how the RRA might operate in certain situations and to provide general guidance on good practice. The code should also not be seen as a substitute for seeking specialist advice on the possible legal consequences of particular situations.

2 THE LEGAL CONTEXT

2.1 The Race Relations Act 1976 (RRA) makes it unlawful to discriminate against, or harass, applicants for employment, workers and former workers, on racial grounds.

Racial grounds and racial groups

2.2 The RRA defines racial grounds as including race, colour, nationality (including citizenship) or ethnic or national origins. Racial groups are groups defined by those grounds. All racial groups are protected from unlawful racial discrimination or harassment under the RRA (see Example 1).

2.3 To comply with the EC Race Directive (2000/43/EC), the government introduced the Race Relations Act (Amendment) Regulations 2003, which give legal protection from racial discrimination and harassment on grounds of race or ethnic or national origins. Since the grounds protected under the original RRA (see para 2.2) differ from those protected under the Regulations, the amended RRA contains disparities in certain definitions and standards, such as indirect discrimination and harassment. However, this does not substantially affect the practical guidance given in this code.

Types of discrimination

2.4 The RRA defines four main types of unlawful discrimination:

a. direct discrimination;

b. indirect discrimination;

c. victimisation; and

d. harassment.

Direct discrimination [Section 1(1)(a) of the RRA]

2.5 Direct discrimination occurs when a person is treated less favourably, on racial grounds, than another person is or would be treated in the same or similar circumstances (see Example 2). Apart from limited exceptions (see paras 2.33–2.36) to the general prohibition of discrimination in the RRA, direct discrimination is automatically unlawful, whatever the reason for it. There can be no justification for the difference in treatment.

2.6 In considering whether there has been less favourable treatment, the employment tribunal will examine evidence of any disadvantage the complainant has suffered as a result of the alleged act of discrimination. This may include evidence that the person has been disciplined or dismissed, or any other evidence that shows that the circumstances in which the complainant has to continue to work are to her or his disadvantage (see Example 3).

531

Appendix 4

Example 1: Racial groups

BBC v Souster [2001] IRLR 150

Mr Souster, a presenter for BBC Scotland's Rugby Special, complained that he had lost his job because he was English and the BBC wanted a Scottish person. Mr Souster claimed that being English was a matter of national origins, while the BBC argued that, since both the Scots and the English share a British passport, there could be no unlawful discrimination between different parts of the one nation. The Scottish Court of Session, which had to decide whether the RRA applies to discrimination between the Scots and the English, ruled that national origins should be interpreted more broadly and flexibly than just by reference to a passport. As England and Scotland were once separate nations, the English and the Scots have separate national origins and therefore the RRA does cover discrimination between them.

On the question of whether the English and Scots are part of a 'racial group', the Court of Session followed the House of Lords' ruling in an earlier case *(Mandla v Dowell-Lee, [1983] IRLR 209)*, to the effect that '… it is possible for a person to fall into a particular racial group either by birth or by adherence'. The court also observed that, if the way the discriminator treats someone is based on her or his perception of that person's national or ethnic origins, then their actual origins, let alone their passport nationality, are irrelevant.

This definition of racial grounds clearly takes into account the complex reality of national identity, where a person may change their nationality by marriage or geographical migration or indeed simply by association, as well as the complexity of racial prejudice, where a person who discriminates may do so in complete ignorance of the victim's actual nationality or national background.

2.7   In cases alleging direct racial discrimination, the way a person has been treated will be compared with the way a person from a different racial group has been, or would be, treated in the same or similar circumstances. The courts have recognised that it may not always be possible to compare the alleged treatment with the treatment of an actual other person, and that a hypothetical comparison might have to be made with a person from a different racial group in a similar situation. The question to be asked is: 'how would a person from a different racial group be treated, in circumstances that are not identical, but not too dissimilar?' (see Example 4).

Example 2: Direct discrimination

Hussain v Alfred Brown (Worsted Mills) Ltd, Case No. 1805479/98

An Asian with 15 years' experience in textile work applied, for the fourth time, for a job as a warper at a textile mill, close to where he lived in Bradford. As before, he did not receive a reply to his application. However, his son, who had applied at the same time, in the name of J A Taylor, and as someone with ten years' experience, was called in for a trial. The employment tribunal upheld his father's claim that he had been discriminated against on racial grounds. The tribunal took account of the fact that, in four years, not one of the company's 70 workers had been from an ethnic minority group, even though the mill was very near Bradford, with its large ethnic minority population, many of whom had considerable skills in the textile trade. The complainant was awarded a total of around £7,000 in compensation, including £2,500 for injury to feelings.

532

Segregation [Section 1(2) of the RRA]

2.8   Segregating a person from others, on racial grounds, automatically means treating her or him less favourably, and constitutes unlawful direct discrimination. The segregation of workers, by racial group, will be unlawful even if they have the same access to promotion, training or pay and conditions as other workers.

Example 3: Proving less favourable treatment

Shamoon v Chief Constable of the Royal Ulster Constabulary (RUC) [2003] IRLR 285

When complaints were made about the appraisal reports written by a chief inspector at the RUC, her appraisal duties were withdrawn. Meanwhile, the other two chief inspectors at her grade continued to carry out appraisals. The RUC argued that carrying out appraisals was not a right, but, at most, a practice; that it was a small part of the complainant's duties; and that she did not suffer loss of rank or any financial disadvantage when the function was removed from her. The chief inspector brought legal proceedings under the Sex Discrimination Act 1975.

In an important case for all discrimination law, the House of Lords held that a reasonable employee might well feel demeaned, both in the eyes of those whom she managed and in the eyes of her colleagues, once it was known that a part of her normal duties had been taken away from her following a complaint. The House of Lords concluded that, if an employee reasonably believes that the circumstances in which they would have to continue to work would put them at a disadvantage, this would be sufficient to prove they had suffered a detriment.

Example 4: A hypothetical comparator

Balamoody v UK Central Council for Nursing, Midwifery and Health Visiting [2002] IRLR 288

The complainant, a Mauritian, was the owner of a nursing home. He was convicted in a magistrates' court of failures in relation to the administration of drugs and staffing at the home. As a result, the UK Central Council for Nursing, Midwifery and Health Visiting found him guilty of professional misconduct and struck him off its register. The complainant blamed his matron, a white woman, for the offences he had been convicted for. He complained that the disparity in their treatment – she had not faced disciplinary proceedings – was due to his race.

In a case of direct discrimination, one has to compare like with like (section 3(4) of the RRA). If the complainant can point to an actual person whose circumstances are sufficiently similar to his or her own, so much the better. In this case, the employment tribunal found that the matron was not an appropriate comparator, and dismissed the claim. The Employment Appeals Tribunal went on to uphold the tribunal's decision. However, the Court of Appeal held that both tribunals had made an error of principle: in those circumstances where it was not possible to find an actual comparator who had been treated less favourably, the tribunal would have to construct a hypothetical comparator, as a benchmark, to show how a person from other racial groups would have been treated. In this case, the court felt there was evidence to allow an inference that the council's refusal to reinstate the applicant on the register was racially discriminatory.

Appendix 4

Indirect discrimination [sections 1(1)(b) and 1(1A) of the RRA]

2.9   The RRA contains two definitions of indirect discrimination, depending on the grounds of discrimination. The definition of indirect discrimination introduced under section 1(1A) to comply with the EC Race Directive applies when the discrimination is on grounds of race or ethnic or national origins, but not colour or nationality. When the discrimination is on grounds of colour or nationality, the original definition under section 1(1)(b) applies (see Example 5).

      a.   *Grounds of race or ethnic or national origins* [section 1(1A) of the RRA]

          This occurs when a provision, criterion or practice which, on the face of it has nothing to do with race or ethnic or national origin, and is applied equally to everyone –

          i.   puts or would put people of a certain race or ethnic or national origins at a particular disadvantage when compared with others; and

          ii.   puts a person of that race or ethnic or national origins at that disadvantage; and

          iii.   cannot be shown to be a 'proportionate means of achieving a legitimate aim'.

      b.   *Grounds of colour or nationality* [section 1(1)(b) of the RRA]

          This occurs when an apparently non-discriminatory requirement or condition which applies equally to everyone –

          i.   can only be met by a considerably smaller proportion of people from a particular racial group than the proportion not from that group who can meet it; and

          ii.   cannot be justified on non-racial grounds; and

          iii.   puts a person from that group at a disadvantage because he or she cannot meet it.

Example 5: Indirect discrimination

Aina v Employment Service [2002] DCLD 103D

A Black African employee applied for the post of equal opportunities manager in his organisation. He was assessed as having the skills and ability for the job. However, his application was rejected because, unknown to him, the post was open only to permanent staff at higher grades than his. Monitoring data showed that the organisation had no permanent Black African employees at the grades in question. The employment tribunal held that there was no justification for the requirement, and that it amounted to indirect discrimination on racial grounds.

2.10   Although the definition of indirect discrimination introduced to meet the EC Race Directive does not apply to grounds of colour or nationality, in practice, a criterion that disadvantaged someone because of his or her colour would also be likely to disadvantage that person because of his or her race or ethnic or national origins.

      ■ **Example A.** A prohibition on workers wearing their hair in locks would disproportionately disadvantage black people, compared with white people, but this prohibition could also be challenged on grounds of ethnic or national origins, for example, Jamaican.

2.11 'Proportionate means' may be defined as means that are appropriate and necessary to achieve a legitimate business or other objective, such as meeting health and safety requirements (see also para 2.12).

> ■ **Example B.** A blanket ban on beards in a food packaging factory might not be a proportionate means of meeting health and safety requirements, if face masks could be used satisfactorily instead.

> ■ **Example C.** Y, a white English woman, applies for a job as a receptionist with a hospital trust in Wales. Under the Welsh Language Act 1993, the trust has drawn up a Welsh Language Scheme, which permits the trust to require applicants for posts involving the provision of services to the public to be able to speak Welsh, or to be prepared to learn it to an acceptable degree within six months. Y does not speak Welsh and is not prepared to learn it. She does not get the job and her complaint that she has been discriminated against on grounds of national origins fails, because the requirement is considered to be a reasonable means of achieving a legitimate aim. It should be noted that Y might have had a stronger case if the post she had applied for had been one of many receptionist posts at the hospital trust, or, if the trust had had enough Welsh-speaking receptionists to do the work. Meanwhile, W, a man of Pakistani origin, who also does not speak Welsh, successfully applies for a post in the trust's finance department; as the post does not involve contact with the public, it carries no Welsh language requirement.

2.12 The test of indirect discrimination is the same under both definitions; it involves drawing an objective balance between the discriminatory effects of the provision, criterion, practice, requirement or condition and the employer's reasonable need to apply it. When assessing the justification for policies and practices that could have a disproportionate effect on some racial groups, it would be useful to consider the following questions:

    a.   Does the provision, criterion, practice, requirement or condition correspond to a real need?

    b.   Does the need pursue a legitimate aim, for example health and safety?

    c.   Are the means used to achieve the aim appropriate and necessary?

    d.   Is there any other way of achieving the aim in question?

    e.   Is there a way of reducing any potentially unlawful discriminatory effect?

2.13 The concept of 'provision, criterion or practice', which was introduced to comply with the EC Race Directive, is broader and less restrictive than the concept of 'requirement or condition' in the original definition of indirect discrimination in the RRA. The concept of 'provision, criterion or practice' covers the full breadth of formal and informal practices in employment.

> ■ **Example D.** M, who is of Nigerian origin, is informed of a vacancy for a managing director. M phones and is told that the company's normal practice is to use head-hunters for recruitment to senior management posts. If M can show that this practice makes it more difficult for people of Nigerian origin than others to get senior management jobs in this company, and that this puts her at a disadvantage, the practice could amount to unlawful indirect discrimination.

Victimisation [Section 2 of the RRA]

2.14 It is unlawful to treat a person less favourably on racial grounds because he or she has:

    a.   brought proceedings under the RRA; or

Example 6: Victimisation

Mann v Gloucester County Council Fire and Rescue Services (1) and Gibb (2) [1997] Case No. 1400859/96

A complaint by an Asian fire fighter that the sub-officer in charge of the station had made racially derogatory remarks was initially upheld during the informal stage of an investigation, but later dismissed. The fire station's divisional officer made recommendations, to make sure there were no recriminations. However, almost immediately, the Asian fire fighter was 'sent to Coventry' and his colleagues refused to speak to him. The tribunal upheld his claim of unlawful victimisation, rejecting the fire authority's claim that it had taken all reasonably practicable steps to prevent this. The tribunal thought it was unrealistic of the authority to expect either of the parties, and everybody else concerned, to rise above the situation before a good deal of skilled counselling had been given to them all.

---

    b.   given evidence or information in connection with any proceedings under the RRA; or

    c.   alleged that an act of unlawful discrimination has been committed; or

    d.   done anything under the RRA in relation to someone, or intends to do so, or is suspected of having done or intending to do so.

2.15   For a claim of victimisation under the RRA to succeed, a complainant would also have to show that:

    a.   he or she has been or would have been treated less favourably, on racial grounds, than others in those circumstances; and

    b.   the treatment was a result of his or her action in relation to allegations or proceedings under the RRA.

Harassment [Section 3A(1) of the RRA]

2.16   The definition of harassment introduced by the 2003 Race Regulations applies when the conduct in question is on grounds of race or ethnic or national origins, but not colour or nationality. Harassment on grounds of colour or nationality involves less favourable treatment and may constitute unlawful direct discrimination (see Example 7, and Examples 19 and 20).

2.17   A person harasses another on grounds of race or ethnic or national origins when he or she engages in unwanted conduct that has the purpose or effect of:

    a.   violating the other person's dignity; or

    b.   creating an intimidating, hostile, degrading, humiliating or offensive environment for that person.

Harassment on grounds of colour or nationality may be recognisable by the same type of behaviour.

2.18   The definition of what is intimidating, hostile, degrading, humiliating or offensive is mainly a subjective one. In considering a claim of harassment, unless the conduct was intentionally hostile, it would only be considered to have the effects described above (see para 2.17) if, after considering all the circumstances, including, especially, the perceptions of the person affected, it was reasonable to do so. This means a court could decide that a complainant was oversensitive and had unreasonably taken offence.

Example 7: Harassment

Anisetti v Tokyo-Mitsubishi International plc Case No. 6002429/98

The Indian-born head of credit derivatives at an international Japanese bank in London resigned, claiming he had been made to feel like a 'second-class citizen' by his Japanese employers. He said he had been humiliated, excluded by workers speaking Japanese and underpaid, simply because he was not Japanese. The bank argued that it was 'natural' for Japanese staff to use their own language among themselves.

An employment tribunal upheld the complainant's claim that he had been discriminated against unlawfully, not because of his Indian national origins, but because he was not Japanese. The tribunal noted that the bank had maintained a practice which had effectively excluded the complainant from various activities, and treated him less favourably than others. The complainant was awarded around £1 million in compensation.

2.19 While the statutory definition of harassment in the RRA applies only to grounds of race or ethnic or national origins, and not to those of colour and nationality, in cases where abuse is overtly directed at a person's skin colour, employment tribunals and courts may interpret 'race' widely, to include colour.

2.20 Similarly, offensive behaviour in relation to a person's nationality may also be regarded as offensive on the grounds of that person's actual or perceived national origins (see Example 1), and would therefore be covered by the statutory definition of harassment in the RRA.

2.21 Employers should note that a single incident, for example a racist joke, on any racial grounds, could be sufficient to cause a person to feel harassed.

Discriminatory advertisements [Section 29 of the RRA]

2.22 It is unlawful to publish, or to be responsible for publishing, any advertisement (see the glossary at Appendix 7) that indicates, or may reasonably be understood to indicate, an intention to discriminate, even if the act of discrimination were lawful.

■ **Example E.** An advertisement in a local newspaper for a Turkish machinist for a dress manufacturing company would be unlawful.

2.23 The test for deciding whether an advertisement indicates an intention to discriminate is whether a reasonable person would consider it to be discriminatory. The definition of advertisement is very wide and includes any form of advertisement or notice, whether public or not; for example, internal circulars or newsletters announcing staff vacancies, emails, displays on notice boards or shop windows, and job advertisements, banners and pop-up windows on websites.

2.24 The RRA allows a small number of limited exceptions, where the advertisement refers to a situation where discrimination is not unlawful; for example, a lawful positive action training measure (see paras 2.33 and 3.43–3.45) or a genuine occupational qualification (see para 2.36). The advertisement should make it clear that the employer is making use of the exception.

Appendix 4

Example 8: Instructions to discriminate

Weathersfield Ltd t/a Van and Truck Rentals v Sargent [1999] IRLR 94

A white woman was told as part of an induction course for her new job as a receptionist that the company, a van and truck rental firm, had a special policy on ethnic minority customers. She was instructed to identify 'coloured or Asian callers' by the sound of their voice and to tell them there were no vehicles available. The woman was so upset by this that she resigned, giving her reasons in a letter. The Court of Appeal ruled that she had been discriminated against on racial grounds when she resigned in response to being given an instruction to discriminate against black and Asian customers.

Pressure to discriminate [Section 31 of the RRA]

2.25   It is unlawful to induce, or attempt to induce, a person to discriminate against, or harass, someone on racial grounds. The pressure may amount to no more than persuasion, and need not necessarily involve a benefit or loss. Nor does the pressure have to be applied directly; it is unlawful if it is applied in such a way that the other person is likely to hear of it. And it is unlawful in itself, even if the person who was put under pressure does not go on to commit an unlawful act of discrimination.

Instructions to discriminate [Section 30 of the RRA]

2.26   It is unlawful for a person who has authority over another person, or whose wishes that person normally follows, to instruct him or her to discriminate against, or harass, someone on racial grounds (see Example 8).

Aiding unlawful acts [Section 33 of the RRA]

2.27   A person who knowingly helps another person to discriminate against, or harass, someone unlawfully, on racial grounds, will be treated as having discriminated similarly themselves. Their only defence would be that they had been told the act would not be unlawful, and it was reasonable for them to believe that statement – it is an offence to make a reckless statement on such matters. In an employment situation, anything a worker does in the course of his or her employment is treated as having been done by his or her employer as well, whether or not the employer knew about it or approved of it. A person who knowingly takes part in an act of unlawful discrimination or harassment will therefore be deemed to have helped his or her employer in acting unlawfully.

Public authorities [Section 71 of the RRA]

2.28   Section 71(1) of the RRA gives public authorities listed in Schedule 1A to the RRA a statutory general duty to have 'due regard' to the need to eliminate unlawful racial discrimination, and to promote equality of opportunity and good relations between people from different racial groups, in carrying out all their functions.

2.29   Most public authorities bound by the general duty must also meet certain specific duties:

a.   to prepare and publish a race equality scheme or policy, which states how they will meet the general duty in the areas of policy and service delivery; and

b.   to monitor specified employment procedures and practices, by racial group (see paras 3.32–3.35).

2.30   The duty to promote race equality also applies to the procurement of goods, facilities and services. Where a public authority's function is carried out, wholly or in part, by an external supplier on its behalf, the authority remains responsible for meeting the duty. Contractors themselves must not discriminate unlawfully on racial grounds, but they do not have the same legal duty to promote equality of opportunity. This means public authorities should build racial equality considerations into the procurement process, to make sure any function that is relevant to the duty meets the requirements of the RRA, regardless of who is carrying out the function.

2.31   A statutory Code of Practice on the Duty to Promote Race Equality was laid before parliament, and came into effect in May 2002.

Burden of proof [Section 54A of the RRA]

2.32   As a result of the amendments required by the EC Race Directive, the burden of proof used by employment tribunals and courts will vary according to the grounds of the discrimination.

a.   *Grounds of race or ethnic or national origins* [section 54A of the RRA]

If a complainant can establish the facts from which an employment tribunal can conclude that an act of racial discrimination or harassment on grounds of race or ethnic or national origins has occurred, the employer will have to prove that any difference in treatment was not due in any way to discrimination or harassment. If the explanation is inadequate or unsatisfactory, the tribunal must find that unlawful discrimination or harassment has occurred.

b.   *Grounds of colour or nationality*

In cases where the discrimination is on grounds of colour or nationality, and section 54A does not therefore apply, if the complainant establishes facts from which an employment tribunal could conclude that he or she has suffered racial discrimination, the tribunal will ask the employer for an explanation. If the explanation is unsatisfactory, the tribunal may find that discrimination has occurred.

When racial discrimination is not unlawful

Positive action [Sections 35, 37 and 38 of the RRA]

2.33   The term 'positive action' refers to the measures that employers may lawfully take to provide access to facilities that meet special needs in relation to education and training or welfare, or to train or encourage people from a particular racial group that is under-represented in particular work (see also paras 3.43–3.45 and Example 10).

National security [Section 42 of the RRA]

2.34   An act of discrimination in employment, on racial grounds, may be permitted if it is done to safeguard national security, and if it can be justified.

Employment for training in skills to be used outside Britain [Section 6 of the RRA]

2.35   Employers may discriminate on grounds of colour or nationality, but not race or ethnic or national origins, in employing a person who does not normally live in Britain for work at an establishment in Britain, in order to train him or her in skills that will only be used outside Britain.

Appendix 4

Genuine occupational requirement and genuine occupational qualification [Sections 4A and 5 of the RRA]

2.36 It is lawful for an employer to discriminate on racial grounds in recruiting people for jobs where being of a particular race or ethnic or national origin is a 'genuine occupational requirement' (GOR), or being of a particular colour or nationality is a 'genuine occupational qualification' (GOQ).

3 THE RESPONSIBILITIES OF EMPLOYERS: A FRAMEWORK FOR ACTION

3.1 The Race Relations Act 1976 (RRA) gives employers a legal duty not to discriminate against or harass applicants for employment, workers (see the glossary at Appendix 7) and former workers, on racial grounds.

What the law says [Sections 4 and 4A of the RRA]

3.2 Employers must not discriminate on racial grounds or subject a person to harassment in:

   a.   the arrangements they make to decide who should be offered employment; or

   b.   the terms on which they offer to employ a person; or

   c.   by refusing or deliberately failing to offer employment.

3.3 It is also unlawful for employers to discriminate on racial grounds against a worker, or to subject him or her to harassment:

   a.   in the terms of employment provided; or

   b.   in the way they make opportunities for training, promotion or transfer, or other benefits, facilities or services, available; or

   c.   by refusing access to such opportunities or benefits, facilities or services; or

   d.   by dismissing the worker or subjecting him or her to some other detriment.

Legal responsibility for discrimination [Sections 32 and 33 of the RRA]

3.4 Legal responsibility for unlawful racial discrimination rests with employers. Discriminatory acts or conduct by workers or agents (for example, contractors) 'in the course of their employment' are treated as having been done by their employer (see also para 2.27), unless the employer can show he or she has taken all reasonably practicable steps to prevent such acts. Employers may be held liable whether or not those acts were done with their knowledge or approval. An employer's liability for racial discrimination may extend to a worker's behaviour when 'off duty', but in a work-related situation, such as a social event for staff, for example a Christmas party. In relation to the police, chief officers will be liable for acts of unlawful racial discrimination or harassment by police officers.

3.5 A worker who discriminates against, or harasses, someone, on racial grounds, in the course of his or her employment may be personally liable for his or her actions. Under the RRA, the employer will also be liable, unless he or she can show that all reasonably practical steps were taken to prevent unlawful racial discrimination or harassment. In this case, the worker may be solely liable for the unlawful act.

3.6 It is unlawful to discriminate against a former worker, on racial grounds, or to subject him or her to harassment, after the employment relationship has come to an end, if the discrimination or harassment has arisen from, or is closely connected with, the employment.

A FRAMEWORK FOR ACTION

3.7 Good employment practice is the key to employers meeting their legal responsibilities, and avoiding claims of racial discrimination or harassment. Employers need to make sure no worker (past, present or future) is treated less favourably than others, on racial grounds.

3.8 A systematic approach to developing and maintaining good practice is the best way of showing that an organisation is taking its legal responsibilities seriously. To help employers and others meet their legal obligations, it is recommended that they:

    a.   draw up an equal opportunities policy in employment; and

    b.   put the equal opportunities policy in employment into practice.

3.9 The policy may apply to all types of equality of opportunity covered by legislation, but it needs to make explicit reference to racial equality and consider all the ways in which employers are likely to be affected by the provisions of the RRA.

A. Draw up an equal opportunities policy on employment

3.10 The aim of an equal opportunities policy in employment is to make sure that:

    a.   no job applicant or worker receives less favourable treatment than another, on racial grounds;

    b.   no job applicant or worker is placed at a disadvantage by requirements, provisions, criteria, conditions or practices, unless they can be justified as a necessary and appropriate means of achieving a legitimate aim; and

    c.   people from under-represented racial groups are given training and encouragement to take equal advantage of opportunities in the organisation.

3.11 An equal opportunities policy in employment should be a written policy, which sets out:

    a.   the employer's commitment to the principle of equality;

    b.   the organisation's ethos and values;

    c.   how the policy applies to the organisation's procedures and practice;

    d.   what is and what is not acceptable behaviour at work;

    e.   how to use the organisation's complaints procedure to raise any concerns or complaints workers might have about discrimination or harassment;

    f.   the rights and responsibilities of all; and

    g.   how the organisation will deal with any breaches of the policy.

3.12 The policy should cover all aspects of employment, including recruitment, terms and conditions of work, training and development, promotion, performance, grievance, discipline and treatment of workers when their contract of employment ends.

3.13 As far as possible, the equal opportunities policy should be drawn up and agreed in consultation with workers and any recognised trade unions or other workplace representatives.

3.14 [refers to an appendix to this Code of Practice not reproduced here for reasons of space].

Appendix 4

B. Put the equal opportunities policy into practice

3.15　Employment tribunals have made it clear that statements of intent or paper policies and procedures alone are unlikely to provide employers with a defence in legal proceedings under the RRA. This means employers need to be able to show that they take their equal opportunities policy seriously, and put it into operation in all aspects of employment in the organisation (see Examples 9 and 10).

3.16　The most systematic, practical and effective way of approaching this is to draw up an equal opportunities action plan. Its aims should be to:

 a. promote the equal opportunities policy;

 b. make sure all workers understand the policy, and provide training for those who have particular responsibilities under it;

 c. monitor workers and applicants for employment, promotion and training, by racial group, and review all employment policies, procedures and practices, to see if they are potentially discriminatory or obstruct equality of opportunity; and

 d. take steps to remove potentially unlawful discrimination, and reduce any significant disparities between racial groups.

Promote the equal opportunities policy

3.17　The equal opportunities policy in employment should be publicised as widely as possible, for example through office notice boards, circulars, email bulletins, contracts of employment, training on equality, induction, internal and external websites, annual reports and staff newsletters and handbooks.

3.18　The policy should be a priority for the organisation, and an essential part of its business or corporate plan. The policy will carry greater force if it has the explicit backing of the chair or director or proprietor, and the board and senior management (where applicable).

3.19　Overall responsibility for the policy, and for reporting regularly on its effectiveness, should rest with a senior manager (where applicable).

Train workers on the equal opportunities policy

3.20　Employers should make sure all their workers understand the organisation's equal opportunities policy, and how it affects them, and that they are aware of any plans for putting it into practice. This could be done by providing basic training and providing written information and guidance on the policy and plan. Some workers may need more advanced training, depending on their jobs. Equal opportunities should also be a standard component of other training courses, at all levels.

Example 9: Putting policy into practice

Baptiste v Westminster Press Ltd t/a Bradford and District Newspapers, Case No. 35945/96 [1996] DCLD 30

An unsuccessful black applicant for a post in the advertising department of a newspaper was told at the interview for the job that the phrase 'black bastard' was commonly used in the organisation. The tribunal dismissed the company's two-page equal opportunities policy and one page code of practice as a classic example of employers believing that the preparation of such documents alone, without any supporting advice or instructions to managers on implementing or monitoring them, was sufficient to meet their legal obligations. The complainant was awarded a total of around £12,000 in compensation.

Example 10: Interview

Umerji v Blackburn Borough Council, Case No. 29273/94 [1995] DCLD 47

An Asian part-time worker on a short-term contract with a local council was one of six candidates interviewed by a panel for the full-time post of welfare officer with the council. He performed better than any of the other candidates, scoring higher than a white council worker. The panel agreed to offer the Asian applicant the job. The panel subsequently reversed its decision and decided to offer the post to the white worker. According to the council, the Asian applicant was not selected because he had failed to meet the criterion of 'written communication' skills, which only became apparent when the application forms were considered after the interview process.

The tribunal upheld the Asian worker's claim of unlawful racial discrimination. It found that he had not only achieved the highest score in both the test of his technical ability and in the interview as a whole, but had also overcome the 'hurdle' of the application form, by being put on the shortlist in the first place. Further, as a council worker, his 'written communication' skills were well known to his employer. The tribunal found the council's replies to the race relations questionnaire to be 'evasive and/or equivocal', and rejected its explanations as 'a cover-up'.

The tribunal criticised the council for failing to follow its own equal opportunities and selection procedures: 'It is quite pointless for the respondent to go to the trouble and expense of creating an elaborate selection procedure and an elaborate equal opportunities policy, if it then breaches that procedure and the policy by following an entirely separate procedure, directed apparently by events, and by the personal whim of individual officers.' The tribunal awarded compensation of around £14,000.

3.21 The training will benefit from consulting workers and their representatives about their needs, and incorporating feedback from any training into future courses.

3.22 Employers should make sure in-house trainers are themselves trained before running courses for other staff. External trainers also need to be fully informed about the organisation's policies, including its equal opportunities policy.

3.23 Employers will find it helpful to give a named manager responsibility for equal opportunities training in the organisation.

3.24 In the event of legal proceedings being brought against them under the RRA, employers may find it easier to defend themselves if they are able to show that the basic equal opportunities training all workers receive includes the following:

a.   the law against racial discrimination and harassment;

b.   the organisation's equal opportunities policy, why it has been introduced and how it will be put into practice;

c.   what is acceptable and unacceptable conduct in the workplace;

d.   workers' responsibilities under the equal opportunities policy to maintain and promote a workplace free of unlawful racial discrimination and harassment; and

e.   how prejudice can affect the way an organisation functions, and the effects that generalisations about racial groups, and bias in day-to-day operations, can have on people's chances of obtaining work, promotion, recognition and respect.

Appendix 4

Example 11: Monitoring

Richards v Brighton Borough Council [1992] Case No. 14213/91 and EAT 431/92 [1993] DCLD 19

A black woman, who had been turned down for the post of information officer in a council's housing department, in favour of a white woman with much less relevant work experience, won her claim of racial discrimination against the council. The tribunal noted the council's failure to monitor its equal opportunities policy.

Monitor workers and applicants by racial group, and review all employment policies, procedures and practices

3.25 Monitoring, by racial group, gives employers the information they need to understand how their policies, practices and procedures in the field of employment affect people from different racial groups.

3.26 Monitoring is a process that involves collecting, analysing and evaluating information, to measure performance, progress and change. It can be done in several ways, including questionnaires, surveys, consultation and feedback. Monitoring, by racial group, will allow employers to:

    a.   determine the composition of their workforce, by racial group, and compare this information with benchmarks, such as census data;

    b.   know how their workforce is distributed across the organisation, by location, type of job and grade;

    c.   uncover any disparities between racial groups, in the workforce as a whole and at different levels of the organisation, and investigate the underlying causes;

    d.   find out whether people from certain racial groups are typically taking longer to obtain promotion;

    e.   examine whether the practices, provisions, criteria, requirements or conditions used to select candidates for employment, training and promotion might be indirectly discriminatory, and why, and consider how they might be changed to avoid any negative effects on candidates from a particular racial group (or groups);

    f.   set realistic targets and timetables for reducing any significant racial disparities, both within the workforce as a whole, and at different levels of the organisation;

    g.   send a clear message to its workers, and to job seekers, that the organisation is serious about achieving fair and equitable participation, and encourage them to cooperate fully; and

    h.   judge whether the equal opportunities policy is achieving its aims.

3.27 Monitoring, by racial group, should cover the following:

    a.   applications for jobs, temporary and permanent, advertised and non-advertised, and success rates at each stage of the process;

    b.   distribution of workers in the organisation, by type of job, location, and grade;

    c.   applications for promotion, transfer and training, and success rates for each;

    d.   results of performance appraisals;

e.   grievances and disciplinary action, including the results, and tribunal decisions involving claims of racial discrimination or harassment; and

f.   terminations of contract (for whatever reason).

3.28   Section 8 of the RRA gives the meaning of employment at an establishment in Great Britain. Employers who have operations or subsidiaries in other countries, or who have outsourced functions to other countries, need to make arrangements to keep their monitoring data for workers at establishments in Great Britain separate (or in a form that is readily identifiable).

> ■ **Example F.** A bank outsources its payroll function to a company in Manila. It transfers a senior manager to Manila from its office in London, to oversee the work. The bank would include the senior manager, but not the payroll workers in Manila, in the monitoring data it keeps to meet the recommendations of this code.

3.29   The information needed for effective monitoring may be obtained in a number of ways. The best course is to ask workers and applicants for jobs, training and promotion to select the racial group they want to be associated with from a list of categories. The 2001 census provides the most comprehensive and reliable data about the population in England, Scotland and Wales, increasingly supplemented by the Labour Force Survey and other survey statistics. Employers should therefore use categories that are compatible with those used in the 2001 census. Employers who wish to include a group that is not separately listed in the census classification should add the group as a sub-group of the appropriate main group in the census classification system. For example, Somali would be a sub-group of Other in the broad Black or Black British category, Sikh a sub-group of Indian in the Asian or Asian British category, and Roma/Gypsy a sub-group of Other in the White category. In response to increasing national consciousness in England, Scotland and Wales, employers may also want to consider offering workers and applicants the opportunity to classify themselves in terms of a national identity. It is important to remember that any aggregation of data, especially when the numbers are small, risks masking significant disparities between sub-groups, for example between Indian and Bangladeshi, if they are considered only as part of the broad Asian group.

3.30   Smaller organisations may only need a simple method of collecting information about workers' and job applicants' racial groups, such as a questionnaire. Larger organisations are likely to need more sophisticated procedures and computerised systems as well, to capture the full picture across their subsidiaries and branches in Britain.

3.31   To ensure the integrity of their monitoring systems, employers should consider the following steps:

a.   consult workers, trade unions and other representatives in the workplace, and make sure they understand the reasons for introducing monitoring, before asking workers for information about their racial group;

b.   assure everyone concerned that information about ethnic or racial background will be treated in the strictest confidence;

c.   analyse the information regularly, preferably together with other available information, for example, on sex, sexual orientation, disability, religion or belief, or age;

d.   review the information periodically, and make sure it is current; and

e.   make sure managers responsible for monitoring, and anyone else involved in the process, are properly trained in data protection and sensitive data processing.

Appendix 4

Public authorities and monitoring

3.32   Most of the public authorities bound by the statutory general duty to promote race equality (see paras 2.28–2.29) also have a specific duty to monitor, by racial group, all their workers, and all applicants for jobs, promotion and training. Public authorities with 150 or more full-time-equivalent workers must also monitor the number of workers from each racial group who:

   a.   receive training;

   b.   benefit or suffer detriment from performance assessment;

   c.   are involved in grievances;

   d.   are subject to disciplinary action; and

   e.   end employment with the organisation (for whatever reason).

3.33   Public authorities must publish the results of this monitoring each year.

3.34   Educational institutions are not bound by the specific duty for public authorities as employers. However, schools do have to give their local education authorities (education authorities in Scotland) information about staff, so that the authorities can meet their duty to monitor, by racial group, employment in the schools they manage, and publish a report on it each year. Further and higher education institutions have a specific duty to monitor, by racial group, the recruitment of staff and their career progress. They are also expected to take reasonable and practicable steps to publish the results of their monitoring each year.

3.35   A statutory *Code of Practice on the Duty to Promote Race Equality* was laid before parliament and came into effect in May 2002. The CRE has also produced nonstatutory guidance for public authorities on different aspects of the duty.

Take steps to prevent unlawful discrimination, and reduce any significant disparities between racial groups

3.36   If the monitoring data show significant disparities between racial groups, employers should investigate the possible causes, and examine all the arrangements, procedures and practices that give effect to their policies in the field of employment, including recruitment, training, promotion, grievance and discipline, performance assessment and dismissal. The absence of disparities for ethnic minorities as a whole, or for one racial group in particular (see para 3.29), should not be taken as evidence that 'discrimination is not a problem'. The aim should be to make sure none of the rules, requirements, procedures or practices used, formally or informally, put any racial groups at a significant disadvantage; for example, indirectly discriminatory eligibility rules for promotion, or restrictive advertising techniques. It is recommended that employers approach this as systematically as possible, taking the following steps:

   a.   review the selection criteria used, to make sure they are strictly related to the job or training opportunity, and do not have an unjustifiable adverse effect on any racial groups;

   b.   examine all decision-making processes, to make sure they are fair, and are followed consistently across the full range of recruitment and assessment exercises;

   c.   review the policy on advertising jobs, and training and promotion opportunities, to make sure the information is reaching any under-represented groups, and that people from these groups feel encouraged to apply;

d.   reassess the labour markets from which they traditionally recruit;

e.   set targets (see paras 3.38–3.42) for employment, training and promotion, as part of a programme of action to reduce any significant disparities between racial groups, and regularly review progress; and

f.   consider whether lawful positive action might be appropriate.

3.37   Larger employers may find it useful to:

a.   nominate a person with specialist knowledge of discrimination and equality to monitor the effectiveness of the organisation's equal opportunities policy, conduct independent investigations of complaints of discrimination and harassment, and advise on, and coordinate, action; and

b.   encourage their branches or subsidiaries to draw up and implement their own equal opportunities action plan, against standards set and controlled centrally.

Racial equality targets

3.38   Employers could consider setting racial equality targets as a means of planning the reduction of any significant disparities between racial groups. A racial equality target could represent improvements in representation for particular racial groups or progress towards equality of treatment. For example, it could show the percentage of workers from a particular racial group (or groups) that an organisation is aiming to have in particular areas or types of work within a certain period of time; or a reduction or elimination of any unfavourable disparity in assessment ratings between racial groups over a certain period of time.

3.39   Racial equality targets are not quotas. Restricting recruitment to people from particular racial groups, in order to improve their representation in the workforce, would be positive discrimination. This is unlawful in Britain. All selection for employment must be, and be seen to be, fair, and based solely on merit.

3.40   Racial equality targets for recruitment, promotion and training should be based on the ethnic and racial composition of the area from which an organisation decides to recruit for particular jobs, and on the ethnic and racial composition of its own workforce. Progress towards racial equality targets can then be monitored against the steps being taken, including positive action training and encouragement (see paras 3.43–3.45 and Appendix 1), to make recruitment and other employment policies and practices fairer and more equal.

3.41   Employers should consider publishing their racial equality targets, for example, in their annual reports, to show how their organisation is working towards fair participation.

3.42   Employers should base their corporate priorities, objectives, approaches and any racial equality targets on the outcomes listed below.

a.   The ethnic and racial composition of the workforce, at each location and level, reflects the composition of the labour markets used for different types of work.

b.   Vacancies attract applications from the full range of qualified candidates in the relevant labour markets, including candidates from ethnic minorities.

c.   The ratio of appointments to applications is proportionate across all racial groups.

d.   The organisation's board and senior management team (where applicable) reflect the ethnic and racial backgrounds of all potential candidates, both internally and externally.

e. Workers from all racial groups are equally likely to apply for, and be offered, training.

f. Applications for promotion and deputising are received from across the full spectrum of workers, irrespective of racial group.

g. Workers spend the same length of time at a particular grade, on average, irrespective of racial group.

h. Progress from one grade to another is unaffected by workers' racial groups.

i. Workers are not disproportionately subject to disciplinary proceedings because of their racial group.

j. Workers from all racial groups benefit equally from bonuses or performance pay.

k. Grievances are not more likely to be brought by workers from particular racial groups.

l. The number of complaints alleging racial discrimination or harassment is negligible.

m. There are no significant disparities between racial groups among staff leaving the organisation, for whatever reason.

Positive action [Sections 35, 37 and 38 of the RRA]

3.43 The RRA recognises that, due to past discrimination or other disadvantages, people from particular racial groups may not have fully realised their potential, and may not have the qualifications or experience to make them eligible for particular jobs. The aim of positive action, as permitted under the RRA, is to give people from a particular racial group (or groups) the opportunity to compete for work in which they have been under-represented or absent. The RRA also allows action to be taken to make facilities or services, such as language classes or training or education in basic work skills, available for people from a particular racial group (or groups) who would otherwise be excluded from opportunities.

3.44 If the results of monitoring show under-representation, or the complete absence of a racial group (or groups) in particular work, for example among senior managers or shop floor supervisors, it is recommended that employers take the following steps:

a. consider positive action training or encouragement;

b. make sure the positive action scheme offers only training or encouragement, and not employment – employers making use of the positive action provisions of the RRA should be especially careful that the training or encouragement provided as a form of positive action does not constitute employment, or lead automatically to employment; for example, 'on-the-job' training or apprenticeships, which are defined as employment, and not training, cannot form part of a positive action programme (see Example 12 below); and

c. inform workers, trade unions and other workplace representatives about their plans, explaining that the aim of positive action training or encouragement is to help create a level playing field, not to favour any particular racial group.

■ **Example G.** A national broadcaster used section 37 of the RRA to set up a mentoring scheme for would-be sports journalists. The scheme gave 12 young people from ethnic minorities a year's training and work placements in the sports broadcasting department, leading to a postgraduate certificate in broadcast journalism from a leading institution. Twelve specially selected and trained senior managers from the sports department were matched with the trainees.

Example 12: Positive action

Hughes and others v London Borough of Hackney (unreported) [1986]

A local authority included a statement in an advertisement for gardening apprentices encouraging young people from 'black and ethnic minorities' to apply, and referring to section 38 of the RRA. Three white people applied for the jobs and were told they were open only to people from ethnic minorities. The employment tribunal upheld their claims that they had been unlawfully discriminated against on racial grounds, pointing out that 'encouragement' under the positive action provisions of the RRA did not extend to providing job opportunities for any section of the community.

3.45 Positive action may, and should, be used to encourage or train workers to compete for jobs where they are under-represented (section 38 of the RRA).

Equal opportunities conditions in contracts

3.46 Employers should encourage companies and other organisations, with whom they have, or propose to enter into, contracts for goods, facilities or services, to take practical steps to promote equality of opportunity in their employment practices. Employers should therefore:

    a.   make acceptance on tender lists, and the award or renewal of a contract, conditional on the organisation's providing information about any findings of racial discrimination or harassment, and adopting the recommendations of this code;

    b.   include terms and conditions in contracts that require contractors to follow the recommendations of this code; and

    c.   encourage individuals and organisations from under-represented racial groups to tender or compete for contracts.

3.47 Most public authorities have a legal duty to promote race equality when carrying out their functions (see also paras 2.28–2.31). The duty applies whether they carry out these functions themselves or contract them out to private businesses or voluntary organisations. While bound by the RRA's general prohibition of unlawful racial discrimination, private businesses and voluntary organisations are not bound by the duty. Public authorities therefore need to make arrangements during the tendering process, and through the contract itself, to make sure contractors are able to meet the duty on their behalf, if it applies to the goods, works, facilities or services being contracted out. The CRE has produced guides to procurement for local authorities and other public authorities.

Appendix 5

Code of Practice on the Duty to Promote Racial Equality

1 INTRODUCTION

1.1 The Race Relations Act places a general duty on a wide range of public authorities to promote race equality. This duty means that authorities must have due regard to the need to:

   a. eliminate unlawful racial discrimination;

   b. promote equality of opportunity; and

   c. promote good relations between people of different racial groups.

1.2 Most public authorities are bound by this duty. Many of them provide major public services, such as education or health. Some of them (for example professional representative organisations, such as the Royal College of Surgeons, or broadcasting authorities) are bound by this duty only so far as their public functions are concerned.

1.3 The duty aims to make the promotion of race equality central to the way public authorities work. Promoting race equality will improve the way public services are delivered for everyone. In most cases, these authorities should be able to use their existing arrangements – such as those for policy making – to meet the duty's requirements. This should help to avoid any unnecessary or duplicated work.

Benefits of the duty

1.4 The duty will help public authorities to make steady progress in achieving race equality. In relation to policy development and service delivery, the duty will:

   a. encourage policy makers to be more aware of possible problems;

   b. contribute to more informed decision making;

   c. make sure that policies are properly targeted;

   d. improve the authority's ability to deliver suitable and accessible services that meet varied needs;

   e. encourage greater openness about policy making;

   f. increase confidence in public services, especially among ethnic minority communities;

   g. help to develop good practice; and

   h. help to avoid claims of unlawful racial discrimination.

1.5 The duty of public authorities to promote race equality in employment will:

   a. help to make the authority's workforce more representative of the communities it serves;

   b. attract able staff;

   c. avoid losing or undervaluing able staff;

   d. improve staff morale and productivity;

   e. improve the way staff are managed;

550

f.   help to develop good practice; and

g.   help to avoid claims of unlawful racial discrimination.

Purpose of the code

1.6   Public authorities can decide how they will meet their duty to promote race equality. The Race Relations Act gives the CRE the power to issue codes of practice, with the approval of Parliament.

1.7   This code offers practical guidance to public authorities on how to meet their duty to promote race equality. It includes guidance on both the general duty (see 1.1) and specific duties imposed by the Home Secretary. The code's aim is to help public authorities to adopt good practice and to eliminate racial discrimination. The code should also help the public understand what public authorities have to do, and the role that the public can play.

1.8   The specific duties imposed by order of the Home Secretary came into effect on **3 December 2001**. Public authorities bound by these duties were required to have properly timetabled and realistic plans for meeting these duties in place by **31 May 2002**.

1.9   This code applies to public authorities in England and Wales and to 'non-devolved' public authorities in Scotland. Chapter 6 of this code applies only to the governing bodies of educational institutions in England and Wales. The Code of Practice for Scotland will apply to devolved public authorities in Scotland.

Nature of the code

1.10   This code of practice is a 'statutory' code. This means that it has been approved by Parliament. It also means that the code is admissible in evidence in any legal action, and a court or tribunal should take the code's recommendations into account. On its own, the code does not place any legal obligations on public authorities. It is not a complete statement of the law, as only the courts can give this. If a public authority does not follow the code's guidance, it may need to be able to show how it has otherwise met its legal obligations under the general duty and any specific duties.

How to use the code

1.11   The code is divided into five parts, seven chapters and six appendices.

a.   Part I (chapters 2 and 3) applies to all listed public authorities, including schools, and further and higher education institutions.

b.   Part II (chapters 4 and 5) deals with promoting race equality in certain public authorities other than educational institutions.

c.   Part III (chapter 6) deals with promoting race equality in educational institutions.

d.   Part IV (chapter 7) deals with the CRE's role, including enforcing this code.

e.   Part V (appendices 1 to 6) lists the public authorities that are bound by the general duty (appendix 1), the public authorities that are required to publish a race equality scheme (appendix 2), the public authorities bound by the employment duty (appendix 3), the public authorities bound by the duties for educational institutions (appendix 4), Scottish public authorities (appendix 5), and other guidance published by the CRE (appendix 6).

Appendix 5

2   THE LEGAL FRAMEWORK

2.1   The Race Relations Act defines direct and indirect discrimination, and victimisation. It outlaws racial discrimination in employment, training, education, housing, public appointments, and the provision of goods, facilities and services. The Race Relations (Amendment) Act 2000 came into force on 2 April 2001 and since then the Race Relations Act (the Act) has covered all the functions of public authorities (with just a few exceptions).

2.2   Section 71(1) of the Act places a general duty on listed public authorities. The Act also gives the Home Secretary power to make orders placing specific duties on all or some of these authorities (section 71(2)). Scottish ministers have a similar power over Scottish public authorities (section 71B(1)). Under the Race Relations Act 1976 (Statutory Duties) Order 2001, the specific duties discussed in this code came into force on **3 December 2001**.

2.3   The Act gives the CRE enforcement powers over the specific duties imposed by the Home Secretary and Scottish ministers. The Act also gives the CRE power to issue codes of practice containing practical guidance on how public authorities can meet the general duty and specific duties. This is a statutory code, issued for this purpose.

The general duty to promote race equality

2.4   This general duty applies to all public authorities listed in Schedule 1A to the Act. The duty's aim is to make the promotion of race equality central to the work of the listed public authorities.

Specific duties to promote race equality

2.5   Specific duties have been placed on some public authorities responsible for delivering important public services. The duties involve making arrangements that will help these authorities to meet the general duty to promote race equality.

    a.   The public authorities listed in appendix 2 [not reproduced here] must prepare and publish a race equality scheme. This scheme should set out the 'functions' or 'policies' that are relevant to meeting the general duty, and the arrangements that will help to meet the duty in the areas of policy and service delivery.

    b.   The public authorities listed in appendix 3 [not reproduced here] must monitor their employment procedures and practice. Some of these authorities have to produce a race equality scheme. They may find it useful to include the arrangements they make to meet their employment duties in their race equality schemes.

    c.   The educational institutions listed in appendix 4 [not reproduced here] have to prepare a race equality policy and put in place arrangements for meeting their specific duties on policy and employment.

2.6   Public authorities that introduce effective arrangements, as required under the specific duties, should be able to show that they are meeting the general duty to promote race equality. Taking action to promote race equality should give authorities the evidence they need to show that they are meeting the general duty.

2.7   Chapters 4, 5, and 6 give guidance on the specific duties.

Liability under the Race Relations Act

2.8   Public authorities are responsible for meeting their general and specific duties. Within each public authority, this responsibility will rest with the groups or individuals who are liable (legally responsible) for the authority's acts or failure to act.

Private or voluntary organisations carrying out a public authority's functions

2.9   When a public authority has a contract or other agreement with a private company or voluntary organisation to carry out any of its functions, and the duty to promote race equality applies to those functions, the public authority remains responsible for meeting the general duty and any specific duties that apply to those functions. The authority should therefore consider the arrangements it will need. If the authority's race equality duties are relevant to the functions it is contracting out, it may be appropriate to incorporate those duties among the performance requirements for delivery of the service. For example, a contractor could be required to monitor service users by their racial group, to make sure the authority is meeting its duties. This would not involve requirements concerning the contractor's internal practices. Whatever action the authority takes, it must be consistent with the policy and legal framework for public procurement.

2.10   In addition to specifications for the general duty and any specific duties, public authorities may promote race equality by encouraging contractors to draw up policies that will help them (contractors) to avoid unlawful discrimination, and promote equality of opportunity. Such encouragement should only be within a voluntary framework, once contracts have been awarded, rather than by making specific criteria or conditions part of the selection process. Public authorities should bear in mind that the general duty does not override other laws or regulations on public procurement. In particular, as above, whatever action the authority takes must be consistent with the policy and legal framework for public procurement.

Partnership

2.11   Public authorities should take account of their general duty to promote race equality – and any specific duties – when they work with other public, private or voluntary organisations. There is no similar obligation on private or voluntary-sector partners.

2.12   Public authorities that are involved in partnership work with other public authorities, or with private or voluntary-sector organisations, are still responsible for meeting their general duty to promote race equality, and any specific duties.

2.13   In practice, this will mean that a public authority working within a partnership will need to seek agreement from its partners to arrangements for planning, funding and managing joint work that will allow it to meet its statutory race equality duties. Public authorities should reflect their partnership work in their race equality schemes.

Inspecting and auditing public authorities

2.14   Agencies that audit or inspect public authorities are bound by the duty to promote race equality. These agencies need to consider how the duty fits with their inspection or audit obligations. In most cases, inspection and audit bodies should be able to use their existing inspection arrangements to promote race equality.

Appendix 5

3   THE GENERAL DUTY

3.1   This chapter explains what public authorities can do to meet the general duty to promote race equality. The duty is set out in section 71(1) of the Race Relations Act (the Act) and it applies to every public authority listed in Schedule 1A to the Act (see appendix 1 of this code). Section 71(1) says:

> Every body or other person specified in Schedule 1A or of a description falling within that Schedule shall, in carrying out its functions, have due regard to the need
>
> a) to eliminate unlawful racial discrimination; and
>
> b) to promote equality of opportunity and good relations between persons of different racial groups.*

---

* For immigration and nationality functions, the general duty does not include the words 'equality of opportunity and' (section 71A(1)).

Guiding principles

3.2   Four principles should govern public authorities' efforts to meet their duty to promote race equality.

   a.   Promoting race equality is obligatory for all public authorities listed in Schedule 1A to the Act.

   b.   Public authorities must meet the duty to promote race equality in all relevant functions.

   c.   The weight given to race equality should be proportionate to its relevance.

   d.   The elements of the duty are complementary (which means they are all necessary to meet the whole duty).

'Obligatory'

3.3   Public authorities listed in Schedule 1A to the Act must make race equality a central part of their functions (such as planning, policy making, service delivery, regulation, inspection, enforcement, and employment). The general duty does not tell public authorities how to do their work, but it expects them to assess whether race equality is relevant to their functions. If it is, the authority should do everything it can to meet the general duty. The duty should underpin all policy and practice, and it should encourage improvement. It is not necessarily a new responsibility for the authority, just a more effective way of doing what it already does.

'Relevant'

3.4   Race equality will be more relevant to some functions than others. Relevance is about how much a function affects people, as members of the public or as employees of the authority. For example, a local authority may decide that race equality is more relevant to raising educational standards than to its work on highway maintenance. Public authorities should therefore assess whether, and how, race equality is relevant to each of their functions. A public authority may decide that the general duty does not apply to some of its functions; for example those that are purely technical, such as traffic control or weather forecasting.

'Proportionate'

3.5   Under section 71(1) of the Act, public authorities are expected to have 'due regard' to the three parts of the duty to promote race equality (see 1.1). This means that the weight given to race equality should be proportionate to its relevance to a particular function. In practice, this approach may mean giving greater consideration and resources to functions or policies that have most effect on the public, or on the authority's employees. The authority's concern should be to ask whether particular policies could affect different racial groups in different ways, and whether the policies will promote good race relations.

3.6   'Due regard' does not mean that race equality is less important when the ethnic minority population is small. It is also not acceptable for a public authority to claim that it does not have enough resources to meet the duty. This is because meeting the general duty is a statutory requirement. In practice, this means that public authorities should draw on work they already do to promote race equality, and build on it, using their existing administrative systems and processes and adjusting their plans and priorities, where necessary.

3.7   The general duty is a continuing duty. What a public authority has to do to meet it may change over time as its functions or policies change, or as the communities it serves change.

'Complementary'

3.8   The general duty has three parts:

    a.   eliminating unlawful racial discrimination;

    b.   promoting equality of opportunity; and

    c.   promoting good relations between people of different racial groups.

3.9   These three parts support each other. And, in practice, they may overlap (for example, promoting equality of opportunity may also eliminate or prevent unlawful racial discrimination, and promote good race relations). However, it is important to remember that the three parts are different, and that achieving one of them may not lead to achieving all three. For example, a new equal opportunities policy that is not clearly explained when it is introduced may improve equality of opportunity, but it may also damage race relations and create resentment if staff do not understand how it benefits everyone.

3.10   Public authorities should consider and deal with all three parts of the general duty.

How to meet the general duty

3.11   Public authorities should consider the following four steps to meet the general duty.

    a.   Identify which of their functions and policies are relevant to the duty, or, in other words, affect most people.

    b.   Put the functions and policies in order of priority, based on how relevant they are to race equality.

    c.   Assess whether the way these 'relevant' functions and policies are being carried out meets the three parts of the duty.

    d.   Consider whether any changes need to be made to meet the duty, and make the changes.

Appendix 5

Identifying relevant functions

3.12   To identify relevant functions, a public authority will find it useful, first, to make a list of all its functions, including employment. It should then assess how relevant each function is to each part of the general duty. As shown in paragraph 3.4, some functions may, by their nature, have little or no relevance.

3.13   A public authority should consider setting priorities, and giving priority to those functions that are most relevant to race equality.

Assessing impact and considering change

3.14   To assess the impact its functions and policies have on race equality, the authority may find it useful to draw up a clear statement of the aims of each function or policy. It should then consider whether it has information about how different racial groups are affected by the function or policy, as employees or users (or possible users) of services. The authority should also consider whether its functions and policies are promoting good race relations. The authority could get this information from various sources; for example previous research, records of complaints, surveys, or local meetings. These methods should help public authorities to assess which of their services are used by which racial groups, or what people think of their services, and whether they are being provided fairly to people from different racial groups. This kind of evidence should help public authorities to decide what they might need to do to meet all three parts of the general duty.

3.15   Public authorities may also need to consider adapting their existing information systems, so that they can provide information about different racial groups and show what progress the authority is making on race equality.

3.16   To assess the effects of a policy, or the way a function is being carried out, public authorities could ask themselves the following questions.

a.   Could the policy or the way the function is carried out have an adverse impact on equality of opportunity for some racial groups? In other words, does it put some racial groups at a disadvantage?

b.   Could the policy or the way the function is carried out have an adverse impact on relations between different racial groups?

c.   Is the adverse impact, if any, unavoidable? Could it be considered to be unlawful racial discrimination? Can it be justified by the aims and importance of the policy or function? Are there other ways in which the authority's aims can be achieved without causing an adverse impact on some racial groups?

d.   Could the adverse impact be reduced by taking particular measures?

e.   Is further research or consultation necessary? Would this research be proportionate to the importance of the policy or function? Is it likely to lead to a different outcome?

3.17   If the assessment suggests that the policy, or the way the function is carried out, should be modified, the authority should do this to meet the general duty.

4   SPECIFIC DUTIES: POLICY AND SERVICE DELIVERY

Relationship between the general and the specific duties

4.1   The specific duties have been introduced to help public authorities to meet the general duty. The specific duties are a means to an end – in other words, steps, methods or arrangements – rather than an end in themselves. Meeting the general duty is the main objective. This means that each time a public authority tackles a specific duty, it must consider whether it is meeting the three parts of the general duty (see 3.8). The authority needs regularly to ask this key question:

What action should we take to:

a. eliminate unlawful discrimination;

b. promote equality of opportunity; and

c. promote good race relations?

Race equality scheme

4.2 This chapter explains what arrangements the public authorities listed in appendix 2 [not reproduced here] must set out and publish as part of a race equality scheme. The arrangements in the scheme are not ends in themselves, but the necessary basic means for meeting the general duty. Some public authorities will already have made good progress towards putting these arrangements in place in carrying out some of their functions. Others may wish to go beyond the necessary minimum.

4.3 The necessary arrangements may not have to be new. Most of the main public services already have systems in place to meet their statutory requirements to collect information on performance, or to have their policies and services examined by independent inspection or audit agencies.

4.4 By publishing a race equality scheme, the public authority is accountable for its proposals for meeting the duty. This is also an opportunity for the authority to explain the values, principles and standards that guide its approach to race equality.

4.5 Under the specific duties, which came into effect on 3 December 2001, the listed public authorities had to publish a race equality scheme by 31 May 2002. The scheme is a timetabled and realistic plan, setting out the authority's arrangements for meeting the general and specific duties.

4.6 The scheme should show how the public authority plans to meet its statutory duties under section 71(1) of the Race Relations Act (the Act) and, in particular, articles 2(2) and 2(3) of the Race Relations Act 1976 (Statutory Duties) Order 2001.

> 2. (2) A Race Equality Scheme shall state, in particular –
>
> (a) those of its functions and policies, or proposed policies, which that person has assessed as relevant to its performance of the duty imposed by section 71(1) of the Race Relations Act; and
>
> (b) that person's arrangements for –
>
> (i) assessing and consulting on the likely impact of its proposed policies on the promotion of race equality;
>
> (ii) monitoring its policies for any adverse impact on the promotion of race equality;
>
> (iii) publishing the results of such assessments and consultation as are mentioned in sub-paragraph (i) and of such monitoring as is mentioned in sub-paragraph (ii);
>
> (iv) ensuring public access to information and services which it provides; and
>
> (v) training staff in connection with the duties imposed by section 71(1) of the Race Relations Act and this Order.

> *(3) Such a person shall, within a period of three years from 31st May 2002, and within each further period of three years, review the assessment referred to in paragraph (2)(a).*

4.7 All public authorities that have to publish a race equality scheme also have specific employment duties. These authorities may find it useful to include the arrangements they make to meet their employment duties in their race equality schemes.

4.8 The race equality scheme can be part of a more general equality strategy or improvement plan, as long as it can be easily identified as meeting all the statutory requirements for this type of scheme.

Identifying relevant functions and policies

4.9 Public authorities must list in their race equality scheme the functions and policies (including their proposed policies) that are relevant to the general duty to promote race equality. They should review this list at least every three years (see 4.6).

4.10 The general principles for identifying functions have already been described under the general duty (see 3.4). To decide whether a function or policy is relevant to the general duty to promote race equality, public authorities should consider whether that function or policy could affect different racial groups in different ways or affect good race relations.

4.11 To make sure they meet the duty, for each function or policy, public authorities might ask:

    a.   whether, and how, each of the three parts of the general duty – eliminating discrimination, promoting equality of opportunity, and promoting good race relations – applies;

    b.   which racial groups are affected; and

    c.   whether there is any reason to believe that people are, or could be, differently affected because of their racial group.

4.12 Public authorities will find it useful to make a list of all their functions, and to assess the relevance of these functions to the duty to promote race equality. In some cases, the assessment will need to consider the relevance and effect of particular policies.

4.13 If the authority is not sure how a particular function or policy might affect race equality, it could consider that function or policy as potentially relevant from the start. The authority should also consider new functions or policies whose effects have not yet been assessed in a similar way.

4.14 In practice, authorities will want to know how relevant each function or policy is to the general duty. They can then give it appropriate priority. For each function or policy, they might ask:

    a.   whether there is already evidence that the function or policy is affecting some racial groups differently;

    b.   whether there is any public concern that the function or policy in question is causing discrimination; and

    c.   whether there is any public concern that the function or policy is damaging good race relations.

4.15 Listing functions in order of priority can help public authorities to organise and plan their action. However, to meet the terms of the Act they will need to look at all relevant functions and policies. The race equality scheme should allow for this review.

Arrangements for assessing, and consulting on, the likely impact of proposed policies

4.16 Public authorities must set out in their race equality scheme their arrangements for assessing, and consulting on, the likely impact of their proposed policies on race equality (see 4.6).

4.17 Public authorities are expected to set out their arrangements for:

 a. assessing the likely impact their proposed policies will have, including their arrangements for collecting data;

 b. consulting groups that may be affected by the policies.

4.18 Public authorities may find that they can use the arrangements they already have in place to carry out the necessary assessments and consultations.

Assessment

4.19 Assessing the likely impact of a proposed policy should help to identify whether that policy might have a different impact on some racial groups, and whether it will contribute to good race relations. The assessment may involve using:

 a. information that is already available;

 b. research findings;

 c. population data, including census findings;

 d. comparisons with similar policies in other authorities;

 e. survey results;

 f. ethnic data collected at different stages of a process (for example, when people apply for a service);

 g. one-off data-gathering exercises; or

 h. specially-commissioned research.

Consultation

4.20 Public authorities already consult people in a number of different ways. However, an authority will raise confidence in its services and improve the way it develops policy if it uses clear consultation methods and explains them to its staff and to the public.

4.21 Public authorities could consult people through:

 a. consultation meetings;

 b. focus groups;

 c. reference groups;

 d. citizens' juries;

 e. public scrutiny; or

 f. survey questionnaires.

Appendix 5

4.22 Whichever consultation method they use, public authorities should try to make sure that:

    a.   they use people's views to shape their decision-making process;

    b.   the exercise represents the views of those who are likely to be affected by the policy;

    c.   the consultation method is suitable for both the topic and the groups involved;

    d.   the exercise is in proportion to the effect that the policy is likely to have;

    e.   the consultation's aims are clearly explained;

    f.   the consultation exercise is properly timetabled;

    g.   the consultation exercise is monitored; and

    h.   the consultation's findings are published.

4.23 If the assessment or consultation shows that the proposed policy is likely to have an adverse impact or harm race equality, the public authority will want to consider how it is going to meet the general duty to promote race equality. The authority might ask itself the following questions.

    a.   If one of our policies leads to unlawful racial discrimination, can we find another way of meeting our aims?

    b.   If one of our policies adversely affects people from certain racial groups, can we justify it because of its overall objectives? If we adapt the policy, could that compensate for any adverse effects?

    c.   If the assessment or consultation exercise reveals that certain racial groups have different needs, can we meet these needs, either within the proposed policy or in some other way?

    d.   Could the policy harm good race relations?

    e.   Will changes to the policy be significant, and will we need fresh consultation?

Arrangements for monitoring policies for adverse impact

4.24 Public authorities must set out in their race equality scheme their arrangements for monitoring their policies for any adverse impact on race equality (see 4.6).

4.25 Knowing that a policy is working as it should is vital to achieving the aims of the general duty. Keeping track of how a policy is working, and whether it is having an adverse impact or harming race equality, depends largely on having an efficient, up-to-date, and relevant monitoring system.

4.26 Under this duty, public authorities should set out their arrangements to monitor all the policies that are relevant to the general duty to promote race equality. These could include a wide range of policies, such as service delivery, as well as regulatory and enforcement functions, such as licensing or 'stop and search'.

4.27 Monitoring allows public authorities to test:

    a.   how racial groups are affected by their policies (for example, how often and why people use a service, how often they experience enforcement or legal action, how often they make complaints and why, and whether they face disadvantage or find that their needs are not met);

    b.   whether people from all groups are equally satisfied with the way they are treated;

c.   whether services are provided effectively to all communities; and

d.   whether services are suitable and designed to meet different needs (for example, whether they recognise language difficulties, individual cultural needs, or long-standing patterns of discrimination or exclusion).

4.28   Arrangements that the authority makes, or changes, to meet the duty should be relevant to the size of the authority, the nature of the policy and its possible effect on the public, particularly on different racial groups. Authorities can use a range of methods to monitor and analyse the effects of their policies on different racial groups, including:

a.   statistical analysis of ethnic monitoring data;

b.   satisfaction surveys (analysed by the racial groups to which the people surveyed belong);

c.   random or targeted surveys; and

d.   meetings, focus groups, and citizens' juries.

4.29   A public authority's arrangements might explain what it would do if its monitoring showed that one of its policies was having an adverse impact on race equality, and that it would prevent the authority from meeting its general duty.

4.30   The authority should ask the following questions.

a.   If one of our policies is leading to unlawful racial discrimination, can we find another way to meet our aims?

b.   If one of our policies is adversely affecting people from certain racial groups, can we justify the policy because of its overall objectives? If we adapt the policy, could that compensate for any adverse effects?

c.   If the policy is harming good race relations, what should we do?

d.   Will changes to the policy be significant, and will we need to consult about them?

Arrangements for publishing assessment, consultation and monitoring reports

4.31   Public authorities must set out in their race equality scheme their arrangements for publishing the results of any assessments, consultations and monitoring they carry out to see whether their policies have an adverse impact on race equality (see 4.6).

4.32   Publishing these results will increase an authority's openness and allow it to show that it is committed to promoting race equality. In time, this should increase public confidence in the authority – across all racial groups.

4.33   An authority's publishing arrangements should be in proportion to its size and the importance of the subject.

4.34   The authority should arrange to include the following points in publishing the results of consultations:

a.   why the consultation took place;

b.   how it was carried out;

c.   a summary of the responses or views it produced;

d.   an assessment of the policy options; and

e.   what the public authority is proposing to do.

Appendix 5

4.35   The authority should set out in its race equality scheme how often, and in what form, the results of its assessments, consultations and monitoring will be published. The authority's publishing arrangements might also take account of how these fit in with its other statutory requirements or demands for published information.

Arrangements for making sure the public have access to information and services

4.36   Public authorities must set out in their race equality scheme their arrangements for making sure that the public have access to information and services they provide (see 4.6).

4.37   To meet this specific duty, public authorities should arrange to make their information and services accessible to everyone. Authorities might consider the following.

a.   Consider access to information and services when they assess their functions. For example, is there enough information available to the public? Is the information user-friendly?

b.   Consider whether a service is not being fully used because people do not have enough information about it, or because they are not confident that the service can meet their particular needs sympathetically or fairly.

c.   Ask whether information is available at the right time and in the right place.

d.   Take steps to improve the information available.

e.   Monitor how effectively information is given to the public, and make improvements, where necessary.

f.   Make sure that staff have the skills, information and understanding needed to deal fairly and equally with all clients.

4.38   Public authorities might also consider how they can improve public access to their services. Possible ways include:

a.   asking local communities what services they need and how they want them provided;

b.   providing 'outreach' services to particular groups in an environment and style they are familiar with;

c.   strengthening cooperation with particular groups;

d.   arranging for interpreters;

e.   taking positive action; and

f.   developing access to computers and internet services.

Arrangements for training staff

4.39   Public authorities must set out in their race equality scheme their arrangements for training their staff in connection with the general duty to promote race equality, and any specific duties (see 4.6).

4.40   Staff training arrangements under this duty should aim to make sure that staff responsible for meeting the general and specific duties are aware of these – and have the skills needed to carry them out. Public authorities should consider what staff at various levels need to know about the general and specific duties, before giving them the training they need. This specific duty also includes meeting the training needs of the staff responsible for managing and delivering the public authority's race equality scheme. Staff training should therefore focus on what the authority needs to do to meet the duties laid down in the Race Relations Act and any specific duties.

5 SPECIFIC DUTIES: EMPLOYMENT

5.1 The specific duty on employment applies to most of the public authorities bound by the general duty. Schools and further and higher education institutions are not bound by the employment duty, as they have separate employment responsibilities. A few, mainly advisory, agencies are also not bound by the employment duty.

5.2 Articles 5(1), 5(2), and 5(3) of the Race Relations Act 1976 (Statutory Duties) Order 2001 say the following:

    5. (1) A person to which this article applies shall,

        (a) before 31st May 2002, have in place arrangements for fulfilling, as soon as is reasonably practicable, its duties under paragraph (2); and

        (b) fulfil those duties in accordance with such arrangements.

    (2) It shall be the duty of such a person to monitor, by reference to the racial groups to which they belong,

        (a) the numbers of –

            (i) staff in post, and

            (ii) applicants for employment, training and promotion, from each such group, and

        (b) where that person has 150 or more full-time staff, the numbers of staff from each such group who –

            (i) receive training;

            (ii) benefit or suffer detriment as a result of its performance assessment procedures;

            (iii) are involved in grievance procedures;

            (iv) are the subject of disciplinary procedures; or

            (v) cease employment with that person.

    (3) Such a person shall publish annually the results of its monitoring under paragraph (2).

5.3 Public authorities that have to produce race equality schemes may find it useful to include their arrangements for meeting their employment duty in their race equality schemes.

5.4 The specific duties on employment are designed to provide a framework for measuring progress in equality of opportunity in public-sector employment. The specific duties are also aimed at providing monitoring information to guide initiatives that could lead to a more representative public-sector workforce. For example, these initiatives could include setting recruitment targets for under-represented racial groups, or targeting management development courses at racial groups that are under-represented at certain levels. The specific duties on employment set minimum standards. Other issues may also be relevant for good employment practice. This will depend on local circumstances.

5.5 Ethnic monitoring is central to providing a clear picture of what is happening during the authority's employment cycle – from applying for a job and joining the authority to leaving it. Monitoring helps to measure overall progress and to show whether the authority's equal opportunities policies are effective. Monitoring is the essential tool to assess progress – or lack of it – in removing barriers to equality of opportunity in the public services.

Appendix 5

5.6   It is important that the authority explains to applicants and existing staff why they are monitoring employment. People will normally only have to give information about their racial group voluntarily, and the authority should explain the conditions of the Data Protection Act 1998 (about processing this information) to them.

5.7   Wherever possible, the authority should build monitoring information into the information systems it already uses. The authority may be able to publish its monitoring results each year through its existing reporting systems. In its published results, the authority should explain how it is dealing with trends or problems highlighted by its monitoring. The authority may also find it useful to combine and analyse ethnic monitoring data with other data; for example on sex and disability.

5.8   To help meet the specific duty on employment, public authorities should:

     a.   collect ethnic monitoring data; and

     b.   publish the results of the monitoring each year.

5.9   To check that they are meeting the general duty, public authorities may want to:

     a.   analyse the data to find any patterns of inequality; and

     b.   take whatever steps are needed to remove barriers and promote equality of opportunity.

5.10   If the monitoring shows that current employment policies, procedures and practice are leading to unlawful racial discrimination, the authority should take steps to end the discrimination. As a first step, the authority should examine each of its procedures closely to find out where and how discrimination might be happening, and then consider what changes to introduce.

5.11   On the other hand, the monitoring may show that current policies, procedures and practice have an adverse impact on equality of opportunity or good race relations (even though they are not causing unlawful discrimination). If this is the case, the authority should consider changing its policies or procedures so that they still meet the same aims, but do not harm equality of opportunity or race relations.

Positive action

5.12   If monitoring reveals that some racial groups are under-represented in the workforce, the authority could consider using 'positive action'. This allows employers and others to target their job training and recruitment efforts at those groups that are under-represented in a particular area of work. However, positive action does not allow discrimination when deciding who will be offered a job.

Ethnic categories and the 2001 census

5.13   Public authorities are encouraged to use the same ethnic classification system as the one used in the 2001 census. Some authorities already have systems in place. If an authority chooses to collect more detailed information, it should make sure that the categories are the same as, or similar to, those used in the 2001 census. Any extra ethnic categories it adds to reflect its particular circumstances should fit in with the 2001 census categories.

5.14   Public authorities should make realistic and timetabled plans to adapt their ethnic monitoring systems to meet the specific duties.

5.15   The 2001 census used different ethnic classifications for England and Wales, and Scotland.

Appendix 6

Disability Rights Commission Code of Practice: Employment and Occupation

2 HOW CAN DISCRIMINATION BE AVOIDED?

Introduction

2.1   Prevention is better than cure. There are various actions which employers can take in order to avoid discriminating against disabled people. By doing so, employers are not only likely to minimise the incidence of expensive and time-consuming litigation, but will also improve their general performance and the quality of their business operations. This chapter sets out some guidance on ways to help ensure that disabled people are not discriminated against.

Understanding the social dimension of disability

2.2   The concept of discrimination in the Act reflects an understanding that functional limitations arising from disabled people's impairments do not inevitably restrict their ability to participate fully in society. Rather than the limitations of an impairment, it is often environmental factors (such as the structure of a building, or an employer's working practices) which unnecessarily lead to these social restrictions. This principle underpins the duty to make reasonable adjustments. Understanding this will assist employers and others to avoid discrimination. It is as important to consider which aspects of employment and occupation create difficulties for a disabled person as it is to understand the particular nature of an individual's disability.

Recognising the diverse nature of disability

2.3   There are around ten million disabled adults in our society. The nature and extent of their disabilities vary widely, as do their requirements for overcoming any difficulties they may face. If employers are to avoid discriminating, they need to understand this, and to be aware of the effects their decisions and actions – and those of their agents and employees – may have on disabled people. The evidence shows that many of the steps that can be taken to avoid discrimination cost little or nothing and are easy to implement.

Avoiding making assumptions

2.4   It is advisable to avoid making assumptions about disabled people. Disabilities will often affect different people in different ways and their needs may be different as well. The following suggestions may help to avoid discrimination:

- Do not assume that because a person does not look disabled, he is not disabled.

- Do not assume that because you do not know of any disabled people working within an organisation there are none.

- Do not assume that most disabled people use wheelchairs.

- Do not assume that people with learning disabilities cannot be valuable employees, or that they can only do low status jobs.

- Do not assume that a person with a mental health problem cannot do a demanding job.

- Do not assume that all blind people read Braille or have guide dogs.

- Do not assume that all deaf people use sign language.

- Do not assume that because a disabled person may have less employment experience (in paid employment) than a non-disabled person, he has less to offer.

Finding out about disabled people's needs

2.5   As explained later in the Code, the Act requires employers to think about ways of complying with their legal duties. Listening carefully to disabled people and finding out what they want will help employers to meet their obligations by identifying the best way of meeting disabled people's needs. There is a better chance of reaching the best outcome if discussions are held with disabled people at an early stage.

2.6   Often, discussing with disabled people what is required to meet their needs will reassure an employer that suitable adjustments can be carried out cheaply and with very little inconvenience.

2.7   Evidence shows that in meeting the needs of disabled employees an organisation learns how to meet the needs of disabled customers, and vice versa. By consulting with disabled employees, an organisation can therefore improve the service it provides to its disabled customers and enhance its business.

2.8   There are various ways in which the views of disabled people can be obtained. Many larger employers have established formal structures for seeking and representing the views of disabled people. Small employers can also consult with disabled employees, although the methods may be less formal.

A large employer sets up a network through which disabled employees can discuss their concerns and make recommendations to management, either directly or via a recognised trade union.

A small employer asks a disabled employee if he has any concerns about how a reorganisation of the business will impact upon him.

Seeking expert advice

2.9   It may be possible to avoid discrimination by using personal or in-house knowledge and expertise – particularly if information or views are obtained from the disabled person concerned. However, although the Act does not specifically require anyone to obtain expert advice about meeting the needs of disabled people with regard to employment, in practice it may sometimes be necessary to do so in order to comply with the principal duties set out in the Act. Expert advice might be especially useful if a person is newly disabled or if the effects of a person's disability become more marked. Expert advice about meeting the needs of disabled people may be available from local Jobcentre Plus offices, or from local and national disability organisations.

Planning ahead

2.10   The duties which the Act places on employers are owed to the individual disabled people with whom they have dealings. There is no duty owed to disabled people in general. Nevertheless, it is likely to be cost effective for employers to plan ahead. Considering the needs of a range of disabled people when planning for change (such as when planning a building refurbishment, a new IT system, or the design of a website) is likely to make it easier to implement adjustments for individuals when the need arises.

2.11   It is good practice for employers to have access audits carried out to identify any improvements which can be made to a building to make it more accessible. Access audits should be carried out by suitably qualified people, such as those listed in the National Register of Access Consultants. Websites and intranet sites can also be reviewed to see how accessible they are to disabled people using access software.

The owner of a small shop is planning a refit of her premises. As part of the refit she asks the designers to comply with British Standard 8300 to ensure that the shop has a good standard of access for a variety of disabled people, whether customers or employees. BS 8300 is a code of practice on the design of buildings and their approaches to meet the needs of disabled people.

An employer is re-designing its website, which it uses to promote the company as well as to advertise vacancies. The employer ensures that the new design for the website is easy to read for people with a variety of access software; has the website checked for accessibility; and invites disabled readers of the website to let the employer know if they find any part of it inaccessible.

Implementing anti-discriminatory policies and practices

2.12   Employers are more likely to comply with their duties under the Act, and to avoid the risk of legal action being taken against them, if they implement anti-discriminatory policies and practices. These are often referred to as equality policies or diversity policies. Additionally, in the event that legal action is taken, employers may be asked to demonstrate to an employment tribunal that they have effective policies and procedures in place to minimise the risk of discrimination. Although large and small employers are likely to have different kinds of anti-discriminatory policies and practices, it is advisable for all employers to take the following steps:

- Establish a policy which aims to prevent discrimination against disabled people and which is communicated to all employees and agents of the employer.

- Provide disability awareness and equality training to all employees. In addition, train employees and agents so that they understand the employer's policy on disability, their obligations under the Act and the practice of reasonable adjustments. People within the organisation who have responsibility for managing, recruiting or training employees are likely to need more specialist training.

- Inform all employees and agents that conduct which breaches the policy will not be tolerated, and respond quickly and effectively to any such breaches.

- Monitor the implementation and effectiveness of such a policy.

- Address acts of disability discrimination by employees as part of disciplinary rules and procedures.

- Have complaints and grievance procedures which are easy for disabled people to use and which are designed to resolve issues effectively.

- Have clear procedures to prevent and deal with harassment for a reason related to a person's disability.

- Establish a policy in relation to disability-related leave, and monitor the implementation and effectiveness of such a policy.

- Consult with disabled employees about their experiences of working for the organisation.

- Regularly review the effectiveness of reasonable adjustments made for disabled people in accordance with the Act, and act on the findings of those reviews.

- Keep clear records of decisions taken in respect of each of these matters.

When a large company introduces a new disability policy, it might ask an external training company to run training sessions for all staff, or it might ask a human resources manager to deliver training to staff on this policy. The external training company might be one run by disabled people.

A small employer introducing a similar policy asks the managing director to devote a team meeting to explaining the policy to her staff and to discuss why it is important and how it will operate.

A large employer trains all its employees in disability equality, the organisation's disability policy and the Disability Discrimination Act. It also trains all occupational health advisers with whom it works to ensure that they have the necessary expertise about the Act and the organisation's disability policy.

A small employer only uses occupational health advisers who can demonstrate that they have knowledge of the Act.

A large employer issues a questionnaire to employees about the organisation's attitude to disability, inviting suggestions for improvements.

A small employer asks disabled employees to feed back views on the employer's approach to disability issues.

Auditing policies and procedures

2.13 Although there is no duty under Part 2 to anticipate the needs of disabled people in general, it is a good idea for employers to keep all their policies under review, and to consider the needs of disabled people as part of this process. It is advisable for employers to do this in addition to having a specific policy to prevent discrimination. Employers are likely to have policies about matters such as:

- flexible working arrangements
- appraisal and performance-related pay systems
- sickness absence
- redundancy selection criteria
- emergency evacuation procedures
- procurement of equipment, IT systems, software and websites
- information provision
- employee training and development
- employee assistance schemes offering financial or emotional support.

> An organisation has a policy to ensure that all employees are kept informed about the organisation's activities through an intranet site. The policy says that the intranet site should be accessible to all employees, including those who use access software (such as synthetic speech output) because of their disabilities.

> An employer has a policy of having annual appraisal interviews for all employees. The policy says that during the interviews, disabled employees should be asked whether they need any (further) reasonable adjustments. This could equally apply to a large or small employer.

> An employer introduces a system for performance-related pay. It takes advice on performance-related pay systems from an employers' organisation, to ensure that the system it introduces is an effective tool for improving performance and is fair to all employees. It also ensures that every year the system is monitored to ensure that disabled people do not, on average, get lower awards.

> A redundancy policy that has sickness absence as a selection criterion is amended to exclude disability-related absence. The sickness absence policy is also changed so that disability-related sickness is recorded separately.

> A new procurement policy requires a number of factors to be taken into account in procuring equipment and IT systems. These factors include cost and energy efficiency. It is good practice for such factors to include accessibility for disabled people as well.

> Emergency evacuation policies and procedures are reviewed to ensure that there are individual evacuation plans for any disabled people who need them.

Monitoring

2.14 Monitoring of employees is an important way of determining whether anti-discrimination measures taken by an organisation are effective, and ensuring that disability equality is a reality within that organisation. Information must be gathered sensitively, with appropriately worded questions, and confidentiality must be ensured. Knowing the proportion of disabled people at various levels of the organisation, and at various stages in relation to the recruitment process, can help an organisation determine where practices and policies need to be improved. The extent to which formal monitoring can be carried out will depend on the size of the organisation.

2.15 Monitoring will be more effective if employees (or job applicants) feel comfortable about disclosing information about their disabilities. This is more likely to be the case if the employer explains the purpose of the monitoring and if employees or job applicants believe that the employer genuinely values disabled employees and is using the information gathered to create positive change.

> Through monitoring of candidates at the recruitment stage an employer becomes aware that, although several disabled people applied for a post, none was short-listed for interview. It uses this information to review the essential requirements for the post.

Appendix 6

2.16   Some organisations, especially large ones, choose to monitor by broad type of disability to understand the barriers faced by people with different types of impairment.

> A large employer notices through monitoring that the organisation has been successful at retaining most groups of disabled people, but not people with mental health problems. It acts on this information by contacting a specialist organisation for advice about good practice in retaining people with mental health problems.

Ensuring good practice in recruitment

Attracting disabled applicants

2.17   An organisation which recognises that suitably qualified disabled people have not applied to work for it may want to make contact with local employment services, including Jobcentre Plus and specialist disability employment services, to encourage disabled people to apply. It is normally lawful for an employer to advertise a vacancy as open only to disabled people.

> By monitoring the recruitment process a small employer notices that very few disabled people apply to work for it. In the light of this information, it decides to notify local disability employment projects of its vacancies.

> A retailer has a number of vacancies to fill. It contacts Jobcentre Plus and arranges an open morning for local disabled people to find out more about working for this employer.

> Through its monitoring process, a medium-sized employer becomes aware of the fact that disabled people are under-represented in its workforce. It is looking for people to fill 3 work experience placements and decides to offer these placements to disabled people only.

> A museum wants to understand the needs of its disabled visitors better. It decides to change its person specifications for posts in the visitor services department to include a requirement to have knowledge of disability access issues. It notifies local employment services for disabled people of these posts.

2.18   It is good practice to consider carefully what information should be included in advertisements and where they should be placed.

> An advertisement which specifies that flexible working is available may encourage more disabled applicants to apply.

> An advertisement that appears in the disability press and a local talking newspaper may encourage disabled applicants to apply.

Promoting a positive image

2.19   It is good practice for an employer to consider its image to ensure that it gives an impression of itself as an organisation that is aware of the needs of disabled people and is striving to create a more diverse workforce.

A large employer ensures that its recruitment brochure includes images of disabled employees, and contains information about its disability policy.

A small employer advertises in a local newspaper. The advertisement states that disabled people are encouraged to apply.

Use of the Disability Symbol

2.20   The Disability Symbol is a recognition given to employers by Jobcentre Plus. An employer displaying the Disability Symbol must commit itself to a number of measures concerning the recruitment, development and retention of disabled people, including offering a guaranteed interview to any disabled person who meets the essential requirements of the job. It is important that employers make clear what those essential requirements are.

Resolving disputes

2.21   Having policies and practices to combat discrimination, together with regular consultation with employees, is likely to minimise disputes about disability discrimination. But when such disputes do occur, it is in the interests of employers to attempt wherever possible to resolve them as they arise. Grievance procedures can provide an open and fair way for employees to make their concerns known, and can enable grievances to be resolved quickly before they become major problems. Use of the procedures may highlight areas in which the duty to make reasonable adjustments has not been observed, and can prevent misunderstandings leading to complaints to tribunals. It is important to ensure that grievance procedures are accessible to disabled people.

2.22   In certain circumstances, employers and employees are required by law to comply with internal dispute resolution procedures before making a complaint to a tribunal. [. . .] Whether or not an attempt at internal resolution of a dispute is made as a result of a legal requirement, it should be carried out in a non-discriminatory way to comply with the Act.

3   THE ACT'S PROVISIONS ON EMPLOYMENT AND OCCUPATION – AN OVERVIEW

Introduction

3.1   This chapter gives an overview of the provisions of the Act relating to employment and occupation. It explains who has rights and duties under those provisions and outlines what is made unlawful by them. Later chapters explain the provisions in greater detail.

Who has rights under the Act?

Disabled people

3.2   The Act gives protection from discrimination to a 'disabled' person within the meaning of the Act. A disabled person is someone who has a physical or mental impairment which has an effect on his or her ability to carry out normal day-to-day activities. That effect must be:

- substantial (that is, more than minor or trivial), and

- adverse, and

- long term (that is, it has lasted or is likely to last for at least a year or for the rest of the life of the person affected).

3.3 Physical or mental impairment includes sensory impairment. Hidden impairments are also covered (for example, mental illness or mental health problems, learning disabilities, dyslexia, diabetes and epilepsy).

3.4 In considering its duties under the Act, an employer should not use any definition of 'disabled person' which is narrower than that in the Act. An employer who is requested to make a disability-related adjustment may ask the person requesting it for evidence that the impairment is one which meets the definition of disability in the Act. It may be appropriate to do so where the disability is not obvious. However, employers should not ask for more information about the impairment than is necessary for this purpose. Nor should they ask for evidence of disability where it ought to be obvious that the Act will apply.

> A woman with ME (chronic fatigue syndrome) asks for time off to attend regular hospital appointments. The employer could legitimately ask to see a letter from the doctor or an appointment card. However, the employer then asks her questions about the likely progress of the illness so that he can bear this in mind when thinking about restructuring the department. This is likely to be unlawful.

People who have had a disability in the past

3.5 People who have had a disability within the meaning of the Act in the past are protected from discrimination even if they no longer have the disability.

> A job applicant discloses on her application form that while at university from 1992 to 1993 she had long-term clinical depression after her father died. It would be discrimination to refuse to interview or recruit her because she has had a disability in the past. The fact that the disability preceded the Disability Discrimination Act 1995 is irrelevant.

More information about the meaning of disability

3.6 For a fuller understanding of the concept of disability under the Act, reference should be made to Appendix B. A government publication, **Guidance on matters to be taken into account in determining questions relating to the definition of disability**, provides additional help in understanding the concept of disability and in identifying who is a disabled person. Where relevant, the Guidance must be taken into account in any legal proceedings.

People who have been victimised

3.7 The Act also gives rights to people who have been victimised, whether or not they have a disability or have had one in the past. (see paragraphs 4.33 to 4.36).

Who has obligations under the Act?

Employers

3.8 Later chapters explain in detail the duties which the Act imposes upon employers. The Act defines 'employment' as employment under a contract of service or of apprenticeship or a contract personally to do any work. Anyone who works under a contract falling within this definition is an employee, whether or not, for example, he works full-time.

3.9   Members of the Armed Forces are excluded from protection under the Act's provisions on employment and occupation. Otherwise, those provisions now apply to all employers in respect of people they employ wholly or partly at an establishment in Great Britain. Protection under the Act extends to employment wholly outside Great Britain, provided that the employment has a sufficiently close connection with Great Britain – and the Act sets out the circumstances in which this will be the case. Certain employment on board ships, hovercraft and aircraft is also covered.

3.10   A person who is recruiting an employee has duties under the Act even if he is not yet an employer (because the new recruit will be his first employee).

People or bodies concerned with certain occupations

3.11   The Act's definition of employment is wide enough to include people who are self-employed but who agree to perform work personally. The provisions of Part 2 also extend to the following occupations which do not fall within the definition of employment:

- contract workers
- office holders
- police officers
- partners in firms
- barristers and advocates
- people undertaking practical work experience for a limited period for the purposes of vocational training.

Many of the principles which apply to employers under Part 2 are equally applicable in respect of these occupations.

Others to whom Part 2 applies

3.12   In addition, the Act's provisions on employment and occupation may also impose obligations upon the following people and organisations:

- trustees and managers of occupational pension schemes
- insurers who provide group insurance services for an employer's employees
- landlords of premises occupied by an employer or other person to whom Part 2 applies
- employees and agents of a person to whom Part 2 applies
- Ministers of the Crown, government departments and agencies.

Providers of employment services

3.13   The Act also contains provisions to prevent discrimination by people or organisations who provide employment services – such as employment agencies and careers guidance services.

Appendix 6

Trade organisations and qualifications bodies

3.14   Finally, Part 2 makes special provision in respect of discrimination against disabled people by trade organisations and qualifications bodies. The nature and effect of the provisions in question is explained in a separate code of practice issued by the DRC.

What does the Act say about discrimination in relation to employment and occupation?

Effect of the Act

3.15   The Act makes it unlawful for an employer to **discriminate** against a disabled person in relation to the recruitment or retention of staff.

3.16   However, the Act does not prohibit an employer from appointing the best person for the job. Nor does it prevent employers from treating disabled people more favourably than those who are not disabled.

Forms of discrimination

3.17   The four forms of discrimination which are unlawful under Part 2 are:

- direct discrimination (the meaning of which is explained at paragraphs 4.5 to 4.23)

- failure to comply with a duty to make reasonable adjustments

- 'disability-related discrimination' (see paragraphs 4.27 to 4.32), and

- victimisation of a person (whether or not he is disabled) – what the Act says about victimisation is explained at paragraphs 4.33 to 4.36.

Aspects of employment in respect of which discrimination is unlawful

3.18   In relation to recruitment, the Act says that it is unlawful for an employer to discriminate against a disabled person:

- in the arrangements made for determining who should be offered employment

- in the terms on which the disabled person is offered employment, or

- by refusing to offer, or deliberately not offering, the disabled person employment.

3.19   In relation to the retention of staff, the Act says that it is unlawful for an employer to discriminate against a disabled person whom it employs:

- in the terms of employment which it affords him

- in the opportunities which it affords him for promotion, a transfer, training or receiving any other benefit

- by refusing to afford him, or deliberately not affording him, any such opportunity, or

- by dismissing him, or subjecting him to any other detriment.

3.20 The Act also makes it unlawful for an employer to discriminate against a disabled person after that person's employment has come to an end.

What else is unlawful under the Act's provisions on employment and occupation?

Harassment

3.21 In addition to what it says about discrimination, Part 2 makes it unlawful, in relation to the recruitment or retention of staff, for an employer to subject a disabled person to **harassment** for a reason which relates to his disability. What the Act says about harassment is explained in more detail at paragraphs 4.38 and 4.39.

Instructions and pressure to discriminate

3.22 It is also unlawful for a person who has authority or influence over another to instruct him, or put pressure on him, to act unlawfully under the provisions of Part 2 (or, insofar as they relate to employment services, Part 3). This covers pressure to discriminate, whether applied directly to the person concerned, or indirectly but in a way in which he is likely to hear of it. However, the Act does not give individual disabled people the right to take legal action in respect of unlawful instructions or pressure to discriminate. Such action may only be taken by the DRC.

Who is liable for unlawful acts?

Responsibility for the acts of others

3.23 Employers who act through agents (such as occupational health advisers or recruitment agencies) are liable for the actions of their agents done with the employer's express or implied authority. The Act also says that employers are responsible for the actions of their employees in the course of their employment. However, in legal proceedings against an employer based on the actions of an employee, it is a defence that the employer took 'such steps as were reasonably practicable' to prevent such actions. It is not a defence for the employer simply to show that the action took place without its knowledge or approval. Chapter 2 gives guidance on the steps which it might be appropriate to take for this purpose.

A shopkeeper goes abroad for 3 months and leaves his son in charge of the shop. While he is away his son picks on a shop assistant with a learning disability, by constantly criticising her work unfairly. The shop assistant leaves her job as a result of this bullying. The shopkeeper is responsible for the actions of his son.

Aiding an unlawful act

3.24 A person who knowingly helps another to do something made unlawful by the Act will be treated as having done the same kind of unlawful act. This means that, where an employer is liable for an unlawful act of its employee or agent, that employee or agent will be liable for aiding the unlawful act of the employer.

A recruitment consultant engaged by an engineering company refuses to consider a disabled applicant for a vacancy, because the company has told the consultant that it does not want the post filled by someone who is 'handicapped'. Under the Act the consultant could be liable for aiding the company to discriminate, in addition to the company's own liability for its unlawful act.

3.25   Where an employee discriminates against or harasses a disabled employee, it is the employer who will be liable for that unlawful act – unless it can show that it took such steps as were reasonable to prevent the unlawful act in question. But the employee who committed the discrimination or harassment will be liable for aiding the unlawful act – and this will be the case even if the employer is able to show that it took reasonable steps to prevent the act.

An employer has policies relating to harassment and disability. It ensures that all employees are aware of the policies and of the fact that harassment of disabled employees is subject to disciplinary action. It also ensures that managers receive training in applying the policies. A woman with a learning disability is humiliated by a colleague and disciplinary action is taken against the colleague. In these circumstances the colleague would be liable for aiding the unlawful act of the employer (the harassment) even though the employer would itself avoid liability because it had taken reasonably practicable steps to prevent the unlawful act.

Enforcing rights under Part 2

3.26   Enforcement of rights under Part 2 takes place in the employment tribunals. Enforcement of rights under the Act in relation to the provision of employment services also takes place in the employment tribunals.

4   WHAT IS DISCRIMINATION AND HARASSMENT?

Introduction

4.1   As noted at paragraph 3.17, the forms of discrimination which the Act makes unlawful in relation to employment are:

- direct discrimination

- failure to comply with a duty to make reasonable adjustments

- disability-related discrimination, and

- victimisation.

4.2   This chapter describes these four forms of discrimination in more detail, and explains the differences between them. It explores, in particular, the distinction between direct discrimination and disability-related discrimination (see paragraphs 4.28 to 4.31). These two forms of discrimination both depend on the way in which the employer treats the disabled person concerned – both require the disabled person to have been treated less favourably than other people are (or would be) treated. However, whether such treatment amounts to one of these forms of discrimination or the other (and, indeed, whether the treatment is unlawful in the first place) depends on the circumstances in which it arose.

4.3   The chapter examines the four forms of discrimination in the order in which they are listed in paragraph 4.1. This is because less favourable treatment which does not amount to direct discrimination can sometimes be justified. (In contrast, neither direct discrimination nor a failure to comply with a duty to make a reasonable adjustment is justifiable. Victimisation cannot be justified either.) In deciding whether the treatment is justified, and therefore whether there has been disability-related discrimination, the Act requires the question of reasonable adjustments to be taken into account (see paragraphs 6.4 and 6.5 where this is explained in more detail). Consequently, although the chapter describes direct discrimination first, it touches on the subject of reasonable adjustments before moving on to disability-related discrimination.

4.4   This chapter also explains what the Act means by 'harassment'. The concepts of discrimination and harassment are relevant not only in relation to employment but also to the application of Part 2 in other situations. The provisions about discrimination and harassment in Part 2 are also relevant to what the Act says about employment services in Part 3.

What does the Act mean by 'direct discrimination'?

What does the Act say?

4.5   The Act says that an employer's treatment of a disabled person amounts to direct discrimination if:

- it is on the ground of his disability

- the treatment is less favourable than the way in which a person not having that particular disability is (or would be) treated, and

- the relevant circumstances, including the abilities, of the person with whom the comparison is made are the same as, or not materially different from, those of the disabled person.

4.6   It follows that direct discrimination depends on an employer's treatment of a disabled person being on the ground of his disability. It also depends on a comparison of that treatment with the way in which the employer treats (or would treat) an appropriate comparator. If, on the ground of his disability, the disabled person is treated less favourably than the comparator is (or would be) treated, the treatment amounts to direct discrimination.

When is direct discrimination likely to occur?

4.7   Treatment of a disabled person is 'on the ground of' his disability if it is caused by the fact that he is disabled or has the disability in question. In general, this means that treatment is on the ground of disability if a disabled person would not have received it but for his disability. However, disability does not have to be the only (or even the main) cause of the treatment complained of – provided that it is an effective cause, determined objectively from all the circumstances.

4.8   Consequently, if the less favourable treatment occurs because of the employer's generalised, or stereotypical, assumptions about the disability or its effects, it is likely to be direct discrimination. This is because an employer would not normally make such assumptions about a non-disabled person, but would instead consider his individual abilities.

A blind woman is not short-listed for a job involving computers because the employer wrongly assumes that blind people cannot use them. The employer makes no attempt to look at the individual circumstances. The employer has treated the woman less favourably than other people by not short-listing her for the job. The treatment was on the ground of the woman's disability (because assumptions would not have been made about a non-disabled person).

Appendix 6

4.9   In addition, less favourable treatment which is disability-specific, or which arises out of prejudice about disability (or about a particular type of disability), is also likely to amount to direct discrimination.

> An employer seeking a shop assistant turns down a disabled applicant with a severe facial disfigurement solely on the ground that other employees would be uncomfortable working alongside him. This would amount to direct discrimination and would be unlawful.

> A disabled woman who uses a wheelchair applies for a job. She can do the job just as well as any other applicant, but the employer wrongly assumes that the wheelchair will cause an obstruction in the office. He therefore gives the job to a person who is no more suitable for the job but who is not a wheelchair-user. This would amount to direct discrimination and would be unlawful.

4.10   In some cases, an apparently neutral reason for less favourable treatment of a disabled person may, on investigation, turn out to be a pretext for direct discrimination.

4.11   Direct discrimination will often occur where the employer is aware that the disabled person has a disability, and this is the reason for the employer's treatment of him. Direct discrimination need not be conscious – people may hold prejudices that they do not admit, even to themselves. Thus, a person may behave in a discriminatory way while believing that he would never do so. Moreover, direct discrimination may sometimes occur even though the employer is unaware of a person's disability.

> An employer advertises a promotion internally to its workforce. The job description states that people with a history of mental illness would not be suitable for the post. An employee who would otherwise be eligible for the promotion has a history of schizophrenia, but the employer is unaware of this. The employee would, neverthe-less, have a good claim for unlawful direct discrimination in relation to the promo-tion opportunities afforded to him by his employer. The act of direct discrimination in this case is the blanket ban on anyone who has had a mental illness, effectively rejecting whole categories of people with no consideration of their individual abili-ties.

4.12   In situations such as those described in the above examples, it will often be readily apparent that the disabled person concerned has been treated less favourably on the ground of his disability. In other cases, however, this may be less obvious. Whether or not the basis for the treatment in question appears to be clear, a useful way of telling whether or not it is discriminatory (and of establishing what kind of discrimination it is), is to focus on the person with whom the disabled person should be compared. That person may be real or hypothetical (see paragraph 4.18).

Identifying comparators in respect of direct discrimination

4.13   In determining whether a disabled person has been treated less favourably in the context of direct discrimination, his treatment must be compared with that of an appropriate comparator. This must be someone who does not have the same disability. It could be a non-disabled person or a person with other disabilities.

578

A person who becomes disabled takes six months' sick leave because of his disability, and is dismissed by his employer. A non-disabled fellow employee also takes six months' sick leave (because he has broken his leg) but is not dismissed. The difference in treatment is attributable to the employer's unwillingness to employ disabled staff and the treatment is therefore on the ground of disability. The non-disabled employee is an appropriate comparator in the context of direct discrimination because his relevant circumstances are the same as those of the disabled person. It is the fact of having taken six months' sick leave which is relevant in these circumstances. As the disabled person has been treated less favourably than the comparator, this is direct discrimination.

4.14 It follows that, in the great majority of cases, some difference will exist between the circumstances (including the abilities) of the comparator and those of the disabled person – there is no need to find a comparator whose circumstances are the same as those of the disabled person in every respect. What matters is that the comparator's **relevant** circumstances (including his abilities) must be the same as, or not materially different from, those of the disabled person.

In the previous example, the position would be different if it were the employer's policy to dismiss any member of staff who has been off sick for six months, and that policy were applied equally to disabled and non-disabled staff. In this case there would be no direct discrimination because the disabled person would not have been treated less favourably than the comparator – both would have been dismissed. Nevertheless, there may be a claim for failure to make reasonable adjustments to the policy, for example by allowing disability leave (see paragraph 4.25). In addition, the employer's policy may give rise to a claim for disability-related discrimination (see paragraph 4.27).

4.15 Once an appropriate comparator is identified, it is clear that the situation described in the example at paragraph 4.8 amounts to direct discrimination:

In the example about the blind woman who is not short-listed for a job involving computers, there is direct discrimination because the woman was treated less favourably on the ground of her disability than an appropriate comparator (that is, a person who is not blind but who has the same abilities to do the job as the blind applicant): such a person would not have been rejected out of hand without consideration of her individual abilities.

4.16 The examples of direct discrimination in paragraph 4.9 also become clearer when the appropriate comparator is identified in each case:

In the example about the disabled person with a severe facial disfigurement who applies to be a shop assistant, there is direct discrimination because the man was treated less favourably on the ground of his disability than an appropriate comparator (that is, a person who does not have such a disfigurement but who does have the same abilities to do the job): such a person would not have been rejected in the same way.

> In the example about the disabled woman who is not offered a job because she uses a wheelchair, there is direct discrimination because the woman was treated less favourably on the ground of her disability than an appropriate comparator (that is, a person who does not use a wheelchair but who does have the same abilities to do the job): such a person would not have been rejected in the same way.

4.17   The comparator used in relation to direct discrimination under the Act is the same as it is for other types of direct discrimination – such as direct sex discrimination. It is, however, made explicit in the Act that the comparator must have the same relevant abilities as the disabled person.

4.18   It may not be possible to identify an actual comparator whose relevant circumstances are the same as (or not materially different from) those of the disabled person in question. In such cases a hypothetical comparator may be used. Evidence which helps to establish how a hypothetical comparator would have been treated is likely to include details of how other people (not satisfying the statutory comparison test) were treated in circumstances which were broadly similar.

> A disabled person works in a restaurant. She makes a mistake on the till and this results in a small financial loss to her employer. She is dismissed because of this. The situation has not arisen before, and so there is no actual comparator. Nevertheless, six months earlier a non-disabled fellow employee was disciplined for taking home items of food without permission and received a written warning. The treatment of that person might be used as evidence that a hypothetical non-disabled member of staff who makes an error on the till would not have been dismissed for that reason.

4.19   It should be noted that the type of comparator described in the preceding paragraphs is only relevant to disability discrimination when assessing whether there has been **direct** discrimination. A different comparison falls to be made when assessing whether there has been a failure to comply with a duty to make reasonable adjustments (see paragraphs 5.3 and 5.4) or when considering disability-related discrimination (see paragraph 4.30).

Focusing on relevant circumstances

4.20   As stated in paragraph 4.14, direct discrimination only occurs where the **relevant** circumstances of the comparator, including his abilities, are the same as, or not materially different from, those of the disabled person himself. It is therefore important to focus on those circumstances which are, in fact, relevant to the matter to which the less favourable treatment relates. Although, in some cases, the effects of the disability may be relevant, the fact of the disability itself is not a relevant circumstance for these purposes. This is because the comparison must be with a person **not** having that particular disability.

> A disabled person with arthritis who can type at 30 words per minute (wpm) applies for an administrative job which includes typing, but is rejected on the ground that her typing speed is too slow. The correct comparator in a claim for direct discrimination would be a person not having arthritis who also has a typing speed of 30 wpm (with the same accuracy rate).

A disabled person with a severe visual impairment applies for a job as a bus driver and is refused the job because he fails to meet the minimum level of visual acuity which is essential to the safe performance of the job. The correct comparator is a person not having that particular disability (for example, a person who merely has poorer than average eyesight) also failing to meet that minimum standard.

A disabled person with schizophrenia applies for a job as an administrative assistant with his local authority, and declares his history of mental illness. The local authority refuses him employment, relying on a negative medical report from the authority's occupational health adviser which is based on assumptions about the effects of schizophrenia, without adequate consideration of the individual's abilities and the impact of the impairment in his particular case. This is likely to amount to direct discrimination and to be unlawful. The comparator here is a person who does not have schizophrenia, but who has the same abilities to do the job (including relevant qualifications and experience) as the disabled applicant: such a person would not have been rejected without adequate consideration of his individual abilities.

4.21 If (as in the above examples) a disabled person alleges that he has been refused the offer of a job on the ground of his disability, it is only appropriate to compare those of his circumstances which are relevant to his ability to do the job. It is not appropriate to compare other circumstances which are not relevant to this issue. The need to focus on relevant circumstances applies not only to recruitment cases of this kind, but also to any other situation where direct discrimination may have occurred.

A disabled man with arthritis applies for an administrative job which includes typing, but is rejected in favour of a non-disabled candidate. Because of his arthritis, the man has a slow typing speed and has difficulty walking. The job is entirely desk-based, and does not require the person doing it to be able to walk further than a few metres within the office. The comparator in a claim of direct discrimination would be a non-disabled applicant with the same slow typing speed (and with the same abilities to do the job – e.g., the same typing accuracy rate, and the same knowledge of word-processing packages) – but it would not be necessary for the comparator to have mobility problems (because the ability to walk further than a few metres is not relevant to the candidates' ability to do the job).

Relevance of reasonable adjustments to comparison

4.22 In making the comparison in respect of a claim of direct discrimination, the disabled person's abilities must be considered **as they in fact are**. In some cases, there will be particular reasonable adjustments which an employer was required by the Act to make, but in fact failed to make. It may be that those adjustments would have had an effect on the disabled person's abilities to do the job. But in making the comparison, the disabled person's abilities should be considered as they **in fact** were, and not as they would or might have been had those adjustments been made. On the other hand, if adjustments have **in fact** been made which have had the effect of enhancing the disabled person's abilities, then it is those enhanced abilities which should be considered. The disabled person's abilities are being considered as they in fact are (and not as they might have been if the adjustments had not been made).

> A disabled person who applies for an administrative job which includes typing is not allowed to use her own adapted keyboard (even though it would have been reasonable for the employer to allow this) and types a test document at 30 wpm. Her speed with the adapted keyboard would have been 50 wpm. A non-disabled candidate is given the job because her typing speed on the test was 45 wpm with the same accuracy rate. This is not direct discrimination, as the comparator is a non-disabled person typing at 30 wpm. (But the disabled person would be likely to have good claims in respect of two other forms of discrimination – failure to make reasonable adjustments and disability-related discrimination – see paragraph 4.37.)

> A disabled person with arthritis who applies for a similar job is allowed to use an adapted keyboard and types a test document at 50 wpm. A non-disabled candidate types at 30 wpm with the same accuracy rate. However, the disabled candidate is rejected because of prejudice and the other candidate is offered the job instead. This is direct discrimination, as the comparator would be a person not having arthritis who could type at 50 wpm.

Can direct discrimination be justified?

4.23   Treatment of a disabled person which amounts to direct discrimination under the Act's provisions on employment and occupation is unlawful. It can never be justified.

Failure to make reasonable adjustments – relationship to discrimination

4.24   For the reason given in paragraph 4.3, it may be necessary to consider whether an employer has failed to comply with a duty to make a reasonable adjustment in order to determine whether disability-related discrimination has occurred.

4.25   Irrespective of its relevance to disability-related discrimination, however, a failure to comply with a duty to make a reasonable adjustment in respect of a disabled person amounts to discrimination in its own right. Such a failure is therefore unlawful. Chapter 5 explains the circumstances in which an employer has such a duty, and gives guidance as to what employers need to do when the duty arises.

4.26   As with direct discrimination, the Act does not permit an employer to justify a failure to comply with a duty to make a reasonable adjustment (see paragraphs 5.43 and 5.44).

What is disability-related discrimination?

What does the Act say?

4.27   The Act says that an employer's treatment of a disabled person amounts to discrimination if:

- it is for a reason related to his disability

- the treatment is less favourable than the way in which the employer treats (or would treat) others to whom that reason does not (or would not) apply, and

- the employer cannot show that the treatment is justified.

4.28   Although the Act itself does not use the term 'disability-related discrimination', this expression is used in the Code when referring to treatment of a disabled person which:

- is unlawful because each of the conditions listed in paragraph 4.27 is satisfied, but

- does not amount to direct discrimination under the Act.

4.29 In general, direct discrimination occurs when the reason for the less favourable treatment in question is the disability, while disability-related discrimination occurs when the reason relates to the disability but is not the disability itself. The expression 'disability-related discrimination' therefore distinguishes less favourable treatment which amounts to direct discrimination from a wider class of less favourable treatment which, although not amounting to direct discrimination, is nevertheless unlawful.

When does disability-related discrimination occur?

4.30 In determining whether disability-related discrimination has occurred, the employer's treatment of the disabled person must be compared with that of a person **to whom the disability-related reason does not apply**. This contrasts with direct discrimination, which requires a comparison to be made with a person without the disability in question but whose relevant circumstances are the same. The comparator may be non-disabled or disabled – but the key point is that the disability-related reason for the less favourable treatment must not apply to him.

A disabled man is dismissed for taking six months' sick leave which is disability-related. The employer's policy, which has been applied equally to all staff (whether disabled or not) is to dismiss all employees who have taken this amount of sick leave. The disability-related reason for the less favourable treatment of the disabled person is the fact of having taken six months' sick leave, and the correct comparator is a person to whom that reason does not apply – that is, someone who has not taken six months' sick leave. Consequently, unless the employer can show that the treatment is justified, it will amount to disability-related discrimination because the comparator would not have been dismissed. However, the reason for the treatment is not the disability itself (it is only a matter related thereto, namely the amount of sick leave taken). So there is no direct discrimination.

A disabled woman is refused an administrative job because she cannot type. She cannot type because she has arthritis. A non-disabled person who was unable to type would also have been turned down. The disability-related reason for the less favourable treatment is the woman's inability to type, and the correct comparator is a person to whom that reason does not apply – that is, someone who can type. Such a person would not have been refused the job. Nevertheless, the disabled woman has been treated less favourably for a disability-related reason and this will be unlawful unless it can be justified. There is no direct discrimination, however, because the comparator for **direct** discrimination is a person who does not have arthritis, but who is also unable to type.

4.31 The relationship between a disabled person's disability and the employer's treatment of him must be judged objectively. The reason for any less favourable treatment may well relate to the disability even if the employer does not have knowledge of the disability as such, or of whether its salient features are such that it meets the definition of disability in the Act. Less favourable treatment which is not itself direct discrimination will still be unlawful (subject to justification) if, in fact, the reason for it relates to the person's disability.

> A woman takes three periods of sickness absence in a two month period because of her disability, which is multiple sclerosis (MS). Her employer is unaware that she has MS and dismisses her, in the same way that it would dismiss any employee for a similar attendance record. Nevertheless, this is less favourable treatment for a disability-related reason (namely, the woman's record of sickness absence) and would be unlawful unless it can be justified.

4.32 The circumstances in which justification may be possible are explained in Chapter 6. However, it is worth noting that the possibility of justifying potential discrimination only arises at all when the form of discrimination being considered is disability-related discrimination, rather than direct discrimination or failure to make reasonable adjustments.

What does the Act say about victimisation?

4.33 Victimisation is a special form of discrimination which is made unlawful by the Act. It is unlawful for one person to treat another ('the victim') less favourably than he treats or would treat other people in the same circumstances because the victim has:

- brought, or given evidence or information in connection with, proceedings under the Act (whether or not proceedings are later withdrawn)

- done anything else under or by reference to the Act, or

- alleged someone has contravened the Act (whether or not the allegation is later dropped),

or because the person believes or suspects that the victim has done or intends to do any of these things.

> A disabled employee complains of discrimination, having been refused promotion at work. A colleague gives evidence at the tribunal hearing on his behalf. The employer makes the disabled person's colleague redundant because of this. This amounts to victimisation. It would also be unlawful to subject a colleague to any detriment where he attends the tribunal not to give evidence but purely to offer support to the claimant – because this would be something which is done by reference to the Act.

4.34 It is not victimisation to treat a person less favourably because that person has made an allegation which was false and not made in good faith.

4.35 However, the fact that a person has given evidence on behalf of an applicant in a claim which was unsuccessful does not, of itself, prove that his evidence was false or that it was not given in good faith.

4.36 Unlike the other forms of discrimination which are made unlawful by the Act, victimisation may be claimed by people who are not disabled as well as by those who are.

How do the different forms of discrimination compare in practice?

4.37 The way in which the different forms of discrimination which are unlawful under the Act's provisions on employment and occupation may operate in practice can be demonstrated by the following series of examples.

A woman with arthritis applies for a secretarial job in a local business. There is a question on the application form about disability, and she indicates that she has arthritis but that it does not affect her typing. The employer rejects her application because it nevertheless wrongly assumes that she will not be able to carry out the job due to her arthritis. This is direct discrimination.

In the situation described above, the woman instead declares on the application form that her arthritis does affect her ability to type. She is called for an interview and is told that a typing test forms part of the selection process. She tells the employer that she will need to use an adapted keyboard in order to take the test, but this is not provided on the day of the interview, and the woman fails the test as a result. As a consequence of failing the test, she is turned down for the job. This is not direct discrimination, as the reason for the employer's rejection of the woman was not her disability, but was the fact that she failed the typing test.

However, in such circumstances the employer has a duty to make reasonable adjustments to its selection arrangements. Depending on the circumstances, it may be a reasonable adjustment for the employer to provide the adapted keyboard or allow the woman to use her own keyboard in order that she is not placed at a substantial disadvantage by the test. If this is the case, then the employer will be unlawfully discriminating against her by failing to make the adjustment.

Although there is no direct discrimination, the employer has still treated the woman less favourably for a reason relating to her disability (namely the fact that she failed the typing test). This will be disability-related discrimination unless the employer can show that it is justified – and the employer will be unable to show this if it would have been reasonable for it to provide her with an adapted keyboard or allow her to use her own in order to take the typing test.

Because of the way in which she has been treated, the disabled woman makes a claim against the employer under Part 2 of the Act. Some time later, however, the same employer advertises a further secretarial vacancy. The woman applies again, but the employer rejects her application because she has previously made a claim under the Act. This is victimisation.

What does the Act say about harassment?

4.38 The Act says that harassment occurs where, for a reason which relates to a person's disability, another person engages in unwanted conduct which has the purpose or effect of:

● violating the disabled person's dignity, or

● creating an intimidating, hostile, degrading, humiliating or offensive environment for him.

4.39 If the conduct in question was engaged in with the intention that it should have either of these effects, then it amounts to harassment irrespective of its actual effect on the disabled person. In the absence of such intention, however, the conduct will only amount to harassment if it should reasonably be considered as having either of these effects. Regard must be had to all the circumstances in order to determine whether this is the case. Those circumstances include, in particular, the perception of the disabled person.

A man with a learning disability is often called 'stupid' and 'slow' by a colleague at work. This is harassment, whether or not the disabled man was present when these comments were made, because they were said with the intention of humiliating him.

A man with a stammer feels he is being harassed because his manager makes constant jokes about people with speech impairments. He asks his manager to stop doing this, but the manager says he is being 'oversensitive' as he habitually makes jokes in the office about many different sorts of people. This is likely to amount to harassment because making remarks of this kind should reasonably be considered as having either of the effects mentioned above.

An employee with HIV uses a colleague's mug. The colleague then makes a point of being seen washing the mug with bleach, which is not something she would do if anyone else used her mug. She also makes offensive comments about having her mug used by someone with HIV. This is likely to amount to harassment.

An employee circulates by email a joke about people with autism. A colleague with autism receives the email and finds the joke offensive. This is likely to amount to harassment.

A woman with depression considers that she is being harassed by her manager who constantly asks her if she is feeling all right, despite the fact that she has asked him not to do so in front of the rest of the team. This could amount to harassment.

What does the Act say about statutory obligations?

4.40   Nothing is made unlawful by the Act if it is required by an express statutory obligation. However, it is only in cases where a statutory obligation is specific in its requirements, leaving an employer with no choice other than to act in a particular way, that the provisions of the Act may be overridden. The provision in section 59 of the Act is thus of narrow application, and it is likely to permit disability discrimination only in rare circumstances.

What evidence is needed to prove that discrimination or harassment has occurred?

4.41   As stated in paragraph 3.26, enforcement of rights under the Act's provisions on employment and occupation takes place in the employment tribunals. A person who brings a claim for unlawful discrimination or harassment must show that discrimination has occurred. He must prove this on the balance of probabilities in order to succeed with a claim in an employment tribunal.

4.42   However, the Act says that, when such a claim is heard by an employment tribunal, the tribunal must uphold the claim if:

- the claimant proves facts from which the tribunal could conclude in the absence of an adequate explanation that the person against whom the claim is made (the respondent) has acted unlawfully, and

- the respondent fails to prove that he did not act in that way.

A disabled employee scores very poorly in a redundancy selection process in comparison with other employees in the same position as himself, getting low marks for skill and performance in his job. The employee has always had good appraisals in comparison with other employees and no action has ever been taken against him in respect of competence. Unless the employer demonstrates a non-discriminatory reason for the low scores, unlawful discrimination will be inferred in these circumstances.

4.43 Consequently, where a disabled person is able to prove on the balance of probabilities facts from which an inference of unlawful discrimination or harassment could be drawn, the burden of proof shifts to the respondent – for example, the disabled person's employer. This means that the employer must show that it is more likely than not that its conduct was not unlawful. This principle applies to allegations in respect of all forms of discrimination, including victimisation, and to harassment. Its practical effect in relation to the three principal forms of disability discrimination can be summarised as follows:

- To prove an allegation of **direct discrimination**, an employee must prove facts from which it could be inferred in the absence of an adequate explanation that he has been treated less favourably on the ground of his disability than an appropriate comparator has been, or would be, treated. If the employee does this, the claim will succeed unless the employer can show that disability was not any part of the reason for the treatment in question.

- To prove an allegation that there has been a **failure to comply with a duty to make reasonable adjustments**, an employee must prove facts from which it could be inferred in the absence of an adequate explanation that such a duty has arisen, and that it has been breached. If the employee does this, the claim will succeed unless the employer can show that it did not fail to comply with its duty in this regard.

- To prove an allegation of **disability-related discrimination**, an employee must prove facts from which it could be inferred in the absence of an adequate explanation that, for a reason relating to his disability, he has been treated less favourably than a person to whom that reason does not apply has been, or would be, treated. If the employee does this, the burden of proof shifts, and it is for the employer to show that the employee has not received less favourable treatment for a disability-related reason. Even if the employer cannot show this, however, the employee's claim will not succeed if the employer shows that the treatment was justified.

4.44 The Act provides a means by which a disabled person can seek evidence about whether he has been discriminated against, or subjected to harassment, under the Act's provisions on employment and occupation. He may do this by using a questionnaire to obtain further information from a person he thinks has acted unlawfully in relation to him. If there has been a failure to provide a satisfactory response to questions asked by the disabled person in this way, inferences may be drawn from that failure.

4.45 In addition, the fact that there has been a failure to comply with a relevant provision of the Code must be taken into account by a court or tribunal, where it considers it relevant, in determining whether there has been discrimination or harassment (see paragraph 1.6).

5 WHAT IS THE DUTY TO MAKE REASONABLE ADJUSTMENTS?

Introduction

5.1   In Chapter 4 it was noted that one of the ways in which discrimination occurs under Part 2 of the Act is when an employer fails to comply with a duty imposed on it to make 'reasonable adjustments' in relation to the disabled person. This chapter examines the circumstances in which a duty to make reasonable adjustments arises and outlines what an employer needs to do in order to discharge such a duty.

5.2   The concept of a duty to make reasonable adjustments is also relevant to the application of Part 2 in other situations.

When does an employer's duty to make reasonable adjustments arise?

5.3   The duty to make reasonable adjustments arises where a provision, criterion or practice applied by or on behalf of the employer, or any physical feature of premises occupied by the employer, places a disabled person at a substantial disadvantage compared with people who are not disabled. An employer has to take such steps as it is reasonable for it to have to take in all the circumstances to prevent that disadvantage – in other words the employer has to make a 'reasonable adjustment'. Where the duty arises, an employer cannot justify a failure to make a reasonable adjustment.

A man who is disabled because he has dyslexia applies for a job which involves writing letters. The employer gives all applicants a test of their letter-writing ability. The man can generally write letters very well but finds it difficult to do so in stressful situations and within short deadlines. He is given longer to take the test. This adjustment is likely to be a reasonable one for the employer to make.

5.4   It does not matter if a disabled person cannot point to an actual non-disabled person compared with whom he is at a substantial disadvantage. The fact that a non-disabled person, or even another disabled person, would not be substantially disadvantaged by the provision, criterion or practice or by the physical feature in question is irrelevant. The duty is owed specifically to the individual disabled person.

Which disabled people does the duty protect?

5.5   The duty to make reasonable adjustments applies in recruitment and during all stages of employment, including dismissal. It may also apply after employment has ended. The duty relates to all disabled employees of an employer and to any disabled applicant for employment. In the case of a provision, criterion or practice for determining to whom employment should be offered, the duty also applies in respect of any disabled person who has notified the employer that he may be an applicant for that employment.

5.6   The extent of the duty to make reasonable adjustments depends on the employment circumstances of the disabled person in question. For example, more extensive duties are owed to employees than to people who are merely thinking about applying for a job. More extensive duties are also owed to current employees than to former employees. The extent to which employers have knowledge of relevant circumstances is also a factor (see paragraphs 5.12 to 5.16).

5.7   In order to avoid discrimination, it would be prudent for employers not to attempt to make a fine judgement as to whether a particular individual falls within the statutory definition of disability, but to focus instead on meeting the needs of each employee and job applicant.

What are 'provisions, criteria and practices'?

5.8   Provisions, criteria and practices include arrangements, for example for determining to whom employment should be offered, and terms, conditions or arrangements on which employment, promotion, a transfer, training or any other benefit is offered or afforded. The duty to make reasonable adjustments applies, for example, to selection and interview procedures and the premises used for such procedures, as well as to job offers, contractual arrangements and working conditions.

A call centre normally employs supervisors on a full-time basis. A woman with sickle cell anaemia applies for a job as a supervisor. Because of pain and fatigue relating to her condition she asks to be able to do the job on a part-time basis. The call centre agrees. The hours of work which are offered amount to an adjustment to a working practice. This is likely to be a reasonable adjustment to the call centre's working practice.

An employer has a policy that designated car parking spaces are only offered to senior managers. A woman who is not a manager, but who has a mobility impairment and needs to park very close to the office, is given a designated car parking space. This is likely to be a reasonable adjustment to the employer's car parking policy.

What is a 'physical feature'?

5.9   The Act says that the following are to be treated as a physical feature:

- any feature arising from the design or construction of a building on the premises occupied by the employer

- any feature on the premises of any approach to, exit from, or access to such a building

- any fixtures, fittings, furnishings, furniture, equipment or materials in or on the premises, and

- any other physical element or quality of any land comprised in the premises occupied by the employer.

All these features are covered, whether temporary or permanent.

The design of a particular workplace makes it difficult for someone with a hearing impairment to hear, because the main office is open plan and has hard flooring. That is a substantial disadvantage caused by the physical features of the workplace.

Clear glass doors at the end of a corridor in a particular workplace present a hazard for a visually impaired employee. This is a substantial disadvantage caused by the physical features of the workplace.

5.10   Physical features will include steps, stairways, kerbs, exterior surfaces and paving, parking areas, building entrances and exits (including emergency escape routes), internal and external doors, gates, toilet and washing facilities, lighting and ventilation, lifts and escalators, floor coverings, signs, furniture, and temporary or movable items. This is not an exhaustive list.

What disadvantages give rise to the duty?

5.11   The Act says that only substantial disadvantages give rise to the duty. Substantial disadvantages are those which are not minor or trivial. Whether or not such a disadvantage exists in a particular case is a question of fact. What matters is not that a provision, criterion or practice or a physical feature is capable of causing a substantial disadvantage to the disabled person in question, but that it actually has this effect on him, or (where applicable) that it would have this effect if he were doing the job at the time.

What if the employer does not know that the person is disabled or is an actual or potential job applicant?

5.12   Although (as explained in paragraphs 4.11 and 4.31) less favourable treatment can occur even if the employer does not know that an employee is disabled, the employer only has a duty to make an adjustment if it knows, or could reasonably be expected to know, that the employee has a disability and is likely to be placed at a substantial disadvantage. The employer must, however, do all it can reasonably be expected to do to find out whether this is the case.

An employee has depression which sometimes causes her to cry at work, but the reason for her behaviour is not known to her employer. The employer makes no effort to find out if the employee is disabled and whether a reasonable adjustment could be made to her working arrangements. The employee is disciplined without being given any opportunity to explain that the problem arises from a disability. The employer may be in breach of the duty to make reasonable adjustments because it failed to do all it could reasonably be expected to do to establish if the employee was disabled and substantially disadvantaged.

An employer has an annual appraisal system which specifically provides an opportunity for employees to notify the employer in confidence if they are disabled and are put at a substantial disadvantage by the working arrangements or premises. This gives the employer the opportunity to find out if an employee requires reasonable adjustments, although it would not mean that the employer should not consider reasonable adjustments for an employee at other times of the year.

5.13   The principle stated in paragraph 5.12 applies equally to a disabled person who is an actual or potential applicant for employment.

An applicant is not short-listed for interview for the position of administrative assistant, a post which mainly involves typing, because he states on his application form that he cannot type. The reason he cannot type is that he has severe arthritis, but this is not stated anywhere on the form. The employer would not be expected to make an adjustment to the typing requirement in these circumstances as it had no knowledge of the disability and could not reasonably be expected to know of it.

5.14 In addition, an employer only has a duty to make an adjustment if it knows, or could reasonably be expected to know, that the disabled person is, or may be, an applicant.

5.15 If an employer's agent or employee (such as an occupational health adviser, a personnel officer or line manager or recruitment agent) knows, in that capacity, of an employee's disability, the employer will not usually be able to claim that it does not know of the disability, and that it therefore has no obligation to make a reasonable adjustment. The same applies in respect of actual or potential applicants for employment. Employers therefore need to ensure that where information about disabled people may come through different channels, there is a means – suitably confidential – for bringing the information together, to make it easier for the employer to fulfil its duties under the Act.

An occupational health adviser is engaged by a large employer to provide it with information about its employees' health. The occupational health adviser becomes aware of an employee's disability, which the employee's line manager does not know about. The employer's working arrangements put the employee at a substantial disadvantage because of the effects of her disability and she claims that a reasonable adjustment should have been made. It will not be a defence for the employer to claim that it did not know of her disability. This is because the information gained by the occupational health adviser on the employer's behalf is imputed to the employer. The occupational health adviser's knowledge means that the employer's duty under the Act applies. If the employee did not give consent for the occupational health adviser to pass on personal information to the line manager, it might be necessary for the line manager to implement the reasonable adjustment without knowing precisely why it has to do so.

5.16 Information will not be imputed to the employer if it is gained by a person providing services to employees independently of the employer. This is the case even if the employer has arranged for those services to be provided.

An employer contracts with an agency to provide an independent counselling service to employees. The contract says that the counsellors are not acting on the employer's behalf while in the counselling role. Any information about a person's disability obtained by a counsellor during such counselling would not be imputed to the employer and so would not trigger the employer's duty to make reasonable adjustments.

Does the duty to make reasonable adjustments apply in other situations related to employment and occupation?

5.17 Paragraphs 5.3 to 5.16 explain when it may be necessary to make an adjustment in relation to employment. Part 2 imposes similar requirements in relation to the occupations it covers, subject to certain differences. Reasonable adjustments may also be required in relation to occupational pension schemes and group insurance services.

What adjustments might an employer have to make?

5.18 The Act gives a number of examples of adjustments, or 'steps', which employers may have to take, if it is reasonable for them to have to do so (see paragraphs 5.24 to 5.42). Any necessary adjustments should be implemented in a timely fashion, and it may also be necessary for an employer to make more than one adjustment. It is advisable to agree any proposed adjustments with the disabled person in question before they are made.

Appendix 6

The Act does not give an exhaustive list of the steps which may have to be taken to discharge the duty. Steps other than those listed here, or a combination of steps, will sometimes have to be taken. However, the steps in the Act are:

- making adjustments to premises

An employer makes structural or other physical changes such as widening a doorway, providing a ramp or moving furniture for a wheelchair user; relocates light switches, door handles or shelves for someone who has difficulty in reaching; or provides appropriate contrast in decor to help the safe mobility of a visually impaired person.

- allocating some of the disabled person's duties to another person

An employer reallocates minor or subsidiary duties to another employee as a disabled person has difficulty doing them because of his disability. For example, the job involves occasionally going onto the open roof of a building but the employer transfers this work away from an employee whose disability involves severe vertigo.

- transferring the person to fill an existing vacancy

An employer should consider whether a suitable alternative post is available for an employee who becomes disabled (or whose disability worsens), where no reasonable adjustment would enable the employee to continue doing the current job. Such a post might also involve retraining or other reasonable adjustments such as equipment for the new post.

- altering the person's hours of working or training

This could include allowing a disabled person to work flexible hours to enable him to have additional breaks to overcome fatigue arising from his disability. It could also include permitting part time working, or different working hours to avoid the need to travel in the rush hour if this is a problem related to an impairment. A phased return to work with a gradual build-up of hours might also be appropriate in some circumstances.

- assigning the person to a different place of work or training

An employer relocates the work station of a newly disabled employee (who now uses a wheelchair) from an inaccessible third floor office to an accessible one on the ground floor. It would be reasonable to move his place of work to other premises of the same employer if the first building is inaccessible.

- allowing the person to be absent during working or training hours for rehabilitation, assessment or treatment

An employer allows a person who has become disabled more time off during work than would be allowed to non-disabled employees to enable him to have rehabilitation training. A similar adjustment would be appropriate if a disability worsens or if a disabled person needs occasional treatment anyway.

- giving, or arranging for, training or mentoring (whether for the disabled person or any other person)

This could be training in particular pieces of equipment which the disabled person uses, or an alteration to the standard employee training to reflect the employee's particular disability. For example, all employees are trained in the use of a particular machine but an employer provides slightly different or longer training for an employee with restricted hand or arm movements, or training in additional software for a visually impaired person so that he can use a computer with speech output.

An employer provides training for employees on conducting meetings in a way that enables a deaf staff member to participate effectively.

A disabled man returns to work after a six-month period of absence due to a stroke. His employer pays for him to see a work mentor, and allows time off to see the mentor, to help with his loss of confidence following the onset of his disability.

- acquiring or modifying equipment

An employer might have to provide special equipment (such as an adapted keyboard for someone with arthritis or a large screen for a visually impaired person), an adapted telephone for someone with a hearing impairment, or other modified equipment for disabled employees (such as longer handles on a machine). There is no requirement to provide or modify equipment for personal purposes unconnected with an employee's work, such as providing a wheelchair if a person needs one in any event but does not have one. The disadvantage in such a case does not flow from the employer's arrangements or premises.

- modifying instructions or reference manuals

The format of instructions and manuals might need to be modified for some disabled people (e.g. produced in Braille or on audio tape) and instructions for people with learning disabilities might need to be conveyed orally with individual demonstration.

- modifying procedures for testing or assessment

A person with restricted manual dexterity would be disadvantaged by a written test, so the employer gives that person an oral test instead.

- providing a reader or interpreter

A colleague reads mail to a person with a visual impairment at particular times during the working day. Alternatively, the employer might hire a reader.

- providing supervision or other support

> An employer provides a support worker, or arranges help from a colleague, in appropriate circumstances, for someone whose disability leads to uncertainty or lack of confidence.

5.19 It may sometimes be necessary for an employer to take a combination of steps.

> A woman who is deaf-blind is given a new job with her employer in an unfamiliar part of the building. The employer (i) arranges facilities for her guide dog in the new area, (ii) arranges for her new instructions to be in Braille and (iii) trains colleagues to communicate with her, and provides disability equality training to all staff.

5.20 As mentioned above, it might be reasonable for employers to have to take other steps, which are not given as examples in the Act. These steps could include:

- conducting a proper assessment of what reasonable adjustments may be required

- permitting flexible working

- allowing a disabled employee to take a period of disability leave

> An employee who has cancer needs to undergo treatment and rehabilitation. His employer allows a period of disability leave and permits him to return to his job at the end of this period.

- participating in supported employment schemes, such as Workstep

> A man applies for a job as an office assistant after several years of not working because of depression. He has been participating in a supported employment scheme where he saw the post advertised. As a reasonable adjustment he asks the employer to let him make private phone calls during the working day to a support worker at the scheme.

- employing a support worker to assist a disabled employee

> An adviser with a visual impairment is sometimes required to make home visits. The employer employs a support worker to assist her on these visits.

- modifying disciplinary or grievance procedures

> A woman with a learning disability is allowed to take a friend (who does not work with her) to act as an advocate at a meeting with her employer about a grievance. The employer also ensures that the meeting is conducted in a way that does not disadvantage or patronise the disabled woman.

- adjusting redundancy selection criteria

> A woman with an autoimmune disease has taken several short periods of absence during the year because of the condition. When her employer is taking absences into account as a criterion for selecting people for redundancy, he discounts these periods of disability-related absence.

- modifying performance-related pay arrangements.

> A disabled woman who is paid purely on her output needs frequent short additional breaks during her working day – something her employer agrees to as a reasonable adjustment. It is likely to be a reasonable adjustment for her employer to pay her at an agreed rate (e.g. her average hourly rate) for these breaks.

5.21 Advice and assistance (which may include financial assistance) in relation to making adjustments may be available from the Access to Work scheme.

5.22 In some cases a reasonable adjustment will not work without the co-operation of other employees. Employees may therefore have an important role in helping to ensure that a reasonable adjustment is carried out in practice. Subject to considerations about confidentiality (explained at paragraphs 8.21 to 8.23), employers must ensure that this happens. It is unlikely to be a valid defence to a claim under the Act that staff were obstructive or unhelpful when the employer tried to make reasonable adjustments. An employer would at least need to be able to show that it took such behaviour seriously and dealt with it appropriately. Employers will be more likely to be able to do this if they establish and implement the type of policies and practices described at paragraph 2.12.

> An employer ensures that an employee with autism has a structured working day as a reasonable adjustment. As part of the reasonable adjustment it is the responsibility of the employer to ensure that other employees cooperate with this arrangement.

5.23 [refers to sections not reproduced here for reasons of space].

When is it 'reasonable' for an employer to have to make adjustments?

5.24 Whether it is reasonable for an employer to make any particular adjustment will depend on a number of things, such as its cost and effectiveness. However, if an adjustment is one which it is reasonable to make, then the employer must do so. Where a disabled person is placed at a substantial disadvantage by a provision, criterion or practice of the employer, or by a physical feature of the premises it occupies, the employer must consider whether any reasonable adjustments can be made to overcome that disadvantage. There is no onus on the disabled person to suggest what adjustments should be made (although it is good practice for employers to ask) but, where the disabled person does so, the employer must consider whether such adjustments would help overcome the disadvantage, and whether they are reasonable.

> A disabled employee has been absent from work as a result of depression. Neither the employee nor his doctor is able to suggest any adjustments that could be made. Nevertheless the employer should still consider whether any adjustments, such as working from home for a time, would be reasonable.

5.25   Effective and practicable adjustments for disabled people often involve little or no cost or disruption and are therefore very likely to be reasonable for an employer to have to make. Even if an adjustment has a significant cost associated with it, it may still be cost-effective in overall terms – and so may be a reasonable adjustment to make. Many adjustments do not involve making physical changes to premises. However, where such changes do need to be made, employers may need to take account of the considerations explained in Chapter 12 [not reproduced here] which deals with issues about making alterations to premises.

5.26   If making a particular adjustment would increase the risks to the health and safety of any person (including the disabled person in question) then this is a relevant factor in deciding whether it is reasonable to make that adjustment. Suitable and sufficient risk assessments, such as those carried out for the purposes of the Management of Health and Safety at Work Regulations 1999, should be used to help determine whether such risks are likely to arise.

5.27   The Act lists a number of factors which may, in particular, have a bearing on whether it will be reasonable for the employer to have to make a particular adjustment. These factors make a useful checklist, particularly when considering more substantial adjustments. The effectiveness and practicability of a particular adjustment might be considered first. If it is practicable and effective, the financial aspects might be looked at as a whole – the cost of the adjustment and resources available to fund it. Other factors might also have a bearing. The factors in the Act are listed below.

The effectiveness of the step in preventing the disadvantage

5.28   It is unlikely to be reasonable for an employer to have to make an adjustment involving little benefit to the disabled person.

> A disabled employee cannot physically access the stationery cupboard at work. It is unlikely to be reasonable for the employer to have to make the cupboard accessible, unless distribution of stationery was a significant part of the employee's job.

5.29   However, an adjustment which, taken alone, is of marginal benefit, may be one of several adjustments which, when looked at together, would be effective. In that case, it is likely to be reasonable to have to make it.

The practicability of the step

5.30   It is more likely to be reasonable for an employer to have to take a step which is easy to take than one which is difficult. In some circumstances it may be reasonable to have to take a step, even though it is difficult.

> It might be impracticable for an employer who needs to appoint an employee urgently to have to wait for an adjustment to be made to an entrance. How long it might be reasonable for the employer to have to wait would depend on the circumstances. However, it might be possible to make a temporary adjustment in the meantime, such as using another, less convenient entrance.

The financial and other costs of the adjustment and the extent of any disruption caused

5.31 If an adjustment costs little or nothing and is not disruptive, it would be reasonable unless some other factor (such as practicability or effectiveness) made it unreasonable. The costs to be taken into account include those for staff and other resources. The significance of the cost of a step may depend in part on what the employer might otherwise spend in the circumstances. In assessing the likely costs of making an adjustment, the availability of external funding (such as funding by Access to Work) should be taken into account.

> It would be reasonable for an employer to have to spend at least as much on an adjustment to enable the retention of a disabled person – including any retraining – as might be spent on recruiting and training a replacement.

5.32 The significance of the cost of a step may also depend in part on the value of the employee's experience and expertise to the employer.

5.33 Examples of the factors that might be considered as relating to the value of an employee would include:

- the amount of resources (such as training) invested in the individual by the employer
- the employee's length of service
- the employee's level of skill and knowledge
- the employee's quality of relationships with clients
- the level of the employee's pay.

5.34 It is more likely to be reasonable for an employer to have to make an adjustment with significant costs for an employee who is likely to be in the job for some time than for a temporary employee.

5.35 An employer is more likely to have to make an adjustment which might cause only minor inconvenience to other employees or the employer than one which might unavoidably prevent other employees from doing their job, or cause other significant disruption.

The extent of the employer's financial or other resources

5.36 It is more likely to be reasonable for an employer with substantial financial resources to have to make an adjustment with a significant cost, than for an employer with fewer resources. The resources in practice available to the employer as a whole should be taken into account as well as other calls on those resources. For larger employers, it is good practice to have a specific budget for reasonable adjustments – but limitations on the size of any such budget will not affect the existence of the employer's duties to disabled employees. The reasonableness of an adjustment will depend not only on the resources in practice available for the adjustment but also on all other relevant factors (such as effectiveness and practicability).

> If a shop is part of a retail chain, the total resources of that business would be taken into account when assessing whether an adjustment is reasonable. Competing demands on those resources will also be taken into account.

Appendix 6

5.37 It is more likely to be reasonable for an employer with a substantial number of staff to have to make certain adjustments, than for a smaller employer.

It would generally be reasonable for an employer with a large staff to make significant efforts to reallocate duties or identify a suitable alternative post or provide supervision from existing staff. It may also be reasonable for a small company to make these adjustments but not if it involved disproportionate effort.

The availability to the employer of financial or other assistance to help make an adjustment

5.38 The availability of outside help (such as advice and assistance from Access to Work) may well be a relevant factor.

A small employer, in recruiting a disabled person, finds that the only feasible adjustment is too costly for it alone. However, if assistance is available e.g. from the Access to Work scheme or a voluntary body, it may well be reasonable for the employer to make the adjustment.

5.39 A disabled person is not required to contribute to the cost of a reasonable adjustment. However, if a disabled person has a particular piece of special or adapted equipment which he is prepared to use for work, this might make it reasonable for the employer to have to take some other step (as well as allowing the use of the equipment).

An employer requires its employees to use company cars for all business travel. One employee's disability means she would have to use an adapted car or an alternative form of transport. If she has an adapted car of her own which she is willing to use on business, it might well be reasonable for the employer to allow this and pay her an allowance to cover the cost of doing so, even if it might not have been reasonable for it to provide an adapted company car (because of the additional expense), or to pay an allowance to cover alternative travel arrangements in the absence of an adapted car. This would be a reasonable step to take because it would be cost-effective for the employer, easy to implement and would remove the disadvantage to the disabled employee immediately.

A disabled woman employed as a computer engineer uses a piece of communications equipment that she obtained through the Access to Work scheme. Her employer pays the cost of repair when it breaks down.

The nature of the employer's activities, and the size of its undertaking

5.40 As explained in paragraphs 3.9 and 3.10, Part 2 now applies to all employers (except for the Armed Forces), irrespective of their size. However, the size of an employer's undertaking and the nature of its activities may be relevant in determining the reasonableness of a particular step.

A small manufacturing company making chairs employs a craftswoman who becomes disabled and can no longer carry out her job, even after adjustments have been considered. The only jobs available in the company are production-based as the company owner herself carries out all other functions, such as marketing and running the office. Given the nature of the business, it is not likely to be reasonable for the employer to provide an alternative job for the employee.

In contrast, a business of the same size which designs, manufactures and retails games is likely to have a wide range of jobs. In these circumstances, if an employee were no longer able to work in a production role it might be reasonable for the employer to provide an alternative job.

A sales assistant in a small shop who has a mental health problem requests time off each week to attend a psychotherapy appointment. It would be more likely to be reasonable for her employer to agree to this if there were other sales assistants who could cover for her absence.

In relation to private households, the extent to which taking the step would disrupt the household or disturb any person residing there

5.41 The duty to make reasonable adjustments may apply in respect of disabled people who work in private households. However, even if the financial cost would be minimal, it might not be reasonable to take a particular step if doing so would entail disruption to the household or disturbance to people who live there.

A man employs a deaf cleaner in his house. They communicate with each other by writing notes. It is likely to be a reasonable adjustment for him to communicate with her in this way.

A person with a severe dust allergy applies for the position of nanny. When she is interviewed it becomes apparent that she can only work in an environment which is dust free. The prospective employers take the view that this would be too disruptive to their home life. It is unlikely to be reasonable for them to have to make the adjustments needed to employ this person.

Other factors

5.42 Although the Act does not mention any further factors, others may be relevant depending on the circumstances. For example:

- effect on other employees

A disabled person wants to work in a cold office as heat aggravates his skin condition. This is not reasonable in the open plan office where he works because it would be uncomfortable for other employees to have to work in these conditions. Moving him to a small office on his own may be a reasonable adjustment in these circumstances.

> A disabled woman working as a baker in a small bakery wants to avoid night shifts because disturbances to her sleep patterns trigger her migraines. Other employees would also like to avoid night shifts, for reasons unrelated to disability. This is unlikely to be a relevant factor for the employer in considering whether it is reasonable to allow the disabled employee's request.

- adjustments made for other disabled employees

> If an employer has a number of staff with mobility problems this may mean that it would be reasonable to make significant structural changes to their workplace.

- the extent to which the disabled person is willing to co-operate

> An employee with a mobility impairment works in a team located on an upper floor to which there is no access by lift. Getting there is very tiring for the employee, and the employer could easily make a more accessible location available for him. Following a workplace assessment the employer decides to move the employee to the alternative location, but the employee refuses to co-operate. If there is no other adjustment that the employer can reasonably make, it does not have to do any more.

Can failure to make a reasonable adjustment ever be justified?

5.43   The Act does not permit an employer to justify a failure to comply with a duty to make a reasonable adjustment. This is a change in the law (see Appendix A).

5.44   Clearly, however, an employer will only breach such a duty if the adjustment in question is one which it is reasonable for it to have to make. So, where the duty applies, it is the question of 'reasonableness' which alone determines whether the adjustment has to be made.

6   JUSTIFICATION

Introduction

6.1   Most conduct which is potentially unlawful under Part 2 of the Act cannot be justified. Conduct which amounts to:

- direct discrimination
- failure to comply with a duty to make a reasonable adjustment
- victimisation
- harassment
- instructions or pressure to discriminate, or
- aiding an unlawful act

is unlawful irrespective of the reason or motive for it.

When does the Act permit justification?

6.2   Paragraph 4.27 explains that one of the forms of discrimination which is unlawful under Part 2 is disability-related discrimination. However, an employer's conduct towards a disabled person does not amount to disability-related discrimination if it can be justified. This chapter explains the limited circumstances in which this may happen.

6.3 Where less favourable treatment of a disabled person is capable of being justified (that is, where it is **not** direct discrimination), the Act says that it will, in fact, be justified if, but only if, the reason for the treatment is both material to the circumstances of the particular case **and** substantial. This is an objective test. 'Material' means that there must be a reasonably strong connection between the reason given for the treatment and the circumstances of the particular case. 'Substantial' means, in the context of justification, that the reason must carry real weight and be of substance.

A man who has severe back pain and is unable to bend is rejected for a job as a carpet fitter as he cannot carry out the essential requirement of the job, which is to fit carpets. This would be lawful as the reason he is rejected is a substantial one and is clearly material to the circumstances.

6.4 In certain circumstances, the existence of a material and substantial reason for disability-related less favourable treatment is not enough to justify that treatment. This is the case where an employer is also under a duty to make reasonable adjustments in relation to the disabled person but fails to comply with that duty.

6.5 In those circumstances, it is necessary to consider not only whether there is a material and substantial reason for the less favourable treatment, but also whether the treatment would still have been justified even if the employer had complied with its duty to make reasonable adjustments. In effect, it is necessary to ask the question 'would a reasonable adjustment have made any difference?' If a reasonable adjustment would have made a difference to the reason that is being used to justify the treatment, then the less favourable treatment cannot be justified.

An applicant for an administrative job appears not to be the best person for the job, but only because her typing speed is too slow as a result of arthritis in her hands. If a reasonable adjustment – perhaps an adapted keyboard – would overcome this, her typing speed would not in itself be a substantial reason for not employing her. Therefore the employer would be unlawfully discriminating if, on account of her typing speed, he did not employ her or provide that adjustment.

6.6 In relation to disability-related discrimination, the fact that an employer has failed to comply with a duty to make a reasonable adjustment means that the sequence of events for justifying disability-related less favourable treatment is as follows:

- The disabled person proves facts from which it could be inferred in the absence of an adequate explanation that:

  a. for a reason related to his disability, he has been treated less favourably than a person to whom that reason does not apply has been, or would be, treated, and

  b. a duty to make a reasonable adjustment has arisen in respect of him and the employer has failed to comply with it.

- The employer will be found to have discriminated unless it proves that:

  a. the reason for the treatment is both material to the circumstances of the particular case and substantial, and

b.   the reason would still have applied if the reasonable adjustment had been made.

Can health and safety concerns justify less favourable treatment?

6.7   Stereotypical assumptions about the health and safety implications of disability should be avoided, both in general terms and in relation to particular types of disability. Indeed, less favourable treatment which is based on such assumptions may itself amount to direct discrimination – which is incapable of justification (see paragraph 4.5). The fact that a person has a disability does not necessarily mean that he represents an additional risk to health and safety.

> An employer has a policy of not employing anyone with diabetes because it believes that people with this condition are a health and safety risk. A person with diabetes applies to work for this employer and is turned down on the basis of her disability, without regard to her personal circumstances. A stereotypical assumption has been made which is likely to amount to direct discrimination and is therefore unlawful.

6.8   Under health and safety law it is the duty of every employer to ensure, so far as is reasonably practicable, the health, safety and welfare at work of all employees. Part of this duty is a requirement for all employers to assess the risks to the health and safety of all employees in the workplace and then to put in place measures that reduce the risks to as low a level as can reasonably be achieved. Genuine concerns about the health and safety of anybody (including a disabled employee) may be relevant when seeking to establish that disability-related less favourable treatment of a disabled person is justified. However, it is important to remember that health and safety law does not require employers to remove all conceivable risk, but to ensure that risk is properly appreciated, understood and managed. Further information can be obtained from the Health and Safety Executive.

6.9   It is the employer who must decide what action to take in response to concerns about health and safety. However, when an employer has reason to think that the effects of a person's disability may give rise to an issue about health and safety, it is prudent for it to have a new risk assessment carried out by a suitably qualified person. This is because:

- If an employer treats a disabled person less favourably merely on the basis of generalised assumptions about the health and safety implications of having a disability, such treatment may itself amount to direct discrimination – which is incapable of justification.

- Even where there is no direct discrimination, an employer which treats a disabled person less favourably without having a suitable and sufficient risk assessment carried out is unlikely to be able to show that its concerns about health and safety justify the less favourable treatment.

> A pilot develops a heart condition, and his employer asks him to undertake a risk assessment to be carried out by an appropriate consultant. This is likely to be justifiable.

6.10   Nevertheless, an employer should not subject a disabled person to a risk assessment if this is not merited by the particular circumstances of the case.

A person with a learning disability has been working in a shop for many years, stocking shelves without any problems. A new manager is appointed who insists that a risk assessment is carried out for her but not for all the other shelf stackers. This is unlikely to be warranted – and indeed it is likely to amount to direct discrimination.

6.11 A risk assessment must be suitable and sufficient. It should identify the risks associated with a work activity, taking account of any reasonable adjustments put in place for the disabled person, and should be specific for the individual carrying out a particular task. It is therefore unlikely that an employer which has a **general** policy of treating people with certain disabilities (such as epilepsy, diabetes or mental health problems) less favourably than other people will be able to justify doing so – even if that policy is in accordance with the advice of an occupational health adviser.

6.12 A 'blanket' policy of this nature will usually be unlawful. This is because it is likely to amount to direct discrimination (which cannot ever be justified) or to disability-related less favourable treatment which is not justifiable in the circumstances – ie disability-related discrimination.

6.13 Reasonable adjustments made by an employer may remove or reduce health and safety risks related to a person's disability. A suitable and sufficient assessment of such risks therefore needs to take account of the impact which making any reasonable adjustments would have. If a risk assessment is not conducted on this basis, then an employer is unlikely to be able to show that its concerns about health and safety justify less favourable treatment of the disabled person.

Can medical information justify less favourable treatment?

6.14 Consideration of medical information (such as a doctor's report or the answers to a medical questionnaire) is likely to form part of an assessment of health and safety risks. In most cases, however, having a disability does not adversely affect a person's general health. In other cases, its effect on a person's health may fluctuate. Although medical information about a disability may justify an adverse employment decision (such as a decision to dismiss or not to promote), it will not do so if there is no effect on the person's ability to do the job (or if any effect is less than substantial), no matter how great the effects of the disability are in other ways. Indeed, less favourable treatment of a disabled person in a case where his disability has no effect on his ability to do the job may well amount to direct discrimination – which is incapable of being justified.

An employer requires all candidates for a job as a technician in a chemical plant to complete a medical questionnaire. Medical information about one candidate shows that she has a degenerative condition which is likely to affect her ability to walk. This is not relevant to her ability to do the sedentary job in question. It would be unlawful for the employer to reject her on the ground of her disability as her disability is irrelevant to her ability to do the job. This would amount to direct discrimination.

The same employer is looking for a technician to work on a specific project for two years. A medical questionnaire shows that a candidate has a degenerative condition which could mean that he would not be able to work for that long. Because of this, further medical evidence is requested from his doctor and this confirms that he would not be able to work for two years. It is likely to be lawful to reject this candidate if the two-year requirement is justified in terms of the work and if there are no reasonable adjustments that could be made.

6.15 In addition, where medical information is available, employers must weigh it up in the context of the actual job, and the capabilities of the individual. An employer should also consider whether reasonable adjustments could be made in order to overcome any problems which may have been identified as a result of the medical information. It should not be taken for granted that the person who provides the medical information will be aware that employers have a duty to make reasonable adjustments, what these adjustments might be, or of the relevant working arrangements. It is good practice, therefore, to ensure that medical advisers are made aware of these matters. Information provided by a medical adviser should only be relied on if the adviser has the appropriate knowledge and expertise.

> An occupational health adviser recommends that an administrative assistant cannot carry on in her current job because she has been diagnosed with Repetitive Strain Injury. The employer has another member of staff who uses voice recognition software, and considers this technology may be of relevance. The employer asks the adviser to review his conclusion taking this into account. The adviser revises his opinion and concludes that, with appropriate software, she can continue in her role.

6.16 In any event, although medical evidence may generally be considered as an 'expert contribution', it should not ordinarily be the sole factor influencing an employer's decision on employment related matters. The views of the disabled person (about his own capabilities and possible adjustments) should also be sought. In addition, and subject to considerations about confidentiality, other contributions could come from the disabled person's line manager (about the nature of the job and possible adjustments). It may also be possible to seek help from disability organisations or from Jobcentre Plus, who have staff trained to advise about disability issues in the workplace. Ultimately, it is for the employer – and not the medical adviser – to take decisions as to whether, for example, to reject a job applicant or to maintain a disabled person's employment.

> An employer receives advice from an occupational health adviser stating simply that an employee is 'unfit for work'. In spite of this the employer must consider whether there are reasonable adjustments which should be made.

APPENDIX A: CHANGES TO THE ACT

The table below summarises the main changes to the Act's provisions on employment and occupation taking effect on 1 October 2004. It does not include all the changes occurring on that date, and is not a full explanation of the law.

	Position before 1st October 2004
Scope	• DDA covered employers with 15 or more employees. • Some occupations (e.g. police & firefighters) were not covered.
Types of Discrimination	Three kinds of discrimination: • Less favourable treatment. • Failure to make reasonable adjustments. • Victimisation.

	Position before 1st October 2004
When is Justification relevant?	Justification was of relevance in cases about: • Less favourable treatment. • Failure to make reasonable adjustments.
Harassment	Covered, but no separate provisions on this.
Claims	Most claims covered by the Code were brought in the employment tribunal, apart from those involving trustees and managers of occupational pension schemes and claims about employment services.

Position after 1st October 2004

- All employers are covered by the DDA except for the Armed Forces.
- New occupations such as police and partners in firms are covered.
- Practical work experience, whether paid or unpaid, is covered.
- There are new provisions on discriminatory advertisements.
- Employment services are covered.

Four kinds of discrimination:
- Direct discrimination.
- Failure to make reasonable adjustments.
- 'Disability-related discrimination'.
- Victimisation.

Justification is NOT relevant in cases about:
- Direct discrimination.
- Failure to make reasonable adjustments.

Justification is relevant in cases about:
- Disability-related discrimination.

New provisions on harassment.

All claims covered by this Code are brought in the employment tribunal.

APPENDIX B:THE MEANING OF DISABILITY

This appendix is included to aid understanding about who is covered by the Act and should provide sufficient information on the definition of disability to cover the large majority of cases. The definition of disability in the Act is designed to cover only people who would generally be considered to be disabled. A Government publication 'Guidance on matters to be taken into account in determining questions relating to the definition of disability', is also available.

When is a person disabled?

A person has a disability if he has a physical or mental impairment, which has a substantial and long-term adverse effect on his ability to carry out normal day-to-day activities.

Appendix 6

What about people who have recovered from a disability?

People who have had a disability within the definition are protected from discrimination even if they have since recovered.

What does 'impairment' cover?

It covers physical or mental impairments; this includes sensory impairments, such as those affecting sight or hearing.

Are all mental impairments covered?

The term 'mental impairment' is intended to cover a wide range of impairments relating to mental functioning, including what are often known as learning disabilities. The Act says that a mental illness must be a clinically well-recognised illness in order to amount to a mental impairment. A clinically well-recognised illness is one that is recognised by a respected body of medical opinion.

What is a 'substantial' adverse effect?

A substantial adverse effect is something which is more than a minor or trivial effect. The requirement that an effect must be substantial reflects the general understanding of disability as a limitation going beyond the normal differences in ability which might exist among people.

What is a 'long-term' effect?

A long-term effect of an impairment is one:

● which has lasted at least 12 months, or

● where the total period for which it lasts is likely to be at least 12 months, or

● which is likely to last for the rest of the life of the person affected.

Effects which are not long-term would therefore include loss of mobility due to a broken limb which is likely to heal within 12 months and the effects of temporary infections, from which a person would be likely to recover within 12 months.

What if the effects come and go over a period of time?

If an impairment has had a substantial adverse effect on normal day-to-day activities but that effect ceases, the substantial effect is treated as continuing if it is likely to recur; that is if it is more probable than not that the effect will recur.

What are 'normal day-to-day activities'?

They are activities which are carried out by most people on a fairly regular and frequent basis. The term is not intended to include activities which are normal only for a particular person or group of people, such as playing a musical instrument, or a sport, to a professional standard or performing a skilled or specialised task at work. However, someone who is affected in such a specialised way but is also affected in normal day-to-day activities would be covered by this part of the definition. The test of whether an impairment affects normal day-to-day activities is whether it affects one of the broad categories of capacity listed in Schedule 1 to the Act. They are:

- mobility
- manual dexterity
- physical co-ordination
- continence
- ability to lift, carry or otherwise move everyday objects
- speech, hearing or eyesight
- memory or ability to concentrate, learn or understand, or
- perception of the risk of physical danger.

What about treatment?

Someone with an impairment may be receiving medical or other treatment which alleviates or removes the effects (though not the impairment). In such cases, the treatment is ignored and the impairment is taken to have the effect it would have had without such treatment. This does not apply if substantial adverse effects are not likely to recur even if the treatment stops (i.e. the impairment has been cured).

Does this include people who wear spectacles?

No. The sole exception to the rule about ignoring the effects of treatment is the wearing of spectacles or contact lenses. In this case, the effect while the person is wearing spectacles or contact lenses should be considered.

Are people who have disfigurements covered?

People with severe disfigurements are covered by the Act. They do not need to demonstrate that the impairment has a substantial adverse effect on their ability to carry out normal day-to-day activities.

What about people who know their condition is going to get worse over time?

Progressive conditions are conditions which are likely to change and develop over time. Examples given in the Act are cancer, multiple sclerosis, muscular dystrophy and HIV infection. Where a person has a progressive condition he will be covered by the Act from the moment the condition leads to an impairment which has some effect on ability to carry out normal day-to-day activities, even though not a substantial effect, if that impairment is likely eventually to have a substantial adverse effect on such ability.

What about people who are blind or partially sighted?

People who are registered as blind or partially sighted, or who are certified as being blind or partially sighted by a consultant ophthalmologist are automatically treated under the Act as being disabled. People who are not registered or certified as blind or partially sighted will be covered by the Act if they can establish that they meet the Act's definition of disability.

Are people with genetic conditions covered?

If a genetic condition has no effect on ability to carry out normal day-to-day activities, the person is not covered. Diagnosis does not in itself bring someone within the definition. If the condition is progressive, then the rule about progressive conditions applies.

Appendix 6

Are any conditions specifically excluded from the coverage of the Act?

Yes. Certain conditions are to be regarded as not amounting to impairments for the purposes of the Act. These are:

- addiction to or dependency on alcohol, nicotine, or any other substance (other than as a result of the substance being medically prescribed)

- seasonal allergic rhinitis (e.g. hayfever), except where it aggravates the effect of another condition

- tendency to set fires

- tendency to steal

- tendency to physical or sexual abuse of other persons

- exhibitionism

- voyeurism.

Also, disfigurements which consist of a tattoo (which has not been removed), non-medical body piercing, or something attached through such piercing, are to be treated as not having a substantial adverse effect on the person's ability to carry out normal day-to-day activities.

Appendix 7

Disability Rights Commission Code of Practice: Trade Organisations and Qualification Bodies

3. DISCRIMINATION BY TRADE ORGANISATIONS AND QUALIFICATIONS BODIES – AN OVERVIEW

Introduction

3.1 This chapter gives an overview of those provisions of the Act which are relevant to trade organisations and qualifications bodies. It explains who has rights and duties under those provisions and outlines what is made unlawful by them. Later chapters explain the provisions in greater detail.

Who has rights under the Act?

Disabled people

3.2 The Act gives protection from discrimination to a 'disabled' person within the meaning of the Act.

A disabled person is someone who has a physical or mental impairment which has an effect on his or her ability to carry out normal day-to-day activities. That effect must be:

- substantial (that is, more than minor or trivial), and

- adverse, and

- long term (that is, it has lasted or is likely to last for at least a year or for the rest of the life of the person affected).

3.3 Physical or mental impairment includes sensory impairment. Hidden impairments are also covered (for example, mental illness or mental health problems, learning disabilities, dyslexia, diabetes and epilepsy).

3.4 In considering its duties under the Act, a trade organisation or a qualifications body should not use any definition of 'disabled person' which is narrower than that in the Act. If such an organisation or body is asked to make a disability-related adjustment, it may ask the person requesting it for evidence that the impairment is one which meets the definition of disability in the Act. It may be appropriate to do so where the disability is not obvious. However, it is not appropriate to ask for more information about the impairment than is necessary for this purpose. Nor should evidence of disability be asked for where it ought to be obvious that the Act will apply.

People who have had a disability in the past

3.5 People who have had a disability within the meaning of the Act in the past are protected from discrimination even if they no longer have the disability.

More information about the meaning of disability

3.6 [...] A government publication, *Guidance on matters to be taken into account in determining questions relating to the definition of disability*, provides additional help in understanding the concept of disability and in identifying who is a disabled person. Where relevant, the Guidance must be taken into account in any legal proceedings.

People who have been victimised

3.7   The Act also gives rights to people who have been victimised, whether or not they have a disability or have had one in the past.

Who has obligations under the Act?

Trade organisations

3.8   The Act defines a trade organisation as an organisation of workers or of employers, or any other organisation whose members carry on a particular profession or trade for the purposes of which the organisation exists. Bodies like trade unions, employers' associations, chartered professional institutions are all trade organisations because they exist for the purposes of the profession or trade which their members carry on. Examples of trade organisations include the Law Society, the Royal College of Nursing, the Swimming Teachers' Association, the Society of Floristry, the British Computer Society, and the Institute of Carpenters. The Act applies to all trade organisations, no matter how many (or how few) members they may have.

Qualifications bodies

3.9   The Act defines a qualifications body as an authority or body which can confer, renew or extend a professional or trade qualification. For this purpose a professional or trade qualification is an authorisation, qualification, recognition, registration, enrolment, approval or certification which is needed for, or which facilitates engagement in, a particular profession or trade. [. . .] Qualifications bodies include examination boards, the General Medical Council, the Nursing and Midwifery Council, and the Driving Standards Agency. Other examples are City and Guilds, the Institute of the Motor Industry, the Hospitality Awarding Body and the Guild of Cleaners and Launderers.

3.10   Nevertheless, certain bodies are not regarded as qualifications bodies for the purposes of Part 2, even though they may perform some of the functions mentioned in paragraph 3.9. These are listed in the Act. Broadly speaking, they comprise local education authorities in England and Wales, education authorities in Scotland, and other bodies having responsibility for schools and colleges. This is because discrimination by such bodies is the concern of Part 4 of the Act, which relates to discrimination in the provision of education. The DRC has issued two separate codes of practice giving guidance on the operation of Part 4.

3.11   Clearly, certain trade organisations (such as the Law Society) also confer professional or trade qualifications. Consequently, the same organisation or body can be both a trade organisation and a qualifications body. Where this is the case, the application of the Act's provisions depends upon the capacity in which the organisation or body is acting at the time in question. For example, if an alleged act of discrimination relates to conferring, renewing or extending a professional or trade qualification, the relevant provisions are those relating to discrimination by qualifications bodies – the fact that the body is also a trade organisation is irrelevant in this context.

Employers and others to whom Part 2 applies

3.12   The primary focus of Part 2 is, of course, on the duties of employers to disabled people. [H]owever, that is not the subject of this Code. Guidance on the application of the Act to employers (as well as its application to people and bodies concerned with certain occupations and to persons such as the trustees or managers of occupational pension schemes and the providers of group insurance services) is given in a separate code of practice issued by the DRC. It has already been noted that, as employers themselves, trade organisations and qualifications bodies have duties under Part 2 in respect of disabled people whom they employ, or who apply to them for employment. Those duties are governed by the employment provisions of the Act.

What does the Act say about discrimination by trade organisations and qualifications bodies?

Effect of the Act

3.13   The Act makes it unlawful for a trade organisation to **discriminate** against a disabled person in relation to membership of the organisation or access to membership benefits. The Act also makes it unlawful for a qualifications body to **discriminate** against a disabled person in relation to conferring professional or trade qualifications.

3.14   However, the Act does not prevent organisations or bodies from treating disabled people more favourably than those who are not disabled.

Forms of discrimination

3.15   The four forms of discrimination which are unlawful under Part 2 are:

- direct discrimination

- failure to comply with a duty to make reasonable adjustments

- 'disability-related discrimination', and

- victimisation of a person (whether or not he is disabled).

Discrimination by trade organisations

3.16   The Act says that it is unlawful for a trade organisation to discriminate against a disabled person:

- in the arrangements it makes for the purpose of determining who should be offered membership of the organisation, or

- in the terms on which it is prepared to admit him to membership, or

- by refusing to accept, or deliberately not accepting, his application for membership.

3.17   The Act also says that it is unlawful for a trade organisation to discriminate against a disabled member:

- in the way it affords the member access to any benefits or by refusing or deliberately omitting to afford access to them, or

- by depriving the member of membership, or varying the terms of his membership, or

- by subjecting the member to any other detriment.

3.18   It should be noted that the Act does not protect corporate members of trade organisations, even if a disabled person is a representative of a corporate member.

A trade organisation in the building industry has both individual and corporate members. A disabled employee of a company which is a member of this trade organisation would not have protection from discrimination by the trade organisation under Part 2, whereas an individual member of the organisation would have such protection.

Discrimination by qualifications bodies

3.19   In relation to conferring, renewing, or extending professional or trade qualifications (abbreviated to 'conferring'), the Act says that it is unlawful for a qualifications body to discriminate against a disabled person:

- in the arrangements it makes for the purpose of determining upon whom to confer a professional or trade qualification, or

- in the terms on which it is prepared to confer such a qualification, or

- by refusing or deliberately omitting to grant any application by him for a professional or trade qualification, or

- by withdrawing such a qualification from him or varying the terms on which he holds it.

What else is unlawful under the relevant provisions of the Act?

Harassment

3.20   In addition to what it says about discrimination, Part 2 makes it unlawful for either a trade organisation or a qualifications body to subject a disabled person to harassment for a reason which relates to his disability.

Instructions and pressure to discriminate

3.21   It is also unlawful for a person who has authority or influence over another to instruct him, or put pressure on him, to act unlawfully under the provisions of Part 2. This covers pressure to discriminate, whether applied directly to the person concerned, or indirectly but in a way in which he is likely to hear of it. However, the Act does not give individual disabled people the right to take legal action in respect of unlawful instructions or pressure to discriminate. Such action may only be taken by the DRC.

A trade union is holding a conference. The conference organiser, who is a paid employee of the union working in the events department, instructs the branch representatives not to send any wheelchair users to the conference as the venue is not wheelchair accessible. This is likely to be unlawful as it is an instruction to discriminate.

Discriminatory advertisements

3.22 The Act does not prevent advertisements for membership of trade organisations or for professional or trade qualifications from saying that applications from disabled people are welcome. However, it does say that it is unlawful for those seeking members for an organisation (or seeking candidates for qualifications) to publish an advertisement (or cause it to be published) which indicates, or might reasonably be understood to indicate:

- that the success of a person's application may depend to any extent on his not having any disability, or any particular disability, or

- that the person determining the application is reluctant to make reasonable adjustments.

3.23 This applies to every form of advertisement or notice, whether to the public or not. However, an advertisement may still be lawful even if it does indicate that having a particular disability will adversely affect an applicant's prospects of success. This will be the case where, for example, the particular circumstances are such that the trade organisation or qualifications body is entitled to take the effects of the disability into account when assessing the suitability of applicants.

> A qualifications body in the tourism industry advertises in a trade publication, inviting readers to apply to take a course leading to a qualification accredited by that body. The advertisement says that candidates 'must have excellent written and spoken English'. This would exclude people who used British Sign Language as their first language, or people who had dyslexia, and may be unlawful.

> However a qualifications body advertising a course in tree surgery, would not be discriminating by stipulating that candidates 'must not be afraid of heights', even if this would exclude people who had vertigo as a result of their disability.

3.24 It is good practice to consider carefully what information should be included in advertisements and where they should be placed.

3.25 The Act does not give individual applicants for membership of trade organisations or applicants for professional or trade qualifications the right to take legal action in respect of discriminatory advertisements. Such action may only be taken by the DRC.

Who is liable for unlawful acts?

Responsibility for the acts of others

3.26 Trade organisations and qualifications bodies who act through agents are liable for the actions of their agents done with the express or implied authority of the organisation or body in question – this can include the actions of unpaid union representatives in the workplace. The Act also says that trade organisations and qualifications bodies are responsible for the actions of their employees in the course of their employment. For example, a trade union is responsible for the actions of its salaried officials in the course of their employment.

3.27 However, in legal proceedings against a trade organisation or qualifications body based on the actions of an employee, it is a defence that the organisation or body took 'such steps as were reasonably practicable' to prevent such actions. It is not a defence simply to show that the action took place without the knowledge or approval of the organisation or body.

A trade union has a disability policy which states that it will pay for sign language interpreters to interpret at branch meetings, should the need arise, from a central union fund. This policy, and the arrangements available for paying for sign language interpreters (and for other adjustments), is explained to all branch representatives are required to undergo basic training in the policy. A deaf union member requests a sign language interpreter for a branch meeting, but the branch representative who has undergone this training says that this is not possible as there are insufficient funds in the branch to pay for this adjustment. In this case the union could demonstrate that it had taken 'such steps as were reasonably practicable' to prevent such actions and it is likely that it has not acted unlawfully. The branch representative, however, is likely to be acting unlawfully (see paragraphs 3.28 and 3.29).

Aiding an unlawful act

3.28   A person who knowingly helps another to do something made unlawful by the Act will be treated as having done the same kind of unlawful act. This means that, where a trade organisation or qualifications body is liable for an unlawful act of its employee or agent, that employee or agent will be liable for aiding the unlawful act of the organisation or body.

3.29   Where an employee of a trade organisation or qualifications body discriminates against or harasses a disabled person, it is the employing organisation or body which will be liable for that unlawful act – unless it can show that it took such steps as were reasonable to prevent the unlawful act in question. But the employee who committed the discrimination or harassment will be liable for aiding the unlawful act – and this will be the case even if the trade organisation or qualifications body is able to show that it took reasonable steps to prevent the act.

In the previous example, where the union has taken steps to ensure that disabled members can participate in branch meetings, it is likely that the branch representative would be acting unlawfully in aiding an unlawful act by the union, even though the union itself has avoided liability by taking reasonably practicable steps.

Enforcing rights under Part 2

3.30   Enforcement of rights under Part 2 takes place in the employment tribunals.

Appendix 8

EU Recommendation on Sexual Harassment

EQUAL TREATMENT FOR WOMEN AND MEN

PROTECTION OF THE DIGNITY OF WOMEN AND MEN AT WORK

Editorial note: These recommendations were issued by the European Union.

1) Objective

To promote greater awareness of the problem of sexual harassment at work and its consequences: to draw attention to the code of conduct and recommend application of the same.

2) Community Measures

Commission Recommendation 92/131/EEC of 27 November 1991 on the protection of the dignity of women and men at work.

3) Contents

1. The Member States are recommended to take action to promote awareness that conduct of a sexual nature, or other conduct based on sex and affecting dignity, is unacceptable.

2. Sexual harassment is defined as:

   conduct which is unwanted, unreasonable and offensive to the recipient; the fact that a person's rejection of, or submission to, such conduct on the part of employers or workers (including superiors or colleagues) is used explicitly or implicitly as a basis for a decision which affects that person's access to vocational training, access to employment, continued employment or salary; any conduct which creates an intimidating, hostile or humiliating work environment for the recipient.

3. Such conduct may, in certain circumstances, be contrary to the principle of equal treatment within the meaning of Articles 3, 4 and 5 of Council Directive 76/207/EEC on equal treatment.

4. Member States are called on to take action in the public sector to implement the Commission's code of conduct, with such action serving as an example to the private sector. Member States should also encourage employers and employee representatives to develop measures to implement the code of conduct.

5. The Commission is to draw up a report based on the information forwarded by the Member States concerning the measures taken, with the Commission having to be notified of these within three years of the date on which the Recommendation is adopted.

4) Deadline for Implementation of the Legislation in the Member States

Not applicable.

Appendix 8

5) **Date of Entry Into Force (if different from the above)**

6) **References**

Official Journal L 49, 24.02.1992

7) **Follow-up Work**

Declaration on the implementation of the Recommendation adopted by the Council on 19 December 1991.

8) **Commission Implementing Measures**

EQUAL TREATMENT FOR MEN AND WOMEN

PREVENTING SEXUAL HARASSMENT AT WORK

1) **Objective**

To seek the opinion of the social partners on the question of protecting the dignity of men and women at work (referred to as "sexual harassment").

2) **Community Measure**

Commission communication of 24 July 1996 concerning the consultation of management and labour on the prevention of sexual harassment at work.

3) **Contents**

1. In accordance with Article 4 of the Recommendation of 27 November 1991 (see summary, 9.14a), the Member States informed the Commission in 1994 and in 1995 of measures taken to promote awareness of the fact that sexual harassment is unacceptable. These are the elements used in drawing up the "Evaluation report concerning the Commission Recommendation on the protection of the dignity of men and women at work" which is attached to the communication.

2. As sexual harassment is an affront to the dignity of the individual and a hindrance to productivity within the European Union, it constitutes an obstacle to an efficient labour market in which men and women work together.

3. Some specific groups are particularly vulnerable: divorced or separated women, new entrants to the labour market, those with irregular or precarious employment, women with disabilities, women from racial minorities, homosexuals and young men.

4. Given the growing trend towards men and women working together at similar levels, many cases of sexual harassment now take place between persons at the same level in the hierarchy, not always between employees and their superiors.

5. Sexual harassment has adverse consequences for all:

    - workers subject to it, in terms of health, confidence, morale, performance and career prospects;

    - workers not themselves the object thereof but who are witness to it or have knowledge of it, in terms of working environment, etc;

    - employers, in terms of economic efficiency, negative publicity and possible legal implications.

6.   The problem of sexual harassment has in recent years been acknowledged in a majority of the Member States and has resulted in the enactment or preparation of legislative acts in Belgium, France, Germany, Italy, Ireland, the Netherlands and Spain and in collective agreements in some sectors in Spain, the United Kingdom, the Netherlands and Denmark.

7.   The evaluation report concludes, however, that the Recommendation and the code of practice have not led to the adoption of sufficient measures to ensure a working environment where sexual harassment can be effectively prevented and combated. Since it deals with an affront to the dignity of the individual and an obstacle to productivity, the problem deserves to be tackled at European level.

8.   The evaluation report underlines the need for a global approach:

- to highlight points of agreement and differences between different national policies;

- to enable the social partners to play a part in elaborating any form of future action;

- to work towards the adoption of a binding instrument setting out a common plan to be adapted to each country's achievements, needs and preferences.

9.   The practical knowledge and experience of the social partners in implementing measures to combat sexual harassment are widely recognised. Their action could take the form of a collective agreement at European level. In the light of their reaction to this communication, the Commission will consider what further action is required.

4)   Deadline for Implementation of the Legislation in the Member States

Not applicable.

5)   Date of Entry Into Force (if different from the above)

6)   References

Commission communication COM(96) 373 final

Not published in the Official Journal.

7)   Follow-Up Work

On 19 March 1997, the Commission adopted a communication initiating the second-stage consultation of management and labour on the prevention of sexual harassment at work [SEC(97) 568 final, not published in the Official Journal].

In the first round of consultations, which began in July 1996, replies were received from 17 of the 39 employer and trade union organisations consulted. A majority recognised that sexual harassment is a widespread problem which must be prevented in the workplace for the sake of both the individual and the company.

However, opinions differed on the best ways of dealing with the problem:

- the employers' organisations regarded the steps taken at national level as a good basis for further action, in line with the principle of subsidiarity;

- the trade union organisations considered that very little had been done at national level and that this would also be the case in future if a binding Community instrument was not adopted.

Appendix 8

In the consultation document, the Commission presents evidence of the occurrence of sexual harassment and highlights the ineffectiveness of the national legislation, which is primarily repressive and thus provides remedies, by either civil or penal procedures, only for severe isolated cases of sexual harassment. The Commission favours a comprehensive prevention policy, with rules and procedures that are specifically applicable to the context of the workplace.

The proposal on which the Commission seeks the opinions of the social partners covers three points:

- a legal definition of sexual harassment;
- a framework of minimum standards setting out the main steps to be taken to prevent harassment;
- a system of help and advice for victims (with the appointment of counsellors at the workplace).

The Commission has already stated its commitment, should the social partners be unable to conclude an agreement at European level, to seeking other ways of preventing sexual harassment (possibly involving the adoption of a binding legal instrument). However, it will not take a final decision until it has considered the comments received during the consultation procedure.

8)   Commission Implementing Measures

EQUAL TREATMENT FOR WOMEN AND MEN

CODE OF PRACTICE – DIGNITY OF WOMEN AND MEN AT WORK

1)   Objective

To provide practical guidance to employers, trade unions and employees with a view to clamping down on sexual harassment, and to ensure that adequate procedures are readily available to deal with the problem and prevent its recurrence. To encourage men and women to respect one another's human integrity.

2)   Community Measures

Commission code of practice on sexual harassment.

3)   Contents

1.   The Commission restates the general definition of sexual harassment contained in its Recommendation. National judges will still have to decide whether cases brought to their attention fall within this category and are to be regarded as a criminal offence, an infringement of statutory obligations (especially in health and safety matters) or a contravention of obligations imposed on employers by contract or otherwise. It calls on employers in the public and private sectors, trade unions and employees to follow the guidelines of the code and to include appropriate clauses in collective bargaining agreements.

2.   Recommendations to employers

    a)   Prevention

        Employers should issue a policy statement which expressly states that sexual harassment will not be permitted or condoned and that employees have a right to complain about it should it occur. The policy statement should leave no doubt as to what is considered inappropriate behaviour which may, in certain circumstances, be unlawful. It should also explain the procedure to be followed for making a complaint or obtaining assistance, and should specify the disciplinary measures applicable. It should provide assurance that complaints will be dealt with seriously, expeditiously and confidentially, and that complainants will be protected against victimization. Once it has been drawn up, the statement must be communicated to everyone concerned, so as to ensure the widest possible awareness. Managers are to explain the organization's policy to their staff, and are expected to take appropriate measures, act supportively towards victims and provide any information required. The provision of training for managers and supervisors is an important means of combating sexual harassment.

b) Procedures

Clear and precise procedures must be developed, giving practical guidance on how to deal with this problem. Such guidance must draw the employees' attention to their legal rights and to any time limits within which they must be exercised. Employees should be advised to try first of all to resolve the problem informally by explaining, either themselves or through a third party, that the behaviour in question is not welcome, offends them and interferes with their work. If the unwelcome conduct persists, there will be grounds for making a complaint. To this end, it is recommended that a formal procedure for dealing with complaints be set up, in which employees can place their trust and which specifies the person to whom the complaint should be brought. It is also recommended that someone be designated to provide advice and assistance. The complainant and the alleged harasser have the right to be represented by a trade union representative, a friend or a colleague. Employers should monitor and review these procedures in order to ensure that they are working effectively. Investigations of complaints are to be carried out with sensitivity by independent persons, with due respect for the rights of the complainant and the alleged harasser. Complaints must be resolved speedily and confidentially at the end of an investigation focusing on the facts. Any violation of the organization's policy should be treated as a disciplinary offence. Disciplinary rules should make clear what is regarded as inappropriate behaviour and should indicate the range of penalties. Any victimization or retaliation against an employee bringing a complaint in good faith is to be considered as a disciplinary offence.

3. Recommendations to trade unions

Sexual harassment is a trade union issue which must be treated seriously and sympathetically when complaints arise. Trade unions are expected to formulate and issue clear policy statements on sexual harassment and to take steps to raise awareness of the problem, in order to help create a climate in which sexual harassment is neither condoned nor ignored. They should declare that sexual harassment is inappropriate behaviour and should inform staff about its consequences. It is also a good idea to ensure that there are sufficient female representatives to support women subjected to sexual harassment.

4. Employees' responsibilities

Employees have a clear role to play in discouraging any form of reprehensible behaviour and making it unacceptable. They can contribute to preventing sexual harassment through awareness and sensitivity towards the issue and by ensuring that standards of conduct for themselves and for colleagues do not cause offence. Employees should lend support to victims of harassment and should inform management and/or their staff representative through the appropriate channels.

4)   Deadline for Implementation of the Legislation in the Member States

Not applicable.

5)   Date of Entry Into Force (if different from the above).

6)   References

Official Journal L 49, 24.02.1992.

7)   Follow-up Work

Declaration on the implementation of the code adopted by the Council on 19 December 1991.

8)   Commission Implementing Measures

Appendix 9

ACAS Guidance on Commonly Practised Religions

GUIDANCE ON COMMONLY PRACTISED RELIGIONS

The Regulations cover religion, religious belief and similar philosophical beliefs. Until the Courts and Tribunals have had an opportunity to consider which religions or beliefs are covered by these Regulations, it is not possible to provide definitive guidance. However, those listed below are some of the most commonly practised religions and beliefs in Britain. They are listed in alphabetical order for ease of reference only. However, there are many more and this list should not be considered to be exhaustive.

The information is intended for guidance only. It may assist employers to plan and implement policies and systems which meet the needs of both the employer and employee. Calendars indicating festivals in world religions are available from a number of sources.

Not all members of each religion follow all the practices and observances. Neither will every member of each religion request time off for each and every festival. In some instances, an adjustment to the working day to allow time to attend a prayer meeting before or after work may be all that is requested. In many instances nothing will be requested. Whilst employers are encouraged to be flexible where reasonable and appropriate, employees should recognise that they also have a responsibility to be reasonable and to consider the needs of the business in which they are employed.

Reminder: The Working Time Regulations 1998 provide most workers with an entitlement to 4 weeks' annual leave per year; that is 4 weeks × normal working week. If a worker normally works a 6 day week his/her leave annual entitlement is 24 days per year. If a worker works a 2 day week his/her annual leave entitlement is 8 days. The Working Time Regulations do not apply to workers on board sea-going fishing vessels, to certain sea-farers nor to workers on board most ships which operate on inland waterways. In addition, the annual leave entitlement does not apply to the armed forces, police nor to certain specific activities in the civil protection services; to mobile staff in civil aviation; nor, until 1 August 2004, to doctors in training. Under the Regulations this leave entitlement is not additional to bank holidays, unless otherwise stated in the worker's Terms and Conditions.

Employers can set the times that staff take their leave, for example, for a Christmas shutdown. However, employers should consider whether setting times for annual leave may be discriminatory because of religion or belief.

Under the Working Time Regulations an employer can require an employee to give twice as many days notice of annual leave as the number of days to be taken as annual leave. Therefore two days' annual leave may require four days' notice.

Further information on the Working Time Regulations is available from Acas or the DTI.

Baha'i

Baha'is should say one of three obligatory prayers during the day. Prayers need to be recited in a quiet place where the Baha'i will wish to face the Qiblih (the Shrine of Baha'u'llah, near Akka, Israel), which is in a southeasterly direction from the UK. Two of the prayers require movement and prostrations.

Baha'is are required to wash their hands and face before prayers but can use a normal washroom facility for this purpose.

Festivals: Baha'i festivals take place from sunset to sunset and followers may wish to leave work early in order to be home for sunset on the day prior to the festival date. Baha'is will wish to refrain from working on the key festival dates.

The Baha'i Fast	2 March – 20 March

Baha'is refrain from eating or drinking from sunrise to sunset during this period. Baha'is working evening or night shifts will appreciate the opportunity to prepare food at sundown. There are exemptions from fasting for sickness, pregnancy, travelling and strenuous physical work.

Naw-Ruz (Baha'i New Year)	21 March
Ridvan	21 April – 2 May

Ridvan is the most important of the Baha'i festivals and includes three holy days on which Baha'is would wish to refrain from working. They are:

1st Day of Ridvan	21 April
9th Day of Ridvan	29 April
12th Day of Ridvan	2 May
Declaration of the Bab	23 May
Ascension of the Baha'u'llah	29 May
Martyrdom of the Bab	9 July
Birth of the Bab	20 October
Birth of Baha'u'llah	12 November

Food: As a matter of principal most Baha'is do not take alcohol. Otherwise there are no dietary restrictions.

Bereavement: Burial should take place as soon as possible after legal formalities and funeral arrangements can be put in hand. The body should be transported no more than one hour's journey from the place where the person died, so funerals take place relatively close to the place of death. The usual arrangements for compassionate leave should generally suffice. Baha'is have no specific period of mourning.

Buddhism

Festivals: There are a number of different traditions in Buddhism arising from different cultural and ethnic backgrounds. Different traditions will celebrate different festivals. Some Buddhist traditions do not celebrate any festivals. Buddhist members of staff should be asked which festivals are important to them.

Festivals follow the lunar calendar and will therefore not take place on the same day each year.

Saindran Memorial Day	January
Parinirvana	February

Magha Puja Day	February/March
Honen Memorial Day	March
Buddha Day (Vesak or Visakah Puja)	May
The Ploughing Festival	May
Buddhist New Year	Varies according to tradition
Asalha Puja Day (Dhamma Day)	July
Ulambana (Ancestor Day)	July
Abhidhamma Day	October
Kathina Day	October
The Elephant Festival	November
Loy Krathorg	December
Bodhi Day	December
Uposatha	weekly on the lunar quarter day
Avalokitesvara's Birthday	

Food: Most Buddhists are vegetarian reflecting their adherence to the precept of non-harm to self and others. Many would not want to prepare or serve meat for others. Buddhists upholding the precept to avoid intoxication may not wish to drink alcohol, or serve it.

Clothing: Many Buddhists would prefer to wear clothing which reflects their adherence to non-harm eg not wearing leather clothing and leather shoes.

Christianity

There are a wide variety of Christian Churches and organisations all of which have their own specific needs, rituals and observations.

Festivals:

Christmas Day	25 December
Ash Wednesday	Feb/March
	(date set by lunar calendar)

This is a day of fasting/abstinence for many Christians.

Maundy Thursday	March/April
	(date set by lunar calendar)
Good Friday	March/April
	(date set by lunar calendar)
Easter Sunday	March/April
	(date set by lunar calendar)
All Saints Day	1 November
Christmas Eve	24 December

In addition there are a number of 'holy days of obligation' when Christians may wish to attend a church service and request a late start to the working day, or early finish in order that they can attend their local church. Many practising Christians will wish to attend their Church on Sundays throughout the year.

Food: Some Christians avoid alcohol.

Clothing: Some Christian churches forbid the use of cosmetics and require their female members to dress particularly modestly.

Bereavement: No special requirements beyond normal compassionate leave.

Hinduism

Festivals: Hinduism is a diverse religion and not all Hindus will celebrate the same festivals.

Makar Sakranti	14 January
Maha Shiva Ratri	February
Holi	March
Ramnavami	April
Rakshabandham	August
Janmashtami	August
Ganesh Chaturthi	August/September
Navaratri	September/October
Dushera (aka Vijayadashmi)	September/October
Karava Chauth	October
Diwali	Late October/Early November
New Year	Late October/Early November

There are a number of occasions through the year when some Hindus fast.

Clothing: Hindu women will often wear a bindi which is a red spot worn on the forehead and denotes that she is of the Hindu faith. In addition, many married Hindu women wear a necklace (mangal sutra) which is placed around their necks during the marriage ceremony and is in addition to a wedding ring.

A few Orthodox Hindu men wear a small tuft of hair (shikha) similar to a ponytail but this is often hidden beneath the remaining hair. Some Orthodox Hindu men also wear a clay marking on their foreheads known as a tilak.

Food: Most Hindus are vegetarian and will not eat meat, fish or eggs. None eat beef.

Bereavement: Following cremation, close relatives of the deceased will observe a 13 day mourning period during which they will wish to remain at home. The closest male relatives may take the ashes of the deceased to the Ganges, in India. They may therefore request extended leave. Close male relatives of the deceased may shave their heads as a mark of respect.

Islam (Muslims)

Observant Muslims are required to pray five times a day. Each prayer time takes about 15 minutes and can take place anywhere clean and quiet.

Prayer times are:
    At dawn (Fajr)
    At mid-day (Zuhr) in Winter sometime between 1200 – 1300hrs and in
    Summer between 1300 – 1600hrs
    Late Afternoon (Asr) in Winter 1430 – 1530
    After Sunset (Maghrib)
    Late Evening (Isha)

Friday mid-day prayers are particularly important to Muslims and may take a little longer than other prayer times. Friday prayers must be said in congregation and may require Muslims to travel to the nearest mosque or prayer gathering.

Before prayers, observant Muslims undertake a ritual act of purification. This involves the use of running water to wash hands, face, mouth, nose, arms up to the elbows and feet up to the ankles, although often the washing of the feet will be performed symbolically.

Festivals: The dates of festivals are reliant on a sighting of the new moon and will therefore vary from year to year. Whilst approximate dates will be known well in advance, it is not always possible to give a definitive date until much nearer to the time.

Ramadan, which takes place in the ninth month of the Muslim lunar calendar, is a particularly significant time for Muslims. Fasting is required between dawn and sunset. Most Muslims will attend work in the normal way but in the winter they may wish to break fast with other Muslims at sunset. This could be seen as a delayed lunch break. For those working evening or night shifts, the opportunity to heat food at sunset and/or sunrise will be appreciated.

Eid Al-Fitr – three days to mark the end of Ramadan – most Muslims will only seek annual leave for the first of the three days.

Eid Al-Adha takes place two months and 10 days after Eid Al-Fitr and is a three-day festival. Again, most Muslims will usually only seek leave for the first of the three days.

All Muslims are required to make a pilgrimage to Mecca once in their lifetime. Muslims may therefore seek one extended leave period in which to make such a pilgrimage.

Clothing: Muslims are required to cover the body. Men may therefore be unwilling to wear shorts. Women may wish to cover their whole body, except their face, hands and feet.

Food: Muslims are forbidden to eat any food which is derived from the pig, this includes lard which may be present in bread or even ice cream. In addition they are forbidden to eat any food which is derived from a carnivorous animal. Meat that may be consumed must be slaughtered by the Halal method. Islam also forbids the consumption of alcohol which includes its presence in dishes such as risotto or fruit salad.

Bereavement: Burial must take place as soon as possible following death and may therefore occur at short notice.

Other:

1. Any form of gambling is forbidden under Islam.

2. Observant Muslims are required to wash following use of the toilet and will therefore appreciate access to water in the toilet cubicle. Often Muslims will carry a small container of water into the cubicle for this purpose. By agreement with other staff and cleaners, these containers could be kept in the cubicle.

3. Physical contact between the sexes is discouraged and some Muslims may politely refuse to shake hands with the opposite sex. This should not be viewed negatively.

Jainism

Jains are required to worship three times daily, before dawn, at sunset and at night. Jains working evening or night shifts may wish to take time out to worship or take their meals before sunset.

Festivals: Jain festivals are spiritual in nature.

Oli   April and October

Appendix 9

Eight days semi-fasting twice a year when some take one bland, tasteless meal during day time.

Mahavira Jayanti	April	

Birth anniversary of Lord Mahavira.

Paryusan   August/September

During this sacred period of fasting and forgiveness for eight days Jains fast, observe spiritual rituals, meditate and live a pious life taking only boiled water during day time.

Samvatsari   September

The last day of Paryushan when Jains ask for forgiveness and forgive one another.

Diwali   October/November

Death anniversary of Lord Mahavira, includes a two-day fast and listening to the last message of Mahavira.

Food: Jains practice avoidance of harm to all life – self and others. They are, therefore, strict vegetarians including the avoidance of eggs; some may take milk products. Many also avoid root vegetables. Jains do not eat between sunset and sunrise. Jains do not drink alcohol.

Bereavement: Cremation will take place as soon as practical after death (usually three to five days). There is no specified mourning period and normal compassionate leave arrangements will suffice.

Judaism (Jews)

Observant Jews are required to refrain from work on the Sabbath and Festivals, except where life is at risk. This includes travelling (except on foot), writing, carrying, switching on and off electricity, using a telephone and transactions of a commercial nature (that is buying and selling). The Sabbath and all other Festivals begin one hour before dusk and so practising Jews need to be home by then. Sabbath begins one hour before dusk on Friday.

Festivals:

Passover	March/April	2 sets of 2 days
Pentecost (Shavuoth)	May/June	2 days
New Year	Sept/Oct	2 days
Day of Atonement	Sept/Oct	1 day fasting
Tabernacles (Sukkot)	Sept/Oct	2 sets of 2 days

Clothing: Orthodox Jewish men keep their head covered at all times. Orthodox Jewish women will wish to dress modestly and may not want to wear trousers, short skirts or short sleeves; some may wish to keep their heads covered by a scarf or beret.

Food: Jews are required to eat only kosher food (which has been treated and prepared in a particular manner).

Bereavement: Funerals must take place as soon as possible following the death – the same day where possible – and therefore take place at short notice. Following a death, the immediate family must stay at home and mourn for seven days (Shiva). Following the death of a Father or Mother, an observant Jewish man will be required to go to a Synagogue to pray morning, afternoon and evening for 11 months of the Jewish calendar.

Muslim (*see* Islam)

Other Ancient Religions

These include religions covered by the Council of British Druid Orders and examples are Druidry, Paganism and Wicca.

Festivals: Some examples of Festivals

Candlemas	2 February
Spring Equinox*	21/22 March
Beltaine	30 April
Summer Solstice*	21/22 June
Lughnasadh	2 August
Autumn Equinox*	21/22 September
Samhain	31 October
Winter Solstice*	21/22 December

*Dates moveable due to astronomical times set in accordance with GMT.

Food: Generally vegetarian or vegan, although not always.

Clothing: Some items of jewellery as associated with Pagan faiths such as ankh, pentagram, hammer and crystal.

Bereavement: No specific requirements beyond that of normal compassionate leave.

There are also other ancient religions such as Astaru, Odinism and Shamanism.

Parsi (*see* Zorastrianism)

Rastafarianism

Festivals:

Birthday of Haile Selassie I	23 July
Ethiopian New Year	11 September
Anniversary of the Crowning of Haile Selassie I	2 November
Christmas	25 December

Food: Vegetarian including the avoidance of eggs. Many Rastafarians eat only organic food as close to its raw state as possible.

Clothing: Hair is worn uncut and plaited into 'dreadlocks'. It is often covered by a hat which is usually red, green and gold.

Other: Whilst the faith supports the smoking of ganga (marijuana) this practice remains unlawful in the UK, and is unaffected by the Employment Equality (Religion or Belief) Regulations 2003.

Bereavement: No specific requirements beyond that of normal compassionate leave.

Appendix 9

Sikhism

Festivals:

Birthday of Guru Gobind Singh	5 January
Vaisakhi	14 April
Martyrdom of Guru Arjan Dev	16 June
Sri Guru Granth Sahib Day	1 September
Divali (Diwali)	October/November (date set by lunar calender)
Martyrdom of Guru Tegh Bahadur	24 November
Birthday of Guru Nanak	November

Food: Sikhs do not eat Halal meat. Some do not eat beef and many are vegetarian.

Clothes: Practising male Sikhs observe the 5 Ks of the faith. These are:

Kesh	Uncut hair. Observant Sikhs do not remove or cut any hair from their body. Sikh men and some women will wear a turban.
Kangha	Wooden comb usually worn in the hair.
Kara	Metal bracelet worn on the wrist.
Kachhahera	Knee length underpants.
Kirpan	Short sword worn under the clothing so that it is not visible.

Bereavement: Sikhs are cremated and have a preference for this to take place as soon after the death as possible. There is no specified mourning period and normal compassionate leave arrangements will suffice.

Zoroastrians (Parsi)

Zoroastrians are required to pray five times during the day, saying a special prayer for each part of the day.

Hawab	(sunrise to midday)
Rapithwin	(midday to mid-afternoon)
Uzerin	(mid-afternoon to sunset)
Aiwisruthrem	(sunset to midnight)
Ushahin	(midnight to dawn)

Prayers should be said in front of a fire – or a symbolic replica of fire.

In addition, a ritual is performed each time a Zorostrain washes his/her hands although the ritual is not always strictly performed in all its detail. When it is performed, the individual will stand on the same spot and must speak to no one during the ritual. No special facilities are required.

A prayer will also be said before eating.

Festivals: Dates follow the lunar calendar and will therefore vary from year to year.

Khordad Sal	The Prophet's Birthday
Fravardigan	Remembrance of departed souls

628

Tiragan	Water Festival
Mehergan	Harvest Festival
Ave roj nu Parab	Water Festival
Adar roj nu Parab	Fire Festival
Jashn-e-Sadeh	Mid Winter Festival
Zardosht no Disco	Death of the Prophet
Maktad	Festival of All Souls
NoRuz	New Year

In addition there are six seasonal festivals

Maidyoizaremaya	Mid Spring
Maidyoishema	Mid Summer
Paitishahya	Early Autumn
Ayathrima	Mid Autumn
Maidhyairya	Mid Winter
Hamaspathmaedaya	Pre-Spring

Clothes: Zoroastrians, both male and female, wear two pieces of sacred clothing. The Sudreh (shirt) and the Kusti (cord) which is a string which passes loosely around the waist three times and is tied in a double knot at the back.

It is the Kusti which is ritualistically retied each time the hands are washed.

Bereavement: Following the death of a close family member there is a mourning period of 10 days followed by a ceremony to mark the first month, the sixth month and the twelfth month of bereavement.

Appendix 10

Guidance on Matters to be Taken into Account in Determining Questions Relating to the Definition of Disability

STATUS AND PURPOSE OF THE GUIDANCE

This guidance is issued by the Secretary of State under section 3 of the Disability Discrimination Act 1995, as amended[1]. In this document, any reference to 'the Act' means the Disability Discrimination Act 1995 (as amended).

This guidance concerns the definition of disability in the Act. Section 3 of the Act enables the Secretary of State to issue guidance about matters to be taken into account in determining whether a person is a disabled person. The guidance gives examples.

This guidance does not impose any legal obligations in itself, nor is it an authoritative statement of the law. However, section 3(3) of the Act requires that an adjudicating body[2] which is determining for any purpose of the Act whether a person is a disabled person, must take into account any aspect of this guidance which appears to it to be relevant.

This guidance applies to England, Wales and Scotland. Similar but separate guidance applies to Northern Ireland.

PART 1 INTRODUCTION

The Disability Discrimination Act

1.   The Disability Discrimination Act prohibits discrimination against disabled people in a range of circumstances, covering employment, education, transport, and the provision of goods, facilities, services and public functions. Only those people who are defined as disabled in accordance with section 1 of the Act and the associated schedules and regulations made thereunder, will be entitled to the protection that the Act provides.

Using the guidance

2.   This guidance is primarily designed for adjudicating bodies which determine cases brought under the Act. However, it is also likely to be of value to a range of people and organisations.

3.   **In the vast majority of cases there is unlikely to be any doubt whether or not a person has or has had a disability, but this guidance should prove helpful in cases where the matter is not entirely clear.**

4.   The definition of disability has a number of elements. The guidance covers each of these elements in turn. Each section contains an explanation of the relevant provisions of the Act which supplement the basic definition. Guidance and examples are provided where relevant. Those using this guidance for the first time may wish to read it all, as each part of the guidance builds upon the part(s) preceding it.

---

1   Including by the Special Educational Needs and Disability Act 2001, the Disability Discrimination Act 1995 (Amendment) Regulations 2003, and the Disability Discrimination Act 2005.
2   Section 3(3A) states that an 'Adjudicating body' means a court; a tribunal; and any other person who, or body which, may decide a claim under Part 4.

5. Throughout the guidance, descriptions of statutory provisions in the legislation are immediately preceded by bold italic text and followed by a reference to the relevant provision of the Act or to Regulations made under the Act. References to sections of the Act are marked 'S'; references to schedules are marked 'Sch'; and references to paragraphs in schedules are marked 'Para'.

Other references to 'disability'

6. The definition of disability set out in the Act and described in this guidance is the only definition relevant to determining whether someone is a disabled person for the purposes of the Act. References to 'disability' or to mental or physical impairments in the context of other legislation are not relevant to determining whether someone is a disabled person under this Act.

7. There is a range of services, concessions, schemes and financial benefits for which disabled people may qualify. These include, for example, local authority services for disabled people; the Blue Badge parking scheme; tax concessions for people who are blind; and disability-related social security benefits. However, each of these has its own individual eligibility criteria and qualification for any one of them does not automatically confer entitlement to protection under the Act. In order to be protected by the Disability Discrimination Act, a person must meet the Act's definition of disability as explained below.

PART 2 GUIDANCE ON MATTERS TO BE TAKEN INTO ACCOUNT IN DETERMINING QUESTIONS RELATING TO THE DEFINITION OF DISABILITY

Section A: General

Main elements of the definition of disability

A1. *The Act defines* a disabled person as a person with 'a physical or mental impairment which has a substantial and long-term adverse effect on his ability to carry out normal day-to-day activities' **(S1)**.

A2. This means that, in general:

- the person must have an impairment that is either physical or mental *(see paragraphs A3 to A8 below)*;

- the impairment must have adverse effects which are substantial *(see Section B)*;

- the substantial adverse effects must be long-term *(see Section C)*; and

- the long-term substantial adverse effects must be effects on normal day-to-day activities *(see Section D)*.

This definition is subject to the provisions in **Schedule 1 (Sch1)** and **Schedule 2 (Sch2)**.

Meaning of 'impairment'

A3. The definition requires that the effects which a person may experience arise from a physical or mental impairment. The term mental or physical impairment should be given its ordinary meaning. In many cases, there will be no dispute whether a person has an impairment. Any disagreement is more likely to be about whether the effects of the impairment are sufficient to fall within the definition. Even so, it may sometimes be necessary to decide whether a person has an impairment so as to be able to deal with the issues about its effects.

Appendix 10

A4. Whether a person is disabled for the purposes of the Act is generally determined by reference to the *effect* that an impairment has on that person's ability to carry out normal day-to-day activities. It is not possible to provide an exhaustive list of conditions that qualify as impairments for the purposes of the Act. Any attempt to do so would inevitably become out of date as medical knowledge advanced.

A5. It is important to remember that not all impairments are readily identifiable. While some impairments, particularly visible ones, are easy to identify, there are many which are not so immediately obvious.

A6. A disability can arise from a wide range of impairments and can include:

- sensory impairments, such as those affecting sight or hearing;

- impairments with fluctuating or recurring effects such as rheumatoid arthritis, myalgic encephalitis (ME), chronic fatigue syndrome (CFS), and fibromyalgia;

- progressive conditions such as motor neurone disease, muscular dystrophy, forms of dementia and lupus (SLE);

- cardiovascular diseases including thrombosis, stroke and heart disease;

- developmental impairments such as autistic spectrum disorders (ASD), dyslexia and dyspraxia;

- mental impairments including mental illnesses such as depression, schizo-phrenia, eating disorders and some self-harming behaviour.

A7. It may not always be possible, nor is it necessary, to categorise a condition as either a physical or a mental impairment. The underlying cause of the impairment may be hard to establish. There may be adverse effects which are both physical and mental in nature. Furthermore, effects of a mainly physical nature may stem from an underlying mental impairment, and vice versa.

A8. It is not necessary to consider how an impairment was caused, even if the cause is a consequence of a condition which is excluded. For example, liver disease as a result of alcohol dependency would count as an impairment, although alcoholism itself is expressly excluded from the scope of the Act. What is important to consider is the effect of an impairment not its cause – providing it is not an excluded condition. *See also paragraph A12 below (exclusions from the definition).*

Mental illness

A9. The Act previously required that where any impairment arose from, or consisted of, a mental illness, that illness had to be clinically well-recognised in order for it to be regarded as a mental impairment for the purposes of the Act. The Disability Discrimination Act 2005 amended the original Act to remove this requirement with effect from December 2005. However, anyone who has a mental illness will still need to meet the requirements of the definition as set out in paragraph A1, in order to demonstrate that they have a disability under the Act.

Persons deemed to be disabled

A10. The following people are deemed to meet the definition of disability without having to show that they have an impairment that has (or is likely to have) a substantial, adverse, long-term effect on the ability to carry out normal day-to-day activities:

- A person who has cancer, HIV infection or multiple sclerosis (MS) **(Sch1, Para 6A)**. *See also paragraphs B16 to B19 below (progressive conditions).*

- A person who is certified as blind or partially sighted by a consultant ophthalmologist, or registered as such with a local authority[3].

A11. Anyone who has an impairment which is not listed above will need to meet the requirements of the definition as set out in paragraph A1, in order to demonstrate that they have a disability under the Act.

Exclusions from the definition

A12. Certain conditions are not to be regarded as impairments for the purposes of the Act. These are:

- addiction to or dependency on alcohol, nicotine, or any other substance (other than in consequence of the substance being medically prescribed);

- the condition known as seasonal allergic rhinitis (e.g. hayfever), except where it aggravates the effect of another condition;

- tendency to set fires;

- tendency to steal;

- tendency to physical or sexual abuse of other persons;

- exhibitionism;

- voyeurism.

A13. Also, disfigurements which consist of a tattoo (which has not been removed), non-medical body piercing, or something attached through such piercing, are to be treated as not having a substantial adverse effect on the person's ability to carry out normal day-to-day activities[4].

A14. A person with an excluded condition may nevertheless be protected as a disabled person if they have an accompanying impairment which meets the requirements of the definition. For example, a person who is addicted to a substance such as alcohol may also have severe depression. While they would not meet the definition on the basis of having an addiction, they may still meet the definition as a result of the effects of the depression.

People who have had a disability in the past

A15. **The Act says** that Part 1 of the Act (disability), Part 2 (the employment field and members of locally-electable authorities), Part 3 (discrimination in other areas[5]), Part 4 (education), and Part 5A (public authorities[6]) also apply in relation to a person who has had a disability as defined in paragraphs A1 and A2 above. For this purpose, those Parts of the Act are subject to the provisions in Schedule 2 to the Act **(S2, Sch2)**. This means that someone who is no longer disabled, but who met the requirements of the definition in the past, will still be covered by those parts of the Act listed above. For example, a woman who, four years ago, experienced a severe mental illness that had a substantial adverse and long-term effect on her ability to carry out normal day-to-day activities but who is now recovered, is still entitled to the protection afforded by the Act, as a person with a past disability.

---

3 The Disability Discrimination (Blind and Partially Sighted Persons) Regulations 2003.
4 The Disability Discrimination (Meaning of Disability) Regulations 1996.
5 Part 3 covers goods, facilities, and services; public authorities; private clubs; and premises.
6 Part 5A covers the *duties* of a public authority, as opposed to the *functions* of a public authority, which are dealt with in Part 3.

Appendix 10

A16.   A particular instance of someone who is treated under the Act as having had a disability in the past is someone whose name was on the register of disabled persons under provisions in the Disabled Persons (Employment) Act 1944. The introduction of the employment provisions in the Disability Discrimination Act coincided with the abolition of the Quota scheme which had operated under the Disabled Persons (Employment) Act 1944. *The Act says* that anyone who was registered as a disabled person under the Disabled Persons (Employment) Act 1944 and whose name appeared on the register both on 12 January 1995 and on 2 December 1996 (the date the employment provisions came into force) was to be treated as having a disability for the purposes of the Disability Discrimination Act during the period of three years starting on 2 December 1996. This applied regardless of whether the person otherwise met the definition of 'disabled person' during that period. Those who were treated by this provision as being disabled for the three-year period are also treated after this period has ended as having had a disability in the past **(Sch1, Para 7)**.

Section B: Substantial

Meaning of 'substantial adverse effect'

B1.   The requirement that an adverse effect on normal day-to-day activities should be a substantial one reflects the general understanding of disability as a limitation going beyond the normal differences in ability which may exist among people. A substantial effect is more than would be produced by the sort of physical or mental conditions experienced by many people which have only minor effects. A substantial effect is one which is more than 'minor' or 'trivial'. This section looks in more detail at what 'substantial' means. It should be read in conjunction with Section D which considers what is meant by 'normal day-to-day activities'.

The time taken to carry out an activity

B2.   The time taken by a person with an impairment to carry out a normal day-to-day activity should be considered when assessing whether the effect of that impairment is substantial. It should be compared with the time it might take to complete an activity by a person who did not have the impairment.

> A ten-year old child has cerebral palsy. The effects include muscle stiffness, poor balance and unco-ordinated movements. The child is still able to do most things for himself, but he gets tired very easily and it is harder for him to accomplish tasks like eating and drinking, washing, and getting dressed. Although he has the ability to carry out everyday activities such as these, everything takes longer compared to a child of the same age who does not have cerebral palsy. This amounts to a substantial adverse effect.

The way in which an activity is carried out

B3.   Another factor to be considered when assessing whether the effect of an impairment is substantial is the way in which a person with that impairment carries out a normal day-to-day activity. The comparison should be with the way the person might be expected to carry out the activity if he or she did not have the impairment.

Cumulative effects of an impairment

B4.   An impairment might not have a substantial adverse effect on a person's ability to undertake a particular day-to-day activity in isolation, but its effects on more than one activity, taken together, could result in an overall substantial adverse effect.

B5. For example, a person whose impairment causes breathing difficulties may, as a result, experience minor effects on the ability to carry out a number of activities such as getting washed and dressed, preparing a meal, or travelling on public transport. But taken together, the cumulative result would amount to a substantial adverse effect on their ability to carry out these normal day-to-day activities.

> A woman with depression experiences a range of symptoms that include a loss of energy and motivation that makes even the simplest of tasks or decisions seem quite difficult. For example, she finds it difficult to get up in the morning, get washed and dressed, and prepare breakfast. She is forgetful and cannot plan ahead. As a result she has often run out of food before she thinks of going shopping again. Household tasks are frequently left undone, or take much longer to complete than normal. Together, the effects amount to a substantial adverse effect.

B6. A person may have more than one impairment, any one of which alone would not have a substantial effect. In such a case, account should be taken of whether the impairments together have a substantial effect overall on the person's ability to carry out normal day-to-day activities. For example, a minor impairment which affects physical co-ordination and an irreversible but minor injury to a leg which affects mobility, taken together, might have a substantial effect on the person's ability to carry out certain normal day-to-day activities.

Effects of behaviour

B7. Account should be taken of how far a person can reasonably be expected to modify their behaviour to prevent or reduce the effects of an impairment on normal day-to-day activities. If a person can behave in such a way that the impairment ceases to have a substantial adverse effect on his or her ability to carry out normal day-to-day activities the person would no longer meet the definition of disability. For example, while it would be reasonable to expect a person who has back pain to avoid extreme activities such as parachuting, it would not be reasonable to expect them to give up a job that involved activities that exacerbated the problems (such as long hours sitting at a computer desk).

B8. However, account should also be taken of where a person avoids doing things which cause pain or fatigue; or because of a loss of energy and motivation; or because they have been advised by a medical practitioner to behave in a certain way. It would not be reasonable to conclude that a person who did employ an avoidance strategy was not a disabled person. It is important to consider the things a person cannot do, or can only do with difficulty, rather than focussing on those things a person can do.

B9. Where a disabled person is advised by a medical practitioner to behave in a certain way in order to reduce the impact of the disability that advice might count as treatment to be disregarded. *See paragraphs B12 to B15 below (effects of treatment). Also, see paragraphs C8 (likelihood of recurrence) and D11 (indirect effects).*

B10. In some cases, people have coping strategies which cease to work in certain circumstances (for example, where someone who stutters or has dyslexia is placed under stress). If it is possible that a person's ability to manage the effects of an impairment will break down so that effects will sometimes still occur, this possibility must be taken into account when assessing the effects of the impairment.

Appendix 10

Effects of environment

B11. Environmental conditions may exacerbate the effect of an impairment. Factors such as temperature, humidity, the time of day or night, how tired the person is or how much stress he or she is under may have an impact on the effects. When assessing whether adverse effects are substantial, the extent to which such environmental factors are likely to have an impact should also therefore be considered. *See also paragraphs C4 to C7 below, meaning of 'long-term' (recurring or fluctuating effects).*

> A woman has had rheumatoid arthritis for the last three years and has difficulty carrying out day-to-day activities such as walking, undertaking household tasks, and getting washed and dressed. The effects are particularly bad during autumn and winter months when the weather is cold and damp. Symptoms are mild during the summer months. The effect on her ability to carry out normal day-to-day activities fluctuates according to the weather conditions, but because the effect of the impairment is likely to recur, this person meets the definition of disability requirement on the meaning of 'long-term' (**Sch1, Para 2(2)**).

Effects of treatment

B12. *The Act provides* that where an impairment is being treated or corrected the impairment is to be treated as having the effect it would have without the measures in question (**Sch1, Para 6(1)**). The Act states that the treatment or correction measures to be disregarded for these purposes include medical treatment and the use of a prosthesis or other aid (**Sch1, Para 6(2)**).

B13. This applies even if the measures result in the effects being completely under control or not at all apparent.

B14. For example, if a person with a hearing impairment wears a hearing aid the question whether his or her impairment has a substantial adverse effect is to be decided by reference to what the hearing level would be without the hearing aid. And in the case of someone with diabetes which is being controlled by medication or diet, whether or not the effect is substantial should be decided by reference to what the condition would be if he or she was not taking that medication or following the required diet. *See also paragraph C9 below, regarding medical or other treatment that reduces or removes the effects of an impairment.*

B15. *The Act states* that this provision does not apply to sight impairments to the extent that they are capable of correction by spectacles or contact lenses. In other words the only effects on ability to carry out normal day-to-day activities to be considered are those which remain when spectacles or contact lenses are used (or would remain if they were used). This does not include the use of devices to correct sight which are not spectacles or contact lenses (**Sch1, Para 6(3)**).

Progressive conditions

B16. A progressive condition is one which is likely to change and develop over time. *The Act gives* examples of progressive conditions, including cancer, multiple sclerosis, and HIV infection. It should be noted that, following the amendments made by the Disability Discrimination Act 2005 (**see paragraph A10**), persons with cancer, multiple sclerosis or HIV infection are all now deemed to be disabled persons for the purposes of the Act.

B17. All other progressive conditions are, however, still subject to the special provisions set out in **Sch1, Para 8**, which provide that a person with a progressive condition is to be regarded as having an impairment which has a substantial adverse effect on his or her ability to carry out normal day-to-day activities before it actually does so. In addition to the conditions listed in the Act, other examples of a progressive condition include systemic lupus erythematosis (SLE), various types of dementia, rheumatoid arthritis, and motor neurone disease. Medical prognosis of the likely impact of the condition will be the normal route to establishing protection under this provision.

B18. Where a person has a progressive condition, he or she will be treated as having an impairment which has a *substantial* adverse effect from the moment any impairment resulting from that condition first has *some* effect on ability to carry out normal day-to-day activities. The effect need not be continuous *(see also paragraphs C4 to C7 on recurring or fluctuating effects)*, and need not be substantial. The person will still need to show that the impairment meets the requirements of **Sch1, Para 2** (meaning of long-term).

B19. For this rule to operate, medical diagnosis of the condition is not by itself enough. The requirement is that in the particular circumstances of the person concerned, the condition is *more likely than not* to progress to a point where the effects become substantial.

A young boy aged 11 has been experiencing muscle cramps and some weakness. The effects are quite minor at present but he has been diagnosed as having muscular dystrophy. Eventually it is expected that the resulting muscle weakness will cause substantial adverse effects on his ability to walk, run and climb stairs. Although there is no substantial adverse effect at present, muscular dystrophy is a progressive condition, and this child will still be entitled to the protection of the Disability Discrimination Act under the special provisions in **Sch1, Para 8** of the Act if it can be shown that the effects are likely to become substantial.

A woman has been diagnosed with lupus (SLE) following complaints to her GP that she was experiencing mild aches and pains in her joints. She had also been feeling generally unwell, with flu-like symptoms, and unusual fatigue. The initial symptoms are quite minor and could not be said to have a substantial adverse effect. However, SLE is a progressive condition, with fluctuating effects. She has been advised that the condition may come and go over many years, and in the future the effects may become substantial, including severe joint pain, inflammation, stiffness, and skin rashes. Providing it can be shown that the effects are likely to become substantial, she will be entitled to the protection of the Act under the special provisions in Sch1, Para 8.

B20. A person with a progressive condition which has no effect on day-to-day activities because it is successfully treated (for example by surgery), may still be covered by **Sch1, Para 8** if treatment for the condition results in an impairment which has some effect on normal day-to-day activities and the effects of the progressive condition are likely to become substantial in the future. For example, a person who has an operation for prostate cancer may develop urinary incontinence. The effect of the incontinence should be taken into account as an effect arising from the original impairment. Whether the effects of any treatment can qualify for the purposes of **Sch1, Para 8** will depend on the circumstances of the case.

Appendix 10

Severe disfigurements

B21. **The Act provides** that where an impairment consists of a severe disfigurement, it is to be treated as having a substantial adverse effect on the person's ability to carry out normal day-to-day activities. There is no need to demonstrate such an effect (**Sch1, Para 3**). Regulations provide that a disfigurement which consists of a tattoo (which has not been removed) is not to be considered as a severe disfigurement. Also excluded is a piercing of the body for decorative purposes including anything attached through the piercing[7].

B22. Examples of disfigurements include scars, birthmarks, limb or postural deformation (including restricted bodily development), or diseases of the skin. Assessing severity will be mainly a matter of the degree of the disfigurement. However, it may be necessary to take account of where the disfigurement in question is (e.g. on the back as opposed to the face).

Section C: Long term

Meaning of 'long-term effects'

C1. **The Act states** that, for the purpose of deciding whether a person is disabled, a long-term effect of an impairment is one:

- which has lasted at least 12 months; or

- where the total period for which it lasts, from the time of the first onset, is likely to be at least 12 months; or

- which is likely to last for the rest of the life of the person affected (**Sch1, Para 2**).

For the purpose of deciding whether a person has had a disability in the past, a long-term effect of an impairment is one which has lasted at least 12 months (**Sch2, Para 5**).

Meaning of 'likely'

C2. It is likely that an event will happen if it is more probable than not that it will happen.

C3. In assessing the likelihood of an effect lasting for 12 months, account should be taken of the total period for which the effect exists. This includes any time before the point when the alleged discriminatory behaviour occurred as well as time afterwards. Account should also be taken of both the typical length of such an effect on an individual, and any relevant factors specific to this individual (for example, general state of health or age).

Recurring or fluctuating effects

C4. **The Act states** that if an impairment has had a substantial adverse effect on a person's ability to carry out normal day-to-day activities but that effect ceases, the substantial effect is treated as continuing if it is likely to recur. In other words, it is more likely than not that the effect will recur. (In deciding whether a person has had a disability in the past, the question is whether a substantial adverse effect has in fact recurred.) Conditions with effects which recur only sporadically or for short periods can still qualify as an impairment for the purposes of the Act, in respect of the meaning of 'long term' (**Sch1, Para 2(2); Sch2, Para 5**).

---

7 The Disability Discrimination (Meaning of Disability) Regulations 1996.

C5.   For example, a person with rheumatoid arthritis may experience substantial adverse effects from the first occurrence for a few weeks and then have a period of remission. *See also example on page [636] above*. But, if the substantial adverse effects are likely to recur, they are to be treated as if they were continuing. If the effects are likely to recur beyond 12 months after the first occurrence, they are to be treated as long-term. Other impairments with effects which can recur or where effects can be sporadic, include mental illnesses such as schizophrenia, certain types of depression, and epilepsy.

A young man has depression. It has been diagnosed as a recurring form of depression. The first episode occurred in months one and two of a 13-month period. The second episode took place in month 13. This man will satisfy the requirements of the definition in respect of the meaning of long term, because the adverse effects have recurred beyond 12 months after the first occurrence and are therefore treated as having continued for the whole period (in this case, a period of 13 months).

A young woman also has recurring depression, but her second episode took place in months ten and 11. At that stage she will not be covered by the Act as the effects of her impairment have not yet lasted or recurred beyond a 12-month period after the first occurrence.

C6.   It is not necessary for the effect to be the same throughout the relevant period. It may change, such as where activities which are initially very difficult become possible to a much greater extent. It might even disappear temporarily. Or other effects on the ability to carry out normal day-to-day activities may develop and the initial effect may disappear altogether.

C7.   Regulations specifically exclude seasonal allergic rhinitis (e.g. hayfever) except where it aggravates the effects of an existing condition[8]. *See also paragraph A12 (exclusions)*.

Likelihood of recurrence

C8.   Likelihood of recurrence should be considered taking all the circumstances of the case into account. This should include what the person could reasonably be expected to do to prevent the recurrence; for example, the person might reasonably be expected to take action which prevents the impairment from having such effects (e.g. avoiding substances to which he or she is allergic). This may be unreasonably difficult with some substances. In addition, it is possible that the way in which a person can control or cope with the effects of an impairment may not always be successful because, for example, a routine is not followed or the person is in an unfamiliar environment. If there is an increased likelihood that the control will break down, it will be more likely that there will be a recurrence. That possibility should be taken into account when assessing the likelihood of a recurrence. *See also paragraphs B7 to B10 above (effects of behaviour, including coping strategies and medical advice), paragraph B11 (environmental effects), and paragraphs B12 to B15 (effect of treatment)*.

C9.   If medical or other treatment is likely to cure an impairment, so that recurrence of its effects would then be unlikely even if there were no further treatment, this should be taken into consideration when looking at the likelihood of recurrence of those effects. However, if the treatment simply delays or prevents a recurrence, and a recurrence would be likely if the treatment stopped, then the treatment is to be ignored and the effect is to be regarded as likely to recur.

---

8   The Disability Discrimination (Meaning of Disability) Regulations 1996.

Appendix 10

Assessing whether a past disability was long-term

C10. **The Act provides** that a person who has had a disability within the definition is protected from some forms of discrimination even if he or she has since recovered or the effects have become less than substantial. In deciding whether a past condition was a disability, its effects count as long-term if they lasted 12 months or more after the first occurrence, or if a recurrence happened or continued until more than 12 months after the first occurrence **(S2, Sch2, Para 5).** *For the forms of discrimination covered by this provision see paragraph A15 above. For examples of how this provision works, see above at C5.*

SECTION D: NORMAL DAY-TO-DAY ACTIVITIES

List of 'capacities'

D1. **The Act states** that an impairment is to be taken to affect the ability of a person to carry out normal day-to-day activities only if it affects that person in respect of one or more of the following **(Sch1, Para 4):**

- mobility;

- manual dexterity;

- physical co-ordination;

- continence;

- ability to lift, carry or otherwise move everyday objects;

- speech, hearing or eyesight;

- memory or ability to concentrate, learn or understand; or

- perception of the risk of physical danger.

For the purposes of this guidance, the above list will be referred to as a list of 'capacities'.

D2. The list of capacities should be looked at in a broad sense, and applied equally to both physical and mental impairments. For example, it is often assumed that for people with a mental impairment the relevant capacity will be 'memory or ability to concentrate, learn or understand'. The capacities of mobility and physical co-ordination for example, are often seen as relevant only where there is a physical impairment. However, in many instances this will not be the case. A person with a mental impairment may also have difficulties carrying out activities that involve mobility or other 'physical' skills, and people with a physical impairment may also have effects that involve mental processes such as the ability to concentrate (for example, as a result of pain or fatigue).

D3. An impairment will only be treated as affecting a normal day-to-day activity if it involves at least one of the capacities set out at D1 above. The substantial effect is determined by looking at the effect on the particular day-to-day activity, not the relevant capacity. So for example, an inability to go shopping because of restricted mobility is in itself a substantial effect on a normal day-to-day activity; it is not necessary to show that all or any other aspects of the capacity of mobility are substantially affected.

Meaning of 'normal day-to-day activities'

D4. **It should be noted that the list of capacities set out in D1 above is not a list of day-to-day activities.** It is not possible to provide an exhaustive list of day-to-day activities, although guidance on this matter is given here. In general, day-to-day activities are things people do on a regular or daily basis, and examples include shopping, reading and writing, talking, watching television, getting washed and dressed, preparing and eating food, carrying out household tasks, walking and travelling by various forms of transport, and taking part in social activities.

D5. The term 'normal day-to-day activities' is not intended to include activities which are normal only for a particular person or a small group of people. In deciding whether an activity is a normal day-to-day activity, account should be taken of how far it is normal for a large number of people, and carried out by people on a daily or frequent and fairly regular basis. In this context, 'normal' should be given its ordinary, every-day meaning.

D6. A normal day-to-day activity is not necessarily one that is carried out by a majority of people – for example, it is possible that some activities might be carried out only, or more predominantly, by people of a particular gender, such as applying make-up or using hair curling equipment, and cannot therefore be said to be normal for *most* people. They would nevertheless be considered to be normal day-to-day activities.

Work-related and other specialised activities

D7. Normal day-to-day activities do not include work of any particular form because no particular form of work is 'normal' for most people. In any individual case, the activities carried out might be highly specialised. In addition, the Act only covers effects which go beyond the normal differences in skill or ability.

D8. The same is true of activities such as playing a musical instrument to a high standard of achievement; taking part in a particular game or hobby where very specific skills or level of ability are required; or playing a particular sport to a high level of ability, such as would be required for a professional footballer or athlete.

D9. However, many types of work or specialised hobby, sport or pastime may still involve normal day-to-day activities. For example; sitting down, standing up, walking, running, talking, writing, making a cup of tea, using everyday objects such as a keyboard, and lifting, moving or carrying everyday objects such as a chair.

A woman plays the piano to a high standard, and often takes part in public performances. She has developed carpal tunnel syndrome in her wrists, an impairment that adversely affects manual dexterity. She can continue to play the piano, but not to such a high standard, and she has to take frequent breaks to rest her arms. This would not of itself be an adverse effect on a normal day-to-day activity. However, as a result of her impairment she also finds it difficult to operate a computer keyboard and cannot use her PC to send emails or write letters. This is an adverse effect on a normal day-to-day activity.

A man works for a factory in their warehouse, loading and unloading stock. He develops heart problems and no longer has the ability to lift or move heavy items at work. This is not a normal day-to-day activity. However, he is also unable to lift, carry or move everyday objects such as a chair, either at work or around the home. This is an adverse effect on a normal day-to-day activity.

D10. The effects on a person as a result of environmental conditions either in the workplace or in other location where a specialised activity is being carried out, should not be discounted simply because there may be a work-related or other specialised activity involved, as there may also be an adverse effect on ability to carry out a normal day-to-day activity.

A middle-aged man works in a factory where chemical fumes cause him to have breathing difficulties, and this has made it impossible for him to continue to do his job. He has been diagnosed with occupational asthma, which has a substantial adverse effect while he is at work. As a result he is no longer able to work where he would continue to be exposed to the fumes. He finds any general exertion difficult and this adversely affects activities which involve the capacities of mobility and ability to lift and carry everyday objects. The effects fluctuate, and when he is not at work his asthma attacks are very infrequent. Although the substantial effect is only apparent while at work, the man is able to demonstrate that his impairment has an adverse effect on normal day-to-day activities and at least one capacity in the list in D1.

Indirect effects

D11. An impairment may not directly *prevent* someone from carrying out one or more normal day-to-day activities, but it may still have a substantial adverse long-term effect on how they carry out those activities. For example:

- pain or fatigue: where an impairment causes pain or fatigue in performing normal day-to-day activities the person may have the capacity to do something but suffer pain in doing so; or the impairment might make the activity more than usually fatiguing so that the person might not be able to repeat the task over a sustained period of time. *See also paragraph B8 above (effects of behaviour)*;

A man has had chronic fatigue syndrome for several years and although he has the physical capability to walk and to stand, he finds these very difficult to sustain for any length of time because of the overwhelming fatigue he experiences. As a consequence, he is restricted in his ability to take part in normal day-to-day activities such as travelling, so he avoids going out socially, and works from home several days a week. Therefore there is a substantial adverse effect on normal day-to-day activities.

- medical advice: where a person has been professionally advised to change, limit or refrain from a normal day-to-day activity on account of an impairment or only do it in a certain way or under certain conditions. *See also paragraphs B12 to B15 above (effects of treatment)*.

A woman who works as a teacher develops sciatic pain which is attributed to a prolapsed intevertebral disc. Despite physiotherapy and traction her pain became worse. As a result her doctor advises her to avoid repetitive bending or lifting, and to avoid carrying heavy items. She takes pain relief medication daily and avoids those activities mentioned by her doctor.

Children with a disability

D12. The effects of an impairment may not be apparent in babies and young children because they are too young to have developed the ability to act in a way which falls within the capacities listed in D1. Regulations provide that where an impairment to a child under six years old does not have an effect in respect of any of the capacities, it is to be treated as having a substantial and long-term adverse effect on the ability of that child to carry out normal day-to-day activities where it would normally have a substantial and long-term adverse effect on the ability of a person aged six years or over to carry out normal day-to-day activities[9].

D13. Children aged six and older are subject to the normal requirements of the definition.

A six-year-old child has been diagnosed as having autism. He is unable to convey anything meaningful through his speech, for example that he is hungry or in pain. If left unsupervised he will often try to run out of the front door and in to the road to look at the wheels of parked or sometimes passing cars, and has no sense of danger at all. When going somewhere new or taking a different route he can become very anxious. This amounts to a substantial adverse effect on his ability to carry out normal day-to-day activities, even for such a young child. The capacities of mobility, speech, and perception of risk are all affected.

D14. Since September 2002, provisions in the Special Educational Needs and Disability Act 2001 have extended Part 4 of the Disability Discrimination Act to cover every aspect of education[10]. The disability discrimination duties provide protection for disabled pupils by preventing discrimination against them at school on the grounds of disability. A pupil must satisfy the definition of disability as described in this guidance in order to be protected by the Disability Discrimination Act. The duties in the Act are designed to dovetail with duties under the Special Educational Needs (SEN) framework which are based on a separate definition of special education needs. Further information on these duties can be found in the SEN Code of Practice[11] and the Code of Practice for Schools[12].

Examples of children in an educational setting where their impairment has a substantial adverse long term effect on ability to carry out normal day-to-day activities:

A 10-year-old girl has learning difficulties. She has a short attention span and has difficulties remembering facts from one day to the next. She can read only a few familiar words and has some early mathematical skills. To record her work in class she needs to use a tape recorder, pictures and symbols.

A 14-year-old boy has been diagnosed as having attention deficit hyperactivity disorder (ADHD). He often forgets his books, worksheets or homework. In class he finds it difficult to concentrate and skips from task to task forgetting instructions. He often fidgets and makes inappropriate remarks in class or in the playground. Sometimes there can be outbursts of temper.

In both of these examples reading, writing and participating in activities in class and/or in the playground, which are all normal day-to-day activities, are adversely affected to a substantial degree. The capacity affected is 'memory, or ability to concentrate, learn or understand'.

---

9 The Disability Discrimination (Meaning of Disability) Regulations 1996.
10 The Special Educational Needs and Disability Act 2001 amends Part 4 of the Disability Discrimination Act to prevent discrimination against disabled people in their access to education.
11 The Special Educational Needs Code of Practice (November 2001), Department for Education and Skills.
12 Code of Practice for Schools: Disability Discrimination Act 1995: Part 4 (July 2002), Disability Rights Commission.

Appendix 10

List of capacities, with examples of normal day-to-day activities

D15.   The following section looks at the **list of capacities**, and provides illustrative examples of normal day-to-day activities which might affect those capacities.

D16.   Examples are given of circumstances where it would *not be reasonable* to regard the effect as substantial. In these examples, the effect described should be thought of as if it were the *only* effect of the impairment.

D17.   The examples of what it would, and what it would not, be reasonable to regard as substantial adverse effects on normal day-to-day activities are indicators and not tests. They do not mean that if a person can do an activity listed then he or she does not experience any substantial adverse effects; the person may be affected in relation to other activities, and this instead may indicate a substantial effect. Or the person may be affected in a minor way in a number of different activities, and the cumulative effect could amount to a substantial adverse effect. *See also paragraphs B4 to B6 (cumulative effects).*

D18.   The examples describe the effect which would occur when the various factors described in Parts A, B and C above have been allowed for, including for example the effects of a person making such modifications of behaviour as might reasonably be expected, or of disregarding the impact of medical or other treatment.

D19.   Some of the examples show how an adverse effect may arise from either a physical or a mental impairment. Where illustrations of both types of impairment have not been given, this does not mean that only one type of impairment could result in that particular effect. **Regard should be given to the fact that physical impairments can result in mental effects, and mental impairments can have physical manifestations.**

Mobility

D20.   This covers moving or changing position in a wide sense. Account should be taken of the extent to which, because of either a physical or a mental impairment, a person finds difficult such day-to-day activities as: getting around unaided or using a normal means of transport; leaving home with or without assistance; walking a short distance; climbing stairs; travelling in a car or completing a journey on public transport; sitting, standing, bending, or reaching; or getting around in an unfamiliar place.

Examples

It would be reasonable to regard as having a substantial adverse effect:

- difficulty in travelling a short journey as a passenger in a vehicle, because, for example, it would be painful getting in and out of a car, or sitting in a car for even a short time, or perhaps, as a result of a mental impairment, the person would become distressed while in the car;

- total inability to walk, or difficulty walking other than at a slow pace or with unsteady or jerky movements;

- difficulty in going up or down steps, stairs or gradients for example because movements are painful, uncomfortable or restricted in some way;

- difficulty using one or more forms of public transport for example as a result of physical restrictions or as a result of a mental impairment;

- difficulty going out of doors unaccompanied for example because the person has a phobia.

A young woman with severe anxiety and symptoms of agoraphobia is unable to go out because she fears being outside in open spaces and gets panic attacks in stressful situations such as shopping or travelling on a route that is less than familiar.

Similarly, a man with Downs Syndrome, a learning difficulty, has difficulty travelling unaccompanied because he often gets lost in areas that are slightly unfamiliar.

In both cases, the inability to travel around unaccompanied affects the capacity of mobility and has a substantial adverse effect on the ability to carry out normal day-to-day activities.

It would not be reasonable to regard as having a substantial adverse effect:

- experiencing some discomfort as a result of travelling in a car for a journey lasting more than two hours;

- experiencing some tiredness or minor discomfort as a result of walking unaided for a distance of about 1.5 kilometres or one mile.

Manual dexterity

D21. This covers the ability to use hands and fingers with precision. Account should be taken of the extent to which a person can manipulate the fingers on each hand or co-ordinate the use of both hands together to do a task. This includes the ability to carry out normal day-to-day activities that involve things like picking up or manipulating small objects, operating a range of equipment manually, or communicating through writing or typing on standard machinery. Loss of function in the dominant hand would be expected to have a greater effect than equivalent loss in the non-dominant hand.

Examples

It would be reasonable to regard as having a substantial adverse effect:

- difficulty co-ordinating the use of a knife and fork at the same time;

- difficulty preparing a meal because of problems doing things like opening cans or other packages; peeling vegetables; lifting saucepans; and opening the oven door;

- difficulty opening doors which have door knobs rather than lever handles, or gripping handrails on steps or gradients;

- difficulty pressing the buttons on keyboards or keypads at the same speed as someone who does not have an impairment.

A woman with tenosynivitis experiences significant pain in her hands and lower arms when undertaking repetitive tasks such as using a keyboard at home or work, peeling vegetables, and writing. The impairment substantially adversely affects these normal day-to-day activities and it has an impact on the capacity of manual dexterity.

Appendix 10

It would not be reasonable to regard as having a substantial adverse effect:

- inability to undertake activities requiring delicate hand movements, such as threading a small needle;

- inability to reach typing speeds standardised for secretarial work;

- inability to pick up a single small item, such as a pin.

Physical co-ordination

D22. This covers balanced and effective interaction of body movement, including hand and eye co-ordination. In the case of a child, it is necessary to take account of the level of achievement which would be normal for a person of the particular age. In any case, account should be taken of the ability to carry out 'composite' activities such as walking and using hands at the same time.

Examples

It would be reasonable to regard as having a substantial adverse effect:

- ability to pour hot water into a cup to make a cup of tea only with unusual slowness or concentration;

- difficulty placing food into one's own mouth with a fork or spoon, without unusual concentration or assistance.

A young man who has dyspraxia experiences a range of effects which include difficulty co-ordinating physical movements. He is frequently knocking over cups and bottles of drink and cannot combine two activities at the same time, such as walking while holding a plate of food upright, without spilling the food. It would be reasonable to regard this as a substantial adverse effect on normal day-to-day activities affecting manual dexterity.

It would not be reasonable to regard as having a substantial adverse effect:

- simple clumsiness;

- inability to catch a tennis ball.

Continence

D23. This covers the ability to control urination and/or defecation. Account should be taken of the frequency and extent of the loss of control and the age of the individual (for example a very young child would not be expected to be able to control urination and defecation).

Examples

It would be reasonable to regard as having a substantial adverse effect:

- infrequent loss of control of the bowels, if it was entirely unpredictable and led to immediate major soiling;

- loss of control of the bladder while asleep at least once a month;
- frequent minor faecal incontinence or frequent minor leakage from the bladder, particularly if it is unpredictable.

> A young woman has developed colitis, an inflammatory bowel disease. The condition is a chronic one which is subject to periods of remission and flare-ups. During a flare-up she experiences severe abdominal pain and bouts of diarrhoea. This makes it very difficult for her to travel or go to work as she must ensure she is always close to a lavatory. This has a substantial adverse effect on her ability to carry out normal day-to-day activities.

It would not be reasonable to regard as having a substantial adverse effect:

- infrequent (less than once a month) loss of control of the bladder while asleep;
- infrequent and minor leakage from the bladder.

Ability to lift, carry or otherwise move everyday objects

D24. Account should be taken of a person's ability to repeat such functions or, for example, to bear weights over a reasonable period of time. Everyday objects might include such items as books, a kettle of water, bags of shopping, a briefcase, an overnight bag, a chair or other piece of light furniture.

Examples

It would be reasonable to regard as having a substantial adverse effect:

- difficulty picking up objects of moderate weight with one hand;
- difficulty opening a moderately heavy door;
- difficulty carrying a moderately loaded tray steadily.

> A man has achondroplasia, which causes unusually short stature, and arms which are disproportionate in size to the rest of his body. He has difficulty lifting or manipulating everyday items like a vacuum cleaner, or bulky items of household furniture, and has difficulty opening moderately heavy doors, and operating revolving barriers at the entrance to some stations and buildings. It would be reasonable to regard this as a substantial adverse effect on normal day-to-day activities.

It would not be reasonable to regard as having a substantial adverse effect:

- inability to carry heavy luggage without assistance;
- inability to move heavy objects without a mechanical aid, such as move a heavy piece of furniture without a trolley.

Speech, hearing or eyesight

D25. This covers the ability to speak, hear or see and includes face-to-face, telephone and written communication. Account should be taken of the extent to which, as a result of either a physical or mental impairment, a person may have the capacity to speak, hear or see, but may nevertheless be substantially adversely affected in a range of activities involving one of these capacities as a result of the effects of their impairment.

(i) Speech

Account should be taken of how far a person is able to speak clearly at a normal pace and rhythm and to understand someone else speaking normally in the person's native language. It is necessary to consider any effects on speech patterns or which impede the acquisition or processing of one's native language, for example by someone who has had a stroke.

Examples

It would be reasonable to regard as having a substantial adverse effect:

- difficulty giving clear basic instructions orally to colleagues or providers of a service;
- difficulty asking specific questions to clarify instructions;
- taking significantly longer than someone who does not have a speech impairment to say things.

A woman has a persistent and severe stammer, which substantially affects her ability to speak clearly. She has considerable difficulty making herself understood to a shop assistant when asking for advice. The stammer becomes much worse when she is under any kind of pressure, for example when she speaks to strangers, or has to ask for something quickly.

A 6-year-old boy has verbal dyspraxia which adversely affects his ability to speak. He is unable to make himself clear to other people, including his friends and teachers at school.

In both cases it would be reasonable to regard these effects as substantial adverse effects.

It would not be reasonable to regard as having a substantial adverse effect:

- inability to articulate fluently due to a minor stutter, lisp or speech impediment;
- inability to speak in front of an audience simply as a result of nervousness;
- inability to be understood because of having a strong accent;
- inability to converse in a language which is not the speaker's native language.

(ii) Hearing

Account should be taken of effects where the level of background noise is within such a range and of such a type that most people would be able to hear adequately. If a person uses a hearing aid or similar device, what needs to be considered is the effect that would be experienced if the person were not using the hearing aid or device.

Examples

It would be reasonable to regard as having a substantial adverse effect:

- difficulty hearing someone talking at a sound level which is normal for everyday conversations, and in a moderately noisy environment;

- difficulty to hear and understand another person speaking clearly over the voice telephone (where the telephone is not affected by bad reception);

- difficulty to hear or understand normal conversations because of interference cause by auditory hallucinations as a result of a mental impairment.

A woman has tinnitus which interferes with, and makes difficult, the ability to hear or understand normal conversation, to the extent that she cannot hear and respond to what a supermarket checkout assistant is saying if the two people behind her in the queue are holding a conversation at the same time. This has a substantial adverse effect on her ability to carry out the normal day-to-day activity of shopping.

It would not be reasonable to regard as having a substantial adverse effect:

- inability to hold a conversation in a very noisy place, such as a factory floor or at a pop concert;

- inability to sing in tune.

(iii) Eyesight

If a person's sight is corrected by spectacles or contact lenses, or could be corrected by them, what needs to be considered is the effect remaining while they are wearing such spectacles or lenses.

If a person's eyesight is impaired sufficiently to warrant registration or certification as a blind or partially sighted person[13], they are deemed to be a disabled person and do not need to prove that they have an impairment which has a substantial adverse long-term effect on their ability to carry out normal day-to-day activities.

Examples

It would be reasonable to regard as having a substantial adverse effect:

- inability to see to pass the eyesight test for a standard driving test (however where this is corrected by glasses, this is not a substantial adverse effect);

- difficulty recognising by sight a known person across a moderately-sized room;

- inability to distinguish any colours at all;

- difficulty reading ordinary newsprint (unless this can be corrected by reading glasses);

- difficulty walking safely without bumping into things.

---

13 The Disability Discrimination (Blind and Partially Sighted Persons) Regulations 2003.

Appendix 10

A man has retinitis pigmentosa (RP), a heredity eye disorder which affects the retina. In RP sight loss is gradual but progressive. It is unusual for people with RP to become totally blind – most retain some useful vision well into old age. In this case the man has difficulty seeing in poor light and a marked reduction in his field of vision (referred to as tunnel vision). As a result he often bumps into furniture and doors when he is in an unfamiliar environment, and can only read when he is in a very well-lit area. It would be reasonable to conclude that the adverse effects of this impairment on normal day-to-day activities are substantial.

It would not be reasonable to regard as having a substantial adverse effect:

- inability to read very small or indistinct print without the aid of a magnifying glass;

- inability to distinguish a known person across a substantial distance (e.g. across the width of a football pitch);

- simple inability to distinguish between red and green, which is not accompanied by any other effect such as blurring of vision.

Memory or ability to concentrate, learn or understand

D26. Account should be taken of the person's ability to remember, organise his or her thoughts, plan a course of action and carry it out, take in new knowledge, or understand spoken or written instructions. This includes considering whether the person learns to do things significantly more slowly than a person who does not have an impairment. Account should be taken of whether the person has persistent and significant difficulty in reading text in standard English or straightforward numbers. The ability to learn or understand includes the ability to understand or make sense of human non-factual information, and non-verbal communication such as body language and facial expressions.

Examples

It would be reasonable to regard as having a substantial adverse effect:

- intermittent loss of consciousness and associated confused behaviour;

- persistent difficulty to remember the names of familiar people such as family or friends;

- difficulty to adapt after a reasonable period to minor changes in work routine;

- inability to write a cheque without assistance;

- persistent difficulty to remember words in common usage;

- considerable difficulty in following a short sequence such as a simple recipe or a brief list of domestic tasks;

- difficulty taking part in normal social interaction.

A man has Asperger's Syndrome, a form of autism, and this causes him to have difficulty communicating with people. He finds it hard to understand non-verbal communications such as facial expressions, and non-factual communication such as jokes. He takes everything that is said very literally, and therefore has great difficulty in making or keeping friends or developing close relationships. It would be reasonable to regard this as an impairment that has a substantial adverse effect on normal day-to-day activities, and which affects the capacity of 'memory or ability to concentrate, learn or understand'.

It would not be reasonable to regard as having a substantial adverse effect:

- occasionally forgetting the name of a familiar person, such as a colleague;

- inability to concentrate on a task requiring application over several hours;

- inability to fill in a long, detailed, technical document without assistance;

- inability to read at faster than normal speed;

- some shyness or timidity;

- minor problems with writing or spelling.

Perception of the risk of physical danger

D27. This includes both the underestimation and overestimation of physical danger, including danger to well-being. Account should be taken, for example, of whether the person is inclined to neglect basic functions such as eating, drinking, sleeping, keeping warm or personal hygiene; reckless behaviour which puts the person or others at risk; or excessive avoidance behaviour without a good cause.

Examples

It would be reasonable to regard as having a substantial adverse effect:

- difficulty operating safely properly-maintained equipment;

- persistent difficulty crossing a road safely;

- inability to nourish oneself (assuming nourishment is available);

- inability to tell by touch that an object is very hot or cold.

A man has had paranoid schizophrenia for five years, and one of the effects of this impairment is an inability to make proper judgements about activities that may result in a risk to his personal safety. For example, he will walk into roads without checking if cars are coming. This makes normal day-to-day activities such as shopping very difficult.

A woman has had anorexia, an eating disorder, for two years. She is unable to fully grasp that failure to eat properly will result in a risk to her well-being. She is convinced that she is still fat despite being very underweight, and as a result her physical health has deteriorated to the extent that she finds it very difficult taking part in normal day-to-day activities such as shopping, travelling to see friends, or carrying out general household tasks.

In both cases, these people have an impaired appreciation of danger which results in a substantial adverse effect on their ability to carry out normal day-to-day activities.

Appendix 10

It would not be reasonable to regard as having a substantial adverse effect:

- fear of significant heights;

- underestimating the risk associated with dangerous hobbies, such as mountain climbing;

- underestimating risks – other than obvious ones – in unfamiliar workplaces.

Appendix 11

Immigration and Asylum Act 1999, s 22: Code of Practice for All Employers on the Avoidance of Race Discrimination in Recruitment While Seeking to Prevent Illegal Working

INTRODUCTION

Purpose and status of this Code

1. Illegal working is a growing, global problem. Many countries around the world have laws to deal with illegal employment. However, it is important to remember that the population of the United Kingdom is ethnically diverse. Most people from ethnic minorities are British citizens and most non-British citizens from the ethnic minorities are entitled to work here.

2. Section 8 of the Asylum and Immigration Act 1996 ('the 1996 Act'[1]) aims to ensure that employment is offered only to those entitled to live and work in the UK.

3. This Code aims to provide all employers with guidance on avoiding conviction under Section 8 in a way that does not result in unlawful race discrimination[2].

4. In 1996, the Home Office issued detailed guidance about what employers must do to avoid a criminal conviction under Section 8[3]. The 1996 guidance reminds employers of their obligations under the Race Relations Act 1976 (the 1976 Act). This guidance applies also in Northern Ireland where employers have similar obligations under the Race Relations (Northern Ireland) Order 1997. There is evidence, however, that some employers may be unlawfully discriminating when seeking to avoid conviction under section 8.

5. This new Code is designed to strengthen the safeguards against discrimination by re-emphasising employers' statutory duty to avoid race discrimination in their recruitment practices.

6. The Code does not impose any legal obligations itself, and it is not an authoritative statement of the law. Failure to observe the Code is not a breach of the law. But failure to observe the Code is admissible in evidence in any proceedings under the 1976 Act or the Race Relations (Northern Ireland) Order 1997 (the 1997 Order) before an Employment Tribunal (Industrial Tribunal in Northern Ireland). The Tribunal must take the Code into account, if it is relevant.

7. This Code outlines your legal obligations under the Race Relations Act 1976, Race Relations (Northern Ireland) Order 1997 and the Asylum and Immigration Act 1996 and provides some best practice in employment procedures that can help you to meet these obligations. It is not comprehensive and it is for employers to operate transparent recruitment practices which are consistent with the law, ensuring fair treatment to all applicants.

---

1 Introduced by (s 22) of the Immigration and Asylum Act 1999.
2 This Code draws heavily on the Commission for Racial Equality's Guide for Employers 'Racial Equality and the Asylum and Immigration Act 1996'. Readers may also find it useful to refer to that publication. Details of how to get it are in Appendix 2.
3 Prevention of illegal working: Guidance for employers, Home Office Communication Directorate, December 1996.

Appendix 11

Your responsibility under the law: Race Relations Act 1976 and Race Relations (Northern Ireland) Order 1997

8. Under the 1976 Act and the 1997 Order it is unlawful to discriminate in recruitment or employment on the following grounds:

    - race or colour

    - nationality (including citizenship) and

    - ethnic or national origin.

    Race discrimination may be either direct or indirect.

    Direct discrimination means treating a person less favourably on racial grounds, for example by rejecting all job applicants who do not have British nationality or by refusing to consider any black job applicants. Treatment based on race or national stereotypes can also constitute direct discrimination.

    Indirect discrimination means imposing a condition or requirement which applies equally to everyone but is harder for people from particular racial groups to satisfy, and which cannot be justified. For example, it could be discrimination to ask for a high standard of English when the job does not require this.

9. It is unlawful to victimise a person because he or she has made, or supported, a complaint of racial discrimination. It is also unlawful to instruct or induce another person to discriminate. It is also unlawful to publish an advertisement or notice that indicates an intention to discriminate.

Employment Agencies

10. An employment agency practising unlawful discrimination will be liable even if it is acting on the instructions of an employer.

Liability for the actions of others

11. Under the 1976 Act and the 1997 Order, discrimination committed by an employee in the course of his or her employment is treated as having been committed by the employer as well as by the individual employee whether or not the employer knew or approved. Employers can avoid liability if they can prove that they took sufficient reasonable steps to prevent such discrimination. A complaint to a Tribunal may be made against both the employer and the individual employee who is alleged to have discriminated.

Right of Complaint

12. Anyone who believes that he or she has been discriminated against on racial grounds by an employer, a prospective employer or an employment agency may bring a complaint before a Tribunal. If the complaint is upheld, the Tribunal will normally order the employer to pay compensation, for which there is now no upper limit.

13. The Commission for Racial Equality and the Northern Ireland Equality Commission can bring proceedings against an employer who publishes a discriminatory advertisement or who instructs or induces another person to discriminate.

Your responsibility under the law: section 8 of the Asylum and Immigration Act 1996

14. Under section 8 of the Asylum and Immigration Act 1996 it is a criminal offence to employ a person aged 16 or over who is subject to immigration control[4] unless:

   - that person has current and valid permission to be in the United Kingdom and that permission does not prevent him or her from taking the job in question (see paragraph 16); or

   - the person comes into a category specified by the Home Secretary[5] where such employment is allowed (e.g. see paragraph 17).

15. In practice, most people seeking work are not subject to immigration control and can be taken on without contravening section 8. Section 8 does not apply to the employment of:

   - British citizens

   - Commonwealth citizens with the right of abode in the UK, and

   - Citizens of any country in the European Economic Area (EEA).

16. It is lawful to employ anyone who is subject to immigration control so long as his or her leave to enter or remain in the UK has not expired and the leave does not prevent him or her from working.

17. It is lawful also to employ asylum seekers, provided they have written permission to work. It is also lawful to employ people awaiting the outcome of an immigration appeal who before their appeal had permission to work, or people who were entitled to work and are awaiting the outcome of a request for an extension to that permission requested before it ran out.

The statutory defence

18. The 1996 Act makes a statutory defence against prosecution available to all employers. If you establish a defence you will not be convicted, even if it turns out that a person you are employing is subject to immigration control and is working without permission. The defence will be valid unless it can be shown that you knew that the person was not entitled to work when you employed them. Any employer who knows they are employing people who do not have permission to work can be prosecuted under Section 8.

19. In order to establish a defence you need to make sure that, before a person starts working for you, you see at least one document which appears to you to be listed in Appendix 1. You should ensure that the document is an original and that it appears to relate to the person that you are intending to employ. You should make either a copy or record of the document or retain it. This last option will normally only be appropriate in the case of Part 2 of a P45. The statutory defence is only established by checking documents before taking on a new employee. There is no requirement to do anything else, even if the person's permission to be in the United Kingdom is not yet permanent. You should not ask existing employees to demonstrate that they have permission to work.

---

4 A person subject to immigration control is a person who, under the Immigration and Asylum Act 1971, requires leave to enter or remain in the UK.
5 The categories are currently listed in the Immigration (Restrictions on Employment) Order 1996 (SI 1996/3325).

20. The checks which you need to make to claim the statutory defence are in most cases straightforward and can be built into your normal recruitment procedures. Such checks are not compulsory but they are advisable. If you do not make them you will not have the statutory defence which they provide. But if you make checks you should ensure that they are made in a non-discriminatory manner.

Avoiding Racial Discrimination

21. As a matter of good practice you should have clear written procedures for recruitment and selection based on equal and fair treatment for all applicants and should make these known to all relevant staff.

22. All job selections should be on the basis of suitability for the post. You should ensure that no prospective job applicants are discouraged or excluded either directly or indirectly because of their appearance or accent. You should not make assumptions about a person's right to work, or immigration status, on the basis of their colour, race, nationality or ethnic or national origins or the length of time they have been in the UK.

23. To avoid prosecution under the 1996 Act you only need to see and either keep or make a copy of one of the documents listed in Appendix 1 before the employment begins. There is no need to ask about an applicant's immigration status, apart from asking if he or she needs permission to work. Such enquiries could mislead you into taking decisions which might constitute unlawful racial discrimination.

24. The best way to ensure that you do not discriminate is to treat all applicants in the same way at each stage of the recruitment process. For example, if you provide information to prospective applicants, or if you supply an application form, you could also include a reminder that the successful applicant will be asked to produce one of the specified documents - and attach the list.

25. You may ask applicants to provide one of the specified documents at any stage before they start work. Depending on your recruitment processes, you may find it most convenient to request a document from all those called to a first interview, or just from those called to a second interview, or only from the person chosen to fill the vacancy. It is perfectly satisfactory to ask for a document only from the person chosen to fill the vacancy if that is most administratively convenient. But if you ask for a document from one applicant make sure you ask for a document from all applicants being considered at that stage.

26. The documents listed in Appendix 1 are of equal status under the 1996 Act. For example, a person who is unable to produce a document showing their National Insurance Number should not be treated less favourably if he or she is able to produce any other document listed. You only need to see one of the specified documents. Rejecting a candidate who does not have a particular document even though they have one of the others could be unlawful discrimination.

27. If a person is not able to produce one of the listed documents, you should not assume that he or she is living or working in the UK illegally. You should refer the person to a Citizens Advice Bureau or other agency for advice. You should try to keep the job open for as long as possible but you are not obliged to do so if you need to recruit someone urgently.

28. As a matter of good practice you should monitor the outcome of recruitment and selection by the ethnicity of job applicants. This will help you to know whether you are treating applicants fairly and without discrimination and can be used in reviewing recruitment procedures.

APPENDIX 1

List of specified documents[6]

- A document issued by a previous employer, the Inland Revenue, the Benefits Agency, the Contributions Agency or the Employment Service (or the Northern Ireland equivalents) which states the National Insurance number of the person named.

- A passport describing the holder as a British Citizen or having the right of abode in - or an entitlement to readmission to - the United Kingdom.

- A passport containing a Certificate of Entitlement issued by or on behalf of the Government of the United Kingdom certifying that the holder has the right of abode in the United Kingdom.

- A certificate of registration or naturalisation as a British Citizen.

- A birth certificate issued in the United Kingdom, the Republic of Ireland, the Channel Islands or the Isle of Man.

- A passport or national identity card issued by a State which is a party to European Economic Area Agreement and which describes the holder as a national of that State.

- A passport or other travel document endorsed to show that the person named is exempt from immigration control, has indefinite leave to enter, or remain in, the United Kingdom or has no time limit on his or her stay; or a letter issued by the Home Office confirming that the person named has such status.

- A passport or other travel document endorsed to show that the person named has current leave to enter or remain in the United Kingdom and is not precluded from taking the employment in question, or a letter issued by the Home Office confirming that this is the case.

- A United Kingdom residence permit issued to a national of a State which is a party to the European Economic Area Agreement.

- A passport or other travel document endorsed to show that the holder has a current right of residence in the United Kingdom as the family member of a named national of a State which is a party to the European Economic Area Agreement and who is resident in the United Kingdom.

- A letter issued by the Immigration and Nationality Directorate of the Home Office indicating that the person named in the letter is a British citizen or has permission to take employment.

- A work permit or other approval to take employment issued by Work Permits (UK) (formerly Department for Education and Employment) or, in Northern Ireland, by the Training and Employment Agency.

- A passport describing the holder as a British Dependent Territories Citizen and which indicates that the status derives from a connection with Gibraltar.

You should ensure that you see the original documents.

---

6   These documents are currently specified in the Immigration (Restrictions on Employment) Order 1996 (SI 1996/3325).

Appendix 11

Other sources of information

Publications

- The Asylum and Immigration Act 1996: Implications for Racial Equality. This guidance is produced by the Commission for Racial Equality and copies are available from CRE Distribution Services, Elliot House, 10 - 12 Allington Street, London SW1E 5EH.

- Race Relations Code of Practice: For the Elimination of Racial Discrimination and the Promotion of Equality of Opportunity in Employment. This Code contains practical guidance to help employers to comply with the Race Relations Act 1976. It is also produced by the Commission for Racial Equality and copies are available from Central Books, 99 Walis Road, London E9 5LN (Telephone 0208 986 4854).

The Commission for Racial Equality

Visit the Commission for Racial Equality website at www.cre.gov.uk .

The Commission for Racial Equality can also advise on particular points. You should consult the office nearest to you for advice:

Birmingham (Midlands & Wales Region)
3rd Floor
Lancaster House
67 Newhall Street
Birmingham, B3 1NA

Tel: 0121 710 3000

Cardiff (Midlands and Wales Region)
14th Floor
Capital Tower
Greyfriars Street
Cardiff, CF1 3AG

Tel: 0122 238 8977
Fax: 0122 2399680

Edinburgh (North of England and Scotland Region)
The Tun
12 Jackson's Entry
off Holyrood Road
Edinburgh, EH8 8PJ

Tel: 0131 240 2600
Fax: 0131 240 2601

Leeds (North of England and Scotland Region)
1st Floor
Yorkshire Bank Chambers
Infirmary Street
Leeds
LS1 2JP

Tel: 0113 389 3600
Fax: 0113 389 3601

London (Head Office / London and South Region)
Elliot House
10-12 Allington Street
London, SW1E 5EH

Tel: 0171 828 7022
Fax: 0171 630 7605 (main)

Manchester (North of England and Scotland Region)
5th Floor
Maybrook House
40 Blackfriars Street
Manchester M3 2EG

Tel: 0161 835 5500
Fax: 0161 835 5501

Equality Commission for Northern Ireland
Racial Equality Directorate
Andras House
60 Great Victoria Street
Belfast BT2 7BB

Tel: 02890 500 600
Fax: 02890 351 993

Northern Ireland Council for Ethnic Minorities
3rd Floor
Ascot House
Shaftesbury Square
Belfast BT2

Tel: 02890 238 645
Fax: 02890 319 485

If you want further advice about general immigration issues you should contact:

Immigration and Nationality Directorate
Lunar House
40 Wellesley Road
Croydon
CR9 2BY

Tel: 0870 606 7766

Index

All references are to paragraph number

661

Index

Allocation of work
detriment, and, 66.3
Alternative dispute resolution (ADR)
ACAS, 8.1
choice of process, 8.2
introduction, 8.1
mediation, 8.3
relationships at work, and, 221
Amendments
generally, 9
Annualised hours
flexible working, and, 109.2
Appeals
amendments, 10
Applicants
age discrimination, and, 5.1
generally, 35
Appraisals
detriment, and, 66.7
generally, 11
Aptitude tests
generally, 12
introduction, 263
Armed forces
age discrimination, and, 5.1
generally, 13
Arrears of remuneration
equal pay, and, 95.10
Assessments
generally, 14
Assistance
generally, 15
Associated employers
generally, 16
Assumptions
generally, 17
Asylum seekers
generally, 18
Authenticity
racial discrimination, and, 115.5
sex discrimination, and, 115.6

B
Back pay
case law, 19.1
equal pay, and, 95.10
statutory provision, 19.2
Bankruptcy
generally, 20
Banter
generally, 141
Barristers
age discrimination, and, 5.1
generally, 3

Beards
and see Personal appearance
generally, 21
racial discrimination, and, 85.3
Behaviour
substantial adverse effects, and, 254.4
Belief, discrimination on grounds of
direct discrimination, 222.3
dress code, and, 85.4
effect, 222.6
genuine occupational requirement, and
generally, 222.7
introduction, 115.2
harassment, 222.5
indirect discrimination, 222.4
introduction, 222.1
jokes and humour, and, 141
meaning, 222.2
overseas work, and, 177
personal appearance, and, 85.4
positive action, 222.8
relevant legislation, 77
victimisation, 222.5
Benefits
age discrimination, 22.4
company cars, and, 44
dependants, for, 65
job duties, and, 135
overtime, and, 178
part-time work, and, 181.1
reasonable adjustments, 22.3
seniority, 22.2
service, 22.2
statutory provisions, 22.1
terms of employment, and, 261
voluntary redundancy, and, 219
Bonuses
post-employment discrimination, and,
197.4
Breastfeeding
checklist, Appendix
generally, 23
Burden of proof
background, 24.1
Court of Appeal guidance
application, 24.3
generally, 24.2
direct discrimination, and, 67.2
evidence of discrimination, and,
103.2
harassment, and, 119.2
questionnaires, and, 207
'But for' test
generally, 25

662

Index

Index

Index

Index

Index

Index

Index

Index

Index

Uniforms
and see Dress code
and see Personal appearance
generally, 277
Unintentional discrimination
generally, 278
stereotypes, and, 251
Unlawful discrimination
disability discrimination, and, 70.4
Unmarried persons
generally, 279
Unreasonable treatment
direct discrimination, and, 67.3
Unsocial hours working
assumptions, and, 17
childcare, and, 31

V
Vacancy notices
general, 2.1
wording, 2.2
Variation of contracts
generally, 280
Veils
and see Personal appearance
generally, 281
Vicarious liability
course of employment, 87.2
general principles, 87.1
generally, 282
introduction, 151
reasonably practicable steps, 87.3
Victimisation
age discrimination, and, 5.4
case law, 283.2
defamation of character, and, 62
direct discrimination, and, 67.2
dismissal, and, 79.5
domestic employment, and, 84
evidence of discrimination, and, 103.1
generally, 283.1
inferences, and, 129
internal investigations, and, 132

Victimisation – *contd*
jokes and humour, and, 141
practical advice, 283.3
racial discrimination, and, 210
recruitment, and, 218.3
religion or belief discrimination, and, 222.5
sexual orientation discrimination, and, 293.7
statutory provisions, 283.1
subconscious discrimination, and, 252
unconscious discrimination, and, 275
unintentional discrimination, and, 278
Vocational training
age discrimination, and, 5.1
rights and duties, 1.4
Voluntary bodies
generally, 284
Voluntary workers
generally, 285
V-time working
flexible working, and, 109.2

W
Wales
generally, 286
Wasted costs orders
generally, 58.5
Whistle-blowing
generally, 287
Without prejudice
generally, 288
Work allocation
detriment, and, 66.3
Working conditions
conditions, and, 49
generally, 291
Working time
health and safety, and, 120.2
generally, 122
night work, and, 169
Works Rules
generally, 292

682